The Best Medicine

THE
BEST
MEDICINE

THE COMPLETE
HEALTH
AND PREVENTIVE
MEDICINE

HANDBOOK

Kurt Butler, M.S.

Lynn Rayner, M.D.

Harper & Row, Publishers, San Francisco
Cambridge, Hagerstown, New York, Philadelphia
London, Mexico City, São Paulo, Singapore, Sydney

Library of Congress Cataloging in Publication Data

Butler, Kurt.
  The best medicine.

  Bibliography: p.
  Includes index.
  1. Health—Handbooks, manuals, etc. 2. Medicine, Preventive—Handbooks, manuals, etc. I. Rayner, Lynn. II. Title. [DNLM:
1. Health—handbooks. 2. Preventive Medicine—handbooks. 3. Preventive Medicine—popular works. WA 39 B985b]
RA776.B956 1985   613   84-48850
ISBN 0-06-250123-2
ISBN 0-06-250124-0 (pbk.)

FIRST EDITION

Designer: Design Office Bruce Kortebein, San Francisco
Charts and graphs Designer: Christy Butterfield
Drawings: Diana Thewlis

85 86 87 88 89 10 9 8 7 6 5 4 3 2 1

Table of Contents

List of Illustrations and Tables   viii

Acknowledgments   ix

Introduction   ix

Part One   Exercise and Fitness   1

Introduction	Born To Move 3	
Chapter 1	Fitness versus Fatness 4	
Chapter 2	How Exercise Improves Health 9	
Chapter 3	How Much Exercise Is Best? 13	
Chapter 4	How Fit or Fat Are You? 17	
Chapter 5	The Best Fitness Activities 23	
Chapter 6	Exercise and Nutrition 29	
Chapter 7	The Prevention and Treatment of Common Sports Injuries 32	
Chapter 8	Sports and Drugs 50	

Part Two   Nutrition Science and Mythology   55

Chapter 1	A Brief History and Introduction 57
Chapter 2	RDAs and the Four Food Groups 59
Chapter 3	The Ideal Diet 62

Chapter 4   Protein and Amino Acids   68

Chapter 5   Carbohydrates and Fibers   72

Chapter 6   Fats   77

Chapter 7   Vitamins   79

Chapter 8   Adelle Davis and Megavitamins   99

Chapter 9   Minerals   102

Chapter 10   Diets, Diets, and More Diets   111

Chapter 11   Behave Yourself   137

Chapter 12   Reducing Gimmicks   140

Chapter 13   "Special" Foods   142

Chapter 14   Food Additives   151

Chapter 15   Food "Poisoning" and Parasites   161

Chapter 16   Air, Water, and Food Pollution   167

Part Three Healthy Sex and Reproduction 173

Chapter 1   Human Sexual Response in Health and Disease   175

Chapter 2   Birth Control Options   192

Chapter 3   Sexually Transmitted Diseases (STDs)   209

Chapter 4   Healthy Pregnancy, Healthy Children   215

Chapter 5   Common Female Problems   231

Part Four   Common Disorders—A
             Preventive Approach   245

Part Five   Drugs and Health   409

Chapter 1   Over-the-Counter Drugs   411
Chapter 2   Prescription-Only Drugs   442
Chapter 3   Herbs and Herbalism   501
Chapter 4   Recreational Drugs   538

Part Six   Controversial Alternatives 595

Part Seven   Consulting a Physician   665

Chapter 1   When To Consult a Physician   667
Chapter 2   Choosing a Physician or
             Health Care Plan   691

             References   695
             Glossary   705
Appendix A   Recommended Daily Dietary
             Allowances   712
Appendix B   Nutritive Values of Common
             Foods   715
Appendix C   Health Information, Counseling, and
             Referral Services   739
Appendix D   Quackery: A $10 Billion
             Scandal   747
             Index   760

List of Illustrations and Tables

Apparent Effects of Aging that Can Be Modified by Exercise   11

An Atheroma in an Artery   274

Blood Alcohol Levels   540

Calories Burned   27

Causes of Birth Defects   216

Clinical Course of a Human Rabies Case   381

Comparing the Diets at a Glance   114

Drug Ingredients

   Basic List for Home Use   438

   Considered Not Safe or Effective for Uses Given   440

   Safe and Effective for Uses Given   435

Exercises for the Lower Back   282

Exercises that Help Prevent Injuries   34

Fatty Food Allowances   66

Fertility (Temperature) Chart   195

Health Information, Counseling, and Referral Services   737

Heart Attack Risk   335

How Fit or Fat? Comparison of a Fit Jogger and a Fat Jogger   6

Immunization of Infants and Children   499

Laetrile Molecule   637

National Fitness Test and Scores   20

Nutritive Values of Common Foods   715

Percentages of Breast- and Bottle-Feeding   225

Quackery   598

Recommended Daily Dietary Allowances (RDAs)   712

Sexually Transmitted Diseases (STDs)   211

Typical Iridology Chart   632

Acknowledgments

Many thanks to all those who helped us in various ways. Specifically, we want to thank:

The health professionals who reviewed sections of this book and provided many useful comments, especially John Mickey, M.D.; Brian Fellmeth, M.D., Ph.D; Willis Butler, M.D.; John Corboy, M.D.; Grant Stemmerman, M.D.; Floyd Barty, D.D.S.; and Marilyn Walsh, R.D.H.;

research assistants Lynn J. Carey and Alicia Leonhard;

and overworked editors Dick Carter and Dessa Brashear.

Finally, many thanks to our agent, Sandra Dijkstra, a highly skilled matchmaker.

Introduction

For most of our existence we humans have regarded diseases as acts of angry gods, the will of God, or simply fate. Only in very recent times have epidemics and chronic illnesses been demystified and explained. The more we have learned about health and disease, the less fatalistic we have become; it is now clear that most of the important health problems can be completely prevented or delayed for decades. By making the right choices in several key areas of living, we can live longer, healthier, and happier lives. We can also save enormous amounts of money that would otherwise be lost to medical care and low productivity; this can help improve other areas of our personal and social lives and generally increase our standard of living.

The purpose of this book is to help you make the right choices on a personal, family, and community level. We all make decisions about diet, exercise, drugs, vaccinations, air and water pollution, and the like that affect not only ourselves but our children and our neighbors. The more these decisions are based on facts, the better off everyone is. We hope the reader wishes not only to stay healthy but to be an informed and responsible citizen as well.

There are, of course, still many disorders that are not well understood and cannot be prevented or even adequately treated at this time; they still seem to be acts of fate, though research will eventually reveal their causes. Moreover, no matter what steps we take, no matter how careful we are, we will still all die. This book, then, is not about absolutes but about risk factors; we cannot make guarantees, but we can help improve your chances of staying healthy.

You can take safety measures such as wearing seatbelts and obeying traffic rules to increase your chance of survival in an automobile, but there is still a small chance that a drunk will plow into you at just the wrong angle at high speed and kill or cripple you. Nevertheless, the risk is smaller with the seatbelt. Similarly, you can be conscientious about nutrition, exercise, and hygiene and still come down with a serious, even deadly disease. But the

xii   chances of this happening are very small compared to the risk of heart disease, cancer, hepatitis, or gastric ulcers from known causes; your odds are very much better if you are informed and take care.

How To Use This Book

The book has seven parts, each with several chapters or sections. In order, they cover fitness, nutrition, sex and reproduction, common disorders, drugs, controversial alternatives, and consulting a physician. There is no particular logic to the sequence, and the parts can be read in any order. The same is true of the chapters within the parts, though it usually helps to read the introduction first. Wherever possible, subjects within parts or chapters are arranged alphabetically for easy reference. Examples include disorders in Part Four, herbs in Chapter 5-3 (Part Five, Chapter 3), other drugs in Part Five, and unorthodox alternatives in Part Six.

Let your interests be your guide. If you want to know whether a popular diet is for you or whether you need certain vitamin supplements, see Part Two. If you wonder about the appeal and hazards of cocaine or marijuana, turn to Chapter 5-4. If close relatives have died at an early age from heart disease, stroke, or cancer, and you think you might be at risk, you'll find what you need to know in Part Four. If you want to know the truth about laetrile, chiropractic, or homeopathy, see Part Six. Read the table of contents and scan the book so you'll know how it's organized.

If you want information about a specific subject, you can find it through the tables of contents or the index. Notice that the table of contents for the whole book is a mere outline and that each of the seven parts has its own detailed list of components.

While not everyone will want to read the entire volume, there are large chunks that are important to all. Almost everyone should read most of Parts One and Two on fitness and nutrition. Most readers will also be interested in parts of Part Three on sex and reproduction; sexually active persons should read Chapter 3-3 on sexually transmitted diseases; and women should read Chapter 3-5, Common Female Problems.

In Part Four you should read about all the disorders you have had or think you might be susceptible to, or that you want to understand because loved ones have them or you are simply curious. In Part Five you should read about all the nonprescription and prescription drugs, medicinal herbs, and recreational drugs you use, are tempted to use, or are curious about.

Part Six covers an area of growing importance, the many unorthodox and controversial alternative methods of preventing, diagnosing, and healing. Here we provide objective critiques of these systems so you can make intelligent decisions about them.

Everyone should at least skim Part Seven, then reread the relevant sections if there is any question about whether to consult a physician. The alphabetical arrangement of symptoms makes for easy reference. There is a glossary at the end to save you trips to the dictionary.

Health maintainence is an art as well as a science, and conclusions are always subject to revision based on more knowledge. The information we provide is for general educational purposes and should not be construed as prescriptions for individuals. You should always take your physician's advice if it seems to contradict what we present here. (In some cases, however, you may want to seek a second medical opinion.)

KURT BUTLER writes two regular newspaper columns entitled "HealthWise" and "Health Advocate." Those columns and this book are an outgrowth of his belief that the need for widespread health education is every bit as important as the need for doctors. Butler holds a bachelor of science degree in physiology from the University of California at Berkeley; he completed a master of science degree in food and nutritional sciences at the University of Hawaii. He has taught in high schools for a number of years, and helped found the Quackery Action Council (QAC, Haleiwa, HI, 96712), a non-profit research and education group.

LYNN RAYNER, M.D., is on the staff of Straub Clinic in Hawaii. Dr. Rayner graduated from the University of California at San Francisco, where she was a member of the honorary medical society Alpha Omega Alpha. She completed her residency in medicine in Hawaii, including a year as chief medical resident, and was board certified in internal medicine in 1976. Besides her work at Straub, she is assistant professor of medicine at the John A. Burns School of Medicine, University of Hawaii.

Both Kurt Butler and Dr. Rayner live on Oahu.

1

Exercise and Fitness

PART ONE

Introduction: Born To Move

Chapter 1   Fitness versus Fatness

Chapter 2   How Exercise Improves Health

Chapter 3   How Much Exercise Is Best?

Chapter 4   How Fit or Fat Are You?

Chapter 5   The Best Fitness Activities

Chapter 6   Exercise and Nutrition

Chapter 7   The Prevention and Treatment of
Common Sports Injuries

Chapter 8   Sports and Drugs

Born To Move

Humans are commonly thought to differ from animals primarily in the areas of tool-making, language, laughter, and other manifestations of intelligence and mental capacity; but human physical feats are just as impressive. There are, of course, swifter and stronger animals, and those that can fly and do other things humans need mechanical aids to accomplish. But what animal could keep up with a physically fit human as he or she runs ten miles, swims three more, climbs a fifty-foot tree, and throws twenty rocks a hundred yards with great accuracy? Just to show off, a short ballet and gymnastics demonstration could be added.

We are clearly as gifted physically as we are mentally, which is not surprising since the human mind and body evolved together; the intelligence to understand what is needed for food and shelter would be worthless without the physical strength, stamina, and dexterity to go get them.

Since the rise of agriculture, and especially since the industrial revolution, most of us no longer need much physical strength and stamina to put food on the table, and we tend to be much more sedentary than our hunting and gathering ancestors. But our biology has not changed in this short time; we are still born to move. Children naturally enjoy roaming and romping, skipping, jumping, running, and climbing. People who lose this natural exuberance and do not get regular exercise become more susceptible to obesity and a variety of health problems, including atherosclerosis and heart disease, osteoporosis, diabetes, hypertension, constipation, hemorrhoids, and mental depressions.

3

1

Fitness versus Fatness

Consider two extremes: a triathlon finisher who swims a couple miles, bicycles about a hundred, then runs twenty-six, all in less than ten hours; and a sedentary office worker who would strain to walk a fast mile. There are visible and invisible differences between them associated with the tremendous differences in performances. Even if they are the same height and weight, if they hold still in a swimming pool the athlete will sink rapidly, while the unfit person will sink slowly or not at all: he has more fat in his body and fat floats. Muscle tissue is denser and it sinks. Sedentary people can get fat without appearing fat. Their muscles lose fibers and become marbled with fat, like the prime steaks (muscles) from grain-fed, penned-up cattle. The sedentary worker, though he may weigh only 175 pounds, may have fifty pounds of fat, while the triathloner at the same weight has only five pounds of fat, which still provides more than enough calories for the event.

Fitness, of course, is a matter of degree, not an all-or-nothing state. Most people fall somewhere along the spectrum between the sedentary office worker and the triathloner. Methods of estimating one's place on the spectrum are outlined in Chapter 1–4.

As fitness increases fatness decreases. There is a fundamental relationship here. Critics of the fitness approach to weight control say the value of exercise is limited because it does not burn enough calories to be effective, especially at the moderate levels most people find practical and enjoyable. They say that running only burns about ten calories a minute, so most people would have to run at least a mile to work off only 100 calories. This argument misses the point. Exercise does use surprisingly few calories, but the fit person has a higher rate of metabolism and burns more fat all the time, not just during exercise. This is because exercise develops muscles, bones, and fat-burning enzymes that gobble up fat; the lean tissue needs to be "fed" around the clock.[1]

Fatness Is Metabolic—but Changeable

This section explains the physiologic difference between fitness and fatness. If you find it rough going, just read the last paragraph, "A fat person can become a fit person," and sail on.

The difference between fitness and fatness is metabolic: not only do fit persons have less fat, they have more capacity to burn it for energy. The challenge for the fat person is to increase his metabolism and change it to a fat-burning system.

Consider a muscle cell. At rest it gets the little energy it needs by simultaneously metabolizing fat and glucose (blood sugar) step by step, with a specific enzyme catalyzing each step. Fat requires lots of oxygen for each step in its metabolism. Glucose requires very little oxygen for the first steps in its metabolism, its breakdown to pyruvate (which provides a small amount of energy), but lots of oxygen to complete the job by converting the pyruvate to carbon dioxide and water. Now, if the muscle is called upon to work (contract), its energy requirement increases enormously. If there is enough oxygen delivered to the cell by efficient heart and lung action, and if the cell has enough fat-metabolizing enzymes, this extra energy requirement can be met by burning mostly fat.

However, if the person is not fit the oxygen cannot be delivered fast enough by the heart and lungs, and the cell's supply of fat-burning enzymes is low, so the cell relies on the essentially anaerobic (non-oxygen-requiring) first steps of glucose metabolism to get the energy needed. The glucose is stored in the muscle and liver as glycogen, which is drawn upon in anaerobic metabolism.

The cell also gets some energy from the anaerobic first steps of the metabolism of amino acids, which are supplied largely by the breakdown of muscle protein. The resulting pyruvate (from both glucose and amino acids) is converted to lactic acid which accumulates until the muscle rests and enough oxygen is available to complete its metabolism to carbon dioxide and water.

In the fat person the inefficient oxygen delivery system and the poor capacity to burn fat force the cells to resort to using the glucose stores and cannibalising other muscle cells for the needed energy. This causes

6 How Fit or Fat?
Comparison of a Fit Jogger and a Fat Jogger

The Fit Person

Efficient respiratory system with high capacity to take up oxygen for delivery to muscles; strong efficient heart with lower pulse at any level of activity

1 Supplies reserved for sprint at end of run

2 Little protein used for energy

3 No build-up except during sprint

4 Large supply of fatty acid oxidase, the fat-burning enzyme; much fat used for energy

5 Efficient respiratory and circulatory systems supply plenty of oxygen for fat breakdown

The Fat Person

Less efficient respiratory system with lower capacity to take up oxygen for delivery to muscles; less efficient heart with higher pulse at any level of activity

1 Supplies used up rapidly in moderate exercise

2 More protein broken down for energy

3 Builds up rapidly; causes muscle fatigue

4 Low supply of fatty acid oxidase, the fat-burning enzyme; little fat used for energy

5 Inefficient respiratory and circulatory systems supply plenty of oxygen for fat metabolism

Here is how a muscle cell derives energy from sugar, amino acids, and fatty acids:

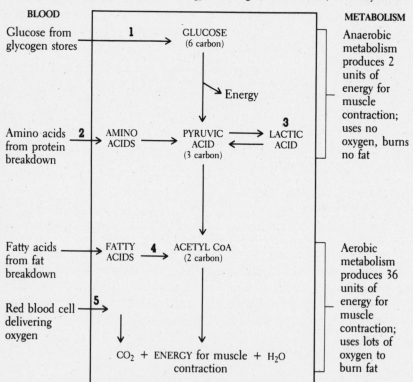

lactic acid build-up and fatigue, which force the end of the exercise before appreciable fat is used up.

In the fit person the oxygen can be delivered rapidly and the cell has a large supply of fat-metabolizing enzymes, so fat is burned to get the energy needed, and the glycogen and protein are largely spared. The exercise can continue for several hours without excessive lactic acid build-up or fatigue.

A fat person can become a fit person. Except in cases of rare genetic disorders, everyone has the potential to increase fitness and decrease fatness. The conversion from fat to fit may be somewhat more difficult in those who were overfed in infancy and early childhood because they have an excess of fat cells,[2] but no one is doomed to be forever fat. The fat person can increase his vital capacity, level of fat-burning enzymes, muscle size, mitochondria (cell-energy factory) concentration, muscle capillary density, blood-flow capacity, and muscle strength.

The Vicious Cycle of Obesity

Here is the bind the fat person is in: exercise is needed to increase fat-burning capacity, but, with little such capacity to begin with, exercise uses up available glucose quickly, blood sugar plummets, and weakness and hunger set in. The exercise ends and the eating begins. This is in sharp contrast to the fit person, who uses fat instead of blood sugar during exercise and does not get tired and hungry. In fact, exercise tends to decrease his appetite temporarily.

The Way Out:
Aerobic Exercise

The vicious cycle of obesity can be broken by a regular program of the right kind of exercise. Suppose the unfit person exercises just hard enough to get the fat-burning machinery working at full capacity but not hard enough to overwhelm it and start using primarily glucose and amino acids for energy. Lactic acid will not accumulate, blood sugar will not drop precipitously, and fatigue and hunger will not set in. At the right pace the body can continue for a long time to burn fat and stimulate muscle DNA to produce more fat-burning enzymes.

If this kind of exercise is done regularly the mass and tone of the muscles increase while the muscle chemistry changes. The metabolic rate increases and more fat is burned off, even during sleep. These changes will

8   continue as long as the mild but prolonged exercise continues. Slack off and the fat-burning machinery will start to degenerate, the muscles will lose their tone, and the body will eventually revert to the glucose burner that gets tired and hungry easily.

Not all exercise is equally beneficial. In dynamic exercise such as walking, running, swimming, and pedaling, there is rhythmic contraction and relaxation of flexor and extensor muscle groups, which promotes blood flow through the arteries as well as venous return to the heart. At the right pace such activities can be continued for long periods.

On the other hand, in isometric exercises (in which muscles are held in contraction for prolonged periods) the sustained contraction limits blood flow by compressing the small arteries and fails to help pump venous blood back to the heart. Moreover, the acute increase of blood pressure associated with isometrics can be very hazardous to persons with heart disease or high blood pressure.

Dynamic exercise is not always aerobic (oxygen using). To be effective the exercise must be vigorous enough to mobilize fat and stimulate fat burning, but not so vigorous as to metabolize glucose and protein for energy.

This happy medium varies a great deal from person to person. The more fit one is, the harder he or she can work out and still burn primarily fat. The less fit must go more slowly to keep the metabolism aerobic and fat-burning. The triathloner can run, swim, and bicycle for several hours at a good speed, burning fat for most of the required energy, while the fat person may slip into anaerobic metabolism walking a fast mile. For more on how vigorous exercise should be, see Chapter 1–3.

2

How Exercise
Improves Health

It has been proposed that proper training at the marathon level provides absolute protection from coronary artery disease and heart attack. There have been some exceptions to this hypothesis, even among those who have apparently trained properly, but they have been few. There can probably never be absolute protection from heart attack, but there is little doubt that fitness does provide an edge. Overweight people tend to be more susceptible to a number of serious health problems[3] (including diabetes, hypertension, heart disease, and gallbladder disorders), and there is no better way to shed fat than to exercise regularly.

The following is a summary of the most important beneficial effects of exercise.

The heart's size, strength, and efficiency are increased. The heart, like any muscle, responds to exercise by growing larger and stronger. The unfit person's heart is small and thin-walled, and it pumps small amounts of blood with each contraction. With proper exercise it can increase in muscle mass, double in chamber volume, and greatly improve in efficiency. Being more efficient, the heart can pump more blood per beat, so it beats less rapidly for a given level of activity.

The resting pulse of a highly trained athlete may be as low as 35 beats a minute, compared to 70 to 100 for an unfit person. If a sedentary person starts exercising at about 75 percent capacity for twenty minutes every other day, his resting and exercise heart rates will decrease about one beat per minute for each week of the program. With prolonged, intensive training, the maximum heart output per minute can be doubled to as much as 40 liters per minute.

10 **Heart muscle circulation is improved.** Oxygen-carrying blood is supplied to the heart muscle by two arteries arising from the aorta (which carries oxygenated blood out of the largest heart chamber, the left ventricle). These coronary arteries branch into smaller and smaller arteries which form a network that can shunt blood to any area of the heart muscle. During heavy exercise these channels open wide.

Animal studies and clinical observations indicate that regular aerobic exercise increases this network of tiny arteries as well as the size of the coronary arteries. Should one of these arteries get plugged (coronary occlusion), a well-developed network can provide adequate blood to the whole heart until the blockage is cleared. Without this detour system, a region of heart muscle could go without blood long enough to damage it and cause a heart attack.[4]

Blood cholesterol can be lowered. Cholesterol is carried in the blood by different proteins, or lipoproteins: high-density (HDL), low-density (LDL) and very-low-density lipoproteins (VLDL). LDL-cholesterol appears to be a significant factor in the formation of fatty plaques, while HDL-cholesterol appears to be protective. Exercise tends to decrease the LDL form and increase the HDL form, thereby reducing the formation of fatty plaques in the arteries.[5]

Clot formation is made less likely by exercise, which enhances fibrinolysis, the body's mechanism for dissolving dangerous blood clots which cause stroke or heart attack.

High blood pressure can often be reduced to safe levels, especially if aerobic exercise is accompanied by proper diet. However, blood pressure may be increased dangerously in those with hypertension, so careful monitoring is essential.

Glucose tolerance, which is poor in diabetes and often heart disease, can be improved. Type 2 diabetes, the more common type, can often be prevented or kept under control without drugs with good nutrition and regular exercise. In this case, staying fit clearly helps prevent or delay blindness, loss of limbs, and other complications of diabetes, including death.

Exercise promotes muscle and bone development by increasing blood levels of anabolic hormones such as growth hormone and testosterone. The risk of osteoporosis developing is greatly decreased by regular exercise. Increased levels of the latter hormone may also tend to increase libido. However, overexercise may decrease bone strength and libido. See Chapter 1-3.

Apparent Effects of Aging That Can Be Modified by Exercise

Increased blood pressure

Decreased cardiac output

Increased tendency to clot formation and thrombotic disease

Increased blood fat and cholesterol

Fatty degeneration of the arteries

Reduced maximum oxygen consumption

Protein wastage; loss of lean body tissue

Calcium wastage; bone weakening

Insensitivity to insulin; poor glucose tolerance

Lower levels of dopamine, norepinephrine, other neurotransmitters

Sleep disturbances

Tendency to depression

Decreased immune function

Lower testosterone levels

Stressful emotions and depression, which some experts believe are factors in coronary artery disease and heart attacks, can be reduced. Studies have shown reduced muscle tension and anxiety levels, and increased self-confidence and emotional stability. Many people exercise simply because it makes them feel good for hours after. Some psychiatrists are prescribing running to their depressed and anxious patients and the results are often very good, with great improvements in mood and ability to function.[6]

Beneficial effects on the mind may also include improved concentration, memory, creativity, and mental speed and stamina. This effect may be due to improved cerebral circulation resulting from general cardiovascular improvement.

Stress resistance is a general benefit of fitness. A person who is fit and strong with muscles full of fat-burning enzymes is more capable of withstanding a sudden illness, injury, surgery, and possibly heavy emotional stress such as grief than a physically weak and unfit person. His or her body is less susceptible to wasting, and if wasting does occur it can continue far longer before causing a crisis. In emergencies requiring prolonged swimming, running, or walking for safety or for help, the fit person has a clear advantage. In short, the reserve of strength and stamina can speed recovery and tip the balance in favor of life in many critical situations.

12   **Added fun** is a major benefit of being fit rather than fat. Whether hiking in the hills, strolling on a beach, or snorkling on a coral reef, the fit person can go much farther and longer and see and do more with much less effort than the fat person.

A decreased rate of aging seems to be the net effect, the sum of the above individual effects, of regular exercise. The degenerative changes common to many body tissues and functions can be slowed by exercise. Nonathletes experience a reduction of "maximum oxygen consumption," probably the most reliable indicator of fitness and life expectancy available, of about 1 percent per year. Proper exercise can reduce this and effectively decrease the rate of aging. Regular exercise maintained over a lifetime holds much more potential as a "fountain of youth" than any drugs or nutritional supplements available or even on the drawing boards.[7]

3

How Much Exercise Is Best?

ost people fall somewhere between the extremes of fitness and fatness discussed in Chapter 1-1 but are not sure where. Guidelines are needed to assure an adequate workout and prevent overdoing it. One approach is to simply walk, run, swim, dance, or bicycle at a steady pace as fast as you can without breathlessness when you talk. Another rule of thumb is that you should feel *good* after the exercise, not exhausted. These guidelines are probably adequate for most people, but some prefer a more precise approach.

The 75 Percent Rule

One widely used rule of thumb is to exercise at a level that makes your heart beat at about 75 percent of its maximum rate, the very fastest it could be driven to beat. Some say 80 percent, but we'll play it safe. Up to the age of 20 the maximum rate is about 200 beats per minute. This decreases to about 150 beats per minute according to the formula

maximum heart rate = 220 minus age

So the proper training rate to aim for is given by the formula

training rate = .75 × (220 − age)

For example, a forty-year-old person should aim for a training rate

14   of 135 beats per minute. If the person is not fit, brisk walking might be all it takes to get there. If he or she is fit, it would take jogging or running.

The Five-Minute and Ten-Minute Rules

If five minutes after you stop exercising your pulse is above 120 beats per minute, you went too hard or too long.

If ten minutes after you stop exercising your breathing rate is more than 16 per minute, you went too hard or too long.

To measure your pulse, use the finger tips rather than the thumb to avoid counting your thumb pulse. Count the beats in ten seconds and multiply by six to get your beats per minute. The pulse can be felt on the inside of the wrist, on the side of the neck, or just in front of the ear in the temple area. It may be necessary to stop the exercise, but with practice the pulse can be measured while walking or jogging. A battery-operated, digital pulse gauge simplifies matters greatly, but before relying on one, test its accuracy against a good watch.

How Often and How Long Should You Exercise?

The benefits of aerobic exercise begin to be significant with regular workouts of about fifteen consecutive minutes every other day. Two eight- or ten-minute workouts are of less benefit than a nonstop fifteen-minute session. The duration and frequency can be steadily increased as fitness improves.

The amount of exercise required for maximum protection from heart disease is a controversial issue. Twenty nonstop minutes of aerobic exercise every other day clearly improves fitness and reduces the risk of cardiovascular disease. While some experts believe that more exercise than this improves the situation only a little, there is evidence that improvement increases at the higher levels, up to about thirty minutes every day and possibly more.[8] However, as exercise increases, so does the risk of harm from overexercise. To be sure of substantial benefits while avoiding the point of diminishing returns, twenty minutes of aerobic exercise every day is a happy medium for most people. Thirty minutes every *other* day is another effective option worth considering.

Why Overexercise Is Harmful   15

It is important not to exceed your capacity for exercise, or you will do more harm than good. Exercising at a level that makes the heart beat at or near its maximum capacity forces the muscles into more anaerobic metabolism which quickly uses up the available glucose and increases the breakdown of muscle tissue. There is always some degree of muscle breakdown during prolonged exercise. Normally the lost tissue is more than replaced over the next twenty-four hours. But if exercise resumes before full recovery, there will be a net loss of muscle tissue rather than a gain.

Repeated for many days, overexercise can result in a significant loss of muscle mass and fat-burning capacity. The older a person is, the more likely this is to occur because tissue repair tends to slow down with age. People who consistently overexercise in a compulsive effort to get in shape end up feeling sore and tired and in worse condition than before they started.

Most important, **overexercise can precipitate a heart attack,** even in apparently healthy persons. Do not ignore symptoms such as tightness or pain in the chest, dizziness, light-headedness, stomach pain, or breathing trouble. This cannot be over emphasized. Failure to heed symptoms with rest and a check-up have cost even experienced runners their lives. For example, the popular fitness writer Jim Fixx, who had a family history of early heart disease, apparently ignored early warning symptoms in the days before his much-publicized fatal heart attack while jogging in July of 1984.

One forty-nine-year-old runner began having chest pains eight kilometers into a race, but kept going. He had a massive heart attack six kilometers later.

Another runner, said by his wife to be obsessed with training, put these words on his T-shirt: "You haven't really run a good marathon until you drop dead at the finish line—Pheidippides." He did just that a week later.

Another man had trouble breathing after running a marathon, yet raced his wife in a final dash home, where he dropped dead.

Careful contemplation of these examples might save your life.

No pain, no gain? This little aphorism, which implies that exercise must make you feel miserable or it is not beneficial, is **absolutely false.** On the contrary, exercise that causes pain and exercising while experiencing pain can lead to severe injuries. True, in intensive body-building programs the muscles one is trying to build should burn after they are worked; but in the moderate to intensive aerobic training programs, which are more beneficial to cardiovascular fitness and general health, there is no reason to experience pain in order to gain.

16 Exercise and Illness

Some people are so enthusiastic about their exercise routines that they will not skip them for anything, not even illness. This is a serious mistake. In illness, even a cold or flu, tissue repair is greatly slowed and exercise causes substantial muscle breakdown. Even the heart muscle can be inflamed and damaged; fatal rhythm disturbances may occur. **Rest is essential when one is sick.**

Proper exercise can be very beneficial for persons with hypertension or diabetes, but a vigorous exercise program should not be started without consulting a physician to discuss the intensity, frequency, and possible adjustments in drug therapy. Persons susceptible to exercise-associated asthma attacks should discuss the problem with their physicians; there is usually no reason to discontinue activities, but some adjustments may be in order.

4

How Fit or Fat Are You?

The upper limit of healthy fat percentage is about 20 to 25 for men and 25 to 30 for women. More fat than this is considered unhealthy, and there are good reasons for substantially lower levels, especially in men. Most athletic men are under 15 percent fat and our triathloner in Chapter 1–1 is only about 3 percent fat. Women who get too thin may develop symptoms of estrogen insufficiency such as anovulation, ameorrhea, and bone thinning (osteoporosis). Problems seem to start at about 20 percent fat for the most susceptible women, but some women can be 15 percent fat or less and remain fertile and healthy.[9] In this sense, it appears that some women are genetically determined to be, or at least allowed to be, less fat than others.

How fat are you? Fat percentage can be estimated by an experienced person, usually a nutritionist, dietician, or nurse, using calipers to measure the thickness of the fat layer under the skin. In the most accurate tests, measurements are done on the back of the upper arm, the back of the thigh, the abdomen, and the back. The results are meaningless unless done by a trained person using standardized procedures.

Fat content can also be estimated by underwater weighing. The person sits on a chair hung from a scale and is lowered into a large water tank. The more he weighs under water, the less fat he has. Some weight reducing clinics, research centers, and college athletic departments have underwater weighing facilities.

To get a rough idea of your fat percentage without an underwater scale, consider these estimates:

18

In *fresh water*, if you float easily your fat content is greater than 25 percent.

If you float only with your lungs full you are about 22 percent fat.

If you sink slowly but definitely even with your lungs full, you are less than 20 percent fat.

In *salt water*, if you sink even with your lungs full you are 13 percent fat or less.

These are rough estimates subject to error due to residual air in the digestive tract and lungs.

Another useful measure of fatness is the waist-to-hip ratio. A tape measure is used and the waist size is divided by the hip size. Ratios greater than .85 in women and .95 in men seem to be associated with a higher incidence of hypertension, diabetes, and other problems related to obesity.

None of these measures of fatness is highly precise, but they can provide useful approximations, especially if more than one is used. More information can be obtained from the measures of fitness, which are generally superior to the measures of fatness.

How fit are you? There are several ways of estimating your level of cardiovascular fitness. Direct measurement of maximum oxygen consumption is the most precise, but the others are also useful. None of the fitness measurements, which are based on averages of real performances, should be taken too seriously in themselves. The important thing is to make steady progress in your performance; the tests are useful guides for measuring your progress.

The Maximum Oxygen Consumption Test. Also known as aerobic power, this is the most precise measure of fitness. The subject walks or runs on a treadmill while his oxygen consumption is monitored. The maximum rate, adjusted for weight, is a clear indicator of the efficiency of the heart and lungs in getting oxygen to the working muscles as well as the capacity of the muscles to use it.

Aerobic power can increase with training for about eighteen months of optimum effort, then it levels off at a plateau probably determined by each person's genes. Further training cannot take a person beyond his genetic capacity for aerobic power.

The Resting Pulse Test. A fast pulse at rest may be a sign of a weak heart. As fitness increases, the heart becomes more efficient (pumps more with each beat) and the resting rate decreases. In very fit athletes it can go as low as 35 beats per minute. More common (and not far from unhealthy) is about

70 for men and 80 for women; 75 and 85, respectively, are clear signs of lack of fitness in apparently healthy persons. Keep in mind, though, that caffeine and other drugs, as well as anxiety and excitement, can speed up the heart.

The Pulse Reduction Test. After prolonged exercise, the heart slows to its resting rate in two stages. The first drop is the largest and most significant and usually occurs within the first minute. The second reduction occurs several minutes to an hour later. The significance of its rate is not clear. The first reduction is used to determine one's level of fitness. A commonly used formula to gauge recovery rate is:

Recovery Rate = exercise pulse − one-minute pulse

The recovery rate is the measure of how fast the pulse slows down after exercise. The exercise pulse is obtained while standing still or walking slowly, immediately after exercise. Count the beats in the first ten seconds after the exercise and multiply by six. This is the exercise pulse. Repeat after one minute for the one-minute pulse.

A recovery rate of less than 20 is considered a sign of poor fitness; 30 is about average. More than 40 is excellent; more than 60 is super.

The Five-Minute and Twelve-Minute Tests. Dr. Kenneth Cooper, the popular fitness advocate, and other physiologists have developed standardized tests and methods of estimating fitness levels. Years of data collecting from thousands of subjects of all ages have led to detailed tables for twelve-minute tests for running/walking, swimming, and cycling. The point of the test is to cover as much ground as you can in twelve minutes (without exceeding about 80 percent of your maximum heart rate unless you are very fit). Other researchers have come up with a five-minute test, which would seem an inferior measure of aerobic capacity, which implies stamina. There will probably be other tests. Most people need consider only the following simple facts.[10]

Assuming the test is for at least five minutes, and preferably more, up to about fifteen minutes, among healthy, nonhandicapped men under sixty, the range of performance is about 140 to 270 yards per minute. The range for women is about 120 to 220.

If you can cover 200 yards a minute (say, 1,000 yards in five minutes), your fitness level is fair if your are a man under fifty, good if you are older. A good performance by a younger man would be at least 220 yards per minute.

For a woman, 200 yards per minute is good if she is in her twenties and excellent if she is in her fifties.

The goal should be to improve fitness until performance is in the "good" range and keep it constant or increasing from year to year. This gets

20 The National Fitness Test

prepared by the National Fitness Foundation

Sit and reach

How far can you reach?
A partner can hold your knees down.
Don't lunge.

Curl-ups

A partner can hold your feet flat on the
floor. Come up only about half
way to the vertical. Come up
smoothly; don't jerk.
Keep hands on floor.

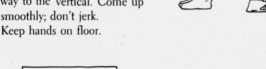

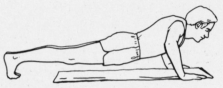

Push-ups

How many can you do in 90 seconds?
Men, keep legs straight, knees off the floor;
lower to 4 inches from the floor.
Women, keep knees on the floor; touch
chest to floor.

Step test

How fit is your heart?
Step onto the bench
24 times per minute
for 3 minutes. Sit
down. Starting 5
seconds after last step,
count your heart beats
in one minute.

Arm hang

How long can you hang on?
Hands face forward.
Bend legs slightly at knees.

National Fitness Test Score

Men	Age	18–29	30–39	40–49	50–59	60-plus
	Push-ups (90 secs.):					
	Gold	50+	45+	40+	35+	30+
	Silver	25–50	22–45	19–40	15–35	10–30
	Bronze	25	22	19	15	10
	Curl-ups (90 secs.):					
	Gold	50+	45+	40+	35+	30+
	Silver	30–50	22–45	21–40	18–35	15–30
	Bronze	0–30	0–22	0–21	0–18	0–15
	Sit & reach (inches)					
	Gold	21+	21+	20+	19+	19+
	Silver	13–21	13–21	13–20	12–19	12–19
	Bronze	0–13	0–13	0–13	0–12	0–12
	3-Minute step (heart rate)					
	Gold	to 75	to 78	to 80	to 85	to 90
	Silver	75–100	78–109	80–112	85–115	90–118
	Bronze	100+	109+	112+	115+	118+
	Arm hang (minutes)					
	Gold	2:00+	1:51+	1:35+	1:20+	1:10+
	Silver	1:00–2:00	:50–1:50	:45–1:35	:35–1:20	30–1:10
	Bronze	0–1:00	0–:50	0–:45	0–:35	0–:30
Women	**Age**	**18–29**	**30–39**	**40–49**	**50–59**	**60-plus**
	Push-ups (90 secs.):					
	Gold	45+	40+	33+	30+	25+
	Silver	17–45	12–40	8–35	6–30	4–25
	Bronze	0–17	0–12	0–8	0–6	0–5
	Curl-ups (90 secs.):					
	Gold	45+	40+	35+	30+	25+
	Silver	25–45	20–40	16–35	12–30	11–25
	Bronze	0–25	0–20	0–16	0–12	0–11
	Sit & reach (inches)					
	Gold	22+	22+	21+	20+	20+
	Silver	17–20	17–22	15–21	14–20	14–20
	Bronze	0–17	0–17	0–15	0–14	0–14
	3-Minute step (heart rate)					
	Gold	to 80	to 84	to 88	to 92	to 95
	Silver	80–110	84–115	88–118	92–123	95–127
	Bronze	110+	115+	118+	123+	127+
	Arm hang (minutes)					
	Gold	1:30+	1:20+	1:11+	1:00+	50+
	Silver	:46–1:30	:40–1:20	:30–1:10	:30–1:00	21–50
	Bronze	0–:46	0–:40	0–:30	0–:30	0–:30

22 harder as the decades go by and inevitably cardiovascular fitness and performance decline. But in the process of trying, many healthy years can be added to life.

The National Fitness Test, prepared by the National Fitness Foundation, measures flexibility and arm strength as well as cardiovascular fitness. The table shows how you rate. To get accurate results, the tests should be done exactly as described below.[11]

The Step Test: Stand facing a bench or table one foot high. Step up onto the bench with one foot, then the other, then down one foot at a time, then up with the other foot first, then down, and so on. Do twenty-four full steps per minute for three minutes, sit down, and count your pulse for one minute starting five seconds after you finish the exercise. Because the pace is critical, this test is difficult to do without a metronome.

Arm Hang: Grasp a bar with palms facing forward, keep your body straight and your feet off the ground. Hang on as long as you can.

Push-ups: Push-ups are done in the usual way with hands directly under shoulders. Women keep the knees on the floor and bend the elbows until the chest touches the floor, then push up until elbows are straight. Men keep the legs straight and knees off the floor, and lower the chest to touch an upright fist (or about four inches from the floor). Do as many as you can in 90 seconds.

Curl-ups: These are modified sit-ups. Lie on your back with your knees bent, feet flat, and hands on thighs. A partner can hold your feet down while you curl your head up, then your shoulders and upper trunk. Come up until fingers touch the middle of the knee-caps, then return. Do as many as you can in 90 seconds.

Sit and Reach: Sit with legs extended and heels about five inches apart. Place a yardstick between your legs with the 15-inch mark on a line between your heels. With a partner holding your knees straight, reach down the yardstick as far as you can with both hands. Do not lunge.

5

The Best Fitness Activities

Dynamic exercise which is rhythmic, steady, moderate in intensity, and prolonged has the most aerobic value and the most potential for improving fitness and health. Isometric exercises tend to inhibit efficient circulation and oxygen consumption, and they have little value in improving cardiovascular fitness. They are also hazardous to persons with atherosclerosis, heart disease, or high blood pressure because they tend to greatly increase blood pressure.

The aerobic value should be considered when choosing activities or exercises for fitness. The lower the value the longer an exercise must continue to provide the same fitness benefits. Of course, other factors are also important such as convenience, cost, practicality, and safety.

Surely the most important consideration in choosing fitness activities is pleasure. An activity that one enjoys will be performed more frequently and consistently than one that is a chore. Even if it has half the aerobic value, in the long run it will be more beneficial.

It is a good idea to switch exercises frequently so different muscles are developed and none is worked beyond its capacity for self-repair. This is especially true for persons over fifty who exercise every day since their tissue regeneration is slower than when they were younger. Switching exercises can also minimize stress injuries and prevent boredom with a single routine. Swimmers and cyclers should jog, jump rope, or dance periodically; a little of these more jarring exercises will help keep the bones strong.

If you are over thirty and have been sedentary for several months or years, you should be especially careful to work up to higher levels of exercise very gradually. Some experts advocate a stress test before embarking on a training program. This question is discussed in Chapter 1–7.

23

24   The following activities are listed approximately in order of their aerobic value and effectiveness in improving cardiovascular fitness.

Cross-country skiing is generally considered to be the very best aerobic exercise. It provides all the benefits of running without the jarring stresses on various tissues. The large leg muscles are used more than in swimming, and very high levels of oxygen consumption can be reached by the fit cross-country skier. Unfortunately, the sport is not accessible or affordable for most people, though it is much cheaper than downhill skiing. Some exercise devices mimic cross-country skiing very well and are excellent for skiers and nonskiers.

Jumping rope is quite strenuous and difficult to do for long periods. It is especially hard on the feet, Achilles' tendons, and knees, and the stress should be minimized by the use of a soft carpet and tennis, basketball, or running shoes, and alternating from foot to foot rather than jumping with both feet. Bouncing on a mini-trampoline is not hard on the joints, but it may not be strenuous enough to provide a good workout for those already in good shape.

Running in place and **jumping jacks** (the sissorslike jumping calisthetics most of us learn in P.E. classes) are convenient for almost everyone, but, like jumping rope, they can be rough on the feet, joints, and tendons. Stress can be minimized by using a soft carpet and good shoes.

Jogging and running are excellent aerobic exercises, but they can be quite stressful and can lead to injuries. During running the body absorbs the shock of about 150 foot-strikes a minute, each one transmitting a force of about four times the runner's weight to his heel, ankle, knee, hip, and lower back. In a survey of 1,000 runners, 60 percent said they had been injured for considerable periods. The most common injuries are of the knee, shin, Achilles' tendon, forefoot, hip, thigh, heel, ankle, arch, and groin, in that order. Almost a forth of those surveyed suffered knee injuries, and only 2 percent had groin injuries. Injury can be avoided by careful choice of shoes, running surfaces, and running habits. Some common running injuries are further discussed in Chapter 1–7.

Polluted air is another hazard to the jogger. Conflicting results have come from studies of strenuous exercise in polluted air, but there are indications that short-term damage can be done to the heart and lungs. The results of one study suggest that running near traffic for a half-hour increases the carbon monoxide in the blood the same amount as smoking ten to twenty cigarettes a day.[12] Yet most researchers feel that the benefits of exercise outweigh the risks except in the heaviest pollution. For urban joggers the best advice is probably to run in the morning and avoid the busiest roads. Warm and windless days tend to be worse. Pregnant women and persons with heart trouble should be especially careful.

Women and jogging. There has been some concern that the stress of the repeated impact of jogging could weaken the connective tissue supporting the uterus and drive it down so that it causes pressure on, and protrusion into, the vagina. These fears are unwarranted; surveys of thousands of women runners indicate the problem does not exist.

However, women who already have a prolapsed uterus (usually caused by giving birth several times) should be aware that running as well as lifting heavy weights and other stressful activities can aggravate the condition. They should be alert for a feeling of pressure on the vagina or leakage of urine when exercising. Running on soft grass with good shoes or on sand lessens the risk.

Jogging can cause breast sagging and pain. This problem can usually be prevented by wearing a sports bra which prevents lateral and spiraling motions of the breasts. The bra should not bind, but should be rigid enough to limit bouncing. It should have wide nonelastic straps, cotton cups, padded seams, and covered metal fasteners.

Women who regularly run or engage in other strenuous exercise and lose too much fat may develop symptoms of estrogen deficiency. This is discussed in Chapter 1–6. Aside from this and the fact that men appear to be more susceptible to heart attack and sudden death during and shortly after exercise than women, the main hazards of running are the same for both sexes, namely, stress injuries to muscles, bones, joints, and connective tissues.

Hiking and hill-climbing are excellent fitness activities, especially with a small pack on the back. Try to maintain a steady, brisk pace for at least a mile between breaks.

Aerobic dancing is a fitness program originally designed for people who find jogging inconvenient or boring. An aerobic dance session resembles a rehearsal for an amateur dance show. Accompanied by Broadway, rock, or disco music, the participants follow the leader in kneelifts, kickjumps, ballet reaches, and rhythmic running, hopping, jumping, stretching, and skipping.

A session should include at least ten minutes of stretching and warming-up exercises, fifteen to thirty minutes of nonstop aerobic movements at a pace determined by one's fitness and the 75 percent rule, and five minutes of cooling down activities such as walking and stretching. It is important to go at your own pace and not try to keep up with the leader or fastest person in the group.

Aerobic dancing can be very effective in improving fitness and shedding fat; even some professional sports teams have taken it up as an integral part of their training. However, the workouts in some commerical aerobic dance programs and some television shows are not intensive enough to provide significant benefits. Remember that, to be of real value, a workout should get your heart beat up to 75 percent of its maximum rate for at least fifteen minutes. Moreover, whether they are intensive enough or not they are stressful and can cause foot, leg, and back injuries, so good shoes and a resilient surface are necessary.

Rowing and paddling are good aerobic activities but not quite as beneficial as those that use the leg muscles more. Persons who enjoy these activities can reach high levels of fitness with a little supplementary running, bicycling, or dancing.

Walking should be brisk, nonstop for at least twenty minutes a session, and engaged in nearly every day. It will not take you to your maximum potential level of fitness, but it is much less likely to cause injuries than any other exercise that improves fitness.

Bicycling is in some ways the best exercise of all, although the peak oxygen load is not as great as with running or cross-country skiing. It is also much less stressful than running and other sports. Cycling has been increasing in popularity because we can fit it into our daily lives, saving energy and parking problems as we cycle to work, school, and shopping; but to be of significant benefit you must ride hard enough to increase your heart rate for at least fifteen minutes nonstop, which is often difficult in urban areas.

A human on a bicycle is the most efficient living locomotion system known, capable of moving a pound of flesh a given distance on less energy than a salmon, horse, pigeon, or bee. A large slice of bread can take you about five miles. This efficiency is a disadvantage in terms of fitness value.

A major problem with bicycling is that it is simply too dangerous in many areas. If this is true in your case you might consider a stationary cycle for your home.

Swimming is an excellent aerobic activity, and a regular program can develop a high level of fitness. However, the maximum oxygen capacity generally does not get as high as with running because the large upper leg muscles are not used as much. There seems to be a tendency for regular swimmers to retain upper-body fat. This is apparently an adaptation for warmth and bouyancy and does not interfere with fitness.

Ice and roller skating are aerobically valuable in theory, but all too often the

Calories Burned per Hour by Average Young Adults in Different Activities

These figures are averages useful for comparative purposes. Exact values depend on the person's weight, ambient temperature, and details of the activities.

Activity	Calories Burned per Hour
Sleeping	80
Standing at ease	120
Driving a car	140
Housework	140–250
Walking (2.5–4 mph)	300–350
Canoeing (2–4 mph)	200–450
Bicycling (5–10 mph)	200–450
Swimming (medium to fast)	300–700
Ping pong	350
Swimming underwater with fins, wetsuit	400–1,000
Skating (roller, ice)	400
Tennis	450
Hill climbing	500
Handball, racquetball	600
Jogging	700
Walking in loose snow with a 20-pound load	900
Cross-country skiing	600–1100

skating area is too small, crowded, and dangerous to allow a high-speed, prolonged workout.

Tennis, racquetball, basketball, and Ping Pong can be very tiring, but they consist largely of bursts of action, and are not as aerobically valuable as steady, smooth, continuous movements. It has been estimated that jogging at the proper rate for fifteen minutes is worth an hour or more of these sports, but this depends on how fast and vigorously the games are played.

Baseball, football, and volleyball are even less effective since they consist mostly of standing around between short bursts of mostly anaerobic move-

28 ments. However, a brisk game of two-on-two volleyball can be valuable, especially if played on sand between players good enough to keep long volleys going. Baseball and football players keep in shape with jogging, sprinting, and other exercises during practice, not by playing their games.

Can work be good exercise? Some people think they get enough exercise because they do a lot of housework, gardening, carpentry, or other strenuous work. However, such work is usually done in short bursts rather than in sustained output at a proper training rate and, strenuous though it may be, has little aerobic value. The muscular construcion worker is often unfit because he feels too tired to exercise after work. However, some workers, such as pedestrian letter carriers and longshoremen with the more active jobs, do gain substantial aerobic benefit from their work. And even some domestic chores, such as lawn-mowing, raking, and mopping, can be good workouts if they raise the heart rate to the training level for at least twenty minutes.

6

Exercise and Nutrition

he many books, articles, and commercials about special diets and supplements athletes supposedly need are largely nonsense. Does a moderate fitness program or accelerated training for a marathon change a person's nutritional requirements? Yes and no. For the most part, athletes in training should eat the same food less active people eat but more of it. The exceptions to this can be summed up in a few short paragraphs.

Water is the nutrient most affected by exercise. Dehydration can cause headache and fatigue and progress to heatstroke, collapse, and if the condition is severe and untreated, even death. Ample amounts of water should be drunk before, during, and after prolonged exercise, especially in hot weather. In general, enough water should be taken to keep the urine clear or slightly yellow; this will usually be more than is dictated by thirst, at least one cup for each fifteen minutes of exercise. Bright yellow urine is a sign of inadequate fluid intake unless it is caused by a recent large dose of B vitamins or brewer's yeast.

Some people advise against taking ice-cold drinks during and after exercise. They believe the cold may set off reflexes that result in spasms of the coronary arteries, heart arrythmias, and heart attack. There is no good evidence for this belief and we are unaware of any reported cases. The biggest hazard seems to be a wave of nausea or brief headache.

Salt lost from sweating needs to be replaced, but salt tablets should generally not be taken even if it is hot and you sweat a lot. This is because too much salt can upset the electrolyte balance and promote heat stroke. It is better to

30 drink lightly salted water (a quarter-teaspoon per quart) and moderately salt your food if you have a craving for it. Persons with hypertension who want to exercise regularly should discuss with their physicians their need to take or avoid salt.

Calorie intake generally must be increased if exercise is increased. The exception is the obese person who wants to combine moderate exercise with moderate calorie restriction. Those who are not fat and maintain a constant calorie intake while involved in an accelerating exercise program risk losing lean tissue, especially muscle mass, and thereby becoming less fit and less strong.

Women especially are likely to be harmed by heavy exercise and inadequate calorie intake. Continued over several months the combination can lead to estrogen deficiency symptoms, including anovulation, amenorrhea, and insidious bone thinning. No special diet or supplements are required to prevent the problems, just an increased intake of all the good foods one presumably eats.[13]

Protein requirement is not increased by moderate exercise, but heavy exercise can result in excessive protein breakdown and nitrogen loss, in which case extra protein might be of value. High-level training that significantly adds to muscle mass may slightly increase the protein requirement, but the added food intake that comes naturally usually takes care of it. There is no need to gorge on high-protein foods, nor are protein supplements (powders, pills, liquids) necessary or desirable. However, vegetarians, especially vegans (vegetarians who avoid dairy and other animal products), would be prudent to eat more high-protein foods like tofu, nuts, and seeds.

Potassium must be replenished daily to prevent weakness, fatigue, irritability, and other signs of deficiency. Problems are especially likely for those taking diuretics or suffering from diarrhea. The best sources of potassium are fruits and vegetables and their juices. Persons with hypertension who want to exercise regularly should discuss their potassium needs with their physicians.

Iron is sometimes in low supply in athletes, especially marathoners and women.[14] Prolonged exercise tends to increase the excretion of iron in the sweat, urine, and feces. Anemia itself, the lack of adequate hemoglobin in the blood, is not very common, but low blood stores, determined by blood ferritin levels, can cause some of the same problems as anemia, including reduced performance, fatigue, headache, and muscle cramping. Once the condition occurs, iron supplements and careful monitoring of blood ferritin will be necessary. It can usually be prevented with a good diet (see Part Two), but supplements may be in order for those who train at the marathon level. Because excess iron can accumulate in the liver and muscles, where it is toxic, doses larger than the RDA (10 milligrams for men, 18 for women) should not be taken without consulting a physician.

Magnesium is excreted in the stool in large amounts if one exercises heavily, and deficiency can cause cramps and chronic fatigue. Good sources are nuts, seeds, leafy greens, whole grains, and magnesium-oxide tablets. We would advise against dolomite unless the manufacturer can guarantee it to be lead-free.

Vitamin requirements are not increased by exercise beyond what increased food consumption will provide. There is no evidence that massive doses of vitamin E or any other nutrient can improve athletic performance or stamina. There is no need for anyone to take commercial vitamin preparations supposedly formulated for athletes and other active persons.

Carbohydrate loading is a popular method of increasing stamina for extreme endurance competition. While fit persons burn fat very effectively for energy, it is desirable to have large reserves of glucose (stored as glycogen in the muscles and liver) available for anaerobic metabolism in the stretch. Training increases muscle glycogen storage capacity, which promotes stamina and sprint capacity for the end of the race.

The idea in carbo loading, as it is commonly called, is to pack the muscle cells with as much glycogen as possible just before the race. One method that seems to work is to exercise to full capacity and eat your normal diet for a week before the race; then exercise lightly for three days on the same diet; then exercise lightly for three days on a very-high-carbohydrate diet; then rest and splurge on carbos on the last day. It's best to eat lots of whole grains, potatoes, beans, fruits, and vegetables, and not fill up on sugary foods. Contrary to the common belief, athletic performance is not improved by a high-sugar snack just before exercise. In fact, the sugar may prevent optimum performance and promote early fatigue.[15]

Before the three-day high-carbohydrate diet, some people insert three days of carbohydrate depletion, which supposedly increases carbohydrate storage capacity. This is unproven, and the practice, accomplished by fasting or a high-protein and high-fat diet, followed by carbohydrate loading for three days before the marathon, may cause muscle or liver damage or abnormal heart metabolism and rhythms.

Carbo loading can cause substantial weight gain due to water retained with the glycogen. This presents no problems; it is quickly lost in the competition.

The very fit person burns about 80 percent fat during a marathon and probably does not benefit from carbohydrate loading.

7

The Prevention and Treatment of Common Sports Injuries

hile exercise can be beneficial, there are also certain hazards, some of them serious. With awareness and care the risks can be minimized. Most injuries and health problems associated with exercise have the same basic cause, the overstressing of muscles, tendons, ligaments, bones, or other tissues. There are certain general principles to follow in all exercises to avoid many kinds of injuries. The most important is to know your body's limits and warning signals and not push yourself too hard. The following principles are also very important.

Drink plenty of water. Before, during, and after prolonged exercise (more than fifteen minutes), drink enough water to keep the urine clear or light yellow. Otherwise there is a risk of dehydration and heat stroke, especially in hot weather.

Do not eat a heavy meal within a couple hours of starting heavy or prolonged exercise. After eating, blood concentrates in the digestive organs, and not enough is available to keep the skeletal muscles and heart going at a fast clip for long. Exercising hard soon after (or before) eating can lead to indigestion, stomach cramps, and side stitches. In extreme cases, especially if coronary artery disease is present (though perhaps silent so far), eating and exercising too close together can contribute to a heart attack. On the other hand, you don't want to go into prolonged exercise on the verge of hunger, so plan ahead.

Stretching muscles and tendons is appropriate before most activities in order to prevent a variety of stress injuries, especially tendon rupture. Stretching should always be done slowly and gently, especially in the morning when muscles are cooler and more susceptible to injury. (See illustrations.)

Warming up slowly before exercising hard is very important in avoiding stress injuries, especially muscle cramps, pains, and strains. Proper warm up involves the use of the muscles in the same way as in the main event, but much slower and with less stress. Joggers should walk for several minutes, then jog slowly before hitting their stride. Sprinters should walk and jog first. Exercises that do not use the same muscles as the main event are of little value for warming up.

Cooling down properly after heavy exercise is one of the most important and least appreciated rules of fitness training. After a hard run or other workout, you should slowly walk or otherwise keep moving for a few minutes and not stand still. You also should not jump into a hot bath or shower. Why? Because the demands on the heart will continue for a while and the heart muscle itself must be supplied, but being still or applying heat suddenly will cause the blood to pool in the large muscles, especially the legs.

 Moreover, the enormous increase in norepinephrine and epinephrine associated with exercise continues for several minutes after the exercise stops. These hormones can induce dangerous arrhythmias, especially when standing still. Persons with known or suspected cardiovascular problems should be especially alert to these dangers.[16]

RICE? Many stress and sports injuries, especially strains and sprains, have traditionally been treated with RICE: rest (often with immobilization), ice, compression, and elevation. The point of all four steps is to reduce movement, blood flow, inflammation, and pain. There are some arguments against immobilization, and sometimes controlled movement along with ethyl chloride is perferred in order to prevent stiffness and weakness which complicate the injury. Pains is usually a good guide to how much movement is safe.

 Ethyl chloride spray, which cools the tissue, is convenient to use. It will not relieve pain and allow movement in severe sprains with ligament rupture or severe fractures, so it is safe. The spray is applied directly over the painful area, which is carefully flexed and moved. The pain is followed with

34   Exercises that Help Prevent Injuries

The following simple exercises strengthen and stretch muscles and thereby help prevent sprains and strains. Try them all, then choose those you like best or need the most and do them regularly and carefully.

Each exercise should last two to five minutes, but serious athletes may benefit from longer stationary stretches, especially of the calf and hamstring.

If you do these in the morning upon arising, be extra careful and start slowly. Your muscles are at their coldest and stiffest and are easily injured. It is good to at least walk around a little and perhaps take a hot shower before working out.

These exercises should be done to the point of mild stretching discomfort or muscle fatigue, not pain or exhaustion.

Groin stretch

With soles of the feet together, lower your head and trunk while pressing down on your legs with your elbows.

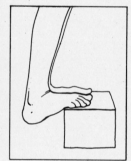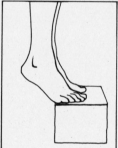

Calf stretch and strengthener

Let your heels drop over the edge of a block or step. Stay in the low position for stretching. Go up and down for strengthening.

Back-leg stretch

Keep your hands on the wall and your feet flat on the ground while slowly moving away from the wall.

Quadriceps stretch

Support yourself with one hand and grab a foot with the other. Pull the foot up to increase the stretch.

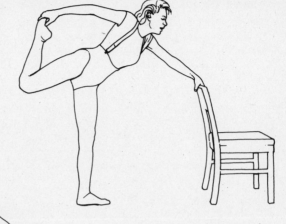

Hamstring stretch

Put one foot up on the back of a chair or a railing and grasp your toes. Straighten the knee and bend the body forward.

Hamstring stretch

Lie on your back. Bring one leg up and grasp the toes with your hands. Slowly straighten your leg as much as possible and pull head up toward the knee.

Hamstring stretch

Cradle your leg with your hands clasped and gently pull it toward your body. Gently twist to left and right.

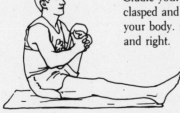
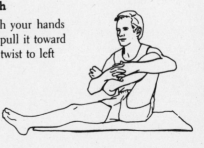

Side leg lifts

Lie on one side with both legs straight. Lift
the upper leg about 45 degrees; lower.
Repeat several times. Do both sides.

Rocking sit-ups with knees bent

Use adequate padding to protect your
spinal column. This type of sit-up is
less likely to cause stress
injury of abdominal
and back muscles
than standard sit-
ups with legs
held down.

Bicyling on your back

Move your legs in a circling
fashion, as if cycling. This is
an excellent toner of the
abdominal muscles.

Single leg lift

Start flat on your back. Now lift one leg while
bringing your head up. Lower your leg and
head. Now lift the other leg, and
so on. Inactive leg can be
straight or bent.

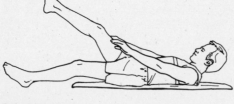

The poor person's weight gym

A stout piece of surgical tubing, an inch or two in diameter and five or six feet long, can be used for a variety of strengthening exercises. You may want to work with two at a time. Be sure to fasten the ends securely, or you'll risk a painful whack.

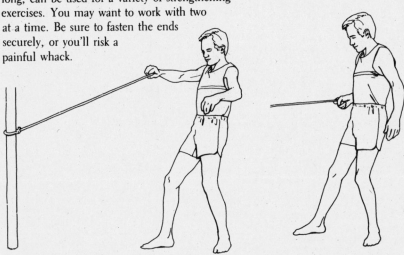

Full arm flex

Stand still and pull tubing forward using only your arm, not your body. Let back slowly. Do both arms.

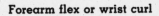

Forearm flex or wrist curl

Pull the tubing foward using only your wrist. Alternate with full arm flex. Excellent for prevention of tennis elbow and thrower's elbow. Do both arms to prevent an imbalance of development.

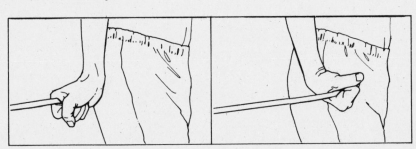

38 the spray until it is reduced or gone. It is believed to work by relieving the muscle spasms that usually accompany strains and sprains; this allows movement and reduces swelling.

Ice is cheaper, more likely to be available to most people, and probably just as effective as ethyl chloride. An ice cube in a plastic bag wrapped in cloth can be applied to the painful area for ten to twenty minutes (no more!) several times a day. It should reduce pain, swelling, and muscle spasms.

Summing up, there is agreement on the value of cooling, whether by ice or ethyl chloride, and on elevation of the injured area to prevent the pooling of blood and increased inflammation and pain. The only question concerns movement, which is apparently harmless and probably beneficial in nonsevere injuries if done carefully. However, in no case should injured tissue be stretched. Rest is surely necessary, even if some movement does help. So, we are left with cooling, movement (careful!), elevation, and rest, or CMER, for stress injuries that can benefit from home treatment. In more severe injuries a physician should be consulted.

See a physician for any obvious or apparent fracture, if a limb is crooked, cold, numb, or blue, if a joint is deformed or moving abnormally, or if you are limping.

Heart Attack

Everyone, no matter how fit, is more likely to have a heart attack while active than while doing nothing. The risk is especially great for those who rarely exercise and it can be decreased by regular exercise.[17] Other risk factors also increase the danger of exercise overloading the heart muscle and precipitating a heart attack. These include being a man over forty (though women are not immune), smoking, high cholesterol levels, high blood pressure, obesity, and a family history of heart disease or sudden death. The risk can be minimized in the following ways.

Drink adequate amounts of *water* and *warm up* and *cool down* properly as described above.

After warming up, exercise at a *moderate pace*; the 75 percent rule is a good guideline (see Chapter 1–3). Be especially careful if you are just starting an exercise program or otherwise greatly increasing your activity level. Start out slowly and gradually increase the length and intensity of your workouts. If you are under a physician's care for hypertension, angina, asthma, or other chronic condition, discuss with your doctor any large change in your activity level.

No matter how healthy you think you are or how careful you think you have been, always be alert for signs of trouble such as chest pains, nausea, dizziness, and difficult breathing. If any of them occurs, stop exercising and sit down. If it continues, **call a physician.**

Do you need a stress test? In order to detect early silent heart disease, some people should have a stress test, an examination of the heart's function during exercise. The most common stress test is treadmill electrocardiography in which an ECG is taken while the person walks or jogs on a treadmill. More sensitive tests using radioactive tracers and computer imaging are done when the stress ECG gives ambiguous results.

A stress test is generally advisable before a major increase in activity for all persons with risk factors for coronary artery disease (see above), including all men over forty and all women past menopause. Some physicians advocate that all exercisers past these milestones have a treadmill ECG every year or two. This may be excessive for those with no risk factors except age, but it makes sense for others.

Heat Stress

Exercise in the heat, especially if inadequate water is drunk, can lead to heat fatigue, heat syncope (fainting), heat cramps, heat exhaustion (sometimes with headache, dizziness, profuse sweating and vomiting), and heat stroke. All of these problems except heat stroke can be dealt with by rest in a cool environment and plenty of water. Slight elevation of the feet helps in syncope. Heat stroke, which is characterized by extreme fatigue, collapse, confusion, headache, and hot, dry skin, requires immediate cooling and hospitalization.

Heat stress can be prevented by avoiding overexercise, especially in hot weather, and drinking plenty of water before, during, and after a workout. Young athletes are still sometimes subjected to water restriction by their coaches in the erroneous belief that this improves stamina. This practice should not be tolerated by youngsters or their parents.

Acclimation is very important; if you move to a warmer climate or if it suddenly gets much hotter than you are used to, give yourself a couple weeks to acclimate before exercising at your normal level. Heat stress can happen to anyone, but among the most susceptible people are children, the obese, the very thin, diabetics, heart patients, and those taking diuretics, antihistamines, stimulants, antidepressants, atropine, or phenothiazines.

Impingement Syndrome

Also known as swimmer's shoulder, bursitis, and rotator cuff tendonitis, impingement syndrome occurs when the shoulder is repeatedly raised over the

40 head as in swimming, throwing, or playing volleyball. The upper-arm bone (humerus) impinges upon the top of the shoulder-joint bone (acromion) in such a way that the tendons, bursa, and other soft tissue are squeezed, causing inflammation and pain.

Aspirin and ice are usually sufficient, but other remedies such as ultrasound or cortisone may be necessary in severe cases. The activity that causes the problem should be minimized; if it must be continued, aspirin before and ice after should help. A coach in the problem sport may be able to improve your technique or style so that less stress is put on the soft tissues of the shoulder. A physiatrist familiar with the problem may be able to prescribe helpful exercises.

Knee Injuries

The knee is a common site of injury because it is an unstable joint where two long, weight-bearing bones are held together only by ligaments and tendons. There is no ball and socket to fit the bones together, and the ligaments allow movement in only one plane. When the knee is severely stressed by a blow, a fall, overuse, or excessive lateral force, injuries of various degrees can occur to one or more of the ligaments, tendons, bones, cartilages, muscles, or bursi in or near the knee. These stresses are all possible in various sports.

Knee injuries that are not properly treated can lead to a lifetime of problems such as those commonly known as "trick knee," in which the knee locks, collapses, clicks, pops, or otherwise annoys and incapacitates. The nature of the "tricks" depends on the exact location and extent of the injuries.

Sprains (ligament tears) are the most common knee injuries. Depending on the direction and force of the blow or the nature of the stress, different ligaments suffer varying degrees of damage.

Knee cap (patella) injuries such as dislocation, fracture, and tendonitis often affect runners and dancers. Chondromalacia, a degenerative process (often due to an earlier injury), can lead to arthritis. Water on the knee is not really water but an excess of synovial fluid in the joint, a sign of inflammation due to injury.

Runner's knee usually refers to chronic tendonitis or chondromalacia. These problems can be very stubborn, and patience is required to prevent further injury. Running on hard surfaces like concrete and asphalt should be avoided; grass and dirt are much better. The safety of running on sand is debatable. Sand is an excellent shock absorber and a beach is usually a nice place to run. However, the inclination toward the water, uneven surface, and softness may promote or aggravate ankle sprains, shin splints, or hamstring strains. A lot depends on the texture of the sand, the size of the grains, and the tilt of the beach. Try it with caution and awareness of the potential hazards.

Jumper's knee is very painful tendonitis of the patellar tendon just above the kneecap. It is caused by overstressing the tendon, which attaches the thigh extensors (the quadriceps) to the kneecap, by repeated vertical jumping such is common in basketball and volleyball.

TREATMENT
Many knee injuries can be treated with CMER (see page 38) and, when pain and inflammation have subsided, proper exercise. But if you have severe, persistent, or recurring knee pain you should see a physician. Special exercises, surgery, or other treatment could save you years of knee troubles. The proper exercises to help speed rehabilitation depend on the exact nature of the injury. For example, stair climbing is helpful in some injuries, but can aggravate others such as chondromalacia. It is important that the injury be properly evaluated so a rational exercise program can be used.

PREVENTION
Always warm up slowly and train patiently and properly for your sport with attention to the areas of major stress. For example, if you play volleyball and spike a lot, you should strengthen your quadricep muscles with appropriate exercises such as straight-leg raises while lying on your back (raise one leg at a time to avoid back stress). Beware the deep-knee-bend, or full squat. It is sometimes recommended for strengthening the quadriceps and developing flexibility, especially in dancing and gymnastics, but it can produce cartilage tears and wearing of the kneecap. In short, it tends to age the knee joint.

If you participate in football, baseball, basketball, volleyball, skiing, or other sports where falling or a blow to the knee is possible, wear knee pads. If you are about to be hit, shorten your stride; running in short choppy steps lessens the chance of being hit while you have a foot on the ground, and thereby the risk of serious injury. Wearing cleats tends to increase the chance of injury and its severity by anchoring the foot during a blow.

Muscle Cramps

Muscle cramps, whether constant or intermittent, can be painful and incapacitating. The causes include muscle fatigue, excessive loss of body fluids or minerals, an injury such as a strain, and blood supply obstruction by prolonged isometric exercise.

42

TREATMENT

Relax the affected muscle, the whole body, and the mind, and gradually stretch the muscle. It often helps to flex the muscles opposing the ones in spasm. For example, if a calf muscle is cramping, flex your foot towards your shin.

PREVENTION

Warm up carefully before exercising hard, and avoid overworking any muscles.

Eat plenty of fruits, vegetables, and grains to get adequate minerals. Drink water before and during exercise. Salt tablets should not be taken, but eating salty foods is okay if you do not have hypertension.

Do not use rubberized exercise suits or heavy clothes; they promote excessive water and mineral loss.

Muscle Strain

A muscle strain (or pull) is a tearing of a muscle or its tendon or both. The injury can range from a few torn muscle or tendon fibers to a complete rupture. For example, runners often pull hamstring muscles (leg flexors in the rear thigh) and swimmers pull shoulder muscles. Strains are caused by excessive tension on a muscle-tendon complex, by trying to do more than strength allows.

TREATMENT

If the injury is severe, with nearly complete loss of function, **consult a physician** right away. Surgery may be required. Milder cases can be treated with CMER for two or three days followed by mild stretching and range-of-motion exercises. The muscle and tendon must be thoroughly rehabilitated before full resumption of activity, or re-injury is certain.

PREVENTION

Always warm up properly by playing slowly and gently before working out hard. Increase your training level gradually and do not work out hard too often. Each vigorous exercise session causes some damage to the muscle, which must heal before being stressed again.

Muscles should be balanced in strength with their opposing muscles. For example, hamstring pulls are common in running sports because the quadriceps (the knee extensors in the front thigh) are usually much stronger than the hamstring and during running they exert tremendous tension on the hamstrings and may stretch them to the point of tearing.

Be sure you are properly nourished for exercise; inadequate minerals can predispose muscles to injury.

Plantar Fasciitis

A fascia is a sheet of strong connective tissue which surrounds and supports a muscle, tendon, or other organ. Most of the body's organs are covered by fasciae, which are subject to injury from stress or trauma.

Probably the most common fascia injury is plantar fasciitis, a stress-induced tear of the plantar fascia, which covers the muscles of the bottom of the foot. The plantar fascia can withstand only so much pressure or stretching. When the pressure is great enough to flatten the arch or spread the toes, the fascia may tear. A sharp pain in the bottom of the foot may occur at the moment of injury or it may develop slowly over hours or days. It will then be most painful while taking the first steps in the morning and with each step in running, which can cause further tearing if done too vigorously.

TREATMENT

The affected foot must be rested to allow healing. Switch to a nonrunning sport for awhile or run gently and not to the point of pain. Inflammation is rare but ice may still help relieve pain. Cortisone and other drugs should not be used to allow continued training because this could lead to further injury, and the cortisone may directly weaken the fascia. Taping and friction massage may help, but the proper methods should be shown by an expert. Sometimes foot imbalances are responsible and must be corrected with orthotics in the shoes. In rare cases surgery is necessary.

PREVENTION

Wear the proper shoes for your feet and for the surface you are running on. A shoe with inadequate arch support and too much flexibility can transmit too much pressure to the fascia. A shoe that is too stiff in the sole requires too much force to bend; when the foot strike is hard, the fascia may give before the sole does.

Persons with flat feet, which tend to pronate (turn inward) excessively when they walk or run, may need extra arch supports or orthotics, shoe inserts which must be specially made for each individual.

Shin Splints

Shin splints are painful cramps in the overstressed shin muscles (which pull the foot up). The spasms may squeeze off the veins and cause the injured muscles to become engorged, swollen, and hard. Depending on the extent of the injury and the care taken not to aggravate it, it should clear up within

44 one to three weeks. The problem is most common in joggers, basketballers, and other runners.

TREATMENT

Rest or move gently and use ice massage until the pain and hardness are gone. If this takes more than three weeks or so, you should see a sports physician or orthopedic surgeon. If the pain occurs while just walking, you should see a physician right away to check for stress fractures.

PREVENTION

Warm up by walking, stretching, and slow jogging before vigorous workouts. Train patiently, work your way up gradually, and heed pain and fatigue as warning signs that you may be overstressing your legs.

Minimize your activities on hard surfaces, and wear good shoes that will cushion the repeated shocks involved in running, aerobic dancing, and jumping rope. Persons with low arches may need arch supports or orthotics.

Strengthen and stretch your shin muscles with ankle and toe exercises and stretch your calf muscles and Achilles' tendons. Vary your speed to strengthen all the tissues of the lower legs. Always running at the same speed is believed to contribute to shin stress.

Knee-high socks or leg warmers may help by improving blood supply and waste removal during exercise.

Sprains

A sprain is an overstretching, tear, or complete rupture of a ligament. Swelling, pain, and dysfunction are proportional to the degree of injury. Ligaments hold bones together and stabilize joints. While they are very strong, they are not designed to withstand the strong side forces that occur in many sports requiring sudden changes of direction. The sprained ankle is one of the most common athletic injuries and usually involves the foot turning inward under the ankle. Sprains also occur in the knees, elbows, fingers, and other joints.

TREATMENT

If you suddenly develop a pain in a joint, stop exercising. If the pain persists, apply CMER. A mild sprain will heal in a few days. But severe pain should be evaluated by a physician to check for torn ligaments and broken bones. Crutches, immobilization, even surgery may be necessary.

As a sprain heals, the exercise of the joint should be gradually increased. With an ankle sprain, for example, activity can increase from bending the joint up and down to walking and standing on the toes, to slow jogging, then short runs and long runs.

PREVENTION

Strengthen the muscles of the lower legs and feet to decrease the stress on the ankle ligaments. Always warm up slowly before running hard.

When walking, jogging, running, or hiking, watch out for ruts and holes.

If you are susceptible to ankle sprains because of pronated or flat feet or other reasons, you may need arch supports or high-top shoes.

Stitches—Side Pains

A stitch is a sharp pain on the left or right side of the upper abdomen which usually occurs during running. The weekend athlete is more likely to experience stitches, but even highly-trained persons can get them. There are two common causes. The most common is cramping of the diaphragm or the muscles of the rib cage when they are forced to produce deep, rapid breathing. This is often due to pushing too hard and running while out of shape.

The other cause is accumulation of gas in the colon. Exercise increases peristalsis, which pushes gas toward the rectum. If it does not escape, pressure builds up.

TREATMENT

Sometimes the pain will stop if you push your fingers deep into the affected area while you keep running. But usually you must slow down or stop and rest for a few minutes. If the pain continues, lift the arm of the affected side high and stretch that side, or bend forward at the waist and stretch both arms over your head. Also, try deep breathing while at rest.

Stitches go away by themselves and do not require medical help. But if pain occurs in the chest, shoulders, neck, or arms, stop exercising and see a physician.

PREVENTION

Run within the limits of your fitness level; do not push too hard.

Do not eat just before working out. This takes blood from the breathing muscles and makes them more likely to cramp. Eat more high-fiber food, which is less likely to form hard stools that block gas in the colon.

Be alert for signs of milk intolerance. Some people otherwise unaffected get gas and cramps from milk only upon exercising.

Stress Fractures

Stress fractures are shallow cracks, most commonly in the bones of the feet, legs, and hands. Running, basketball, football, baseball, skiing, and skating

46 are some of the sports which often lead to stress fractures. Sharp pain from walking or pressing the bone with a finger is an indication of a possible stress fracture.

X-rays usually cannot detect these injuries until about three weeks later when they have substantially healed, but ultrasound can sometimes help diagnose the problem early. A cast is rarely required and carries the risk of atrophying the muscles. The activity that caused the fracture should be suspended, but fitness can be maintained without extending the crack by switching to another sport such as swimming or bicycling.

PREVENTION

As is the case with most sports injuries, stress fractures can usually be prevented by using proper equipment (such as good shoes and running surface) and by being aware of the stresses and alert to your body's warning signals.

Tendonitis

Tendonitis is inflammation of a tendon with swelling and pain. The pain tends to be worse in the morning and it subsides as the tendon is used. This encourages abuse, which may aggravate the problem.

Tendonitis commonly occurs in the Achilles' tendon in runners, the elbows in tennis players, and the shoulders in swimmers and throwers. It is caused by overstressing the tendons with exercise when the muscles are tight.

TREATMENT

Apply an ice massage for the first two days or so, and do gentle stretching and movement. Stretch slowly and hold; jerky stretching could cause further irritation and injury.

Rest the affected area or risk further injury. For example, running with Achilles' tendonitis could rupture the tendon, a serious injury that could lay you up for months.

Cortisone injections can relieve pain due to tendonitis, but they can be risky because they mask the pain and allow continued activity, and may directly weaken the tendon.

PREVENTION

Strengthen your muscles so they will take stress off the tendons. Always warm up properly before working out. Exercise within your limits and heed your body's signals. If you can avoid muscle tightness you can generally prevent tendonitis.

If you are prone to tendonitis in a certain area or if you plan on increasing your exercise level and the stress on certain tendons, then you should regularly do tendon stretching exercises for several minutes before heavy workouts. For example, to stretch your Achilles' tendons, stand on a board inclined toward a wall with your heels and your back against the wall for up to twenty minutes. Gradually increase the incline. Or lean against a wall with your heels on the floor. Move your feet farther and farther from the wall.

Tendon Rupture

A tendon rupture is a complete tear in a tendon or, more commonly, a rupture of a tendon's attachment to a bone or muscle. There is often an audible pop and very severe pain. The area becomes swollen, painful, and black and blue. The most common site by far is the Achilles' tendon, in which case the heel cannot be lifted.

The cause of a tendon rupture is usually a forceful contraction of a muscle in a sport such as sprinting, skiing, handball, or tennis. A rupture is more likely if the attached muscle is tight, fatigued, or weak.

TREATMENT

Immobilize the injured tissue, apply ice or ethyl chloride, and call a physician right away. Partially torn tendons reattach and heal by themselves, but complete ruptures usually require surgery and immobilization, especially if the tendon recoils too far or tears a piece of bone off.

PREVENTION

A rupture in an Achilles' tendon is usually preceded by a partial tear or by Achilles' tendonitis. These painful conditions are clear warnings to rest or risk the more serious danger of rupture.

Strengthen your calf muscles so they will take some stress off the tendons. A good exercise is to walk with an exaggerated tiptoe bounce. Or stand on a step or book with your heels hanging over. Lower your heels then push up on your tiptoes. Repeat until fatigued.

Always stretch and warm up slowly before working up a sweat or making sudden strenuous movements.

Tennis Elbow

This refers to pain in the elbow and the forearms which is aggravated by any action involving gripping or rotating the wrist. In severe cases simple acts like shaking hands, turning a door knob, or brushing one's teeth can be agonizing.

In the strict sense tennis elbow refers to an inflammation at the site

48 of attachment of the forearm extensor muscles to the humerus (upper-arm bone) at the elbow. But the term is often used for similar injuries to other elbow tissues because the causes, symptoms, therapy, and preventive measures are much the same.

The cause of tennis elbow is almost always overuse of a poorly conditioned forearm and hand, such as sporadically playing tennis vigorously with little other arm exercise. Chopping wood, swinging a hammer, beating a rug, paddling a canoe, throwing a ball or javelin, and many other activities can precipitate the condition. The tendons and their points of attachment to the bones are subjected to enormous stresses time and again. Strong, properly conditioned forearm muscles can help absorb the shock, but in weaker arms the tendons and their bone attachments are easily irritated by the stress.

TREATMENT

In the acute situation, right after the injury and for two or three days, immobilization and intermittent cold packs are recommended. Aspirin may reduce the pain and inflammtion. If the pain is very severe, consult a physician; injection of a long-acting local anesthetic or cortisone usually brings relief. The arm should be immobilized to avoid aggravating the injury. Movement can be gradually increased as the pain decreases. Friction massage properly done can be useful. A physiatrist should be consulted for this.

If simple treatment does not bring relief and the condition persists for some weeks, surgery may be required to remove granulation from the areas of inflammation.

PREVENTION

If you play tennis or similarly stress your forearm, always warm up slowly and don't overdo it. Heed the symptoms of fatigue and tightness.

Develop stronger forearms with exercises such as wrist curls or swinging a weighted racket. Improve your stroke with more shoulder and body action and less wrist action. Hit back-handed with two hands at least until your forearm is strong.

Improve your racket. In general, greater weight, more string tension, and a larger handle diameter put more stress on the muscles and tendons. You may want to try the Gripper, a racket with a slightly bent handle. It clearly puts much less stress on the muscles and tendons of the forearm and, if it is widely used, could result in far fewer elbow injuries.

Thrower's Elbow

Almost everything we said about tennis elbow applies to thrower's elbow, but the affected site is the medial epicondyle rather than the lateral epicondyle. This is the point of attachment of the forearm's flexor muscles on the inside of the elbow, rather than the extensor muscle attachment at the outer elbow which is affected in tennis elbow. Thrower's elbow is generally more serious than tennis elbow because of the nearness of the ulnar nerve ("funny bone"), the involvement of which can cause severe pain and disability.

Throwing too hard or with improper warm-up is the most common cause. But just as throwing can precipitate tennis elbow, so playing tennis can cause thrower's elbow. The causes, treatment, and prevention are essentially the same, but thrower's arm is more likely to require surgery due to ulnar nerve involvement.

PREVENTION
Prevention is far preferable to treatment and can be accomplished by properly warming up before throwing hard and strengthening the forearm with wrist curls and other arm exercises (see the Poor Person's Weight Gym, p. 37).

8

Sports and Drugs

any drugs are used in professional and amateur athletics in the belief that they will provide a shortcut in training or an edge in competition. In spite of laws forbidding this and studies showing the drugs to be mostly ineffective and dangerous, doping for sports remains popular. Here we discuss the drugs most commonly used and their effects on athletes. All the drugs are further discussed in Part Five.

When athletes consider taking a drug because others say it helps, they should keep in mind the tremendous power of the placebo effect; even the most sophisticated people can be fooled by their hopes and expectations. And if they are still convinced that a certain drug will do wonders, they should ask themselves whether the long-term costs are worth the short-term gains. Should the purpose of athletics be to help you live a healthy, happy life or to win some medals and money regardless of the cost to your health and sanity?

Amphetamine and its relatives such as methylphenidate (Ritalin) are potent stimulants and mood elevators and are among the most commonly abused drugs in sports. They produce self-confidence, aggressiveness, and delusions of outstanding performance. They tend to mask pain and reduce the perception of fatigue. This increases the risk of injury and heatstroke, a very serious hazard for amphetamine users in strenuous competition. Deaths have occurred. Moreover, the user takes longer to recover from workouts and competition, and is prone to depression and lethargy unless he or she takes more of the drugs, all of which are addicting.

50

Anabolic steroids—See "Testosterone analogues" below.

Androgens—See "Testosterone analogues" below.

Antibiotics do not go well with heavy exercise because the stress can provoke a reaction to the drug, such as diarrhea or vomiting, which otherwise might not occur. Moreover, if you have an infection worthy of antibiotics it could be serious enough to cause a reaction to heavy exercise, which increases susceptibility to bacterial toxins.

Blood packing is also called blood doping, but this is a poor term since no drugs are used. It involves removing a couple of pints of one's blood, training for a few months to bring the red cell level back up to the normal 45 percent (40 in women), and transfusing the removed red cells back before the competition. This is done to elevate the number of red cells and increase the oxygen-carrying capacity of the blood in order to improve performance in endurance events.

      The concentration of red cells increases to about 50 to 52 percent (45 in women) and studies indicate that it works, but not very well. The result is similar to training for several months at a high elevation before competing at sea level. There is a slight risk of the thickened blood slowing circulation and even clogging capillaries. The practice is illegal in most competition but practically impossible to detect.[18]

Caffeine and its relatives in coffee, tea, colas, and various nonprescription drugs are among the more innocuous drugs used by athletes to get a lift for working out or competing. For most people they are harmless in moderation, but some people will experience a racing heart or palpitations. They should cut out the caffeine or theophylline and consult their physicians. However, for athletes susceptible to asthma brought on by exercise, theophylline, taken an hour or so before exercising, is an effective and safe treatment. It is also approved for use in competition, as are cromalyn sodium and albuterol. Very large doses of caffeine are banned, but the illegal amounts are enough to make most people feel sick.

Cocaine is one of the big scandal drugs of the eighties with hundreds of proven or suspected users in professional and amateur sports. Its effects and hazards are nearly identical to those of amphetamines. (See above. See also Chapter 5–4.)

Cortisone and its relatives can do wonders when injected into areas with stubborn, painful, incapacitating inflammation. But it can mask pain and even directly weaken some tissues, so it must be coupled with rest. A cortisone shot to allow use of injured tissue carries a risk of severe injury.

52

Ephedrine is a stimulant related to adrenalin with effects similar to those of amphetamine but usually without the mood elevation. Heatstroke is a potentially lethal hazard.

Human growth hormone, extracted from cadavers, has effects similar to those of testosterone derivatives (below) and is in much demand by athletes because the extra amounts cannot be detected in the blood or urine. The hazards include abnormal glucose metabolism (similar to diabetes), abnormal growth of some tissues, and severe reactions to pig and cow hormones passed off as human-growth hormone. Moreover, the demand for the drug, with some athletes paying hundreds of dollars a month for it, has driven the price out of sight for many dwarf children who could be helped by it. In this respect, the use of this hormone is perhaps the most reprehensible of all the efforts athletes make to gain an edge with chemicals.

Psychedelics such as LSD, peyote, mescaline, and psilocybin mushrooms are sometimes used in long-distance running and other events that test one's stamina. However, the effects are too unpredictable for most people and such use is not very common. (See Chapter 5-4.)

Speed   See **Amphetamines, Caffeine, Cocaine, Ephedrine.**

"Steroids" are a group of hormones and other biochemicals with a particular chemical similarity. Cortisone, other adrenal hormones, and sex hormones are examples of steroids. Since these have very different and sometimes opposing functions, it is better to specify the substance in question rather than speaking of "steroids" as such.

Testosterone analogues are the focus of much scandal and controversy. Testosterone is responsible for the rapid increase in muscle mass in boys at puberty and variants of the hormone are used to prevent muscle atrophy in patients immobilized after surgery. Now, many weightlifters, body builders, and football players take large doses of these synthetic analogues of the male sex hormone to help build up their muscles. They get them from doctors, health club owners, drug companies, pharmacists, and other athletes. It appears that the vast majority of athletes in some sports, especially body building, spend hundreds of dollars a month on the injections and pills.

There seems to be an increase in the size of muscle fibers with the use of these drugs, but this appears to be due to the retention of fluid in the tissues. There is no evidence that in trained athletes and other normal people there is an increase in strength. The dubious benefit should be weighed against a host of side effects. Here are the most important ones reported or suspected so far:[19]

> *Atrophy of the testicles* with decreased libido and sperm count
>
> *Chemical hepatitis* and possibly liver and kidney cancers
>
> *Neurological and behavioral symptoms* such as increased aggressiveness, headaches, fainting, and dizziness
>
> *Greatly decreased HDL-cholesterol* (the "good" type) and an increased risk of atherosclerosis and heart disease (especially given the high-fat diets many body builders are on)
>
> *"Bitch tits,"* the growth of the nipples and surrounding tissue, which often requires cosmetic surgery
>
> *Masculinization of females*, mostly irreversible, with increased facial and body hair, baldness, acne, and leathery skin

2

Nutrition Science and Mythology

PART TWO

Chapter 1 A Brief History and Introduction

Chapter 2 RDAs and the Four Food Groups

Chapter 3 The Ideal Diet

Chapter 4 Protein and Amino Acids

Chapter 5 Carbohydrates and Fibers

Chapter 6 Fats

Chapter 7 Vitamins

Chapter 8 Adelle Davis and Megavitamins

Chapter 9 Minerals

Chapter 10 Diets, Diets, and More Diets

Chapter 11 Behave Yourself

Chapter 12 Reducing Gimmicks

Chapter 13 "Special" Foods

Chapter 14 Food Additives

Chapter 15 Food "Poisoning" and Parasites

Chapter 16 Air, Water, and Food Pollution

1

A Brief History and Introduction

The science of nutrition, the study of foods and their effects on health, is many thousands of years old. Early humans tried various plant, animal, and mineral matter and learned what was poisonous and what was edible, tasty, and filling, and perhaps what promoted growth in their children. The nutritious plants were cultivated and the animals domesticated; the science of nutrition grew hand in hand with the science of agriculture.

Early medical science was helped along when certain foods were found to prevent or cure certain disorders. For example, Hippocrates advocated liver for night blindness. And in 1753 James Lind, a Scottish naval surgeon, published his famous report of experiments done in the British Navy proving that lemons and oranges prevent and cure scurvy. This disease had been written about as early as 1500 B.C. and was one of the most mysterious and feared in all Europe. Ironically, more than 200 years before Lind's report, the French explorer Jacques Cartier and his men had been saved from scurvy by Canadian Indians who taught them to brew the growing tips of spruce and other trees. This was reported in Europe, but the European medical establishment could not bring itself to learn from "ignorant savages," so thousands died needlessly.

Nutritional science remained empirical and rudimentary until the development and application of modern chemistry and biology in the last 200 years. Among the earliest nutrients recognized and chemically identified were proteins, carbohydrates (starch, glycogen, and sugars), fats, and minerals such as calcium and iodine. By the 1900s scientists were doing animal studies in labs around the world and filling in bits of the giant puzzle.

58   As chemical techniques developed, it became clear that animals could not survive on artificial mixtures of purified carbohydrates, proteins, fats, and minerals. As various extracts of different foods were withheld or fed to animals and their growth and health studied, clear patterns emerged. Removing certain elements from the foods caused certain symptoms, although the amounts were so small that their removal did not significantly affect the weight or caloric value. Gradually these factors, the vitamins and trace minerals, have been identified and their biochemical roles sketched out. Besides adequate calories and water, there are now about forty-five substances known to be required in the diet for health.

Although nutritional science is now developed, mature, and making important and useful discoveries almost daily, progress has been gradual. Because of the complexity of the subject and the need for a great deal more information, responsible scientists have generally been cautious and tentative in their advice. But Americans want bold, exciting, and definitive answers right away. So as nutrition science has plodded along and issued rather vague advice that sounds like Grandmother's "Eat a balanced diet," a host of self-proclaimed nutritionists, health spa owners, chiropractors, naturopaths, herbalists, philosophers, and purveyors of various diets, supplements, potions, pills, and powders have stepped in to fill the void. They promote their miraculous healing and reducing diets and nostrums with a religious zeal which many find persuasive. In fact, many people have a sort of religious faith in the nutrition philosophy they have converted to, whether it be macrobiotics or megavitamins.

In the following chapters we present our concept of the ideal diet, discuss the major dietary components and who needs supplements of what, critically review all the popular diets, weight-loss gimmicks, and "special" foods, and take a look at food additives and contaminants and at so-called food poisoning. Finally, there is a brief chapter on air and water pollution, since we ingest contaminants when we eat, drink, and breathe.

2

RDAs and the Four Food Groups

 nutrient is any ingested substance that is used in the normal metabolism of the body. The classes of nutrients are proteins, amino acids, carbohydrates, fats, vitamins, and minerals. Water and oxygen are also considered nutrients, but they are discussed in Part One. An essential nutrient is one whose role cannot be replaced by another and without which serious health problems will develop.

Recommended Dietary Allowances

The Food and Nutrition Board of the National Research Council (NRC) periodically publishes a revised set of Recommended Dietary Allowances (RDAs) based on the latest information from thousands of studies around the world.[1] The RDAs are considered to be adequate for practically all healthy persons, but are not applicable in infections, metabolic disorders, chronic diseases, or other abnormalities (such as premature birth and drug use) that require special dietary treatment. The RDAs have been established for almost one-half of the known required nutrients. They are calculated using several safety factors to insure adequacy for close to 100 percent of the healthy population, and they are substantially higher than the World Health Organization standards for most nutrients. Most people will not develop deficiency symptoms unless their intake falls below two-thirds the RDA for a nutrient for several weeks.

60

RDAs and food value tables are widely used by nutritionists and dieticians to determine whether nutrient intake of groups and individuals is adequate, borderline, or inadequate. Using a one-, two-, or three-day dietary recall, the intake of protein, amino acids, ten vitamins, and six minerals is estimated. If necessary, dietary changes or supplements are then suggested.

The RDAs are often abused by food processors who use them to make inflated nutritional claims about their products. NRC publications caution that the RDAs are based on a variety of common foods in order to provide other nutrients for which they have not been determined. The reasonable assumption here has been that if we eat a variety of common, whole, natural foods such that the RDAs for half the known nutrients are met, the requirement for the other half will probably also be met.

However, food processing often removes trace minerals, amino acids, fibers, and other important food components for which no RDA has yet been set because of insufficient data. The processors then add back a few of the "popular" nutrients, those for which RDAs are known, and call the product "enriched." Because "a variety of common foods" is often taken to mean a diet of "enriched" Snacky Poppies, Lunchy Munchies, and Snow White Rice, which can meet many of the RDAs, the RDAs alone, without consideration of the food itself, cannot be taken as guides to good nutrition. For example, one could meet almost all the RDAs by eating a fortified breakfast cereal with milk and nothing else, but it would be a very poor diet.

Nevertheless, the RDAs are determined by scientists who are experts in their fields, have access to all the latest research data, and use reasonable methods to come to their conclusions. Used with some qualifications, the RDAs provide reasonable estimates of the adequacy of nutrient intake. We will refer to them often. See Appendix A for complete table of RDAs (p. 712).

The Four Food Groups

The Four Food Group System was developed by the United States Department of Agriculture as a guide to nutritious and practical meal planning in institutions and homes. It gives recommended numbers of daily servings for each of the food groups as follows.

> **milk:** two glasses for adults, three for children, and four for teenagers, or the equivalent in cheese, yogurt, or ice cream
>
> **meat:** two or more servings, or equivalent in poultry, eggs, fish, legumes, or nuts
>
> **dark green and yellow vegetables** and **citrus fruit** or tomatoes: five or more servings
>
> **enriched or whole grains:** four or more servings

This is a simple and convenient system but it is not perfect. One problem is the reliance on milk, which many people cannot tolerate. Labeling milk an official, basic food helps promote the milk industry's false propaganda that "everyone needs milk," "milk has something for every body," and "milk drinkers make better lovers." For some 65 million Americans milk offers gas, cramps, diarrhea, exzema, nasal congestion, asthma, and other symptoms of intolerance or allergy. For millions more it is a major source of fats and cholesterol, which threaten cardiovascular health.

Another problem is the encouragement of the use of "enriched" grain products, which are actually impoverished because only some of the nutrients removed in milling have been replaced.

Moreover, the system does not encourage balance and quality. A person could eat lots of eggs, fatty meats, greasy salted nuts, ice creams, and white bread with lots of butter, and still meet these guidelines for a "good" diet.

3

The Ideal Diet

Because of the inherent complexities of nutritional science, we will never know what is perfect. However, we do know what is better. As Professor D.M. Hegsted of the Harvard School of Public Health told the McGovern Committee (see below) the increasingly rich diet (fats, cholesterol, sugar) "which affluent people generally consume, is everywhere associated with a similar disease pattern—high rates of ischemic heart disease, certain forms of cancer, diabetes and obesity. These are the major causes of death and disease....They are epidemic in our population. We cannot afford to temporize."[2]

Skeptics demand absolute proof before recommending even moderate changes in our eating habits. The mountains of circumstantial evidence are not enough for them. But the current American diet evolved from decades of food processing for profit, unchecked by nutrition considerations, and from food advertising not balanced by nutrition education. The risks associated with the highly refined diet have been demonstrated to be large. As Hegsted has pointed out, the question should not be, Why should we change our diet? but, Why shouldn't we?

The U.S. Senate Recommendations

The diet of the nation is so important to national health, health care costs, and agricultural policies that the United States Senate has taken an intense interest in it. In 1977 the Select Committee on Nutrition and Human Needs (the McGovern Committee) held extensive hearings and issued its conclusions in the now-famous *Dietary Goals for the United States*.

It has been estimated that the potential reduction of the nation's 63
health bill possible with dietary changes alone is about 33 percent. This
could mean an annual savings of almost $100 billion, or nearly $500 for
every man, woman, and child in the country. This doesn't include the
benefits of increased creativity and productivity and decreased suffering.[3]

The changes favored by the Senate committee are:

Increase consumption of whole grains, vegetables, and fruits

Increase consumption of fish and poultry

Decrease consumption of red and fatty meat

Decrease consumption of foods high in fat, and partially substitute polyunsaturated fat for saturated fat

Decrease consumption of butter, eggs, and other high cholesterol foods; substitute nonfat milk for whole milk

Decrease consumption of sugar and sugary foods

Decrease consumption of salt and salty foods

The Ideal Diet

Americans get a tremendous amount of nutritional and dietary advice from
various government agencies, private research institutions, and independent
writers of books and magazine articles. Some of it, such as the Four Food
Groups System and the Senate's "Dietary Goals," is good but incomplete.
Some of it is good but too complex and detailed for most people; the "California Diet" is an example (see Chapter 2–10).

Our effort to provide concise but complete guidelines for an ideal
diet is made simple by the fact that the advice from all the responsible
agencies and writers, besides being based on sound science, is largely the
same. On the other hand, the faddish, gimmicky, extreme, and "miraculous" diets and nutrition schemes all contradict each other. The Atkins and
Macrobiotic diets, for example, give precisely opposing advice on fat, carbohydrate, and vitamin content of the diet, but they both claim to produce
"biochemical miracles" that cure and prevent practically all the major serious diseases.

From the considerations in Part Four, especially those relating to
cancers, diabetes, high blood pressure, heart disease, hemorrhoids, diverticular disease, and dental disease, we can improve the Four Food Groups
System to make it a concise guide to meet basic nutritional needs (as discussed in the following pages) and be in general agreement with the Senate
committee's recommendations and those of the American Cancer Society,
the American Cancer Institute, the American Heart Association, the American Diabetes Association, and the American Dental Association.

64

We suggest a daily intake of the following.

Starch. Four or more servings of whole grain foods such as oatmeal, brown rice, corn, buckwheat, millet, whole wheat, cracked wheat, or breads and cereals made from them, or similar unrefined starchy foods such as potatoes and yams.

Produce. Five or more servings of a variety of dark green and yellow vegetables, fruits, and tomatoes, preferably fresh.

Protein. Two or more servings of fish, legumes, seeds, nuts (fresh and free of added oils and salts), poultry, eggs, or lean meat. Fish is superior to pork, lamb, eggs, and beef. It has higher quality protein, fewer undesirable fats, and more unsaturated oils (omega-3 fatty acids) believed to help lower cholesterol and fat levels in the blood. Even the most fatty fish has far less of undesirable fats than most other meat. Poultry is intermediate in value since it has less fat but more cholesterol than most meats.

Calcium. Two to four glasses of milk per day or the equivalent in cheese, yogurt, almonds (not oiled or salted), sesame seed butter, leafy greens, or other high-calcium foods. The dairy products are preferably nonfat or lowfat. Lactase-deficient persons who want to drink milk can buy lactase and add it to milk, but the cost is high, about one-third the cost of the milk. Most lactase-deficient persons can tolerate substantial amounts of yogurt (not the commercial types with added lactose).

In summary, eat a wide variety of whole, fresh, minimally processed foods from the starch, produce, protein, and calcium groups. Minimize or avoid fatty and high-cholesterol meat, charcoal-broiled or smoked meat and fish, burned foods, reheated cooking oil, sugary snacks, pickled vegetables, alcohol, and excessive salt if it tends to raise your blood pressure. (The problems with these foods are discussed in detail in Part Four under Atherosclerosis and Cancer.)

Do You Need Supplements?

If the above regimen is followed, the risk of any deficiency developing is practically nil for healthy people. The following detailed look at individual nutrients will help you decide whether you want to take supplements. There is no evidence and no reason to believe that taking disproportionately large amounts of isolated nutrients or classes of nutrients (such as vitamins or minerals) has any beneficial effects for normal persons, and in some cases it is harmful.

A useful rule of thumb is to take supplements based on the day's dietary intake. For example, if you don't eat two or three vitamin C foods during the day, then take a supplement equal to what you might have easily gotten, anywhere from 50 to 300 milligrams. Remember, though, that it is always better to eat whole foods to get all the nutrients available, including fiber and trace minerals. If you take a multivitamin and mineral supplement, take one with moderate amounts of each required nutrient, about 100 percent of the RDA. Especially avoid those with excessive amounts (more than 200 percent of the RDA) of vitamins A and D, niacin, and zinc for reasons discussed in the pages ahead.

Controlling Fat Intake

If you follow the guidelines for the Ideal Diet, about 60 to 65 percent of your calories will come from carbohydrates, 25 percent from fats, and 10 to 15 percent from proteins. The hardest part for most people is the fat limitation. Americans generally get almost half their calories from fat, a dangerously high level. Reducing this to a reasonable amount means eating more bread, potatoes, pasta, and rice, and less butter, cheese, sour cream, meat, and gravy.

Unless you are a diabetic or an obsessive-compulsive person, you will not go through life weighing your food and consulting nutrition tables to be sure you fall within the guidelines of the Ideal Diet or any other nutrition plan. We will always be guided by taste, cost, and convenience more than by diet dogma. It is usually enough to eat a variety of foods from the four groups and minimize or avoid the less wholesome foods mentioned. You can use the following fat allowance table to help limit your fat and cholesterol intake.

The fat-allowance table is based on the needs of a moderately active person under age seventy who weighs 150 to 160 pounds, or would weigh that if not obese, and has, or should have, a colorie intake of 2,500 to 2,800 calories per day. The fat and cholesterol allowances are based on maximum daily intakes of 75 grams and 250 miligrams, respectively. Some foods (such as eggs) are limited more by their high cholesterol content, some (such as butter) by their high fat content. The allowances are a little higher for foods with more polyunsaturated and fewer saturated fats. Smaller persons with a lower ideal weight should decrease the allowances, and larger and more active persons can increase them.

Don't be misled by labels that indicate certain meat is "lean." For example, "10% fat" on ground beef means that by weight the product is 10 percent fat. But fat has 9 calories per gram, compared to 4 for protein and zero for water, and the product is about 50 percent fat by calories.

66 Fatty Food Allowances

Each of the following is *one fat serving*, though in some case you wouldn't really eat that much at once. Avoid a total of more than *three per day* of these.

The fish, poultry, and meat weights are before cooking. Although some fish have more fat and cholesterol than others, they also have more unsaturated fats that tend to lower cholesterol levels; so the allowance is about the same for all fish.

T = Tablespoon
oz = ounce
lb = pound

Food	One fat serving
Butter	2 T
Bakery sweets	2 to 3 oz
six average cookies, one-half a cream puff, two small pieces of cake or pie, 1½ doughnuts, 1½ cups custard	
Caviar (fish roe)	1 oz
Cheese	
cheddar, swiss, provolone, most others	3 oz
mozarella, ricotta, other low-fat	6 oz
Clams	1 dozen
Crab	⅔ cup
Cream	½ cup
Chocolate (milk chocolate)	3 oz
Eggs (no limit on egg whites)	½ small
Fish	6 oz
Ice cream	
high-fat variety	1⅓ cup
others	1⅔ cup
Lard	2 T
Lobster	⅔ cup
Meat (of four-legged animals)	
beef, pork, most cuts, well trimmed	4 oz
lamb, most cuts, well trimmed	3 oz
sausages, hot dogs, luncheon meats	3 oz
bacon	1½ oz
heart, chopped	⅓ cup
brain	½ T

Food	One fat serving	67
Milk		
regular	3 cups	
low-fat	5 cups	
non-fat	no limit	
Nuts, peanuts, seeds	½ cup	
Poultry		
light or dark meat without skin, bones, or organs	⅓ lb, about 5 oz	
if cooked in oil and skin	reduce allowance by half	
Oysters	one dozen	
Shrimp	½ cup	
Vegetable oils		
margarine	2½ T	
safflower or corn oil	3 T	
Yogurt	same as milk	

4

Protein and Amino Acids

The proteins we eat are digested down to amino acids, small, nitrogen-containing molecules that are absorbed into the blood. Our cells then reassemble the amino acids into the appropriate proteins such as enzymes, hormones, and muscle fibers. There are twenty-two amino acids, but some can be made from others, so only eight are required in the diet. If your protein intake is low, the necessary amino acids will not be presented to the cells, the essential proteins will not be made, and symptoms will eventually appear. Early signs of deficiency include poor growth in children, poor nail and hair growth, poor weight gain in pregnancy, fatigue, slow wound healing, and sluggish immune response with increased susceptibility to infections. Later signs include anemia, edema (swelling), muscle wasting, weight loss, and poor digestion.[4]

The Recommended Dietary Allowance (RDA) for protein ranges from about 10 grams for infants to 75 grams for pregnant women. Nonpregnant women are said to need about 45 grams, men about 55. These include generous safety factors to assure adequacy for those who have higher than average requirements, and in case the quality of protein is less than perfect, that is, protein that does not provide enough of one or more of the essential amino acids. The RDAs also assume adequate calorie intake; if more energy is spent than calories replace, some of the amino acids provided are used for energy rather than building proteins.

Many Americans eat almost twice as much protein as they need. More than 40 percent of it comes from meat (including poultry and fish). This implies that most people could eliminate most of the meat from their diets without becoming protein deficient. This could save money and decrease fat and cholesterol intake.

Protein Quality   69

At least eight of the twenty-two dietary amino acids are essential, and diets lacking any of these cannot support good health: isoleucine, leucine, lysine, methionine, phenylalanine, threonine, tryptophan, valine. Infants, and perhaps adults, also require histidine, which would make nine. An atypical amino acid, taurine, which does not occur in proteins, may also be a required nutrient; studies are under way.

Food proteins are rated according to their amino acid content and value in supporting life and growth. They are each given a score, called the Net Protein Utilization (NPU), from 0 to 100.

Grains, legumes, nuts, and seeds have NPUs of about 40 to 70; tofu, beef, and poultry about 65; fish, milk, and eggs greater than 80. Leafy greens and brewer's yeast rate about 50. Many substantial vegetable sources have not been adequately studied and rated.

A protein is only as strong as its weakest link. Human proteins cannot be assembled from proteins that lack even one of the essential amino acids. The relatively high NPUs of the animal proteins compared to the generally lower scores of the plant proteins reflects the fact that the human protein patterns resemble those of other animals more than those of plants.

Combining Foods To Improve Protein Quality

Grains, nuts, and other seeds are generally limited in protein value because they are low in lysine, and sometimes isoleucine. Legumes generally have low levels of tryptophan and methionine. If grains, nuts, or seeds are eaten with legumes, the protein value of the combination is substantially greater than that of the individual foods.[5] They should be eaten at the same meal for the maximum increase in value. Examples include beans and rice, hummus (garbanzo beans with sesame seed butter), and beans and tortillas. Peanut butter (from a legume) on whole wheat bread is also good.

Brewer's yeast has a mediocre NPU due to its fairly low methionine content. But it has a high concentration of lysine and isoleucine, so makes an excellent complement to grains, nuts, and seeds. It can be added to nut loaves, casseroles, and the like.

Milk protein is not only excellent in itself but combines effectively with grains, nuts, and seeds because of its high lysine content, and with legumes because of its substantial tryptophan content.

70

Fish is an excellent protein source and, because of its high lysine content, combines well with grains.

Green vegetables are often low in methionine. Their protein value is increased by combining them with sesame seeds, mushrooms, and Brazil nuts, which have high levels of this amino acid.

Many excellent recipes based on these principles are presented in Frances Lappe's *Diet for a Small Planet* (Ballantine, 1975). These recipes are especially recommended for persons who don't use many concentrated protein sources such as eggs, fish, and meat, and want to get the maximum value from the plant proteins they do eat.

Lappe, however, makes an error which leads to large mistakes in estimating the protein value of some foods. Her error is to rate the protein concentration of a food as a percentage of its total weight rather than of its total calories. This exaggerates the value of dry foods and underrates the value of juicy foods. For example, she says snap beans and tomatoes *"cannot* [her emphasis] be considered protein sources because they contain less than 2 percent protein."

A hundred grams of snap beans has about 2 grams of protein (8 calories) and a total of 32 calories. This is 25 percent protein, one of the richest sources we have. Tomatoes, by a similar calculation, are a very impressive 20 percent protein, far from the nonprotein status assigned them by Lappe. An avid tomato and snap-bean lover, as many home gardeners are, might eat over two pounds a day and get almost 20 grams of protein, along with lots of vitamins, minerals, and fiber. Broccoli, cabbage, squash, and other vegetables can also make a significant contribution to protein nutrition if large amounts are eaten.

Protein Supplements

Concentrated protein powders are commonly advertised as helpful for developing muscles and fitness. But these mixtures of purified soy, milk, and egg proteins are more likely to do harm than good. Like refined grains and sugar, they provide calories without the vitamins, minerals, and fibers that normally accompany them. Unlike the other refined foods, they are very expensive. They also taste bad, though not as terrible as liquid amino acid products.

The idea of pushing protein in order to increase muscle mass in untenable. The small amount of extra protein that may be needed because of an accelerated fitness or weight-lifting program can be easily provided by the extra amounts of nutritious foods one normally eats. Excessive protein, especially from concentrated supplements, can cause excessive calcium excretion and poor zinc absorption, which can be especially serious problems for growing children and for women susceptible to osteoporosis.[6] When substantially higher protein intake is needed, such as after major surgery, injury, or other severe physical stress, it is far preferable to increase the intake of high-quality, high-protein foods.

Amino Acid Supplements

Several amino acids are sold in pill form and some rather fantastic claims are being made for them. In general, these claims are mere marketing ploys and there is little evidence to support them. (See "The Pearson-Shaw Longevity Theory" in Part Six for a look at some of the more outlandish claims.) Nevertheless, sometimes amino acids supplements may be useful. Tryptophan, for example, appears to help insomniacs and may help relieve chronic pain, and tyrosine may be useful in depression. Studies on these effects are in progress. Because of the potential hazards of amino acids (such as hyperacidity and decreased absorption of the unsupplemented amino acids), they should not be taken for more than a couple days without consulting a physician, registered dietician, or nutritionist.

5

Carbohydrates and Fibers

Carbohydrates are simple sugars, such as glucose and fructose; double sugars, such as sucrose and lactose; and polysugars, such as starch and glycogen. The polysugars and double sugars must be broken down to simple sugars before they can be absorbed into the blood. The word carbohydrate means hydrated (watered) carbon; all carbohydrates are derived from simple sugars, which consist of carbon, hydrogen, and oxygen in the ratio of one H_2O molecule to one carbon atom. Here we discuss the different carbohydrates important in the diet. The indigestible carbohydrate cellulose is discussed with fibers, below.

Simple Sugars

Fructose is present in many fruits and in honey. It is the sweetest of all sugars and commonly used in soft drinks and candies. It loses some of its sweetness with heating, so its use in food processing is limited.

Fructose enters the liver where it is converted to glucose or glycogen; it provides the same amount of energy as ingested glucose. Fructose is heavily promoted (by health food magazines and stores and by mail-order retailers) as a "miracle food" which provides all the benefits of sugar without the disadvantages. It is said to provide instant energy and to cure insomnia, fatigue, anxiety, and other problems. It is also claimed to be better for diabetics than glucose. There is no evidence for any of this. Its only advantage

72

over sucrose appears to be more sweetening power per calorie (about 50 percent) when not heated. This is a slight advantage since the cost of fructose is usually several times the cost of sucrose.

Galactose, the least sweet of the common sugars, is one half of the double sugar lactose (milk sugar); the other half is glucose. Galactose is converted to glucose in the liver; it provides the same amount of energy as glucose.

Glucose is the basic fuel of the body, the carbohydrate which is freely soluble in blood and cell fluids and available to all tissues for their energy needs. Only small amounts of glucose are ingested, but all foodstuffs except fatty acids are converted to glucose before being used for energy. Blood-sugar levels refer to blood glucose.

Glucose is present in honey and some fruits. As a food additive it is often called *dextrose*. It is less sweet than fructose or sucrose, so there is little use for it in making sweet foods.

Double Sugars

Lactose is milk sugar, the major carbohydrate provided by mammals to their offspring and a major source of energy for milk drinkers. It is also a common food additive, though it is the least sweet of the double sugars. Lactose is digested to glucose and galactose before absorption into the blood. Many people, especially blacks and Orientals, gradually lose their lactase, and therefore their ability to digest lactose, as they mature. Too much lactose can cause gas, bloating, cramps, and diarrhea. Because of this intolerance, lactose is the only major carbohydrate that is not universally acceptable as a food, except for very rare genetic intolerance to sucrose, galactose, and fructose.

Maltose is a sugar formed when starch is partly digested, such as when grains are sprouted or corn starch is partly hydrolyzed. It consists of glucose linked to glucose, two molecules at a time, and is somewhat less sweet than sucrose. It is used in malted milk, some breakfast cereals, and other products.

Sucrose is common table sugar, the sweetest of the double sugars. In digestion it is broken down to glucose and fructose, which are absorbed into the blood and used for energy or stored as glycogen or fat. Sucrose is very widespread in plants and reaches high concentrations in the sweeter fruits, which frequently also contain fructose and glucose from broken down sucrose. Most table sugar is extracted from sugar cane and sugar beets.

74 Sugar—Villain or Scapegoat?

In recent years sugar has taken a terrific beating in the health food press. Books and articles accuse sugar of causing a list of diseases a mile long, including heart disease, ulcers, hypoglycemia, diabetes, and insanity. Many people now shy away from sugar as if it were a poison. But is it?

The natural foods with high concentrations of sugar, far from poisoning us, are among the most nutritious. Some fruit lovers get half or more of their calories from the sugars of fruit and they are clearly not poisoned. The popular tirades against sugar do not hold up very well under careful scrutiny. William Dufty's *Sugar Blues*, for example, describes how he lost weight, lost his hemorrhoids, and generally felt better after giving up sugar. He also gave up cocaine, caffeine, and aspirin and started to exercise at the same time, but still blames his previous health problems on sugar.

Another point to consider is that sugar often gets the blame for fat. People will gorge on ice cream, cookies, candies, pastries, and the like, which frequently have more calories from fat than sugar, and they will blame sugar if they get pudgy. High fat consumption is generally more damaging to health than sugar.

The problem with sugars is that food manufacturers use them to make candies and other snacks and desserts that are almost invariably less nutritious than nature's sweet treats. They have fewer vitamins (unless fortified), minerals, trace elements, and fiber, and more oils and fats. They usually stick to the teeth more than the natural foods, so tend to cause tooth decay. Moreover, high sucrose intake may, especially if combined with high sodium intake, aggravate hypertension.

Sugar, then, is a natural component of the diet, not a poison. The problem is not sugar itself but the inferior artificial foods it is used to create. The average American now consumes almost a third of a pound of refined sucrose per day in the form of semisynthetic foods. If most of that sugar were taken in the form of fresh fruits instead, our health would surely benefit.

Polysugars

Starch is formed by chains of glucose molecules and is the energy store in seeds (including beans and grains) and tubers (potatoes and such). When moistened and heated, the starch granules absorb water, swell, and burst, rendering the starch more digestible. It is broken down to glucose, which is absorbed into the blood. High-starch foods include grains such as rice, wheat, and corn, and beans, peas, potatoes, yams, tapioca, and poi.

Starchy foods have long been erroneously considered "fattening" and generally not very wholesome. It is now clear that the problem is not bread and potatoes but the butter and sour cream we put on them. Eating mostly refined grains like white rice and bread promotes constipaton and hemorrhoids, not because of the starch but because the fiber has been removed. Far from being fattening and unwholesome, unrefined starchy foods generally provide vitamins, minerals, trace elements, and fiber, as well as energy. Most Americans would do well to include more starchy vegetables, grains, and beans in their diet but without excessive butter, oils, and salt.

Glycogen is animal starch, the stored form of glucose in the liver and muscles. It is essentially identical to starch, but the chains of glucose are shorter and the molecule is more branched than starch. It is broken down to glucose as needed for energy. Only small amounts are present in most meats, but oysters and other shellfish may contain up to 5 percent of their weight in glycogen.

Fibers

Cellulose, hemicellulose, pectin, lignin, and other structural components of plants are frequently present in fruits, vegetables, grains, and beans. They are important in the diet because they swell with water and provide the roughage which stimulates peristalsis and keeps the contents of the intestines moving along. As intestinal bacteria multiply on the fiber, a gelatinous mass is formed and laxative compounds are generated. A diet low in fiber usually causes some degree of constipation and increases the likelihood of hemorrhoids.

A high-fiber diet helps prevent hemorrhoids, diverticular disease, and possibly appendicitis. Moreover, by increasing transit speed, fiber decreases the contact of carcinogens generated in the gut with the gut wall, and thereby decreases the risk of bowel cancer. Rural Africans who eat lots of fibrous fruits, vegetables, and tubers eliminate about a pound of feces a day and have very little colon cancer; while Englishmen on a refined food diet eliminate less than a fourth of a pound a day and have a high incidence of colon cancer.[7]

Fiber in the diet helps diabetics, prediabetics, and the obese by decreasing the speed of eating and digestion, moderating the insulin response, and increasing the satiety value of the food, thereby inhibiting overeating. Fiber may also help prevent atherosclerosis by decreasing cholesterol absorption. In one study, normal subjects eating a large carrot every morning while otherwise maintaining the same diet had significantly lower cholesterol.[8]

76 Who Needs Fiber Supplements?

If you eat plenty of whole grains, vegetables, and fruits, extra fiber is not likely to help. But if your consumption of such foods is meagre, adding unprocessed bran could be beneficial. It is best to sprinkle small amounts into several dishes or drinks each day rather than taking it all at once. Two to six tablespoons a day is the usual dose.

CAUTION
Excessive fiber supplementation can cause flatulence, bowel rumblings, frequent defecation, constant awareness of bowel activity, and possibly excessive excretion of calcium, zinc, iron, and other minerals.

6

Fats

Fats, like carbohydrates, are made of carbon, hydrogen, and oxygen, but they take more oxygen to metabolize and they pack more energy. One gram of fat is good for nine calories, while one gram of carbohydrate or protein releases only four calories when oxidized. Fats are the most fattening components of foods because smaller amounts fulfill our energy needs. The nature of a fat is determined by the nature of the bonds between the carbons. If all the bonds are single, meaning no more hydrogen can be accepted, the fat is said to be *saturated* and is solid at room temperature. If the fat has double bonds it is not fully hydrogenated, is said to be *unsaturated*, and is liquid (oil) at room temperature. Animal fats are mostly saturated and vegetable fats are mostly unsaturated. Vegetable oils are made into semisolid margarines by hydrogenation. Saturated fats tend to raise cholesterol levels, which increases the heart disease risk, so efforts to decrease fat intake generally concentrate on animal fats.[9]

Linoleic acid, an essential nutrient, is a component of many fats and oils in both plants and animals. It is required for the production of the structural fats of cellular membranes, for regulating cholesterol metabolism, and for the synthesis of prostaglandins, which regulate many physiological functions throughout the body.

Deficiency is very rare, but has occurred in hospitalized patients fed intravenous solutions without any fat and in infants fed fat-free formulas. The first obvious symptom is dry and flaking skin. Borderline deficiency, detectable by blood test, inhibits the transport, breakdown, and excretion of cholesterol.

The requirement for linoleic acid is about 2 percent (3 percent for infants) of total caloric intake. Most Americans consume at least twice this amount. The most concentrated sources are various nuts, seeds, and vegeta-

78 bles and their oils, especially corn and soybean oils. Margarine, olive oil, and shortening are fair sources. Coconut has no linoleic acid.

The functions of fats in the diet are to provide linoleic acid, to promote absorption of the fat-soluble vitamins A, D, E, and K, to provide a concentrated source of energy, to make food tasty, and to promote satiety, that is, to make food filling. A diet too low in fat may be low in the fat-soluble nutrients and in calories, which is especially hazardous to children. Most people find meals with little fat (less than 10 percent of total calories) less palatable and less satisfying than those with more.

Most Americans eat too much fat, not too little. The average diet is 40 to 45 percent fat. Because of the association of high-fat diets with cardiovascular disease, some cancers, obesity, and other problems, responsible authorities and experts agree that this is far too much fat intake and it should be reduced. There is debate on how much fat would be best, with estimates ranging from 10 to 35 percent; 20 to 25 percent is probably a good compromise for most people, though persons at higher risk for atherosclerosis might go a little lower.

High-fat foods include butter, margarine, oils; whole milk, cheese, and other dairy products; most red meats, especially bacon and sausages; nuts, seeds, and peanuts. Significant amounts of "hidden" fats are contributed by foods usually thought of as carbohydrate foods such as doughnuts, pies, cakes, and other pastries, as well as many candies.

Cholesterol is not really a fat but a complex alcohol that occurs in foods from animals. It is important as a precursor of vitamin D, sex hormones, and other substances, but the liver makes it and it is not required in the diet. High blood levels are associated with atherosclerosis and heart disease.

7

Vitamins

People and other animals cannot live on just proteins, carbohydrates, fats, the macrominerals calcium, phosphorous, sodium, chloride, potassium, and magnesium, and water. Although these components provide all the calories and more than 99.9 percent of the weight of our foods, there are at least twenty-five other substances that are required in the diet in very tiny, sometimes invisibly small, amounts. They help keep the metabolic machinery of the cells running by serving as cofactors, or enzyme helpers, in protein synthesis, energy production, and all the other cellular processes of life. About half of them are complex organic molecules and they are called *vitamins*. The rest are simple elements, the trace minerals (see Chapter 2–8). (See Part Four, Dental and Gum Disease, for a particularly vital role vitamins and minerals play in one's health.)

Vitamin A (Retinol)

One of the roles of vitamin A is to combine with a protein (opsin) to form the light-sensitive chemical rhodopsin. One of the first symptoms of vitamin A deficiency is night blindness. Eber's Papyrus, an Egyptian medical treatise from about 1500 B.C., prescribes ox liver or chicken liver for night blindness. This works very well because of the high vitamin A content.

      If deficiency continues after night blindness develops, xerosis (drying) of the conjunctiva and cornea occur, then corneal distortion and irreversible changes in the retina. The cornea may become ulcerated and the lens may be destroyed, causing blindness. Worldwide, vitamin A deficiency is one of the greatest causes of blindness, affecting many thousands of children each year.

      Vitamin A is also necessary for proper growth, resistance to infec-

80 tion, and skin health, probably because of its role in regulating the structure and function of cell membranes. In a deficiency, all the body's mucus membranes, especially those lining the digestive and respiratory tract, degenerate, stop their mucus production, and lose their cilia. Sinus, throat, respiratory, mouth, and ear infections are common results. Tooth and gum health also depend on adequate vitamin A.

Sources Good sources of vitamin A and beta-carotene, which the body converts to vitamin A, include yellow, orange, and green vegetables and fruits such as carrots, sweet potatoes, broccoli, melons, squash, corn, pumpkin, peaches, apricots, cherries, prunes, plums, mangoes, papayas, lettuce, chard, green pepper, tomatoes, kale, spinach, and collard greens. Liver, eggs (yolk), butter, fish, and fish oils are also rich sources. Whole milk is a fair source, as is skim milk, which is usually fortified.

The vitamin A content of these foods varies enormously, so there is no point in measuring portions and consulting tables to determine adequacy on a daily basis. For example, carrots vary from 2,000 to 12,000 and sweet potatoes from 1,500 to 7,700 International Units (IU) per 100 grams. By eating an average of two or three medium servings a day of a variety of these foods, vitamin A adequacy can be assured. For example, one half of a medium size yam or mango, or five fresh apricots, can supply 6,000 IU, more than adequate for almost everyone.

Who Needs Supplements? If you don't eat several of the above foods on a regular basis, you might benefit from vitamin A supplements. An average of 6,000 IU a day should be more than adequate for healthy persons. However, some serious diseases such as cancer, chronic infections, hepatitis, cirrhosis of the liver, and kidney and prostate diseases often cause massive urinary excretion of vitamin A; larger supplements are then in order. Blood tests can determine the need.

Those who eat more foods with vitamin A and beta-carotene appear to be less susceptible to lung cancer than those who eat less, but there is no evidence of further benefit from massive doses of supplements.[10]

The Hazards Excessive vitamin A can be toxic to the brain, liver, skin, muscles, and bones. Symptoms can include severe headaches, nausea, vomiting, diarrhea, fatigue, lethargy, weight loss, abdominal pain, insomnia, restlessness, brittle nails, hair loss, constipation, irregular menses, emotional distress, mouth fissures, bulging eyeballs, and rough, dry, scaly skin. Bone decalcification, fragility, and pain may also occur. In extreme cases recovery can take months.

The toxic dose of vitamin A varies a great deal. Healthy adults may develop symptoms on a regular total intake of 50,000 IU per day. But liver disease or regular alcohol intake can reduce the toxic dose substantially. Infants have developed severe symptoms after one month of 25,000 IU per day. And pregnant women are taking a chance at 20,000 IU a day, which could deform the fetus.[11] There is no benefit to such high levels. The RDA for pregnant women is 10,000 IU, and is surely adequate in normal circumstances.

Excessive intake of beta-carotene from huge amounts of vegetables, such as a quart or two of carrot juice a day, can cause the skin to turn yellow-orange. This is a benign effect, and the potential for toxicity is much less than with vitamin A itself.

Vitamin B-1 (Thiamin)

Thiamin, the antiberiberi factor, is a required cofactor in several energy-producing reactions and is especially important in sugar and amino acid metabolism. Deficiency symptoms include muscle wasting, lassitude, weakness, numbness, paralysis, loss of appetite, mental disturbances, neuritis, and disturbed heart function.

Studies have shown an association of low blood thiamin with a wide variety of so-called functional or neurotic symptoms, such as sleep disturbances, night terrors, depression, dizziness, headaches, chronic fatigue, and loss of appetite. Persons with these problems often eat no breakfast, snack on soda pops and candies, and eat lunches and dinners with low thiamin contents. This borderline beriberi can easily be prevented by proper diet.[12]

Good sources include whole grains, nuts, seeds, beans, peanuts, wheat germ, brewer's yeast, potatoes, dairy products, fish, and lean meat.

Who Needs Supplements? Chronic alcoholism and poor eating habits, especially during pregnancy, growth, surgery, illness, and other stresses, are common causes of low and borderline levels. If refined grain products were not fortified, beriberi would probably be widespread. Fortification of alcoholic beverages is advocated by some. This would probably decrease the incidence of serious nervous disorders in alcoholics.

The RDA is .5 mg per 1,000 calories, or about 1 to 1.5 mg per day. Doses a hundred times this, used by some as an insect repellant, are apparently neither effective nor toxic, but subtle effects from long-term use have not been ruled out.

Injection of huge doses kills animals by respiratory depression. Rarely, large doses of thiamin in humans has caused serious hypersensitivity reactions resembling anaphylactic shock. Several hundred milligrams may cause drowsiness in some people.

82 Vitamin B-2 (Riboflavin)

Like thiamin, riboflavin is a coenzyme involved in oxidation and energy-releasing reactions in every cell of the body. Deficiency causes poor growth, sore mouth, tongue, and throat, sinus and eye lesions, dimness of vision, burning eyes, general debility, and possibly cataract.

Sources Riboflavin is very widespread and often found with thiamin. It is present in almost all plant foods but is more concentrated in milk and less in grains than thiamin. Nuts, leafy vegetables, legumes, and lean meat are good sources. Fruits contribute appreciable amounts. Cooking with baking soda destroys riboflavin.

Who Needs Supplements? The RDA is about 1 to 2 mg and is easily obtained in a varied diet of unrefined foods. Persons with generally poor diets are likely to be deficient. Brewer's yeast and wheat germ are excellent concentrated sources. Single doses many hundreds of times the RDA are apparently not toxic, but long-term effects are unknown.

Vitamin B-3 (Niacin)

Niacin is a coenzyme involved in energy-producing reactions in the metabolism of carbohydrates, proteins, and fats. Pellagra, which causes the Four Ds, dermatitis, diarrhea, dementia, and eventually death, occurred in some areas of Europe and the southern United States for many years before a nutritional cause was established in 1915 in experiments with volunteer convicts.

Sources Good sources include whole grains, nuts, seeds, beans, vegetables, fish, lean meat, and eggs. The amino acid tryptophan can be converted to niacin and provide part of the need, so protein foods are generally good sources. Diets with lots of corn and little else are deficient in niacin and tryptophan and have been a major cause of pellagra.

Who Needs Supplements? The RDA is about 15 to 20 milligrams and it is easily met by a varied diet of natural foods. Niacin is heavily pushed by the megavitamin advocates, mostly on the dubious strength of its use in psychiatry. Even if it were effective in psychosis, that would not be evidence that everyone should take huge doses of it every day. Large doses of niacin are also used in efforts to lower blood-cholesterol levels. Results have been mixed.

Hazards Niacin is the most toxic of the water-soluble vitamins. Toxic symptoms include flushing, itching, nausea, diarrhea, stomach bleeding, ulcer promotion and aggravation, severe dermatitis, insomnia, depression, elevated blood sugar, headaches, elevated uric acid (caution, gout patients), liver damage and jaundice, a shocklike drop in blood pressure, cardiac arrhythmias, and profound abnormalities in heart muscle metabolism. This last effect involves a shift from the normal use of fats as the heart's major energy source to the use of primarily carbohydrates. These changes are greatly magnified by exercise and could seriously affect heart function, especially in persons in fitness training programs.[13]

Vitamin B-6 (Pyridoxine)

Vitamin B-6 is a coenzyme in the energy-producing metabolism of glucose and in the interconversion of amino acids and carbohydrates, which is important in building proteins and body tissue and in breaking amino acids down for energy. Deficiency symptoms include irritability, depression, insomnia, and other personality and mental changes, abnormal electroencephalogram (EEG), poor growth, anemia, mouth sores, seborrhea around the nose and mouth, difficult walking, abnormal tryptophan metabolism, and various other biochemical changes.

Sources The richest sources are walnuts, peanuts, brewer's yeast, sunflower seeds, soy beans, wheat germ, bananas, avocados, liver, lean meat, and fish, followed by whole grains, beans, sweet and white potatoes, almonds, and a very wide variety of other natural foods.

Who Needs Supplements? The RDA is 1.5 to 2 mg, easily obtained from moderate amounts of whole natural foods, especially raw. A diet with plenty of the foods mentioned could supply 20 mg a day.

Supplements greatly exceeding the RDA can be helpful in B-6 dependency states such as certain anemias (very rare), alcoholism, and isoniazid treatment for tuberculosis. Depression and abnormal tryptophan metabolism in oral contraceptive users can sometimes be rapidly corrected by about 50 mg a day.

Doses up to 150 mg have been used successfully in the above conditions, and with more variable results in the treatment of skin problems, premenstrual syndrome, neuromuscular and neurological disease, and nausea and vomiting in pregnancy. Large doses have also been used with some success in recurring oxalate kidney stones, chorea, and loss of muscle tone due to L-dopa therapy in Parkinson's disease. The latter use may reduce the drug's effectiveness. Supplements may prove useful in the prevention of

84 atherosclerosis and coronary artery disease in persons with low dietary intakes.

Hazards Vitamin B-6 is apparently safe in amounts several times the RDA, but the very large doses recommended by some orthomolecular and megavitamin advocates are hazardous. There are reports of severe, crippling nerve damage in persons who took 500 to 2,000 milligrams per day for extended periods. Much smaller doses might be harmful to a fetus, so pregnant women should not take more than about 100 milligrams a day without a compelling reason.[14]

Large doses of supplements (over 100 milligrams a day) have been reported to suppress lactation. This has not been firmly established, but women with problems lactating might try reducing or eliminating vitamin B-6 supplements.

Even small doses of pyridoxine can interfere with L-dopa, a drug used in Parkinsonism.

Vitamin B-12 (Cobalamine)

Like folacin, cobalamine is a coenzyme in the synthesis of nucleic acids and DNA. It is also involved in nerve myelin production, protein synthesis, and other processes. Deficiency causes anemia, due to inadequate red blood cell production, and myelin destruction with numbness and tingling in the hands and feet, poor muscle coordination, mental slowness, depression, confusion, poor memory, and sometimes full-blown psychosis with delusions and hallucinations.

Sources The only source of vitamin B-12 in nature is synthesis by microorganisms, including those in the digestive tracts of most animals. All animal foods (meat, fish, eggs, dairy products) are good sources. Plant foods are devoid of cobalamine unless bacteria-containing root nodules in legumes are included. In some poorer countries grains and vegetables are contaminated with enough insect parts and dirt to prevent deficiency in strict vegetarians. Vitamin B-12 has even been reported in some rain water, probably due to dust particles in the clouds. Brewer's yeast does not contain cobalamine unless it has been added.

Who Needs Supplements? The dietary requirement for vitamin B-12 is extremely small, partly because it is recycled (excreted in the bile and reabsorbed from the intestine) many times. And, unlike the other water-soluble vitamins, an excess is not all flushed right out, but is stored (mostly in the liver) so efficiently that after all dietary sources are withdrawn, it takes two to ten years before symptoms are seen. By then it may be too late to reverse the damage to the nervous system.

The evidence indicates that .1 microgram (a tenth of a millionth of a gram) per day will sustain normal functions in a healthy person. The RDA is set at 3 to 4 micrograms, thirty to forty times the minimum requirement. The average intake is higher still, about 15 micrograms a day. Deficiency due to dietary lack is very rare. However, there have been a few cases of breast-fed infants of strictly vegetarian mothers who developed B-12 deficiency anemia even though the mothers were fine. In one case the baby went into a coma and fell several months behind in its development.

Strict vegetarians who use no milk or other animal products, especially pregnant and lactating women, should take supplements.

Persons lacking intrinsic factor (a substance required for B-12 absorption) usually receive monthly injections of the vitamin for life.

Others who often require supplements include persons with malabsorption disorders, hyperthyroidism, or liver disease, and those who have had a gastrectomy. Chronic alcoholics sometimes develop low levels.

Cobalamine is advocated by some as an appetite stimulant and a remedy in various neurological disoders. Studies point to the placebo effect at work rather than any nutritional or pharmacological benefit. However, cobalamine in the hydroxo form (hydroxocobalamine) does bind cyanide, which may be the tobacco toxin responsible for tobacco amblyopia (dimness of vision). Large doses could theoretically help reduce free cyanide levels and thus reduce the damage.

By the same reasoning, large doses of hydroxocobalamine might help reduce cyanide poisoning due to ingestion of amygdalin (laetrile), either accidently in the diet or deliberately as an anticancer agent (which it isn't; see Part Six). To be of benefit in these cases, the B-12 must be in the hydroxo form, that is, unattached to cyanide.[15]

Hazards Simultaneous ingestion of large doses (100 micrograms) of vitamin B-12 with vitamin C has been reported to cause nose bleed, ear bleeding, dry mouth, and decreased ejaculate volume. These may signify serious internal changes.[16]

Folacin

Folacin (folic acid and related compounds) is a coenzyme in the synthesis of nucleic acids which become components of DNA. It is therefore essential for normal growth, reproduction, blood production, and replacement of all tissue with a high turnover rate, such as that of the digestive tract.

Deficiency causes macrocytic anemia, in which red blood cells are few in number and larger than normal due to failure of the young cells to mature in the bone marrow. Early symptoms of deficiency include gastrointestinal disturbances, such as diarrhea and a smooth red tongue. Although

86 folacin deficiency does not damage the nerve myelin, it often causes irritability, forgetfulness, hostility, and paranoid behavior; these symptoms usually improve dramatically within twenty-four hours of folacin therapy.

Sources As indicated by the name, foliage is an excellent source of folacin. Other good sources include asparagus, broccoli, citrus fruits, nuts, seeds, beans, whole grains, wheat germ, and liver. The richest source is brewer's yeast. A tablespoonfull can provide almost half the RDA. Heating, even to normal cooking temperatures, destroys up to two-thirds of the folacin.

Poor sources include most meats, eggs, root vegetables, most fruit, refined grains, and processed milk (especially dried milk). A diet heavy in these foods with very little from the above group can cause deficiency, especially in pregnant and lactating women.

Who Needs Supplements? The minimum requirement is believed to be about .1 to .2 mg a day, and the RDA is set at .4 mg.

Deficiencies are most common in malabsorption syndromes, infants with low birth weight, alcoholism, pregnancy, various diseases including liver disease, and in the use of such drugs as Dilantin, barbiturates, primidone, cycloserine, possibly oral contraceptives, methotrexate, and various antibiotics.

Women with cervical dysplasia—abnormal and possibly precancerous cells identifiable by the Pap smear—may benefit from folate supplementation of about 10 mg a day, which may prevent the progression to cancer.[17]

Hazards Large doses of folacin are rapidly excreted. Single doses hundreds of times the RDA are apparently without harmful effects, but prolonged use could lead to precipitation of folacin crystals in the kidneys which may damage them. There is no benefit from such large doses, and they can mask vitamin B-12 deficiency by lessening the anemia while allowing the irreversible nerve damage of B-12 deficiency to continue. Strict vegetarians should not take folacin without also taking vitamin B-12.

Supplementation to counter the folate-destroying effects of some anticonvulsants must be discussed with one's physician.

Choline

Not exactly a vitamin for humans, choline is a constituent of phospholipids (such as lecithin) which aid in the transport and metabolism of fats. It is also part of acetylcholine, an important neurotransmitter, and plays a role in the synthesis of some hormones.

Dietary choline is required for normal growth in some animals, but clear-cut deficiency has not been produced in humans because other substances, such as betaine and the amino acid methionine, can do choline's job to some extent.

Sources Good sources are whole grains, legumes, wheat germ, brewer's yeast, vegetables, and milk. Fruits have little choline. A mixed diet of natural foods provides about .5 to 1 gram of choline a day.

Who Needs Supplements? Choline supplements, usually as lecithin, are being tested in age-related memory loss, tardive diskinesia (a neurological disorder often associated with certain antipsychotic drugs) and other neurological disorders, with some successes and some failures reported.

Fatty liver is common in alcoholics and persons with severe protein deficiency. Choline has been used to mobilize the fat out of the liver, but results have generally been disappointing. Large doses, unless taken as lecithin, can cause foul, fishy-smelling stools.

Biotin

This water soluble B-vitamin is required in the synthesis of fatty acids, in the production of energy from carbohydrates, and in the synthesis of DNA, glycogen (glucose storage), and some amino acids. Deficiency causes depression, lassitude, muscle pains, loss of appetite, nausea, anemia, dermatitis, grayish pallor, elevated blood cholesterol, and ECG abnormalities.

Sources Biotin is abundant in natural foods with other B-vitamins. It is stable to heat, processing, and storage. Large amounts are also produced by intestinal bacteria.

Who Needs Supplements? The average intake of biotin in the U.S. is about 2 milligrams per day. At least twice this much is made in the intestines. Because intestinal synthesis of biotin is sufficient to meet the human requirement and because it is widespread in food, deficiency is almost unheard of and difficult to produce in volunteers. However, a deficiency can be induced in about one month by eating eight or more raw egg whites a day and eating only highly refined foods. Raw egg whites contain a protein, avidin, which blocks biotin absorption.

A diet high in natural foods can easily supply several milligrams a day. Even the most potent supplements supply less than 1 milligram, so they are usually a waste of money. However, some success has been reported using them to treat seborrheic dermatitis in infants.

88 Pantothenic Acid

This water-soluble B vitamin is essential for the production of coenzyme A, one of the most important substances in the body, essential for the synthesis and metabolism of proteins, fats, carbohydrates, and several hormones. Deficiency in humans causes fatigue, headache, insomnia, nausea, personality changes, impaired coordination, numbness and tingling of the hands and feet, and loss of antibody production. Experimental deficiency in volunteers is induced with a highly refined diet (supplemented with other vitamins) plus the use of a chemical antagonist to pantothenic acid, without which it would take many months to produce deficiency. Such well-defined deficiency does not occur naturally; a very poor diet causes other deficiencies which confuse the picture. (This is true to some extent with most nutrients.)

Sources Pantothenic acid exists in all living cells and is therefore present in all natural foods. Its very name means "from everywhere." Freezing and canning destroy up to half of it and cooking at moderate temperatures up to about 30 percent.

Who Needs Supplements? No RDA has been set, but 5 mg per day seems to be a borderline amount. Fifty mg can be easily obtained from a diet of natural foods.

Persons who eat a lot of refined foods or drink a lot of alcohol and those under severe stress due to injury, surgery, or illness, may benefit from supplements. Brewer's yeast, wheat germ, and legumes are especially rich sources and are preferable to pantothenic acid pills because they contain several B-vitamins and other nutrients.

While deficiency causes graying in some animals, large doses do not prevent or reverse graying of hair in humans.

Vitamin C (Ascorbic Acid)

Ascorbic acid is an essential cofactor in the synthesis of collagen, a protein important in the formation of connective tissue, skin, tendon, and bone. It helps maintain blood vessel strength and is involved in the formation of hemoglobin, the absorption of iron, and the secretion of adrenal hormones. It appears to have a role in amino acid and carbohydrate metabolism, but this is still unclear. Vitamin C is also an antioxidant, like vitamins E and A, and helps protect essential oils from oxidation.

Vitamin C deficiency causes (roughly in order of appearance) fatigue, rough skin with many small hemorrhages under the surface, hemorrhages in the eye, coiled hair, swollen and bleeding gums, pain in the joints, loss of dental fillings, dental caries, tender mouth, and hair loss. Susceptibility to infections and bacterial toxins increases. Children fail to grow properly.

Sources Fruits and vegetables are by far the most important sources of vitamin C. Fresh and fresh-frozen produce have higher concentrations than cooked or canned, but even these are left with significant amounts intact. Prolonged storage and drying decrease the vitamin C content.

   Some of the richest sources, approximately in order of vitamin C concentration, are: black currants, chili peppers, sweet peppers, broccoli, brussels sprouts, collards, guavas, kale, parsley, cabbage, cauliflower, oranges, lemons, limes, passion fruit, strawberries, papayas, mangoes, spinach, watercress, asparagus, lima beans, swiss chard, grapefruit, okra, bananas, tangerines, potatoes, tomatoes, peas, melons, pineapple, squash, corn.

   To minimize losses, use produce promptly or store it in the refrigerator. After preparation (cooking or cutting up), serve right away. Don't overcook or reheat. Use as little water as possible in cooking; steam or broil in preference to boiling. Never add baking soda, and don't thaw produce before cooking.

Who Needs Supplements? It has been determined that the minimum amount of ascorbic acid required to prevent scurvy in most people is approximately 5 to 10 milligrams per day. To provide a margin of safety, the recommended allowance in some countries is 20 to 30 mg. To provide a greater safety margin, the Food and Nutrition Board RDA is 50 to 60 mg, about the amount in an average orange or medium mixed salad.

   There is no question that certain factors increase the need for vitamin C by increasing its excretion or decreasing its absorption. Severe mental stress may be one such factor. In an interesting study, six convict volunteers were specially housed and fed for the purpose of studying vitamin C metabolism.[18] Radioactive-labeled vitamin C was given daily and the rate of excretion measured. It was remarkably constant at about 45 mg per day.

   Several weeks into the experiment, two of the prisoners escaped. Their roommate remained behind and, after pressure was applied, he "squealed" to the authorities. Several hours later, the other prisoners told him that he would probably be killed for squealing when they returned to the prison after the experiment. He became very apprehensive, pale and tremulous, and remained in a state of anxiety for the next two weeks. To their surprise, the researchers found that this prisoner's ascorbic acid excretion almost tripled during this period.

   Then the warden promised the prisoner parole and safe conduct

90 into civilian life at the conclusion of the experiment. He immediately became calm and relaxed, and his vitamin C excretion rate returned to normal.

Cigarette smoking has been shown to increase the vitamin C requirement, not by increasing excretion but by decreasing absorption into the blood. To maintain an equivalent blood level, the heavy smoker needs almost twice as much in the diet as the nonsmoker. The claim made by some vitamin promoters that smoking one cigarette "destroys" 25 mg of vitamin C is a gross exaggeration. If this were true, a pack-a-day smoker would lose 500 mg every day, about a third of the body stores, and would die of scurvy within weeks of starting the habit. But smoking one pack of cigarettes may block the absorption of about 25 mg of the vitamin.[19]

Aspirin, alcohol, and other drugs seem to increase the vitamin C requirement. By how much is not known, but the effect is not as significant as with cigarette smoking.

Nitrates in food are suspected of forming carcinogenic nitrosamines in the stomach. Vitamin C, whether taken in the food or added, tends to inhibit this reaction. The increased consumption of fresh produce may be responsible for the decline of stomach cancer in the United States over the last several decades.

Large doses (about 1.5 grams a day) may inhibit serious side effects of long-term cortisone therapy, such as the demineralization of bone and the decreased formation of collagen, which can result in osteoporosis and depressed growth.

Large doses are useful in combating urinary tract infections (see UTIs in Part Four). They also have some antihistamine effect and may be useful in colds and allergic reactions, especially hay fever. Huge doses (several grams a day) on a regular basis are recommended by some for the prevention and treatment of influenza and the common cold. Many studies have been done and the results have been mostly negative. It appears that some relief is obtained because of the antihistamine effect, but there is no convincing evidence that vitamin C supplements can prevent or cure colds.

In recent years some authors have advocated large doses of ascorbic acid to prevent and even reverse atherosclerosis. Some studies do indicate a strong correlation of low vitamin C intake with both ischemic heart disease and stroke, but the levels of intake associated with a risk are less than the RDA. Persons at risk, especially older persons, smokers, and those with hypertension and high cholesterol levels, should be sure to get at least the RDA and perhaps two or three times that. But there is no evidence of increased protection from taking megadoses.

Hazards Chewable vitamin C, even in moderate doses, may cause severe dental erosion and should be avoided.

Many people cannot take megadoses of vitamin C for long because they cannot bear the loose bowels and intestinal cramps that so often occur.

At least 10 percent of American blacks, Sephardic Jews, and some persons of Mediterranean and Middle Eastern ancestry are deficient in an important red-blood-cell enzyme, glucose 6-phosphate dehydrogenase, and are highly susceptible to drug-induced hemolytic anemia (red-cell destruction). Megadoses of vitamin C act as a powerful reducing agent and can cause potentially fatal anemia.[20]

Excessive vitamin C can cause excessive absorption of iron and consequent iron poisoning, especially if iron intake is also high. At least one young man has died of severe heart failure apparently due to this effect.

Persons with sickle-cell disease are likewise vulnerable because the vitamin C converts their oxidized hemoglobin to reduced hemoglobin, which takes the sickle shape, clogs capillaries, and causes severe illness. Without treatment, they may die.

Diabetics must be careful with vitamin C. Megadoses can cause the Testape test for urine sugar to be falsely negative, and the Clinitest to be falsely positive. This could lead to underdose or overdose of insulin, and consequent diabetic crisis or insulin shock.

The strong reducing action of mega-C can also distort the occult blood test for colon cancer. Because of the large number of people who take megadoses, this is becoming an important problem in older persons and those deemed at risk for the disease.

Ascorbic acid is normally converted to oxalic acid, which is broken down and excreted in the urine. Some people's bodies can't break down the oxalic acid fast enough, and prolonged use of megadoses of vitamin C increases the susceptibility to oxalate kidney stone formation.

Vitamin C deficiency can impair immunity, but extra amounts do not confer extra benefits; they may, in fact, impair the bactericidal power of leucocytes.

Perhaps the strongest argument against the use of megadoses of ascorbic acid is the development of an increased rate of catabolism and excretion of the vitamin, which leaves the person more vulnerable than ever to deficiency symptoms should the intake be reduced to natural levels. Several studies have demonstrated this effect. For example, one scientist took 10 to 15 grams per day for two weeks. Four weeks after discontinuing the supplements his gums began to swell and bleed, his teeth loosened, his skin became rough, and his muscles ached.[21] Such symptoms don't normally occur until several months after total withdrawal of all vitamin C.

Some studies have shown this effect from as little as 2 grams per day. Cases of infantile scurvy, in spite of an intake of at least 60 mg per day, have been attributed to excessive doses taken by the mothers during pregnancy.

Another very disturbing effect of mega-C has been reported.[22] A

92 thirty-five-year-old chemist took 1 gram of vitamin C and 100 micrograms of vitamin B-12 every day. After only one week he experienced nose bleed, spontaneous bleeding from the external ear, dry mouth, and decreased ejaculate volume. Several repetitions of the experiment by him and others confirmed the effect. This illustrates the complex, and sometimes dangerous, interactions of megadoses of nutrients.

How Much Is Safe? No one knows for sure. It depends largely on the individual's blood chemistry and, as shown by the B-12 experiment, the use of other supplements. Probably no one is immune to the development of tolerance from taking large doses.

Several large servings (five to ten) of vitamin-C-rich foods could provide about a gram (1,000 milligrams) a day. This probably wouldn't cause adverse interactions with vitamin B-12 or other side effects because the vitamin C would gradually enter the blood throughout the day rather than in one huge dose. But it is far more than most bodies could use, and most would be excreted unused.

Dr. Linus Pauling suggests up to 9 grams on a regular basis, since this amount could theoretically be obtained from foods alone. But to get this amount from food, you would have to eat nothing but chili peppers, sweet peppers, and black currants, not exactly a natural diet.

If you already eat lots of vitamin-C-rich foods, supplements would just increase destruction rate and make you more susceptible to deficiency. If you are not eating such foods and want some protection from your smoking, aspirin use, emotional stress, and so on, 500 mg per day (fifty times the minimum to prevent scurvy) would surely be all your body could use on a regular basis. It should be considered an upper limit of regular supplementation in almost all cases. If more is used, say for its antihistamine effect, two or three days should be the limit. Large amounts should be spread throughout the day, not taken all at once. This decreases the likelihood of adverse reactions occurring.

Vitamin D (Cholecalciferol)

Vitamin D is necessary for the absorption of calcium from the intestine and for normal bone metabolism. Without it, bone mineralization is impaired and rickets (in children) or osteomalacia (in adults) occurs. It has been known for almost a hundred years that sunshine is a specific cure for rickets, although vitamin D was not discovered until the 1920s.

Sources The precursor of vitamin D, dehydrocholesterol, is present in the lubricating oily material in and on the skin of animals and humans. When ultraviolet radiation from the sun falls on the skin, one of the four rings of the molecule is broken, forming the three-ringed cholecalciferol, or vitamin D, which is absorbed into the circulation.

Vitamin D occurs naturally in fatty fish (such as tuna, sardines, herring), eggs, liver, butter, and other animal foods. A large number of packaged foods are fortified, such as milk, breakfast cereals, and margarines.

One hundred International Units (IU) per day prevents rickets and ensures normal mineralization and growth in practically all children, but the RDA is set at 400 IU (for all ages) to allow a large safety margin. This amount can be synthesized on the skin by exposure of only the arms to moderate intensity sunshine for about twenty minutes. Clouds decrease the effectiveness only a little, unless they are very thick and the sky quite dark, because the ultraviolet penetrates the clouds; on the other hand, it is blocked by glass and reduced by air pollution.

Who Needs Supplements? Vitamin D is one of the most potent vitamins; the RDA of 400 IU is only 10 *micrograms*, a barely visible speck. It is also toxic, oil soluble, and cumulative. No one denies the toxicity of large doses, but there is confusion about what is large.

Certain conditions, such as long-term corticosteroid therapy and vitamin-D-resistant rickets due to a rare genetic defect, usually call for supplementation. Persons who don't get a daily dose of sunlight or vitamin D foods should consider a supplement. A good example would be a vegetarian who doesn't eat fortified foods and lives in Alaska. Lactating women, infants, and children are especially at risk; this much is not disputed.

However, some vitamin promoters advocate doses many times the RDA and contend that they are harmless.

Hazards These people are apparently not familiar with several reports of devastating consequences that excessive vitamin D has had for some persons. Infants given excessive doses have developed generalized hardening of the arteries; severe mental retardation; a peculiar facial structure with large ears, a high narrow palate and irregular, carious teeth; kidney damage; recurrent infection; loss of appetite; and failure to grow. Discontinuing the vitamin D leads to dramatic improvement if it is not too late.

In England in the 1950s there was a rash of such cases associated with excessive fortification with vitamin D of dried milk and other welfare foods. Several hundred children, many of whom died, were affected. The intake in these cases was generally only 1,000 to 2,500 IU, much less than the tenfold increase over the RDA said by some to be safe. In 1957, the Ministry of Health recommended a 70 percent reduction of vitamin D in fortified milk and cereals.[23]

Adults are by no means exempt from these problems. Combined with moderately high calcium intake, excessive vitamin D can cause calci-

94

um deposition in vital organs. The kidneys are especially vulnerable to damage. Animal studies also indicate dangerous increases in cholesterol and triglyceride levels.

The widespread fortification of foods in sunny climes for consumption by sun-loving whites is highly questionable. Consider, for example, a white person of Northern European ancestry who tans poorly, lives in a sunny area, surfs, eats fortified breakfast cereal with fortified milk (which he drinks a half gallon of a day), takes a multivitamin pill with D in it and antacids with calcium carbonate. This amounts to twenty or more times the vitamin D RDA in a sensitive person with a very high calcium intake, and it spells Danger. The sun exposure alone would unquestionably be more than adequate. All the rest increases, rather than decreases, the risk to the health.

Vitamin E (Tocopherol)

In 1922 it was learned that rats fed mostly rancid lard with adequate amounts of the known vitamins could not bear offspring. The fetuses would be resorbed and the males would become sterile prematurely. Adding a fat-soluble substance from lettuce or wheat germ prevented resorption. Chemical analysis revealed alpha tocopherol and six other tocopherols, all less potent than the alpha. Many thousands of studies in the decades since have not elucidated the biochemical roles of vitamin E as definitely as has been done for other vitamins. This is partly because of the baffling array of abnormalities produced in deprived animals, including injury to the reproductive, nervous, muscular, and circulatory systems.

It has been established that vitamin E is an antioxidant, protects vitamin A and unsaturated fats from oxidation, and prevents cell membrane damage from naturally occurring peroxides, which are highly reactive "free radicals." This general antioxidant effect may account for the many different symptoms of deficiency. However, some experts believe it must have a more specific function, perhaps as a coenzyme, like the B vitamins.

In healthy humans obvious deficiencies are very rare. In cases of sprue, cystic fibrosis, or other malabsorption problems, deficiencies may cause impaired red-cell survival, elevated platelet count, skin lesions, and other changes.

A high intake of polyunsaturated fatty acids increases the vitamin E requirement. Deficiency symptoms have been reported in premature infants given polyunsaturated fats, iron, or oxygen supplementation.

Sources Vegetables, seeds, grains, and their oils are the best sources of the tocopherols. Fruits, meats, beans, eggs, and dairy products contribute significant amounts, as do most margarines, salad oils, and shortenings. Freezing foods destroys substantial amounts of vitamin E.

Who Needs Supplements? There is no question that most premature infants and persons with malabsorption problems should have supplements. Beyond that, controversy rages. The Food and Nutrition Board says 30 International Units (IU) is plenty for everyone and that adequate amounts are found in a varied diet. Although increasing vegetable oil consumption increases the requirement, the oil almost always provides that extra vitamin E.

But magazine writers, vitamin industry spokespersons, and a few physicians advocate up to 2,000 IU, about sixty-five times the RDA, on a regular basis to prevent and cure a long list of ailments including heart disease, varicose veins, phlebitis and other circulatory disorders, cancer, menopausal symptoms, leg cramps, shingles, arthritis, and diabetes. It is also used in efforts to promote wound (especially burn) healing, physical performance, stamina, fertility, and libido.

The advocates say that our food supply is stripped of vitamin E, that vegetable oils increase the need more than they fill it, and that our requirements are higher because of air pollution and years of poor diet.

So far, all the dramatic claims of cures have been anecdotal, not scientific. Careful studies are required to determine whether supplements really help in the various disorders it is claimed useful for. Several such studies have failed to detect any benefits.

The placebo effect is always a possibility when people report improvement after taking vitamin E. Ironically, an article by Richard Passwater (*Prevention*, April 1976), an ardent mega-E advocate, inadvertently supports the conclusion that the placebo effect is the major source of positive reports. This highly biased survey of *Prevention* readers who use vitamin E would be expected to show spectacular improvements.

More than 6,000 heart disease sufferers, aged sixty to sixty-nine, responded to the survey. The duration of heavy supplementation ranged from less than a year to thirty years. The largest percentage of positive responses (indications of improved heart conditions since taking vitamin E) came from those who had used the supplements less than a year, and even in this group fewer than 25 percent reported benefits, which is about what might be expected from the placebo effect. The longer they had taken the vitamin, the less favorable were the reports, as would be expected from the placebo effect, which generally erodes with time.

Is the RDA Adequate? Here is some strong evidence that it is: the plasma level shown to be borderline and hazardous to maintain for more than a year

96   is .5 mg per 100 milliliters of blood (.5 mg percent, as this measure is called). No deficiency symptoms have been observed above this level. In a study of college women eating in a university dining hall and not taking supplements, the average vitamin E intake was slightly below the RDA for about 70 percent of the women. Yet their plasma levels were about 2 mg percent, four times the borderline level.[24]

Can Extra Vitamin E Help Athletes? A very thorough study of this question was done at Tulane University.[25] Forty-eight members of the swimming team were put into two groups matched for age, sex, and swimming ability. For six months one group was given 900 IU of vitamin E, the other group an identical-looking pill with none. No one, not even the coaches or research assistants, knew who was getting which pill until the study was completed. As it turned out, there was no detectable difference in performance, endurance, or improvement between the two groups. Several other studies have come to similar conclusions.

To our knowledge, this study has never been reported in a health food magazine. This is not surprising, for the purpose of these publications is to sell supplements, not to tell the truth about them.

The Sex and Youth Vitamin? Vitamin E's reputation as the "reproduction vitamin" or "sex vitamin" is without foundation. All essential nutrients are required for normal reproduction and any of them could just as logically be given these lofty titles. It just happens that vitamin E's role in reproduction was the first of its roles to be discovered.

Nor is its reputation as a "youth vitamin" based on fact. Animals given large doses for life show no delay in aging and do not live longer than nonsupplemented animals on the same diet. In fact, rats receiving large doses have developed cholesterol deposits in the liver, and those given alcohol plus megadoses of vitamin E have developed much worse liver damage than rats given only alcohol.

The Hazards Vitamin E, like the two vitamins well known to be toxic in excess, A and D, is oil-soluble, and an excess is not readily excreted. This alone is grounds for caution. Even the Shute brothers, physicians and originators of the current mega-E movement, although advocates of large doses in specific circulatory diseases after thorough medical work-up, do not advocate indiscriminate dosing and warn of the dangers of excesses in persons with hypertension.

Excessive vitamin E has been shown to reduce blood thyroid levels in some people. This may account for some of the reported side effects of megadoses, which include headaches, severe fatigue, nausea, blurred vision, dizziness, inflammation of the mouth, chapped lips, muscle weakness, low blood sugar, increased bleeding tendencies, inhibited wound healing, increased blood fats (especially in women), increased cholesterol levels, and gastrointestinal disturbances. The elevated fat and cholesterol could promote heart disease, which is ironic in view of the claims that vitamin E can prevent atherosclerosis. Some people who suffer fatigue and weakness from large doses (800 IU per day) excrete large amounts of creatinine, indicating possible skeletal muscle damage.[26]

In conclusion, eating a varied diet with plenty of whole, natural foods provides adequate vitamin E for normal, healthy persons. Those who take supplements without the advice of a physician should not exceed about 100 IU, the most that could be obtained by eating nothing but foods very rich in the vitamin.

Vitamin K

Vitamin K is necessary for the synthesis of prothrombin and other blood clotting factors in the liver. A deficiency causes poor clotting and hemorrhage.

At least half the requirement is met by production by intestinal bacteria. The rest comes from food such as leafy greens, soybeans, egg yolks, and liver.

Who Needs Supplements? It is difficult to produce a deficiency by dietary restriction alone. But combined with antibiotics, which destroy intestinal bacteria, poor diet can lead to a deficiency and poor blood clotting.

Newborn infants, especially if premature, are sometimes deficient before the establishment of the intestinal flora. Breast milk has adequate vitamin K, as do all the commonly used milk-based formulas. But poor feeding in the first week or so can lead to deficiency.

Chronic fat malabsorption, characteristic of certain uncommon ailments, can lead to deficiency, and liver disease sometimes increases the requirement.

Toxicity The natural forms of vitamin K, K-1 (phylloquinone), and K-2 (menaquinone) are apparently completely safe, even in very large doses. The synthetic K-3 and its various derivatives can be toxic even in moderate doses.

98   **Bioflavinoids,** such as rutin and hesperidin, are widely distributed in natural foods, especially those containing vitamin C. They are not considered vitamins because no deficiency state has been induced or discovered in humans or animals. However, they may potentiate vitamin C, allowing a smaller dose to protect from scurvy, although this is debatable. They have been reported helpful in several circulatory problems, such as retinal hemorrhage, diabetic retinopathy, and strokes. But other reports indicate no benefit.

Para-Aminobenzoic Acid (PABA). Although it is an important growth factor for lower animals, PABA is not a required nutrient, not a vitamin. It is an excellent sun screen when applied to the skin but not when taken internally. Large doses can cause adverse changes in the liver, heart, and kidneys, and a drop in white blood cell count. The marketing of PABA supplements is highly questionable since they provide no benefit and can be hazardous.

Inositol, or myoinositol, is a sugarlike substance that is very widespread in natural foods and is a constituent of certain phospholipids, but the human body makes it and it is no longer considered a vitamin. Inositol pills are sold, but they are quite expensive and there is no known benefit from taking them.

8

Adelle Davis and Megavitamins

s the science of nutrition has progressed, the dramatic power of essential nutrients to cure deficiency symptoms has captured the popular imagination. In many current books on nutrition the guiding philosophy is that if a little scientific magic is good, ten times as much must be ten times as good.

Adelle Davis was among the first to develop and promote this concept. Her books consist of elaborate arguments for more, more, more of each and every known nutrient, and her followers take handfuls of pills, drink quarts of nutrient-rich, milk-based concoctions, and eat lots of high-protein (and high-fat, high-cholesterol) foods. Her recommended daily intake ranges from about three to thirty times the RDAs.

Davis made many false assertions, such as: large doses of vitamin E during pregnancy prevent miscarriages, mental retardation, congenital heart disease and other birth defects; lots of milk prevents cancer (of which she died); lobster is a great stamina food; and so on. There is no evidence for these claims, which are mostly speculations based on misinterpretations of animal and test-tube studies.

Davis instills an unwarranted fear in her followers of going a few hours or, God forbid, a whole day without ingesting several times the RDA of every known nutrient. On the positive side, she has steered many people away from highly-refined foods, and she vigorously supports breast feeding. On the balance, however, she has been a bad influence and some of her advice is dangerous. For example, an infant died after being given potassium chloride for colic, as she suggests in one of her books. She recommends doses of vitamin A which, if taken by pregnant women, can cause birth

100 defects of the urinary tract. Perhaps most harmful is the high-fat and high-cholesterol levels of her recommended diet; the amounts of whole milk, eggs, red meats, and liver and other organ meats she advocates are potentially lethal, especially for those with other risk factors for atherosclerosis and heart disease.

More recent writers, such as Richard A. Passwater, in *Supernutrition* (Pocket Books, 1975), have taken the more-is-better concept much further than even Adelle Davis. Ten times the RDA? Why, that's practically deficient; let's make it fifty to a hundred times. Passwater provides "supernutrition curves" illustrating the supposed increasing benefit of increasing doses of vitamins. According to the curves, anything less than the RDA is definitely deficient and harmful and causes "toxicity disease." Strangely enough, he believes natural amounts to be toxic and very large amounts, many times a natural dose, to be beneficial. As the intake increases above the RDA, the benefits accelerate. One's progress can be measured every few months, he says, by monitoring one's pulse, blood pressure, weight, bowel regularity, stamina, mood, blood chemistry, and frequency of various aches, pains, and disorders.

Passwater suggests starting one's supernutrition program with supplements of two to ten times the RDA, gradually increasing and adjusting the dose and, by regularly measuring all the above parameters, finding the right amount of each vitamin. The curves show the "saturation points," the doses of maximum benefit for most people, to be 50 to 100 times the RDA, but one must constantly experiment and measure the result of varying each nutrient until the optimum amount of each one is found.

The absurdity of this approach is obvious. As Passwater admits, one can vary the dose and study the effects of only one nutrient at a time. One could experiment for weeks with one nutrient before finally deciding that a certain dose is optimal. Then the next nutrient would be taken and its supposed effects studied for weeks, and so on. If one studied all the known nutrients this way, it could take ten years of intense self-study and rigid nutrient control to finally settle on one's "supernutrition level" and this doesn't even take into account the likely interactions of the massive doses.

There is not the slightest evidence that increasing the intake of vitamins, as suggested by Passwater and other megavitamin advocates, can alter one's stamina, pulse, mood, or any of the other conditions he mentions. Taking a pill for fitness, health, and happiness is a very American idea, but it does not work.

The fundamental flaw of the megavitamin theory, which reveals a misunderstanding of the biochemical role of vitamins, is the assumption that increasing vitamin concentrations somehow increases or improves the reactions the vitamins are involved in. Vitamins are enzyme cofactors which help catalyze cellular reactions necessary to life. Vitamin molecules, like enzymes, are reused millions of times before being excreted. If an excess is supplied it is excreted or stored until needed; it cannot push the reactions faster or improve them in any way.

Megavitamin advocates largely ignore the hazards and cost of excessive vitamins and minerals. Some of them work for supplement manufacturers to whom vitamins in the sewer mean money in the bank. More than 95 percent of most megavitamin doses is excreted within a few hours without ever having entered a cell. The cost of a megavitamin program can easily reach several hundred, even a thousand dollars a year and, including interest, over $100,000 in a lifetime, not counting medical costs and lost work time due to toxicity and adverse reactions.

Unfortunately, the megavitamin advocates have so persuaded the public that they are right, and have so inspired supplement manufacturers with visions of greater profits, that it is sometimes difficult to find inexpensive supplements with just the RDA of vitamins and minerals. There seems to be endless competition among the makers of stress, superstress, and supermegastress formulations to see who can pack the most vitamins and minerals into one pill. This silliness has even spread to fortified foods, with breakfast cereals supplying the RDA of ten vitamins in a few bites and tasting more and more like vitamin pills. TV commercials for one brand even show the cereal flakes falling out of vitamin capsules.

9

Minerals

Nutrient minerals are basic chemical elements present in the earth and in plants, and required in the diet for normal growth, reproduction, and health. They are often classified as "major" or "trace" minerals, depending on the amounts required. Although requirements for calcium and phosphorous are many thousands of times greater those for iodine, chromium, and other trace minerals, the minerals in the middle range are difficult to classify. Moreover, the distinction may imply that the major minerals are more important than the others and this is not true. Therefore, we simply discuss the minerals in alphabetical order, with chloride discussed under sodium chloride and "other trace minerals" discussed last.

Calcium

Calcium is required for normal bone development, blood clotting, muscle tone, nerve transmission, and heart muscle function. If insufficient amounts are ingested, the blood level is maintained (by parathyroid hormone) at the cost of bone calcium. Poor growth and poor bones and teeth result.

The richest sources are milk, hard cheese, dark green leafy vegetables, and soft-bone fish. Other good sources include legumes, broccoli, string beans, artichokes, almonds, sesame seeds, soft cheeses, and figs. Fair sources include cottage cheese, nuts, whole grains, carrots, eggs, oranges, dates, and prunes. Most meats, fruits, and vegetables are poor sources.

Who Needs Supplements? One cup of milk provides about 300 mg which, along with another 200 to 300 mg from vegetables and other sources, is enough to keep lacto-vegetarian adult males in calcium balance, but is less

102

than one-fifth the requirement for pregnant or lactating, meat-eating teen-agers. These are the two extremes on the spectrum of calcium requirement. The RDA is 800 mg for most children and adults, but 1200 for teenagers and another 400 for pregnancy or lactation. The RDA is set at these high levels in recognition of the abundance of protein and phosphorous in the typical American diet, which usually leads to the excretion in the stool of about three-fourths of ingested calcium. The actual requirement can be reduced by up to about half by reducing intake of protein, phosphorous, and probably coffee and other drinks containing caffeine.

Infants, children, and pregnant and lactating women should eat generous amounts of calcium-containing foods, especially if they eat meat every day. Even though the RDA is the same for men and nonpregnant, nonlactating women, the latter (except blacks; see Osteoporosis in Part Four) could probably benefit from a higher intake because of their susceptibility to osteoporosis after menopause.[27] It is best for them to develop the densest possible bones before menopause, and some women may require more than the RDA to accomplish this.

If these guidelines cannot be followed, supplements may be in order. Food sources are much preferable, though, and supplements should probably not be taken for "insurance" if the diet is adequate because they can affect the absorption of other minerals and because calcium supplements, such as powdered oyster shell, bone meal, and dolomite often contain lead, cadmium, and mercury.

The safest supplements are probably pure calcium carbonate. In general no more than 50 to 100 percent of the RDA should be taken. Prolonged excessive calcium intake can cause calcification of soft tissues, especially if vitamin D is also taken. Most people should avoid total calcium intake of more than 2 grams per day.

Copper

Copper is involved in the formation and functions of blood, bones, nerves, reproductive organs, and various enzymes. Deficiency can cause anemia, skeletal defects, degeneration of the nervous system, elevated cholesterol levels, and possibly cardiovascular disease.

Sources of copper include various meats, nuts, seeds, peas, grains, beans, and many whole, unprocessed foods. Dairy products are a poor source.

Supplements of up to 5 milligrams a day should be taken by persons who eat poorly and those who take supplements of zinc or vitamin C, both of which decrease the availability of copper.

104 Fluoride

Fluoride is incorporated into the teeth and bones and greatly increases resistance to tooth decay. It is essential to growth.

Sources of fluoride include almost all foods and drinking water, but the amounts present may be less than necessary to prevent dental decay.

Supplements are advisable for people whose drinking water is deficient; fluoridation has proven to be a safe and very effective way of reducing the incidence of dental caries. (See Dental and Gum Disease in Part Four for more on this.)

Iodine

Iodine is a component of the metabolism-regulating hormone thyroxin. When iodine is lacking, the thyroid gland enlarges, sometimes to a volume greater than the whole head. In spite of simple and inexpensive means of prevention, endemic goiter is possibly the most common single deficiency disease in the world, with more than 200 million persons affected. Most of them are in developing nations, isolated villages of Europe, northern India, and South and Central America.

The best sources of iodine used to be seafoods, including seaweed, which the Chinese have used to treat goiters for 5,000 years. The ancient Egyptians and Incas also used this remedy.

The biggest source of dietary iodine in the United States now is dairy products. Farmers feed cows lots of iodine in the belief (unproven) that this prevents foot rot. Moreover, many iodine-containing chemicals are used as antiseptics to clean and sanitize milking machines, storage vats, transport tankers, and other equipment.[28]

The use of iodine chemicals in cleaning food processing equipment has also led to high levels in grain products, sugars, and sugar products such as candies, jams, and puddings. Other important sources include iodized salt, fast foods, nutritional supplements, and erythrosine (food coloring Red #3), which is more than 50 percent iodine.

Iodine deficiency was once a problem in the midwest United States where the soil and the foods grown in it have little of the mineral. This led to the widespread use of iodized salt to prevent goiters. But now most Americans get far more iodine than they need, typically five to ten times the RDA, which is 150 micrograms for adults. These high levels are safe for most people but pose certain hazards for some, especially those with hyperthyroidism and other thyroid problems. Extremely high intakes, fifty or more times the RDA, is common among seaweed gatherers in Japan and causes many of them to develop goiters.

Who Needs Supplements? Strict vegetarians who do not eat dairy products or processed grain or sugar products, and whose vegetables and fruits are grown in noncoastal areas, should use iodized salt or take supplements. One gram of the salt provides about half the RDA.

Iron

Iron is an essential component of metabolic enzymes in every cell of the body. Most of it is present in the blood cells as hemoglobin. Deficiency causes anemia with weakness, pallor, shortness of breath, lack of appetite, and a general slowing of vital functions. Mild deficiency in children has been linked to clumsiness, inattentiveness, and other problems.

Sources: Good sources include lean meats, fish, eggs, legumes, nuts, dried fruits, whole grains, all leafy greens, and molasses. Almost all whole, natural foods provide significant amounts of iron. Cow's milk is a poor source, while human milk is generally much better.

Iron deficiency is possibly the most common nutritional deficiency in the United States, though some trace elements may rival iron for this distinction.[29] The main cause of the problem is the widespread consumption of highly processed foods.

A varied diet of whole natural foods easily supplies the required amounts. For example, 2,500 calories worth of potatoes, broccoli, whole grains, carrots, and other mediocre iron sources supplies the generous RDA (18 mg) for women of child-bearing age. The requirement for men is about half that for women, so is even more easily met.

Who Needs Supplements? The body uses iron very economically, absorbing it much more efficiently when stores are low and storing large amounts of reserves, which last for months, when the intake is large. Therefore, deficiency develops only after a long period of unusually high need, such as in pregnancy and growth, and after severe blood loss, such as in active ulcers, hemorrhoids, and excessive menstrual flow. Borderline intake in young girls for months or years prior to the onset of menses may result in deficiency when blood loss begins. Repeated pregnancies are especially costly to the woman's iron stores. In these situations, supplementation is usually advisable. IUD users and other women with heavy menstrual flow often need supplemental iron.

Ferrous sulfate, fumarate, and gluconate are all well absorbed. If one causes gastrointestinal distress, another can be tried.

106 **Hazards** There is no advantage to taking very large doses of iron unless anemia is present or stores are very low. Prolonged intake of 250 mg per day can cause serious problems due to iron build-up. While 60 mg per day is a common therapeutic dose, even this amount, if not needed, can decrease absorption of zinc and possibly other trace minerals, and can be toxic if vitamin C intake is high.

Magnesium

Magnesium is an essential cofactor in the metabolism of carbohydrates, the maintainence of DNA and RNA, protein synthesis, normal calcium and potassium metabolism, and other important biochemical processes. It is involved in the regulation of body temperature and in nerve and muscle function.

Symptoms and signs of deficiency include low blood calcium, loss of appetite, nausea, apathy, tremors, convulsions, and coma. Chronic deficiency may be a factor in atherosclerosis, but this has not been proven.

Sources: Magnesium tends to parallel protein and phosphorous in food, but meat and milk are poor sources. The best sources are whole grains, nuts, beans, peanuts, leafy greens, wheat germ, and brewer's yeast. Hard water and most fruits and vegetables have fair amounts, which can add up to a lot. For example, a mixed fruit salad would contain about 200 mg per 1,000 calories, or 500 mg per 2,500 calories. The RDA is 300 to 450 mg, the largest amount being required during lactation. Clearly, a diet with generous amounts of natural foods easily provides the requirement. Diets heavy in refined foods may present a problem; for example, brown rice has about 250 mg per 100 grams, but white rice has only 25 mg.

Who Needs Supplements? Persons most likely to need supplements are alcoholics, malnourished infants, pregnant or lactating women on poor diets, persons taking large doses of diuretics for long periods, persons who fast frequently, those on highly refined diets, and heavy exercisers on mediocre diets. The best supplement is probably pure magnesium oxide since dolomite often contains toxic heavy metals. Excessive magnesium can cause diarrhea and may affect the absorption of other minerals, so no more than the RDA should be taken.

Phosphorous

Phosphorous combines with calcium to mineralize bones and teeth. Small amounts are also essential to almost every reaction in the body. Deficiency causes stunted growth and poor quality bones and teeth.

Sources: Phosphorous is widely distributed, especially in protein-rich foods such as meat, fish, and milk, but also in whole grains, vegetables, and fruits.

Who Needs Supplements? Because of its widespread availability, deficiency is almost unheard of, except in cases of very poor diet and heavy, prolonged use of aluminum-containing antacids. Strict vegetarians (vegans) might also have borderline intakes.

Isolated phosphorous supplementation is almost never desirable. Calcium and phosphorous intake should be roughly equal. Excessive phosphorous from a heavy meat diet with lots of soda pop can induce a relative calcium deficiency.

Potassium

Potassium is the major intracellular element, and deficiency results in muscle weakness, even paralysis. Potassium is widely distributed in both plant and animal foods. The best **sources** are fruits and vegetables and their juices.

Potassium is lost in fasting, severe protein deficiency, injury, diuretic use, and diarrhea. Endurance athletes should be especially careful to get adequate amounts.

Supplements, such as potassium chloride, can be **hazardous;** an excess may cause death by depression of heart function. Most persons who need large amounts should drink fruit and vegetable juices.

Sodium and Chloride

These essential nutrients are important in the electrolyte and water balance of cells, nerves, muscles, and the body as a whole. Chloride is also a component of gastric acid (hydrochloric acid). Depletion causes muscle cramping, loss of appetite, and, progressively, apathy, convulsions, coma, and death.

Sodium chloride—common table salt—is widely distributed in foods, and depletion is very rare except from prolonged vomiting, diarrhea, or diuretic use, which can cause large chloride losses, and heavy sweating, which causes large sodium losses.

Who Needs Supplements? Moderate to heavy work in hot conditions can increase the sodium requirement by several grams a day. Salt should be added to food, not taken as tablets. It can also be added to water, but no more than a half teaspoon (2 grams) per liter. If there is little sweating, little sodium is required, and there is usually no need to salt foods, most of which already have some sodium. Excessive salt intake is believed to be a major factor in hypertension in sensitive persons.

Zinc

Zinc is an essential coenzyme in a long list of reactions in the body such as the synthesis of RNA, DNA, and proteins. Deficiency causes dwarfism, failure of sex glands to mature, anemia, abnormal hair and nail growth, decreased pancreatic enzymes, decreased hormone synthesis, decreased alcohol tolerance, poor wound healing, and impaired immunity.

Sources: Zinc is very widely distributed in plant and animal tissues. All natural foods have some, but fruits and green vegetables tend to have less than whole grains, legumes, and nuts. These latter sources, however, have high levels of phytates, which tend to bind much of the zinc and prevent its absorption. The richest sources of available zinc are wheat germ, fish, and meats. Nuts are generally better than beans and grains. Sprouting grains and seeds reduces the phytate activity and increases zinc availability. Making bread with yeast and allowing it to rise eliminates much of the phytate activity and greatly increases zinc availability.

Who Needs Supplements? Premature infants, slow-growing children, especially if they eat poorly or are strict vegetarians, and those with sickle-cell anemia often benefit from daily supplements of about 1 milligram per kilogram body weight (about .5 mg per pound). The zinc directly promotes growth and may also improve the appetite.

Supplements are usually needed by those who:

> drink heavily or have kidney or liver disease
>
> have malabsorption disorders or the rare disease acrodermatitis enteropathica
>
> are on highly refined diets, since refining removes about 80 percent of the zinc from grains
>
> eat a lot of soybeans or whole grains, especially unleavened whole wheat bread, and very little of the richer zinc sources
>
> are under heavy stress from severe injury or surgery or have active ulcers or take corticosteroids or large amounts of alcohol

White spots on the nails, especially in children and teenagers, may indicate zinc deficiency, though this association has not been firmly established. The diet should be checked and, if intake is low, supplements should be taken.

The RDA is 15 mg for adults, 25 mg for lactating women, and 3 to 10 mg for children, depending on age.

CAUTION

While up to 150 mg per day have been used in cases of deficiency, alcoholism, acne, and ulcers, such doses should not be taken by normal healthy persons for prolonged periods because excessive zinc may cause nausea, vomiting, low blood copper, and anemia, and it might promote atherosclerosis by interfering with copper function, increasing LDL-cholesterol, and decreasing HDL-cholesterol. It may also inhibit immune responses.[30] Large doses taken by pregnant women may induce premature birth.

Other Trace Minerals

Recent research reveals that tiny amounts of the unlikeliest elements are essential nutrients without which reproduction, growth, and health are not possible. Who would have guessed, for example, that we have a dietary requirement for tin, chromium, or nickel? Others proven or strongly suspected of being essential include manganese, molybdenum, vanadium, and silicon. Selenium deficiency may damage heart muscle, promote cancer, and weaken the immune system. Even cadmium may have a biological function, though it is toxic in larger amounts, as are the others.

As with so many other essential nutrients, these elements are very widely distributed and present in hundreds of natural foods but are largely removed by refining. For example, in milling wheat 40 to 90 percent of the chromium, manganese, zinc, molybdenum, and copper are removed. Other trace nutrients are also lost. "Enriched" bread is a consumer fraud since it contains added amounts of only a few of the many nutrients removed by processing. Besides trace minerals, amino acids, fiber, vitamin E, and other components are lost and not replaced. This is yet another reason to eat more natural and fewer refined foods.

Since the presence of trace elements varies a great deal and is dependent on soil content, a variety of foods from different areas should be eaten. Dependence on locally grown foods, as advocated by macrobiotics, can contribute to deficiencies, as dramatically illustrated by the high incidence of goiter in many areas of the world where the iodine content of the soil is poor, and high cancer incidence where selenium levels are low.

Who Needs Supplementation? Many trace element preparations are on the market and people wonder if they should take them. If one has a highly refined diet, trace mineral supplements might be of value, but it would make a lot more sense to eat a variety of natural foods. Particularly rich sources are brewer's yeast (not torula yeast, which lacks chromium), wheat germ, kelp,

110 and fish. Taking large doses of trace elements can be dangerous. For example, as little as two weeks of high-potency selenium can cause hair loss, fatigue, vomiting, and other symptoms of toxicity.[31]

What About Hair Analysis?

Some commercial labs claim they can determine your trace-mineral needs by analyzing your hair. Such claims are false. Many variables affect hair mineral content, and no clear association of hair levels with tissue levels or nutritional needs has been established. However, hair analysis may reveal high levels of lead, mercury, and other toxic heavy metals. (See Part Six.)

10

Diets, Diets, and More Diets

Because of our omnivorous nature and the great variety and complexity of foods, an almost infinite number of diets can be conceived—and they are. Dozens of women's magazines and tabloid newspapers have been announcing brand new miracle diets every week for decades, and there is usually at least one book on the best seller lists. The diets are promoted mostly for weight loss but also for skin beauty, stamina, sexual energy, and the healing of various diseases.

It would take volumes to review in detail all the diets advocated in the last few years, but this is not necessary since many are copycat versions of other high-fat, high-protein, high-starch, and prudent diets. We take a close look at the original formulations. We also review popular diets that have unique (and sometimes hokey) twists that shape the meal plans as much as the fat, protein, or starch content. These discussions provide the tools for judging the vast majority of those one is likely to encounter.

It should be noted that we focus on the original versions, not the many modifications made by the authors after the initial best-seller to correct obvious flaws or simply to cash in on a new diet book. For example, the original Atkins, Stillman, and Pritikin diets are prototypes of, respectively, extreme low-carbohydrate, high-protein, and high-starch diets. Their later versions are less extreme and closer to the Ideal Diet. The great thing about the business of writing diet books is that you can first make lots of money and a name for yourself with outlandish theories and claims remarkable for their absurdity, gimmickry, and acceptance by gullible millions; then you can write sensible books that people will buy because you are rich and famous—

112 even if they just tell you what the American Heart Association or American Cancer Society will tell you for free.

Who Needs To Lose Weight?

No one needs to lose weight, per se, but some people need to lose fat. Obesity, which increases the risk of high blood pressure, heart disease, diabetes, gallbladder disease, and some cancers, is inevitable when calorie intake exceeds calorie expenditure for extended periods. Men whose body weight is more than 20 percent fat and women over 25 percent are close to obese; 25 and 30 percent, respectively, are definitely obese. (See Chapters 1–1 and 1–4.)

The Metropolitan Life Insurance Company tables of desirable weights for men and women of different heights and "body frame size" (small, medium, and large) are widely used and taken as gospel by many dieticians, nutritionists, and physicians, and by the general public. Unfortunately, the data are outdated and their validity open to question. They are nothing but average values for men and women who took out life insurance policies at standard premium rates. Nowhere is frame size defined and there is no acceptable method of determining which category one belongs to. The new, revised Metropolitan Life tables have been shifted up, so fewer people are considered obese, but the basic problem remains: the tables tell us nothing about fat.

Some studies have failed to find a consistent relation between weight and death rates for the moderately "overweight," and some indicate that there are fewer deaths among this group than among those at or below their "ideal" weights. Skinny people seem to die more often of peptic ulcers, ulcerative colitis, and some other problems. This has puzzled researchers, and it has been suggested that moderate fatness has some protective value. This may be true, but it seems more likely that most of the data relied on for these studies are worthless because of the arbitrary assignment of frame size according to height. There is no evidence that a person of a given height and weight necessarily has more fat than a person of the same height and less weight. Many "moderately obese" subjects may not be fat at all, and some "normal" subjects may have high percentages of fat.

A scale will not tell you about fat percentage or fitness. It is better to simply feel and look at the fat around your waist and thighs and to try the fitness and fatness tests in Chapter 1–4. They are not perfect, but if they all point in the same direction you will know where you stand. If you are still not sure whether you should lose some fat, discuss it with a physician, preferably one who understands fitness and does not just use the Metropolitan tables.

The Problem with Dieting for Weight Control

Those interested in diets for fat reduction and control should keep in mind some important limitations. First, calories ingested do not count by themselves; they must be weighed against calories expended. Most obese persons do not overeat so much as they underexercise, which gives them a slow metabolic rate and poor fat-burning capacity. When they go on low-calorie diets their metabolism drops even lower and their fat-burning capacity decreases more. When the diet inevitably ends the fat will pile back up. For reasons explained in Part One, adequate exercise is probably the single most important factor in fat control.

Keep in mind, too, that the emphasis diet books and articles almost always put on body weight is very misleading; almost any diet with reduced calories or carbohydrates will cause substantial losses of water, glycogen, and lean tissue (muscle mass), all of which contribute to *weight* reduction but not *fat* reduction. The loss of lean tissue decreases fitness, so promotes fatness in the long run. Ignore your weight, then, and consider instead your visible and palpable flab, your stamina in a long uphill walk or jog, your muscle tone, and your vigor and zest. With proper exercise and good nutrition these can be greatly improved.

In general, fit persons eat more than fat persons of the same weight because they have higher metabolic rates, and muscle takes more food to sustain than fat. Clearly then, calorie reduction is not essential to fat reduction and is not desirable in fit persons. Nevertheless, slight or moderate calorie reduction can help in shedding fat, as long as one does not so restrict food intake that exercise and metabolism decrease or that lean tissue is lost.

The most important consideration in choosing a diet or lifelong eating plan is the carbohydrate-fat-protein profile. The average American now gets about 46 percent of his calories from carbohydrate (22 starch, 24 sugar), 42 percent from fat (26 unsaturated, 16 saturated), and 12 percent from protein. The table shows how this compares to the major diets.

High-Fat, Low-Carbohydrate Diets

The idea that eating a lot of fat and little or no carbohydrate can help in weight reduction is at least a hundred years old. It was popularized in Great Britain in the 1860s by a pamphlet written by coffin-maker William Banting, who claimed to have lost about fifty pounds in a year by eating a lot of meat and very little sugar, bread, and potatoes, and drinking little beer.

114 Comparing the Diets at a Glance

	% Carbohydrate	% Fat	% Protein
Atkins Diet Revolution (1) Start at 0% carbohydrate. No calorie limit.	5	75	20
California Diet and Exercise Program(3) Balance calorie intake with activity level. Minimize refined sugar and grains, saturated fat and cholesterol.	58	30	12
Edelstein's Women's Diet (2) Couple with liberal use of diuretics and appetite suppressants.	20	30	50
Fast Foods; typical fare at average hamburger drive-in High in sugar, saturated fats, cholesterol. Low in fiber.	25	60	15
The Ideal Diet At least half of fat calories from plant sources. At least 75% of carbohydrate calories from whole grains, fruits, vegetables.	60–65	25	10–15
Macrobiotic Diet (3) Start with 100% brown rice diet. No dairy products, eggs, or meat. Occasional fish.	80	10	10
Prudent Diet Favor unsaturated over saturated fat. Avoid high cholesterol foods.	40	35	25
Stillman Diet (2) Drink lots of water.	5	10	85
Pritikin Diet (3) (almost vegetarian) Practically no animal products except skim milk. No high-fat vegetables. No refined grains or sugar.	78	10	12

(1) Hi Fat, Lo Carbo   (3) Hi Starch, Lo Fat
(2) Hi Pro, Lo Carbo

In 1950, Dr. Alfred Pennington, duPont's company physician, wrote up the "duPont Diet" for *Holiday* magazine. This version of the diet was popular for a few years but it faded.

In 1961 Herman Taller, M.D., took vegetable oils with his meals in an effort to reduce his blood cholesterol. When he found his weight dropped as well as his cholesterol levels, he proclaimed his dietary principles in *Calories Don't Count*, which sold about two million copies. Taller claimed that eating two tablespoons of safflower or corn oil before each meal stimulates the production of hormones which work to mobilize fats stored around the body.

When he got involved in the marketing of C.D.C. (for "calories don't count") brand safflower capsules, the federal government prosecuted him for mail fraud and violating federal drug laws. He was fined $7,000 and placed on probation for two years. This seems harsh considering the dangerous diets others have more recently pushed with impunity.

The next high-fat prophet was Robert Atkins, M.D. We discuss his diet in detail since it is the most popular version and is representative of the genre. Other diets in the high-fat category are the Paul Michael's Weight-loss Plan and The Drinking Man's Diet.

Dr. Atkins' "Diet Revolution" Robert C. Atkins, M.D., author of *Dr. Atkins' Diet Revolution* (Bantam, 1972), says thousands of his patients have lost weight without counting calories, without diet pills, without a single pang of hunger, and without elevated serum cholesterol or triglyceride levels. In fact, he claims this diet is the medical treatment of choice for most people with adult-onset diabetes and cholesterol problems.

You may eat as much as you want as often as you want, including such rich foods as heavy cream, butter, eggs, bacon, seafoods, mayonnaise, cheeses, and meats. You may eat 5,000 calories a day, be sedentary, and still lose weight and feel better than ever with more energy than ever. If this sounds like a miracle, it is, Atkins says—a "biochemical miracle" to be exact.

The key is a zero or near-zero carbohydrate diet. In the first week, during which not a gram of carbohydrate is allowed, ketone bodies will appear in the urine as a by product of fat metabolism. Then carbohydrates are gradually added until the ketone excretion stops, then the dieter keeps the carbohydrate intake just below this level, and eats as much fat and protein as he wants. This induced ketosis causes "hundreds of calories to be sneaked out of the body every day in the form of ketones and a host of other incompletely broken down molecules of fat" in the urine and in the breath.

There are some difficulties with this theory. Several studies have shown that people fasting or eating only fats and proteins excrete very little ketones in the breath and urine: the maximum is about 3 grams per day. The caloric value of ketones is about 4.5 calories per gram. So the maximum loss would be less than 15 calories a day, the equivalent of about a third of a teaspoon of butter, much less than the hundreds he claims are sneaked out of the body and certainly not enough to account for the weight losses he claims.[32]

Another problem with Atkins' theory is that it does not take into account weight loss by water loss. It has been shown that carbohydrate in the diet helps retain water, and that high-fat, high-protein diets cause water loss. The obese need to lose fat, not water.

More important than these theoretical objections to Atkins' "diet revolution" are the potential hazards involved with it, especially to diabetics and others prone to heart disease. Atkins encourages a high intake of cholesterol and saturated fats, which can dangerously increase blood levels. Many studies have shown that elevated serum cholesterol is associated with an increased risk of heart disease. Many long-term, carefully controlled studies have shown lower heart attack and fatality rates in humans on low-fat, low-cholesterol diets. Increased fatty acids can disturb heart rhythm and provoke a heart attack if one has cardiovascular disease.

There are also the hazards of fatigue and hypotension. In one study ten healthy, normal adults were placed on diets of 1,500 or 2,000 calories and zero carbohydrate. After two days, all complained of fatigue which was aggravated by physical activity. Relief was immediate upon taking glucose.[33]

The diet often causes increased uric acid in the blood, which can be hazardous to those with gout. Moreover, there is increasing evidence that this type of diet can promote some cancers (see Part Four).

Atkins says there is no need for carbohydrates in the diet because the body can convert fat to carbohydrate and thus keep the blood-sugar level normal. However, except for the glycerol portion of fat, glucose cannot be derived from this source. Glycerol is only about 10 percent of the fat, so fat cannot be considered a good source of glucose, the normal fuel of the brain and nervous system.

Another serious hazard is the possibility of inducing negative calcium balance. A diet so high in meat, and thus in phosphorous and protein, can cause calcium problems. Diet soda pop, also recommended in the diet, is high in phosphorous and has no calcium. Excessive protein intake increases urinary calcium excretion and can result in the loss of a great deal of calcium from the bones.

The ratio of calcium to phosphorous in the diet should be about 1. A lower ratio may predispose the person to osteoporosis. Postmenopausal women are especially at risk.

In one experiment, two men lived for a year on a diet of beef, veal, lamb, pork, and chicken. The protein intake was 100 to 145 grams a day and the carbohydrate only 7 to 12 grams. A persistently negative calcium balance resulted, about a third of a gram every day, a very significant amount.[34]

In conclusion, Atkins' "biochemical miracle" diet is unbalanced and hazardous and it is not recommended.

There are many variations on the high-fat theme. The "Non-Glue Food" Diet, for example, was invented by chiropractor James Van Fleet. Carbohydrates are "glue foods," he says, while fats are energy foods which keep the body well shaped, the skin supple, and "sexiness" high. This is a nonsense diet with no basis in fact.

The "drinking man's diet" is recycled from time to time, especially in magazine articles. It allows all fatty foods plus whiskey, beer, and wine "in moderation," but very little carbohydrate. It foolishly restricts fluids to a quart and a half a day. This restriction plus the alcohol (a diuretic) promotes even more dehydration than the Atkins diet, so leads to a rapid but illusory weight loss. Such water restriction on a ketogenic diet can lead to high ketone levels in the blood. This is essentially the Atkins diet plus alcohol: double trouble.

Because of the illusory rapid weight loss due to water and muscle loss, high-fat, low-carbohydrate diets will probably always be in vogue in one form or another. Be alert for recycled versions.

High-Protein, Low-Carbohydrate Diets

There are several popular high-protein diets now and there will be more in the future. Here is the theory behind them.

Protein is the most essential of the three types of caloric nutrients, being required for the synthesis and maintenance of all tissues, enzymes, blood proteins, antibodies, hormones, and other vital components. Since for weight reduction we want to lose fat and not tissue and blood protein, we want to favor protein over fat.

A similar argument favors protein over carbohydrate, which is not a structural component of tissue. And since carbohydrate tends to stimulate insulin secretion, fat-tissue synthesis, and hunger, protein should be favored over starch and sugar, which should be kept to a minimum.

So, instead of the typical American diet with 12 percent protein, these diets are anywhere from 40 to 90 percent.

Another advantage of protein is that it requires more energy to digest and metabolize than carbohydrate or fat, and up to a third of the calories of protein are consumed in the process, or so the theory goes. This is known as the specific dynamic action (SDA) of protein, and it allows a higher calorie intake.

Critique of the High-Protein Theory As with any low-carbohydrate diet, the

118 initial rapid weight loss is primarily due to water loss, not fat metabolism. This may be psychologically beneficial but the advantage is short term.

Moreover, the SDA of protein is not nearly as large as the protein pushers claim. Far from the 25 to 30 percent of protein energy they say goes for protein digestion and metabolism, the real figure is closer to 10 percent. So, of 100 grams of protein, only 10 grams, or 40 calories, will be "negated." This is a very small advantage, equivalent to a small cookie.

The assumption of a protein-sparing advantage is also unproven and very dubious. Many studies have shown that in people on very-low-calorie diets, nitrogen retention (a measure of protein and tissue retention) is proportional to added calories, and not to the amount of protein provided. That is, the loss of muscle tissue is not inhibited significantly by large amounts of protein, which is practically all rapidly used for energy.[35]

In fact, there is evidence that carbohydrate fed simultaneously with protein is even more sparing of body protein than pure protein is because it quickly provides available precursors for rapid synthesis of some of the "nonessential" amino acids. These are essential for protein synthesis, but are not required in the diet because the body makes them from "scraps" of carbohydrate and from other amino acids.

Granted, there is some evidence that high protein intake inhibits appetite and food intake in both animals and humans. This is probably the strongest advantage of these diets. Unfortunately, in most cases the effect is significant only when protein is in the extreme range of about 70 percent or more of the caloric intake.

One problem with a very high protein intake is that the metabolism of a calorie of protein requires seven times as much water as a calorie of fat or carbohydrate. Moreover, the production of amino acid metabolites such as urea and ammonia is greatly increased. These factors can irritate and stress the kidneys. Large amounts of water must be taken, more than indicated by thirst. The consequent frequent urination can be an inconvenience.

These diets are usually very monotonous, which can discourage long-term compliance. And the very low carbohydrate intake (less than 100 grams) common to most of these diets can cause fatigue, weakness, and depression.

High-protein diets are usually based on animal protein, and often include large amounts of cholesterol and saturated fats and little unsaturated fats. This can lead to dangerous increases in blood cholesterol.

The diets are generally deficient in vitamins and minerals, and supplements are a must. For example, the Stillman diet is deficient in vitamins A, B-1, B-2, C, and E, and in folic acid and several minerals.

Moreover, for unknown reasons, a high protein intake greatly increases calcium excretion in the urine. The calcium comes from the bones, and this can be very hazardous, especially to postmenopausal women, who are already at a high risk for developing osteoporosis.

Also, high-protein diets can cost a great deal of money, many thousands of extra dollars in a lifetime; more balanced diets are cheaper as well as healthier.

In conclusion, while these diets are generally preferable to those high in fat, and may help in weight reduction by decreasing appetite, they are nutritionally poor, expensive, and hazardous for long-term use.

If you decide to try one anyway, you should see a physician before and during, so that blood and urine analysis can be used to monitor cholesterol, calcium, uric acid, ketones, creatine, and other key substances. Vitamin and mineral supplements are usually recommended, and fiber and water intake should be high.

The following are popular high-protein diets, in order of decreasing desirability.

Hayden's High-Protein Diet Naura Hayden, actress and cook, provides high protein recipes in her book, *Everything You've Always Wanted to Know About Energy, But Were Too Weak To Ask* (Hawthorn Books, 1976). Some are for protein drinks with brewer's yeast and milk. Others are for thick, high-protein soups with soy protein, cottage cheese, and yogurt, and high-protein breads and desserts using wheat germ, sunflower seeds, and other nutritious ingredients.

This is better than most high-protein diets, with less cholesterol and saturated fat and more fiber and vitamins; flexible and tasty enough to encourage long-term use; enough carbohydrates to prevent ketosis (too fast but incomplete fat metabolism), and adequate essential oils.

The recipes are good, but if you plan to eat less than a thousand calories worth a day for more than a week, you should see a physician.

Edelstein's Women's Diet Dr. Barbara F. Edelstein's thesis in *The Woman Doctor's Diet for Women* (Prentice-Hall, 1980) is that women are so biologically different from men that diets that work for men do not work for women. The higher estrogen levels in women keep them padded with more fat as a source of calories, protection, and warmth in the event of pregnancy. She claims that "men burn calories twice as fast as women for the same amount of exercise." This calls for strong measures, including the following:

Cut calories drastically. Her basic diet has 1,000 calories per day, but she says some women do not lose weight even on 500 calories.

About half of the caloric intake should be from protein because it tends to satisfy hunger and because calories are used up in protein metabolism. Carbohydrate intake should be low because fat women's bodies handle it "inefficiently" and use fewer calories in digesting and metabolizing it. The core diet menu includes fish, beef, fowl, eggs, melba toast, salads, cooked vegetables (excluding peas and corn), fresh fruit (excluding grapes and cherries), and lots of gelatin.

Combat water retention by drinking more water (apparently to flush out water-retaining salt), lying down after drinking fluid (which she says almost doubles water excretion), and using such diuretics as caffeine-containing drinks, camomile tea, and prescription diuretics if your doctor will prescribe them.

She also says, use diet pills to control your appetite; do not let male physicians lay fear and guilt trips on you about this.

There are serious problems with Edelstein's theory. For example, if men really burned calories twice as fast as women doing the same work, an enormous savings of food and energy could be realized by having women do all the work. But men and women belong to the same species, and there is no evidence of such a drastic difference in efficiency. Her contention that some women do not lose weight even on 500 calories a day is impossible to believe, since the basal energy requirement for a petite woman in her seventies and lying perfectly still is almost twice that amount. Everyone else has a much higher energy requirement.[36]

Edelstein greatly exaggerates the significance of the SDA of protein, and says obese women handle protein "more efficiently" than carbohydrates. She apparently means "less efficiently"; it is the loss of calories during the relatively inefficient digestion and metabolism of protein that makes proteins attractive to the diet theorist.

Her emphasis on weight as opposed to fat leads to an irrelevent preoccupation with water retention. The low carbohydrate intake, diuretics, and other gimmicks that cause water excretion may provide a short-term psychological boost, but they do nothing to get rid of excess fat or improve health, and they can be harmful.

Diet pills have never been shown to help people lose fat in the long run, and there are significant hazards in using them. See Part Five for details.

Like most other high-protein diets, Edelstein's is low in calcium and also causes its excretion in the urine, and low in fiber and B vitamins. The low carbohydrate content can cause fatigue and weakness.

The Scarsdale Diet Dr. Herman Tarnower, in *The Complete Scarsdale Medical Diet* (Rawson-Wade, 1978), presents a two-week program which provides between 600 and 1600 calories a day. While the menu is very rigid and no substitutions are allowed, the amounts are left open. But "overloading the stomach" is not permitted. Meat is the mainstay. Alcohol is not allowed.

Rapid weight loss may occur at the lower caloric levels, and much of it is due to loss of water. There is rarely any benefit to such short-term programs. Once the diet is abandoned, the weight starts to creep back up; yet it is too rigid and nutritionally poor to be long-term.

The Scarsdale diet allows more fruits and vegetables than the Stillman diet, and is an improvement for this reason.

The Stillman Diet Dr. Irwin M. Stillman, in *The Doctor's Quick Weight Loss Diet* (Dell, 1968), encourages you to eat all the lean meat, poultry, eggs, sea foods, and low-fat cheeses you want while avoiding starchy and sweet foods. Like Dr. Atkins, he believes that calories can be sneaked out of the body in the form of ketones, incompletely metabolized fats excreted in the urine. He also believes that proteins take an enormous amount of energy to digest and should therefore be favored by the dieter.

Two partial truths do not add up to a whole truth. Whether during fasting or a zero-carbohydrate diet, only very few calories' worth of ketones (mainly acetone) will leave the body in the urine. And the extra energy required to digest protein is only barely significant at very high levels of protein intake. These minor factors cannot account for the dramatic successes claimed by Stillman and some of his adherents. The apparent biochemical miracle is really just a dramatic loss of water from the body, especially the muscles, because of the loss of glycogen (which holds large amounts of water) and sometimes muscle protein. It doesn't matter if you drink as much water as Stillman advocates; the body can't hold onto it.

People who are obese need to lose fat, not water. They can also do without losing calcium from their bones, which high-protein, high-phosphorous intake tends to cause. The Stillman diet is especially dangerous to nonblack women over forty, most of whom are susceptible to osteoporosis. It is also difficult to get enough fiber from a diet lacking whole grains. This can lead to constipation, hemorrhoids, and other problems. In short, this very-high-protein, low-carbohydrate diet, like Dr. Atkins' "Diet Revolution," is gimmicky, unrealistic, and potentially hazardous.

From Metrecal to Cambridge and Cousins Since the late 1950s there have been many formula diets on the market; their popularity seems to go in cycles. They generally claim to provide all the necessary nutrients and are designed to be the exclusive food for several weeks, though they are often used in conjunction with a solid-food diet. The formulas are mostly high-protein powders from milk, eggs, and soybeans, plus vitamins, minerals, flavors, and colors. Their selling points are simplicity (no special meal preparation or calorie counting), alleged nutritional adequacy, and "guaranteed" weight loss.

The formula diets are patented, copyrighted, and mass marketed, often by multilevel marketing methods, especially during times of high unemployment. Slick brochures promise a "revolutionary" reducing diet which results in "miraculous weight loss." The absolutely new, unique, and scientifically proven system will bring about weight losses of 30, 40, 50 pounds and more, as shown by before and after pictures and testimonials from dozens of people.

These are the main problems with formula diets. Some of them are simply starvation, providing only 300 to 400 calories per day, an amount that assures the body will cannibalize itself to provide the energy required to sustain functions and activity. Some of the tissue so consumed will be fat, but more than half will be lean tissue. Water loss due to glycogen (glucose reserve) depletion and protein breakdown and excretion accounts for much of the weight loss.

The claims that the formulas provide all necessary nutrients are false, since they lack adequate fiber, trace minerals, possibly unknown nutrients, and enough calories to prevent the use of the protein in the formulas for energy. Since at very low caloric levels practically all protein is used for basal energy requirements, the formulas must be considered protein deficient even if they do barely provide the RDA.

The lack of fiber in the formulas naturally promotes constipation. The dehydration that tends to occur has the same effect. A week or more exclusively on a formula can lead to digestive sluggishness and some problems readjusting to a solid diet.

Anyone who wants to go on a formula diet for more than a few days should discuss it with a physician, especially if daily intake is less than 1,000 calories.

The Liquid Amino Acid Diet This fiasco was popularized by Robert Linn, D.O., in his book (with S.L. Stuart), *The Last Chance Diet* (Bantam, 1977), which sold millions of copies and doubled as an ad for his "Prolinn," a foul-tasting concoction of hydrolyzed protein from cattle and pig hides, horns, and hooves. Similar products are also on the market. The dieter takes no food, just the liquid for a total of about 100 grams of protein and 400 calories. It is supposed to cause weight loss about as rapidly as fasting but without the muscle breakdown and other serious side effects.

Weight loss does occur rapidly, but this is often due to loss of lean tissue and water. Sudden death or death due to intractable cardiac arrhythmias can occur even to people with no history of heart disease, according to the Center for Disease Control. The diet may also cause kidney damage, gallstones, gout flare-up, nausea, weakness, fatigue, diarrhea followed by constipation, dry skin, menstrual irregularities, and other symptoms of malnutrition.

The hydrolyzing of the protein to amino acids has no advantage and makes the taste more repulsive. The free amino acids are even more likely to promote or aggravate ulcers than pure protein would be.

Linn's book and several products featuring liquid amino acids are still in the stores in spite of reports of dozens of deaths associated with the diet. This regimen is the worst extreme of high-protein diets, and definitely not recommended.

Prudent Diets

The forerunner of all the low-calorie, low-fat diets was developed in the 1950s by Norman Jolliffe, M.D., for the New York City Health Department. Iva Bennett and Martha Simon wrote *The Prudent Diet* (Bantam, 1973) after thousands of members of the Anti-Coronary Club of New York City tried it for nearly fifteen years. The Prudent Diet has a good track record of lowering weight, blood pressure, cholesterol levels, and risk of heart attack. It advocates a good balance of a wide variety of foods with an emphasis on reducing calories, saturated fats, and cholesterol. It allows somewhat more total fat than is now considered ideal, but the concepts and meal plans of the Prudent Diet have stood the test of time.

Similar diets include *Redbook*'s Wise Woman's Diet, The New York City Health Department Diet, The Wine Diet, The Yogurt Diet, La Costa Spa Diet, and Weight Watchers International Vegetarian Plan. If you feel you need to follow a strict meal plan to reduce your calorie intake or simply help you eat sensibly, any of these would serve you well. But don't reduce calorie intake below 1,000 for more than a week or two without consulting a physician.

High-Starch, Low-Fat Diets

Until recently few writers have dared to give carbohydrates a prominent place in the diet. Starches and sugars have been erroneously considered the villains, the fattening and unnecessary foods. However, the growing realization of the hazards of diets high in fats and proteins has led to increased interest in high-carbohydrate diets, which are generally vegetarian or nearly so.

Diets in the high-starch category include Macrobiotics, The Pritikin Program, The California Diet and Exercise Program, McDougall's Plan for Super Health, The Beverly Hills Medical Diet (not Mazel's Beverly Hills Diet), and the F-Plan Diet. We discuss the first three here.

The Macrobiotic and Kempner Rice Diets Macrobiotics is one of the oldest of the high-carbohydrate diets and is quite popular in and out of Zen Buddist retreats. It is based on the ancient Oriental concept of balancing the yin and yang (female and male) forces in one's life. A number of popular books and magazine articles by modern macrobiotic gurus George Oshawa and Michio Kushi propound the philosophy.

The basic contention is that the most perfect foods are whole grains such as brown rice, barley, and wheat, and they should constitute 60 to 100 percent of the calorie intake. The balance should be vegetables, beans, a

124

little fish, occasional fruit, and no dairy products. Really healthy people, the theory goes, can live on nothing but brown rice, for when you are perfectly balanced your body makes the vitamin C, iron, and other nutrients lacking in rice. The minerals are said to be made from other minerals by nuclear transformation. Our cells are little nuclear power plants carrying out these reactions.

To balance one's metabolism it is generally necessary to stay on the pure rice for a long time. Brown rice has the perfect balance of yin and yang, whereas most other foods are either too yin or too yang. Yin foods such as fruits, sugars, and vegetables high in potassium are feminizing and cause weakness and susceptibility to disease. Yang foods such as meats and vegetables high in sodium are masculinizing, and an excess causes hair to grow on women's bodies. Fluid intake beyond the bare minimum is also said to be very harmful.

The list of ills supposedly caused by excessively yin or yang diets includes cancer, neurological diseases, venereal disease, glaucoma, and many more. They can all be cured by the macrobiotic diet, we are told. Even inherited conditions such as color blindness, sickle-cell anemia, and blood types are determined by yin and yang in the diet.

Epilepsy is caused by drinking too much water, and it can be controlled by restricting fluids and taking more salt. Epileptics should always carry salt with them and take it whenever they sense an attack coming on. Another nervous system disorder, multiple sclerosis, can be caused by hysterectomy.

During menstruation a woman's excess of feminine essence is discharged through the skin as well as the vagina. She should not bathe or wash her hair during the period, or the "excess" will be drawn away from is normal course of discharge. This would somehow cause her to blush and become very easily upset.

No evidence for the assertions is given, no studies presented. We are supposed to rely on the intuition of the macrobiotic masters. Kushi's "physiology" is generally along these lines: heaven's downward force enters the head through an invisible spiral, presses down on the midbrain, and thereby activates it. Moreover, by interaction of this force with the earth force, saliva is produced. Other biological functions are explained in a similar manner.

The assertion that staying on the rice diet long enough will bring about miraculous changes in one's metabolism is very dangerous. People are encouraged in their voluntary malnutrition with warnings that vitamin C is too yin, and a perfectly balanced body can make its own. Gullible young parents, wanting their children to have the advantages of nuclear metabolism from early on, give their children practically nothing but rice. Only the consequent poor health and growth of the children provoke second thoughts.

A few young people have stayed with the pure rice for many

months, waiting for the miraculous transformation. It never came and they died.

The macrobiotic diet is very high in salt. Soy sauce, miso (fermented salted soy paste), salted plums, gomasio (salted crushed sesame seeds), and other forms of sodium abound. Why isn't this considered too yang? Because most people have too much yin influence from drugs and pollutants, and extra yang helps neutralize it.

This is all rather fantastic, and it's a shame people are harmed by the extreme forms of this system. Ironically, if the promoters would avoid the extreme and not make outlandish claims, the diet could actually be beneficial. A typical meal might include miso soup with tofu (soy bean curd) and seaweed, whole grain bread with sesame seed butter, brown rice with sauteed vegetables, and baked fish. Macrobiotic cookbooks have excellent recipes for soups, breads, vegetable dishes, and more. Studies have shown that people who eat this way for several years have very favorable blood lipid profiles, are rarely obese, and are generally in excellent health.[37]

Even the extreme brown-rice diet might be beneficial if used for short periods under a physician's supervision. Dr. Walter Kempner of the Duke University School of Medicine developed a similar diet in the 1940s for kidney patients. It proved helpful to thousands, not only for kidney disease but for atherosclerosis, diabetes, high blood pressure, and obesity.[38] The Kempner rice diet consists of white rice, fruit, and a little fruit juice. Kempner wisely pointed out the real hazards of the diet and did not try to make a best seller out of it. But this starch-loaded diet, with 2,000 calories, 20 grams of protein, and 3 to 5 grams of fat, is less hazardous than the extreme fat and protein diets which have made their purveyors wealthy.

If Kempner's diet can be helpful for some people, why not a macrobiotic regimen? Brown rice would provide more vitamins, minerals, and fiber than white. Complemented with fresh fruits and vegetables, it should be safer than the Kempner rice diet and just as effective. But it, too, is a drastic step and not recommended without a physician's help and for good therapeutic reasons.

In conclusion, forget macrobiotic theory; it's quite irrational. Avoid the extreme of a pure rice diet except under a physician's care, go easy on the soy sauce, miso, and other salty foods, and forget the admonitions against lots of fluids and vitamin C fruit. But do eat lots of whole grains and do use some of the excellent recipes for breads, soups, and vegetable dishes given in macrobiotic cookbooks.

The Pritikin Program Nathan Pritikin, inventor and lay medical researcher, and his collaborators developed another popular high-carbohydrate diet. Their survey of the world literature on degenerative diseases, especially hypertension, heart disease, and diabetes, led them to some radical conclusions which they present in *The Pritikin Program* (Grosset and Dunlap, 1980) and *Live Longer Now* (Charter, 1974). On the one hand, they fully concur with

126 the cholesterol theory, and reduce cholesterol more sharply than in the Prudent Diet; while most fish, including water-packed tuna, is permitted, shrimp, sardines, most cheeses, and even lean meats are discouraged.

On the other hand, saturated fats are drastically reduced, much more than recommended by the American Heart Association. And, unlike the AHA recommendation, Pritikin recommends a decrease in vegetable oils. This is because the oils, while mostly unsaturated fats, also contain substantial amounts of the saturated fats typical of animal fats. Moreover, large amounts of the unsaturated fats in vegetable oils can, he believes, be harmful. So all oily and fatty foods are drastically reduced; such foods as nuts, seeds, peanuts, and nut butters can be taken only in very small amounts if at all. Even soy beans, which are 37 percent fat, are generally not permitted.

Pritikin points to data that indicate an increase of polyunsaturates is associated with an increase in gallstones and cancer and no decrease in heart attacks. Insulin is less potent and more is required on a high-fat diet. At Pritikin's Longevity Center in Santa Monica, California, half of the adult-onset diabetics on insulin for twenty years or more could eliminate insulin by going on his low-fat regimen, according to Pritikin.

Since protein is usually found in association with fat and cholesterol, high intake is discouraged. So we are left with carbohydrates, not sugary foods or refined carbohydrates but natural starches. The program calls for lots of carrots, cucumbers, sprouts, lettuce, and other low-calorie vegetables plus some whole grains, skim milk, potatoes, beans, and fruit. Fish and lean meat are used more as condiments than dishes in themselves. Nuts, egg yolks, and whole milk are not allowed. Salt and caffeine are restricted. The calorie intake breaks down about like this: 10 percent fats, 10 percent proteins, 80 percent carbohydrates.

One disadvantage of so little fat is the loss of its satiety value. Pritikin says his high-fiber, low-calorie diet more than makes up for this by allowing a very large total intake of food. Even the 650-calorie Maximum Weight Loss program calls for four pounds of food in eight servings. On the maintenance program of about 2,000 calories, enormous quantities of food are eaten. Pritikin says this keeps people from feeling hungry or deprived, and it works because people want to eat and are allowed to eat.

The diet is not protein deficient, as some critics have claimed. The 650-calorie option, with 35 grams of protein, carries the risk of lean tissue breakdown, of course, and should be undertaken only with a physician's help. But, this is true of any very-low-calorie diet, even if it's pure protein, because the protein is used for energy and not to build new tissue. On the maintenance program, the protein intake easily meets the RDA.

Another criticism is that the small fat intake might lead to deficiencies in linoleic acid and the oil soluble vitamins. This is very unlikely, since the diet provides plenty of vitamins A, E, and K, and enough linoleic acid to meet the need for it and facilitate absorption of the fat-soluble vitamins.

A more important criticism is that if the diet is adopted as regular fare for children it could be calorie deficient, so protein would be used for energy and proper growth would be inhibited. The problem is that without eating some fat, it's difficult to get enough calories unless one eats practically all day, especially if the main food is high-fiber vegetables that require a lot of chewing. Moreover, the diet is low in calcium and possibly other minerals, and the high fiber content may inhibit the absorption of some of them. This is especially hazardous to women and children.

Pritikin's Longevity Institute residence program (which includes a lot of walking and other exercise as well as diet) has, according to its supporters, achieved remarkable recoveries in patients with severe atherosclerosis, heart disease, high blood pressure, and other problems. However, there is no evidence that the results are any better than those achieved by other successful fat-reduction programs, such as the Prudent Diet coupled with exercise. Pritikin's critics believe that the success of his program lies in weight loss and body fat reduction, which can be achieved with exercise and lower caloric intake, and does not require the drastic reduction of dietary fat.

It is important to keep in mind that patients at the Longevity Institute are under the supervision of physicians. No one should try Pritikin's 650-calorie program for more than a few days without good reason and a physician's help. Mineral supplements should also be taken. The program can cause a weight loss of over a pound a day, a drastic and hazardous rate. Losing two pounds a week, more than a hundred pounds in a year, is much safer. The implication that obese people benefit from losing weight so fast is the main problem with the Pritikin Program. A popular book read by millions should make it clear that only a tiny minority of people need such rapid weight loss or can benefit from it.

It would seem almost impossible for a diet even lower in fat to be devised. It has been done, however, by John McDougall, M.D., author (with his wife, Mary) of *The McDougall Plan for Super Health and Life-long Weight Loss* (New Century, 1983). The plan is completely vegetarian, without a scrap of animal flesh, eggs, or dairy products; only 5 percent of the calories come from fat. This is an extreme diet and could result in inadequate intake of phosphorous, calcium, zinc, iron, vitamin B-12, and other nutrients. Children may not get enough calories for proper growth.

The California Diet And Exercise Program Dr. Peter Wood's book, *The California Diet and Exercise Program* (Anderson World Books, 1982), is one of the few popular books on weight control which puts at least as much emphasis on exercise as on diet. It clearly explains and thoroughly documents the necessity of this approach. Consider, for example, Dr. Wood's own one-year study of college-age runners which showed positive correlations between miles run and body fat lost, miles run and calories eaten, and, believe it or not, calories eaten and fat lost.

128   The problem with dieting in the usual sense is that it slows the metabolism, promotes muscle catabolism, and otherwise decreases fitness, so it promotes obesity after you tire of the diet. Dieting without exercising almost always causes the weight to yo-yo. Yet moderate calorie restriction may be desirable if you are just starting to get fit. Wood's meal plans of from 1,200 to 2,800 calories are based on the U.S. Senate's Dietary Goals of The United States: reduced fat and sugar, and increased fiber and starch.

The meal plans are eminently sensible, with an abundance of whole grains, fresh fruits, and vegetables, and moderate amounts of lean meat and low-fat milk products. They are based on exchanges (caloric equivalents) of food groups and are therefore very flexible and easy to use.

The exercise plan is likewise based on exchanges or caloric equivalents. The emphasis is on play, on enjoying swimming, biking, walking, hiking, jogging, dancing, racketball, and other aerobic acitivies. The program is flexible and the information is clear and easy to use. Neat, readable graphs present combinations of diet and exercise levels so you can calculate expected fat loss over a year. It seems unlikely, however, that any but the most compulsive people will measure food and exercise carefully enough for the projections to be more than very rough estimates.

Perhaps you wonder why it is called the California program. There appear to be three factors here. Dr. Wood and his associates are based at Stanford Medical School; the recommended food is almost all grown, raised, or caught in California; and California is perceived as innovative, even racy, and this might help to sell books.

Miscellaneous Diets

The Beverly Hills Diet First let's look at the promises author Judy Mazel makes in *The Beverly Hills Diet* (Macmillan, 1979). We are told that the diet was originally a Beverly Hills beauty secret and is a revolutionary approach to losing weight and feeling and looking better without going hungry. It allows us to indulge in cheese cake, ice cream, steak, whatever we want and as much as we want, and still lose weight. There is no calorie counting, no food weighing, and no hunger—just wonderful weight loss.

Mazel tells us she had stubborn weight problems for years, so she read and studied and conferred with experts until she learned the great truth about obesity which can be summarized as follows: obesity is not caused by what or how much you eat, only by adverse combinations. If you know what these combinations are and if you avoid them, you will never get fat.

The adverse combinations are those that cause poor digestion, since only undigested food accumulates and becomes fat. No, it is not a misprint; Mazel emphasizes over and over that fat comes from undigested foods. As long as food is fully digested you will not gain weight. Now, this will come as quite a surprise to those who think that only digested food gets into the blood and into the cells for energy or fat formation. How the food gets from the intestines to the fat cells without being digested is not explained, but Mazel assures us her discovery is the synthesis of the work of scores of scientists, nutritionists, and physicians. These are mostly unnamed, but she does thank God for Herbert Shelton, the hygienist of the early 1900s whose system of food combining she adopted wholesale. Shelton, however, did not believe that undigested foods turned to fat.

Besides eating foods in proper combinations or alone, we must chew them well lest they stay in the stomach "festering, fermenting, rotting and ultimately turning into fat." The combinations to avoid are starches and sugars, and carbohydrates and proteins. Carbohydrates should not even be eaten on the same day as proteins because once you have eaten the slightest morsel of a protein food, your carbohydrate metabolism will be shut down for the day and all sugar or starch you eat will turn to fat. In general, protein foods are the most fattening because they are the hardest to digest.

Using Mazel's system of "conscious combining" you eat proteins with other proteins and with fats, you eat carbohydrates with other carbohydrates and with fats, and you eat fruits alone. If you violate these rules, food gets trapped, does not get digested, and turns to fat.

You must beware of artificial sweeteners. They are not digestible, and are therefore fattening. Milk is also a problem. According to Mazel, milk is digested by an enzyme from the thymus gland. In adults the gland is atrophied, so milk goes undigested and turns to fat. Because it is not digested, we do not get the important nutrients from it, yet somehow the fat sneaks in. Moreover, one drop of milk in your morning coffee will make subsequent carbohydrates undigestible and therefore fattening. And any cheese you eat will be poorly digested and will trap other foods which will also be poorly digested and the whole fermenting mass will turn to fat!

In spite of the promises of gluttony while reducing, the actual diet is highly restrictive. Only after you have achieved your desired weight can you eat anything you want in proper combinations. Until then you eat mostly fruits. For the first week you eat nothing but pineapples, bananas, mangos, papayas, prunes, strawberries, and watermelon. You must wait two hours between different fruit. Gradually, nonfruit items are added and they must not be eaten within three hours of the fruit.

One reason Mazel favors fruits is that they supposedly contain enzymes that aid digestion and actually burn off fat. But to get the full benefits of fruits you must eat their seeds which are, she says, the storehouse of the enzymes and the focus of the nutrients. Yes, you are actually supposed to chew (or grind in a blender) and swallow seeds of watermelons, papayas, apples, grapes, and other fruits. She apparently does not realize that this contradicts her advice not to eat proteins and carbohydrates together. It is also bad advice because the seeds generally taste disgusting and some have various toxins.

Summing up, Mazel has some very strange notions about the body and how it works, most of which are not only false but absurd. To contend that undigested food somehow becomes fat in the body, and is the only source of body fat, betrays a first-grader's level of knowledge of the body and its functions. Her other ideas about protein shutting down carbohydrate digestion, fruit enzymes burning up fat, and the rest are equally nonsensical.

The Bio-Diet In *The Bio-Diet* (Crown, 1980), Dr. Luis A. Guerro promises to change your body chemistry so that you eat less without hunger. The focus is on timing as much as on the food itself. The Bio-Diet is supposed to increase the level of natural appetite suppressants in the body and decrease hunger-producing body chemicals. A low-calorie (800–1,000), low-fat, low-sugar menu is provided to get you down to your desired weight with a minimum of pain.

These are the main prescriptions of the Bio-Diet:

About twenty minutes before each meal have a small cup of fish, chicken, or other soup that has some fat and protein. This will increase the secretion of cholescystokinin (CCK) from the intestinal wall. CCK is a hormone that signals the gall bladder to release bile to help digest the fat, and seems to be involved in appetite control. Eating fruits with citric acid before a meal has a similar effect. The effect is not immediate, so be sure to wait about twenty minutes before having your meal.

Drink lots of water and chew lemons to decrease your sweet tooth. Eat lots of vegetables. Their bulk and fiber give a sense of fullness and stimulate the release of appetite-decreasing hormones such as gastrin into the blood. They also tend to decrease fat absorption.

Avoid concentrated sweets and other foods that tend to yo-yo the insulin level and cause rebound hunger and fatigue.

Take tryptophan, pectin, and safflower oil tablets between meals to curb appetite and decrease fat absorption. These are considered optional and not very important.

Use stress reduction techniques and the relaxation reflex to help control appetite.

The menu provided emphasizes citrus fruits, vegetables, and moderate amounts of lean meat and fish; in spite of the fat at the beginning of a meal, this is a very low-fat diet.

Most of the suggestions are probably of marginal benefit, but taken together they may signifantly help reduce appetite. The recommended foods are good, but the caloric intake is too low. If you want to try this diet for more than a few days, you should consult a physician.

The Body-Type Diet In *The Body-Type Diet* (Bantam, 1981) Dr. Elliot D.

Abravanel presents his theory that we each have a body type which is determined by our "dominant endocrine gland," a concept not defined by the author. Each body type is prone to craving and overeating certain kinds of foods in an effort to stimulate the dominant gland. This is the cause of obesity. The solution is to determine our body and gland type, and to avoid foods which stimulate that gland. By eating nonstimulating foods we strengthen the other glands, overcome the cravings, and lose weight.

There is a long questionnaire which the reader uses to determine his or her body type. The questions involve body appearance, fat distribution, food preferences, and personality traits. Once you have determined your type you then follow the appropriate diet and exercise plan and you drink an herbal tea. Yes, there is an herbal tea to help each body type lose weight. The herbs supposedly sooth the dominant gland and reduce cravings and hunger.

Here is a summary of Abravanel's body types and their characteristics.

The *pituitary type* tends to have a big head, a round, childlike face, and baby fat evenly distributed all over the body. This person invariably craves dairy products, which stimulate the pituitary, and should therefore avoid them and eat more meat in order to stimulate the adrenal glands and the gonads. He or she should also drink fenugreek tea.

The *thyroid type* craves sweets, starches, and caffeine. These eventually exhaust the thyroid gland, which leads to sluggishness and obesity. This person should let the thyroid rest and eat more meats and dairy products in order to stimulate the other glands. He or she should drink raspberry leaf tea.

The *adrenal type* craves cholesterol-rich meats and salty foods which stimulate the adrenals, the most powerful of the glands. The adrenal-type man is solid, strong, broad-shouldered, and steady. The adrenal woman tends to gain weight around the waist and breasts. A vegetarian diet and parsley tea is best.

The *gonadal type* is a woman who tends to gain weight in the legs and butt and is most susceptible to cellulite. She craves fats and spicy foods, which stimulate the gonads. She should eat more plant foods and leaner meat and she should drink red clover tea. There are no gonadal-type men.

The diets given for the different types provide about 1,100 calories per day, and are pretty well balanced except for the lack of dairy products for the pituitary type and the lack of carbohydrates for the thyroid type.

The problem with the theory is that speculation and conjecture are presented as scientific fact. There is no evidence presented by the authors, or anyone else we know of, to support the claims that certain foods stimulate certain glands and eventually exhaust them, that each person has a dominant gland which determines his body type and is at the root of his weight problem, or that herbal teas help in weight control by soothing the dominant gland and moderating its cravings. These are nothing more than wild hypotheses which the reader is supposed to accept on faith.

As with all low-calorie diets the Body-Type Diet should not be followed for more than a week or two without consulting a physician.

Fasting We all fast at night, usually for about twelve hours, and when we are sick we tend to eat much less. This is natural, especially in the early and severe stages of illness, though intake may be large during recovery. But some writers advocate fasting regularly for one day to several weeks. They cite numerous alleged benefits, such as "physiological rest" and "cleaning out the system."

Many newly health-conscious persons fast in order, they say, to flush out chemicals from junk food and drugs. Fasting becomes an atonement for their transgressions. If it makes them feel weak and sick, they believe it is because of the mobilization of poisons for disposal and is a sign that they need to fast.

While it may make sense to greatly reduce or eliminate food intake for a day or two after a bout of overindulgence, such fasting on a regular basis makes no sense and can be hazardous, especially if prolonged, for the following reasons.

The Hazards of Fasting The low supply of glucose for the brain, and the breakdown of muscle and other protein tissue for energy, cause weakness, fatigue, irritability, depression, decreased libido, and often a sick feeling. The by-products of this protein metabolism, ammonia and uric acid, are normally easily handled by the liver and kidney. But these organs are severely hampered by inadequate nutrition. Far from "cleansing the system," fasting decreases the body's ability to destroy and excrete toxins. The increase in uric acid concentration is a threat to persons with gout.

Fasting may lead to rapid loss of water, sodium, and potassium, which causes a decrease in blood volume, postural hypotension (low blood pressure upon standing up), and fainting. Severe potassium depletion can cause heart disturbances and heart failure.

Fasting can kill you. The body can't tell voluntary fasting from starvation, and deaths have occurred even during medically supervised fasts and near-fasts. The cause of death is usually kidney or heart failure. Those who survive prolonged fasts may suffer anemia, decreased resistance to infection, and kidney and liver damage. Depression of digestive functions can continue for weeks or months, with even small amounts of food causing pain and discomfort.

Besides being dangerous, and destructive of lean, calorie-consuming tissue, fasting for weight loss almost never works. Even with large initial weight losses, the return to the prefasting weight is well over 90 percent by most accounts. Obese people need to develop good eating and exercise habits to last a lifetime, not short-term panaceas and miracles.

The Mucusless Diet *The Mucusless Diet and Healing System,* by Professor Arnold Ehret, was first published in 1922, was republished in 1953, and has been read by thousands since then. Ehret also wrote *Rational Fasting.* Both books are easy to find in health food stores, and Erhet still has a substantial following. He wrote with the conviction and tone of a prophet, denouncing all who disagreed with him, and claimed to have revolutionized medicine forever.

Although Ehret received no medical training, he and his followers believed that he was a genius who discovered the cause and cure of all disease. He used the title Professor, although the peak of his academic career was as instructor of drawing in Germany in the years before World War I.

Ehret suffered from kidney disease in his thirties, and apparently gained some relief by eating lots of fruits and vegetables and avoiding high-protein foods. This heavily influenced the theory he developed, which goes like this:

Every disease, regardless of the symptoms or the name, is caused by constipation, not just of the bowels, though it starts there, but of the entire body. The uneliminated feces continually poison the blood stream with mucus derived from undigested, uneliminated, unnatural foods accumulated for years and decades. This mucus lodges in every part of the body, creating mechanical obstructions as well as chemical poisoning of the system.

Every disease is but a manifestation of this central cause, and every disorder, from acne to cancer, tuberculosis, blindness, deafness, and venereal disease is preventable and curable by the Ehret system.

To cure and prevent disease we must get rid of the mucus from the body and always keep it to a minimum. We do this by eating nothing but fruits, nuts, and vegetables, and fasting frequently. The worse a fast makes you feel, the more you need it, since lots of mucus is being mobilized for elimination. Enemas are taken frequently to help eliminate the mucus.

Ehret did not stop with presenting humanity with the cure to all diseases. He went on to revolutionize physiology itself with some astounding discoveries, including the following.

The heart does not pump blood through the body. The lungs do all the pumping; the heart is merely a valve.

White blood cells are not disease-fighting cells, as contended by medical science. Rather, they are decayed mucus in the blood, waste from protein and starch in the diet that causes disease and death.

Symptoms of mental illness are caused by gas pressure on the brain due to mucus decay. There is nothing easier to cure than insanity. Fasting is all that is needed.

Eating rice causes leprosy.

Dandruff is dried mucus, and its production ceases upon elimination of all mucus from the body.

Perspiration is the elimination of waste, and a mucus-free body never sweats, even in the greatest heat.

Nitrogen is the essential part of protein, and adequate amounts can be assimilated from the air, much as legume bacteria take nirogen from the air.

The entire white race is unnatural and pathological. The color is due to the mucus-laden white blood corpuscles which clog the white person's system. (Ehret was a German, as white as any, but he liked to sunbathe and let people think he was an American Indian. He claims he could see the paleness in his complexion the morning after eating one piece of bread.)

The best blood-building food is the juice of a ripe blackberry, black cherry, or black grape. This is obvious from the deep red color of the juice.

Male nocturnal emissions represent efforts by the body to expel mucus. They cease on a mucusless diet.

Menstruation is also an effort to expel filth, and it ceases when a woman sticks to a mucusless diet.

Gonorrhea is not caused by sexual contact but by eating mucus foods. The discharge is a necessary cleansing process, no different from a cold.

The body with clean blood can send and receive electromagnetic radiation through the hair. This is important in sexual attraction. Hairless persons are sexually inferior.

Parents whose bodies are truly clear of mucus during intercourse have a good chance of conceiving a genius, who will always be a boy.

The Dangers of the Mucusless Diet Before joining the Ehretists (as they call themselves) in the endless rounds of starvation and enema-taking, consider whether you can accept the doctrines of Ehret's physiology.

Consider too that if you really want to stop mucus production by your body the best way is to avoid all foods with viamin A. But keep in mind that vitamin A deficiency can lead to death by infection due to inadequate mucus to protect against microbes.

Like macrobiotics, the mucusless diet system promotes a dangerous idea, that the more you suffer during starvation, the more you need to be starved to "cleanse the system." This leads unfortunate victims to cling fanatically to the system and dismiss all signs of malnutrition as signs that poisons are being expelled and the diet is working.

Ehret is apparently telling the truth when he claims that women who go on his diet stop menstruating. We have known several young women this has happened to. They are, of course, nonfertile as long as this continues.

Starvation can also cause decreased semen production in men.

Southampton Diet Dr. Stuart Berger's *Southampton Diet* (Simon and Schuster, 1981) purports to unveil a biochemical miracle which keeps the "beautiful people" beautiful, thin, and superactive. It is, we are told, the most revolutionary weight loss system ever devised and it works for everyone without counting calories. A pound a day can be shed safely and without hunger or fatigue.

The key to the diet is ensuring that the proper amino acids reach the brain in the proper amounts. Different foods contain different amino acids which affect the brain in different ways, so each meal is designed with the right balance of amino acids plus the vehicles to get them into the brain. If this is done, only positive neurotransmitters are produced in the brain, and you feel happy, energetic, and satisfied. Poor eating causes negative neurotransmitter production and consequently depression, fatigue, hunger, and insomnia. The Southamptom diet eliminates any food that could produce a negative neurotransmitter.

"Happy foods" (yes, that's what they are called) contain the amino acids tryptophan and tyrosine plus enough carbohydrates to carry them into the brain. This ensures a good supply of serotonin, dopamine, and norepinephrine, the positive neurotransmitters. Examples of happy foods are milk, turkey, chicken, unripened cheeses, bananas, fish, eggs, whole grains, leafy greens, and various fruits.

"Sad foods" are sugary or fatty or contain the wrong amino acids, those that produce negative neurotransmitters. Chocolate is a sad food because of its sugar, fat, and the amino acid phenylalanine. Lobster, lentils, and chick-peas are sad because they contain the amino acid GABA, which supposedly produces lethargy. Foods containing large amounts of the vitamin choline, such as mayonnaise and lecithin, are sad because the choline contributes to the production of the neurotransmitter acetylcholine, which is considered negative for unspecified reasons.

The menus are very exact with precise measures of each item, and there is no calorie counting only because it has already been done. The caloric intake is quite low, in the neighborhood of 1,000 calories per day.

The problem with the Southampton diet is that it is based on

136 conjecture and dubious theories. The relation between diet and neurotransmitter production is not as simple and clear-cut as the author claims. Nor are the functions and effects of the neurotransmitters. The brain has a complex balance of chemicals that work together to produce feelings, moods, and behavior. To call some transmitters negative and some positive is simply nonsense.

We are told that low serotonin levels tend to produce aggressive behavior, yet monkey studies indicate the opposite, that high levels produce aggression. Acetyl choline is called a negative neurotransmitter, so choline is to be avoided. Yet studies indicate that choline, an essential nutrient, is sometimes of value in improving memory and mood in some elderly patients. There is likewise no evidence to support the idea that phenylalanine, an essential amino acid, contributes to negative moods or behavior. In fact, there are indications that it may be helpful against depression.

In spite of the weakness of the theory, the diet is well balanced and reasonable. A typical day's menu includes unsweetened pineapple, low-fat cottage cheese, whole wheat bread, chicken, fish, vegetable salad, cooked vegetables, fruit, and yogurt. But why burden ourselves with lists of restricted and allowed foods and exact meal plans that are based on nonsensical theories?

It is not advisable to go on such a low-calorie diet for more than a week or two without consulting a physician. Nor is it healthy to lose weight at the rate suggested by the authors. No one needs to lose a pound a day.

11

Behave Yourself

Instead of focusing on food, as diets do, the behavior control approach to obesity concentrates on eating. A typical method is to keep a detailed diary of absolutely everything eaten and the amounts, and an estimate of calorie intake, for several weeks. This is very revealing to most people who try it, and by itself can result in eating less. A more detailed diary includes not only every bit you eat but when you eat it, under what circumstances, and how you feel at the time. This helps you detect bad eating habits and situations in which you unconsciously overeat. Do you snack while reading or watching television? Does tension with your family or house mates send you to the refrigerator for consolation? Do you clean your kids' plates to avoid wasting food? Do you eat when you are disappointed, bored, or angry?

If you are a TV snacker, try knitting, clipping and cleaning your nails, or flossing your teeth instead. If you are a bored or angry eater, find a better way to handle those feelings. Take a walk or bike ride, call a friend, start a new book, take up a challenging hobby; do anything but punish yourself with food you don't need.

It helps to focus fully on eating at mealtime. Don't read, watch TV, or talk business. Concentrate on the sight, smell, texture, and taste of the food and make the meal satisfying. Eat slowly. If you eat too fast, you will likely be starting on your second helping before your brain has time to develop a sense of satisfaction with the first. Chew slowly and put your fork down for a minute or two every few bites. Let ten to twenty minutes pass between courses or servings of a meal. This may not be practical for every meal, but it's worth trying, especially for your largest meal of the day.

Perhaps the most important concept in behavior therapy is to learn to recognize true hunger and eat only in response to that, rather than in response to external cues. The sight, smell, or thought of food doesn't have

138

to trigger "false hunger." Learn to pass it up unless you are hungry. And when you go to a party, don't eat just because the food is there and everyone else is eating.

Here are some other useful suggestions.

Shop for food only with a list and only when you are not hungry. This helps keep snacks bought on impulse out of the house.

Keep food out of sight.

Don't nibble while cooking.

Don't feel you have to "clean your plate." Learn to prepare smaller portions. Develop a left-over strategy so you won't feel you have to eat it to avoid waste.

Weight Control Groups

Compulsive overeating is often an emotional problem, somewhat similar to alcoholism. It is not surprising, then, that therapy groups similar to Alcoholics Anonymous have evolved. Several large nationwide diet clubs, and many smaller regional groups, have helped hundreds of thousands of people lose millions of pounds of fat and keep them off.

The success of group programs is based on group support, encouragement, and contagious evangelistic fervor. Healthy competition between members also helps. Most of the groups provide basic nutrition education and reasonable exercise programs. Regular meetings reinforce the concepts and provide opportunities for people with a common problem, obesity, to discuss it freely and openly with other people with the same problem.

Most people in the United States have access to at least one of these groups. There is no way of knowing which group is best for a given person. It is best to attend a meeting or two before committing yourself. As a rough guide, here are some characteristic features of some of the larger groups.

TOPS (Take Off Pounds Sensibly) is the largest and oldest of the nonprofit diet clubs. Group-therapy leaders are elected by local chapters. The clubs are usually for women only or men only on the theory that this encourages more open discussion of the problems. Meetings involve discussions of diet and self-improvement techniques, and sometimes games and skits. Every chapter crowns a queen each year, and some also crown kings. An International King and Queen are recognized each year. This competition promotes adherence to the program. Each member's diet is medically supervised to prevent over-zealousness from doing anyone harm.

Overeaters Anonymous is closely patterned after Alcoholics Anonymous. The emphasis is on the idea that compulsive overeating is an illness, much like alcoholism, which can be arrested and controlled but never cured. The approach is largely spiritual, with a reliance on an "outside Power" to help where willpower has failed. First names only are used to preserve anonymity. Phone calls between meetings are encouraged to help members keep from going on eating binges. Only general dietary advice is given; specific instruction is supposed to come from one's physician.

The Diet Workshop is the largest private, commercial diet club with about sixty-five franchises in operation. A 1,200-calorie diet is combined with behavior modification, nutrition education, and exercise. Each member gets substantial individual attention. The meetings emphasize member participation rather than lectures. Weight-loss contests provide extra motivation.

Weight Watchers International emphasizes the scientific over the evangelical. Many computer-generated diets are provided for different sexes and ages at different stages of weight loss. No substitutions, additions, or subtractions from assigned diets are allowed. Professionals lead the group discussions. A strong behavior modification program helps members change their bad habits.

Prevention Starts Early

Some researchers and physicians believe that bottle feeding in the first few days and weeks of life upsets the normal appetite control mechanisms and establishes a higher caloric requirement for satisfaction. This, they say, results in a lifetime tendency to obesity. Some studies support this theory. Researchers in Great Britain have found much more obesity among bottle-fed babies than breast-fed. More long-term studies are needed to confirm that breast feeding is a major factor in preventing obesity in later life, but since fat infants are more likely to become fat adults, it seems likely that breast feeding is probably important in this regard.

If a bottle is used, it should be offered, not pushed. If the baby gets too fat, the formula can be diluted a little.

It may help to avoid giving solids too soon.

Babies should be fed food without added sugar or honey.

Children should be encouraged to be active in hiking, swimming, bicycling, and team sports.

Junk food snacks, those that provide plenty of calories and little or no other nutrients, should be kept out of the house, but lots of fruit and vegetable snacks should be on hand.

12

Reducing Gimmicks

Passive spot-reducing gimmicks such as heated belts, pulley belts, rollers, and the like, which supposedly vibrate, knead, and melt fat away, may drive a little water out of the body temporarily but are completely worthless for fat reduction. Steam baths and saunas are similarly worthless for losing fat. The active spot-reducing exercises may help tone certain muscles, but they have no effect on subcutaneous fat in the area. Some intramuscular fat may be used up, but the layer of fat between the muscle and skin is part of the whole body-fat storage. Exercises such as sit-ups and leg-lifts do not expend nearly enough energy to mobilize significant amounts of fat as do such aerobic exercises as running, swimming, and cycling, which use several large muscles all at once.

"Cellulite," the watery, oatmealish fat often seen on the thighs, is no exception to this. It is really no different from other fat, and aerobic exercise is required to mobilize it. Massaging, kneading, and pounding are mere mechanical manipulations, where chemical reactions are required to mobilize and metabolize the fat.

Sweat suits are another worthless gimmick. By increasing loss of water, they create a mirage of losing fat while overheating muscles and decreasing stamina. They increase the risk of heatstroke and are therefore dangerous.

Body-contour creams, so-called, which are supposed to cause fat loss under the skin they are rubbed into, are completely worthless for this purpose. There is no product that can penetrate the skin and melt away fat. If they promote sweating, only water is lost, not fat.

Electrical muscle stimulators (EMS) are devices that stimulate muscle contractions by electrical impulses. They are heavily promoted for body shaping, figure toning, cellulite removal, weight loss, and even wrinkle removal. Some health spas provide sessions with EMS devices for armchair joggers; they advertise that you can read or watch TV while sophisticated machines do all the work. The devices are often sold by mail order; ads in magazines claim they can provide the benefits of jogging for ten miles or doing thousands of sit-ups while you lie flat on your back.

EMS devices have legitimate uses in physical therapy, such as to relax muscle spasms, to prevent blood clots in leg muscles after surgery or a stroke, and to prevent muscle atrophy due to disuse. However, they are not effective for weight loss or body shaping, there are certain hazards in their use, and they are not supposed to be used by unlicensed practitioners. The FDA considers the use or promotion of muscle stimulators for use in homes, beauty salons, and health spas for purposes of weight loss or body toning to be fraudulent, even if a physician or other licensed practitioner is using the device.[39]

EMS devices can cause electrical shocks and burns. They should not be used on pregnant women, persons with heart problems or pacemakers, or anyone with epilepsy or cancer. The electrodes should not be placed where a strong current could pass through the heart, brain, or spinal column.

The profits from EMS devices are so hefty that many companies and individuals are involved in their marketing and use, and the FDA cannot adequately police these activities. One case against a muscle stimulator called the Relaxacisor was banned after forty witnesses testified that they had been injured by the machine, but the trial took five months and cost millions of dollars. New devices and companies proliferate and each must be litigated separately. Clearly, then, consumer awareness is the best defense against this health hoax.

Appetite-suppressant drugs and **starch blockers** are hazardous and of no long-term benefit in obesity. They are discussed in Part Five.

13

"Special" Foods

ere is a brief look at some of the foods and supplements frequently touted as beneficial to health, helpful in weight loss, or otherwise special. **Alcohol** is unique in that it is the only drug that is also a food, that is, has caloric value. A few studies have suggested that moderate alcohol consumption (a drink or two a day) may reduce the risk of heart attack by increasing the levels of HDL-cholesterol. However, there are several types of HDL-cholesterol and, compared to LDL-cholesterol, little is known about their roles and the significance of increased blood levels of the different types. Considering the many known hazards of drinking (see Chapter 5–4), alcohol is a long way from being declared a health food.

Apricot kernals and their extracts are sold in health food stores and by mail. They contain amygdalin (laetrile), the phony cancer cure and preventive, which has been proven ineffective and poisonous. Consumption of these products is extremely hazardous since cyanide poisoning can result. The danger is greatest when the kernals are well chewed, ground up, or blended with fresh fruits or vegetables, because these processes liberate the cyanide. If they are eaten, vomiting should be induced by a finger down the throat or drinking warm salt water. **Call a physician right away.**

Bee pollen is heavily promoted as a superfood especially for boosting athletic performance but with many other health benefits as well. The pollen is gathered by bees and stripped from them by devices placed in the hives. Since the pollen comes from many flowers, its content and nutritional value vary drastically with location and time of year. Sugar is the main component, accounting for at least 50 percent of the weight. Protein, fat, and water are the other major components. Pollen also has some vitamins and minerals.[40]

The nutritional claims frequently border on the outrageous. One health-food magazine article says that 32 grams of pollen (about three tablespoons) supplies all the protein and vitamins one needs daily. A typical batch of pollen contains about 20 percent protein, or about 6 of the 32 grams, a small fraction of the RDA. The DNA, RNA, and enzymes, often cited as "essential biofactors" of great benefit to health, have very little nutritional or other value since they are simply digested and used for energy.

Pollen can cause reactions from sniffles to anaphylactic shock in those allergic to it or any of its many contaminants. Besides containing pollen from several types of flower, the products are often contaminated with insects and their waste and eggs, rodent debris, fungi, and bacteria. Persons allergic to bees are perhaps most at risk since the pollen is mixed with nectar and carried between the insect's legs.

Pollen promoters push hard their claims of athletic benefits. They have lots of anecdotes and testimonials, but no scientific studies. In a study at Louisiana State University, half the members of the swimming team took ten pollen tablets a day for six months. The results revealed no benefit.

Consumers should be skeptical of the far-fetched claims made for pollen as a medicine. Promoters have proclaimed it a cure for many health problems, including hair loss, failing memory, alcoholism, eye problems, diabetes, and much more. They frequently refer to "Russian studies" and "secret documents" to imply that countries in the Soviet bloc use pollen for many purposes, but want to keep it a secret because it gives their athletes, and possibly their soldiers, an edge. However convincing this propaganda may seem, no one should take pollen for severe or persistent symptoms; call a physician instead.

Bran, usually from wheat but also from corn, rice, and other grains, is removed in the making of refined flour. People who eat lots of refined foods can often benefit from bran supplements. One to five tablespoons per day can be sprinkled into cereals, soups, homemade breads, and the like. Coarse bran seems to be more effective than finely ground bran in absorbing water and creating stool bulk, thereby preventing constipation and reducing the risk of hemorrhoids and other problems. Too much bran, especially for those accustomed to a low-fiber diet, can cause unpleasant bowel rumblings, gas, and frequent defecation.

Breakfast "super cereals," that is, the highly processed, heavily fortified cold cereals, are promoted as practically all you ever need to eat. We have all seen the television ads in which the couple at the breakfast table is told they will have to eat four bowls of their Grape-Nuts or corn flakes "to equal the vitamin nutrition in our cereal." Their competitors naturally try to keep up in this Breakfast Cereal Vitamin War. They all argue over which can provide the RDA for ten-vitamins-plus-iron in the fewest bites.

144   These cereals are appealing to people who think that if they get the vitamins in one meal they can eat carelessly the rest of the day. But there are about forty-five known required nutrients, and getting overdoses of eleven of them serves no useful purpose. The cereals with the most added vitamins usually also have the most sugar, salt, and other additives, and the least fiber, trace minerals, and natural flavor. These latter elements are more commonly in short supply in the average American diet than the ten relatively common vitamins.

In short, the cereal makers engaged in the vitamin war are perpetrating a subtle consumer fraud for the purpose of maximizing profits. So if you enjoy Grape-Nuts, corn flakes, shredded wheat, wheat flakes, raisin bran, oatmeal, Wheatena, or other nutritious, tasty, simple cereals, don't be misled by the ads about the ones that are heavily fortified, which usually deliver less value for their price.

Brewer's yeast is an excellent source of all the B-vitamins except B-12, unless it is added. A teaspoon or two a day makes an excellent supplement for pregnant women, alcoholics, people who eat poorly, and others. It can be stirred into orange or tomato juice, milk, or water.

There are many varieties and commercial preparations with widely different flavors from deliciously nutty and sweet to bitter and downright vile. The ones advertised as sources of megavitamins taste especially terrible, probably because of the extra vitamins they add, completely unnecessarily. Some of these products have so much added niacin that even small doses can cause nausea and possibly gastric bleeding.

Brewer's yeast is often touted as a great source of high-quality protein. Adelle Davis and other writers suggest using large amounts in blended milk drinks, meatloafs, breads, and pastries. The idea is to eat as much, and trick your family into eating as much, as you possibly can. Some people get up to two cups a day. These efforts rarely last long because they quickly tire of the strong taste of too much brewer's yeast.

It is not a good idea to eat too much yeast anyway for a number of reasons. First, contrary to common belief, yeast protein is not of very high quality; it fact, it ranks below most grain and bean proteins in its balance of amino acids and its ability to promote growth. So, using expensive brewer's yeast as a source of protein is a waste of money. Second, it is so high in phosphorous and so low in calcium that consuming large amounts could increase the risk, especially for women and children, of developing calcium deficiency. Finally, too much of it can produce intestinal gas and loose stools.

Brewer's yeast may help glucose metabolism in diabetics, perhaps because of the chromium it contains.[41] Diabetics should not suddenly start taking a lot of it without discussing it with their physicians, especially if they are taking insulin or diabetes pills. Brewer's yeast may also lower blood cholesterol.

Carob, that is, powder or syrup from the large seed pods of the carob tree, is promoted as a healthy alternative to chocolate and is used much like chocolate in candies, cookies, and drinks. Compared to cocoa powder, carob has much less fat and more fiber. It is also naturally sweet and does not contain the bitter stimulants present in small amounts in chocolate. It is not surprising that carob does not satisfy the chocolate aficionado, who usually considers it a very poor substitute. It is sometimes added to infant formulas to treat vomiting and diarrhea. Whole carob seed pods are tasty snacks which exercise the jaw and provide lots of fiber.

Diet sodas are touted in television ads featuring slender, beautiful people, as aids in controlling weight. There is no evidence to support this contention. While they are essentially calorie-free, people may drink them instead of water and not instead of consuming high-calorie snacks such as candies and potato chips. Most sodas, the "diet" ones included, contain at least two ingredients that tend to promote calcium excretion: caffeine and phosphoric acid. Heavy consumption can increase the risk of calcium deficiency, especially in women and children. Because there are still some doubts about the artificial sweeteners in these products, their use should probably be avoided or minimized during pregnancy, lactation, and childhood.

DMG (dimethyl glycine) and other products deriving from the pangamic acid/vitamin B-15 hoax are promoted as cure-alls and boosters of athletic performance. There is no such thing as vitamin B-15, and there is no evidence to support the claims for the products; on the contrary, some of them are potentially hazardous. See Pangamic Acid in Part Six for details of the hoax.

Fish oils are promoted by the health food industry as a safeguard against heart disease. Studies have shown that eating a lot of fatty fish (with high levels of omega-3 fatty acids) may help lower cholesterol levels and prevent abnormal blood clotting. These are cited to support the sales efforts. However, the supplements are not a good idea for several reasons. To get the benefits enjoyed by the heavy fish eaters that were studied, you would have to take so much cod liver oil that it would add hundreds of calories and possibly too much vitamin A and vitamin D to your diet. Even the most concentrated sources of the oils cannot be recommended because, to get the amounts consumed by heavy fish eaters, you would have to spend thousands of dollars a year. That money would be better spent on fish itself. They are all good, even shellfish, which have much less cholesterol than previously believed and lots of omega-3 fatty acids.

146

Fructose is heavily promoted as a miracle food for energy and stamina, and as an aid in weight control. It is one half of the sucrose (table sugar) molecule; glucose is the other half. It has the advantage of being a bit sweeter per calorie than other sugars, but this advantage must be weighed against its much higher cost and tendency to lose its sweetening power with heating. Fructose does not promote tooth decay as much as sucrose does, but suggestions that it may be better for diabetics because of its relatively slow absorption may be outweighed by evidence that the sugar tends to increase blood cholesterol levels. (See Chapter 2–5 for more on fructose and other sugars.)

Glandulars are curious products, sort of a combination of homeopathy and eat-brains-to-be-smart superstition. They consist of very tiny amounts (milligrams) of dried pancreas, liver, thymus, and other organs and are taken to strengthen one's corresponding organs. There is no evidence that they are the least bit effective, and the theory behind their use is irrational.

Glucomannan is the trade name for a product made from the tubers of *Amorphophallus konjac*, a plant widely cultivated in the Orient for food. Because the powder contains high levels of fiber which absorbs water and swells, it may be useful in preventing constipation, but there is no evidence for the claim that the product can promote weight loss. The plant is not popular in home gardens because it smells like a rotting animal carcass. Its common name is skunk lily.

Honey is promoted as a "natural" sweetener with numerous nutrition and health advantages compared to other sweeteners, especially refined sugar. In reality, the vitamin and mineral content of honey is insignificant, and it cannot be considered superior to sucrose in that respect. It does have high levels of fructose which has more sweetening power per calorie than other sugars. This should be weighed against the higher cost of honey and the decrease of sweetening power upon heating. **Caution:** honey should not be fed to infants less than one year old because there is a slight risk of botulism poisoning in them.

Lecithin, a phospholipid extracted from soybeans, is sold in granule, liquid, and semisolid forms. It is alleged to lower blood cholesterol levels and to improve memory in normal and demented persons. There is some evidence for the first claim, but the effect may simply be due to its polyunsaturated fat content, in which case it would be much cheaper to simply consume more vegetable oil than to take lecithin. The definitive studies on this question have not been done.

     The other claim, that lecithin can improve memory, is based on the fact that it contains choline, a B-vitamin that is incorporated into a neurotransmitter, acetylcholine, which is involved in thought processes.

Unfortunately, careful studies with normal persons and those with memory deficits have not strongly supported the theory.

Liver is often promoted as a health food because of its high concentration of B-vitamins, protein, vitamin A, iron, and other nutrients. Unfortunately, it is also extremely high in cholesterol. A four-ounce serving contains more cholesterol than two large eggs. Moreover, since the liver is the detoxification center of the body, it may contain higher than average levels of pesticide residues, heavy metals, and other contaminants. Since all the nutrients provided by liver are easily available from other foods, there is little reason to eat it.

Margarine, partially hydrogenated and solidified vegetable fat, is used as an alternative to butter, which it outsells by about ten to one. Some of its popularity comes from its alleged superiority to butter healthwise: it has more unsaturated and less saturated fat and no cholesterol. It is also much cheaper. On the other hand, they both have the same percentage of fat and the same number of calories. On the whole, margarine is probably better for those who use large amounts, especially if they have a specific need to lower and control their cholesterol levels. But those who use small amounts and have no need to lower their cholesterol levels can enjoy butter without worry.

Pectin is a fiber present in apples in large amounts and some other fruits in small amounts. Its jelling properties make it useful in making jams and jellies. It not only provides bulk in the diet and helps prevent constipation and hemorrhoids, it also inhibits the absorption of cholesterol from the intestine and thereby helps control its level in the blood. It may also inhibit the absorption of lead and other toxins. Pectin is available in capsules, but the best way to get the fiber into the diet is to eat apples.

Raw milk, according to the health-food press, is much more nutritious than pasteurized milk because the heat treatment supposedly destroys nutrients. It is true that pasteurization lowers the concentration of vitamin A, but most milk is fortified to restore that loss. No protein or minerals and only very small amounts of B-vitamins are lost. The very small nutritional advantages of raw milk are insignificant compared to the dangers.

The problem with raw milk is that, while tuberculosis and brucellosis can be eliminated from dairy herds, *Salmonella* infections of the herds are common and difficult to control. Once these bacteria get into the milk, only pasteurization can eliminate them. Several varieties in milk can cause severe illness and death. Infection with *S. dublin* is especially virulent in the elderly. *Campylobacter* and other bacteria have also been implicated in raw-milk-borne illnesses.[42]

148   Consumers are often fooled by the "certified" label on raw milk cartons; they believe the milk has been tested and found safe by government agencies. In fact, the certification is done by private groups, such as the American Association of Medical Milk Commissions. Such "certified" milk has a poor safety record, which is not surprising because present technology simply cannot produce raw milk that is guaranteed free of dangerous bacteria. The American Academy of Pediatrics, the U.S. Animal Health Association, and other concerned groups have issued warnings about raw milk. Some experts suggest that raw milk containers carry warning labels, which certainly seems justified.

Superoxide dismutase (SOD) is an enzyme, naturally abundant in most cells, which breaks down the highly reactive and harmful superoxide molecule. As a free radical scavenger, it reduces the rate of wear, tear, and aging in most of the tissues of the body, and thereby may help prevent cataracts, arthritis, and other age-related disorders. It is not surprising that health food stores, drug stores and mail-order distributors do a brisk business in SOD tablets. The product labels make no health claims, but promotional literature makes the pills sound like nothing less than the Fountain of Youth. Unfortunately, SOD, like all proteins, is destroyed in the digestive tract, and ingestion of even enormous doses will not increase tissue levels of the enzyme or decrease one's rate of aging or risk of developing degenerative diseases. We recommend you not waste your money on it.

Spirulina is a blue-green alga, *Spirulina platensis*, which grows in ponds and lakes in warm and temperate areas around the world. It has been used as a food and supplement for many centuries in Mexico and other areas, and is now sold here in powder and tablet form as a superfood and supplement. Mexico is the world's main source of edible spirulina, but production in Israel, Taiwan, and Japan is increasing. Spirulina powder is fairly strong tasting alone but blends well into drinks, soups, breads, and other foods. Some people find the intense green color it gives to food unappetizing.

Spirulina is nutritious, with high concentrations of the B-vitamins, beta-carotene (provitamin A), high-quality protein, and trace minerals. Some reports claim it contains vitamin B-12, but this may due to contamination with insect fragments and filth, which is, not surprisingly, difficult to prevent in open ponds and drying areas. While spirulina can be an important source of essential nutrients to those with poor diets, there is no evidence that it helps people lose weight, provides unusual energy or stamina, or helps cure the numerous ailments it is claimed to. Nor is there evidence to support the similar claims made for other alga products.

Sprouts are sprouted seeds and grains that are often added to salads, sandwiches, and cooked foods. The most popular are alfalfa seeds and mung beans, but wheat, barley, sunflower seeds, soy beans, and chia seeds are also frequently used. Bread made with sprouted grains and seeds is uniquely delicious. Sprouting usually increases the levels of vitamins A and C and some of the B-vitamins, but it does not necessarily destroy the toxins naturally present in many beans; bean sprouts are probably best eaten cooked.

Tofu and **tempeh** are soy products analogous to cheese and yogurt. Tofu is made by cooking soybeans, mashing them, and straining the liquid (soy milk) out. Calcium sulfate or magnesium sulfate is added to precipitate the solids. This curd, the tofu, is pressed into blocks, which are usually diced and cooked with stir-fried vegetables and other dishes. Tempeh is a fermented soybean product made by cooking the beans, mixing in the spores of a white mold, *Rhizopus oligosporus*, and incubating for about twenty-four hours. The finished tempeh can be stir-fried or put in soups, salads, lasagna, and dozens of other dishes. Tofu and tempeh are inexpensive, high-protein, low-fat foods with no cholesterol, and they make excellent additions to any diet.

Wheat germ is a wonderful food—potentially, anyway. It is loaded with B-vitamins, vitamin E, protein, fiber, linoleic acid (an essential oil), and potassium and has very little sodium. Best of all, fresh wheat germ is delicious. The problem is that wheat germ gets stale quickly and is rarely fresh by the time it is eaten. Most people think it is slightly bitter because they have never tasted the truly fresh product. They will add it to cereals, breads, and casseroles as a nutrition booster, but only in small amounts so it can't be tasted. The freshest wheat germ comes from mills immediately after it is made. Fortunately, some mills do retail to consumers. If you get the fresh product, it should be rushed home and put in the freezer. Bottled wheat germ is sometimes very good, but this depends on how old it is, and the bottles are usually not dated. Ask your grocer if you are in doubt.

A potential problem with wheat germ is that it has large amounts of phosphorous and almost no calcium. The two minerals should be ingested in roughly equal amounts, so if you eat large amounts of wheat germ your calcium requirement could increase.

Yogurt and related products are supposed to be health foods that help control body weight, keep the intestinal tract healthy, improve digestion, treat a variety of disorders, and even promote longevity. Yogurt is made by inoculating and incubating warm milk with any of several types of bacteria such as *Lactobacillus acidophilus*, *L. bulgaricus*, or *Streptococcus thermophilus*. These organisms convert the lactose (milk sugar) into acids, such as lactic acid, which curdle the rest of the milk, giving it a thick consistency and tart flavor.

Most of the yogurts on the market are heavily laced with sucrose,

150 lactose, artificial flavors and colors, and other additives. Some consider them little more than expensive junk food disguised as health food. The better brands, with only pure yogurt and real fruit, are prohibitively expensive for most people. However, an equally good and perhaps better product can be made at home with little trouble. Milk is heated to 155°F and cooled to 110°F, at which point a teaspoon or so of pure, clean yogurt is stirred in. The mixture is incubated for about eight hours. It can be wrapped in a towel and left in the sun, placed overnight in an oven with a pilot flame, or, for consistent success, placed in an incubator made for the purpose. For a starter, buy the best plain yogurt you can find and use it for a week or so, or use your homemade yogurt after you get it going.

Homemade yogurt has another advantage besides price, and that's flavor. The very best yogurt is less than about twelve hours out of the incubator, and commercial yogurt is never that fresh. It seems that before the lactose is converted to acids it is broken down to glucose and galactose, which are then slowly converted to sour acids. These simple sugars make the yogurt much sweeter than the milk, at least for a few hours. But acids are already being produced, so the young yogurt has a very pleasant sweet-sour flavor which cannot be matched by commercial yogurt.

What about the health claims? Yogurt, like milk, is an excellent source of protein, calcium, phosphorous, and some vitamins. However, it provides the same amount of fat and calories as the milk it is made from and it cannot perform miracles on obesity. The rich, creamy yogurt made from whole milk is a high-fat product.

On the other hand, there may be a grain of truth to some of the health claims made for yogurt. It is certainly a boon for the millions of people who are lactase-deficient and get gas, cramping, and diarrhea from milk. The predigestion of the lactose by the yogurt bacteria (both in the container and in the intestine) reduces the problem and permits a healthy intake of calcium, protein, and milk's other nutrients. This is very important since the vast majority of blacks are lactase-deficient by age ten and many Orientals, Jews, and American Indians are also affected. At least 10 percent of American whites are lactose-intolerant and can benefit from yogurt.

There is little agreement about what then becomes of the bacteria after they are eaten, though it is clear that they live long enough to help digest the lactose they accompany into your mouth. Some promoters of yogurt-related products claim that they colonize the gut, crowd out undesirable bacteria, and thereby improve digestion and alleviate intestinal disorders. Other promoters say no, only their special strain of X-ophilus survives and improves intestinal ecology and health. No one knows for sure; no one has proven that the expensive yogurt tablets people take to treat chronic digestive disorders, skin problems, and allergies are not a complete waste of money.

14

Food Additives

he complex chemical names on food labels sometimes cause people to wonder whether they are being slowly poisoned. Food additives are nothing new, of course. Since prehistoric times, smoke, salt, spices, herbs, plant dyes, thickeners made from seaweed, and flavor enhancers extracted from fish have been used. But recent application of modern chemistry and technology to food production has given rise to an enormous proliferation of semiartificial foods made from refined starch, sugar, and fat, plus thickeners, emulsifiers, moisturizers, flavors, stabilizers, colorings, preservatives, and other additives, several thousand in all.

In most cases the additives are harmless in themselves, but a long list of them in a food indicates a lot of processing, often with nutritional losses at each step, in spite of so-called "enrichment." Highly processed foods tend to be high in fat, sugar, and salt and low in fiber, vitamins, and minerals. This is generally of more significance to the consumer than any toxicity of additives.

Nevertheless, some of the additives are potentially harmful, even some of those on the FDA's GRAS (Generally Regarded As Safe) list. Most of these substances are on the list only because they have been used for a long time with no obvious problems. But cancer, birth defects, and special problems for certain population groups cannot always be easily correlated with additives without expensive, long-term studies. Several substances have been removed from the GRAS list after careful studies demonstrated significant hazards. No doubt a few more will be removed in the future.

The following brief discussions focus on the nature, sources, uses in foods, and potential health hazards, if any, of some of the most common additives. [43]

Acetic acid is vinegar acid, and is used to flavor and preserve. It is completely harmless.

152 **Agar** is a nondigestible carbohydrate extracted from seaweed. It is used in low concentrations as a thickening agent in jam, ice cream, whipped cream, and in baking to prevent icings from drying out. No hazards have been revealed in animal studies and several decades of human use.

Alginate is a seaweed derivative used as a texturizer and thickener. It is not absorbed by the body, and is probably completely safe. **Propylene glycol alginate** is an artificial derivative of alginate and is used for the same purposes, especially in acidic foods since it is acid-stable, which alginate is not. It is also used as a beer foam stabilizer and is also probably safe.

Alpha tocopherol is vitamin E, an excellent and safe antioxidant.

Amylases are proteins that naturally occur in plants as well as in our own digestive juices. They break down starch to dextrin and sugar and are sometimes used by bakers. A small amount of alpha-amylase is added to bread dough to covert a little of the starch to dextrin and sugar, which helps drive the fermenting yeast and improves the bread's texture and flavor. As used in food processing, amylases are completely safe.

Antioxidants—BHA, BHT, propyl gallate. These substances protect fats and oils from oxidation (rancidity) and are very common ingredients in processed foods. How well they work, their necessity, and their safety are controversial subjects. In the body BHA and BHT spare (protect) vitamin E to some extent. In food they all spare vitamin E and unsaturated oils, and under certain conditions they appear to protect animals from some cancers.

Animal tests have failed to consistently show toxicity at high levels of consumption, but there are reports of liver damage in rats given very large amounts. These are synthetic chemicals, they do accumulate in body fat (Americans have particularly high levels), and some experts think they have not been adequately tested for carcinogenicity, fetus-deforming effects, and liver damage.

Because of evidence of toxicity in animal studies, Japan has banned BHA. Eventually the United States and other countries may also ban one or more of these substances. Your best bet is to avoid them unless you can't get fresh-tasting cereals, oils, and nut butters without them. Stale oils are probably more hazardous to your health than these preservatives.

Ascorbic acid and **ascorbate** are vitamin C, an excellent and safe antioxidant.

Ascorbyl palmitate is a fat-soluble form of vitamin C and is perfectly safe.

Aspartame is a synthetic combination of two amino acids that are naturally present in many foods. It is almost 200 times as strong as sucrose but loses its sweetness when heated, so it is not useful in cooking. It is added primarily to soft drinks, breakfast cereals, and various low-calorie sweets.

In the body aspartame is metabolized to the amino acids aspartic acid and phenylalanine. The latter cannot be metabolized by persons with the rare genetic disorder phenylketonuria (PKU), so they must avoid aspartame. Some experts believe that even persons without PKU may experience changes in mood, sleep, and appetite (including, paradoxically, a craving for carbohydrate, like sugar) if they consume large amounts of aspartame because the phenylalanine can affect the levels of some brain neurotransmitters.

Small amounts of the toxic alcohol methanol may also be produced in the metabolism of aspartame, and this has led to complaints by consumer activists and demands that the product be removed from the market; but its proponents say it is the most tested additive ever used and is perfectly safe. Until there is hard evidence of harm to people the sweetener will stay.

Benzoyl peroxide is a flour bleach, probably harmless in itself but an efficient destroyer of vitamin E.

Beta-carotene is a precursor of vitamin A and is a perfectly safe food coloring.

Caffeine is naturally present in the kola nut which was used to make the first kola (or cola) drinks. This is apparently the reason the U.S. Code of Federal Regulations has long required that caffeine be present in any beverages called colas or pepper drinks, unless specified caffeine-free. Many noncolas also have added caffeine, supposedly as a flavoring (bitter) but perhaps also simply as a stimulant drug which subconsciously enhances the appeal of the products. The effects and hazards of caffeine are discussed in Chapter 5–4, Recreational Drugs.

Calcium propionate is a completely natural substance, present throughout the body and in many foods, such as Swiss cheese. It inhibits mold and bacteria growth and is used as a preservative, especially in baked goods. It is harmless, even slightly nutritious.

Caramel is burnt sugar; it is used as a coloring and flavoring in candy, soft drinks, and some frozen foods. It is a possible carcinogen and may eventually be banned as a food additive.

Carrageenan is a carbohydrate extracted from Irish moss, a red, bushy seaweed. It has been used for centuries as a thickener and stabilizer, now mostly in sour cream, ice cream, and other dairy products. It seems to be safe, but some animal studies indicate that allergic-type reactions with intestinal ulcerations may develop, so there is some doubt about its safety in infant formulas since infants are more susceptible to allergy development. It may eventually be banned.

Casein is nutritious milk protein used to improve texture and as a whitener. It is perfectly safe unless you are allergic to milk. Those who are intolerant to lactose (lactase deficient) need not avoid casein.

Carboxymethylcellulose (CMC) and **microcrystalline cellulose** (MC) are simple derivatives of natural cellulose widely used as stabilizers and texturizers. They are apparently completely safe.

Citric acid is very widely used as a flavoring, acidifier, and antioxidant preservative. It is a natural product of metabolism present throughout the body and is completely safe.

Colors, artificial. These synthetic colors are derived from chemically treated coal tar. Thousands of tons are added to all kinds of processed foods every year. Although they have been used for more than a hundred years, the list of allowable colors keeps shrinking as harmful effects such as cancer and kidney and liver damage are discovered. Some people develop allergic reactions to some colorings. These chemicals are completely worthless nutritionally and serve only to deceive the consumer.

Colors, natural. These include such coloring agents as beta-carotene, paprika, turmeric (oleoresin), saffron, and riboflavin. In general they are harmless but not widely used.

Cysteine is a natural amino acid used to prevent vitamin C destruction and is completely safe.

Dextrin is a mixture of a starch fragments used as a flavoring vehicle and thickener and is perfectly safe.

Dextrose is glucose, the basic sugar present in every living cell, and is used as a sweetener and thickener. It is as harmless as sugar and as harmful in excess.

Dioctyl sodium sulfosuccinate (DSS) is a wetting agent that helps dissolve powders. Very small amounts are used and there is no evidence of potential harm.

EDTA, or ethylenediamine tetraacetic acid, is a metal scavenger which keeps positively charged trace metals from catalyzing the destruction of vitamin C, the oxidation of oils, and the browning of some foods. Only 5 percent is absorbed into the blood, and this is rapidly excreted in the urine. It could theoretically bind trace minerals and prevent their absorption, but this effect has not been proven significant. It is probably safe in the small amounts used.

Ergosterol is a natural steroid which is converted to vitamin D upon irradiation with ultraviolet. It is used as a vitamin D supplement and is safe if the overall vitamin D supply is not too high.

Ferrous gluconate is a natural iron compound used to color olives and as an iron supplement. It is perfectly safe unless iron intake is too high.

Flavors, artificial. Thousands of these are used, some of which are entirely synthetic but most of which are synthetic replicas of natural compounds. These are very leniently regulated and little tested. They are probably as harmless as the substances they imitate, but their presence indicates little or none of the natural foods that would normally supply the flavor.

Flavor enhancers. Monosodium glutamate (MSG), disodium guanylate (GMP) and disodium inosinate (IMP) all occur naturally in many protein-containing foods ("GMP" and "IMP" come from alternative chemical names). They are generally safe, but large amounts of MSG, which is often used in Chinese cooking, should be avoided by those who are sensitive to it. Chinese restaurant syndrome may cause headaches, numbness in the limbs, burning sensations, and tightness in the chest. Pregnant women and infants should ingest a minimum of MSG to decrease the chances of sensitivity developing.

Feeling unwell after eating Chinese restaurant food seems to be fairly common, but it is not always caused by allergy or intolerance to MSG. Chinese food often contains very large amounts of sodium from salt, soy sauce, and flavor enhancers, primarily MSG. Up to five grams of sodium may be ingested in one meal, perhaps ten times one's daily requirement (which varies enormously with sweating). This often causes symptoms for up to about four hours. The main complaints are severe thirst, bloating, and headache.[44]

Fumaric acid is a natural metabolite present in every cell of the body. It is used to flavor and acidify and is completely safe.

Furcelleran is a vegetable gum similar to carrageenan and is also obtained from seaweed. It is used as a thickener and jelling agent and is most likely completely safe.

156 **Glycerin** (glycerol) is a natural metabolite in the body. It is the skeleton of fat molecules and is used as a moisturizer. It is completely safe.

Glycyrrhizin, extracted from licorice root, is fifty times as sweet as sucrose and is widely used to flavor processed foods. It is safe in small amounts, but as little as two ounces of licorice candy a day may cause edema, hypertension, headaches, and other circulatory problems in some people. Licorice candy labels should warn against excessive consumption, especially for hypertensives.

Iodides and iodates are used in bread doughs to make them more managable and the bread lighter. The iodates are converted in the body to iodide, an essential nutrient. Erythrosine (food dye Red #3), iodized salt, nutritional supplements, and traces of iodine disinfectants also contribute to the intake of iodine, which is now very high in the United States.

Lactic acid is used to acidify, flavor, and preserve. It is a natural metabolite present throughout the body and is perfectly safe.

Lactose is the slightly sweet milk sugar and is safe except for persons with lactase deficiency (lactose intolerance), in whom it can cause intestinal bloating, cramping, gas, and diarrhea.

Lecithin is a phospholipid present in many plants and in the body, where it helps maintain cell membranes and transport fats and cholesterol. It is used as an emulsifier and antioxidant and is nutritious and safe.

Licorice flavoring. See **Glycyrrhizin.**

Malic acid is a natural metabolite present in all living cells. It has long been used as an acidifier and flavoring and it is completely safe.

Maltol and **ethyl maltol** are used as flavor enhancers in sweet foods and drinks. They have been used for many years and tested on some animals with no sign of toxicity, but some experts think they should be more thoroughly tested for possible carcinogenicity.

Mannitol is a naturally occurring sugar used in "sugarless" chewing gum and low-calorie desserts. It is poorly digested by bacteria and therefore cannot promote tooth decay. It is also poorly absorbed by humans. What little is absorbed is converted to glucose and burned for energy. It is generally safe, but large amounts may have a laxative effect and even cause diarrhea, especially in children.

Monoglycerides and **diglycerides** are fats naturally present in many foods as well as throughout the body. They are used as texturizers and stabilizers in some foods. While harmless in themselves, they are empty calories, which displace more nutritious components when large amounts are added to foods.

Nitrates and **nitrites** are naturally occurring essential plant nutrients used to form plant proteins. Substantial amounts are found in many vegetables. They are also in water leeched from the soil. Fertilizers are a major source of nitrates in the soil, food, and water. For many centuries nitrates and nitrites have been added to meats, especially canned and cured products, to give them a pink color—they are normally grey-brown. In large amounts they can impair hemoglobin function and accidental overdose is sometimes fatal.

These additives also inhibit botulinum growth, so they aid in the prevention of botulism. But critics charge that some foods they are added to do not harbor the deadly bacteria and their use is purely cosmetic. Since they are strongly suspected of forming carcinogenic nitrosamines in the digestive tract, cosmetic use should not be allowed. (This reaction can apparently be inhibited by vitamin C in foods eaten at the same time as the nitrate-containing foods.)

Oxystearin is a modified fatty acid added to vegetable oils to keep them from clouding up in the refrigerator. There is no evidence of potential hazard.

Pectin is a natural carbohydrate fiber present in many fruits and vegetables. It is used as a thickener and is completely safe.

Polysorbates are emulsifiers that have been added to foods since the 1940s. Their fate in the body is well understood and they appear to be completely harmless.

Quinine, a potent and toxic drug, is used as a bitter flavoring in tonic water (quinine water) and other drinks. A very few people are sensitive to quinine and just a small glassful can cause purpura, in which blood oozes out of superficial vessels and turns the skin purple. One quart of quinine water contains about 15 percent of a usual therapeutic dose for malaria. Critics claim it has not been adequately tested for cancer or birth defect promotion, and it should probably be avoided by pregnant women. In spite of theoretical hazards, there is no evidence of widespread problems.

Saccharin has been used as a calorie-free sweetener for about a hundred years. It is extremely sweet, but it has a slightly bitter aftertaste which is often masked by the addition of the amino acid, glycine. It is absorbed into the

158 blood and excreted unchanged in the urine. Animal studies indicate it might be a very weak carcinogen or cocarcinogen, but extensive study of human users has not revealed a cancer hazard. It has not been shown to help in weight loss or control of diabetes.

Silicates are used in various salts and powders to prevent caking and clumping. What little is absorbed is rapidly excreted. According to the available evidence, silicates are completely safe.

Silicones—methyl silicone and others—are used as stabilizers in various products. They are chemically inert and very likely completely safe.

Sodium benzoate occurs naturally in many fruits and vegetables, and may even be a natural metabolite in the human body. It has been used almost since the turn of the century as a preservative; it effectively inhibits the growth of microbes in acidic foods. There are occasional allergic reactions.

Sodium erythorbate is sprayed on cured meats such as hot dogs, bologna, and pastrami to keep them pink. It has no important advantages over its chemical relative, sodium ascorbate (a form of vitamin C) and, though there is no evidence of a hazard, some critics believe it has not been sufficiently tested for health hazards.

Sodium propionate. See **Calcium propionate,** which is essentially the same, but preferable if sodium must be restricted.

Sorbic acid (or potassium sorbate) is a fatlike substance very effective in preventing the growth of molds and fungi. It is metabolized like any natural fat, and many studies indicate it is safe. However, reports that it may combine with nitrates in the digestive tract to form potential carcinogens are stimulating a closer look.

Sorbitol is a close relative of glucose and almost as sweet. It is slowly absorbed and converted to glucose, and is considered better for diabetics than sugar because of the slow absorption. It is also safer for the teeth than sucrose because it does not stick to them. Many human and animal studies indicate it is safe, although it tends to have a laxative effect and often cause gas, bloating, cramps, and diarrhea. Children seem to be especially susceptible, sometimes to very small amounts, but many adults are also affected. Unexplained chronic abdominal complaints should prompt consideration of sorbitol intake and possible intolerance.

Stannous chloride (tin chloride) is an antioxidant used in some bottled foods and drinks to prevent discoloration and flavor deterioration. Tin appears to be an essential nutrient and the amounts added to foods present no hazards.

Stearyl and isopropyl citrate are oil-soluble forms of citric acid and are used as antioxidants to prevent rancidity in vegetable oils and margarines. They are completely metabolized and animal studies indicate they are safe.

Sulfites and bisulfites (of sodium and potassium) have been used since the ancient Egyptians and Romans preserved wine with them. They are also widely used in beer, soft drinks, bottled and canned fruits, vegetables, soups, and other foods. The largest amounts are used in restaurant salads; vegetables can be cut ahead of time for quick serving during peak hours or they can be left in the salad bar for several hours. Bisulfite destroys thiamin and is banned from foods with large amounts of the vitamin.

      These compounds are rapidly converted to innocuous sulfate, and are apparently safe for most people, but they can cause serious reactions in some, especially if they have asthma. Reactions include nausea, diarrhea, hives, itching, anaphylactic shock (which has led to death in some cases), acute asthma attacks, and loss of consciousness. Up to 1 million of the 10 million asthmatics in the United States may be sulfite-sensitive. All asthmatics should be alert for this sensitivity and should do their best to avoid foods with the preservatives.

      Avoidance is sometimes difficult because the preservatives are often used in restaurant foods and in wines without the consumer knowing it. Don't be afraid to ask; your life may depend on it. **Be especially wary of restaurant salads, fruits, seafoods, and potatoes.** A restaurant meal can supply fifty to a hundred times your usual daily intake of sulfites.

      Nearly one-third of all people sensitive to sulfites are not asthmatics and have no known allergies, so the problem is one of concern to the general population. Increasing reports of adverse reactions from asthmatics and nonasthmatics alike has prompted ongoing review and increasing restrictions on the use of the chemicals. In the future we can expect to see more labeling, including in restaurants, and stricter limitations on the uses and allowed concentrations of sulfites. Ironically, sulfites have been used as preservatives in some asthma medicines, a practice being phased out.

Sulfur dioxide is a gas used in beverages, dried fruits, and other foods. It is easily metabolized and excreted and appears to be safe for most people, but the large amounts present in some wines can provoke severe reactions in sensitive persons.

Tartaric acid occurs naturally in many fruits and is used for its tart flavor. Most of it is destroyed by intestinal bacteria and the remainder is rapidly metabolized and excreted. Even very high levels appear to be harmless.

160   **Xylitol** is a sweetener naturally present in many plants including plums, strawberries, raspberries, and some vegetables. The main sources for commercial use are corncobs and birchwood chips. Xylitol has the same taste, appearance, and caloric value as sucrose, but it does not stick to the teeth, feed bacteria, and promote acid formation and tooth decay; this is naturally considered an advantage for chewing gum and some candies. However, it is rarely used now and may be banned because animal studies indicate it might cause or promote tumors.

15

Food "Poisoning" and Parasites

e have known for a long time that foods can be infested and contaminated with organisms and toxins that cause illness, usually nausea, vomiting, and diarrhea, sometimes very severe and occasionally fatal. While even our ancient ancestors had to contend with visible molds, which they probably recognized as a source of illness, most of the offending organisms and toxins have been identified only in recent decades. The most important ones are bacteria and bacterial toxins, mold toxins, protozoa, viruses, and worms. Their life cycles, and the nature of the illnesses they cause and the means of prevention are well understood, but thousands of people still get miserably sick and a few die each year because of someone's ignorance or carelessness.

People responsible for growing, harvesting, storing, preparing, and serving food should be aware of the potential problems and how to prevent them. Laws and regulations make some important steps mandatory, but bad food still slips through to consumers all too often. Summarized below are the most common and most important food-borne parasites and poisons, and the steps necessary to prevent illness from them.[45]

Bacteria and Bacterial Toxins

There are many bacteria that contaminate foods and, either by infection or poisoning, make us sick. For example, more than 1700 kinds of *Salmonella* bacteria thrive in raw meats, poultry, fish, eggs, and milk and multiply rapidly at room temperature. Within twelve to forty-eight hours after the

161

162 foods are eaten symptoms begin. The nausea, vomiting, diarrhea, abdominal cramps, headache, and fever can last for a week. The infection may be lethal in infants, the elderly, and the infirm.

Staphylococcus aureus, which is also believed responsible for toxic shock syndrome, poisons foods it contaminates if they are left too long at room temperature. Cream-filled pastries, meats, poultry, eggs, tuna, and all the products and dishes made from them are favorite foods for these bacteria. Seemingly minor staph infections of the skin can be the source of the bacteria in food handlers. Typical symptoms include nausea, vomiting, diarrhea, abdominal cramps, and prostration. They usually begin within one to eight hours of eating and last a day or two. The toxin is rarely lethal.

Shigella, Campylobacter, Clostridium, and *Yersinia* are bacteria that have similar sources and produce similar illnesses to those above. Shigellosis is especially troublesome and difficult to get rid of in day-care centers, where good hygeine must always be strived for. *Yersinia*, often from raw milk, can produce symptoms which mimic appendicitis so closely that unnecessary surgery may be done.

Vibrio cholera bacteria cause **cholera.** The symptoms range from mild to very severe diarrhea, which can lead to dehydration and death. The most common sources are fish and shellfish, especially raw oysters, taken from waters contaminated by human sewage.

Botulism is caused by a toxin produced by *Clostridium botulinum* bacteria. The bacteria are widespread but they produce the toxin only in an anaerobic environment of low acidity (high pH). Low-acid foods such as beans, olives, beef, mushrooms, and spinach that are canned without adequate cooking are ideal for botulinum toxin production. The most common source of botulism is home-canned foods. Honey may have large amounts of botulinum spores, which are harmless to adults but can cause botulism in infants. Honey should not be fed to infants.

Botulism is rare, but it must be considered because it is potentially lethal and will occur whenever we get careless about canned foods. Neurotoxic symptoms of botulism start within eight to thirty-six hours after eating and include double vision, difficult swallowing and talking, and progressive paralysis of the respiratory system. The latter leads to death if the person is not treated. *Botulinum* antitoxins are effective if given in time. If the above symptoms appear, get medical help immediately.

Traveler's diarrhea, frequently contracted by American tourists in Mexico, is caused by several food- and water-borne strains of *Escherichia coli* bacteria which attach themselves to the intestinal lining and produce toxins that provoke diarrhea. Doxycycline and other antibiotics are often given to prevent the problem, but they may cause gastrointestinal symptoms, sunlight sensitivity, and other side effects. Their liberal use also contributes to the resistance of bacteria to antibiotics. Pepto Bismol (bismuth subsalicylate) is an effective preventive in most people, but the necessary dose is quite large, about a cup a day, which can be cumbersome and expensive, and can produce constipation. It is also ineffective for about a fourth of those who try it. A vaccine is being developed, but its routine use is years away.

Prevention of illness from bacteria in food: All food must be handled, cooked, and stored properly. Be aware that bacteria are lurking on our skin, nails, and hair, and that they can multiply and produce toxins in foods. Keep in mind that all raw animal products will rapidly breed *Salmonella* and other bacteria when left at room temperature. Be careful to wash cutting boards, plates, knives, and other utensils used with raw poultry or meat before using them again. Do not touch your face, hair, or body while handling food. Don't handle any animals and then food without first washing your hands. Don't drink raw milk; even "certified" raw milk has been associated with serious illness and death. Even cooked foods can breed dangerous bacteria, and they generally must be refrigerated within an hour or two of cooking. Foods should be refrigerated at 40°F or below.

To prevent botulism, do your home canning with the utmost care, and never cut corners, especially by reducing pressure cooking time. Don't eat food from cans (commercial or home-prepared) that are swollen, leaking, or broken.

To prevent traveler's diarrhea, avoid fruits, vegetables, and other raw foods that may have been handled or rinsed with bad water, which is common in Mexico and some other countries. Stick to cooked foods and fruits that you peel yourself. Avoid water and ice if it has not been chlorinated or otherwise treated.

Mycotoxins

Several types of molds establish themselves on a variety of foods, especially grains, beans, peanuts, and their products. Some of them produce toxins which can cause liver and kidney disease. *Aspergillus flavus*, for example, can cause liver cancer.

Prevention of mold poisoning. Don't eat foods with visible mold. Store grains and other susceptible foods in closed containers in a cool, dry place.

Protozoa

Some varieties of these single-cell organisms can infect the human intestinal tract, cause sickness, and be spread through the feces. For example, **giardia-**

164 sis is caused by the flagellate *Giardia lamblia* and **amebiasis** is caused by the ameba *Entamoeba histolytica*. Symptoms of these infections include diarrhea, abdominal pain, gas, anemia, and weight loss. Several effective drugs can usually clear up the infections.

Prevention of protozoal infection: Avoid raw fruits and vegetables in areas where protozoa are endemic. Food handlers must keep their hands clean at all times, especially if food is to be served raw. Sewage must be properly disposed of and local sanitation laws must be obeyed to avoid contamination of drinking water supplies.

Viruses

Several varieties of **enteroviruses, rotaviruses, parvoviruses,** and others exist in human digestive tracts and are expelled in feces, which may then contaminate food and water. Symptoms of infection include severe diarrhea, nausea, and vomiting and usually last less than a week, but they may last longer and respiratory symptoms may develop.

The most important food-borne virus is **hepatitis A.** Primary food sources include shellfish from waters contaminated with human sewage, and foods, usually raw, handled by persons carrying and shedding the virus, whether or not they have symptoms of infection. Hepatitis is discussed in detail in Part Four.

Prevention of diseases from viruses in food. Patients and known carriers of hepatitis A virus should not handle food to be eaten or utensils to be used by others. Food handlers at all levels must make sure their hands are absolutely clean. It is especially important to wash the hands thoroughly after using the toilet. Shellfish from contaminated waters should be avoided, and local sewage disposal laws should be obeyed to avoid contaminating water supplies.

Worms

The worms that make foods hazardous to eat are not the visible insect larvae on our lettuce and in our apples that we mistakenly call worms. Those little beasties are specialized for crop devastation and cannot directly harm humans or animals even if swallowed alive. The worms we are concerned about here are usually microscopic eggs or larvae of real worms, not insects. They occur in the tissues and wastes of cattle, hogs, fish, and other animals, and may grow to prodigious size once the adult form is settled in a host.

Trichinella spiralis is a tiny roundworm that infects swine, rats, bears, walrus, and other wild animals. Young larvae settle in skeletal muscle fibers, grow into the adolescent spiral form, and develop protective shells. They stay largely unchanged for years. If the flesh is eaten, their shells protect them from stomach acid, and they mature and mate in the intestines. They then die and are evacuated, while their larvae bore through the intestinal wall and ride the blood to the muscles.

The severity of symptoms of this worm infection, known as **trichinellosis** (also called trichinosis), depends on the number ingested and the individual's immunity. During the intestinal phase there is rarely more than mild diarrhea, but after the muscles have been invaded symptoms may include muscle pain, fever, nausea and vomiting, headache, facial swelling, and difficult breathing. In severe cases death may occur in about a month, but treatment with the drug thiabendazole is usually successful. Severe illness and death are not common, but experts suspect that a quarter million or so mild cases go unreported each year.

PREVENTION
Don't eat raw or undercooked meat of swine, wild boar, bear, walrus, or other game. Cool spots in meat can leave surviving worms. Microwave oven cooking is especially troublesome in this regard. For microwave cooking of pork and other potential sources of *trichinella*, the USDA recommends that evenly shaped cuts of five pounds or less be cooked at a medium setting (300–350 watts), with frequent rotation, to 170°F throughout, then allowed to sit at least ten minutes under aluminum foil. Swine should not be fed garbage because it sometimes contains raw, trichinella-infected meat.

Tapeworms, most commonly *Taenia saginata* from infected beef, but also *T. solium* from infected pork, develop into adults in the human intestine. Symptoms include diarrhea, frequent hunger pangs (the large worms expropriate what you have eaten for yourself), and chronic indigestion. Their eggs, which can also be consumed in vegetables contaminated with the animals' feces, hatch, and the larvae (of *T. solium* but not *T. saginata*) penetrate to the blood and are carried to soft tissues. In the brain they can grow to large masses and cause death.

PREVENTION
Take the same precautions as for preventing trichinellosis, but cook beef to 160°F.

Fish worms, that is, various roundworms, tapeworms, and flukes consumed in some raw or undercooked fish, can infect humans and cause serious illness. For example, several related roundworms called anisakines exist as larvae in the flesh of many fish. If eaten by humans they anchor themselves to the gastrointestinal tract and cause ulcers, pain, bleeding, and nausea.

166 They sometimes wander up the throat and throughout the body, settle in other tissues, and form granulomas, which are tumorlike masses sometimes misdiagnosed as cancerous. Horrible as this may sound, such infections are rarely life threatening, which is fortunate because there is no cure.

A dangerous fish tapeworm is *Diphyllobothrium latum*, which can grow to 100 feet long in the human digestive tract and cause pernicious anemia. In recent years it has frequently been associated with raw, under-cooked, pickled, and salted salmon, especially in Japan and on the west coast of the United States. Fortunately, the drug niclosamide provides an effective treatment.

PREVENTION
Freeze fish to $-4°F$ for seventy-two hours, or fry at $140°F$ for five minutes, or bake or broil until the meat flakes easily. Don't worry unduly about sushi bars; the chefs are usually well trained in choosing fish unlikely to be infected and in removing larvae should they be present. You are more likely to be infected by eating home-prepared sushi or sashimi, or simply lightly cooked fish, than by eating at a sushi bar.

Ascaris worms are large roundworms that can grow as thick as a pencil and cause severe symptoms in infected humans. The eggs are on fruits and vege-tables grown in contaminated soil or sewage sludge. When swallowed, they hatch in the gut, and the larvae travel to various tissues. Intestinal blockage and an asthmalike condition may develop. The infection is especially severe in children and sometimes lethal in infants. Mebendazole, piperazine, and other drugs help kill and expel the parasite.

PREVENTION
Rinse unpeeled fruits with water and rinse or scrub vegetables before eating them raw.

16

Air, Water, and Food Pollution

The fouling of our air, water, and food supplies has become an enormous problem and a threat to good health. The growth of population and industry and the rise of chemical agriculture have led to the proliferation of hazardous chemicals throughout the thin film covering the earth known as the biosphere. Hundreds of volumes have been written on the complex problems, the answers to which generally require group and community action more than lifestyle changes. Individual awareness is important, however, as a prerequisite to effective political action and is necessary to avoid some of the worst hazards in the environment. The following is a brief survey of some of the more important pollution problems.[46]

Air Pollutants

The major gaseous pollutants are carbon monoxide, nitrogen oxides, hydrocarbons, and sulfur oxides. Liquid and solid particles from smoke, dust, and the like can also pollute the air. All the gases and many of the particles, including asbestos, lead, nickel, selenium, and sulfuric acid droplets, are health hazards. In high concentrations most of them are very toxic and potentially lethal. In the lower concentrations found in polluted air they cause, promote, or aggravate chronic respiratory and circulatory problems and various cancers.

Nature, of course, contributes substantially to air pollution. For example, most of the atmosphere's nitrogen oxide is produced naturally by bacteria, carbon monoxide is produced by volcanoes and electrical storms,

168

and dust, including naturally-occurring asbestos, is kicked up by the wind. However, nature is rarely responsible for the dangerously high concentrations found in urban areas. It is well known that motor vehicles, industrial processes, and the burning of solid wastes are the major sources of air pollution high enough to be a threat to health.

Laws regulating emissions from these sources generally prevent catastrophe, but in some areas special precautions may be in order. This is especially true on days of temperature inversion, when a lack of wind and other factors combine to trap large masses of polluted air in a populated basin or valley.

Individual Remedies. If possible, live away from polluted areas. If not, reduce your activity level on smog alert days, don't jog or bicycle during peak traffic hours or on the busiest roads, and try to avoid long, slow drives in bumper-to-bumper traffic, especially through tunnels. Exercise when you can to help clear particulate matter from your respiratory system. Remember that some air pollutants increase the harm done by cigarette smoke which is a major indoor pollutant especially to the smoker but also to those who share his air. For example, smokers have about five times as much carbon monoxide in their blood as nonsmokers.

If you live in a rural area and use a wood-burning stove, remember that its smoke can be a major air pollutant if too many such stoves are used where there is little wind. Moreover, unless the stoves are installed and used properly they can cause carbon dioxide, carbon monoxide, and other gases to accumulate to potentially dangerous levels inside the home.

Water Pollutants

Water pollution in the United States is caused by agricultural pesticides draining into waterways and seeping into water tables and wells, toxic industrial wastes dumped into streams and rivers or buried where they seep into water supplies, and run-off from mining operations, barnyards, and feed lots. While we have not experienced an epidemic of health problems associated with impure drinking water, there are reasons for concern and action.

For example, tap water in some areas has high levels of chloroform and related carcinogens which are formed when chlorine (added to kill bacteria) reacts with decaying vegetable matter. Preliminary studies suggest that people who drink such water for many years are much more susceptible to bladder and colon cancers. In some communities, farming activities have contaminated the water tables and well water with ethylene dibromide (EDB) and other pesticides. Some water is polluted by dirty air even before it falls as rain—acid rain, that is. Water flowing through pipes, especially if it is acidic, can corrode the metals and take lead, cadmium, and copper to your tap.

Another reason for concern is that, in spite of the growing number of major pollutants and ways they can get into our water, the Environmental Protection Agency (EPA) demands that only a handful of chemicals be checked for by the water utilities, who frequently ignore even these meagre requirements. Moreover, millions of wells, both private and public, have never been tested for any pollutants.

Individual remedies. If we cannot solve the problem of water pollution as a nation by cleaning up dump sites and ending the polluting of waterways and water tables, individuals and families will have to fend for themselves. Millions have already lost faith in their local water supplies and have taken remedial steps. Ask your water utility or your local public health department what is added to the water, what is or might be present as a pollutant, and how the levels compare to EPA safety guidelines.

If you are not satisfied with the information or if you still have questions, call some chemistry labs and get cost estimates for a thorough analysis of your water. Depending on where you live, how old your plumbing is, and other variables, some logical things to check for are lead, cadmium, chloroform and other trihalomethanes, dieldrin and other pesticides, copper, hydrocarbons, and bacteria. If you decide that you and your family should not drink your tap water, then it's time to take action. There are two main alternatives, both fairly expensive but probably worth the cost in many cases.

Bottled water is a fast-growing industry, partly because of concern about water safety. However, there are hundreds of brands on the market, they come from many and varied sources, and there is no guarantee that they are pure and safe. Tests have shown that some bottled water has more chloroform and other pollutants than tap water, some have less, and most have about the same amount. In fact, seltzers and club sodas are almost all simply carbonated tap water and naturally have all the pollutants common to the water they are made of. Some bottled spring waters, especially mineral waters, have small but significant levels of arsenic, barium, and other potential toxins. Other bottled waters have been shown to be completely free of pollutants. The following are only examples; read recent consumer publications for more recent and complete information.

Bottled waters (including some carbonated) found to be free of pollutants include Perrier, White Rock, Evian, Deer Park, White Rose, Waldbaums, Schweppes, No-Cal, Old-Fashioned, and Grand Union.

Home water filters have become a billion-dollar-a-year business. There are many brands on the market and they work in a number of different ways. The most effective systems use activated carbon, made by heating coal or wood to a very high temperature. This etches channels and craters in the

170 carbon, and when water is forced through, the pollutants get trapped in the tiny pockets.

When comparing models of water filters, most of which fit under the sink, check the initial cost (usually $200 to $500), the filter replacement cost ($50 to $150 per year), and the efficiency of the systems. Look for 99 percent removal of trihalomethanes and halogenated organics, and at least 35 percent removal of nonpurgeable total organic carbon (NPTOC).

Food Pollution

Our foods are almost never pure and completely free of potentially harmful contaminants. Even if we grow them ourselves without using chemicals they may pick up lead from the soil or drifting pesticide spray from the neighbors' farms and gardens. The potential for contamination is multiplied when the food is grown on large farms and transported long distances. Insecticides are among the most troublesome of the pollutants because they are so widespread and because heavy exposure can cause or promote serious illnesses, including cancer.

There is no evidence yet that pesticide residues in foods have become a major public health problem, and the hazards to the consumer have been greatly exaggerated by some. Most people are exposed to far more potentially carcinogenic chemicals in the form of natural pesticides that occur in most plants than in the form of synthetic pesticides which contaminate their food. The health hazards of pesticides are mostly to the workers who make and apply them. Nevertheless, there are steps worth taking to minimize your intake of hazardous chemicals with your food.

Individual remedies. Wash your fruits and vegetables with dilute soap or soak them in dilute vinegar (1/4 cup per gallon of water). Even if they have to be peeled, washing may be advisable. For example, oranges are frequently coated with a strong-smelling white crystalline fungicide, which is used to suppress molds during transport. If you peel the orange without washing it first, you inevitably smear the chemical all over the orange and end up swallowing it.

Peel or scrub root vegetables. The soil they were grown in likely contains pesticides and heavy metals. Few nutrients are lost by peeling carrots and the like.

Be wary of produce from Mexico and Central America, where pesticides banned in the United States are sometimes heavily used and government controls are not very tight. The FDA monitors imported foods for pesticide residues, but it can only do sample checks. When other factors are equal, buying American is usually better, though it is not always easy to tell where produce comes from. We're not saying don't buy foreign produce; but be extra thorough in cleaning it if you suspect it was imported.

Grow your own fruits and vegetables and use an absolute minimum of pesticides. Learn how to control pests without using chemicals; read books and ask local gardening and farming experts. If you do have to use pesticides, at least you can be sure to use them in accordance with safety requirements and with the law. If you live in an urban area with very polluted air, especially near heavy traffic, have your garden soil analyzed for lead, most of which comes from vehicle exhaust.

The problem of lead is especially important for children, who can suffer long-term neurological problems, including learning deficits, from excessive exposure. The major sources of lead contamination, in addition to gasoline fumes, are industrial emissions, leaded paint, food grown in soil with lead or exposed to lead-polluted air, and contaminated soil. Tin cans were once a significant source of lead in our food, but techniques have greatly improved, and the cans now impart very little or no lead to the food. Children in high-risk areas (with paint chips and dust in the soil) can be protected by keeping the homes as free of dust and paint chips as possible, keeping their hands clean, and discouraging them from eating nonfoods.

Finally, you can reduce the impact of pesticides, heavy metals, and other pollutants on your health by eating well. Numerous studies have shown that low levels of essential nutrients slow down the metabolism and excretion of the pollutants, while a healthy diet helps to get rid of them.

Healthy Sex and Reproduction

PART THREE

Chapter 1   Human Sexual Response in
             Health and Disease

Chapter 2   Birth Control Options

Chapter 3   Sexually Transmitted Diseases
             (STDs)

Chapter 4   Healthy Pregnancy, Healthy
             Children

Chapter 5   Common Female Problems

1

Human Sexual Response in Health and Disease

All primates learn sexual behavior by imitation or instruction. If a young ape or monkey cannot witness intercourse it will not know what to do when its turn comes. Humans, too, must learn sexual behavior. However, since we prefer privacy our children must be instructed by means other than imitation. There is no possibility of not having sex education. The question is, who will do the educating—the neighborhood children, pornographers, or responsible adults who have some understanding of the many dimensions of human sexuality?

Sex Education

Sexual ignorance causes a great deal of unnecessary suffering from unwanted pregnancies, venereal diseases, confusion, guilt, and sexual dysfunctions in couples who lack understanding of their own or each other's sexuality. Health professionals, teachers, religious leaders, and parents should be prepared to provide knowledge and understanding to those who want and need them.

Humans are born with the capacity for sexual pleasure and most of us die with it, although certain illnesses and drugs, as well as abstinence for long periods in old age, may greatly reduce or eliminate the capacity. Here we discuss the sexual response cycle, common sexual dysfunctions, and important factors that influence sexual activity.

175

176 The Sexual Response Cycle[1]

Sexual response can be a pure reflex to genital stimulation; the reflexive pathway from the genitals to the spinal nerves and back to the genitals is complete without input to or from the brain. But sexual activity is never that simple because psychic input inhibits or stimulates the reflex. For example, fear is a potent inhibitory signal. It prepares a person to fight or flee, which require stimulation of the sympathetic nervous system and inhibition of the parasympathetic. As we shall see, fear plays an important role in the development of common sexual dysfunctions, especially in men.

Sexual response, on the other hand, requires parasympathetic stimulation. Fantasies or memories of pleasure promote anticipation, and the psychic input is stimulating to the parasympathetic system and sexual functions. Because of this intimate association of sex and the mind, the study of human sexuality is enormously complex. Each person is unique in his or her sexual preferences and patterns. Nevertheless, whatever turns you on, the physiological response is pretty much the same for everyone, men and women alike. A complete cycle goes from excitement to plateau to orgasm and resolution.

During **excitement** there is an increased heart rate and blood pressure. Muscle tension increases, especially in the abdominal and genital areas. The woman's, and sometimes the man's, nipples become erect and breast size increases. The clitoris and penis are engorged with blood and increase in diameter and length. Vaginal lubrication appears, the vagina expands (regardless of insertion of penis), the labia thicken, and the uterus may be elevated. In the man, the scrotum and testes are elevated.

During **plateau,** nipple erection and breast enlargement continue. Heart rate, blood pressure, and muscle tension increase further. The clitoris withdraws beneath the clitoral hood. The penis increases in circumference. The uterus becomes fully elevated, and the labia swell further. The testes swell to about one and a half times their unstimulated state and further elevate.

During **orgasm,** voluntary muscle control is lost and involuntary contractions and spasms occur. Heart rate and blood pressure peak and breathing is rapid. The uterus and the muscles in and around the vagina and pelvic floor contract in a rapid series; the pelvis seems to throb. The muscles of the penis and lower pelvic area contract in expulsive spasms.

During **resolution,** there is a return to normal, with the blood receding from engorged pelvic and genital areas; this process is much more rapid in men than in women. The heart and respiratory rates decrease and muscles relax. Deep relaxation and sleep may follow. A film of perspiration usually appears, especially on women.

Women have the physiological potential to return to plateau after orgasm and to experience more than one orgasm before full resolution. Some women experience this, but most do not. Men usually cannot return to plateau and another orgasm without full resolution and several minutes to several hours interval.

Although a complete cycle involves each of the above phases, cycles vary a great deal in the length and intensity of each phase and, for some women, the return to plateau. Moreover, excitement and plateau frequently occur without the orgasm which hastens resolution. Prolonged plateau without orgasm and consequent return to normal blood flow patterns can cause severe and prolonged pain in the abdomen and genitals in both men and women. Such experiences may also result in prolonged psychic tension.

Sexual Dysfunctions[2]

Certain factors tend to be common among those with major sexual dysfunctions. There is often a history of early strict religious training, with sex considered sinful and to be reserved for procreation. Prolonged problems with self-esteem are also common. Many times the main problem is persistent lack of communication between partners.

Preorgasmic Women

Having never experienced orgasm is a common complaint among women with sexual dysfunction. The woman enters the excitement phase and may go in and out of plateau, but does not experience orgasm. This is known as preorgasmia. Resolution is slow and she may experience abdominal and genital pain, as well as frustration. However, some women say they are satisfied with just the pleasure of closeness and stimulation.

CAUSES
There are several common causes of preorgasmia. In many cases parental influence discouraged sexual behavior, seductive dress, nudity, and discussions of sex. Menstruation was taught to be dirty. Repeated emphasis on not "going too far" may have caused the girl to habitually suppress her sexual feelings for many years. The mother is often nonorgasmic and may have taught her daughter that her primary function is to satisfy her husband.

Some preorgasmic women have never had adequate stimulation either self-induced or with a partner. It is estimated that a third to a half of all women require direct clitoral stimulation to achieve orgasm. (For others, penile thrusting is enough, and direct stimulation may be irritating.)

REMEDIES WORTH TRYING

Avoid deceiving your partner, such as faking an orgasm, and don't blame your partner. Communicate your needs and desires. Avoid scheduled sex and demands for performance on either partner. The focus should be on prolonged pleasure and affection as goals in themselves, not as means to the goal of intercourse and satisfaction. Try variety and innovation in time, place, and positions. Become aware of your own body by self-exploration to orgasm if possible. Learn what you like, then guide your partner.

The Situational Nonorgasmic Woman

Some women can experience orgasm, but not in certain situations, such as with a light on, in the daytime, with someone else or even an animal in the house or, most commonly, during intercourse. This could be a sign of unresolved conflicts with ones partner, boredom with routinized sex, or general disappointment with the relationship.

A woman's partner may be too quick, insensitive, and uncaring. On the other hand, even if he is not, she may receive inadequate clitoral stimulation during intercourse. Penile thrusting is insufficient for many women. Some women are nonorgasmic because of their partners' dysfunction. For example, a woman may not experience adequate stimulation because of her partner's premature ejaculation, which prevents prolonged sex play and intercourse.

REMEDIES WORTH TRYING

Try to identify the factors in the situation or about your partner that turn you off. Be open and honest; communicate your needs and desires. If necessary, help him overcome his own dysfunctions. If you are bored, try variety and innovation. If you are too tired in the evening, try the morning.

Couples seeking therapy because the woman is secondarily nonorgasmic are often successfully led through a process such as the following.

The woman establishes full orgasmic capacity by self-stimulation. She then guides her partner in stimulating her the same way to orgasm. This is done several times before intercourse is attempted. Once this is well established, intercourse commences during her high plateau with continued manual stimulation to orgasm. Eventually, the manual stimulation may be unnecessary. But, due to normal anatomical variation, many women continue to require direct clitoral stimulation.

Vaginismus

During sexual excitement the vagina normally expands to easily accept even the largest penis, but involuntary tightening of the paravaginal muscles, vaginismus, can prevent penetration by even the smallest. The tightening may also occur during pelvic examination or tampon or diaphragm insertion.

CAUSES

Vaginismus may have its roots in excessive control and sexual repression by the parents. The woman may fear the pain of intercourse after their repeated warnings about it.

Vaginismus may also be subsequent to her partner's insensitivity during their first intercourse, which may have been very painful to her. Or she may have been raped or otherwise sexually abused.

Vaginismus is sometimes associated with a recent painful vaginal infection.

REMEDIES

The woman and her partner must recognize the problems as a reflex response, not a conscious process. The goal of treatment is to desensitize the woman to vaginal insertion. Using a lubricant if necessary, the woman first inserts one finger. When that can be done comfortably, she inserts two, then three, then four.

Then her partner inserts a finger, and works up to four. When this is comfortable, he inserts his penis. The process may require great patience and understanding. Recriminations and blaming can retard the progress.

Painful Intercourse

Common causes include vaginal and cervical infections, endometriosis, complications of surgery, tears in vaginal ligaments, an IUD, a rash from contraceptive creams, foams, douches, and diaphragms. However, the most common cause is probably inadequate lubrication due to inadequate sexual arousal or estrogen deficiency after menopause or removal of the ovaries. A water-soluble lubricant can be used but not petroleum jelly. Persistant pain during intercourse should be discussed with a physician.

Primary Erective Impotence

In this condition, the man has never attained an erection sufficient for vaginal penetration while with a woman.

180

CAUSES

There are several. The parents may have been very strict, punishing the boy for any sexual activities, and providing no sex education. The child may have slept in bed with the mother as an adolescent, and the suppression by the incest taboo may have become deeply rooted and associated with being in bed with any female. The man's first sexual experience with a woman may have been traumatic; she may have pressured him to perform, then laughed at him. Or he may be a homosexual and not know it or want to admit it to himself. Homosexuality itself is not considered a disease or disorder by most physicians and psychologists, but it can give rise to sexual complications and dysfunctions in those who do not recognize or cannot accept their orientation.

TREATMENT

Treatment aims at decreasing anxiety about performing and developing the idea that the goal is not erection per se but enjoyment of closeness, warmth, and pleasurable sensations in all parts of the body. Usually it is best to stop all sexual activity and efforts temporarily. Daily sessions of massage and body exploration are recommended, but without genital stimulation or attempts at intercourse should erection occur.

After exploration and the establishment of pleasurable stimulation of nongenital areas, the couple progresses to genital contact. He must be aware of, and indicate to her, what he enjoys most. He may use self-exploration first to determine how to guide her. Again, the goal is not erection but development of awareness. This is continued daily with the resolution not to engage in intercourse even if erection occurs.

Only after erection has been established in several such sessions, progress to this: with the woman on top, establish erection and insert the penis. Without movement, concentrate on vaginal containment. After a minute or so, begin slow pelvic thrusting.

Secondary Erective Impotence

This is repeated lack of erection after previous successes. It can be very disturbing; unlike a woman, a man cannot fake it. The problem may be situational; for example, the man has no problem with prostitutes or one-night lovers but cannot achieve erection with a woman he loves. More commonly, he does not develop an erection for any woman.

CAUSES

They may be psychological or physical, such as diabetes, atherosclerosis, or drug use. If erections do occur—in dreaming, for example—the lack of response with a woman is very likely psychological. But if erections never occur, the cause is probably physical. Many sleep laboratories are equipped to determine whether erections happen during sleep.

Fear is the most common psychological factor in secondary impotence. Fear and sexual arousal are not compatible. The fear can be caused by a single past failure, perhaps due to excess alcohol, marijuana, cocaine, or other drug. Memories of the failure induce fear of failure the next time. The fear suppresses the libido, and the second failure is more upsetting. Subsequent efforts are more difficult as the fear of failure grows with each time it happens.

TREATMENT OF PSYCHOGENIC IMPOTENCE
Be aware, if possible, of erection during sleep and at other times. This will assure you that the problem is psychological, not physiological.

Stop all alcohol, marijuana, cocaine, amphetamines, and other unnecessary drugs. If you are taking a medicine you suspect is interfering with your sex life, discuss the problem with your doctor.

In relaxed sessions with your partner, focus on total enjoyment, not performance and not erection. If you do experience erection, don't rush to intercourse; let it come and go in several sessions. This should firmly associate your partner with pleasure while reducing pressure to perform.

As with the procedure for primary impotence, it is useful to avoid movement after penile insertion and to focus on vaginal containment for a minute or so before commencing slow pelvic thrusting.

TREATMENT OF IMPOTENCE DUE TO PHYSICAL CAUSES
This requires a physician's care. The cause may be atherosclerosis of the penile arteries. These blood vessels become so clogged with plaque that they cannot deliver enough blood to sustain erection. This has been seen even in men in their thirties and is probably more common than previously believed. The condition can be largely prevented, or delayed for years or decades, by the same things that help prevent general atherosclerosis: proper diet, physical fitness, and no smoking.

Impotence may be due to diabetes, which promotes blood vessel damage, as well as general fatigue. Diabetes often goes undetected. In stubborn cases of impotence without erection even during sleep, diabetes should be considered a possible cause. Impotence can also be caused by testosterone deficiency due to aging.

Premature Ejaculation

This is the most common sexual dysfunction in men. When a man ejaculates within a few minutes of sex play and cannot delay long enough to satisfy

182   his partner, tension and frustration for both can result. There is no clear definition of "premature," but if a man consistently ejaculates within a few seconds of insertion, or even before, he clearly has a problem. Consistent early ejaculation may be a problem for some couples but not for others.

POSSIBLE CAUSES

His early experiences may have been with prostitutes or in other forbidden situations. He may have always had to hide and hurry to avoid detection. He may have indulged in lots of petting to ejaculation without intercourse, thereby developing an association of foreplay with orgasm. Or there may be a history of practicing coitus interruptus for birth control, and he may be conditioned to ejaculating outside the vagina. The cause may also be more psychic than reflexive. Early ejaculation may be an expression of hostility, fear of deep involvement, or guilt. It can also be provoked by anxiety and fear about one's sexual adequacy.

TREATMENT

Explore the cause. If it is due to unexpressed or unconscious hostility, resentment, fear, or guilt, counseling may be helpful.

Otherwise, the squeeze technique works well for many. This is best done with the woman on top. She manually stimulates just before the point of inevitable ejaculation. To stop it, she presses her thumb against the frenulum (the skin fold on the underside of the penis, just back of the opening) with her first two fingers opposite the thumb above and below the coronal ridge. Sufficient pressure stops ejaculation.

Stimulation resumes, again just before the point of inevitability before applying the squeeze. This is pacticed for several sessions without intercourse or ejaculation until the couple is confident of control. Then she stimulates him as before, applies the squeeze and inserts his penis, though it may be only semi-erect after the squeeze. They remain still at first, then begin slow pelvic thrusting.

If ejaculation seems to be coming, she pulls away, applies the squeeze, and reinserts the penis. This is repeated until control during intercourse is established. Patience and care usually bring success.

Products with topical anesthetics are available. By decreasing stimulation they may delay ejaculation. However, it is difficult to control the amount of numbing and repeated use may become irritating to the skin. Condoms may also help by reducing sensitivity.

Ejaculatory Incompetence

Inability to ejaculate in the vagina, in spite of strong libido and ability to ejaculate outside the vagina, is not very common, but it does occur.

There is usually a history of strict, puritanical parents severely cautioning against sexual activities. The vagina is sometimes thought of as an unclean, dangerous organ; vaginal teeth may be fantasized. Psychological counseling may be necessary, but this simple conditioning procedure sometimes works.

Sitting astride him, the woman manually stimulates him to the point of orgasm, at which time she quickly inserts his penis. If ejaculation occurs this way several times, he may come to associate intercourse with pleasure and orgasm.

Priapism

This is a continuous, painful erection, sustained without erotic stimulation or desire for erection. It usually involves a serious dysfunction of erective mechanisms and may be a symptom of leukemia or other disease, or a side effect of drugs or hormones. It can cause permanent damage and impotence. Amputation of the penis may be required. A physician should be consulted right away.

Shared Dysfunctions

Often both partners have sexual dysfunctions that are related and need solving together. For example, in vaginismus, impotence may occur in the man after weeks or months of fruitless efforts at intercourse. And in premature ejaculation, the woman may become nonorgasmic.

Choosing a Sex Therapist

If simple measures taken on your own do not solve your problem, you may benefit from the guidance of a sex counselor; but be careful. There are many unqualified operators and outright rip-offs in this new field. A family physician, gynecologist, psychiatrist, nurse, social worker, or clergyman may be able to recommend a good therapist or may *be* a good one. Most urologists are trained to evaluate and treat sexual dysfunctions or refer the patient to an appropriate therapist.

If you have doubts about qualifications, ask about the therapist's training, degree, and certification. A master's, Ph.D., or M.D. degree is a good sign. Certification is better. For a certified sex therapist in your area, contact the American Association of Sex Educators, Counselors, and Therapists. (See Appendix B.)

184

Some therapists use biofeedback devices which are reported very helpful in some cases, especially in erective impotence.

In some cases, it may be better to seek psychotherapy rather than sexual therapy as such. For example, severe depression involves reduced levels of many physical functions, apparently due to depletion or dysfunction of brain neurotransmitters. Sexual dysfunction is just one of several depressed functions, and it would be fruitless to attempt cure of one symptom.

Similarly, if an individual or couple has severe emotional conflicts, the relatively simple techniques of the sex counselor are not likely to improve their sex lives, which cannot be isolated from their relationship as a whole.

Sexercises

Women can do certain exercises to increase the tone of muscles involved in sexual response and thereby increase their own and their partners' pleasure.

To increase the tone of the pubococcygeal muscles, tense the muscles in the vaginal area, including those in the lower abdomen and those used to check urine flow or bowel movement. Tense and relax them several times for a minute or so; repeat several times a day, less often for maintainence once desired tone is acheived.

The levator ani muscles often lose tone after childbirth; this may decrease orgasmic response. To increase their tone, the exercise is the same as above.

There is no general agreement on whether men can gain more control over ejaculation by similar exercises, though some men say they have, and Tantric yoga sometimes uses such exercises in preparation for prolonged ritual intercourse without ejaculation.

CAUTION
Overindulgence in these exercises can promote constipation and hemorrhoids. This possibility is reduced by favoring rapid flex and relaxation, rather than the more isometric sustained contractions.

Mechanical and Chemical Sex Aids

Electric vibrators are for women who wish more intense genital stimulation. Not all women enjoy the rapid vibration these devices generate. They are generally effective only if the woman is otherwise orgasmic, but sometimes they are effective for women who had been preorgasmic.

Fears that women might develop a fetish for the device at the expense of her lover are unfounded. This almost never happens, perhaps because its overuse can traumatize the nerves and desensitize them, dulling the pleasure, sometimes for days or weeks. A few cases of bruises and cuts have been reported, but vibrators are generally safe. The should never be inserted into the vagina while turned off, then turned on; they should be turned on before insertion.

"Ticklers" are condoms with rubber projections which are supposed to increase vaginal stimulation. They are generally ineffective. Touch and pressure receptors are relatively scarce deep within the vagina, and erotic sensation is usually focused on the area of the labia and clitoris.

Spanish fly is a strongly irritating and blistering powder made from the cantharides beetle. Although it sometimes produces a sensation somewhat resembling sexual stimulation, it is dangerous and not conductive to pleasurable sexual response. It **should be avoided.** Similar preparations include such things as camphor, menthol, oleoresin, and cayenne pepper. These are also hazardous and should be avoided.

Herbal stimulants. Many herbs have long been reported to be aphrodisiacs. These are usually stimulants such as damiana, yohimbe, and garlic, which is often forbidden in yoga and Buddhist sects because of its reported power to stimulate sexual appetite.

Sex During Menstruation

Some religious groups and some primitive cultures forbid intercourse during menstruation. There are no health or medical reasons for this restriction. Some women desire sexual activity to orgasm during menstruation in order to help relieve pelvic congestion and pain. Some women prefer sexual intercourse during menstruation in the belief that pregnancy is not possible, but this is not always true.

Sex During Pregnancy

There is usually a general decline of sexual drive and activity during pregnancy, sometimes associated with first trimester nausea. But some women experience an increase of sexual tension, especially during the second trimester, which may be related to the increased pelvic congestion. There is

186 some debate about whether intercourse can increase the risk of infection and premature labor. This should be discussed with one's physician. Orgasm during late pregnancy has not been implicated in premature labor, but may be a consideration if there is a history of miscarriages.

Sex After Childbirth

It may be several months before a woman feels up to sex, but some women are ready right away and there is no reason to wait. Intercourse may resume as soon as a woman has no pain and the episiotomy, if performed, has healed. Milk may spurt out during sexual activity, especially during late plateau and orgasm. This is no cause for concern.

Breast feeding can offer substantial protection against pregnancy. The sucking stimulus decreases the pituitary hormones responsible for lactation. However, it must be the almost exclusive nutrition of the infant. Even then it isn't foolproof; pregnancies can occur.

Sex and Sports

Many people believe that sexual activity before an athletic event wastes energy and inhibits performance, but facts indicate otherwise. Runners and other athletes often perform extremely well the day after, or even an hour after, energetic sexual activity to orgasm. Casey Stengel, the legendary New York Yankee manager, was probably right when he said it's not the catching that causes the problem for athletes, but the chasing.

Exercise, some researchers claim, tends to increase testosterone levels in both males and females, and testosterone tends to increase libido in both sexes. Physically fit athletes also tend to have high libidos because they are generally healthy. It seems unreasonable to expect them to abstain from enjoying some of the fruits of their labor. It should be noted, however, that overexercise to the point of chronic low-level fatigue can decrease libido.

The **frequency** of sexual activity to orgasm is sometimes a matter of concern. People wonder if they are normal being so active or so inactive. Frequency depends on many factors and can range from a few times a year to several times a day and not be considered abnormal. The ages of the partners and the age of the relationship are probably the two most important factors. A new couple in their teens or early twenties might have intercourse two or three times a day for weeks. The rate declines as they age. It commonly levels off at about once or twice a week, and remains there for decades.

Sexual Activity in Later Life   187

People are born with a capacity for response to erotic stimuli and they usually die with it. Less than 5 percent of the population actually loses all sexual responsiveness as they age. But while our culture tends to applaud virility or lustiness in a twenty-five-year-old man or woman, the sexually active sixty year old is often considered an oddity.

      While libido may be reduced with age, it remains a significant force in one's life and it is sometimes increased, especially in women. The elderly should not feel ashamed or suppress their sexuality. If they do so for long enough, dysfunction and atrophy may occur. In spite of desire for union, the body may fail to respond with lubrication or erection.

Menopause

In the United States, most women stop menstruating between forty-five and fifty. Ovarian function slows, estrogen levels decrease, and various physiological changes take place. These are usually mild, but the loss of reproductive capacity may create emotional turmoil. Changes may include thinning of the vaginal epithelium, decreased lubrication during sexual arousal, painful tetany of the uterus during orgasm, and hot flashes due to circulatory instability. Most postmenopausal changes can be prevented or treated with the proper use of estrogens and lubricants. (See Osteoporosis in Part Four.)

      Women's sex drive is not affected by the decrease of estrogen. In menopause libido may increase, probably due to testosterone from the adrenals, and psychological factors such as the loss of fear of pregnancy.

Male Climacteric

The middle years, from about forty-five to sixty, are considered "critical years" for men. Suicide, and death from cardiovascular disease, peak in these years. Testosterone levels decrease and this may be associated with decreased libido, less easily provoked erection, decreased force of ejaculation, and less pleasure associated with orgasm. Hot flashes may occur, especially during stress and anxiety. Some men become less forceful in dealing with others.

      Oral and injectible testosterone may be used if plasma levels are low, but regular administration reduces one's own testosterone production by suppressing the luteinizing hormone from the pituitary gland. This hormone increases testosterone secretion, and is itself suppressed by testosterone. (This feedback is common in biological systems.)

188

Some symptoms may not be due to low testosterone but to boredom with years of routine, and feeling threatened by competition from younger men. While his libido may be decreasing, his wife's may be increasing. With nagging self-doubts haunting him, he needs emotional support. Often his wife does too, and cannot provide him with enough. He may deal with the stress by having affairs or becoming an alcoholic or drug abuser.

Sex in Illness

Normal sexual function depends on coordination of normal functioning nerves, endocrine glands, cardiovascular system, and intact genitals. Disease or injury to any of these can cause sexual dysfunction. (Rarely, injury or disease of the brain can increase libido.)

Sex and the heart patient. During sexual activity, heart rate and blood pressure increase substantially, and survivors of heart attacks are often concerned about the possible danger of sexual activity. There is a certain hazard, especially for men with much younger women, and especially during clandestine meetings which increase the stress.

However, generally speaking, the cardiovascular stress imposed by sexual activity is not excessive. The energy expenditure of intercourse is about the same as walking three or four miles an hour, or more slowly up a flight of stairs. If one can do this without excessive increase of blood pressure or ECG changes, there should be no problem with intercourse.

Sex and hypertension. Persons with uncontrolled hypertension (above 180/ 110 mm Hg) should be cautious about all physical exertion, including sexual. The degree of risk varies with each patient and must be discussed with one's physician.

In any case, the main problem here is that many antihypertensive drugs interfere with erection or ejaculation. The worst offenders seem to be guanethidine and reserpine, but they are not used much. Methyldopa is also a problem for some. Hydralazine, propranolol, and clonidine evidently carry less risk but they, too, can cause problems.

Sometimes after drug use stops, psychic impotence replaces drug-induced impotence because of the anxiety created by unsuccessful efforts at intercourse. In this case the man might benefit from the remedy for secondary impotence described above.

Sex and diabetes. Many diabetic men and women experience some degree of sexual dysfunction. Optimum control of blood sugar with diet, exercise, and insulin, if necessary, can improve sexual function.

Testes removal or absence at birth does not preclude sexual activity, even if both testes are involved. Testosterone, the "libido hormone," is made by the adrenal cortex as well as the testes, and sufficient amounts are often available. If not, testosterone supplements can help.

Mastectomy or **hysterectomy** usually does not affect the libido, but an associated decrease in self-esteem may cause depression and subsequent decrease in sexual functions.

Vaginal surgery may alter sexual function. Surgical reconstruction may restore normal function.

Prostatectomy can cause impotence, but fewer than one-third who have this operation experience any change in sexual functions. This is important to keep in mind because the belief that impotence is a necessary or likely consequence may itself cause impotence. If there is a change, it is not always impotence; sometimes the bladder sphincter is damaged, so that during orgasm ejaculate is forced into the bladder rather than out the penis. But sometimes nerve supply is damaged and true impotence does occur.

Liver disease usually decreases libido. This is probably due to an increase in circulating estrogens which the ailing liver cannot metabolize fast enough.

Sex during hospitalization. Hospitalization for weeks or months often causes problems for those who want to be, and are physically capable of being, sexually active. The main problem is lack of privacy. Even if a person has a private room or curtain for the bed, nurses and others generally do not respect the need for privacy. Some prisons and state hospitals have arrangements for conjugal visits and passes; perhaps general hospitals could have as much. Long-term patients could at least have a "Do Not Disturb" sign which they can use with confidence.

Sex and mental illness. There is a long history of supposed relations between mental disorders and sexual problems. In ancient times hysteria was attributed to a "wandering womb" and Hippocrates prescribed sexual intercourse. Masturbation was long believed to cause insanity. Sigmund Freud and the psychoanalysts developed theories relating neuroses to sexual dysfunctions. Wilhelm Reich took this to an extreme and concluded that disturbed sexual function was at the root of practically all neuroses, psychoses, and even cancer. A "perfect orgasm" was, for Reich, a sign of perfect mental health.

Mental illness, whatever the cause, may contribute to altered sexual functioning by directly affecting the brain's sexual pathways and by disturbing relations with other people. The former is not surprising; the brain's neurotransmitters (chemical messengers), which are involved in libido and

190 sexual response, are often disrupted in psychotic disorders. In some cases, the process works the other way: a sexual problem may become a precipitating stress in the development of mental illness.

Vicious circles sometimes develop. For example, a minor sexual problem may cause a great deal of anxiety and guilt, which cause decreased libido, which provokes more anxiety and guilt, and so on until the emotional disturbance is severe.

Early and mild schizophrenia may be associated with increased libido, and hypersexuality sometimes occurs in the manic phase of manic-depression. But moderate to severe depression usually causes a greatly decreased interest in sex.

As with other hospitalized patients, the mentally ill need some measure of privacy, especially when their partners visit them.

Sex and Drugs[3]

Drugs can strongly influence sexual response by their effects on the brain, nerves, endocrine glands, hormones, and the cardiovascular system. All drugs being used should be considered suspect when sexual dysfunction occurs; the most important drugs which often affect the sexual response are discussed here.

Regular consumption of **alcohol** greatly increases destruction of testosterone in the liver. This can decrease libido in both males and females. Chronic alcoholic men with liver disease experience atrophy of the testes and breast enlargement. Alcohol can also cause impotence by damaging peripheral nerves and decreasing sensitivity to touch.

Antihypertensives, such as reserpine, guanethedine, methyldopa, and others may cause decreased libido, erective impotence, lack of ejaculation, or retro-ejaculation. Women may also experience sexual dysfunction.

Antihistamines, used in cold and allergy medicines, can cause depression of the parasympathetic nervous system with consequent erectile dysfunction or vaginal dryness.

Oral contraceptives sometimes cause decreased libido, apparently by decreasing testosterone levels. Adjustments in dosage may eliminate the effect.

Phenothiazine tranquilizers such as chlorpromazine (Thorazine) and trifluoperazine (Stelazine) can diminish libido by altering pituitary function and increasing estrogen levels. Some of these drugs may also cause the painful and dangerous priapism.

Narcotics, sedatives, and sleep aids can decrease libido by their general depressant effects. The regular heroin and barbituate users often become virtually asexual.

Estrogen given to men can cause testicular atrophy, greatly decreased libido and frequency of erection, increased breast size, darker nipples, fatter hips and buttocks, decreased muscle strength, softer skin, sparse beard, and decreased aggressiveness. It is sometimes given to men to help control certain cancers and, in England and a few other countries, to control libido and aggressiveness in sex offenders.

Testosterone given to women (to control certain cancers) can cause amenorrhea and atrophy of the ovaries, hairiness, increase in muscle strength and size, decrease in hip and buttock fat, deeper voice, balding, hypertrophy of the labia and clitoris, and increased libido.

Progesterone tends to decrease testosterone and libido in males and females.

Cocaine, amphetamines, Ritalin, and other powerful stimulants can greatly decrease libido, probably by excessive stimulation of the sympathetic nervous system. Cocaine has been reported to cause the painful and dangerous priapism in some men, but much more often it causes erective impotence.

Marijuana, used regularly for long periods, may decrease libido, possibly by decreasing testosterone levels, but this is in dispute. It has a tendency to dry the vaginal mucosa and thereby diminish sexual pleasure. Some people experience paranoid or panic reactions inimical to sexual response.

Psychedelics such as LSD, mescaline, and psilocybin, have variable effects on sexuality but often decrease libido by inducing anxiety.

Tobacco tends to decrease libido, possibly by decreasing testosterone levels.

The above are all generalizations subject to some exceptions. For example, in certain situations, and for some people, alcohol, marijuana, cocaine, and even small doses of narcotics or tranquilizers may tend to increase libido by decreasing inhibition. But long-term regular use of any of these drugs tends to have negative effects on sexuality. See Chapter 5–4.

2

Birth Control Options

Pregnancy and childbirth are hazardous to the health, much more so than even the riskiest birth control methods. The development of effective contraceptive methods has given women the choice of whether and when to risk pregnancy. It has also freed them to seek work and fulfillment outside the home, and it has helped slow the worldwide population explosion. Few scientific breakthroughs have provided so much benefit for the risk.[4]

There are risks, however, especially with oral contraceptives and IUDs. A woman should familiarize herself with the pros and cons of each method so she can make an intelligent decision for herself and not be pushed into using one of her lover's or physician's choosing. A man should also be aware of the methods since some of them require his cooperation, and the condom and vasectomy are his alone.

Note on effectiveness ratings: if a contraceptive method is said to be 99 percent effective, this means one woman could expect one pregnancy in 100 years (if she were fertile that long and used only that method). Put another way, of 100 women using the method, one will get pregnant each year. A 90 percent effective method would yield ten pregnancies.

Condoms

Penile sheaths have been used for hundreds of years to prevent pregnancy and venereal disease. The early ones were made of linen and animal intestines. Now the most effective and widely used condoms are made of latex rubber.

Used concientiously, condoms are very effective in preventing conception. One estimate is that in twenty-five years of regular use, latex condoms will fail to protect a couple only one time. If spermicide is also used, less than one pregnancy in a hundred years can be expected. But in the real world, they are not always used concientiously and women who rely on their partners to use condoms often get pregnant.

Condoms have the important added benefits of decreasing the spread of venereal disease, decreasing the risk of cervical cancer, and inhibiting premature ejaculation.

FDA standards assure strength and lack of holes in the latex condoms. Lamb intestine condoms do not meet such high standards but, combined with spermicide, they can be very effective. Some men prefer them because they are extremely thin, and using one is a little less like "taking a shower with a raincoat on," as the standard complaint goes.

Most people have no significant problems with condoms, but occasionally a couple simply cannot use one without breaking it, no matter how lubricated she or the condom is and no matter how careful they are. Because of the possibility of breakage, it is wise to use a spermicide the first few times, especially around midcycle. It is also a good idea to always have spermicide on hand, preferably the foam type. If a condom breaks, it may help to immediately apply a very generous amount.

Diaphragms

These round rubber domes fitted to cover the cervix are not very effective by themselves, but they greatly increase the effectiveness of spermicides. Properly fitted and used, a diaphragm can be expected to fail a woman only once in thirty-five to fifty years. As with condoms, diaphragm use is not always concientious, and women who rely on them exclusively during the first year of marriage (or other passion-filled times) often get pregnant.

A diaphragm must be fitted by an experienced nurse or physician. If it is too small it will not be effective; if it is too large, if it can be felt in the body, it may cause pain or difficulty urinating when left in for hours (as it must be).

Success depends greatly on proper instruction in its use at the time of fitting. It must be properly inserted at the right time and left in place for long enough. The woman should practice insertion at the time of fitting to be sure she is doing it right. The following are the key points to remember.

Check the diaphragm regularly for defects by running water over it.

Before insertion, apply spermicidal cream or jelly around the rim and in the center on the cervical side of the diaphragm.

After insertion, intercourse should take place within an hour or two, or more spermicide should be applied (leaving the diaphragm in place).

After intercourse, the diaphragm must be left in place at least seven hours. If it is removed too soon, live sperm could enter the uterus.

One adverse effect of a diaphragm, which occurs in very few women, is stubborn cystitis (bladder inflammation) in spite of a good fit. Another occasional problem is allergic sensitivity to the spermicide in the man or woman. Changing brands often helps. Rarely, sensitivity to the diaphragm latex itself occurs.

While diaphragms do not protect from other venereal diseases, they may provide some protection from cervical cancer, especially in women who are active from a young age with more than one partner.

Finally, it is interesting that the diaphragm is the most popular contraceptive among women physicians.

Fertility Awareness

A woman is fertile only a few days of each cycle. If intercourse is avoided on these days, she will not get pregnant. The challenge is in determining which days are safe. Three techniques are available and they are often used in combination. They are most effective for women who are very regular in their cycles. The crux of the problem is the fact that the sperm often remains viable for about three days in the female, and intercourse must be avoided for at least three days before ovulation, which occurs at variable times in the cycle.[5]

The **calendar rhythm method** is the oldest of the fertility awareness methods. It depends on the fact that ovulation occurs about two weeks before the start of each period. With a record of the last eight to twelve cycles, a woman can estimate the day of ovulation and avoid intercourse (or use a contraceptive) for three or four days before and after.

If the start of the period is taken as day one, the last infertile day before ovulation is approximately day $S-21$, where S is the shortest complete cycle the woman has recorded in the last year or so. For example, if the shortest cycle was twenty-six days, then day five of the cycle is probably the last safe day before ovulation.

The first safe day after ovulation is approximately day $L-10$, where L is the longest period recorded in the last year or so. For example, if

Fertility Chart No. __6__

Name __SUSAN__   **Months** __NOV./DEC.__   **Year** __1984__

Based on __5__ **cycles   This cycle** __30__ **days   Cycle Variation** __29/31__

Day and Date	Cycle Date	Basal Body Temperature — Usual Time __7 A.M.__ Temp O __X__ V ___ R ___	Coitus Contraception	Mucus Descrip. — Wet, dry, consistency, color, etc.	Cervix	Notes — Disturbances, schedule changes, pains, moods, etc.
12/T	1	9 97 1 2③4 5 6 7 8 9 9 8 1 2 3 4 5 6 7 8 9 99 1		MENSES		
13/W	2	9 97 1 2 3④5 6 7 8 9 9 8 1 2 3 4 5 6 7 8 9 99 1		MENSES		
14/Th	3	9 97 1 2 3 4⑤6 7 8 9 9 8 1 2 3 4 5 6 7 8 9 99 1		MENSES		
15/F	4	9 97 1 2 3 4⑥6 7 8 9 9 8 1 2 3 4 5 6 7 8 9 99 1	✓ N	MENSES		
16/S	5	9 97 1 2 3 4 5 6 7⑧9 9 8 1 2 3 4 5 6 7 8 9 99 1		DRY		SLEPT LATE
17/Su	6	9 97 1 2 3 4 5⑥7 8 9 9 8 1 2 3 4 5 6 7 8 9 99 1		DRY		
18/M	7	9 97 1 2 3 4⑤6 7 8 9 9 8 1 2 3 4 5 6 7 8 9 99 1		STICKY		
19/T	8	9 97 1 2 3 4 5⑥7 8 9 9 8 1 2 3 4 5 6 7 8 9 99 1	✓ N	STICKY		
20/W	9	9 97 1 2 3④5 6 7 8 9 9 8 1 2 3 4 5 6 7 8 9 99 1		GETTING STRETCHY		
21/Th	10	9 97 1 2 3 4⑤6 7 8 9 9 8 1 2 3 4 5 6 7 8 9 99 1		STRETCHY, WHITE		
22/F	11	9 97 1 2 3 4⑤6 7 8 9 9 8 1 2 3 4 5 6 7 8 9 99 1	✓ D	STRETCHY, WHITE		
23/S	12	9 97 1 2 3④5 6 7 8 9 9 8 1 2 3 4 5 6 7 8 9 99 1		STRETCHY, SLIPPERY	o	
24/Su	13	9 97 1 2 3 4⑤6 7 8 9 9 8 1 2 3 4 5 6 7 8 9 99 1		STRETCHY, SLIPPERY	o	
25/M	14	9 97 1 2 3 4⑤6 7 8 9 9 8 1 2 3 4 5 6 7 8 9 99 1	✓ D	"	o	
26/T	15	9 97 1 2 3 4 5⑥7 8 9 9 8 1 2 3 4 5 6 7 8 9 99 1		"	o	
27/W	16	9 97 1 2 3 4 5 6⑦8 9 9 8 1 2 3 4 5 6 7 8 9 99 1		"	o	
28/Th	17	9⑨⑦1 2 3 4 5 6 7 8 9 9 8 1 2 3 4 5 6 7 8 9 99 1		CLEAR, SLIPPERY	o	SORE BREASTS
29/F	18	9 97 1 2 3 4 5 6⑦8 9 9 8 1 2 3 4 5 6 7 8 9 99 1	✓ D	CLEAR, WET, SLIPPERY	o	CRAMPS
30/S	19	9 97 1 2 3 4 5 6 7 8 9⑨⑧1 2 3 4 5 6 7 8 9 99 1		STICKY, STRETCHY	o	
1/Su	20	9 97 1 2 3 4 5 6 7 8 9 8 1②3 4 5 6 7 8 9 99 1		"	o	
2/M	21	9 97 1 2 3 4 5 6 7 8 9 8 1 2 3④5 6 7 8 9 99 1		STICKY		
3/T	22	9 97 1 2 3 4 5 6 7 8 9 8 1 2③4 5 6 7 8 9 99 1		STICKY		
4/W	23	9 97 1 2 3 4 5 6 7 8 9 8 1 2 3④5 6 7 8 9 99 1	✓ D	STICKY		
5/Th	24	9 97 1 2 3 4 5 6 7 8 9 8 1 2 3 4⑤6 7 8 9 99 1		DRY		
6/F	25	9 97 1 2 3 4 5 6 7 8 9 8 1 2 3 4⑥6 7 8 9 99 1		DRY		
7/S	26	9 97 1 2 3 4 5 6 7 8 9 8 1 2 3④5 6 7 8 9 99 1	✓ D	DRY		
8/Su	27	9 97 1 2 3 4 5 6 7 8 9 8 1 2③4 5 6 7 8 9 99 1		DRY		BAD SKIN
9/M	28	9 97 1 2 3 4 5 6 7 8 9 8 1 2③4 5 6 7 8 9 99 1		WET		BAD SKIN
10/T	29	9 97 1 2 3 4 5 6 7 8 9 8①2 3 4 5 6 7 8 9 99 1		WET		CRAMPS
11/W	30	9 97 1 2 3 4 5 6⑦8 9 9 8 1 2 3 4 5 6 7 8 9 99 1		MENSES		
12/Th	31	9 97 1 2 3 4 5 6 7 8 9 9 8 1 2 3 4 5 6 7 8 9 99 1				
	32	9 97 1 2 3 4 5 6 7 8 9 9 8 1 2 3 4 5 6 7 8 9 99 1				
	33	9 97 1 2 3 4 5 6 7 8 9 9 8 1 2 3 4 5 6 7 8 9 99 1				

Note: Under "Coitus", **n** means no contraceptive; **d** means diaphragm.

196 Fertility Chart No. _____

Name _____ Months _____ Year _____

Based on ___ cycles   This cycle ___ days   Cycle Variation _____

Day and Date	Cycle Date	Basal Body Temperature Usual Time _____ Temp O ___ V ___ R ___	Coitus Contraception	Mucus Descrip. Wet, dry, consistency, color, etc.	Cervix	Notes Disturbances, schedule changes, pains, moods, etc.
	1	9 97 1 2 3 4 5 6 7 8 9 98 1 2 3 4 5 6 7 8 9 99 1				
	2	9 97 1 2 3 4 5 6 7 8 9 98 1 2 3 4 5 6 7 8 9 99 1				
	3	9 97 1 2 3 4 5 6 7 8 9 98 1 2 3 4 5 6 7 8 9 99 1				
	4	9 97 1 2 3 4 5 6 7 8 9 98 1 2 3 4 5 6 7 8 9 99 1				
	5	9 97 1 2 3 4 5 6 7 8 9 98 1 2 3 4 5 6 7 8 9 99 1				
	6	9 97 1 2 3 4 5 6 7 8 9 98 1 2 3 4 5 6 7 8 9 99 1				
	7	9 97 1 2 3 4 5 6 7 8 9 98 1 2 3 4 5 6 7 8 9 99 1				
	8	9 97 1 2 3 4 5 6 7 8 9 98 1 2 3 4 5 6 7 8 9 99 1				
	9	9 97 1 2 3 4 5 6 7 8 9 98 1 2 3 4 5 6 7 8 9 99 1				
	10	9 97 1 2 3 4 5 6 7 8 9 98 1 2 3 4 5 6 7 8 9 99 1				
	11	9 97 1 2 3 4 5 6 7 8 9 98 1 2 3 4 5 6 7 8 9 99 1				
	12	9 97 1 2 3 4 5 6 7 8 9 98 1 2 3 4 5 6 7 8 9 99 1				
	13	9 97 1 2 3 4 5 6 7 8 9 98 1 2 3 4 5 6 7 8 9 99 1				
	14	9 97 1 2 3 4 5 6 7 8 9 98 1 2 3 4 5 6 7 8 9 99 1				
	15	9 97 1 2 3 4 5 6 7 8 9 98 1 2 3 4 5 6 7 8 9 99 1				
	16	9 97 1 2 3 4 5 6 7 8 9 98 1 2 3 4 5 6 7 8 9 99 1				
	17	9 97 1 2 3 4 5 6 7 8 9 98 1 2 3 4 5 6 7 8 9 99 1				
	18	9 97 1 2 3 4 5 6 7 8 9 98 1 2 3 4 5 6 7 8 9 99 1				
	19	9 97 1 2 3 4 5 6 7 8 9 98 1 2 3 4 5 6 7 8 9 99 1				
	20	9 97 1 2 3 4 5 6 7 8 9 98 1 2 3 4 5 6 7 8 9 99 1				
	21	9 97 1 2 3 4 5 6 7 8 9 98 1 2 3 4 5 6 7 8 9 99 1				
	22	9 97 1 2 3 4 5 6 7 8 9 98 1 2 3 4 5 6 7 8 9 99 1				
	23	9 97 1 2 3 4 5 6 7 8 9 98 1 2 3 4 5 6 7 8 9 99 1				
	24	9 97 1 2 3 4 5 6 7 8 9 98 1 2 3 4 5 6 7 8 9 99 1				
	25	9 97 1 2 3 4 5 6 7 8 9 98 1 2 3 4 5 6 7 8 9 99 1				
	26	9 97 1 2 3 4 5 6 7 8 9 98 1 2 3 4 5 6 7 8 9 99 1				
	27	9 97 1 2 3 4 5 6 7 8 9 98 1 2 3 4 5 6 7 8 9 99 1				
	28	9 97 1 2 3 4 5 6 7 8 9 98 1 2 3 4 5 6 7 8 9 99 1				
	29	9 97 1 2 3 4 5 6 7 8 9 98 1 2 3 4 5 6 7 8 9 99 1				
	30	9 97 1 2 3 4 5 6 7 8 9 98 1 2 3 4 5 6 7 8 9 99 1				
	31	9 97 1 2 3 4 5 6 7 8 9 98 1 2 3 4 5 6 7 8 9 99 1				
	32	9 97 1 2 3 4 5 6 7 8 9 98 1 2 3 4 5 6 7 8 9 99 1				
	33	9 97 1 2 3 4 5 6 7 8 9 98 1 2 3 4 5 6 7 8 9 99 1				

Note: Under "Coitus", **n** means no contraceptive; **d** means diaphragm.

L is thirty days, then day twenty, would be the first safe day after ovulation. In this example, abstinence is required from day six to day twenty, about two weeks.

The success of this method depends on a high degree of regularity. An unusually early or late ovulation will greatly increase the risk of pregnancy.

The **temperature method** of fertility awareness relies on the slight rise in the basal body temperature caused by the appearance of progesterone after ovulation. The woman takes her temprature each morning while still in bed, preferably with a basal body thermometer for easy, accurate reading. When the temperature has been elevated by .5° to 1.0°F for three days in a row, the fertile phase is probably over for that cycle, and intercourse is safe. If a woman is very regular, she can consider the six days before the expected temperature rise to be fertile and days before that safe. Vaginal or rectal temperature is probably more accurate than oral. Whatever method is used, it must be used consistently; you cannot skip around.

The problem with the temperature method is that the temperature rise is not always abrupt and easy to detect, and various stresses, such as a poor night's sleep, alcohol, and cigarettes, can throw it off. Using only the temperature method, a woman can expect failure (pregnancy) about once every five years, or one chance in five each year. If she abstains completely before ovulation, the method is much more effective.

The **cervical mucus method** depends on hormone-induced changes in the amount and consistency of the mucus. As ovulation approaches, the cervical glands secrete an increasing amount of thin, stretchable mucus, similar in consistency to raw egg white. This secretion peaks at about the time of ovulation, and it is favorable to sperm life and mobility. Intercourse is avoided from the time the thin mucus is first noticed to about four days after it peaks. Do not check mucus consistency during sexual arousal. Vaginal lubrication is from different glands, and is not related to fertility. These related changes are often seen at ovulation.

> An opening of the cervical os (seen using a speculum and flashlight)
>
> A soft, rubbery consistency of the cervix (it is usually firm, like the tip of the nose)
>
> An increase in the sugar content of the mucus. This can be detected using yellow Testape (used by diabetics). It is held on the finger with a rubber band, touched to the cervical os, and withdrawn. If it turns dark blue, ovulation has recently occurred. Bluish green indicated less sugar and no ovulation.
>
> Some women regularly experience painful ovulation. Learning to recognize this can be very useful.

198   Unfortunately, the mucus method cannot be considered reliable because almost a third of all women do not experience clear-cut mucus changes on a regular basis. Moreover, the mucus is often affected by other factors such as a minor case of vaginitis. Even women with mucus changes regular enough to use this method can expect an unwanted pregnancy about once every four years. But a very regular woman with definite, regular mucus changes can get better results, especially if the other fertility awareness methods are also used.

Intrauterine Devices

An intrauterine device (IUD) is a small loop, coil, or T-shaped device which is inserted just inside the uterus. It is made of polyethylene plastic, sometimes with copper, sometimes with progesterone, and always with a barium coating for detection by X-ray and a nylon tail which hangs into the vagina. The proliferation of different types is a consequence of searches for more effectiveness and greater safety, and the workings of the patent laws.

The IUD apparently works by stimulating an inflammatory reaction in the endometrium (uterine lining) which kills the sperm or prevents implantation of the fertilized egg. It is about 97 to 98 percent effective. For more protection, a backup method (spermicide, condom) can be used around midcycle.

To facilitate insertion and to make sure it is not done during pregnancy, which is dangerous, the IUD should be inserted during the woman's period, in the first week following a period, immediately after an early abortion, or six to eight weeks after childbirth or a late abortion. Insertion at other times increases the risk of perforation of the uterus.

The plastic IUDS can be left in place for many years, as long as no problem occurs. Copper ones should be changed every three years because the spermicidal and contraceptive power is slowly lost. Those containing progesterone must be replaced every year. An IUD should be removed within a few months of menopause.

Insertion must be done by a physician or nurse using sterile procedures. At this time the woman is instructed on how to feel for the IUD tail to be sure it is in the right place.

If the woman has previously given birth, little pain is likely to occur. If she has not, there may be mild to very severe cramps and aching, which may last several hours. Cramps and spotting between periods may occur sporadically for the first few weeks, and the first three or four periods may be unusually heavy. A mild mucus discharge for a month or two is normal, but if it is heavy or foul-smelling, *a physician should check for infection*.

During the first week, the tail should be checked several times.

After the first period and then once a year, the IUD should be checked by a physician or nurse. In general, the string should be checked before intercourse and after each period. During the first three months, a backup contraceptive method should be used, since IUDs are frequently expelled during this time.

Problems with IUDS

About one-third of the women have the IUD removed (or expel it) within a year. In almost all cases the reason is pain, infection, bleeding, or perforation of the uterus. The skill of the inserter is much more important than the type of device in determining success or failure so it is best to choose a very experienced physician or nurse.

The risk of **pelvic infection** is substantial, and such infection may damage the Fallopian tubes and cause sterility. IUD users have roughly double the risk of pelvic inflammatory disease compared to women who use no contraceptive, and an even greater risk compared to women who use oral contraceptives or barrier methods, both of which provide some protection against pelvic disease.

Blood loss during menstrual periods is generally much higher for IUD users. An iron supplement may be needed.

Septic (infected) pregnancy, and sometimes death, may result if the IUD is left in place for months after pregnancy occurs. Physicians usually recommend removal as soon as possible, certainly by the end of the third month.

Etopic (tubal) pregnancy occurs in about 5 percent of those for whom the IUD fails. The symptoms of this very dangerous condition are abdominal pain, bleeding, and irregular menstruation. A physician should be seen right away.

For all the trouble, pain, and risk, the benefits are not spectacular; the failure rate is almost 3 percent. Nevertheless, IUDs are sometimes the best choice for older women who have had children and have little risk of pelvic inflammatory disease or sexually transmitted disease.

An IUD should not be inserted if a woman has large fibroid tumors, a recent history of pelvic infection, or tubal damage. Women who bleed heavily or have severe menstrual cramps should consider other methods first, since an IUD is likely to aggravate the problems.

Symptoms suggesting pelvic infection, which should send the IUD user to her physician, are vague lower abdominal pain, a foul-smelling yellowish discharge, pain with intercourse, a temperature above 99 degrees,

200 chills, unexplained fatigue, or flu-like aches and pains. If the cause of such symptoms is in doubt, the IUD should be removed immediately.

Morning-After Methods

If a woman has intercourse and thinks conception may have occurred, in a emergency she can prevent pregnancy by taking one of several available high-dose estrogen products which prevent implantation of the fertilized egg in the endometrium. These powerful drugs are available by prescription only, and must be started within about three days of intercourse and taken for about a week.

All these drugs, especially diethylstilbestrol (DES), carry the **risk of causing fetal abnormalities** should they fail to prevent the pregnancy. Nausea vomiting, headaches, and other adverse effects often occur. Nausea medicines may help.

Certain copper IUDs may prevent implantation if inserted within a few days of intercourse. Ask a physician.

Menstrual extraction is a relatively safe, effective method of preventing pregnancy after conception. It must be done within about two weeks of intercourse. It involves inserting a cannula (small tube) into the cervix and, with a suction syringe, removing the lining of the uterus. Only an experienced physician can do this. In some states menstrual extraction is considered an abortion. It is sometimes called a miniabortion.

Spermicidal Barriers

Spermicidal foams, jellies, creams, and suppositories are available without a prescription. Foams are probably the most effective. If a woman uses nothing but foam and uses it properly and without fail, she can expect less than one pregnancy in twenty-five years, or four chances in 100 of a pregnancy in any given year. Suppositories are probably almost as effective. With creams or jellies, the rate approaches one pregnancy in ten years.

Women who have recently given birth and those who have had many children should use a double dose of the product.

Suppositories generally must be inserted ten minutes or more before intercourse. Follow the instructions for the product.

The contraceptive should not be removed by douching or bathing for at least six hours after intercourse.

The jellies are water insoluble and do not distribute very well. They are much more effective with a diaphragm.

Sensitivity reactions occur in some women, and men. These are generally not serious. Different products can be tried.

An added benefit is that spermicides seem to protect against some venereal diseases.

Sponge contraceptives work by releasing a spermicide during intercourse and by absorbing and blocking sperm. The contraceptive effect lasts up to twenty-four hours after insertion, but the sponge should be left in place for at least six hours after intercourse for maximum protection. The sponge is an over-the-counter product (Today) and does not have to be fitted like a diaphragm. Unfortunately, it is only about 85 percent effective, so fertility awareness may be in order. As with other spermicidal products, irritation and allergic reactions may occur. There is also a very slight risk of toxic shock syndrome (see Part Four), so follow the instructions on the box.

Sterilization

Fallopian tube surgery is the method of choice for most women who want to permanently end the possibility of becoming pregnant. It assures that the eggs will not travel down the tubes and unite with sperm. While reversal is sometimes possible, it cannot be counted on, and the surgery should be considered final. There are different methods of performing this surgery.

In a **laparotomy** an incision is made in the abdominal wall and the tubes are tied or cut. This is sometimes done on an outpatient basis on thin women, but it usually requires a short hospital stay.

In **laparoscopy**, a device is used to visualize the tubes through a small incision near the navel. They are then cauterized or clipped shut. The method is fast and easy and leaves just a very small scar near the navel. A general anesthetic is used, and two or three liters of carbon dioxide are injected into the abdomen to expand it to make visualization and cauterizing of the tubes easy. The procedure takes less than an hour and can sometimes be done without hospitalization. Many physicians consider this the simplest and safest method, all things considered.

In a **colpotomy,** the incision to get at the tubes is made through the vaginal wall between the rectum and uterus. It is a simple procedure and leaves no scar, but bleeding and infection are more likely to be a problem. Intercourse and douching should be avoided for about five weeks afterward.

A **coldoscopy** is like a colpotomy, but a coldoscope, similar to a laparoscope, is used to visualize the tubes.

A **vasectomy** is cutting off the vas deferens, the tubes which carry semen from the testicles. It is generally considered the safest of all sterilization methods, those for women included. Most vasectomies are done by urologists in their offices or clinics. Some family doctors and general surgeons also do the operation.

In the procedure, a local anesthetic is given and either one or two small incisions are made in the scrotum. The tubes are pulled out and cut, then closed with clips, sutures, or cauterization. Normal activities can be resumed within a couple of hours, though coitus, heavy lifting, and strenuous athletic activities should be avoided for about a week. An athletic supporter may prevent swelling and pain.

Because viable sperm may remain in the upper part of the tubes, several ejaculations (about a dozen) are required before the man can be considered sterile. The doctor must examine ejaculate specimens until two in a row are free of sperm. Until then, usually about a month, other contraceptive methods are necessary.

Possible complications of vasectomy include hemotoma (blood clot) at the site of the surgery, inflammation of the testicles, and sperm granuloma, a painful lump at the site of the surgery due to a local immune reaction to leakage of dead sperm products through the walls of the cut tubes. It may take weeks or months to resolve and may have to be surgically removed. All of these complications are rare, especially sperm granuloma.

Antibodies against the dead sperm products absorbed into the blood develop in about half of all men in the year following vasectomy. They soon subside to very low levels, and there is no evidence they cause any problems.

Contrary to common misconceptions, vasectomy does not in any way decrease libido, sexual pleasure, masculinity, or health. Ejaculate volume is reduced by less than 10 percent.

Oral Contraceptives[6]

"The pill" is the most commonly used form of birth control in the United States; almost a third of all women between eighteen and forty-five years of age currently use some form of oral contraceptive. The principle attractions are simplicity and effectiveness.

There are two basic types of oral contraceptives, the combination pill containing estrogen and a progestogen, and the minipill with progestogen only. The combination pill is more than 99 percent effective and the minipill is about 97 percent effective.

Before oral contraceptives can be prescribed there should be a complete evaluation, including a physical examination and medical history, to determine the safety of the hormones for each woman. Complete candor is important. Perhaps the strongest risk factors are cigarette smoking, hypertension, and cardiovascular disease. If you are judged not at risk, ask for pills with the lowest possible dose, since these provide all or most of the benefits and are safer than the larger doses, which may eventually be banned.

How They Work

The **combination pills** inhibit the pituitary hormones, follicle-stimulating horomone (FSH), and luteinizing horomone (LH), which normally stimulate the growth of ovarian follicles and trigger ovulation. The pills also change the endometrium to prevent implantation, should fertilization occur. Progestogen also makes the mucus thick and difficult for the sperm to penetrate.

The **minipill** must be taken every day, without interruption, even during one's period. If one is forgotten, the risk of pregnancy is much greater than is the case with the combination pills. Another disadvantage is that about half of the women who use it experience unpredictable bleeding, and this is a common reason for changing to a combination pill. Moreover, a backup method of birth control is often recommended during the first six months of minipill use because of the higher risk of pregnancy during this time.

During lactation, the estrogen in the combination pill may decrease the quantity of milk, so the minipill is often used at this time. But the risk to the infant of the progestogen (which chemically resembles the male horomone, testosterone) is unknown and considered too high by some physicians.

How soon does the combination pill work? If it is started on or before day five of the cycle, on the day after an abortion, or three or four days after childbirth it is effective immediately, and no backup method is required.

CAUTION
Vomiting, diarrhea, and the use of some antibiotics, anticonvulsants, and other prescription drugs may decrease the effectiveness of the pill. Check with your doctor. If in doubt, use a backup method for the cycle.

If the pill is forgotten, take two the next day. Missing one pill rarely results in pregnancy, unless it's the minipill. If you miss two pills in a row, take two for two days. To be extra safe, use a backup method for the rest of the cycle.

To alter your cycle, you can stop taking the pill seven days or less before the end of the cycle and discard the rest of them. The period will come early. Start the new pills as usual, five days later.

204 Bonus Benefits
of Oral Contraceptives[7]

Besides preventing pregnancy and allowing anxiety-free sexual activity, the right oral contraceptives for the right women can provide some very significant health benefits. In general, oral contraceptive users have substantially less risk of developing ovarian cancer and cysts, endometrial cancer, benign breast disease, pelvic inflammatory disease, even rheumatoid arthritis, and perhaps breast cancer. The hazards of the hormones have been much publicized, but for the vast majority of women who do not smoke or have cardiovascular problems the health benefits outweigh the risks.

Side Effects and
Hazards of Oral Contraceptives

There are many side effects associated with the use of oral contraceptives, some of them serious (but rare), some trivial. The long list of potential problems and proscriptions should be kept in perspective; most women have only minor problems or none at all. The doses of hormones are much smaller than in the early pills and the risk groups are clearly defined. If women at risk (see below) are excluded and the hazards of pregnancy and childbirth are taken into account, it is generally safer to use an oral contraceptive than not. Nevertheless, it is wise for users to be aware of the hazards and alert for side effects. These are discussed below, approximately in order of increasing seriousness. Many of the problems can be alleviated by switching to another formulation.

Bleeding when the period is not due occurs most commonly on the minipill or low-dose combination. It is an inconvenience but not a health problem.

Scanty periods, sometimes just spotting, may occur because the buildup of the endometrium (uterine lining) is suppressed by the pill. This should not cause concern. However, if the period is missed for two months in a row (and no pills have been missed), you should probably get a pregnancy test and possibly change pills.

Breast tenderness is normal for a month or two, but if it is severe or long-lasting, see a physician about changing pills.

Breast size may increase or decrease, but this should not cause concern unless it involves one bra size or more, in which case the pill should be stopped.

Acne and oily skin may be promoted by progestogen. Estrogen tends to counter this effect.

Facial hair may increase while head hair may thin. This is rare and not clearly associated with pill use.

Alcohol metabolism is slowed by the pill, which makes it easier to get drunk and stay drunk.

Nausea sometimes occurs, especially in the first few cycles. It may help to take the pill right after a meal.

Vaginitis due to monilia infection may be aggravated by the pill. Lower doses of progestogen may help.

Weight gain sometimes happens. The progestogen tends to increase appetite while the estrogen tends to increase fluid retention.

Depression with fatigue and decreased libido sometimes results, apparently because estrogen decreases the brain level of serotonin by increasing the requirement for vitamin B-6. A supplement of 50 milligrams per day of vitamin B-6 sometimes helps, but a lower estrogen dose may be necessary.

Mild headaches may be relieved by switching pills.

Bladder infections are slightly more common in oral contraceptive users.

Skin changes, such as darker moles and greater susceptibility to sunburn, may appear. Theoretically, this could increase the risk of skin cancers, but data on this are not available yet.

Changes in vision due to changes in the shape of the eyeball and cornea may be caused by the estrogen. Contact lens discomfort may result.

Amenorrhea and infertility may follow stopping the pill and may last a year or two. A physician should be consulted. Increased fertility sometimes occurs.

Birth defects may be caused by the pill being taken during pregnancy. That is why it is so important to be sure you are not pregnant before starting on the pill. If a period is missed after a pill is missed, get a pregnancy test before starting a new cycle. If the pill is stopped, it is advisable to use another method of birth control for three months before getting pregnant.

Gallstones requiring surgery are much more common among user of oral contraceptives; apparently the hormones concentrate the bile.

Migraine headaches are sometimes aggravated, even initiated, by oral contraceptives. This is potentially very serious and you should stop using the pill.

Chemical diabetes, with increased blood sugar and insulin, occurs in about one-third of all pill users. There are usually no symptoms, but the long-term effects are unknown. Prediabetics and borderline cases may be pushed over the line.

Fertility reduction persists for a year or so after stopping use of the pill in about a fourth of those who use it. This can make pregnancy planning difficult, but it should not cause undue concern.

Tumors of the breast and uterus, both benign and cancerous, can theoretically be promoted by estrogen. However, the small doses used in oral contraceptives have not been shown to be associated with excess cancer of the breast, and some studies indicate the pills decrease the risk. There is some evidence of more cervical cancer in women who used the pill when younger, but this can be accounted for by the earlier and less monogamous sexual experiences of the pill users. The exposure of the more susceptible teenage vaginal mucosa to herpes and other viruses is believed to be a major factor in subsequent development of cervical cancer.

Does this prove that the pill is safe only as long as you are not sexually active? Not quite, but sexually active teenage girls would probably be better off in the long run if they used diaphragms and sponges or their partners used condoms, especially if there is more than one partner.

Liver disease can be aggravated by the pill. Hepatitis and other liver diseases should be completely cleared before resuming use of the pill.

Liver tumors are sometimes caused by oral contraceptives. If a pain or lump occurs under the right rib cage, stop taking the pill and see a physician.

Hypertension develops in about 5 percent of all pill users. Almost all of them experience some increase in blood pressure, but normal levels are usually not exceeded.

Blood clot promotion is probably the greatest hazard. The pill increases the concentration of some clotting factors in the blood, increasing the probability of heart attack, stroke, pulmonary embolism (lung clot) and thrombo-phlebitis (inflamed vein due to a clot, usually in the leg). In cases of leg swelling or pain, abdominal pain, chest pain or shortness of breath, cough without apparent reason, severe headaches, or visual problems, stop taking the pill and see a physician.

Coronary artery disease risk factors may be increased by oral contraceptives. Estrogens tend to increase serum fats, while progestogens tend to increase cholesterol levels. These effects can be very serious when coupled with smoking, hypertension, and other risk factors. It is a good idea to have your blood-lipid levels checked before and periodically during use of the pill, especially if your family has a history of coronary artery disease and heart attacks.

Who Should
Not Use the Pill?

It is generally agreed that a woman should not take oral contraceptives if she:

has a history of heart attack, stroke, phlebitis, severe varicose veins, or other blood clotting disorders

has hypertension

smokes cigarettes, especially after age 30

is over age 40

has elevated blood fats or cholesterol

has had cancer of the breast or uterus, or large fibroid tumors of the uterus

has frequent or severe migraine headaches

has liver disease or dysfunction as shown by blood tests

has sickle-cell anemia

has grossly irregular periods

is breast feeding

Many physicians also believe a woman should not take oral contraceptives if she:

has diabetes or a strong family history of diabetes, hypertension,

208

stroke, blood-clotting disorders, very lumpy breasts, or breast cancer

has a history of toxemia of pregnancy or kidney disease with hypertension (pill use here is usually safe with careful blood pressure monitoring)

has epilepsy, severe eye problems, or a history of Sydenham's chorea

has any type of severe chronic disease

is severely overweight

was exposed to DES before birth (there is little evidence for this proscription)

3

Sexually Transmitted Diseases (STDs)

A bout twenty diseases are transmitted by sexual contact, oral and manual as well as regular intercourse.[8] The most important in the United States are, in approximate order of prevalence, nongonococcal urethritis (NGU, mostly chlamydia infections), gonorrhea, genital herpes, cytomegalovirus, trichomoniasis, nonspecific bacterial vaginitis, and syphilis. Hepatitis B and AIDS are important STDs discussed separately in Part Four. Ano-genital warts are important because of their increasing incidence and their apparent association with cervical cancer.

Nongonococcal urethritis (NGU) is now even more common than gonorrhea. It is caused by several strains of *Chlamydia trachomatis* and possibly other bacteria. Nearly 10 percent of all sexually active women have chlamydial infections. Inner-city clinics report an incidence of nearly 25 percent. The infection can result in ectopic pregnancy, miscarriage, female sterility, and pneumonia and eye infections in the newborn. Men may develop inflammation and pain of the testes, sperm ducts, urethra, and prostate.

Symptoms are often mild, just a slight discharge and slight urinary pain. Sometimes, especially in women, there are no symptoms. When found or strongly suspected, treatment is usually with tetracycline. Penicillin is ineffective. All sexual partners should also be treated or reinfection is likely.

Because the infection can have serious consequences in women

209

210 and newborn babies, some physicians advocate routine screening of pregnant women for chlamydia in selected populations at high risk. The most likely candidates include women who are unmarried and pregnant, less than twenty years old, live in an inner city, have other STDs, have a sex partner with NGU, or report late for prenatal care. The main obstacle to mass screening is that chlamydial cultures are expensive and not widely available.

Some strains of chlamydia are responsible for a chronic eye inflammation called trachoma that is one of the world's leading cause of blindness. It is most common in some parts of Africa, the Middle East and Southeast Asia where sanitary conditions are poor. It is not a venereal disease and is usually contracted in childhood by personal contact.

Gonorrhea ("the clap," "getting burned") is caused by *Neisseria gonorrhea* bacteria which infects the mucus membranes of the reproductive organs, urethra, rectum, eyes, and throat. Sterility can result from infection of the prostate or sperm ducts in men, or the Fallopian tubes or ovaries in women. Generalized gonorrhea can cause arthritis, liver disease, and serious skin rashs. Infection of an infant's eyes during birth can cause blindness. This is the reason for the silver nitrate or penicillin eyedrops at birth.

Most women and some men who have the disease show no symptoms in spite of severe infection which is damaging internal organs and being spread to others. This is why sexually active, nonmonogamous people, especially women, should be tested for gonorrhea once or twice a year. Routine gynecological examinations should include a gonorrhea culture and check for pelvic inflammatory disease (PID).

When symptoms do occur, they may include burning urination, vaginal or penile discharge, irritation of the vulva, pain on defecation, or abnormal anal discharge. Untreated cervical gonorrhea can lead to PID with Fallopian tube infection which can cause fever, nausea, vomiting, burning during urination, heavy vaginal discharge, and severe lower abdominal pains. Any of these symptoms, whether they occur in you or in any of your sexual contacts, should send you running to a clinic.

The preferred treatment is penicillin. Tetracycline is usually given to those allergic to penicillin. Persons with PPNG (penicillinase-producing Neisseria gonorrhoeae) infection, caused by a "superbug" resistant to penicillin, are usually treated with spectinomycin. In general, all partners of infected persons should be assumed to be infected and should be treated. Because chlamydial infection is so common in persons with gonorrhea, there is a trend toward treating gonorrhea patients for chlamydia too.

Genital herpes infections are caused by the Herpes simplex virus-1 (HSV-1) and increasingly by HSV-2, which causes oral herpes (cold sores). The lesions can be quite painful and recur periodically in anywhere from 5 to 25 percent of the cases. However, contrary to some scare stories, herpes does not destroy

Sexually Transmitted Diseases (STDs)

Cause	Symptoms	Usual Treatment	Possible Consequences
AIDS Acquired Immune Deficiency Syndrome			
Virus	persistent swollen lymph nodes, night sweats; infections, neoplasms	antibiotics, anticancer drugs	usually fatal
Chlamydia			
Bacteria (tiny, similar to viruses)	Slight discharge, mild to severe pain; often no symptoms	tetracycline	ectopic pregnancy, miscarriage, female sterility; eye damage and pneumonia in newborn
CMV Cytomegalovirus			
Virus	usually no symptoms; sometimes fever, malaise; joint pain	none	severe illness, death in infants
Gonorrhea			
Bacteria	burning urination, discharge; very often no symptoms in women	penicillin (plus tetracycline if chlamydia likely)	pelvic inflammatory disease; sterility in females, males; arthritis, liver disease; blindness in infants
Hepatitis B			
Virus	jaundice, malaise, loss of appetite; carrier state without symptoms very common	rest, balanced diet	liver cirrhosis, liver cancer
Herpes			
Virus	painful blisters that break into open sores; recurrence may be preceeded by tingling, burning and malaise	symptomatic; acyclovir for first attack	cervical cancer; severe eye damage; brain damage, death in infants; miscarriage
NSV Nonspecific Vaginitis			
Several bacteria	vaginal itch, smelly discharge	various antibiotics	premature labor, miscarriage, infertility
Syphilis			
Bacteria	painless sore which disappears, followed by rashes, more sores; swollen lymph nodes	penicillin	heat, brain damage
Trichomoniasis			
Flagellate	vaginal itch; urinary pain and frequency; a smelly discharge; usually no symptoms in men	metronodazole	
Wart, Ano-genital			
Virus	warts on or around the genitals or anus	removal	cervical cancer

212 sex lives and mental health, and recurrences are generally much less severe than the original outbreak. For the majority of affected persons, the affliction is a relatively trivial problem.

Nevertheless, herpes is a growing problem and a serious one because it can promote cervical cancer in women and severe brain damage and death in infants. It sometimes causes serious eye infections and is a major threat to persons with compromised immune systems. For these reasons herpes needs to be better controlled. A vaccine may help in the future, but for now the best way to slow down the spread of the virus is for the public to understand it and the disease it causes and take preventive measures.

Herpes sores are painful blisters that break and form crusty sores. They shed millions of viruses and are extremely contagious. During a recurrence viruses may be shed before sores appear. There is often tingling, burning, or itching in the affected area, and sometimes general malaise and a feeling of impending illness. This is called the *prodrome*.

The **single most important preventive measure** is to recognize the lesions and the prodrome and to strictly avoid sexual contact while they are present. This includes oral-genital contact because the virus that causes cold sores can also cause genital herpes and vice versa.

Herpes outbreaks can be treated by keeping the area clean and dry, avoiding tight clothing which irritates and traps moisture, and ointments and topical anesthetics. Acyclovir (Zovirax) is an expensive prescription drug that reduces symptoms in the initial outbreak and sometimes in recurrences. Vitamins, zinc, lysine, dye-light exposures, DMSO, and nonprescription drugs are ineffective, as are smallpox and other vaccines.

The question of nonsexual transmission of herpes arises because studies have shown that the virus can live for several hours on plastic, glass, clothes, towels, and other surfaces as well as in unchlorinated water. But this does not mean it can infect people. Without mechanical friction infection is highly unlikely to occur, and nonvenereal transmission is very rare. But until we know more, it is considered prudent for persons with herpes sores or the prodrome to use separate towels, silverware (for oral herpes), and the like, and to be careful about sharing objects with infants and young children.

Preventing herpes in the newborn is especially important. This can usually be accomplished by Cesaerean section if genital herpes lesions are present at the time of birth. But sometimes the lesions are small and go unnoticed, and sometimes the virus is shed when there are no lesions. Until a more sensitive test for shedding viruses is available, the best tool is careful examination of pregnant women who have had herpes or whose sex partners have had it.

Cytomegalovirus (CMV) is a very common virus in the herpes family which produces symtoms in only a few of those it infects. Most people acquire the infection sometime during their lives and it is the most common known infection of fetuses and the newborn; but disease from the infection is not common. The most severe occurs in infants, for whom damage to the liver, bone marrow, or brain is usually fatal. The virus crosses the placenta to the fetus if the mother has the infection. She rarely has any symptoms or knowledge that the virus is present. Sometimes symptoms suggesting mononucleosis appear, in which case tests for "mono" and CMV should be done. The symptoms include sudden onset of fever, malaise, and muscle and joint pain.

The virus can apparently be passed on by any close contact, including sexual intimacy, and by blood transfusions. It has been found in semen, milk, urine, feces, saliva, cervical secretions, and blood. Promiscuous homosexuals have a very high incidence of infection. Persons with AIDS, those receiving immune suppressing drugs after organ transplant, and those with otherwise compromised immune systems are at high risk for serious disease from the infection. Unfortunately, there is no effective treatment for CMV disease. The best hope for future prevention is a vaccine being developed.

Trichomoniasis is caused by a parasitic flagellate, *Trichomonas vaginalis*, which can survive on wet objects such as douching equipment, sponges, and washclothes, but is usually sexually transmitted. The symptoms in women include vaginal itch, bad-smelling, yellow-green frothy discharge, burning pain, and frequent urge to urinate. Men usually have no symptoms in spite of harboring the parasite and passing it on to women.

Treatment is with metronidazole (Flagyl), except for pregnant women, who can get some symptomatic relief with vaginal suppositories, vinegar douches, and other measures. Women's sex partners must also be treated. Condoms should be used until both partners are cleared of the infection.

Bacterial Vaginitis is caused by *Gardnerella vaginalis* and other bacteria. The symptoms include itching, a fishy-smelling, grayish, flour-paste-like discharge, and sometimes a mild burning sensation. The common infection has been thought to be a relatively minor nuisance, but there is now evidence it can cause premature labor and infertility. Women who use IUDs have a much higher incidence than those who don't. Oral contraceptives seem to have a protective effect. Treatment is usually with metronidazole.

Syphilis is less common but more serious than most other STDs. It is caused by the *Treponema pallidum* bacteria, which can penetrate the thin skin around the genitals, anus, and mouth, spread to the nervous system and heart, and cause brain damage, insanity, paralysis, heart disease, and death.

The symptom in the first stage is a painless sore or ulcer on the genitals, lips, breast, fingers, or around the rectum. It appears one to several

214 weeks after contact. Without treatment the sore disappears, but in most cases a rash appears all over the body or just on the hands and feet. Wartlike growths may occur around the ano-genital area. There may be fever and swollen lymph nodes. This second stage also clears up and the latent phase with no symptoms begins. It may last a few weeks to twenty years, with occasional relapses to the second stage. Eventually the third stage begins with the infection of the heart and brain.

Because of the long incubation period, the seemingly minor nature of the initial lesion, and the long latent period, syphilis is often not detected and treated early. It is important for sexually active persons, especially homosexuals, who are the most likely victims, to be aware of the symptoms and see a physician if syphilis is suspected. The blood test is very accurate in detecting infection and should be taken once a year by anyone who has more than one sexual partner. If the test is positive, all partners should be treated. The usual treatment is with Bicillin, a long-acting penicillin. In allergic persons, tetracycline or erythromycin is used.

PREVENTION OF VENEREAL DISEASE

Know your sex partner(s). **Minimize multiple contacts.**

See a physician about treatment if a partner has an STD.

Use **condoms.**

Use **spermicidal foam, cream, or jelly.** Besides killing sperm, they may kill gonorrhea and syphilis germs.

Urinate and wash genitals after intercourse.

4

Healthy Pregnancy, Healthy Children

The earliest suspicion of pregnancy usually occurs when a fertile woman has intercourse without using any birth control method, then misses her period. Confirmation can be made with a pregnancy test which detects human chorionic gonadotropin (HCG), a hormone made by the placenta from the first day of implantation of the fertilized egg in the womb. Pregnancy test kits are available for home use from drug stores and by mail order.

Once pregnancy is confirmed, a woman should select a physician or nurse-midwife with whom she feels she can work for about a year. Accessibility, responsiveness, readiness to answer all questions, and personal and philosophical compatibility are important considerations. A nurse-midwife should be certified by the American College of Midwifery and have a physician on call for backup. The advantage of a nurse-midwife is that she is frequently more knowledgeable about, and available for dealing with, the many normal but often distressing symptoms of pregnancy, and she can often provide more thorough and personalized coaching in exercises and other preparations for birth. She can also usually labor-sit, that is, be at the woman's side through most or all of the labor, and later coach her in breast feeding.

Routine Prenatal Care

Routine care during pregnancy, which generally requires an obstetrician or gynecologist, will include a complete medical history and physical examina-

215

216 Causes of Birth Defects

The preponderance of each group of causes is proportional to the segments of the circle. The goals of research are to decrease the unknown category and to learn to prevent the damage due to the known causes.

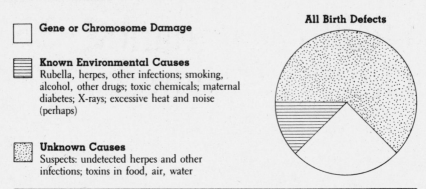

All Birth Defects

☐ **Gene or Chromosome Damage**

▤ **Known Environmental Causes**
Rubella, herpes, other infections; smoking, alcohol, other drugs; toxic chemicals; maternal diabetes; X-rays; excessive heat and noise (perhaps)

▨ **Unknown Causes**
Suspects: undetected herpes and other infections; toxins in food, air, water

tion, preferably within about ten weeks of conception; a pelvic exam; a Pap test; a gonorrhea smear; blood pressure checks; weight checks; urine tests for sugar and protein; and blood tests for syphilis, blood type, and nutritional status. Rubella and genetic disorders common to certain ethnic groups are checked for. After about twelve weeks the fetal heartbeat can be monitored and the fetus visualized with ultrasound devices.

Nutritional considerations are very important during pregnancy. A balanced diet with all the essential nutrients and calories in adequate supply is crucial to the health of both the mother and the developing fetus. Pregnancy is no time to go on a diet to lose weight; the mother-to-be must eat for two people. How much weight should she gain? Through most of the twentieth century, up until about the mid-sixties, weight gain was strictly controlled with diet, salt restriction, and sometimes diuretics and even appetite suppressants in the belief that this would help prevent preeclampsia and toxemia of pregnancy. This practice generally results in smaller, less healthy, less intelligent babies and has been largely abandoned. The consensus now is that the optimal weight gain is about twenty-five to thirty pounds. A little more may be all right for some women, but too much may predispose a woman to hypertension, diabetes, and fatigue.

There is no special diet recommended for pregnancy, but it is more important than ever to eat as well as possible and substantially more than usual. See Chapter 2–3 for guidelines to a balanced diet. The nutrients most likely needing attention are protein, iron, folic acid, and calcium. The requirements for these increase by 50 to 100 percent. The intake of high *protein* and high *calcium* foods should be increased substantially. Supplements of *iron* and *folic acid* are usually advisable. Other vitamin and mineral supplements may be taken, but it is best not to exceed the RDAs, especially for vitamins A and D. It is wise to be especially careful to avoid potential sources of natural *toxins* such as moldy foods and sprouting potatoes.

Preventing Birth Defects and Mental Retardation[9]

It is a great tragedy that 3 to 4 percent of all children born to normal parents develop serious birth defects, genetic disease, or mental retardation. This is about 100,000 per year in the United States, which already has over 6 million retarded persons. Millions more will later develop inherited diseases that cause early death or disability. Contrary to some newspaper headlines claiming that birth defects are more common now, the vast majority are about as common as they were a generation ago, though babies with certain serious problems are more likely to live now. There are many fewer incidences of neural tube defects and Down's syndrome than there were two decades ago, but the reasons for this are unclear.

It is one of the great hopes of preventive medicine that most of these tragedies can eventually be avoided by the application of medical genetics and good prenatal care. Progress has been slow, however, because the cause of most birth defects is unknown. About 25 percent result from defects in chromosomes and genes and another 5 to 7 percent from drugs, chemicals, infections, and other known environmental factors. It is only these cases, which comprise approximately one-third of all birth defects, that we can theoretically prevent, at least until we know more about the causes.

This is an important point to understand because mothers often blame themselves and suffer needless and unjustified guilt in the false belief that if they had done something different the child might have been healthy. Similar considerations hold for **miscarriage,** which is, contrary to popular belief, not caused by physical or emotional stress, travel, or exercise. Most miscarriages are the result of a genetic or anatomical abnormality of the fetus which cannot be prevented with our present knowledge.

Chromosome defects, such as too many or too few, are responsible for Down's syndrome (mongolism), hermaphroditism, and other disorders. Effective contraception for women over age thirty-five probably accounts for some of the decrease in incidence.

Molecular diseases, also known as inborn errors of metabolism or genetic diseases, are often due to a single defect in a single gene which causes a

218 metabolic block. Depending on what gene is affected, the block affects the metabolism of amino acids, fats, carbohydrates, nucleic acids, or other biochemicals. The unmetabolized substance then accumulates to toxic levels and damages the brain, eyes, or other tissue. In other cases the metabolic block prevents the formation of a necessary protein or the removal of a waste product. Hundreds of these genetic diseases have been identified, and they account for almost one-third of hospitalized children in the United States. Treatment is often basically palliative and involves lifelong institutionalization. In other cases early recognition of the defect and proper treatment from birth or even before can prevent the worst. Some examples follow.

Phenylketonuria (PKU). The amino acid phenylalanine accumulates in the blood, causing mental retardation. Blue-eyed blonds are most often affected. Early diagnosis and avoidance of more than the required amount of the essential amino acid can prevent brain damage.

Galactosemia. The sugar galactose (from lactose), though absorbed, cannot be metabolized, and ingested lactose causes vomiting, diarrhea, jaundice, cataracts, and mental retardation. Early diagnosis and avoidance of the sugar can prevent illness and brain damage.

Sickle-cell anemia. The hemoglobin molecule is defective by one amino acid, which distorts the shape of the red blood cell and makes it a very poor oxygen carrier. Blacks are most commonly affected.

Tay-Sachs disease causes abnormal lipid build up, brain destruction, blindness, and eventually death. It affects Ashkenazic Jews almost exclusively.

Hemophilia is a bleeding disease due to a missing clotting factor. It is transmitted by the carrier mother to half her sons.
    Other genetically determined defects include clubfoot, hip dislocations, cleft palate, and pyloric stenosis, an abnormality of the opening between the stomach and intestine. More complex genetic disorders include cystic fibrosis, dwarfism, gout, Wilson's disease, glaucoma, high blood pressure, progressive muscular dystrophy, diabetes, and some types of hypercholesterolemia, very high cholesterol levels which can lead to early heart attacks. Most of these conditions can be treated to improve the quality and length of life.

Drug use during pregnancy can cause serious birth defects and mental retardation. Everyone knows about the thalidomide tragedy, which the United States was spared thanks to an alert FDA official. Now other tranquilizers such as Librium, Valium, and meprobamate are suspected of causing subtle brain defects to the fetus if taken during pregnancy. Bendectin, an antinausea drug prescribed for pregnant women since 1957, is no longer made because of suspicions that it may cause birth defects. Aside from prescription drugs, women should be cautious about all drug use, including ointments and other topical drugs, antacids, cough and cold medicines, laxatives, antihistamines, pain killers, and all recreational drugs.

A fetus can be harmed at any time during pregnancy, and care is always in order. However, it appears that the most *critical period*, during which the fetus is most sensitive and vulnerable to harm, is day eighteen to day twenty-eight, approximately the third and fourth weeks of pregnancy. Therefore, this is a reasonable rule of thumb: a woman should assume she is pregnant from the day she has had intercourse without protection or, even if she has been careful, from the first day her period is due. During this time she should avoid anything that has been implicated as a cause of birth defects.

Drugs known to cause fetal harm include alcohol, diethylstilbestrol (DES), heroin, nicotine and other constituents of cigarette smoke, some anticancer and anticonvulsant drugs, methadone, lithium, testosterone and related steroids, progestins, overdoses of vitamins A and D, and warfarin.

Drugs suspected of causing fetal harm include antibiotics (including sulfa drugs), aspirin, cortisone-type drugs, various diuretics, oral diabetes drugs, various tranquilizers, phenylmercuric acetate, LSD, marijuana, and excessive doses of iodine and trace minerals. Extremely high doses of the B vitamins and other nutrients might also be harmful. Caffeine, anesthetic gases (occupational exposure), bromocriptine, Bendectin (now banned), and the spermicide nonoxynol-9 are suspected by some, but the weight of evidence does not strongly support any association of these with birth defects.

The question of **alcohol** use during pregnancy deserves further comment. The fetal alcohol syndrome, with such symptoms as a flat face, a short, upturned nose, small eyes and head, facial asymmetry, and lower intelligence, was only recognized in the 1970s after more than twenty-five centuries of alcohol use. This is because the effect is too rare to detect without careful statistical analysis of expertly obtained data.

The question of how much alcohol during pregnancy may cause the syndrome is still hotly debated. Since no safe level of intake has been firmly established, many physicians say the less the better and none is best. Others say this is going too far, that it is unnecessarily restrictive since there is no evidence of harm from light, occasional drinking, meaning the equivalent of a beer or two a few times a month. However, light drinking plus cigarette smoking appears much riskier than either alone.

Occupational hazards to the fetus include exposure to benzene, cadium, lead, chloroprene, various insecticides, and perhaps surgical anesthetics. All due care should be taken, but there is no cause for alarm at the increasing numbers of women in the work force; there has not been an associated epidemic of birth defects, which some feared might occur.

X-rays during early pregnancy, especially large doses to the bowel, back, or kidney may cause fetal defects. They should be avoided except for the most urgent medical reasons, when there is any possibility of being pregnant.

Some infections during pregnancy can cause very serious birth defects. Often the mother is only mildly ill with slight malaise and low-grade fever or none at all. The main culprits are rubella, cytomegalovirus, herpes virus, and toxoplasmosis from cats or birds or undercooked beef or pork. Pregnant and possibly pregnant women should avoid handling cats and birds and their litter and avoid eating undercooked meat. They should not attend infants or children with rubella or undiagnosed illness. Girls should be vaccinated against rubella before menarche and not while pregnant or possibly pregnant. If a history of vaginal herpes is present, the mother must be checked frequently for a recurrence near delivery time.

Toxemia of pregnancy, also known as **eclampsia,** is a serious complication of pregnancy. In the early stage, known as preeclampsia, there is high blood pressure, excessive edema (swelling) of the hands, feet, and face, and protein in the urine. These are dangerous signs. If they progress to eclampsia, blood pressure soars and there may be visual changes including partial blindness, severe headaches, dizziness, vomiting, kidney and liver damage, convulsions, shock, coma, and death of the mother and fetus. If the infant survives it will be small, even if full term, and may suffer varying degrees of brain damage and possible mental retardation, epilepsy, cerebral palsy, or other neurological disorders.

      Toxemia of pregnancy has been recognized for centuries and is known as the "ancient enigma of obstetrics." Leading theories of the cause focus on a possible virus infection, liver and kidney problems, and malnutrition. One theory is that malnutrition leads to liver dysfunction, consequent decreased protein synthesis, and decreased detoxification of hormones, metabolic products, and toxins from the intestinal flora. The theory has not been proven, but prenatal clinics that emphasize good nutrition generally have lower toxemia rates.

Rh disease. The Rh factor is a protein found on the blood cells of about 85 percent of the population. If the mother is Rh-negative and the father is Rh-positive, the fetus may be Rh-positive and its blood may sensitize the mother's, that is, prime it to react against Rh-positive blood. In subsequent pregnancies this could cause a serious, even fatal, reaction in an Rh-positive fetus. If it survives it could develop mental retardation. Blood transfusions in the uterus and at birth may save the infant's life and prevent retardation.

Rh disease can be prevented in Rh-negative women by an injection of immune globulin after any incident in which Rh-positive cells may have entered her blood, including giving birth to an Rh-positive child, an abortion, miscarriage, or ectopic pregnancy, or amniocentesis for chromosome testing. The immune globulin prevents the woman from developing antibodies to Rh-positive cells in her blood by destroying the cells quickly.

Incest and inbreeding greatly increase the risk of birth defects. Everyone carries about three to six defective genes. Such genes are "recessive" and may be carried for generations without showing up as a disease or malformation. But if two people with the same defective gene mate, the children may develop the defect. The chances of having the same defective recessive gene are much greater with blood relatives. Groups that are isolated geographically or culturally, such as the Amish and certain communities in the Appalachians, have a high incidence of inbreeding and high rates of mental retardation, congential deafness, dwarfism, and other genetic disorders.

Because many of the recessive genes are much more common to some ethnic groups than others, marrying outside the group may decrease the probability of these disorders occurring. The evidence in favor of outbreeding, hybridizing, and inter-ethnic marriages is infinitely stronger than arguments for "racial purity."

Ultrasound imaging in pregnancy has been used for about twenty years and is growing in popularity; it is now available in almost all hospitals and many physicians' offices. While no harmful effects have been reported so far, a panel of experts under the auspices of the National Institutes of Health concluded that ultrasound should be used only in cases of high-risk or complicated pregnancies and not for routine screening or determining the sex of the fetus. This is because animal studies have suggested that the procedure might retard fetal growth, impair immune response, and damage cells, which could cause subtle damage.

A high-risk pregnancy is one that occurs in a woman in such poor health that the pregnancy carries a much higher than average risk of harm to the mother and the child. Women in the high-risk groups should consider the hazards carefully before deciding to have a child, and should carefully follow their doctors' advice should they become pregnant. High-risk conditions include alcoholism or any other kind of drug addiction, cancer, diabetes, hypertension, kidney disease, heart disease, and congenital anemias such as sickle-cell disease.

222   Another line of defense against congenital disorders is **early detection** of abnormalities in the fetus. There are several methods for this. A blood test for alphafetoprotein (AFP) helps detect neural tube defects, and amniocentesis is used to identify chromosomal and genetic defects. A new procedure, chorionic villi sampling, may provide very early diagnosis without the inconvenience and risks of amniocentesis. Instead of fetal cells being analyzed, genetically identical cells can be taken from the placenta by inserting a catheter through the vagina into the uterus. Anesthesia is unnecessary and the test results are known quickly.

Amniocentesis is done fourteen to sixteen weeks into pregnancy. Amniotic fluid is removed by a needle inserted into the womb. The fluid contains some live cells shed by the fetus, and these are cultured in a special medium and examined for chromosomal and genetic defects. When disorders are detected, they may be treated during pregnancy or soon after birth. In some cases, such as Down's syndrome, the woman often chooses to terminate the pregnancy.

Amniocentesis is not a routine procedure every pregnant woman should submit to. While it is quite safe, facilities are only barely adequate to handle the cases which clearly call for the test. The likely candidates are women who

> are Rh-negative sensitized and have Rh-positive mates
>
> have suffered repeated miscarriages
>
> become pregnant after age thirty-five (there is about a 10 percent chance of chromosomal abnormality; the relevence of the father's age is being studied)
>
> have a family history of hereditary disease or a mate with such history
>
> have had an affected child
>
> have a parent with an unusual or abnormal chromosome, or a mate with such a parent

Common Discomforts and Disorders of Pregnancy

Pregnancy involves large hormonal changes and substantial physical and psychological stresses. It is not surprising that there are a number of physical complaints that frequently accompany pregnancy.[10] Most pregnant women experience at least one or two of the problems. A few experience none, and a few experience several and are quite miserable for some weeks. These problems are generally of no serious consequence to the health of either the mother or fetus, but symptoms that are severe or persistant should be discussed with a physician. Some of the more common are considered here.

Nausea and vomiting, so-called morning sickness, can occur any time of day, mostly during months two and three but sometimes throughout pregnancy. Remedies worth trying include nibbling on crackers or dry toast, sipping carbonated beverages, sipping warm water, and eating small meals frequently. Vitamin B-6 is sometimes recommended, but its value has not been proven. If it is tried, doses of more than 200 milligrams per day should be avoided because of the theoretical possibility of damage to the fetal nerves. Vitamin K has been reported helpful in nausea and vomiting of pregnancy. Its use should be discussed with one's physician.

Heartburn and belching are common because the stomach cannot hold as much food. Pressure from the fetus and perhaps hormonal effects on the smooth muscles of the esophagus cause stomach juices to back up into the esophagus, which is burned and irritated. It may help to eat small meals slowly and carefully and to avoid gas-producing foods like cabbage and cucumbers and those that increase stomach acid, like coffee and tea.

Dental and gum problems are sometimes aggravated by pregnancy, especially if the diet is poor. Routine dental care should be continued but general anesthesia should be avoided.

Constipation, hemorrhoids, and varicose veins are common in pregnancy because of the growing pressure in the lower body and the increased blood volume. Proper diet with adequate fiber and water, and adequate exercise, especially walking, can help minimize these problems. If iron supplements seem to be causing constipation, try another type. If necessary, bulk stool softeners such as psyllium seed can be used occasionally.

Urinary tract infection is one of the most common problems in pregnancy because of hormonal, mechanical, and immune changes. It can lead to premature delivery, slowed fetal growth, and life-threatening kidney infection in the mother, so it must be treated. Antibiotics known to be safe for the fetus are used. Unfortunately, an infection may be present without the usual symptoms such as urinary frequency and urgency, and pain. Because of this, pregnant women who have ever had a urinary tract infection should be screened for such. Eventually this may become routine for all pregnant women.

It should be noted here that simple urinary frequency is very common because of the pressure of the uterus on the bladder. This is normal and

224 should not be treated; fluid intake should not be decreased. However, if pain or fever also occurs, a physician should be seen at once.

Cardiovascular changes such as increased heart rate and occasional palpitations, nosebleeds, and dizziness due to postural hypotension (from standing suddenly) are common because of increased blood volume, pressure in the abdominal area, and hormonal changes. These are usually not serious.

Spotting and **abdominal cramping** are common in early pregnancy. Occasional bleeding during the first three months is no cause for concern, but continued or heavy bleeding should be discussed with a physician.

Headaches, fatigue, insomnia, and **depression** are very common and quite normal considering the physical and emotional stresses of pregnancy. They can be minimized by common sense measures like adequate exercise, rest, and diet, and a supportive environment with frequent contact with friends and loved ones. Drugs to relieve the symptoms should not be taken without a physician's advice.

Edema (swelling) of the feet is very common, especially in late pregnancy, and is mostly due to increased blood volume and slowed blood flow. Excessive salt intake, tight garters, and prolonged standing can aggravate the problem. It helps to elevate the feet often. Edema in the face and hands in the morning may be a sign of toxemia and should be discussed with a physician.

Backaches are common in late pregnancy, especially for women with a history of back pain. They can be largely prevented by an exercise program begun before pregnancy or early in pregnancy. This is discussed further in Part Four.

Other changes that frequently occur during pregnancy and should not cause alarm include dry, itching skin, changes in hair distribution and texture, a watery vaginal discharge, leg cramps, skin pigmentation (especially on the face), mild shortness of breath, and tender breasts.

Sympathetic sickness in the husband, the *couvade syndrome,* is apparently quite common. Perhaps 20 percent of all fathers-to-be suffer from nausea, loss of appetite, or abdominal pain severe enough for them to seek medical care, and for no apparent reason other than that their wives are pregnant. To avoid unnecessary medication, men with such symptoms should let their physicians know if their wives are pregnant. A little reassurance may be all that is needed.

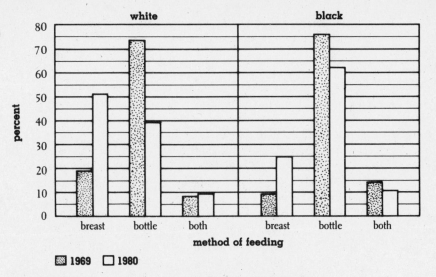

Percentages of Breast- and Bottle-Feeding

Among white and black women, United States, 1969 and 1980*
*National Natality Survey, National Center for Health Statistics
From Center for Disease Control, *Morbidity and Mortality Weekly Report*, 33:153, 1984.

Infant Nutrition

Breast feeding for at least the first several months is the preferred source of infant nutrition in most cases. In the 1940s about 65 percent of United States infants were breast fed; in the late sixties it was only 15 percent. Now breast feeding is making a comeback and more than 50 percent are breast fed. The American Academy of Pediatrics and the Canadian Pediatric Society have issued a joint statement strongly encouraging physicians to recommend breast feeding. With care, formula and solid feeding can be very nutritious, but breast feeding is considered generally superior for the following reasons.

At birth the infant emerges from an almost germ-free environment into a world teeming with staphylococcus, streptococcus, and other bacteria, as well as viruses, fungi, and other infectious organisms. The immune system at birth is not well developed, and the infant is especially susceptible to intestinal and respiratory **infections** and to allergy development for about a year. Fortunately, mother's colostrum, a watery yellowish fluid released by the breast during the first few days, and mother's milk itself are rich in antibodies the infant lacks. The colostrum and milk are also very rich in infection-fighting white blood cells, mostly the very efficient "killer" macro-

226 phages. The incidence of respiratory, intestinal, ear, and other infections is generally much lower among breast-fed infants.

Widespread bottle feeding in developing countries, where sanitation is poor and formulas often diluted for economy, has contributed to high infant mortality rates. Some countries have declared baby bottles a health hazard and banned their sale without a health worker's prescription. Two years after the ban went into effect in Papua, New Guinea, the average weight of young children had increased significantly.

Breast feeding provides substantial protection from **allergic** problems. The very young intestinal wall does not always manage to absorb only digested nutrients and keep out large protein fragments. When such undigested molecules are absorbed sensitization may occur, in which case allergic problems with that food will appear in the future. Moreover, some infants are allergic to cow's milk and suffer lung disorders, anemia, severe diarrhea, and other problems. This is rare, and allergy to mother's milk is even rarer. (In one such case the starving baby, allergic to everything tried, was finally saved by poi, the Polynesian staple made from taro root.)

The **psychological benefits** to the infant and mother of early, close, prolonged contact are enhanced by nursing.

Breast feeding may provide some protection from **obesity** because the infants tend to stop when they are full and are not encouraged to continue beyond the point of satisfaction in order to finish what has been prepared. It is also a great help in controlling the weight of the mother, since it can use about 1,000 calories a day.

The protein, mineral, and fat composition of mother's milk is quite different from cow's milk. The **protein** content of cow's milk is so high that it is dangerous to feed to an infant without dilution. Human milk has more unsaturated fatty acids (like vegetable oils) and fewer saturated fatty acids. However, most commercial milk-based formulas are modified to resemble human milk in these respects.

The **iron** in human milk is better absorbed and capable of meeting the infant's needs for at least the first six months of life.

Breast feeding is generally **less expensive** than bottle feeding. It is also much **more convenient,** since it does not require bottles, cans, sterilization, and so on.

Breast feeding also **speeds maternal recovery** by stimulating the uterus to recover its tone and shape.

Breast feeding is not adequate, of course, when the mother is malnourished. She should have a balanced diet of whole, natural foods without excessive supplements. Vegetarians should be certain to get adequate vitamin B-12, either from dairy products or supplements.

Many drugs taken by the mother are excreted in the milk and may be harmful to the infant. Especially important to avoid while breast feeding are: oral contraceptives, reserpine, atropine, steroid hormones, diuretics, anticoagulants, antithyroid drugs, barbiturates, tetracyline, and various anti-cancer drugs. Marijuana, alcohol, caffeine, cigarettes, narcotics, tranquilizers, and stimulant laxatives should also be avoided or minimized.

Certain foods eaten by the mother may cause colic in the nursing infant. Milk, garlic, onions, and vegetables in the cabbage family are common culprits, but this is highly variable.

When to start solid foods is a much-debated subject, and no hard rules can be given. Solid feeding too early may increase the susceptibility to allergies, but most infants have low iron reserves, and mother's milk does not supply as much iron as some solid foods. A safe bet is to exclusively breast feed for about three to seven months, then start giving small amounts of solids. There is no need to buy baby food. The regular family fare, preferably unsalted and without strong seasonings, can be pureed.

As teeth develop, larger, chewy morsels can be given. However, care must be taken not to serve food that can be choked on. Asphyxiation by food kills a child in the United States about once every five days. Be especially careful with hot dogs, candies, nuts, grapes, beans, and apples. These should be mashed or cut or broken into safer forms.

Infants under one year of age should not be fed honey. Even "pure" or "filtered" honey often contains botulism spores, which can produce the deadly toxin in infants.

Children of allergic parents should not be given cow's milk, eggs, chocolate, citrus fruit or juice, wheat, or other commonly allergenic foods for the first year.

Parents who bottle feed their infants or give them rubber-nipple pacifiers should boil the nipples five or six times, changing the water after each boil. This will reduce the level of carcinogenic nitrosamines in the rubber. The Consumer Product Safety Commission and the FDA are forcing the gradual reduction of the nitrosamine levels, but it will be years before they are negligible.

Sudden Infant Death Syndrome (SIDS)

In SIDS an infant, usually less than six months of age, for no apparent reason suddenly stops breathing, the heart stops, and death ensues. In the United States there are about two cases per 1,000 live births. The vast majority of infants are not in danger, but the problem causes a great deal of anxiety because of its seeming arbitrary nature.

SIDS, by definition, cannot be treated, for death is final. However, progress is being made in preventing it. This is possible because the syndrome is not as arbitrary as it seems; some infants are much more at risk

228 than others. These include siblings (especially twins) of SIDS victims, premature or unusually small infants, and those with a history of "almost SIDS," that is, one or more episodes of cessation of breathing (apnea). Such infants can be monitored at home with electronic equipment on loan from a hospital. Parents should be alert for breathing problems, prolonged staring spells, feeding difficulties, sleep disturbances, rigid posturing, and pallor or a gray appearance. A physician should be consulted for any of these.

The risk of SIDS can be reduced if the mother avoids smoking during pregnancy and in the presence of the infant, and by protecting the infant from cold and flu germs. SIDS is most likely after a recent virus infection, during winter months, and at two or three months of age.

Questions and Issues in Pregnancy and Childbirth

Exercise during pregnancy is important to maintain general fitness, to improve circulation, to relieve swelling, to prevent back pain, and to prepare for childbirth. There is no reason a healthy pregnant woman should "take it easy" and become sedentary. The same activities enjoyed before pregnancy can be continued, but with extra care not to fall, especially in the later months. Walking, swimming, and abdominal exercises (such as sit-ups with bent knees) are especially good. Very heavy exercise may deprive the fetus of some blood flow and nutrients, and some evidence suggests that marathoners who train hard during pregnancy may have smaller babies. It is probably safer not to push beyond 70 percent of the maximum heart rate, or .70" (220 – age) beats per minute. (See Chapter 1–3 for more on this formula.)

Hot tubs, suanas, and steam baths should be avoided or used with care, especially during the first trimester of pregnancy. If the body's core temperature exceeds 102°F, the fetus may suffer brain, nerve, or other damage.

Sexual intercourse during pregnancy is generally safe, but not if there is a risk of the woman contracting a venereal disease. Also, she should urinate after intercourse to lessen the risk of a urinary tract infection.

Caesarean section, named for Julius Caesar who was said to have been cut from his mother's womb, is surgical opening of the abdominal wall and uterus and removal of the baby and the placenta. The uterus and abdomen are then closed with sutures. The surgery can save lives when the baby's head is too big or not properly positioned for normal delivery; when the mother has active genital herpes or is seriously ill and cannot carry the baby to term without great risk; when fetal monitoring shows a depressed or irregular heart beat; and when previous Caesarean section or other uterine surgery has been done. Sometimes a normal birth can follow a Caesarean delivery.

The most controversial C-sections are those done on the basis of fetal monitoring without other evidence of a risk to the baby or mother. The percentage of babies delivered by C-section has increased dramatically, along with the increase in fetal monitoring (with devices attached to the mother's abdomen and, in late labor, the infant's scalp). Once there are signs of fetal distress, most physicians prefer not to risk harm to the fetus by waiting, which may be much riskier than a C-section. It is difficult to say, after the fact, whether the surgery was necessary or delivery could have been normal.

Nevertheless, some physicians are a bit too quick with the knife, as indicated by their very high rates of delivery by C-section. This is usually a matter of sincere judgment, not shady practice; there is plenty of room for honest differences of opinion. Some women very much want to have a natural birthing experience and are deprived of it, as well as being subjected to unnecessary pain and injury, on the basis of inconclusive data from electronic devices. A woman who is worried about being pressured into a last-minute, unnecessary C-section should discuss her concerns with her physician and inquire about his or her philosophy on delivery by the surgery.

Chemical pain relief during childbirth. Most women these days want to avoid or minimize the use of pain-relieving drugs out of fear they might harm the child and a desire to have a more natural childbirth, an experience they can participate in and appreciate. However, women vary enormously in their pain thresholds and tolerance. Some experience pain beyond their capacity to withstand, and there is usually no reason they should not be given pain-relieving drugs; carefully selected and used, they do not threaten the health of mother or child.

General anesthesia is not usually indicated for a normal delivery because the woman who is asleep cannot push and help along the labor, which may be prolonged. It also puts the baby to sleep and may depress its breathing and heart rate to the point of threatening the oxygen supply to the brain.

Analgesics and tranquilizers, usually given by injection or inhalation (nitrous oxide), can ease pain enough to allow rest and relaxation between contractions. This can greatly improve the quality of the experience for the mother. Small doses are used; the purpose is not to induce sleep or to affect the baby. Excessive sedation can lengthen the early phase of labor.

Nerve blocking injections, such as saddle block, epidural anesthesia, and caudal anesthesia, numb the lower areas with procaine-type drugs like those used in dentistry. If you are allergic to these be sure your doctor knows it.

230   **Home delivery** is an attractive option to many women because of the warm, congenial atmosphere compared to the often cold, uninviting air of the labor and delivery rooms. Unfortunately, home delivery is risky even in healthy low-risk pregnancies because serious complications, such as fetal distress or hemorrhage, can occur without warning. Hospitals are equipped to save lives in such emergencies. While the odds are against complications if the woman is healthy, if the baby or mother is harmed it will seem a very high price to pay for the luxury of a home birth. A better alternative is a family-oriented childbirth center with a homelike atmosphere, which many hospitals are setting up and encouraging husbands to participate in. If home delivery is nevertheless preferred, backup arrangements should be made with a nearby hospital and transportation should planned.

Circumcision, the surgical removal of the foreskin of the penis, is done on about 90 percent of all baby boys a day or two after birth, in spite of the position of the American Academy of Pediatrics that there is no good medical reason for the procedure. There is no evidence that it can prevent infections, penile cancer, or cervical cancer in mates any more than simple hygiene can. For example, in most European countries circumcision is done much less often than in the United States with no associated increase in cervical cancer.

The reasons for the persistence of the practice include custom, habit, religion, the false belief that circumcision is good preventive medicine or hospital policy, and the profitability of the surgery to physicians and hospitals. Physicians sometimes try to talk parents out of the surgery if their beliefs are not based on religion, but these efforts are often in vain.

The case against circumcision is that it is a painful, frightening, traumatic, unnecessary, and somewhat dangerous mutilation. The baby is strapped to a table called a Circumstraint, his genital area is washed with cold Betadine, and the foreskin (which usually has not yet separated) is forced back causing some bleeding; then clamps and hemostats are used to crush the foreskin to prevent bleeding before cutting it away with a surgical knife. All this is done without anesthesia, and the baby is invariably enraged at the pain and insult. There is also a danger of excessive bleeding, infection, and even mutilation, though this is rare.

5

Common Female Problems

omen have a much larger role in reproduction than men, they have a more complex reproduction system, and, not surprisingly, they have far more problems involving reproductive organs than men do. It is valuable for women to be aware of the more common and important of these problems, to understand their causes, and to recognize their early signs and symptoms. This makes prevention and effective treatment more likely.[11]

Breast Cancer

Breast cancer is a major cause of death among women. The risk can apparently be reduced by reducing fat consumption. Early detection is very important. See Cancer in Part Four.

Cervical Erosion

Cervical tissue sometimes erodes because of irritation or trauma from tampon insertion, intercourse, or infection. There is usually pain during tampon insertion and intercourse, and a thick mucus discharge, sometimes containing pus. Cervical erosion makes the cervix more vulnerable to infection, but if no infection develops the symptoms of cervical erosion are often minimal and go unnoticed.

DES women (those who were exposed to diethylstilbestrol while in

232 the womb) are more susceptible to cervical erosion than others. Some estrogen-containing pills may aggravate the condition, but they do not cause it.

Treatment, which is not necessary in mild cases, consists of vinegar and water douching. However, if itching, burning, or other signs of infection occur, a physician should be consulted. It may be necessary to stop using estrogen and to administer antibiotics. Recurrent infections associated with cervical erosion may call for cryosurgery (freezing) or cautery (electrical burning) to destroy some of the troublesome cervical tissue. The treatments are generally painless and do not affect fertility.

Prevention might be achieved in some cases by being more careful during tampon insertion and perhaps by avoiding excessively violent intercourse, especially when you are not physically ready and receptive. Every DES woman should be under the care of a gynecologist who does frequent examinations and carefully monitors changes in the cervix.

CIN—Cervical Intraepithelial Neoplasia

In CIN, also called cervical IN, the outer cells of the cervix show abnormalities under a microscrope. These changes sometimes precede cancer and are graded from I (mild) to III (severe), also called carcinoma in situ, which takes ten years or so to become malignant. CIN causes no symptoms and is detected by a Pap smear. If the abnormalities are found, other procedures to examine the cervix may be done.

TREATMENT

Treatment of CIN, which is an important cancer prevention measure, usually consists of elimination of the abnormal tissue with laser or cryosurgery. The cure rate is over 90 percent and there are no long-term adverse effects. In severe cases (grade III), older women who do not want more children may choose hysterectomy (removal of the uterus) as a CIN cure and cancer preventive. However, more limited surgery (such as cone biopsy) may obviate the need for a hysterectomy.

PREVENTION

Prevention can be accomplished, or CIN made less likely to occur, by avoiding and preventing the factors which are strongly associated with it, namely early (teenage) sexual intercourse, intercourse with many different men, genital herpes, and cigarette smoking.

Cervicitis

Cervicitis is an inflammation of the cervical glands with profuse mucus production. It is often accompanied by vaginitis, the treatment of which clears the cervicitis. Otherwise, it usually clears without treatment, especially in the minor cases which often occur shortly after childbirth. However, it may progress to cervical erosion. (See above.)

Cystitis

See Urinary Tract Infections, below and in Part Four.

Endometrial Hyperplasia

This is an excessive build up of the endometrium (lining of the uterus) associated with failure to ovulate. Since the egg is not released, the woman stays in the proliferative (estrogenic) phase of her cycle. Eventually, frequent or profuse menstrual bleeding occurs. The problem is most common in girls who have just begun puberty and in women around menopause. The cause is not clear, but sometimes estrogenic drugs are a factor.

TREATMENT
Treatment depends mostly on the age of the woman and the severity of the problem. It may include stopping estrogen use, taking progestins, and undergoing dilation and curettage. In persistant cases hysterectomy may be necessary to prevent uterine cancer from occurring later.

Endometriosis

Endometriosis is a strange, puzzling disorder in which endometrial tissue (menstrual tissue) appears outside the uterus. It becomes attached to the outside of the Fallopian tubes, ovaries, bladder, and other organs in fibrous, adhesive patches which still respond to monthly hormonal cycles. Like normal endometrial tissue, these patches thicken with blood during the latter part of the cycle. If nerves are nearby they are stimulated and pain occurs.

The symptoms of endometriosis include severe menstrual pain, pain during intercourse, infertility (due to Fallopian tube adhesions), chronic pelvic pain, and prolonged and irregular periods. Most of these should be present before endometriosis is suspected. The condition is confirmed by laparoscopy, in which the abdominal cavity is viewed with a scope through a small incision near the navel.

The cause of endometriosis is not known. One theory is that some menstrual tissue backs up and out the Fallopian tubes into the abdominal cavity. Another is that endometrial cells get into the lymph and blood and thereby wander to other organs, sometimes as far as the lungs.

TREATMENT

Treatment depends on severity, age, and other factors. In about a third of the cases the condition subsides without treatment, in another third it stays the same, and in another third it gets worse. In cases of severe pain or unwanted infertility, the treatment options include estrogens, progestins, cautery, laser surgery, and hysterectomy. If the woman plans to have a child sooner or later, sooner might be better, both to treat the endometriosis by suspending the monthly cycle and to have the child before the problem causes infertility.

Fibroid Tumors

A fibroid tumor is a noncancerous growth of muscle tissue on or inside the uterus. They are quite common and affect about one in four women, usually in their thirties or forties. Their cause is unknown, but their growth is stimulated by oral contraceptives that contain estrogen, and they recede with menopause. Although they sometimes grow very large, they usually are no bigger than a marble, produce no symptoms, and require no treatment. But if a fibroid tumor causes pressure on other organs in the pelvis or if it causes pain or heavy bleeding or contributes to infertility, it can be surgically removed. In some cases this can be done without affecting fertility, but sometimes the uterus must be removed. Fibroid tumors are the most common reason for hysterectomy.

Lumpy Breasts (Fibrocystic Breast Changes)

Nearly half the women in the United States will have lumpy breasts sometime in their lives, usually between ages eighteen and fifty, while the ovaries are functioning. The lumps are either long fibers that form a solid, scarlike mass or small pockets filled with fluid or semisolid material. The breasts may become heavy, painful, and tender. The pain and discomfort may be continuous, but is often most severe during the week or so before the menstrual period.

CAUSE

Women with lumpy breasts tend to have high levels of prolactin, a hormone from the pituitary gland that controls the movement of fluid into breast tissue. High estrogen levels may also be a factor. Caffeine and nicotine might promote the fibrocystic changes, but this has not been proven.

TREATMENT

Relief can be obtained by wearing a supporting bra.

Needle aspiration or surgical removal of the lumps may help substantially, but these procedures often must be repeated and do not really solve the problem.

Vitamin E supplements of about 600 IU per day for several weeks appears helpful in some cases. If no response is apparent within two menstrual cycles, continued use is not likely to help.

Avoiding all xanthine stimulants (caffeine, theophylline, theobromine) seems to help in some cases. This means not using coffee, tea, colas, chocolate, or any of the numerous headache, cold, and stimulant pills on the market. Stimulant herbs such as gotu kola and guarana must also be avoided. (Regular users of any of these products should withdraw gradually to avoid headaches and other symptoms.) Stopping smoking may also help.

Oral contraceptives seem to help in some cases, but they aggravate the condition in others.

Danazol, a drug used primarily for endometriosis, has proven effective for some cases of lumpy breasts. It is quite expensive and may cause masculinization, so it should be considered only in severe cases.

Bromocriptine, a drug used primarily for decreasing lactation after birth, is sometimes helpful, but it may cause nausea and low blood pressure.

PREVENTION

Many women might never develop lumpy breasts if they avoid xanthines. Coffee, tea, and colas are the major sources in most cases. Avoiding smoking may also help. But these ideas are not proven.

Menstrual Problems

Each month, under the influence of the ovarian hormones estrogen and progesterone, the endometrium (uterine lining) thickens, proliferates, and is prepared for the implantation of the fertilized ovum (egg). When fertilization does not occur, the estrogen and progesterone output drops, the endometrium is shed, and a new cycle begins.

The cycle is counted from the first day of bleeding to the last day of not bleeding. It is normally twenty-one to thirty-five days long, with the flow occurring for one to seven days and requiring one to ten tampons or pads per day.

Menstrual Irregularity. Young women are usually quite irregular in the first

236

one to three years of menstruation because they have not yet started ovulating; this is generally nothing to worry about. In the more mature woman the length of the cycle and the period and the total blood flow per period are pretty constant, but they may vary from one woman to the next. Large changes in these patterns should be discussed with a physician.

The cycle can be affected by travel, emotional stress, and illness. This is because the pituitary and ovarian hormones governing the cycle are controlled by the hypothalamus, a part of the brain directly connected with the pituitary and easily influenced by other brain activity.

Hypermenorrhea (Excess Menstrual Flow). Excessive menstrual bleeding can be inconvenient and even frightening. It should be investigated by a gynecologist because it can lead to iron deficiency anemia and may be a sign of a infection, IUD complications, ectopic (tubal) pregnancy, cancer, hormonal disturbances, or other serious problems.

Amenorrhea Missing several periods in a row is common and usually normal in girls who have not yet started to ovulate regularly. But if a woman who is normally regular misses her period two months in a row, she should have a physical and gynecological examination. The most likely causes are pregnancy, malnutrition (fasting, extreme dieting, poor eating habits, anorexia nervosa, overeating), excessive exercise without an adequate increase in caloric intake, and emotional stress. Rare disorders of the pituitary gland or ovaries are much less common causes. Amenorrhea due to diet and exercise should not be taken lightly or seen as convenient birth control; it can be associated with the development of osteoporosis, a very serious disorder (see below).

Dysmenorrhea This is the most common cause of loss of work days for women. Symptoms are pain (aching and cramping) in the lower abdomen and sometimes radiating to the back or inner thighs. There may also be nausea, vomiting, diarrhea, headache, dizziness, breast tenderness, fatigue, and muscle pain. There may be some discomfort a day or two before the period begins, but the most severe pain usually occurs on the first day of menstruation. It may last several hours to three days.

Dysmenorrhea occurs in all age-groups of menstruating women, but it is more common in the late teens and early twenties and in women who have never given birth. It declines sharply in the mid-twenties. Obesity and menstrual irregularity are also associated with dysmenorrhea.

CAUSES

Psychological factors such as immaturity, ambivalence about one's femininity, and unresolved sexual conflicts have long been blamed for dysmenorrhea, but such theories are mostly discredited. Nevertheless, emotional stress can sometimes aggravate menstrual discomfort.

In most cases the primary cause of dysmenorrhea appears to be an excess of prostaglandins. These hormones promote the uterine contractions and blood vessel constrictions that lead to menstrual flow. Excessive amounts cause painful contractions and can create the other symptoms.

Other possible causes are infections, cysts, endometriosis, and intrauterine devices.

TREATMENT AND PREVENTION

If dysmenorrhea is severe or occurs for the first time after age twenty-five it may be secondary to a more serious problem. A physician should be consulted. Primary dysmenorrhea (not due to organic lesions) can usually be treated effectively by one or more of the following:

> **Exercise,** such as swimming, bicycling, walking, or jogging, may help by improving circulation and relaxing muscles. Sit-ups (with knees bent), leg-lifts (one leg at a time), and yoga exercises may also help.

> **Sexual orgasm** may help by improving circulation and relieving pelvic congestion. Sexual arousal without orgasm can aggravate discomfort.

> **Heat** application with a hot-water bottle, heating pad, or hot bath, can help relieve pain.

> **Massage** and deep thumb pressure around the middle of the back on either side of the spine is sometimes good for several hours of pain relief.

> **Aspirin** and other salicylates, which are mild prostaglandin antagonists, often provide relief, especially if taken before cramps begin. Acetaminophen does not affect prostaglandins, but it may relieve the pain of cramps and headaches.

> **Anti-inflammatory drugs** like ibuprofen and indomethacin decrease prostaglandin levels very effectively and can greatly reduce symptoms of dysmenorrhea. Ibuprofen is now available over the counter, but discuss it with your physician. See p. 423.

> **Magnesium and vitamin B-6** supplements, about 200 milligrams of each, sometimes decrease the intensity of the uterine contractions and the cramps that go with them.

238

Oral contraceptives with a combination of estrogen and progestin often prevent or alleviate dysmenorrhea, apparently by lowering prostaglandin levels. Naturally, their effects and side effects must be considered.

Herb teas are sometimes helpful. Black cohosh (squaw root) contains salicylic acid, which slightly lowers prostaglandin levels and reduces cramping and other symptoms. Ginger and pennyroyal are believed to promote menstrual flow and relieve congestion, but oil of pennyroyal is dangerous and should not be used.

Premenstrual Syndrome (PMS). About a week to ten days before menstruation many women experience a variety of symptoms such as bloating and weight gain due to water retention, tender or swollen breasts, headaches, backaches, irritability, depression, anxiety, lethargy, joint pain, hives, craving for sweets, and decreased tolerance to alcohol. In most cases the symptoms are short-lived and merely a nuisance, but sometimes they are severe enough to disrupt normal functioning.

CAUSE

The leading theories of the cause of PMS are estrogen excess, progesterone deficiency, and decreased levels of the neurotransmitters (brain chemicals) dopamine and serotonin. These chemical changes are believed to lead to sodium and water retention, hypoglycemia, and other consequences that account for the symptoms of PMS.

TREATMENT AND PREVENTION

Reduce intake of salt and concentrated sugars to reduce water retention and symptoms of hypoglycemia.

Exercise regularly to improve the general sense of well-being and to decrease water retention.

Avoid excessive alcohol intake in the days before the period begins.

Take vitamin B-6 supplements every day. This is a controversial remedy because the doses reputed to be effective approach those that can cause severe neurological damage and which may be harmful to a fetus, should a woman be pregnant without knowing it. Doses up to 200 milligrams (100 times the RDA) are probably safe, but more should not be taken without consulting a physician. See p. 84 for other hazards.

Diuretics can help reduce water retention and bloating. The nonprescription diuretics in products for PMS are generally not strong enough to have much effect. If a diuretic is prescribed, be sure to follow instructions, especially those regarding diet; potassium depletion can lead to weakness and other symptoms. Keep in mind that withdrawal after regular heavy use of diuretics may cause rebound water retention, more diuretic use, and a vicious cycle.

Natural progesterone from plant sources, given by rectal or vaginal suppository for five days or so before the period, is widely used in England and claimed to be very effective, although carefully controlled studies to prove the treatment works have not been done. It has not been approved by the FDA, which considers the doses dangerously high, so be wary of progesterone suppositories sold in the United States; they may have been illegally manufactured.

Calcium supplementation for a week or so before menstruation is claimed by some to reduce symptoms, but this is questionable because blood and soft tissue levels of calcium are normally kept very constant by hormones.

Osteoporosis

Because it is common, costly, painful, crippling, and even lethal, osteoporosis demands very careful attention. It can occur in men, but for hormonal reasons it is much more common in women (other than blacks). Women should be aware of the problem and how to prevent it. See Part Four.

Ovarian Cysts

These are growths on the ovaries which can cause sharp abdominal pains, sometimes during intercourse, but which sometimes produce no symptoms. One type, the retention cysts, also called functional cysts, is associated with temporary disorders of the egg follicle, and they recede after one menstrual cycle. Other cysts do not, and some of these are malignant. In either case they must be surgically removed to keep them from growing to enormous size. If a cyst proves to be malignant, chemotherapy will probably also be necessary.

Polyps

Polyps are benign growths on stalks which develop on the cervix or within the uterus. The cause is unknown. The cervical type can cause bleeding

240 during intercourse, between periods, and after menopause, or they may cause no symptoms. The uterine polyps can cause excessive menstrual flow, irregular periods, and even infertility.

TREATMENT
Treatment, which is not necessary unless the polyps cause problems, consists of removal by dilation and curettage, a careful scraping.

Toxic Shock Syndrome

Any woman can suffer toxic shock syndrome, but the vast majority of cases are associated with tampon use during menstruation. Women who use tampons should be aware of the symptoms and know what to do if they occur. See Part Four.

Urinary Tract Infections

Bacterial infections of the bladder or urethra can occur in anyone, but for anatomic reasons they are much more common in women. Women should be aware of the symptoms and understand how the problems can be prevented and treated. See Part Four.

Vaginitis

Vaginitis, or inflammation of the vagina with itching, burning, and pain during intercourse, is often caused by the overgrowth of a fungus, *Candida albicans*, also known as *monilia*. Vaginitis can also be caused by *Trichomonas vaginalis* (protozoan flagellates) as well as *Chlamydia* and the bacterium *Gardnerella vaginalis*. These infections are discussed under Sexually Transmitted Diseases in Chapter 3–3. Here we discuss candida infections, sometimes called *yeast infections* because of the yeasty odor of the cottage-cheese-like discharge.

CAUSE
Normally, several different microorganisms inhabit the vagina and keep each other in check. But hormonal or acidity changes and other factors can kill off some of the organisms and encourage others, leading to an imbalance. Factors that can promote candida overgrowth include some antibiotics, oral contraceptives especially when first started, pregnancy, diabetes, and premenstrual hormonal changes. Also suspected are excessive douching, using

so-called feminine hygiene sprays, and wearing tight pants or underwear and wet swim suits.

TREATMENT

Mild cases of candida often resolve spontaneously, especially if the provoking factors are removed. A dilute vinegar douche (one tablespoon vinegar in a quart of water) may help in the very early stage of overgrowth but rarely once symptoms are severe.

Direct application of yogurt and lactobacillus culture are used by some on the theory that they will help restore the floral balance of the vagina. There have been reports of success, but clear proof is lacking. If attempted, clean, fresh, plain yogurt should be used.

The surest remedy is antifungal cream or tablets with nystatin or clotrimazole. These are very effective and safe.

PREVENTION

Candida can usually be prevented with simple precautions. Keep the vaginal area dry. Wipe after urination. Cotton underwear is preferable to synthetic since it promotes air circulation and dryness. Panties usually should not be worn to bed. Prescribed antibiotics should be taken strictly according to instructions and any sign of vaginitis associated with their use should discussed with your physician. If you use a diaphragm be sure it is clean. In chronic cases of monilia infection the diaphragm should be replaced or soaked in an antiseptic solution. Uncircumcised men should wash under their foreskin before intercourse.

Fertility Problems

Not all women in the usual child-bearing years can have children, and not all men are capable of fertile union. Moreover, some couples are infertile with each other although fertile with others. It appears that almost 15 percent of all young couples in the United States have fertility problems. Of these, about one-third can be traced to men, one-half to women and one-sixth to incompatibility between sperm and female fluids and tissues.

When we consider the complexity of the events that lead to fertilization, gestation, and birth, it is not surprising that things can go wrong. Both men and women must be sound anatomically and physiologically for everything to go smoothly. The man must produce an adequate amount of healthy semen and sperm, which must travel without obstruction or impediments through almost twenty feet of his tubes and a foot of hers to reach the egg; moreover, it must be chemically compatible with the woman.

The woman's ovaries must produce healthy eggs (about one a month) which are transported through the Fallopian tubes and, if fertilized,

242 implanted in the uterus. Hormones from the pituitary, ovaries, and uterus must work in concert to support the healthy development of the fetus until the birth of the child. There is a potential for problems at every step in this long process. Fertility specialists can often find the cause of the trouble and prescribe effective therapy. However, this can be time-consuming, inconvenient, unpleasant, and expensive, so couples should consider and try a number of simple remedies before seeking help.

REMEDIES WORTH TRYING

There are several simple things to try when there is no obvious problem such as infection or lack of periods. **The man** should avoid exposure to pesticides, marijuana, tobacco, and other unnecessary drugs, and eschew jockstraps, tight pants, frequent and prolonged baths, and other causes of overheated testes. If he works in a hot kitchen or factory he should wear the coolest possible clothes. He might increase his intake of vitamin C foods or even take supplements up to 500 mg per day for a couple weeks; the vitamin seems to decrease sperm agglutination (clumping). This is not likely to help men who have adequate vitamin C in their blood, but may benefit those who have been short-changed for months or years.

The woman should, of course, be having periods. Even so, she still may not be ovulating. She should take and faithfully record her basal temperature every morning for several months (before rising or being active) and determine whether the average increases by .5° to 1°F during the latter half. If it does not increase for several days in about the third week of the cycle, ovulation may not be occurring. She should also note the length of the second half of the cycle. If her temperature increases normally but her period starts within a week instead of two weeks of ovulation, she can suspect that her corpeus luteum (a part of the ovary) is not producing enough hormones. Making these observations before seeing a specialist can save time and money.

The woman should maintain good general health, avoid exposure to chemicals and drugs, and make sure she is not exercising or dieting so much that her periods stop. She should not use lubricating jelly before intercourse, and she should stay in bed for up to a half-hour afterwards and not douche. She can try a mild baking soda douche (one or two tablespoons per quart of water) before intercourse to counter semen that is possibly too acidic.

The couple should have intercourse several times a month on various days of her cycle for at least a year. Most women are fertile around midcycle, about fourteen days from the first day of each period. The couple should make sure ejaculation occurs deep in the vagina, which usually entails his being on top. They can try abstinence for four to seven days or for the first half of her cycle in order to increase his sperm concentration.

Seeking professional help. If a solid year of effort and home remedies does not bring results, a couple should carefully select a fertility specialist, based on advice from their family physician, her obstetrician, and friends who have been successfully treated. If possible, consult a physician who is certified by the American Board of Obstetrics and Gynecology as a specialist in fertility. They are usually associated with medical schools.

What to expect. Couples will be questioned about their sexual activity, its timing during her cycle, and their family and medical histories. She can expect a pelvic exam, Pap smear, tests for venereal disease, and basal temperature testing (if she has not already done it). Further tests are done to check the health and functioning of her reproduction organs. An endometrial biopsy (a painless scraping of the uterus lining) can help determine whether ovulation is taking place, whether hormone activity is normal, and whether infection is present. A histerosalpingogram (a dye and X-ray technique) and other methods can detect cysts, tumors, and scars in the tubes and uterus.

Men usually have their semen analyzed for normal volume and viscosity and for adequate numbers of healthy, motile sperm. If the count is low or the sperm are abnormal, a testicular biopsy (done under local anesthesia) may be indicated. A complete urological examination to detect diseases and abnormalities of the male reproductive system is routine.

The most common successful treatments are drugs, surgery, and artificial insemination. The most commonly used fertility drugs are clomiphene (Clomid) and a mixture of follicle-stimulating hormone and luteinizing hormone called Pergonal. These can stimulate ovulation in women with hormonal deficiencies that prevent normal cycles. They are best administered by very experienced specialists to increase the chances of success and decrease the probability of multiple births. In cases of corpus luteum insufficiency (above), vaginal progesterone suppositories used in the second half of the cycle may promote proper implantation of the fertilized egg. In cases of infections, antibiotics often restore fertility.

Surgery can remove scarring, adhesions, tumors, and other growths (see endometriosis, above) that block the tubes or uterus or interfere with their functions.

If the man is the source of the problem, there is usually a low concentration of sperm in his semen, and they may be weak or defective. Sometimes physical causes, such as diabetes,, varicose testicular veins, or bacterial infections can be found and treated.

If the woman is having abnormal immunological reactions against

244 her mate's sperm, it sometimes helps to use condoms for several months to drive down her concentration of antibodies, then to have intercourse without condoms around the middle of her cycle. If the man is reacting abnormally to his own sperm (autoimmunity) the hormones testosterone and corticosteroids may help.

Other options include artificial insemination, either with the partner's sperm or an anonymous donor's, and *in vitro* fertilization, in which an egg from the mother is fertilized with sperm in a laboratory, then reimplanted into her uterus.

4

Common Disorders— A Preventive Approach

PART FOUR

Introduction
Acne
AIDS
Allergies
Alzheimer's Disease
Anemia
Anorexia Nervosa
    and Bulimia
Appendicitis
Asthma
Atherosclerosis
Backaches
Boils
Bronchitis
Cancers
Chickenpox
Colds
Cold Sores
Constipation
Dental and Gum Disease
Diabetes
Diverticular Disease
Emphysema
Epilepsy
Fungus Infections
Gallstones
Gout
Headaches
Hearing Loss
Heart Disease
Hepatitis
Hernia
Hypertension
Hypoglycemia

Influenza
Insomnia
Kidney Disease
Kidney Stones
Malaria
Measles
Mental and Emotional
    Disturbances
Mononucleosis
Multiple Sclerosis
Mumps
Osteoarthritis
Osteoporosis
Peptic Ulcers
Pneumonia
Prostatitis
Psoriasis
Rabies
Rheumatoid Arthritis
Rubella
Scoliosis
Shingles
Sinusitis
Spastic Colon
Strep Throat
Strokes
Toxic Shock Syndrome
Tuberculosis
Ulcerative Colitis
Urinary Tract Infections
Varicose Veins
Vision Loss
Warts

Introduction

This part of the book is a primer of the most common and important diseases and disorders, those that almost everyone will encounter in themselves or in friends and relatives. A few less common disorders are also discussed because they are of special interest for various reasons. Rabies, for example, is not common in humans, but the animal reservoir of the disease is growing, control is getting more expensive, and public education can help reduce the risk and the cost. Note that some very common and important disorders such as sexually transmitted diseases and common female problems are discussed in Part Three.

The emphasis is on clear and simple explanations of the basis of each disorder so that the principles of prevention and treatment can be understood. As you peruse these pages, keep in mind that the power of suggestion can be great, and if you find yourself thinking you have symptoms of this or that disease remember that most students of medicine experience a phase of hypochondria that fades soon enough. Rather than attempt self-diagnosis (except for obvious problems like mild acne and constipation), use the symptoms guide to consulting a physician in Part Seven. Use this Part for general information on disorders and as a guide to personal and social preventive medicine.

248 Acne

In this disfiguring and distressing condition the openings of the sebaceous (oil producing) glands become plugged with enlarged dead cells. This traps the oil that normally covers the skin and protects it from drying out or becoming infected with certain fungi. As the oil accumulates the plug grows toward the skin surface. This whitehead, which becomes a blackhead from exposure to the air, is called a *comedo*. It cannot be washed off since it is slightly below the surface.

Often these comedos will ooze out without being noticed. But sometimes bacteria (*Corynebacterium acnes*) will break down the oil into free fatty acids that irritate the tissue and cause inflammation. This pimple is usually resolved by the body's defenses, or it drains and heals. But sometimes it grows, damages surrounding tissue, and results in permanent scarring.

Normal hormones, especially testosterone and progesterone, trigger acne development. Nothing can be done about this, but the aggravating factors can be minimized.

Keys to Control

Keep your face clean with two or three gentle washings a day using mild soap and warm water. Vigorous scrubbing can aggravate acne by injuring and plugging the drainage canals of the sebaceous glands. Soaking the face with a hot clean washcloth or steaming it with a pot of boiling water before washing may help.

Don't squeeze comedos. This can injure the skin and cause blemishes and scars. Sometimes mechanical comedo extractors are effective, but many brands are not. An experienced physician or nurse can advise on their selection and use, but in most cases they are not necessary. Pimples that have come to a head can be gently pressed after a hot compress.

Keep oily hair away from acne-prone skin. Cutting or restyling may be necessary. Greasy hair itself does not cause or aggravate acne, but the oil can be transferred to the face.

Avoid touching the affected areas. Habitual touching, rubbing, or resting the face on the hands can aggravate acne.

Avoid oily cosmetics, lotions, creams, and hair products. They can promote plugging of the openings. It has been estimated that half of all cosmetics are capable of provoking acne. Avoid harsh shampoos and keep all hair products away from the face.

Many drugs can cause and aggravate acne including the cortisone group, oral contraceptives (especially those with progesterone), dilantin, and amphetamines.

Diet has long been linked to acne in folklore. Oily foods, chocolate, nuts, cheeses, iodine, and sugar are most often blamed. The very word *comedo* is derive from the Latin word for glutton. Careful studies have thrown some doubt on these beliefs, but people do vary. If any food seems to aggravate the condition it can be avoided on a trial basis. (Most of us would do well to cut down on the suspected foods anyway.)

Do Supplements Help?

Zinc has been reported helpful in some cases, even for persons not helped by tetracycline.[1] A couple reports, even from reliable sources, are not proof, but there is no harm in trying this remedy. Fifty to 150 mg per day can be taken for two to three months. However, pregnant women should not take this much.

Vitamin B-6, up to 200 mg per day before and during menstruation, seems to help some women. Higher doses may be hazardous, may even cause nerve damage. See p. 84 for other cautions. There is no evidence that vitamin A is effective, and the large doses sometimes used are hazardous.

Acne Medicines

Many over-the-counter acne products are a waste of money, and those with a greasy base or salve can aggravate the problem. A few medicines can be helpful, especially if they have **benzoyl peroxide** which helps dry and peel the skin and decrease the population of the responsible bacteria. Always apply it to a thoroughly dry skin and carefully avoid the eyes, mouth, and nostrils. Start with a 5 percent gel once a day, then twice a day, then try a 10 percent gel. If your skin becomes irritated, go back to the 5 percent. The first week of use may result in a worsening condition, so be patient. Products containing **resorcinol** with sulfur can help, but they should be avoided by blacks since the chemical can discolor their skin.

Vitamin A acid, or **tretinoin,** available only by prescription, is very effective when used properly. Some experts consider it the most effective and underused of the acne medicines. The skin must be absolutely dry before applying, or the acid will penetrate too deeply and cause intense stinging and

250 irritation. The acne may seem worse after several weeks of treatment, but this is because the drying and peeling action of the acid has uncovered hidden comedos. Two or three months may be required, after which dramatic improvement can be expected.

CAUTION

Tretinoin increases susceptibility to sunburn and skin cancer, so if you go out in the sun use a sunscreen such as PABA and apply the acid only after sun exposure is over.

Several topical **antibiotics** are available by prescription. Oral antibiotics, especially tetracycline, can help in severe cases, but there are hazards such as stomach upset and vaginal yeast infections.

The most potent of all acne medicines appears to be a synthetic vitamin A relative called **isotretinoin** (Accutane). It can have very serious side effects including birth defects, visual problems, and excess calcium in the blood, which can damage the kidneys and other organs. It is reserved for severe cystic acne. Pregnant women must not take it. Users must not donate blood to blood banks.

AIDS

Acquired immune deficiency syndrome (AIDS) is a highly lethal disease first recognized in male homosexuals in 1979. Victims become vulnerable to rare cancers and to infections usually seen only in genetic immune deficiency or as a result of a steroid treatment to prevent rejection of a transplanted organ or chemotherapy for cancer.

More specifically, AIDS patients come down with severe cases of Pneumocystis carinii pneumonia (PCP), thrush (an oral fungus infection), virulent herpes which attacks internal organs, atypical tuberculosis, toxoplasmosis, and other infections which intact immune systems usually handle with ease. They are also prone to such cancers as Hodgkin's disease and other lymphomas, and Kaposi's sarcoma. The latter was, until recently, a mild skin cancer that affected mostly the elderly but is now aggressive and lethal in young AIDS patients.

While the number of cases of AIDS increased from a handful in 1979 to several thousand a few years later, the epidemic is not explosive as is often true with influenza or bubonic plague. Very few persons outside the clearly defined risk groups have contracted AIDS, and the risk for the general population is about zero, even if there is prolonged closeness with AIDS patients at work or in school.

The Risk Groups[2]

> Sexually active **homosexual or bisexual men with multiple partners;** the more partners, the greater the risk
>
> Present or past **abusers of intravenous drugs**
>
> **Sexual partners** (male or female, homosexual or heterosexual) of persons with AIDS
>
> **Sexual partners of any of the above** (though female to male transmission has occurred only rarely)
>
> **Hemophiliacs** who use a lot of blood products intravenously

Haitian entrants to the United States are often included on this list, but those stricken probably have one of the above risk factors.

CAUSE[3]

AIDS is caused by a type of human T-cell leukemia virus called HTLV-3, or simply the AIDS virus. This virulent speck of DNA and protein apparently destroys T-lymphocyte helper cells, blood cells that promote immune function. The victim is left highly vulnerable to ""opportunistic" infections and malignant disorders. (Similar viruses HTLV-1 and HTLV-2 stimulate excessive growth of the same cells and thereby cause leukemia.)

The virus is passed with blood among intravenous drug users and with semen in intimate sexual contact. In hemophilia drugs and sex are not the problem. Most "bleeders" now use a freeze-dried clotting agent called Factor VIII concentrate, which is mixed with water and injected to stop a bleeding episode. It works beautifully, but each dose is made from the pooled plasma of nearly 20,000 donors, which greatly increases the risk of exposure to infected plasma.

It is important to note that the national blood supply is not contaminated and blood transfusions are not risky. Unfortunately, ignorance and hysteria are so widespread that in some areas blood donations have fallen off severely because many people fear that giving blood somehow carries a risk of contracting AIDS. This is 100 percent false. Receiving blood is also very safe. More than 3 million transfusions are performed in the United States every year, and since 1979 only a dozen or so cases of AIDS have been linked to receiving blood. This is fewer than one in a million. Even so, efforts are underway to decrease the risk further.

TREATMENT

The treatment for AIDS depends on the specific infections or malignancies, and may include antibiotics, anticancer drugs, and interferon. Typically,

252 there will be a series of infections, a new one raging in as the old one subsides with treatment.

While each manifestation of the disease must be specifically treated as it occurs, two things can strengthen the body and the will to live, which may falter in those who are very sick and feel abandoned. One is proper nutrition. There is no special diet, but AIDS patients should be encouraged to eat nutritious, balanced meals to the extent possible. The other is emotional support. One of the worst things that can happen to an AIDS patient is to be shunned by friends and family. For this reason we emphasize that there is no danger in casual contact with an AIDS patient.

PREVENTION

Avoid promiscuous homosexual intimacy, intravenous drug abuse, and sex with people in the risk groups. Promiscuous homosexual males can greatly reduce their risk by limiting sexual activity to one person or a closed circle of healthy partners.

Members of AIDS risk groups should refrain from donating blood and plasma. Recently developed tests for AIDS virus markers are not adequate and decisions should not be based on them.

Those with risk factors and symptoms suggestive of early AIDS such as night fevers, persistant swollen lymph glands, and unexplained fatigue or weight loss should see a physician.

A vaccine is in the works and may be ready in a decade or so.

It should be noted that AIDS is not necessarily a homosexual disease but an epidemic among sexually promiscuous persons, so far mostly men. There is no reason why women should not also be affected, and some have been—apparently due to injecting drugs or to sexual contact with bisexual men who contracted the virus. Some experts fear the virus is essentially the same as the hepatitis B virus in its habits, including its transmission by saliva, and that it will sooner or later spill over into the general population. In Zaire AIDS appears to be a sexually transmitted disease much like any other, with no preference for male homosexuals, but probably a higher incidence in promiscuous persons.[4]

Allergies

An allergic reaction is an inappropriate response of the immune system that produces antibodies (proteins that bind to other molecules) against harmless substances. There are many types of antibodies and reactions, so allergies can involve the skin, the blood, the lungs, and other organs. Symptoms range in severity from mild hives to severe wheezing, cardiovascular collapse, and shock.

Adverse drugs reactions, lactose intolerance, and aversion to certain foods (common in children) should not be confused with true allergies.

The allergic person's body reacts to common harmless substances as if they were deadly microbes. The antibodies combine with the offending substance (antigen), and histamine and other chemicals are released into the tissues causing swelling, redness, itching, respiratory distress, or gastrointestinal symptoms.

The hereditary factor is strong; the predisposition to allergies in general (not specific allergies) tends to run in families. Emotional stress, tension, anxiety, and fatigue increase sensitivity. In some cases extreme temperatures may also predispose to attacks.

An allergy can usually be diagnosed by the symptoms, but identifying the culprits is often difficult and time-consuming. We know when we have hay fever, hives, or asthma, but we don't always know what triggers it. The methods used include a careful search for associations between symptoms and the environment, skin tests in which small amounts of suspected allergens are introduced into the skin, and the RAST (radioallergosorbant technique) test, which measures specific antibodies in the blood.

PREVENTING ALLERGIES (as opposed to preventing attacks in allergic persons)

Breast feeding for several months may help prevent allergies, especially food allergies, from developing. The lining of the newborn's digestive system is somewhat permeable to undigested proteins. When these are absorbed, whole antibodies may form and the body is then sensitized to the food. New foods should be introduced slowly, in small amounts, and not too early. Children of allergic parents should not be fed eggs, cow's milk, or other commonly allergenic foods, or be exposed to wool, fur, or feathers for the first year.[5] Care should be taken not to expose children to drugs in breast milk, especially if allergies run in the family. Breast-feeding mothers should avoid all unnecessary drugs.

Hay Fever

Also known as allergic rhinitis, hay fever, with sneezing, running nose, and itching eyes, nose, and ears, is brought on by contact with pollens of ragweed, grasses, and trees (especially deciduous, rarely evergreen), mold and fungus spores, house dust, and animal dander. Symptoms may also include headache, insomnia, loss of appetite, and fatigue as well as coughing and wheezing.

TREATMENT AND PREVENTION

Avoid allergens as much as possible. Knowing the seasonal variation of the symptoms and the pollination period of the local plants can help pin down the specific allergens and may help in avoiding them. Use air filters to keep

254 pollens, fungi, and molds out of the house. If a humidifier is used it should be regularly cleaned since it may harbor molds and spread their spores throughout the house. Control house dust with damp mopping and dusting; avoid sweeping and vacuuming. Get rid of, or avoid contact with, offending pets, feather pillows, wool rugs, and the like. Foam pillows and mattresses often contain traces of formaldehyde, which is an allergen to many people. Don't overlook gas leaks and fumes from stoves and furnaces.

Antihistamines can be very helpful but often cause drowsiness and other side effects that vary from person to person. Try several types until the one with the weakest side effects is found; start with a small dose and gradually increase it. See Chapter 5–1 for more on these drugs.

Nasal sprays with corticosteroids usually suppress symptoms within a few days and are a major advance in therapy. While systemic use of these drugs can be quite hazardous, so little is absorbed into the circulation from the nasal sprays that the risk is negligible.

Cromolyn sodium can help. See Asthma Drugs in Chapter 5–2.

Nasal and oral decongestants, on the other hand, are not very useful since they relieve only one symptom, stuffy nose, which is not the main complaint in hay fever. Frequent or prolonged use (more than three days) of the sprays can lead to rebound congestion—if you stop using them the stuffiness may be worse than when you started.

In some cases a large dose of **vitamin C** (500 milligrams or more) inhibits the constrictive effects of histamine on airways for several hours, and substantial relief may be obtained. It seems to work better for some than others, and if used for more than a few days can cause diarrhea and other side effects (see Chapter 2–7).

Skin tests and desensitization shots are often tried. Once the allergens are identified, increasing amounts of them are injected under the skin once or twice a week, sometimes for years. These procedures are time-consuming, expensive, and of dubious value in many cases. They seem to work better against allergies to plants than to animals.

Hives (Urticaria)

In hives the skin erupts into elevated, red, well-defined wheals with blanched centers. They usually itch intensely and last a few hours to several days, though they may last only a few minutes. Common causes are eggs, shellfish, mangos, strawberries, pork, tomatoes, and chocolate. Insect bites and viral and bacterial infections also can precipitate hives. Food additives, especially colorings and preservatives, can cause hives as well as other allergic reactions. In recognition of this, some countries require listing of all additives and their quantities on food labels. Common culprits include tartrazine (yellow dye #5) and the preservative sodium benzoate.

Emotional stress, heat, and cold can bring on attacks, and sun sensitivity causes hives in some.

Many drugs, including aspirin, can cause hives. Whenever this occurs, stop taking the drug at once and consult your physician.

TREATMENT AND PREVENTION
Avoid the allergen, expecially during stress or tension.

Oral antihistamines usually provide some relief. Avoid topical antihistamines, as allergic reactions to them may develop. In severe cases unresponsive to antihistamines, a few days of **corticosteroid** treatment prescribed by a physician usually suppresses the allergic reaction.

In a chronic case of unknown origin, a rigid **elimination diet** may help. The person fasts or goes on a basic hypoallergenic diet which eliminates all suspected foods. Then, one at a time, suspected foods are added and the reactions noted.

Other Food Allergies

Besides hives, food allergies may cause abdominal pain, nausea, vomiting, diarrhea, asthma, headaches, nasal congestion, canker sores, possibly bedwetting in children, and even anaphylactic shock, a life-threatening reaction with brochial spasms, suffocation, and unconsciousness. There is some evidence that food allergies may provoke rheumatoid arthritis flare-ups, but this is controversial and probably rare. Severe food allergies, especially when the allergen is unknown, can lead to anxiety about eating, loss of appetite, and consequent anemia, weight loss, and other signs of malnutrition.

Food allergies are most common in children and can lead to poor growth, fatigue, insomnia, poor school work, irritability, and difficulty getting along with others. An aversion to the more commonly allergenic foods such as milk and eggs is not necessarily a whim and should be taken seriously, especially if there is a family history of allergies, including asthma and hay fever. Fortunately, children tend to outgrow food allergies.

TREATMENT AND PREVENTION
The symptoms can usually be treated with oral **antihistamines** or **corticosteroids.**

The allergens may be identified by keeping a careful **diary** of foods

256 eaten and symptoms or by trial diets that eliminate suspected foods. **Avoid the allergen** if possible. This is often difficult because so many prepared foods have small amounts of eggs, milk, wheat, or other commonly allergenic foods. Additives may also be the source of the problem, so read labels.

Insecticide residues are sometimes to blame. This can be very difficult to recognize and deal with but, fortunately, seems to be rare.

Desensitization may help, but it is difficult and not always effective. One takes a very small amount of the food and gradually increases the amount until resistance is achieved or until it is clear resistance cannot be achieved. This should not be tried without consulting a physician.

Cytotoxic testing is a heavily promoted method of diagnosing food allergies and intertolerances. White blood cells are incubated with suspected antigens and changes in the cells are noted. The method is controversial because studies show it to be somewhere between worthless and slightly useful, yet clinics and labs that offer services directly to the public are popping up like mushrooms. Some of them make wild claims about diagnosing and curing many ailments and charge hundreds of dollars, yet escape all government regulation and licensing procedures by claiming to be simply providing nutrition counseling. We suggest you avoid cytotoxic testing clinics unless referred by a physician to one with proven effective techniques and reasonable cost. (We say this in case accurate cytotoxic methods are developed; there are none as we go to press.)

Drug Allergies

Allergies can be caused by any drug, but they are more likely with some than others. For example, penicillin and phenylbutazone are more commonly allergenic than digitalis or tetracycline. A reaction can be immediate, producing hives, fever, or severe anaphylaxis with wheezing, pallor, low blood pressure, stupor, coma, and even death; or it may become apparent only after weeks or months of using a drug. Allergies to some drugs (such as quinine and sulfas) cause destruction of red blood cells. The reaction usually subsides promptly after the drug is withdrawn but sometimes lasts for weeks or months.

Drug reactions may follow eating foods, especially meat or milk, contaminated with drugs such as penicillin. Sometimes the first medical dose causes a reaction, the person having been previously exposed to the drug in his food and thereby sensitized to it.

TREATMENT AND PREVENTION
Immediate injection of epinephrine is the treatment of choice in severe cases. Oral antihistamines and corticosteroids help control prolonged reactions. Of course, the offending drug must be withdrawn.

Persons with any allergies or even **family history** of allergies should always mention the fact to doctors and nurses treating them.

Contact Dermatitis

In this type of allergy inflammation with itching and burning occurs where the offending substance touches the skin. To test a suspected allergen, put a little on the skin and cover it with a bandage. Check it in a day or two for a small rash. Poison oak and ivy reactions are common and typical examples.

TREATMENT AND PREVENTION
Wash the affected area thoroughly to remove the allergen, being careful not to spread it to other parts of the body.

Herbalists recommend jewelweed juice, plantain, aloe vera, and goldenseal to soothe the itching and dry up the blisters of poison oak and ivy. They are harmless but not proven effective.

The widely used industrial chemical hexavalent **chromium** often causes severe contact dermatitis. A 10 percent vitamin C solution, swabbed on and blotted dry, can nearly eliminate the reaction even if contact with the chemical is continued.

Avoid the offending substance. Poison oak and ivy are almost universal allergens. Others are not so obvious, and alertness is often required to determine the cause of the problem. Common offenders include hair dyes, curling chemicals and rinses, soaps, detergents, shampoos, cosmetics, toothpastes, mouthwashes, nail polishes, perfumes, insect sprays, nasal sprays, furs, leather, fabrics, condoms, douches, toilet paper, antiperspirants, deodorants, lipsticks, rectal suppositories, spectacle frames, hair brush bristles, shoes, socks, and various metals and plastics such as nickel, earrings, wristwatches, telephones, and ballpoint pens.

Eczema (Atopic Dermatitis)

Eczema is an allergic condition with dry, itching skin. In chronic cases with frequent scratching the skin weeps and may become infected; it may eventually become thickened and rough.

Eczema runs in families with hay fever and asthma and can be aggravated by emotional stress, sweating, infection, and food allergies. Common sites in infants and children are the cheeks, arms, and legs. Adults have more trouble with their hands, especially if they are often wet; this removes natural oils and drys out the skin.

258 TREATMENT AND PREVENTION

Those susceptible to eczema may be helped by the following measures.

Avoid dressing too warmly, which causes sweating and may aggravate itching. Wool clothing should be avoided.

Avoid bathing with soap and water, which tends to dry the skin. Look for cleansers with **cetyl alcohol.**

Avoid oily creams, which may increase sweat retention and itching.

Use **aspirin** to relieve severe itching, but use it sparingly to prevent side effects.

Prescription **steroid creams** can relieve severe itching, but a physician's supervision is necessary to prevent thinning of the skin.

If food allergies are suspected, try an **elimination diet** (see food allergies, above).

Reduction of emotional stress is sometimes the most important remedy.

Insect Sting Allergies

Severe allergic reactions to the venom of *Hymenoptera* insects (bee, wasp, yellow jacket, hornet) can cause shortness of breath, heart palpitations, wheezing, coughing, anaphylactic shock, and death. Mild reactions involve swelling and tenderness or numbness of the area around the sting.

TREATMENT AND PREVENTION

The **stinger should be removed** and the victim should not move about since muscular activity increases absorption of the venom. If it's necessary to go for help, walk, don't run. But it's better to sit still while being taken to a physician.

If possible, a **tourniquet** (no longer than fifteen minutes) or **cold compress** or both should be applied to slow absorption. **Epinephrine** should be given subcutaneously, or if the victim is already in shock, intravenously. Anyone with this very serious allergy should get a kit with epinephrine or a similar drug; ask your physician.

If you ever have a very serious reaction to an insect sting, with unusual swelling, pain, sweating, nausea and weakness, BEWARE! The next time could be worse. See an allergist. Hyposensitization treatments are often effective and could save your life.

Alzheimer's Disease

This is the most common cause of dementia (loss of mental capacity) in persons over fifty and one of the top four or five contributing causes of death in the United States. Victims may also be under fifty. Any and all of the typical signs and symptoms of dementia may occur, starting gradually with slight impairment of recent memory, learning, and problem solving. Early signs may go unnoticed as habits sustain social behavior, but eventually the mental deficiency is obvious to all. The person becomes slow, sloppy, and confused, and has difficulty with complex tasks and unfamiliar situations.

The difficulties often cause angry and frustrated emotional outbursts. There is frequently depression, apathy, anxiety, a loss of liveliness, and sometimes delusions and hallucinations. In the late stages of severe cases all mental powers are lost, and the patient does not even know where or who he—or more likely she—is. He or she may suffer seizures and become totally bedridden and dependent on nursing care. Death—due to infections, malnutrion, and other complications of being bedridden—can come within ten years of the onset of severe Alzheimer's. In some cases, however, the dementia is relatively mild and survival much longer.

Diagnosis is generally by exclusion of other causes of the symptoms, such as vitamin B-12 deficiency, severe depression, and syphilis. This is very important because other causes are often curable, whereas there is no effective treatment for Alzheimer's disease.

CAUSE[6,7,8]

There is some question about whether there is an actual loss of brain cells beyond that normally associated with aging. Results from autopsies vary and computerized tomography (a special X-ray technique) of patients does not invariably show shrinkage of brain tissue. But there is no question that there are serious disruptions in the structural and functional connections between the brain cells. Microscopic studies reveal characteristic "neurofibril tangles" and "senile plaques," both apparently signs of damaged and destroyed dendrites and synapses, structures essential to the communication between brain cells (neurons).

The damage seems especially severe to the neurons of the cholinergic system, that is, the areas and cells of the brain that communicate using the neurotransmitter acetylcholine. But some studies indicate that several neurotransmitters may be involved, which could severely complicate the problems of treatment and prevention.

What causes the damage to the cells and their biochemical functions is the subject of intense research and debate. The leading theories are discussed below. Whatever turns out to be the immediate cause or causes,

260 there is strong evidence that the disease tends to run in families. For example, in one study of 125 autopsy-proven cases of Alzheimer's, 40 percent had relatives with the disease. Also, the incidence of Down's syndrome is increased in Alzheimer families, and Down's patients who survive to middle age often develop brain damage identical to that of Alzheimer patients.

It may be that **genetic factors** make some people more susceptible to the immediate cause or causes. There may actually be more than one disease, with different causes in different persons. On the other hand, more than one cause may be involved in the disease in a given patient. For example, perhaps a genetic defect leads to susceptibility to a virus that induces abnormal immune processes, which damage the brain's ability to keep aluminum out of the cells, which leads to the cellular damage and all the symptoms.

A virus is suspected because it has been established that diseases with similar symptoms and brain changes are caused by slow viruses. Examples include kuru, once common in brain-eating cannibals, and scrapie in sheep. There are also reports that extracts of the brains of Alzheimer's patients have caused brain degeneration in chimps, but other researchers have not confirmed this effect. Such transmission would be difficult to prove because the virus may have a very long latent period, perhaps up to thirty years.

An autoimmune disorder, that is, an abnormal immune response that triggers antibodies to attack brain cells, is supported by the finding of brain-active antibodies in Alzheimer patients.

Aluminum toxicity was first suspected when it was found that kidney dialysis patients who got lots of aluminum from the large volumes of water used to flush wastes from the blood, and from aluminum-containing antacids, often developed a severe dementia leading to helplessness and death. The problem has been alleviated by the use of aluminum-free water. Then autopsy showed that Alzheimer patients generally have far more aluminum in their brains than others.

Animal studies have added to the evidence against aluminum. For example, aluminum injected into cats' brains results in behavioral changes similar to some symptoms of Alzheimer's disease, and aluminum fed to rabbits causes similar brain damage.

If aluminum is involved, it is not simply a matter of exposure or ingestion. Alzheimer patients do not have higher intakes or blood levels of the metal than normal people. But they may have a deficiency in the transport system of the brain cells that normally keeps aluminum out. The accumulation of the metal in the neurons could lead to malfunctions such as decreased production of acetylcholine.

TREATMENT

All complicating symptoms and health problems such as nutritional deficiencies, infections, dehydration, and congestive heart failure need to be
effectively treated since they can make the mental condition much worse and
accelerate deterioration.

Tranquilizers, antidepressants, antibiotics, and other drugs are
sometimes essential, but their use and dosages must be strictly minimized to
the extent possible because Alzheimer patients are often much more susceptible to drug toxicity, which can severely increase the symptoms.

Because the patients are often confused and afraid, family members and health professionals involved in their care must be supportive and
accepting, and must take the time again and again to explain and reassure.
Familiar, pleasant surroundings should be maintained as far as possible.
Obligations and pressures to perform and produce must be minimized in
order to minimize confusion, frustration, and emotional outbursts.

More specific treatments, such as those discussed below, are based
on unproven theories and are *strictly experimental*. They may go the way of
discredited treatments such as hyperbaric oxygen, or they may prove helpful;
but unwarranted hope must not be entertained.

Lecithin, which provides the vitamin choline, an essential precursor for the
production of acetylcholine in the brain, is sometimes given in an effort to
boost the brain levels of the neurotransmitter. Physostigmine, a drug that
inhibits the breakdown of acetylcholine, is given for the same reason.

Arginine vasopressin is a neuropeptide, a chain of amino acids with hormonelike activity in the brain. It has been reported to help memory and
learning in some Alzheimer patients.

Aluminum reduction is the goal of some therapy, and this involves reducing
intake as well as removing what's already there. The main sources to avoid
are medicines (antacids, buffered aspirin, hemorrhoid preparations, antiperspirants), foods (leavening agents, baking powders, cake mixes, processed
cheese, nondairy creamers, noncaking table salt, and some city water supplies.

Partial removal of the metal from the body can be achieved with
regular doses of sodium fluoride, which chelates aluminum and carries it out
of the body. The drugs deferoxamine and EDTA are also used.

PREVENTION

Until the cause is found there can be no certain preventive measures. However, it would not hurt and it may eventually prove helpful to minimize
aluminum intake. After all, the metal has no function in the body, and large
amounts are known to be toxic to the brain. About 10 to 20 percent of

262 ingested aluminum is absorbed into the blood. A typical daily intake from all sources is about 10 mg but it can reach 2,000. If Alzheimer's disease has occurred in a blood relative, it would seem prudent to restrict aluminum intake to the lower levels. The most important sources to avoid would be antacids that contain aluminum, powdered foods (read labels), and processed cheese. Pots, pans, and beverage cans are a relatively minor source of aluminum in the diet.

If a middle-aged or elderly relative shows obvious signs of reduced mental capacity such as inability to dress him- or herself, carry on a rational conversation, or do simple arithmetic, take him or her to a neurologist, preferably one recommended by your personal internist or family physician.

Anemia

Anemia is a condition of insufficient red blood cells or hemoglobin, which can cause fatigue, weakness, a tendency to fainting, decreased libido, headache, irritability, pallor, shortness of breath, amenorrhea, and other symptoms. Fatigue is usually the earliest, with others appearing as the anemia worsens.

Anemia may be due to blood loss, increased red-cell destruction, or decreased red-cell formation. Each of these has many possible causes, so anemias take many forms, each with a different treatment.

The anemias discussed below are the most common ones. Because of the complexity, the many possible causes, and the necessity of precise treatment, it is important not to try to diagnose and treat oneself.

Iron-deficiency Anemia

The body must have adequate iron for the formation of hemoglobin and red blood cells. Small amounts of iron are normally lost in the urine, sweat, and feces and replaced in the diet. Almost all iron-deficiency anemia in adults is due to loss of blood. A large loss due to trauma or hemorrhage, or a regular, small loss from an ulcer, hemorrhoids, or heavy menstrual flow can lead to anemia, especially if the iron intake is low.

Other causes include repeated pregnancies, chronic diarrhea, malabsorption disease, regular aspirin use, intestinal tumors, diverticuli, excessive blood donations, and excessive exercise (see Chapter 1–6).

TREATMENT

The cause of the iron loss must be determined and dealt with, and the lost iron replaced. Iron-rich foods could be used, but supplements assure faster recovery. The most effective oral supplements are ferrous sulfate, ferrous gluconate, ferrous succinate, and ferrous citrate. If absorption is poor due to intestinal disease, injections may be used, but they are painful and potentially hazardous.

PREVENTION

Prevent or treat all causes of blood loss, such as hemorrhoids, ulcers, chronic diarrhea, and heavy menstrual flow (more than twenty tampons per period); some people have to avoid aspirin.

Be sure to get enough **iron.** It is widely distributed in foods, and a varied diet assures enough for most people. Red meat, especially liver, is the most abundant source, but green vegetables, sweet potatoes, nuts and seeds, beans, and fruits such as apricots, prunes, figs, and raisins are also excellent sources. For example, a half-cup of spinach plus a half-cup of peas have more iron than a large hamburger.

The persons most at risk are women of child-bearing age. If calories are being restricted in order to lose weight, a supplement is advisable. **Infants and young children** are also at high risk because of their rapid growth and because milk is a poor source of iron. **Vegetarians** need to be more careful than meat eaters.

Pernicious Anemia

In addition to the usual signs of anemia, pernicious anemia causes a loss of appetite, a smooth, sore tongue, and neurological symptoms such as "pins and needles" in the feet, memory defects, and even psychosis. It is important that these symptoms be recognized and treated early or they may not be reversible.

Vitamin B-12 is necessary for the manufacture of red blood cells in the bone marrow. Dietary deficiency is very rare, but some people lack a substance called *intrinsic factor* which is required for B-12 absorption. This deficiency, which rarely occurs before age thirty-five, is apparently genetically determined. It is much more common in persons of English, Irish, and Scandinavian descent, and is very rare in Orientals. It can also be acquired by gastric or intestinal surgery.

TREATMENT

Vitamin B-12 injections, once a week at first then once a month for life, prevent anemia and nervous system degeneration and all their complications. Very large oral doses may be adequate for some.

264 Folate-deficiency Anemia

Folic acid, a B vitamin, is required for the manufacture of red blood cells; without it, anemia occurs. The most common cause is inadequate diet, especially in connection with alcoholism and pregnancy which greatly increase the folate requirement. If the pregnancy involves twins, the requirement is greater still.

Those with sprue or malabsorption often develop anemia from folate deficiency; though it may be ingested, it does not get into the blood. Sometimes persons with epilepsy develop this anemia because their anticonvulsants increase the folate requirement.

TREATMENT

Folic acid supplements, about 1 to 5 mg per day, bring the blood back to normal. In sprue or malabsorption syndrome, injections may be necessary. Because folic acid can mask neurological symptoms of pernicious anemia, proper diagnosis is critical; **self-treatment of suspected anemia with folate is not recommended.**

PREVENTION

Eat two or more servings of food with folic acid every day. Good sources are raw leafy vegetables, fresh asparagus, broccoli, oranges, nuts, and, best of all, wheat germ, and brewer's yeast. Cooking and canning destroy folic acid, so eat fresh, raw foods.

Aplastic Anemia

In this very serious condition the blood-forming cells of the bone marrow are damaged, so red cells, white cells, and platelets are reduced; anemia is accompanied by reduced resistance to infection and a tendency to bleeding.

The damage to the cells in the bone marrow may be caused by many different drugs and chemicals, including phenylbutazone, chloramphenicol, cancer chemotheraphy, benzene, hair dyes, and insecticides, and by excessive radiation and sometimes viral and bacterial infections.

TREATMENT

Exposure to all suspected medications and chemicals must be stopped. Transfusions may be necessary. Infections and bleeding must be treated vigorously.

PREVENTION

Avoid unnecessary exposure to **drugs** and **chemicals,** especially those known to be capable of depressing marrow function.

Acquired Hemolytic Anemia

In this case the anemia is due to destruction of red blood cells (hemolysis). In addition to the common symptoms, there is usually some jaundice because the hemoglobin of the destroyed cells is converted to yellowish pigments.

Various industrial poisons and drugs and even some plants may be responsible. Aniline, lead, snake venom, sulfonamides, quinine, castor beans, and fava beans are capable of causing hemolysis in sensitive persons. This may be why Pythagoras, the ancient philosopher and mathematician, forbade his followers to eat beans. Malaria, various bacterial infections, enlarged spleen, and some cancers can also cause this form of anemia.

TREATMENT

Therapy depends on the exact cause but usually includes transfusions of red cells and corticosteroids to slow or stop the hemolysis.

PREVENTION

Avoid unnecessary exposure to drugs and chemicals. A large number of blacks, Orientals, and Mediterranean and Middle Eastern people are deficient in red-cell enzyme, glucose-6-phosphate dehydrogenase. They should be very careful about taking any drugs since many (including sulfa drugs, megadoses of vitamin C, and antimalarial drugs) may cause red-cell destruction. Screening tests are available and should be used on persons from susceptible populations before suspect drugs are given. Some of these people must avoid fava beans and pollen, whose natural chemicals can cause mild to severe hemolysis.

Sickle-Cell Anemia

This is a hereditary hemolytic anemia with abnormal red cells and inefficient hemoglobin. It affects those with two genes for the trait, about one in 500 blacks in the United States. It causes recurrent attacks of fever and pain in the arms, legs, and abdomen. In crises, symptoms are treated and transfusion is usually necessary. The disease is often fatal.

Sickle-cell carriers (about one in ten blacks), those with only one gene for the trait, are usually healthy, but anoxic stress (high altitudes, overexercise) may cause severe illness since half the red cells are abnormal. It is believed that the sickle-cell gene is prevalent in some areas because the trait confers resistance to malaria. This protection for the many (the sickle-cell carriers) comes at the cost of severe illness (sickle-cell anemia) in about 2 percent of them.

266 PREVENTION

Carriers of the gene may want genetic counseling to weigh the risk of having affected children. Marriage to other carriers will be risky. In early pregnancy amniocentesis can determine whether the fetus is effected.

Anorexia
Nervosa and Bulimia

Anorexia nervosa is a puzzling and stubborn eating disorder which seems to defy logic and understanding. Normal, successful young people (about 90 percent females) develop an obsession with their weight, dieting, and often exercise. They frequently use laxatives, diuretics, and enemas to increase the appearance of thinness. They are afraid of food and eating and become prisoners of eating-related activities and thoughts, compulsive rituals, and endless planning designed to rigidly control and minimize food intake. Many end up looking like starvation victims, all the while denying that they are unusually thin.

More than 95 percent of anorexics are white North Americans, Western Europeans, or Australians mostly between thirteen and twenty-two, although the condition may begin at practically any age over ten. Two stressful growing-up milestones tend to trigger it: the onset of menses and graduation from high school.

Because of the compulsive rituals (such as precisely cutting food into tiny pieces) and the necessity of being in complete control of food preparation and intake, eating becomes a private affair. Social contact is shunned because it tends to encourage eating. So the anorexic becomes reclusive at an age when social contacts and skill are normally expanding. Her sexuality quotient is low and she shies away from intimacy. A sense of inferiority and inadequacy is common, and in chronic cases severe depression can be a serious complication, often leading to suicide.

The anorexic is often too deluded and confused to understand the gravity of her situation. The obsession with thinness, the fear of eating, and the delusional thinking about her "fatness" are the prominent psychological features. The physical consequences generally include significant weight loss, decreased body temperature, lowered blood pressure, slower pulse, loss of menstrual periods, shrinking breasts, thinning hair, constipation, dry skin, and excessive growth of downy body hair.

The condition may last for a few months or it may wax and wane for years. Death is a frequent outcome; estimates range as high as 5,000 a year in the United States, perhaps 10 percent of the cases. Many survivors suffer years of weakness and sickness due to starvation-induced damage, often to the liver, kidneys, and heart. Diabetics are especially vulnerable to serious harm.

CAUSE[9]

The epidemiology of anorexia nervosa strongly suggests that it is associated with, and largely a result of, the **cult of thinness** which began in the 1960s. A generation of American, European, and Australian women has been indoctrinated by the fashion industry, and now there is an epidemic. Another theory is that the young woman fears her physical maturation and emerging sexuality so much that she starves away her breasts, hips, and menstrual periods.

Since most girls and women do not become anorexic, some must be more susceptible than others. Their psychological profile includes insecurity, a sense of powerlessness and inferiority (often in spite of high achievement), a lack of spontaneity, rigidity and extremity in behavior with no appreciation of moderation, and general immaturity. There is often little positive feedback or affection from the parents, especially the father, who tends to be cold and aloof.

The cult of thinness provides the person with an opportunity for precise self-control of her behavior as well as extreme achievement. She sees reducing as a form of competition she can win and as an attention-getting device.

TREATMENT

There are two goals here, first of all to save the anorexic's life; and in the long run to cure her of her delusional affliction, usually a slow process. This calls for a physician to work with a psychotherapist.

Severe cases often require long-term hospitalization. The patient often must be fed through a tube inserted through the nose and into the stomach. In extreme cases total parenteral nutrition may be required to save the patient's life. This involves inserting a tube into a vein in the chest and pumping in nutrients.

The psychotherapy can be long and difficult. It is too soon to conclude that a specific approach will or should become standard treatment, but one widely used, often successful method stresses a nurturing, authoritative, non-neutral but friendly posture toward the patient.[10] She is repeatedly reminded of the seriousness of her condition and encouraged to face reality and give up her delusions; yet there is always empathy and consideration for the real fears of the anorexic. Strong rapport and trust are developed, hopefully leading to self-trust, self-esteem, growth, and maturity. The barrier and habit of solitude are broken. Group sessions with family members and with other anorexics often help achieve these ends.

PREVENTION

Our concept of beauty changes with the times. The pendulum seems to be swinging away from the ultra-thin look to a more robust, athletic look, and this is encouraging.

Biology classes at the intermediate and high school levels should emphasize human physiology and anatomy, and include discussions of the functions of normal fat: keeping the body warm, providing a padding for sitting and lying, and helping keep women fertile by playing a role in estrogen storage and activation.

Good parenting can help. Firm, intelligent guidance and lots of affection and positive strokes can help children develop a sense of security, self-esteem, and confidence. Fathers should continue healthy expressions of affection as their daughters mature.

Parents of adolescent girls should be able to **recognize the early signs** of anorexia nervosa and quickly take steps, preferably with professional guidance, to meet the problem before it becomes entrenched. Some signs to watch for are dieting and fasting, excessive concern with bodily appearance and thinness, refusal to eat with the family, social isolation, a sense of inadequacy, and the use of diuretics and laxatives.

Bulimia

Persons afflicted with this eating disorder indulge in truly enormous binges of overeating (bulimia) and vomiting. For most people an average meal is about 1,000 calories. Bulimics consume anywhere from 2,000 to 50,000 calories in one session of a few hours. It may be vomited in several episodes or all at once when the eating binge is over. The amount of food eaten and retained is variable, so bulimics may be emaciated or normal in weight.

The frequent vomiting can cause severe acid burns to the esophagus, gum recession, and dissolution of the enamel of the teeth, leading to rampant tooth decay. It can also cause chloride and potassium deficiencies, which can lead to heart arrhythmias and heart damage. Moreover, the problem can become very time-consuming and, because of the large quantities of food eaten, very expensive. Shop-lifting is often resorted to. Bulimia can be as serious as anorexia and sometimes alternates with it. Compared to other anorexics, the bulimic type are generally more socially mature and sexually active. They often smoke, drink, experiment with drugs, and show other signs of addictive behavior.

Bulimia can also occur without anorexia. In this case there is no loss of appetite or fear of food and frequently no personality disorder. But there is much overeating and vomiting. The latter often starts casually as a diet substitute and continues as the person becomes addicted to the sensuous muscular convulsions. The body's satiety mechanisms become disordered and ever larger meals are required for satisfaction. These lead to more vomiting, and so on.

Like anorexia nervosa, bulimic disorders generally call for extensive psychotherapy, and sometimes hospitalization with supervision to prevent vomiting.

Appendicitis

The appendix is a hollow, dead-end structure two to three inches long at the juncture of the small and large intestines. If it becomes infected and inflamed, severe abdominal pain is felt, especially below and to the right of the navel. Nausea, vomiting, constipation, and slight fever usually occur. The appendix may rupture and release bacteria and their poisons into the abdominal cavity. This is called peritonitis and is extremely serious.

CAUSE

In appendicitis the opening into the appendix is obstructed by a fecalith (a stone crystalized in the intestine), a foreign body, a neoplasm, parasites, or perhaps inflammation due to viral infection. The swelling blocks blood flow in the appendix, resulting in stasis and gangrene. If untreated, swelling continues until the wall of the appendix bursts.

TREATMENT

Consult a physician if severe abdominal pain lasts two or three hours. Surgical removal of the appendix before it bursts is critical. To prevent rupture, don't take laxatives or enemas, or apply heat to the abdomen. Don't eat or drink anything. If the appendix does rupture, surgery must be postponed for several days of bed rest, antibiotic treatment, and intravenous feedings.

PREVENTION

High fiber diets may decrease the incidence of fecaliths and thereby reduce the possibility of appendicitis.

Removal of the appendix would, of course, prevent appendicitis, but this is major surgery and is not recommended unless a person is having abdominal surgery for some other reason and appendectomy would not add risk to that procedure.

270 Asthma

An asthma attack occurs when the soft muscular walls of the bronchial airways go into constrictive spasms and the delicate lining of the walls (the mucosa) swells and pours mucus into the airways. The mucus sometimes hardens into plugs that block the tubes. Breathing is difficult and loud. Attacks vary in severity and may last minutes, hours, or days. Extreme attacks can end in death.

Many children who have asthma outgrow it by late adolescence. A few continue to suffer attacks throughout life, particularly if they had eczema in infancy. Adult-onset asthma also tends to improve with age, but sometimes it becomes chronic, and bronchitis develops (see Bronchitis). Unless such complications develop, asthmatics are not sick or incapacitated except during an attack.

CAUSE

Most asthma has an allergic basis, and the bronchial airways are hyperreactive to a wide variety of irritants that cause them to constrict. In the most common type of asthma, the antigen (offending substance) combines with the antibodies on the surface of the bronchial *mast cells*, causing them to release *spasmogens* such as histamine, which prompt the bronchial muscle spasms and mucus production. Physical exertion, respiratory infections, and emotional stress or excitement can precipitate attacks by increasing the hypersensitivity of the bronchi.

Common allergens are grass and tree pollen, mold spores, fungi, animal feces, house dust (including insect fragments and feces, and entire tiny insects), and industrial and household chemicals. Even ocean spray can trigger attacks. The offending substance can often be recognized because of the immediacy of the reaction, especially in young people; but sometimes the allergen is not obvious, especially in adults.

Attacks are sometimes caused by foods such as eggs, chocolate, shellfish, oranges, milk, and cereal grains. However, this is not common, and such foods are more likely to cause hives or gastrointestinal symptoms for people allergic to them. Aspirin, penicillin, and other drugs can precipitate attacks in sensitive persons.

Some asthmatics are sensitive to sharp changes in temperature, air pressure, and perhaps even ion levels, which may trigger attacks (ions are electrically charged particles in the air).

Susceptibility to asthma runs in families. If both parents have asthma or many allergies their children have about a 50 percent chance of developing asthma.

TREATMENT

All known allergens should be removed from the person's vicinity, and he should try to rest and stay calm. Children should be comforted and reassured.

Attacks can usually be aborted by promptly inhaling bronchodilator aerosols, which relax the bronchial muscles. Other drugs are taken more or less continuously to prevent attacks (see Chapter 5–2). Your physician will determine which is best for you. It is important that they be used correctly for the most benefit with the least side effects. It is not a good idea to treat yourself with nonprescription asthma drugs (see Chapter 5–1).

In severe cases doctors often turn to cortisone-type drugs to suppress the allergic reaction. They are usually quite effective, but long-term therapy is fraught with dangers including addiction, growth suppression, increased susceptibility to infections, impaired wound healing, skin problems, and psychological disturbances. A major advance is the development of cortisone aerosols, which act directly on the airways and minimize systemic effects of the drug.

Attacks are often preceded by a runny nose and coughing. Antihistamines are sometimes used to relieve these symptoms, but they may cause drowsiness. Vitamin C in large doses (up to half a gram an hour during an attack) has an antihistamine effect without causing drowsiness, but it can cause diarrhea and other problems. Vitamin B-6 taken in large doses for several weeks has been reported to decrease the frequency and severity of attacks in children with severe asthma, but it is potentially hazardous. See Chapter 2–7 for more on the hazards of megavitamins.

Herbalists often recommend desert tea (ephedra), which contains ephedrine, an adrenaline-like substance that reduces the bronchial spasms. However the dose is unpredictable, and more effective remedies are available. Teas and herbal vapor baths of pleurisy root, mullein, and elecampane are sometimes recommended by herbalists to help loosen mucus and ease cough.

PREVENTING ASTHMA ATTACKS

Don't smoke. Avoid air pollution.

Avoid irritants. Reduce house dust, especially in the bedroom. Control home ventilation to reduce pollens. Avoid chemical fumes, fresh paint, hair sprays, pets and their hairs, feathers and dander, and animal hair and feathers in pillows and furniture.

Keep home humidity around 50 percent and the air not too cool. Always keep warm. Dress well from head to toe in the cold and try not to breath cold air.

272 **Eat moderately,** slowly, and never just before going to bed; digestive disturbances increase the likelihood of an attack. Eat balanced, nutritious meals to help maintain resistance to infections.

Avoid aspirin if you are intolerant; it causes attacks in about a fifth of all asthmatics.

Avoid excessive emotional stress and overexcitement. Anger can provoke an attack, so parents of asthmatic children must delicately balance firmness and leniency. Relaxation treatment with biofeedback may be helpful. In one study twenty-two asthmatic children were taught to be aware of facial tension with the aid of biofeedback. They learned to relax and suffered fewer and milder attacks than the controls. Relaxation training through hypnosis has also been reported helpful. (See Part Six for a detailed look at hypnosis.)

Exercise programs may help increase breathing efficiency by building up the diaphragm and other breathing muscles. Deep breathing with complete exhalation lets stale air out of the lower lungs and loosens and strengthens breathing muscles. Whistling and blowing bits of paper across a table are often recommended. The yogic "cleansing breath" has similar effects. (See Part Six for more on yoga.)

Playing a wind instrument such as a clarinet, recorder, flute, trumpet, or tuba is among the most beneficial of the exercises. This can increase vital capacity, improve lung function, and help promote relaxation. Perhaps most important, especially for child asthmatics, is the psychological benefit of being active, normal, and "included."

General exercise can also be helpful, but strenuous activity for too long can provoke an attack in some, including a few nonasthmatics. The ideal activity is moderate, and vigorous only in short spurts up to two or three minutes. Hiking, baseball, and swimming are generally better than basketball, tennis, or marathon running, though the latter are certainly not ruled out.

Skin testing and **desensitization shots** are sometimes recommended. This may help, but the expense, discomfort, and frequency of error make it a questionable procedure for many. The shots are generally more successful against allergies to plants than to animals.

Some writers have recommended bee pollen and honey for controlling asthma and hay fever. There is no evidence for this and it does not make much theoretical sense; pollen allergies usually involve the windblown pollens of drab-colored flowers, not the bee-carried pollens of colorful flowers. In any case, consuming allergens can be dangerous.

PREVENTING ASTHMA

Breast feeding for at least four to six months may help prevent asthma itself, as opposed to preventing asthma attacks. Breast-fed children are less likely to develop allergies. New foods should be introduced in small amounts, slowly and not too early. Children of allergic parents should not be fed eggs or other commonly allergenic foods, or exposed to wool, fur, or feathers for the first year. Minimizing exposure to dust, smoke, and fumes may also help.

Atherosclerosis

Atherosclerosis, the presence of atheromas (fatty streaks and plaques on the inner walls of the arteries) causes or contributes to more deaths in the United States than all other diseases and accidents combined. The gradual injury to and clogging of the arteries feeding the heart muscle, the brain, and the kidneys leads to heart attack, stroke, and kidney failure.

There is a spectrum of disorders, depending on the extent of artery damage. In the case of the coronary arteries (those feeding the heart muscle) angina pectoris may be the first sign of trouble. This is pain in the chest upon exertion due to the lack of sufficient blood and oxygen supply to the heart muscle. It may last a few seconds to several minutes, and may or may not progress to a myocardial infarction (MI), a heart attack, when the heart muscle is deprived of blood for so long that a portion of it is permanently damaged. Recovery depends on the extent of damage and the adequacy of treatment; some die and some go on to lead normal lives.

Treatments for atherosclerosis and its manifestations include removal of atheromas by surgery or laser, widening of affected arteries using small balloons (angioplasty), and the use of various drugs (see Chapter 5–2). Treatment also includes diet, treating high blood pressure, and not smoking —measures which might have prevented the problem if started some years sooner.

CAUSE [11,12,13]

Atherosclerosis often begins early in life, sometimes before puberty, though the disease usually remains silent, producing no signs or symptoms until after age forty or fifty. The earliest change is believed to be a slight injury to the inner lining of the artery, which allows blood to penetrate into the artery wall. There, in a complex series of events involving platelets (small blood cells that initiate clotting), the muscle cells of the artery wall accumulate abnormal amounts of cholesterol. These cells swell to form large plaques (atheromas) that protrude into the artery channels and impede the flow of blood. The atheromas also make the artery wall rigid so it doesn't contract and dilate normally, and they roughen the surface of the inner wall, increas-

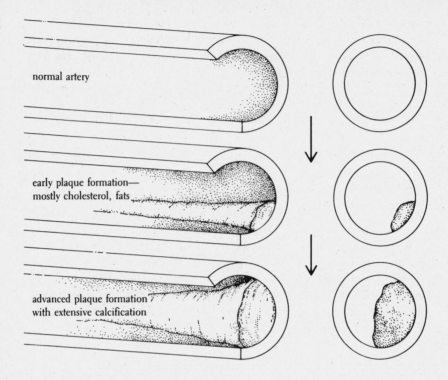

normal artery

early plaque formation—
mostly cholesterol, fats

advanced plaque formation
with extensive calcification

An Atheroma in an Artery

In atherosclerosis there are many such atheromas in the arteries. If the risk factors are not eliminated, this process continues until the artery is completely blocked or until damage to the artery stimulates thrombosis, dangerous clot formation.

ing the likelihood of clot formation. A clot can plug an artery and cause a heart attack or stroke.

The exact nature of the initial lesion which allows the blood and cholesterol to enter the artery wall is not fully understood, but high blood pressure almost surely contributes to the injury and the continuing artery destruction.

A theory gaining wide interest sees the development and spread of the atheromas as a cancerlike process in which the factors that cause the initial injury to the artery wall and changes in the artery muscle cells also transform the cells into aberrant, rapidly-dividing, cholesterol-grabbing freaks.

Whatever the details of the pathology, a great deal of data gathered from many sources over decades of research incriminate several risk factors and point to some protective measures. These factors are additive. For example, a high cholesterol level is more dangerous if blood pressure is also high, and the risk is greater still if the person smokes. Reducing or eliminating these factors (when possible) is important in both treating and preventing atherosclerosis and its serious consequences.

Risk Factors

The following are listed approximately in order from the most powerful predictors of atherosclerosis to those less consistently associated with the disease but believed to significantly increase the risk.

Age. This is not necessarily a cause if other risk factors are controlled. If not, atherogenesis, the formation and development of atheromas, can begin in pre-teen years. It appears that the effect of age is mostly due to the accumulated effects of the other risk factors.

Smoking tobacco (and possibly marijuana). Smokers have about three times the chance of suffering a heart attack as nonsmokers. Smoking causes a lot more heart disease than it does lung cancer.

Maleness. Higher levels of estrogen and possibly certain prostaglandins (powerful hormones) seem to reduce the susceptibility of the female's arteries to injury. After menopause, however, women tend to catch up with men in incidence of atherosclerosis and heart disease.

Hypertension. High blood pressure increases the risk of developing atherosclerosis, probably by promoting injury to the artery walls, forcing blood into the slightest lesion, and inhibiting the healing of lesions.

High cholesterol levels. *LDL-cholesterol* is cholesterol attached to low-density lipoproteins for transport to and deposition into cells. High levels in the blood are associated with a higher risk of heart disease. *HDL-cholesterol* is a less abundant form attached to high-density lipoproteins. It is believed to collect excess cholesterol, possibly even from cells, and transport it to the liver for excretion. High levels of HDL-cholesterol are apparently favorable to the health of the arteries, but much less is known about this than about the hazards of high levels of LDL-cholesterol.

      Cholesterol is necessary for adrenal and sex hormone production, but it is synthesized in the liver and is not needed in the diet. Many studies have shown that consuming lots of cholesterol increases its accumulation in the blood and thereby increases the risk of atherosclerosis. Saturated fats (mostly from animal fats) also increase cholesterol levels; polyunsaturated fats (mostly from vegetable oils) tend to lower them.

276 **A rich diet,** with generous amounts of meat, butter, whole milk, cheese, eggs, and lots of calories, tends to promote atherosclerosis. In countries occupied during World War II by the Germans, and in postwar Germany itself, heart attacks and other evidence of atherosclerosis greatly decreased. On the other hand, Japanese, Indians, Italians, and others who move to the United States and switch from a simple, low-fat diet to a rich, American diet greatly increase their odds of developing heart and blood vessel disease. Japan has about one-tenth the rate of coronary artery disease as the U.S.

International studies, some sponsored by the United Nations, have consistently shown a correlation between consumption of cholesterol and saturated fats, and death from coronary artery disease (CAD). The Seven Country Study looked at eighteen populations with markedly different rates of CAD and showed a high correlation among saturated fat intake, total serum cholesterol, and CAD incidence. The Oslo Study showed that dietary changes in high-risk, middle-aged men can greatly lower cholesterol levels and decrease the risk of heart attack.

Genetics. Excessive build up of blood cholesterol is sometimes a genetic disorder which must be controlled from childhood to prevent early death. *Type II hyperlipidemia* is the most common of these disorders. Weight control and strict limitations of cholesterol and fat intake are usually effective.

Diabetes. About half of all diabetics die prematurely of heart attacks. Blood vessel destruction seems to be a basic aspect of diabetes, though it can be minimized by good control of blood sugar in most cases.

Obesity. This plague is often associated with hypertension, elevated blood fats, low HDL-cholesterol, and diabetes, which predispose to atherosclerosis and heart disease. As a group, obese people are less likely to be free of atherosclerosis than lean people.

Poor physical fitness. Lack of exercise is consistently associated with a high ratio of total cholesterol to HDL-cholesterol and a high level of blood fats. Moreover, fitness increases vital (lung) capacity, which is inversely related to heart attack incidence.

Many other factors, mostly nutritional, have been implicated in heart disease by various studies and theories. None of them has been proven to be involved, but there is circumstantial evidence, and they deserve further study. In brief summary:

Dietary fibers such as cellulose, pectin, lignin, and other indigestible components of whole grains, legumes, fruits, and vegetables appear to reduce cholesterol. In one study, eating about a quarter pound of raw carrots at breakfast for three weeks reduced serum cholesterol by an average of 11 percent, a substantial drop for such a minor dietary change. The effect persisted for three weeks after the carrots were discontinued. The mechanism of the effect is not clear, but the fiber may decrease intestinal absorption of cholesterol.

Vitamin B-6 deficiency has been suggested as a cause of the initial lesions which lead to atheromas. The theory is that the lesions are caused by a toxic substance, homocysteine, a breakdown product of the amino acid methionine. But if adequate vitamin B-6 (pyridoxine) is available the toxin is rapidly broken down. There is some evidence in favor of the theory.

Vegetarians are known to be less susceptible to atherosclerosis. This has long been thought to be a consequence of their lower fat and cholesterol intake. But it could be partly due to their high pyridoxine and low methionine consumption. Plant foods are generally much richer in pyridoxine, and animal foods are much richer in methionine. Meat eaters who also eat lots of processed and sugary foods and little fresh produce usually have very low pyridoxine consumption.

It is important to understand that methionine is an essential amino acid and cannot be eliminated from the diet. Proponents of the theory advocate a better balance of methionine and pyridoxine intake, which means eating less meat and more fruits, vegetables, whole grains, and beans.

Vitamin C deficiency may be a factor. Some studies have shown a decreased rate of conversion (in the liver) of cholesterol to bile acids and a consequent increase in liver and blood cholesterol in guinea pigs deficient in vitamin C. Other studies indicate vitamin C supplements may increase HDL-cholesterol in the animals. However, human studies have yielded mixed results, and the effect of vitamin C on total cholesterol and HDL-cholesterol in humans is uncertain.

However, the role of vitamin C in maintaining the health of capillaries is well known. Deficiency leads to tissue fragility, capillary hemorrhage, and defective wound healing, all of which might be expected to predispose to atherosclerosis. After all, the walls of the larger arteries are themselves fed by capillaries. In atherosclerosis these capillaries frequently rupture and produce small hemorrhages in the artery wall. This injury attracts platelets, which adhere and promote thrombus (clot) development.

Humans who are definitely deficient in vitamin C are susceptible to this process, but there is no proof that it is a factor in the vast majority of cases of coronary artery disease where vitamin C intake is sufficient to prevent signs of scurvy. One study in Great Britain showed a strong negative correlation between vitamin C consumption and both coronary artery disease and cerebrovascular disease; but dietary fat, pyridoxine, fiber, and other possible factors were not taken into account. Nevertheless, the evidence is strong

278   enough to conclude that regular consumption of at least the RDA of vitamin C is probably beneficial to circulatory health.

Magnesium and potassium deficiencies may play a role in heart attacks. Studies have shown very low levels of these elements in the hearts of men who died suddenly of heart attacks. Areas with magnesium-rich drinking water, such as Nebraska, have lower heart attack rates. There is evidence that very low blood magnesium can cause artery spasms and dangerously erratic heart rhythms, which can cause angina and heart attack.

Other minerals, including chromium, copper, zinc, calcium, and silicon, may be involved in maintaining the health of the blood vessels and heart. See Part Two for more on these minerals.

Lecithin supplements may help lower blood cholesterol levels in some people. For example, in one study twenty-one patients with elevated cholesterol were given soybean lecithin for three months. All but two of them had followed a low-fat diet for one to ten years without satisfactory lowering of cholesterol and various drugs had also failed. Six of the original twenty-one quit the study because they could not tolerate the six tablespoonsful (36 grams) of the oily granules a day; three did not respond at all. The remaining twelve patients showed a striking decline of serum cholesterol of 41 percent.[14]

Other studies have indicated lecithin may increase HDL-cholesterol and inhibit platelet clumping. Both effects are considered favorable for cardiovascular health. Test tube studies indicate that lecithin helps dissolve cholesterol, which suggests it might keep it from accumulating in the walls of the arteries.

Lecithin is expensive, but plenty is available from unblanched soy flour, seeds, nuts, whole grains, and cold-pressed vegetable oils, all of which have other important nutrients as well. Taking large amounts of lecithin supplements daily can contribute to obesity since one gram has nine calories; a few spoonfuls can supply several hundred calories. (Products vary, so we can't be more specific; read labels!) The phosphorous content is also high and probably increases the calcium requirement somewhat.

Soy protein, according to some research, can substantially lower cholesterol levels independently of the fat, cholesterol, or fiber in the diet. If these studies are borne out, tofu and other soy products will be high on the list of foods that combat atherosclerosis.[15]

Vitamin E supplementation has long been advocated for the prevention and treatment of atherosclerosis and heart disease by Drs. Evan and Wilfrid

Shute, who originated the concept, and by health food magazines. However, there is inadequate evidence to support their claims. (See Chapter 2–7.)

Garlic may help lower blood pressure and cholesterol levels (see Chapter 5–3). Onions and cayenne pepper may have a similar though probably weaker effect.

Hypothyroidism tends to increase the fat levels in the blood. Persons with this hormonal disorder should carefully follow their physicians' advice.

Psychosocial stress may contribute to atherosclerosis and heart disease. In their book *Type A Behavior and Your Heart* (Fawcett Crest, 1975), Drs. Meyer Friedman and Ray Rosenman describe the personality type they believe to be the most prone to heart disease as a hard-driving, impatient, irritable person who walks, talks, and eats fast and feels guilty about relaxing. They call this condition "hurry sickness" and say it results in hormonal changes, such as increased adrenalin and insulin, which may promote atherosclerosis. The authors say that such harmful behavior patterns can be changed, and they provide exercises designed to help people slow down, calm down, and reduce their "floating hostility."

There are several problems with this theory. Behavior is difficult to measure, and it is usually not clear whether someone is a type A. Even if fool-proof psychological tests could be developed (highly unlikely), they would undoubtedly be long, complex, and expensive to administer and score —much costlier than simple blood pressure and cholesterol measurements. Moreover, large-scale studies have not clearly linked personality types with risk of heart disease as has been done with cholesterol levels, hypertension, cigarette smoking, and diabetes.

More convincing along these lines is the evidence that profound emotional stress can trigger a coronary artery spasm or heart arrhythmia which can result in a heart attack. Such "death from a broken heart" is more likely in those who aready have atherosclerosis, but it may happen (though very rarely) to healthy people. (See Mental and Emotional Problems later in this Part.)

Aspirin has an anticlotting effect which might prevent heart attacks and strokes in those with atherosclerosis. Small amounts are used, generally a tablet a day or less. However, the drug can produce serious side effects, and it should not be used for this purpose without the advice of a physician.

HOW TO PREVENT ATHEROSCLEROSIS AND CORONARY ARTERY DISEASE

Much remains to be learned and there are no certain answers. But the wealth of information accumulated over the last hundred years or so provides

280 strong circumstantial evidence that the risk of developing atherosclerosis, and of its progressing once it has developed, can be substantially reduced by the following measures.

Don't smoke.

Prevent or control hypertension.

Prevent or control diabetes.

Keep fit with regular exercise; don't let obesity creep up on you.

Eat right. Most Americans should eat more whole grains, fish, beans, and fresh produce, and less fatty meat, eggs, whole milk, cheese, butter, and refined, sugary foods. This type of diet helps keep cholesterol and fat levels down, and vitamins C and B-6, magnesium, and potassium levels up. It may also be beneficial to include generous amounts of garlic, onions, cayenne, and tofu and other sources of soy protein.

Birth control pills should not be taken by some women (see Chapter 3–2).

Children at high risk, those with a family history of high cholesterol or heart attack before age fifty, should have blood fats and cholesterol checked at age two or three, then once every three to five years. They may have to be very careful about dietary fat and other risk factors to avoid an early death.

Children at average risk should have their cholesterol levels checked at about age ten. They should be taught the dangers of atherosclerosis and the importance of eating right, not smoking, and keeping fit. Atherosclerosis prevention should be a major focus of health and physical education classes in primary and secondary schools.

Adults should have their cholesterol and fat levels checked every three to five years or as suggested by their physicians.

Death due to coronary artery disease is slowly but steadily declining, probably due to increasing awareness and application of some of the above measures.

Backaches (Low-Back Pain)

Chronic low-back pain is extremely common; the majority of Americans have an episode at least once in their lives. The muscles, ligaments, tendons, and intervertebral discs (cartilage cushions between the vertebrae) are responsible for supporting the spinal column. Injury to any of these tissues can cause mild to severe pain and incapacitation, sometimes for many months.

CAUSES

Almost all low-back pain is caused by strained and torn muscles, ligaments, tendons, and discs. The injury may be apparent immediately, or there may be no pain until hours later. Sometimes the muscles around the injured part go into prolonged contractions or spasms. This may help immobilize the area and prevent further injury, but the spasms themselves may cause severe pain.

Very often it is not clear, even to a specialist, what tissue is involved or how bad the injury is. The question of what percent of low-back problems are due to disc injury is very controversial. The experts' estimates range from 5 percent to 50 percent. The discs tend to compress, become less flexible, and degenerate with age.

The discs have a gelatinous center, the *nucleus pulposus*, which may push out a weakened area of the disc cartilage; this is a prolapsed disc. Or the nucleus pulposus may leak out through the damaged cartilage when the disc is herniated. In either case, pressure on the spinal root of the sciatic nerve may cause severe shooting pains down the back of the thigh along the course of the nerve. This is called *sciatica*. Sometimes the person thinks it is a leg or buttock problem and doesn't suspect a back injury.

Injury to the weakened tissue is usually caused by excessive stress in lifting, twisting, throwing, or other activity. In disc herniation the onset of pain is often sudden and very severe.

Poor posture, often a result of weak back muscles, can cause excessive pressure on the discs and ligaments and contribute to their injury. Poorly designed chairs, couches, and car seats are often to blame.

TREATMENT

By far the most important treatment for most low-back injuries is complete bed rest on a firm mattress for several days, with a gradual return to normal activities. Care must be taken not to stress the injured part; it must heal naturally, and this takes time.

Light massage and heat applications may help, but vigorous manipulations such as twisting and cracking the back can aggravate the injury. In sciatica, traction on the leg or hanging from a chinning bar may help.

Improve the general health with adequate rest, exercise, and good nutrition, including adequate vitamin C, which is critical in collagen formation and connective tissue healing. If your intake of vitamin C has been borderline for a long time, supplements of 200 to 500 mg per day may be in order for a few weeks or months, or until you start to eat better.

Exercise to the extent possible without straining the back. The abdominal and back muscles must be strengthened to decrease the stress and

282 **Spinal flex and extension**

Sit with your hands together and bend your back and neck so your head touches your chest. Come up until you are looking straight up with your hands directly overhead.

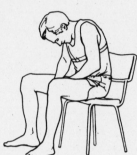

Trunk rotation

With hands on knees, rotate in a circle from the waist.

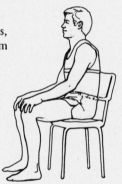

Trunk twist

Twist at the waist and turn your head to one side, then the other.

The cobra

Lie flat on your stomach with your hands about even with your shoulders. Slowly push your torso up while keeping your pubic bone on the ground. Pull your head back and look up. Hold for several seconds; rest; repeat.

This exercise, which stretches the abdominal and hip flexor muscles, can be harmful in certain back conditions; ask your physician if you are being treated for a back problem before trying this.

Whole body stretch and flex

1. Feet flat, head even with the arms

2. Bring head down, leg forward

3. Swing head and leg up while coming to your toes

4. Swing head and legs down to #2 position

5. Repeat

284

strain on weak ligaments and discs. But great care must be taken not to do overly strenuous exercises. Full sit-ups, for example, can aggravate back pain.

The majority of apparent disc injuries resolve without surgery, especially with adequate rest and care. When they do not, a last resort before surgery is chemonucleosis. An enzyme such as chymopapain (a meat tenderizer from papaya) or collagenase is injected into the herniated or prolapsed disc. It dissolves the gelatinous material pressing on the nerve. The success rate has been impressive, but there are some hazards, including occasional severe allergic reactions.

Sometimes symptoms of sciatica can be caused by keeping a wallet in the hip pocket and sitting on it for extended periods. Sitting cross-legged carries the same risk.

Sometimes back pain is more serious than a pulled muscle, strained ligament, or ruptured disc. It could be arthritis, an infection, osteoporosis, a tumor, or a disease of the muscles, nerves, or kidneys. So it is prudent to discuss persistant or unusual pains with a medical doctor; chiropractors know little about these serious conditions.

PREVENTION

Keep your back fit; exercise it and move it in all possible directions every day to keep the muscles strong and all the connective tissues well nourished. Keep the abdominal muscles strong too. Do a little every day; don't indulge in bursts of activity. The following exercises are especially good for the back: spinal flex and extension; trunk rotation; trunk twist; rocking sit-ups.

Lift objects properly, and if you cannot manage with ease don't even try. When lifting things, don't bend at the waist; bend your knees and use your leg muscles, keeping your back straight.

Sit up straight; don't slump or slouch. Aim for vertebral alignment and a slight lumbar (lower back) curve.

Don't wear high heels if they seem to cause pain in your back.

Lose fat if you are obese; the excess weight strains the back.

Boils (furuncles)

A boil is a localized bacterial (usually staphylococcal) abscess of the skin and underlying tissue, which usually starts at the base of a hair follicle. Most boils come to a head and drain spontaneously. Sometimes the infection spreads under the skin and into deeper tissue and forms several interconnected boils. This is called a *carbuncle*.

The bacteria may enter the blood, especially if a boil is squeezed or manipulated, and go on to infect the heart, bones, joints, and other tissue. Boils on the face, especially the nose and upper lip, are quite serious since they may infect the sinuses and even the brain.

CAUSE

The cause of boils is not "bad blood" (systemic infection), as some herbalists and naturopaths claim, but the entrance of staphylococcus bacteria into the skin. If "bad blood" were the cause, we would see infections of internal organs much more often, but these are rare except after long-term serious boils.

Occasional boils, even a few every year, are not serious. But frequent outbreaks can be a sign of poor resistance, poor nutrition, inadequate hygiene of cuts and scratches, or diabetes. The problem should be discussed with a physician.

TREATMENT

The area should be kept clean with several washes a day; injury and irritation should be avoided. To reduce pain and stimulate head formation and drainage, apply very warm salt-water compresses several times a day. **Do not squeeze** or press a boil or attempt to open it. This could cause the infection to spread under the skin and delay healing.

Draining boils are highly contaminated and should be covered with sterile gauze to prevent spreading the bacteria. Hands should be washed before and after dressing the wound.

Antibiotic ointments applied around the boil may help prevent further infection, but they sometimes provoke allergic reactions and aggravate the infection.

Some experts say boils can often be aborted early by applying **rubbing alcohol**. This is harmless and may work for some, but do not rub or press the affected area.

See a physician if you have several boils at once, frequent boils, a carbuncle, or a boil on the nose or upper lip. Incision, drainage, and antibiotics may be necessary.

PREVENTION

Clean all cuts, scratches, and abrasions as thoroughly as possible. Use mild soap and warm water. Remove every particle of dirt, sand, or coral. Antisep-

286   tics such as Mercurochrome and Merthiolate are often painful and irritating and never necessary.

Eat well to help maintain a healthy immune system and strong resistance to infection. Adequate protein, zinc, and vitamins A and C are especially important.

Avoid chemicals and tight clothing which irritate the skin and promote infection.

Bathe with a mild, nonirritating soap, and keep your hands clean.

Bronchitis

This is a long-term condition of persistent coughing with mucus production and repeated respiratory infections. After some years chronic bronchitis may lead to permanent lung damage.

CAUSE

The known causes are cigarette smoking, air pollution, and dusty occupations. Bronchial allergies are sometimes involved. Nutritional inadequacy can increase susceptibility. Vitamin A is especially important for healthy lung tissue. Certain rare inherited conditions can also lead to chronic bronchitis.

TREATMENT

Treatment usually involves stopping smoking; removal of occupational hazards, hair spray, dust, and air pollution if possible; removal of allergens if they are a factor; and administration of antibiotics (usually tetracycline or ampicillan) to control acute flare-ups. Influenza and pneumonia vaccinations are often recommended.

      Drinking a lot of fluids is advisable to help keep the mucus liquid. Soups with hot spices like garlic, peppers (especially cayenne), and curry, and herbal teas with mullein, ginger, and coltsfoot may also help to loosen mucus and unclog the lungs' airways (but see cautions in Chapter 5–3).

PREVENTION
Don't smoke.

Don't inhale dust, aerosols, or fumes, which are often problems on the job. Coal miners, carpenters, factory hands, and other workers should insist on protection such as masks and ventilation and make sure they are properly used. Avoid living in an air-polluted area if possible.

Children should be protected from cigarette smoke and dirty air since these may predispose them to chronic bronchitis later.

Good nutrition is very important in resisting infections. All the essential nutrients are important, but adequate vitamin A is especially critical, so eat plenty of colorful fruits and vegetables such as yams, carrots, spinach, apricots, peaches, melons, papayas, and mangoes.

Cancers

Cancer is the abnormal, excessive growth of cells and their spread to distant organs. The overproduction of certain cells often interferes with vital body functions. About one in four Americans now alive will eventually develop at least one form of cancer. Tremendous efforts in recent decades have led to significant improvements in the detection and treatment of the disease, but it is still among the major causes of death and disability, and the most feared disease in the United States.

A consensus is developing that much more emphasis must be placed on cancer prevention. We already know enough to prevent or significantly delay about two-thirds of all cancers. Now we need to apply our knowledge. The following is a summary of the most important factors involved in cancer development and cancer prevention. Early detection is very important and is discussed at the end of this chapter. Cancer chemotherapy is discussed in Chapter 5–2.

Cancer-Promoting Factors in the Diet

Dietary fats and cancer.[16,17] One of the most significant developments in preventive medicine since the discovery of the links between smoking and lung cancer and between diet and heart disease is the discovery of strong correlations between dietary fat and cancer of the breast, prostate, and colon, all major killers in the United States. Other cancers may also be involved. The evidence has been strong enough for the American Cancer Society and the National Cancer Institute, to issue dietary guidelines recommending less fat—beef, pork, whole-milk products, fried foods, poultry skin, and gravies. The recommendations are consistent with those of the Dietary Goals for the United States issued by the Senate Committee on Nutrition, and with the diet long recommended for reducing atherosclerosis and heart disease (see Chapter 2–3). Here is a sampling of the evidence.

In dozens of countries studied, the incidence of breast, colon, and prostate cancer, are directly proportional to dietary animal-fat intake.

Animal fat in the diet has been shown to increase the nocturnal

288 prolactin surge in women. This pituitary hormone enhances breast tumor formation in animals.

Japanese who move to Hawaii, where they eat more meat, develop more of these cancers. If they move to California, where they eat still more meat, the incidence increases even further.

American blacks, who eat much more animal fat than Africans, have two to three times their rate of these cancers.

Vegetarians, who are less likely to get cancer, produce a lot fewer bile acids (secreted by the gall bladder) than nonvegetarians. Some bile acids are proven carcinogens (cancer causers) and would be banned if they were food additives.

Seventh Day Adventists in the United States eat much less meat than the average and have much lower than average rates of breast, colon, prostate, and other cancers. Those who are strict vegetarians have the lowest rates.

The production of known mutagens (very likely carcinogens) in human stools can be greatly decreased by reducing dietary fat. This reduces the exposure of the intestine to the mutagens.

Many studies have shown that broiled, charred, and smoked meats have large amounts of carcinogenic substances.

Obesity, which is promoted by fat in the diet, increases the risk of uterine cancer up to ten-fold. The risk of kidney and other cancers may also be increased.

What about vegetable oils? Some animal studies have shown a cancer-promoting effect of large amounts of vegetable oils in the diet. Results have been inconsistent and tend to be contradicted by human studies. For example, Japanese women have much more linoleic acid in their fat tissue but only one-fifth the breast cancer rate; they suffer fewer other cancers as well. However, rancid oils are probably cancer promoters, so caution is advised. Vegetable oils for deep frying should not be used over and over, a practice common in some fast food restaurants.

Saccharin is a weak carcinogen in some animals, but several thorough studies have failed to find an increased cancer risk among users. Still, the heavy consumption of diet soft drinks with saccharin by youngsters and pregnant women should be discouraged.

Nitrates and nitrites, used for centuries to preserve various processed meats, are suspected of combining with amines (amino acid fragments) to form carcinogenic nitrosamines. Eating vitamin C foods with those that contain nitrates probably greatly reduces the cancer risk.

Natural plant carcinogens.[18] Many people are concerned about pesticide residues in food and believe they are causing many cancers. So far these fears appear to be unfounded; while heavy exposure to some pesticides may promote some cancers in farmers and chemical workers, there is no evidence that the traces found in foods can cause disease. However, studies have shown that many edible plants contain natural pesticides, many of which are mutagenic and carcinogenic. The levels of the toxins are especially high in plants bred for resistance to insects and fungi; some new varieties have been banned for this reason. At this point it appears that our consumption of nature's pesticides is several thousand times greater than our intake of synthetic pesticides.

The task of identifying the toxins and estimating their potential for harm has only just begun. Many food plants contain both carcinogens and anticarcinogens such as vitamins A and C and are beneficial on balance. Others will be shown to have such high levels of toxins that prudent people will use them in moderation, if at all. Until more details are available, the best advice is to eat moderate amounts of a wide variety of foods, favoring those with known or suspected anticancer potential. This will minimize the intake of any given toxin.

The following examples illustrate the problem. Safrole and related compounds known to cause cancer in rats are present in sarsaparilla (used for herb tea and root beer) and black pepper; hydrazine and related carcinogens are present in large amounts in edible mushrooms, including the popular false morel and common commercial mushrooms; psoralen derivatives are carcinogens present in celery, parsley, and related plants; gossypol, a probable carcinogen, is present in large amounts in cottonseed oil, which is added to some margarines, cooking oils, and sesame butters; nitrates, which form carcinogenic nitroso compounds, are present in beets, celery, lettuce, spinach, and other vegetables.

Nutrition Against Cancer

Several food elements are believed to boost resistance to cancer when provided in adequate amounts.[19,20,21] There is no evidence that very large doses provide extra protection, and in some cases such doses can be dangerous. Most of the elements are further discussed in Part Two.

Carotene, a precursor of vitamin A, and other carotenoids have been shown to be anticarcinogenic in rodents and appear to provide some protection from lung cancer in humans. These substances are present in all plants with chlorophyll.

Vitamin C may help prevent the formation of carcinogenic nitrosamines if taken with meals containing nitrites. The amount required is believed to be small. Eating some vitamin C food with every meal is a good idea. The increased consumption of vitamin C foods in the last few decades may be largely responsible for the plummeting stomach cancer rate in the United States. Vitamin C supplements have been reported to reduce the incidence of rectal polyps, which are linked to rectal and colon cancer, and to inhibit bladder tumor formation.

Vitamin E is a scavenger of highly reactive free radicals that can damage DNA and may provide some protection from cancer initiation.

Selenium inhibits the induction of many kinds of tumors in animals and is believed to be an important anticancer factor in the diet. Whole grains are usually a good source.

Vitamin B complex and **iron** deficiencies have been linked to a precancerous condition of the mouth, pharynx, and esophagus known as Plummer-Vinson syndrome.

Cruciferous vegetables (those of the mustard family), including broccoli, Brussels sprouts, cauliflower, cabbage, and turnips have been reported to stimulate liver, intestinal, and lung enzymes which detoxify carcinogens in animals and increase their resistance to cancer. Studies indicate that the more cruciferous vegetables people eat, the less likely they are to get colon cancer.

In other studies, cabbage, asparagus, radish, and other vegetable juices have been reported to inhibit the ability of tobacco smoke to cause mutations (genetic changes that likely cause cancer). The raw juices were more potent. The substances responsible for the effect have not been isolated.

Fiber in the diet may help protect against cancer. People with lots of fiber in their diets tend to have lower rates of colon cancer. It is theorized that fiber exerts its protective effect by creating bulk as it absorbs water in the intestine and thereby dilutes carcinogens and speeds transit through the bowel. It may also favorably influence intestinal flora and decrease the conversion of bile acids to carcinogens.

BHA and BHT, the antioxidants used as food preservatives, have been shown to inhibit some chemically induced cancers in animals and may have contributed to keeping the stomach cancer incidence low in the United States. They are still under suspicion as possible liver toxins and should not be consumed as "supplements," as recommended by some writers.

Drugs that Promote Cancer

A number of drugs, including recreational drugs, and hormones have a tendency to cause or promote various cancers. Tobacco is the most important of these, but the others are also significant.

Tobacco. Smoking, snuffing, and chewing tobacco have long been linked with mouth, nasal, lip, esophageal, laryngeal, lung, bladder, and pancreatic cancers. More recently a strong association has been found between smoking and cancer of the cervix. The use of tobacco increases the risk of these cancers by up to ten times. Cigar and pipe smoking are about one-third to one-half as risky as cigarette smoking. Snuffing and chewing tobacco are less risky than smoking but can cause oral cancer. The danger of smoking is significantly increased by exposure to many environmental and occupational pollutants such as asbestos, coal, rubber, textile, dust, chemicals, and uranium.

Marijuana. Smoking marijuana may carry a significant risk of developing lung, mouth, and throat cancers, and possibly others.

Alcohol. The risk of esophageal cancer among alcoholics is about seventeen times the average. For heavy drinkers, those who average about six beers, five small glasses of wine, or two ounces of liquor per day, the risk of cancer of the mouth or esophagus is two to five times the risk for nondrinkers. The risk of pancreatic cancer is also higher for drinkers. Alcohol also promotes the cancer-causing effects of tobacco.

DES (diethystilbestrol), the synthetic estrogen, was used in the 1940s and 1950s for menopausal symptoms, pregnancy testing, pregnancy nausea, and threatened miscarriage. By 1971 it was clear that exposure in the uterus fifteen to twenty years earlier was the cause of a rash of cases of the very rare adenocarcinoma of the vagina in young women. Hundreds of thousands of women born in the United States between 1947 and 1971 had been exposed and are considered at risk; they should have semiannual checkups. DES mothers may also be at risk; they should have an annual pelvic examination and Pap test and should minimize further estrogen exposure.

Postmenopausal estrogens may increase the risk of endometrial cancer in some women. However, new dose regimens and combination with progestins seem to have a protective effect, especially against breast cancer. Discuss the risks and benefits with your physician.

Anabolic steroids, the testosterone analogues that are widely used by weight

292 lifters, body builders, and other athletes, may promote liver and other cancers.

Immunosuppressants, used in kidney transplants and some serious diseases, are suspected of increasing cancer risk by inhibiting immunologic resistance to cancer cells.

Amphetamines are suspected of increasing the risk of Hodgkin's disease and other cancers.

Other drugs, including some tranquilizers, antibiotics, and antihistamines, have been linked with various tumors in laboratory animals. These studies are suggestive only and do not prove these drugs cause cancer in humans, but they provide another reason to keep drug intake to a minimum.

Occupational Cancer Hazards

It is estimated that somewhere between 5 and 20 percent of all cancers in the United States are due to exposure to cancer-causing substances on the job. The list includes nuclear radiation, arsenic, coal tar pitch, dry cleaning chemicals, gasoline, benzens, benzidine, asbestos, PVC, nitrobiphenyl, wood dust, and coke-oven emissions. If you work in an industrial, chemical, or nuclear plant or uranium or other mine, it is very important to follow all the safety rules and to report violations to your union or to the Occupational Safety and Health Administration (OSHA). Keep in mind that simultaneous exposure to cigarette smoke and asbestos greatly increases the already high risk of exposure to either. The same may be true of smoking and other industrial carcinogens.

X-Rays

It has been known for decades that radiologists have a high risk of developing leukemia if they don't take precautions to reduce their exposure to X-rays. We also know that infants exposed to X-rays in the uterus are more likely to develop cancer. There is no doubt that X-ray exposure promotes the development of cancer and should be minimized to the extent possible without risking health. The FDA has been trying to reduce that exposure, and it recommends the discontinuation of the following.

> All routine chest X-rays made to uncover diseases (such as tuberculosis, lung cancer, and heart problems) in apparently well persons

All routine prenatal screening examination by X-ray

Routine chest X-rays given solely because of admission to a hospital

Mandatory chest X-ray for employment

Repeated X-ray examination of TB reactors (those with positive TB skin tests), asymptomatic TB patients, and persons in nursing homes and chronic disease hospitals

Dentists are also guilty of unnecessary exposure. Full-mouth X-rays are rarely necessary more often than once every five to ten years, but many dentists take them far more often.

Chiropractors use X-rays irrationally and expose people unnecessarily. Some even offer them free as an inducement to make an appointment. (See Part Six for more on chiropractic.)

It is a good idea to always ask the physician or dentist who proposes an X-ray to explain its benefit and whether a previous film might suffice. Keep a record of your exposure, including the name of the doctor, the type of exam, and the purpose. Request a copy of the X-rays if you are moving or going to another doctor.

Cooperate with the operator during X-ray exposure to avoid the need for retakes. If necessary, request lead shielding for your chest and reproductive organs, or for those of your child.

Beware of old X-ray machines, especially the type with the short, pointed plastic cone. Ask whether the equipment has been inspected by a licensing agency or professional organization. The results of these inspections are open to the public. For more information, ask your State Radiological Health Agency.

When X-rays are recommended, be sure to tell your doctor if you are pregnant or might be.

These considerations should not frighten you away from prudent X-ray use. For example, mammography delivers very low doses, and the benefits are much greater than the risks for women over thirty-five.

Nuclear Radiation

Nuclear radiation has long been known to cause cancer by damaging cellular reproductive and control mechanisms. Japanese survivors of the atomic bombing of Hiroshima and Nagasaki have been dying of leukemia and other cancers at a very high rate for thirty years. United States servicemen exposed to nuclear explosions for test purposes in the 1950s say they have been developing leukemia, bone cancer, and other malignancies. Marshall Islanders

294   and residents of Southern Utah exposed to dust from nuclear tests report high cancer rates. Should nuclear war occur, many survivors would die of cancer in the following years. It is clearly in everyone's interest that all atmospheric testing of nuclear weapons be ended and that nuclear war be prevented.

The widespread construction of nuclear power plants, especially plutonium breeder reactors, could greatly increase the cancer risk. Plutonium remains deadly for a half million years. Aside from the catastrophic effects a meltdown would have, there are the dangers of theft, sabotage, and leakage from mines, plants, waste burial grounds, and transportation accidents. According to some nuclear physicists, if the United States continues to build nuclear plants, even with 99.9 percent containment perfection and none of the dangers above, by the end of the century we will have an additional 100,000 cancer deaths a year. This, however, is a highly controversial conclusion, and other estimates are much lower.

Air and Water Pollution

The dumping of industrial wastes into the nation's air and water supplies has increased the cancer risk in some areas. Cigarette smokers in cities downwind from sulfur-emitting power plants have a greater risk of developing lung cancer than smokers in less polluted areas. Some researchers believe that the sulfuric acid increases the carcinogenicity of cigarette smoke.

Pesticides and herbicides in water supplies are a source of constant concern. Industrial wastes in the drinking water have been linked to increased cancer mortality in Louisiana and other states. One of the problems is that the chlorine added to water to disinfect it often combines with organic industrial chemicals and decaying plant material to form the carcinogenic chloroform.

The Environmental Protection Agency is gradually (too gradually) forcing the clean up of the nation's waters. The individual can remain alert to political efforts to slow the clean-up, and drink unchlorinated spring water if his tap water is chlorinated and contaminated with industrial wastes or decaying plant matter. Small amounts of chlorine without industrial wastes are probably not hazardous. The individual can also report suspected illegal dumping of chemicals into waterways to the local police or the state Attorney General's Office. A favorite trick of some industrial polluters who need to get rid of tons of chemical waste cheaply is to send it out in tanker trucks on rainy days with the drains open enough to leak it onto the roads.

The problem of cancer and other diseases caused by man-made toxins grows steadily with industrialization. Developed nations and those struggling to catch up cannot ignore this. Politicians and industrialists concerned about the economic cost of pollution control must include in their calculations the health care costs and lower productivity which result from not controlling pollution.

The Sun and Skin Cancer

So-called aging of the skin is largely a result of irreversible sun damage, not time. The changes in sun-damaged skin commonly precede malignant changes. Premalignant lesions are usually hard, dry scales on a red base, or a persistent sore or ulcer. They may eventually develop into squamous cell or basal cell cancer. Untreated, these can extend to the underlying bone and eventually cause death. However, when detected early these cancers are usually successfully treated with surgery, freezing, burning, or chemosurgery.

Basal cell cancer is the most common skin cancer. It usually occurs on the face, neck, and top of the hands. It starts as a small pearly pimple, sometimes with tiny blood vessels on the surface. Later it develops a crust that bleeds easily if irritated.

Squamous cell cancer occurs most often on the head but may appear on the hands or elsewhere. It may look like a basal cell cancer or it may appear as sharply outlined red scaly patches. While sun exposure is the cause of most of these cancers, they can also be caused by exposure to coal tar, pitch, arsenic, paraffin oil, and X-rays.

Malignant melanoma is an increasingly common, often deadly cancer of the melanin-producing cells (melanocytes) of the skin. It may result from the transformation of a mole or develop by itself. Females get it somewhat more often than males, the older more often than the young, and lighter skinned persons, especially the blue-eyed, poor tanners who freckle and burn easily, much more often than darker persons. Malignant melanoma is usually dark brown or black with irregular borders and surface. It grows and may ulcerate and bleed easily if injured. The original color may turn into shades of blue, red, and even white.

    The most common sites of melanoma are the face, head, neck, the back (especially males), and the legs (especially females). Metastases to vital organs occurs early and rapidly; delay in diagnosis and removal can be fatal. Susceptibility seems to be hereditary. Members of affected families often develop dysplastic nevi, moles with a tendency to become malignant. Such moles should be monitored carefully for changes in size, color, and shape, as well as bleeding, scaling, and itching or burning of the surrounding skin.

Sunlight is by far the most common trigger for all skin cancers. Their incidence in populations is proportional to closeness to the equator, to skin

296 exposure, and to skin lightness. Pigment protects the cells from the mutagenic ultraviolet rays of sunlight. Incidence is high among descendents of northern Europeans living in the southern U.S. and northern Australia, especially sunbathers and farmers, fishermen, and laborers who like to work with a minimum of clothing. Sporadic heavy overexposure is more hazardous than smaller exposures every day. Contrary to some reports, fluorescent lights emit far too little ultraviolet light to be a hazard.

The fair-skinned sunbather or unprotected worker often suffers *solar elastosis*, a degeneration of the skin which starts as a yellowish mottling, changes to pigmented blotches, and gives rise to malignant changes. Even teenagers can develop solar elastosis. Affected areas should be watched for life for signs of malignancy, especially if exposure to the sun continues. The damage done by ultraviolet radiation to the skin cells is cumulative and cannot be reversed or healed, only prevented from progressing.

HOW TO PREVENT SKIN CANCER

Avoid excessive exposure to the sun, especially if you are fair skinned. Ignore the tanning fad. Use protective clothing and a sunscreen agent such as PABA, oxybenzone, or sulisobenzone. These have all been proven effective in blocking ultraviolet (UV) radiation. Protect yourself when skiing. Snow reflects about 80 percent of UV radiation. Don't be fooled by cloudy days; UV radiation penetrates clouds very well.

The year of 1980 was a year of heavy sunspot activity characterized by huge flares and greatly increased UV radiation. We will probably be seeing a bumper crop of skin cancers, including tragic melanoma cases, in the 1980s. The next sunspot peak year is 1991.

Watch for solar elastosis, as described above. See a dermatologist soon if you suspect it. Remember, only an expert can tell for sure if a growth, lesion, or pigmented area is cancerous or precancerous. The latter lesions can often be treated and cancer prevented by application of 5-fluorocil. This powerful drug is available by prescription only; a physician must supervise its use.

Sex and Cancer

Hepatitis B and AIDS both of which most commonly affect homosexual men, can lead to cancers. They are discussed in detail elsewhere (hepatitis in this section, AIDS in Chapter 3–3).

Cancer of the cervix has a strong association with sexual activity. Virgins and celibates have little chance of getting it. Those who start having intercourse before the age of twenty have about twelve times the risk of those who refrain until after twenty. The risk seems to be increased by multiple partners. Prostitutes have the highest incidence of all.[22]

Genital herpes and genital warts may promote cervical cancer. Using a condom or diaphragm probably decreases the risk, but it is no guarantee. Women who have genital herpes or warts should get frequent Pap smears to detect any precancerous conditions, which can then be treated with simple cryosurgery (freezing) and other methods.

Circumcision has been recommended as a cancer preventive by some popular health writers. It is suggested that male smegma, the thick secretion that accumulates under the foreskin of the penis if hygiene is poor, may have something to do with cervical cancer in women who have intercourse with uncircumcised men. On the basis of this hypothesis, routine circumcision during infancy is advocated. The evidence is not convincing, however, and painful surgery should not be based on speculation. See Chapter 3–4 for more on circumcision.

Psychological Factors

Psychological stress has been shown to alter levels of hormones, especially ACTH, cortisone, and other "stress hormones." These prepare the body for action, but also suppress immune responses and increase vulnerability to viruses, bacteria, and possibly cancer cells.[23,24] Some studies show a higher cancer incidence in rats and mice raised in very noisy or otherwise stressful environments.

Major psychological upheaval has been reported to induce cancer. Such results are highly unlikely because it usually takes years for cancer to develop. Other reports link cancer with personality types, especially the nonassertive, noncompetitive, anger-suppressing person who rarely shows strong emotions. These theories are far from proven.

A low incidence of cancer has been reported in the mentally retarded and in certain types of psychotics. On the other hand, paranoid schizophrenics are reported to have a normal to high cancer incidence. Perhaps one of the most significant findings is that single, widowed, and divorced men and women have higher rates of almost every type of cancer than married persons. It is theorized that prolonged stress is the common factor in these cases, that unmarried persons, paranoids, and those who repress their emotions experience more stress than the retarded, expressive, and married persons. But it may simply be that lonely people have more bad habits such as drinking and smoking.

298 Miscellaneous Factors

Asbestos is a hazard not only to those who work with it every day but to anyone who breathes it. Workers tearing down old buildings should be very cautious with any insulating materials and avoid breathing the dust from it.

Trail biking can be very hazardous in some parts of the country. Studies have shown that the dust churned up is sometimes almost pure asbestos, which is a natural mineral fiber and not always an industrial pollutant.

Urinary tract infections (UTIs) may increase the risk of bladder cancer, though this is controversial. The infecting bacteria produce dimethynitrosamine, a powerful carcinogen, in the urine. However, no clear link between UTIs and actual bladder cancer cases has been shown. Nevertheless it is important to treat such infections promptly and prevent their recurrence (see discussion of UTIs later in this section).

Some **hair dyes** contain chemicals shown to be carcinogenic in animals. Small amounts are absorbed through the skin of the user and hair dresser. Several epidemiological studies have failed to show any increased cancer risk to humans, so it must be small. Still, warning labels may be placed on the products.

Laetrile (amygdalin) and "vitamin B-15" (DMG) have been shown to be mutagenic and possibly carcinogenic by the Ames test. See Part Six for more on these dangerous hoaxes.

Breast feeding has long been suspected of reducing the risk of breast cancer, but extensive studies have failed to show a protective effect.

Early Warning Signs

The sooner a cancer is recognized, the more likely treatment is to succeed. So it is important to be familiar with the early warning signs and know how to look for them.

Unusual bleeding or discharge between periods, especially during or after menopause, may indicate uterine cancer. The American Cancer Society (ACS) recommends a **Pap test** every three years for women over twenty, and for those under twenty but sexually active, after negative tests in two consecutive years. It recommends a pelvic exam every three years from twenty to forty and annually thereafter. The American College of Obstetricians and

Gynecologists disagrees, and recommends an annual Pap smear. Women who have had genital warts or herpes should have Pap smears at least once a year.

A breast self-examination once a month should become a lifetime habit. Breast cancer is a major threat to women over thirty-five and early detection definitely saves lives. The ACS recommends three exams, one in the shower, one before a mirror, and one lying down. It should be done about one week after the menstrual period when temporary hormonally induced changes will be minimal.

> **In the shower,** use flat fingers over every part of each breast to check for any lump or thickening. Use the right hand for the left breast and vice versa.

> **Before a mirror,** look for changes in the contour of each breast such as swelling, dimpling, puckering, skin irritation; or changes in the nipples such as whitish scale or distorted shape. Do this with arms at your sides, then with arms raised high overhead, then with hands on hips and pressing down firmly to flex your chest muscles. Finally, gently squeeze each nipple; report any discharge to your physician immediately.

> **Lying on your back,** put a pillow or folded towel under your right shoulder and your right hand behind your head. With flat fingers of the left hand, press gently in small circular motions, systematically covering every part of your breast, including the nipple. Repeat for the left breast. Report any lump you discover to your physician.

> **Know your family history;** regular breast self-examination is especially important for women who have close relatives who had breast cancer.

Mammography is recommended once between the ages of thirty-five and forty, then every other year up to fifty and yearly thereafter. Women at high risk may need earlier and more frequent examination. Careful palpation by an experienced physician is also a very sensitive detection method. Early detection not only saves lives; it allows less extensive surgery, so reduces trauma and costs.

Breast implants, usually made of silicon and inserted for cosmetic purposes, can make early detection of cancer difficult. This should be considered, especially if a woman's relatives have had breast cancer.

300   **A nagging cough** or hoarseness should be discussed with a physician. The ACS no longer recommends annual chest X-rays or sputum cytology tests for heavy smokers without symptoms because early detection by these methods has not reduced mortality. In fact, the annual OK may give false assurance and encourage continued smoking. Coughing up blood should always be reported to a physician.

Rectal bleeding or changes in bowel habits unexplained by dietary or other changes should be reported to a physician. Rectal bleeding is usually due to hemorrhoids or ulcers, but it can be caused by cancer. The ACS no longer recommends routine annual sigmoidoscopic exams for those over forty, but recommends one every three to five years for those over fifty, provided negative exams have been recorded for two consecutive years. An annual test for blood in the stool is recommended for those over fifty. Persons who have ever had ulcerative colitis or rectal polyps, or a strong family history of bowel cancer, are at high risk for colon cancer and should discuss more frequent tests with a physician.

Urinary difficulties such as pain, frequency, or weak or interrupted flow; persistent pain in the lower back, pelvis, or upper thighs; or blood in the urine may signal prostate or bladder cancer. Every man over forty should have a rectal examination of the prostate once a year.

A testicular lump or enlargement should be reported to a physician. Monthly self-examination can save lives because these cancers spread rapidly. After a warm shower or bath, examine each testicle between the thumb and fingers and feel for hard lumps, slight enlargement, or a change in the consistency. Testicular cancer is primarily a young man's disease. Self-examination is especially important between the ages of fifteen and thirty-five and should be taught in high school health and physical education classes. Undescended testes have a very high risk of developing cancer. Parents should have their infant sons checked for this.

Difficulty swallowing or a lump on or near the thyroid gland should be reported to a physician. If you have had X-ray treatments of the head or neck, discuss with a physician how often you should be examined for possible thyroid cancer.

Stomach pain or digestive discomfort that continues for two weeks or more should be discussed with a physician. Persons with pernicious anemia or lack of hydrochloric acid are at higher risk for stomach cancer and should have regular checkups.

Moles, freckles, or warts that have changed in color or shape or that bleed should be examined by a dermatologist.

A lump, white spot, or scaly area on the lip or in the mouth should be seen by a physician. Those who suck on tobacco should regularly and thoroughly examine the mouth area for signs of cancer. Feel with your fingers the sides of your neck and under your jaw. Look at and feel the lip area, inside and outside the mouth, for color changes and lumps. Look and feel for white scaly areas and lumps all over the inside of the mouth including the gums, cheeks, roof, and floor. Pull the tongue out and hold it to the right, then left and look for lumps and growths. Use a good light for this examination and do it at least once a month so you really know your mouth and will quickly notice any changes.

A swollen lymph gland in the neck, armpit, or groin that lasts three weeks or more should be seen by a physician.

Persistent fatigue, weight loss, fever, itching, night sweats, nausea, repeated infections or easy bruising should be discussed with a physician.

Children who are easily fatigued, listless, drowsy, pale, or who experience persistant nausea, nosebleeds, headaches, double vision, or stumbling should be examined.

Chickenpox

Chickenpox is a highly contagious virus infection that few children escape. It is generally a mild illness with low-grade fever and a rash with clusters of raised red spots. These become blisters which collapse and scab over. New crops of blisters erupt for three or four days. The major complaint is itching. The rare adult case is usually much more severe.

The incubation period is about two to three weeks. The virus can be transmitted in the fluid from the easily broken blisters or in droplets from the mouth or throat. It is contagious for about a week after the blisters first appear. The scabs are not contagious.

In otherwise healthy children, complications such as encephalitis and severe bacterial infection of the lesions are very rare. On the other hand, if a child is undergoing treatment for cancer the virus can run rampant and cause fatal infection of the brain and other organs.

One episode of chickenpox confers lifelong immunity against the disease, but in most cases the virus manages to survive in a latent form in the nerve roots and can cause shingles years or decades later. The varicella-zoster (chickenpox-shingles) virus belongs to the herpes family, other members of which also remain latent in nerve roots and cause outbreaks later as they move down the nerves to the skin.

302

TREATMENT

If the fever is high (103°F or more), bed rest and lots of fluids are essential. Acetaminophen can help reduce fever and itching.

Scratching should be discouraged and nails trimmed to prevent infection. The hands should be washed several times a day and the affected skin kept clean. Bathing with baking soda in the water may relieve itching.

Although serious symptoms are very rare, they can occur. It is very important to **see a physician immediately** if there are convulsions, a stiff neck, severe lethargy or headache, or rapid breathing.

Call a physician if the lesions seem to be infected by bacteria, with large areas of redness or draining pus. Treatment over the phone is preferable to an office visit in order to prevent the spread of the disease.

PREVENTION

A vaccine is now available and may become widely used. Until then, some physicians believe it may be better not to prevent chickenpox in otherwise healthy children because it is so mild for them and can be more severe for adults. Exposure is almost inevitable, especially for children. Still, it is probably best to limit it in children since prolonged or heavy exposure (such as wrestling with an infected pal) can result in more severe cases.

Colds

The symptoms of colds are variable but usually include two or more of the following: weakness and malaise, loss of appetite, raspy or sore throat, sneezing, copious nasal discharge, nasal stuffiness, coughing, and sometimes mild fever. Colds rarely last more than a week or so and are rarely serious except in the chronically ill or debilitated.

Is It a Cold or Flu?

The common cold is often confused with influenza (flu), which is generally much more serious. (See Influenza.) The confusion causes unnecessary clinic visits for colds as well as delay in seeking help for the flu in high-risk groups. Colds usually come on gradually, do not cause high fever, and produce symptoms mostly in the upper respiratory system. Influenza comes on suddenly with fever, muscle pain, headache, sore and red eyes, and a dry cough. Colds occur any time of year, while flu comes in epidemics in the winter, usually with local publicity.

CAUSE

Colds are caused by **viruses** (more than 200 types of rhinoviruses, adenoviruses, and other) which escape the action of the cilia in the upper respiratory tract, penetrate the protective layer of mucus, attach themselves to living cells and inject their genetic material. The cells' resources are then turned to making more viruses which destroy them and burst out to attack those that surround them.

In self-defense the cells release interferon and other antiviral chemicals, as well as histamine, which dilates capillaries and promotes congestion and mucus secretion. Nerve endings in the nose and trachea are stimulated by the extra fluid and congestion and initiate a sneeze or cough reflex. The miseries of a cold are primarily caused by the defensive reaction to the infection.

Colds are spread when the viruses are passed on to the mucus membranes of other people. Research suggests that most colds are *caught with the hands*, not through the air. A person with a cold sheds millions of the viruses and can easily leave a trail of them on whatever or whomever he or she touches. They can then be picked up by shaking hands, or touching a door knob, hand railing, money, or other object; then introduced onto the mucus membranes by rubbing the eyes or nose. Cold viruses can probably also be spread by kissing, sharing eating utensils, and inhaling droplets in the air from sneezing and coughing, but these modes of transmission seem less important than hand-to-hand inoculation.

People usually have fewer colds as they get older. Young children, who have no immunity to most of the viruses, average three or four colds a year. Those in their sixties average fewer than one a year, probably because they have already been infected by most of the common cold viruses and are immune to them.

Does Cold Cause Colds?

Colds can occur any time of year, in warm weather or cold. One cannot catch a cold by getting caught in a downpour or being exposed to a draft. Why, then, the common beliefs to the contrary, which are strong enough to give the illness its very name? Perhaps the stress of exposure to the cold lowers resistance to the virus and makes illness more likely if exposure does occur. Perhaps the viruses survive longer on colder objects. No one knows for sure.

TREATMENT

Certain types of interferon (a natural antiviral agent) may eventually be used to cure colds, but for at least the remainder of the 1980s there will be no

304

cure. Nevertheless, proper treatment is important because it can prevent complications and speed recovery.

Heed the symptoms early. Do not try to brave your way through them or ignore them. Greatly reduce your activity level. Rest, relax, and get extra sleep. In severe cases, stay in bed for a day or two.

Drink extra fluids, especially soups and fruit and vegetable juices. Soups and teas with chicken, cayenne, garlic, ginger, mullein, or peppermint help loosen mucus and clear the nasal passages.

Blow your nose gently, if at all, to avoid forcing infected mucus deep into the sinuses and to minimize the risk of spread to the middle ear.

Vitamin C supplements, up to 10 grams a day, apparently decrease symptoms by an antihistamine effect. Such large doses should not be taken for more than a few days.

Regardless of what the commercials may claim for cold pills, it almost never makes sense to take one, not even aspirin, for a cold. The only appropriate, safe, and effective products are certain single-ingredient nasal sprays, drops, and inhalers, and these should be used sparingly and for no longer than three days. They should never be shared, since they may contain viruses sucked into the bottle. Commercial cold "remedies" are discussed in detail in Chapter 5–1.

When To Consult a
Physician for Coldlike Symptoms

Persons with diabetes or diseases of the heart, lung, liver, or kidney should inform their physicians when they develop symptoms. So should those who have had their spleens removed.

An otherwise healthy person who develops a high fever (101°F or 38.3°C), sharp chest pains, coughing up thick phlegm, a severe sore throat, or difficult breathing should see a physician.

Children with throat pain should be seen by a physician, as should adults if there is also pus on the throat or tonsils, fever, swollen glands in the neck, a rash, a history of rheumatic fever, or exposure to someone known to have strep throat. Symptoms, other than a runny nose, that last longer than a week may be signs of a complication; a physician should be consulted.

Preventing Colds

Persons with colds should be aware that they are **shedding millions of viruses** that can infect other people. They should wash their hands often and avoid touching others or sneezing or coughing around them. It apparently helps to use "Killer Kleenex" (Avert), a tissue impregnated with citric acid, which is harmless to humans but deadly to the cold viruses.

Wash your hands before touching your eyes, nose, or mouth, especially if you have been around someone with a cold or in a public building touching railings, door handles, and other objects.

Stay in good general health; eat right, exercise, and get adequate rest and sleep.

Don't smoke and don't expose others, especially children, to smoke, which damages the cilia of the respiratory system and otherwise harms the body's defenses.

Does Vitamin C Prevent Colds?

Adequate intake of all the essential nutrients is important for optimum resistance to infections, but the evidence indicates that taking massive doses of vitamin C does not prevent colds, though it may provide some symptomatic relief. See Chapter 2–7 for more about the vitamin.

Cold Sores (Labial Herpes)

Cold sores, also known as fever blisters, are caused by *Herpes simplex virus type 1* (HSV-1), a close relative of HSV-2 which is responsible for most genital herpes. Cold sores usually occur around the outside of the mouth, but they may erupt anywhere and are highly contagious. They are painful, stinging blisters or ulcers, sometimes in groups of several and often recurrent. Each attack can last a week or two. Cold sores are usually not serious, but if the cornea is infected blindness can result and infections in infants can be life-threatening. The infection can spread to the genitals by the hands or by sexual contact and take on all the characteristics of genital herpes.

TREATMENT
There are many folk remedies and commercial products for herpes sores, but none of them speeds healing. Amino acids, especially lysine, and various vitamins and minerals are often used, but they have not been shown to be effective.

For pain relief there are various products with tannic acid, benzoin, phenol, camphor, menthol, and benzocaine. Myrrh dissolved in alcohol may help.

Do not use neomycin or other topical antibiotics; they don't affect the virus or relieve pain, and they may cause irritation and allergic reaction. Do not use steroid creams; they may spread the virus and make future flare-ups worse. Do not accept a smallpox vaccination for herpes infection. The vaccine is not effective against the virus or any other infection or condition.

See a physician right away if an eye becomes inflamed while a cold sore is present or if the sores spread from the original site. If you have painless mouth sores, they could be something more serious than herpes, such as cancer or syphilis. Consult a physician.

PREVENTION
Cold sores shed millions of viruses in the watery fluid that oozes from them. Avoid contact with persons with active infections, and if you have a cold sore avoid touching it since you could spread the virus to other parts of your body and to other persons. Wash your hands before using the toilet or touching your genitals, or your cold sore may become genital herpes. Be careful about sharing lipstick, drinking glasses, and so on. Be especially careful about touching infants and sharing objects with them if you have a cold sore.

Constipation

Infrequent, difficult bowel movements with dry, hard stools is a common complaint. This is not surprising considering the excessive fat most people eat, the heavy use of refined sugar and grains, and the low fiber content of the average diet. But some people think they are constipated when they are not, because of misconception passed on by health writers.

One popular book, *Back to Eden* by Jethro Kloss, says that the bowels should move three or four times every day, at least once following every meal. If they do not, you must drink various teas (including the poisonous mandrake) and exercise. There would seem to be little time for anything but eating and sitting on the toilet—or preparing to sit on the toilet.

One bowel movement a day is normal and most common, but more or less is not necessarily abnormal. The need to strain over stool is probably the best criterion of constipation, which should be dealt with to prevent hemorrhoids, diverticular disease, and possibly cancer of the colon.

CAUSES
Common causes include insufficient roughage and fluid in the diet, lack of exercise, excessive use of laxatives or antacids, and lack of regular bowel habits.

TREATMENT

Try deep breathing and walking.

Exercise the abdominal muscles. While holding the breath, pull the abdomen in and out rhythmically to stimulate the colon. Massage the abdomen. Use stroking, tapping, clapping, and kneading all over the abdomen.

Eat high-fiber foods (whole grains, fruits, and vegetables); eat prunes and figs and drink their juices. Drink a lot of water and take bran.

Many commercial laxatives are available. Only a few of them (the bulk remedies) can be recommended (see Chapter 5–1).

Consult a physician for persistant changes in bowel habits, bleeding, or pencil-thin stools.

PREVENTION

Eat more fruit, vegetables, and whole grains. Avoid refined, concentrated foods. Drink more water. Too much juice is not a good idea; it is better to eat the whole orange, apple, or carrot which contains the fiber.

Be active; take walks, bike rides, and swims. Tone up the abdominal muscles with leg lifts (one leg at a time), sit-ups (with knees bent), and other exercises.

If you must use aluminum-containing antacids, use the type with magnesium too, and drink plenty of water. Avoid using laxatives and enemas.

Dental and Gum Disease

Dental and gum disease, the most common health problem in the United States, is costly, painful, inconvenient, and even deadly; the spread of bacterial infection from cavities to the blood can promote certain kinds of heart and kidney disease. It is widely believed that dental health is peripheral to general health and that losing one's teeth is no big problem since dentures can be worn. But natural teeth exert enormous pressures while dentures produce, at best, one fifth of this biting and chewing force. Considering the nutritional value of whole natural foods which require plenty of chewing, perhaps this is why it is often said that dentures can cost ten years of one's lifespan.

causes

Caries (decay and decalcification) is caused by an attack and invasion by organized, highly concentrated colonies of bacteria, mostly *Streptococcus mutans* and *Lactobacillus acidophilus*. Disorganized and free-floating, these germs are harmless, and the latter may even be beneficial in the intestine. But when they manage to adhere to the surface of the teeth the trouble begins. They excrete a sticky, transparent film of dextran, multiply by the millions, and deposit more dextran.

This whitish-yellowish film of germs and dextran is called plaque and feels furry to the tongue. When the plaque is thick enough it shields the bacteria from oxygen and they begin to produce acids that eat away the tooth enamel. Soon a cavity is formed.

When plaque hardens at the gumline, germs colonize beneath it and evolve fermentation products that irritate and inflame the gums. This inflammation is known as **gingivitis,** and it can be aggravated by various irritants including broken, malformed teeth, improperly placed or overhanging fillings, poorly constructed crowns and bridges, and inadequate vitamin C in the diet.

When hardened calculus or tartar develops from plaque, its rough surface causes tiny breaks in the gum tissue and gum infection sets in. Pockets of infection form and they reach deeper toward the base of the teeth. The tiny connective tissue filaments anchoring the teeth to the gums are attacked and destroyed. This is **periodontal disease** or gum disease, once known as pyorrhea. Eventually even the jaw bone may become infected.

Genetic susceptibility to dental and gum disease varies substantially. Some people get very few cavities in spite of relatively poor eating habits and oral hygiene, while others who take more care get more cavities. But whatever one's given level of resistence, controllable factors determine the degree of damage done. In almost all cases, the disease is totally preventable, though some will have to work more at it than others.

Nutritional factors during tooth development in fetal growth, infancy, and childhood can have significant effects. Poor nutrition leads to weakness in the microstructure of the calcified tissues and vulnerability later in life, in spite of improved nutrition. Clearly, dental and gum disease prevention should begin early in life, preferably in the uterus.

The most important nutrients during and after tooth development, the lack of which commonly causes problems sooner or later, are vitamins A, C, and D and calcium, phosphorous, and fluoride. Vitamin A deficiency in the fetus or during infancy causes abnormal tooth structure, poor calcification, and reduced enamel formation.

Vitamin C deficiency causes weakening of the collagen connective tissue. The gums are spongy, bleed easily, and may ulcerate. Dentin formation is decreased. (Dentin is the bonelike bulk of the tooth, just under the harder enamel, the visible layer.) Deficiency of vitamin D, calcium, or phosphorous causes delayed eruption of teeth, poor positioning, decreased dentin and enamel, and increased susceptibility to decay. Mild deficiency of B vitamins, most commonly folate and niacin, can weaken the soft tissues and tooth-supporting structures and increase their vulnerability to infection.

Fluoride deficiency causes defective calcification and vulnerable teeth. The mineral is an essential nutrient required in growth and development. The first sign of slight deficiency is increased tooth decay. In extreme deficiency, which is very rare because practically all food and water has some fluoride, poor growth is seen.

In order to produce the sticky dextrans and the corrosive acids, the bacteria need carbohydrates. Whenever a starchy or sugary food is eaten, bacteria metabolize the residue left in the mouth and produce acid. Depending on the food, after about an hour or two (the *clearance time*) the acid level returns to normal. The sugar and starch of candies and breads have the longest clearance times and lead to the most damage.

Saliva is very important in preventing decay; it constantly washes away debris, neutralizes acid with its bicarbonate, ammonia, and arginine, and decreases bacterial acid production with its sialin, a tetrapeptide (chain of four amino acids). It also provides a constant bath of fluoride, calcium, and phosphorous for direct absorption into the enamel.

Animals with their salivary glands removed and humans with low saliva production usually experience a tremendous increase of tooth decay. This may partly explain the known action of some drugs such as amphetamines and some tranquilizers of increasing tooth decay. There is some suspicion that marijuana may have a similar effect, since it is known to cause dry mouth. Habitual mouth breathing can also lead to dry mouth and increased dental disease.

Smokers have a higher rate of jawbone decalcification and more loose teeth. This is consistent with an increased risk of osteoporosis among smokers.

Poor dental care itself can promote dental disease. Poorly placed or overhanging fillings and crowns can create crevices and areas vulnerable to plaque build-up, gum irritation, and infection.

Thumbsucking generally does *not* cause dental problems unless it continues past age four.

Early Warning Signs

Any of the following should be discussed with a dentist; they should also remind you to clean your teeth well every day.

Sensitivity to heat, cold, or sweets

Pain when chewing

310

Brown spots or little holes on a tooth

Swelling or pus around the gumline, or gums that bleed or are red or tender

A change in your bite, the way your teeth fit together

Bad breath unresponsive to thorough brushing and flossing and not due to sinus infection

Loose adult teeth

Persistant pain in the mouth or sinus area

Toothaches are rather late signs and require attention within a day or two. The best way to relieve a toothache is to clean out the cavity as thoughly as possible using a brush and vigorous rinsing. Keep food debris away from the affected tooth. Then, of course, see a dentist.

TREATMENT

Any substantially decayed area of a tooth must be scraped and drilled out, and the hole must be filled. The most common fillings are amalgams of silver, mercury, tin, and other metals; half the United States population has at least one. There is increasing concern about the health problems mercury may cause—not only for those who are allergic to the heavy metal (perhaps 5 percent of the population) but for anyone who has too much mercury in the body from all sources combined. It has been claimed that mercury in fillings can cause all kinds of psychiatric and neurological problems. So far there is only scant evidence for these claims. Nevertheless, mercury is a toxin and, if only for the protection of dentists, their aids, and sensitive patients, the trend to other materials such as plastics and ceramics is certainly a good one.

Proper treatment of dental and gum disease also involves thorough cleaning and instruction in self-care. The advice should be carefully followed in order to prevent further problems and costly and painful treatments.

Treatment of severe gum disease often involves surgery to clean the roots of the teeth. The controversial *Keyes method*, developed by dental researcher Dr. Paul Keyes, attempts to eliminate the bacteria responsible without surgery. The teeth are cleaned of plaque and the infected pockets treated with certain salt solutions which supposedly destroy bacteria. The person is taught to use an irrigating device and to clean the teeth with bicarbonate of soda, salt, and peroxide. An oral antibiotic such as tetracycline is often prescribed and the bacteria in the mouth carefully monitored.

Critics say the method can mask symptoms while the infection continues, and they criticize the use of the antibiotics as unnecessary and potentially hazardous. They also deny that the method can reduce the need for surgery. The jury is still out on the Keyes method. If you have gum disease, discuss the latest findings with your dentist. Meanwhile, keep in mind that pulsating irrigators can do serious harm if used improperly; on the other hand, a baking soda slurry used as a rinse after cleaning might be helpful and can't hurt.

PREVENTION
Long-term studies involving thousands of people prove that we now have the ability to essentially wipe out this serious infectious disease. Here we summarize the necessary steps.

Assure the best nutrition from gestation through old age. Adequate amounts of all the essential nutrients are necessary, but calcium, phosphorous, fluoride, and vitamins A, C, and D are the most important.

Eat whole natural foods. Whole grains, beans, and fresh fruits and vegetables, besides providing important nutrients, require plenty of chewing. This exercises, stimulates, and strengthens the teeth, gums, jawbones, and chewing muscles. The coarse fiber in raw produce helps clean the teeth. Lime-soaked tortillas actually help repair tiny cavities, as the calcium from the lime plugs the holes and is incorporated into the structure of the teeth.

Presweetened cereals are among the worst foods for dental health. Some have well over 50 percent sucrose, as well as refined flour, and crunchiness that forces the sticky mass between the teeth. Unfortunately, the largest group of consumers of these products, young children and teenagers, are the least likely to floss the stuff out. Chewy candies and raisins and other dried fruit can cause similar problems.

Use fluoride drinking water, rinses, and toothpastes. The fluoride greatly strengthens the teeth and even promotes remineralization of early enamel lesions. The fluoride also has an antibiotic action against the bacteria that cause decay and infect the gums.

Brush and floss carefully at least once a day, preferably before bed. No matter how well you eat, this is essential. Good, natural foods often have plenty of carbohydrate and long enough clearance times to contribute to plaque build up. Hygiene is also most important during tooth growth; a tooth kept free of plaque and decay in its early months will be less vulnerable years later.

The principle of plaque control is simple. Every surface of every tooth, including areas below the gum line in the sulcus (crevice), surfaces touching

312   other teeth, and fissures on the tops of molars must be scraped clean regularly. Thoroughness is more important than frequency. This is illustrated by a study in which volunteers ate their regular diets and did not brush or floss. Thorough cleaning by professionals every two weeks prevented all tooth decay. Such infrequent cleaning is not recommended since no one, not even a hygienist, can clean his or her own teeth this well after two weeks of plaque build up. Daily cleaning is most effective since it easily disrupts young colonies of decay-causing bacteria before they are firmly established.

    Some tooth surfaces must be cleaned with a brush; others require floss. The toothbrush should be soft. A hard or even medium brush can cause gum recession and tooth sensitivity. Soft polished nylon bristles are best. They soften up under warm water and don't have the sharp, jagged edges of boar bristles, which can put holes in your gums and promote infection.

    Toothpaste is not necessary for cleaning, though it can be useful in fluoride application. Certainly the highly abrasive type advertised as good for getting teeth very white should be avoided. Teeth are not naturally white but various shades of yellow. Heavy use of abrasive toothpaste can cause enamel thinning and tooth sensitivity. A quick brushing with a zesty toothpaste can give an illusion of a good cleaning. Some dentists recommend flossing, then brushing well with water only, then brushing with fluoride. Since fluoride cannot penetrate the bacterial plaque, it makes sense to remove the plaque before applying the fluoride.

    When brushing, systematically clean as many tooth surfaces as you can. To clean below the gum line, hold the brush at about a 45-degree angle (midway between horizontal and vertical) where the gum meets the teeth. Gently vibrate the brush to dislodge plaque between the teeth and gums.

    Now use dental floss or ribbon to clean areas you missed with the brush. Gently ease the ribbon between the teeth and insert it between the gum and each tooth, as far down as it will go. Scrape up and down a couple times. Be gentle with your gums.

    Every few months use a disclosing wafer after cleaning (they are available in drug stores) to check how good a job you are doing. The wafer releases a red dye that clings to any remaining plaque and shows areas you may have missed.

    While all this may seem like a lot of trouble, remember that one thorough cleaning a day is far more effective than two or three superficial jobs which could add up to more time and effort. In fact, one very thorough cleaning every few days is preferable to thrice daily scrubbing of the visible surfaces that leaves plaque undisturbed below the gum line and between the teeth. But daily cleaning is best and if done properly the rewards are enormous: a fresh, clean mouth, and freedom from cavities, gum disease, and all the inconvenience, pain, and often enormous expense involved.

Sealants made from a clear plastic bonding resin can seal crevices on the biting surfaces of teeth, keep bacteria out, and prevent decay. This is one of the most effective, yet underutilized preventives available. The tooth enamel is etched with acid, the sealant is applied, and light is used to harden it. It is usually applied to molars, whose rough biting surfaces are not always well-protected by fluoride. The treatment is simple, painless, and inexpensive, and it can protect for about five years.

Water-irrigation devices are recommended by some dentists in spite of the lack of evidence of benefit. If improperly used, these devices can aggravate and even cause gum disease by weakening the tissue and forcing bacteria and their byproducts into the gum. Those who use such a product should be instructed in its safe use; be especially careful about the higher settings. The spray should never be directed at an area of inflammation, irritation, or pain.

Protecting primary **baby teeth** is important since the last of them don't come out until about age thirteen. Children whose baby teeth rot away early are more likely to have speech problems, psychological problems, and a need for expensive orthodontic treatment. One of the most important preventive measures is to not put the baby to bed with a bottle of milk or juice after the teeth start erupting. All too often the fluid pools around the teeth and sits there for hours while the child sleeps. The sugars (including milk sugar) feed the bacteria which destroy the teeth.

Chlorinated pool water is often far too acid and can cause enamel erosion, with gritty, painful, chalky, or transparent teeth, in persons who swim laps frequently or otherwise spend a lot of time in the pool. The pH should be read three times a day and kept at 7.2 to 7.8. If you swim often in a pool, do not hesitate to ask the pool manager about pH readings, which are very easy to do. If in doubt, get some pH paper from a drug store, pool supply store, gardening shop, or chemical supply store and do the measurements yourself. The paper is inexpensive and simple to use; just follow the directions on the box.

Vaccines against tooth decay are being tested. The idea is to stimulate the body's production of antibodies against the *Streptococcus mutans* bacteria, which are responsible for most tooth decay.

See a dentist and hygienist regularly. Ask for specific instructions on cleaning areas you may not be doing well. Ask about sealants and fluoride treatments, especially for children.

314   Choosing a Dentist

No matter how well you eat and clean your teeth, you should see a dentist periodically to check your teeth and gums and repair damage that may have occurred. Choosing the right dentist can be very important to your oral and general health, as well as your bank account. Some dentists are much more prevention oriented than others. You want to find one who will help you prevent problems by pointing out areas you aren't cleaning well and, if necessary, showing you how to brush, floss, and use disclosing tablets. Dental hygienists can be very helpful in this area.

You also want a dentist who is not too fast with the drill. In many cases, especially if fluoride rinse or toothpaste is used, remineralization occurs and no drilling and filling is necessary. The dentin-forming cells in the tooth continue to produce dentin at a slow rate throughout the life of the tooth, and this process is speeded up when a cavity is nearby. In other words, teeth can heal themselves to some extent, especially if kept clean and well nourished.

You want a dentist who recognizes this and will "wait and see" with the smaller cavities, rather than reach for the drill, make bigger holes, and fill them with amalgam which could irritate the gums and create new zones vulnerable to plaque build-up and decay. In one important study in England, where all adults are entitled to a free dental exam every six months, those who took advantage of this were compared with those who did not. It was shown that the regular attenders had fewer healthy teeth. They had more fillings than the irregulars had decayed spots, which was attributed to overtreatment.[25]

How often you should visit your dentist is an individual matter. Most children up to about twelve should have their teeth examined and cleaned about every six months. Adults with few problems should see a dentist every year or two. But most adults can profit from twice yearly cleanings because even the most conscientious persons usually have a few isolated areas which are hard to clean and where soft plaque can change to hard calculus in a matter of weeks.

Beware the gold merchants. When considering extensive and expensive work proposed by a dentist, it is prudent to get at least one more opinion. This is especially true with gold work, about which there is much disagreement within the dental profession. It often happens that a dentist will strongly recommend several gold caps and crowns, with the prediction that teeth will be lost and gum disease will develop if the work is not done soon. The patient sees another dentist who recommends limited work and no gold, and years later the teeth are all sound, and a mortgage on the house has been avoided.

Should Drinking
Water Be Fluoridated?

In the early 1900s it was widely known that people in some southern states commonly developed brown dental stains or mottling known as "Texas teeth." In 1931 fluoride naturally present in the drinking water was found to be responsible for the dental discoloration. Thought was given to ways to remove the mineral from the water until it was found that the mottled teeth were highly resistant to tooth decay. Studies were done comparing the fluoride levels in the drinking water of various cities and the incidence of tooth decay, and they all pointed to a strong protective effect of fluoride.

A fluoride level that is too high can cause mottling, but at about 1 ppm the mineral protects the teeth without staining them. The natural concentration is much greater (up to 8 ppm) in some areas, especially in the southwest, but in other areas, particularly the northeast, the fluoride levels are often less than .1 ppm. The target level of fluoridation programs is 1 ppm. The programs have uniformly resulted in improved dental health in the affected communities, and they are strongly supported by the American Dental Association as well as the World Health Organization (WHO) and dental and medical associations around the world.

Nevertheless, strong oppositon from vocal groups has frightened many communities in the United States and Europe away from fluoridation of their water supplies. Most of the opposition comes from the National Health Federation (NHF), a group founded in the 1950s by Fred J. Hart after a United States District Court ordered him to stop distributing phony electronic treatment devices. His electronic Medical Foundation did diagnosis by mail using dried blood spots sent in from all over the country, mostly by chiropractors.

Throughout its history the NHF has, under the guise of promoting "freedom of choice" in health matters, opposed pasteurization of milk, vaccination against virulent diseases, fluoridation of water, and other public health programs. It has promoted the laetrile and pangamic acid hoaxes and has served as an umbrella group and rallying point for all manner of quackery.

The NHF's antifluoride campaign has been especially vicious and effective. The organization has sponsored and published questionable studies purporting to show that fluoride causes cancer and other health problems. These propaganda tracts have created enough fluoridation phobia to deprive millions of the benefits of the nutrient.

The 1970 WHO report (*Fluorides and Human Health*) reviewed the information from thousands of studies around the world on every aspect of

316 fluoride and found no evidence of any ill effects. Studies done by the National Cancer Institute, the U.S. Center for Disease Control, the Canadian Health and Welfare Ministry, and other leading scientific organizations have refuted the claims of a cancer-fluoride link.

Fluoridation of drinking water does not cause birth defects either. American and British studies of millions of people who drink fluoridated water have shown no link with Down's syndrome, cleft palate, clubfoot, or any other birth defect. Studies with mice have revealed no chromosomal damage even at 50 ppm of fluoride for several generations.

What about slow poisoning? Fluoride is, afterall, a poison, as are many other essential nutrients when consumed in excess. This is an important point since fluoride poisoning (fluorosis) does occur if the level is much over 10 ppm, as is the case in some areas of India. At such high levels, especially if the intake of calcium, protein, and vitamin C is low, the bones become brittle and crippling fractures occur. But the concentration in fluoridated water is a small fraction of these levels and slow poisoning is not a problem.

This is not to say there is absolutely no risk. There are examples of widespread supplementation programs resulting not only in the virtual disappearance of deficiency but in the appearance of toxicity syndromes. The vitamin D tragedy in England comes to mind (see Chapter 2–7), and iodine consumption in the United States verges on excessive for some people. So it is prudent to consider the possibility of fluoride overdosing.

Let's consider a person who eats lots of seaweed, fish, and canned and frozen foods processed with fluoridated water. Suppose he drinks a lot of tea and uses fluoridated toothpaste. Suppose also that he does not drink much milk and has a fairly low intake of calcium and other minerals, a situation which promotes fluoride absorption from the gut. This adds up to a relatively high fluoride intake and it might be argued that fluoridating this person's drinking water could push his intake too high. This is unlikely, however, because so very little is added to the water, just a drop in the bucket compared to the other sources.

To avoid excessive fluoride follow these precautions. Ask your local health or water department how much fluoride is in your drinking water. If it has more than .7 ppm, avoid supplements and excessive tea and seaweed. Children who drink fluoridated water should not use fluoridated mouthwash and should use pea-size dabs of fluoridated toothpaste. Make sure you get enough calcium, phosphorous, and magnesium in your diet; these help moderate fluoride absorption if excessive amounts are ingested.

If you live in a low-fluoride area where the political climate makes water fluoridation impossible, you can still get the benefits of the mineral by brushing and rinsing with fluoridated toothpastes and rinses. A community-wide alternative is the fluoridation of milk, which has proven spectacularly successful in reducing dental decay in school children. The milk can be

labeled so people have a choice and no hysterical arguments about Big
Brother poisoning the citizens can stand in the way.

Diabetes

Diabetes mellitus is a disease in which there is insensitivity to or inadequate
amounts of the hormone insulin, which may be slightly altered and less
potent than normal. This leads to disturbances of carbohydrate, fat, and
protein metabolism. There is often some degree of damage to blood vessels,
kidneys, eyes, and nerves, and a tendency to atherosclerosis, especially of the
heart, leg, and brain arteries. There is also increased susceptibility to infection.

There are really two types of diabetes mellitus, the insulin-dependent, ketosis-prone *type I* and the non-insulin-dependent, more stable *type
II*, often called NIDDM. Of course, we are all dependent on insulin; the terms
refer to the usual treatment for the two types. Ketosis is the state the diabetic
falls into when the blood sugar is not properly controlled.

Type I (which can occur at any age but most often begins in childhood) accounts for about 10 percent of the cases and usually has a sudden
onset with increased thirst and hunger, weight loss, weakness, fatigue, increased urination, blurred vision, irritability, and other symptoms. There is
sugar in the urine (glucosuria) because of excessive sugar in the blood (hyperglycemia). The basic problem is a severe lack of insulin, which is required
for the entry of glucose into muscle and other cells. No matter how much is
eaten the glucose does not enter the cells but accumulates in the blood and
spills into the urine.

Fat is mobilized to feed the starving cells, but their use leaves a
flood of their breakdown products, the ketones (acetone and others), in the
blood. This is *ketosis* and it is responsible for many of the symptoms and
complications of the disease. Type I diabetes is called "brittle" because ketosis is more likely than in type II. It carries a higher risk of severe complications, including blindness, kidney disease, heart disease, and nerve damage.

Type II diabetes usually affects overweight persons over thirty-five.
The onset is milder than with insulin-dependent diabetes and may include
one or more of the following symptoms: excessive thirst and urination, decreased libido, blurred vision, headache, itching, loose teeth, infection, ab-
scessed gums, weakness, and fatigue. Sometimes there are no symptoms.
Tests show hyperglycemia and sometimes glucosuria. The basic problem is
insufficient insulin and relative insensitivity to it. There is a risk of severe
visual, circulatory, and nerve complications, though not as great as in type I.

Several million Americans have type II diabetes and don't know it.
If you are over forty and fat, see a physician for a general physical examination, including a blood pressure check and possibly a blood sugar check. If

318   you have any unexplained symptoms such as unusual thirst, hunger, or fatigue, or frequent infections, let your doctor know.

CAUSE

The primary cause of insufficient insulin production is not known but is the subject of intense research. A theory rapidly gaining support is that the insulin-producing beta-cells of the pancreas are damaged by an autoimmune reaction, perhaps triggered by a virus. The abnormal production of antibodies to the beta-cells gradually destroys them until, years after the process began, the disease becomes apparent. Certain chemicals may also damage the cells and trigger diabetes; streptozotocin is the standard diabetes inducer used in labs around the world. Related substances, nitrosamines, are present in smoked meat and are suspected of being diabetes triggers on the basis of animal studies; the disease can be induced in offspring by feeding the parents smoked meat before mating.

TREATMENT

The choice of one's physician is very important because the diabetic and the physician must work together for many years and they must feel completely comfortable and confident with each other. The basic care involves the proper balancing and timing of food intake, exercise, and insulin dose, if any. Too much food and too little exercise or insulin can cause hyperglycemia, ketosis, and coma. Too little food and too much exercise or insulin can cause hypoglycemia and insulin shock.

Besides understanding these relationships, there is a need for extra care in personal hygiene, prevention and treatment of infections, and avoidance of cigarette smoking. Attention to proper nutrition and exercise is critical if one is to minimize complications.

In type I diabetes replacement of insulin is usually necessary for life, and the doses must be carefully timed and balanced with eating and physical activity. The insulin user should always have a supply (as well as some sugar) nearby and should carry an identification card or wear a bracelet with his or her insulin dose and doctor's phone number.

In type II diabetes, there is usually a good chance of achieving control by diet and exercise alone, without insulin or diabetes pills. The main goal is usually to lose fat. Many obese diabetics have more insulin than nondiabetics, but their excess fat makes their bodies resistant to it. For tips on losing fat and getting fit, see Part One.

There is considerable controversy regarding the various oral hypoglycemic agents (diabetes pills). Certainly exercise and diet are safer, but they do not always work, and some patients are not motivated enough to stick with a weight-loss program. In such cases, and when a patient refuses or is unable to inject insulin (which cannot be taken by pill), diabetes pills can be appropriate (see Chapter 5–2).

Although the subject is controversial, it appears that the risk of diabetic retinopathy, blindness, and other complications can be substantially reduced by rigid control of blood sugar levels, especially in type I diabetes. This may require the use of an insulin pump or careful self-monitoring of glucose levels and multiple insulin injections. It is also very important to control hypertension in all diabetics.

A new drug, *sorbinil*, is credited with preventing and reversing nerve damage and cataracts by preventing the accumulation of sorbitol (which occurs when blood sugar is high). It may be available soon.

Cyclosporine and other immune-suppressing drugs seem to help in some cases. This supports the autoimmune theory.

Beta-cell transplants, the insertion of healthy insulin-producing cells into the pancreas, is a promising experimental technique; it could gain wide acceptance.

The Recommended Diet

In general, the recommended diet for persons with diabetes is the same as for nondiabetics: lots of whole grains, beans, fruits, vegetables, and fish; much less beef, pork, and other red meats; low-fat dairy products are fine, but the others should be avoided. The difference is that persons with diabetes must be more regular in their eating habits and much more careful to avoid binges of consuming excess calories, fat, or sugar.

Some starchy foods cause the blood sugar to rise almost as fast as sugar does, especially if eaten alone. Individuals have different responses to different foods. In general, it is best for diabetics to eat carbohydrate foods with other foods to slow their absorption. A good meal would be a salad, rice, and fish; a small dessert may be OK as long as the calorie intake is not excessive. Alcohol should be avoided or used sparingly.

The diabetic's diet should be low in sugar, fat, and cholesterol, and high in protein, starch, and fiber. The question of sugar is controversial, but it is clear that the calorie count is more important. The reduction of fats and cholesterol is prudent since fats in the bloodstream make the cells less sensitive to insulin, and because diabetics run a very high risk of developing atherosclerosis, which is promoted by high fat and high cholesterol levels. Calories usually must be restricted and kept nearly the same from day to day.

Studies of insulin-taking diabetics show that the addition of fiber to the diet often results in lower blood sugar levels and lower insulin requirements.[26] Switching to a high-carbohydrate, high-fiber diet can reduce the insulin requirement even without weight loss. Blood fat and cholesterol levels also decline. If you are a diabetic and want to reduce or eliminate drug use, it is very important to discuss any change in your diet or exercise habits with your physician in order to avoid serious complications.

320 **PREVENTION**
Genetic susceptibility is an important factor in diabetes. However, most persons prone to the disease can greatly reduce the risk and postpone the expression of the genetic tendency by attention to the provoking factors. These are the most important triggers:

Poor diet and obesity. Excessive calories, fat, and sugar and insufficient fiber are all risky.

Poor fitness. Lack of proper exercise is conducive to fatness and insulin resistance.

Certain drugs. Oral contraceptives, ACTH, cortisone, and other drugs sometimes contribute by causing abnormal glucose tolerance.

Smoked meat and fish *might* be factors; pregnant women and even couples who want to be parents would be prudent to avoid these items, especially if they have a family history of diabetes, at least until the question is cleared up.

Breast feeding may prove to have a protective effect; if a virus is involved, the antibodies from the mother's milk might disarm them and prevent damage to the pancreatic beta-cells.

Diverticular Disease

A diverticulum is an abnormal sac or pouch in the wall of the digestive tract, most commonly in the colon. *Diverticulosis* is the presence of diverticula without symptoms; it is very common. *Diverticulitis* is an inflammation of the sacs; it is rare. In acute cases ("left-sided appendicitis") there may be severe abdominal pain, fever, constipation, nausea, gas, and other symptoms. Abcess formation, gangrene, and perforation may occur. Diagnosis is by barium enema X-ray.

In chronic diverticulitis, the walls of the bowels may thicken, constipation gets worse, and intestinal obstruction may occur. Diverticula may bleed, slowly or rapidly. This is usually painless.

CAUSE
The exact cause is not known. Genetic susceptibility seems to be a factor. Also, diverticula occur less frequently in populations who eat a lot of high-fiber foods. Lack of fiber apparently increases pressure in the colon and this increases the tendency for diverticula to be pushed out through weak areas of

the wall. Inflammation may be caused by fecaliths (trapped, hardened masses of feces), as sometimes occurs in appendicitis. Low dietary fiber may increase the formation of fecaliths since fiber holds water and keeps the stool soft.

TREATMENT

In diverticulosis, continued use of a high-fiber diet with plenty of whole grains, fruits, and vegetables and added bran may reduce the formation of new diverticula. In diverticulitis, liquid diet and antibiotics may be necessary to prevent serious complications.

PREVENTION

Eat a high-fiber diet, that is, one with plenty of fruits and vegetables and whole grains. Compensate for a low-fiber diet with bran or other roughage.

Drink adequate fluids, a bit more than enough to avoid thirst.

Don't strain while defecating.

Emphysema

In this progressively debilitating disease the lungs lose elasticity and the alveoli (air sacs) are distended or ruptured. These destructive changes make respiration, especially expiration, difficult. In extreme cases the subject is short of breath upon the slightest exertion, or even at rest.

Early detection is elusive, since considerable lung damage may occur before it shows up on X-ray and before respiration becomes difficult. It can be strongly suspected though, if there is shortness of breath and a history of smoking or chronic bronchitis.

CAUSES

Emphysema seems to result from inherited susceptibility combined with insults to the lungs. Chronic bronchitis, smoking, smog, and dust cause low-grade inflammation. This results in the release of proteases (protein destroyers) from leukocytes (white blood cells) which have converged on the area. These proteases are normally limited in their actions by inhibitors, especially alpha-I antitrypsin (AAT). But some people are genetically deficient in AAT and therefore more susceptible to tissue destruction by the proteases. Preparations of AAT are being experimented with and may eventually be effective preventives.

322

TREATMENT

Treatment usually consists of removal of the insults to the lungs to the extent possible, humidification of the air, drainage of mucus from the lungs, antibiotics for bronchial infections, sometimes drugs to break up the mucus, and sometimes bronchodilators.

Herbalists and some physicians recommend hot spices such as peppers, curry, and garlic, and teas with ginger, elecampane, coltsfoot, and cowslip to help keep the lungs clear. These may be helpful, but the potential hazards of heavy consumption are not known, so moderation is in order.

The greatest dangers in emphysema are bronchial infections and smog or smoke, which can increase bronchial secretions and block the airways to the point of suffocation. Coughing, humidification of the air, and physiotherapy may help in the crisis; but aminophylline (intravenous), tracheal suction, or oxygen may be required. Because of the great danger infections present in emphysema, influenza and pneumonia vaccination are usually recommended.

Emphysema is generally considered irreversible, and treatment is usually aimed at slowing its progress and preventing and dealing with complications. But some physicians believe that daily aerobic exercise can arrest emphysema and chronic bronchitis, improve well-being, and permit increased activity. The question whether exercise actually improves lung function is still controversial. But at the very least it can decrease the pulse and increase the efficiency of oxygen consumption.

Alpha-I antitrypsin (AAT) is the first recombinant DNA product to be granted FDA orphan drug status and about to be tested on humans. It is a protein produced in the livers of most people, and one of its functions is to inhibit the action of elastase, an enzyme that helps combat bacteria in the lungs. In some emphysema victims (a minority) the AAT is lacking, apparently due to a genetic defect; the elastase becomes overactive and attacks the lung tissue itself.

PREVENTION

Above all, don't smoke. Smoking increases the risk of emphysema ten to twenty times. Don't wait for symptoms before stopping. You could destroy more than half your lungs before you are aware of it.

Protect children from cigarette smoke and deal with their respiratory infections promptly.

Avoid dust, fumes, aerosols, and air pollution.

Treat bronchial infections promptly; use antibiotics if necessary.

Epilepsy

In these neurological disorders the persons suffer recurrent attacks of abnormal nerve discharges due to disturbed brain functions. There are about twenty types of seizure with different causes and characteristics. They may be mild and hardly noticeable, perhaps just a blank stare and detached feelings; or they may involve convulsions and loss of consciousness. Attacks are often preceded by a peculiar feeling or aura. The victim may fall, bite the tongue, pass urine, and froth at the mouth; or may appear to stop breathing and turn blue before the attack is over. Severe seizures are often followed by sleepiness or confusion.

CAUSES

Most cases involve one or a combination of the following: genetic predisposition, localized brain damage, or increased cerebral excitability due to metabolic disturbance.

A major contributing cause is head injury which "scars" brain tissue and causes abnormal electical activity. Sometimes the brain lesion is acquired before, during, or shortly after birth and produces epileptic symptoms years later. Trauma, infection, tumors, and impaired circulation are some of the causes. Sometimes the cause is not identifiable.

Hypoglycemia (low blood sugar) is one of the metabolic disturbances that may increase cerebral excitability and predispose to an attack, which can also be triggered by emotional stress or overexcitement.

Nonepileptic seizures can be caused by various insults, including withdrawal from alcohol, heroin, methadone, or barbiturates; deficiency of vitamin B-6 or magnesium (especially in infants); and lead poisoning.

TREATMENT

In an acute attack the head should be positioned for easy breathing. The person should lie on his side, not his back. Tongue biting may be prevented by placing a pad between the teeth, but be sure it is too large to swallow, like a folded handkerchief. However, you should not put a finger in the mouth of a person experiencing a seizure; a serious bite could result.

Seizures almost always stop by themselves. If they continue one after another without consciousness returning, immediate medical attention is required. Moreover, anyone who has a seizure for the first time should see a physician immediately.

In general, the patient should:

Maintain a well-balanced diet with plenty of fiber and fluids to prevent constipation

Avoid alcohol, psychedelic drugs, and strobe lights

Be active but avoid excessive fatigue or overexcitement and get plenty of rest and sleep

Carry a card or wear a bracelet indicating the problem and how to handle it

Avoid very hazardous occupations and recreations such as solitary swimming and rock climbing; driving and operating heavy machinery may be restricted by law.

There are many drugs used to control the several types of epilepsy; the right one must be carefully chosen and its concentration in the blood carefully monitored. Proper choice and use of anticonvulsants usually prevents seizures, but there can be serious side effects. Benefits and risks must be weighed. (See Chapter 5–2 for more on anticonvulsants.)

Family understanding and support are very important in helping the person live with epilepsy and lead a normal life. Moreover, by decreasing emotional stress, plenty of love and affection may decrease cerebral excitability and so decrease attacks, and help prevent psychological complications as well.

Sometimes epilepsy clears up spontaneously. Sometimes surgery is necessary to remove a tumor or a focal area that triggers attacks.

PREVENTION

Prevent head injuries. Wear seat belts in cars and helmets on motorcycles. Young children should be securely strapped into safety seats even for short trips.

Prevent measles with vaccinations.

Prevent toxemia and other complications of pregnancy. The most important factors here are good diet, avoidance of unnecessary drugs, and delivery in a hospital where facilities are available to deal with complications.

Prevent drug abuse, especially of narcotics, alcohol, barbiturates, and amphetamines, all of which have been associated with convulsions.

Genetic counseling may be in order in severe cases, but the genetic factor is rarely so strong or clear-cut that persons with epilepsy should consider not having children.

Fungus Infections

Various kinds of fungus can infect the skin on the scalp, head, trunk, nails, hands, and feet. Reddish or greyish patches with itching, stinging, and scaling are the usual symptoms. On the trunk and scalp the lesions appear ringlike. Sometimes the hair falls out or is easily pulled out. Treatment can ease discomfort, forstall possibly serious complications, and prevent infecting others.

CAUSE
Several fungi produce this type of infection, which is spread by contact with infected persons or their clothing or from infected pets, especially cats.

In the case of athlete's foot, moist areas in showers and around swimming pools can harbor and spread the fungi, but they are very widespread, perhaps on everyone's feet most of the time. Some people are much more susceptible than others, for unknown reasons.

TREATMENT
Avoid scratching, rubbing, or even touching the area. Keep the skin clean, cool, and dry. It may be necessary to decrease activity in order to decrease heat and moisture. Stimulants like coffee, tea, and colas may increase perspiration. Wear only clean, dry, loose clothing.

For athlete's foot, wash between the toes and dry well twice a day. A drying agent like calamine or talcum powder will help keep the area dry. Put on clean socks after washing. Whenever possible go barefoot or wear sandals to allow maximum ventilation.

These simple measures are often effective without resorting to drugs. It is important to apply them and try to avoid the drugs because the raw, infected skin is highly sensitive to irritation, and allergic reaction to the medicines and other ingredients in the preparations is very common.

Nevertheless, drugs are sometimes needed and some very effective ones are available, particularly tolnaftate and miconazole. Benzoic acid with salicylic acid, undecylenic acid, and aluminum chloride (30% solution) are helpful and less expensive.

Allergic persons should test the medicine on a small area of skin before using. It is important not to overtreat if irritation and dermatitis are to be avoided.

In very stubborn cases, a physician may prescribe oral griseofulvin, which gets into the skin via the blood and kills the fungi. It is especially effective when the face, neck, trunk, and nails are affected.

PREVENTION
Infected persons and animals should be treated to prevent infecting others.

326   Avoid sharing clothes, towels, hairbrushes, combs, and caps, especially if you know you are susceptible.

Use rubber or wood sandals in public or communal showers.

Keep your skin clear, dry, and cool. Use cotton clothes, especially socks, in preference to synthetics, which tend to trap the moisture on the skin.

Wear sandals, slippers, or other open footwear whenever possible to decrease moisture and heat. Don't wear airtight shoes or clothes.

Gallstones

The gallbladder is a small sac under the liver which stores bile from the liver and releases it into the duodenum, where it helps digest fats. The bile contains bile acids, cholesterol, lecithin, calcium, and other substances. Sometimes these become too concentrated, or supersaturated, and stones crystallize in the sac.

Nearly a third of all women and a fifth of all men past forty have gallstones, but few of them experience any symptoms. A stone may block the bile duct or cause it to spasm; this can be very painful and cause nausea, vomiting, fever, and jaundice. Severe complications can ensue, and the problem must be treated. Diabetics are particularly prone to develop infections at the site of gallstones.

CAUSE

Why does the bile become supersaturated and give rise to stones? Unfortunately, we do not know. Genetics, age, obesity, and pregnancy are predisposing factors. Hemolytic anemia sometimes promotes gallstone formation.

Dietary protein and fat stimulate bile production. Fat also stimulates release of the bile into the intestine. But the role of diet in gallstone formation is poorly understood. Moderate alcohol consumption may decrease gallstone formation, while excessive sugar and calories, as well as birth control pills and other sources of estrogen, tend to promote it, as do fasting and the drug chlorfibrate, which lowers blood lipids.

TREATMENT

It is generally agreed that treatment is necessary if the stones cause symptoms or if the victim is diabetic. Beyond that there is controversy.

Some physicians believe stones always call for surgical removal of the gallbladder, even if there are no symptoms. This is because once stones appear they are likely to continue to form, and sooner or later they are bound to cause trouble. In addition, the presence of stones increases the risk of gallbladder cancer. Thus, it is argued that it is better to remove the gallbladder when the person is young and healthy than to wait until surgery is riskier.

The organ is not essential; if it is removed, bile goes straight from the liver to the intestine.

Others argue that such major surgery should be avoided unless absolutely necessary, that the risk of cancer of the colon is greater with surgery than without, possibly because of prolonged contact of the bile acids with the intestinal lining.[27] Moreover, surgery does not always solve the problem anyway, since stones can form in the duct that carries bile from the liver to the intestine. Each case must be considered with a physician on the basis of the severity of the problem, age, general health, and the level of risk for colon cancer (family history, fat content of diet, and other factors).

In a few cases treatment consists of avoiding fatty, greasy foods and taking chenodeoxycholic acid ("cheno"), a natural bile acid which increases the solubility of cholesterol in the bile. Unfortunately, the drug does not work on the majority of stones (they tend to recur) and it can cause liver disease.

PREVENTION

Avoid obesity, but don't fast. Beyond this, diet has not been proven to be an important factor in gallstone formation. Nevertheless, it seems reasonable to keep cholesterol levels low since most stones are made mainly of cholesterol. Moreover, a high fiber intake may decrease the cholesterol concentration in the bile. Therefore, it would seem prudent to avoid a lot of animal fat and to eat whole grains, vegetables, and fruit. Soy protein has an effect similar to that of fiber, so tofu, tempeh, and other soy products might help prevent gallstone formation.[28]

Gout

One of the most painful of ailments, gouty arthritis is credited with inspiring John Milton's writing of the torments of Hell in *Paradise Lost*. The sixteenth century English physician Thomas Sydenhan, a victim for thirty-five years, described the pain as "a violent stretching and tearing of the ligaments, a gnawing pain with pressure and tightening. One cannot bear the weight of the bedclothes nor the jar of a person walking in the room. The night is spent in torture and sleeplessness."

The pain is caused by the build up of needle-shaped uric acid crystals in the joints—especially in the big toe—and the inflammatory reaction to these crystals. If untreated, permanent deformity of the joint may result.

CAUSE

The disease is usually caused by an inherited predisposition to excessive uric acid in the blood, either because of overproduction or deficient excretion of

328 the acid. Not everyone with the excess suffers from gout—for unknown reasons only about one in six of them gets the deposits in the joints and all the consequences.

The usual victims are men over thirty-five. The sedentary and obese are more likely victims than the active and slender. Injury and stress to joints, such as wearing shoes that are too tight, can precipitate attacks. So can acute illness such as heart attack or pneumonia.

TREATMENT

Drugs are very important here: anti-inflammatory agents such as colchicine, NSAIDS, and corticosteroids are effective in acute attacks; uric acid removers such as probenecid and sulfinpyrazone increase its excretion in the urine; allopurinol decreases uric acid production. These prescription drugs are described in Chapter 5–2. **Do not take aspirin.**

Rest is important during a flare-up. The joint should be elevated on a pillow. A high liquid intake is very important to help remove the uric acid.

Proper nutrition is important: preventing obesity helps keep uric acid levels down; moreover, foods rich in purines should be avoided, at least during an attack, since they are broken down to uric acid. These foods include glandular meats, liver, anchovies, sardines, shellfish, brewer's yeast, and asparagus. Alcohol may also aggravate the problem by increasing uric acid levels.

Eating cherries is an old folk remedy, but there is no hard evidence it works. Studies are needed. Eating cherries would certainly be preferble to taking gout drugs if it did help.

PREVENTION

The condition is usually genetically determined, and it can't be prevented in a fundamental sense. But most acute attacks can be prevented by moderation in eating and drinking and careful use of the appropriate drugs.

Headaches

Possibly the most common of human pains, headaches are almost always due to dilation, constriction, spasm, irritation, or inflammation of arteries or muscles of the head and neck. Sometimes more than one of these factors is at work. The type of pain is determined by the cause.

Tension headaches, or muscle contraction headaches, are the most common. The pain, usually tightness and pressure without exact location, involves the sustained constriction of scalp, neck, and face muscles. Poor pos-

ture on the job (computer, desk, cash register, assembly line), with prolonged flexion of the neck can trigger such a headache. Depression, fatigue,
mental tension, and emotional stress can also be factors.

Remedies include rest, quiet, warm bath, gentle massage, aspirin and other
pain relievers (see Chapter 5–1), and meditation and relaxation exercises (see
Part Six). The frequent victim needs more rest and relaxation and less emotional and mental stress.

A modern acupressure technique may help. It involves pressing
hard on certain nerves; this jams circuits to the brain and relieves the pain.
The hard edge of the thumbnail should be used and the points pressed hard
enough to hurt for fifteen to thirty seconds. This is repeated several times.
For details see Acupuncture and Acupressure in Part Six.

Migraine headaches are often preceded or accompanied by visual and psychological changes and sometimes nausea and vomiting. The pain, which is
usually limited to one side, is pounding and often incapacitating. Migraines
are fairly common, especially among young women; they affect perhaps
8 percent of the United States population and tend to run in families.

Migraine headaches are apparently caused by vascular changes—
first constriction of certain arteries, then dilation and traction (stretching) of
the nerves surrounding them; throbbing pain coincides with the pulse. Hormonal and allergic factors have been blamed for the painful series of events,
but the exact cause has not been pinned down.

TREATMENT
Treatment includes relaxation, certain drugs, biofeedback, acupuncture, and
acupressure. At the first sign of an attack it is important to sit or lie in a
quiet, dark room. Two to four aspirin or the prescribed dose of ergotamine
tartrate or other medication, taken right away, may abort the attack. More
potent drugs are used in severe cases; consult your physician.

> **Relaxation and biofeedback** seem to help some.[29] The person
> learns to increase blood flow to the extremities at the first sign of an
> attack. Practice this technique several times, then apply it when
> you sense a headache coming on: close your eyes and relax as well
> as you can under the circumstances; as vividly as you can, imagine
> your hands and feet warming up, then getting hotter and hotter,
> until they feel on fire; at the same time, visualize your head and
> neck packed with ice or snow.

> **Acupuncture** may help. Needles are inserted into various points
> on the head. The treatment may work by changing blood flow
> patterns, increasing relaxation, promoting endorphin release, or by

suggestion. (Endorphins are powerful morphinelike hormones produced in the brain.) **Acupressure** may also be worth trying (see Part Six).

Suspected precipitating factors include certain **foods** (especially cheeses, wine, beer, chocolate, vinegar, pickles, organ meats, preserved fish and meat, soybeans, lima beans, onions, spinach, and foods with MSG or nitrates), **niacin** in large doses (which can dilate the blood vessels), **alcohol, caffeine, nicotine, estrogen** (naturally during the menstrual cycle or from oral contraceptives or estrogen replacement therapy), **excessive sun,** and **chemicals** (fumes and vapors). [30]

Emotional stress seems to be very important in provoking migraines. Personal problems must be dealt with, with the aid of a counselor if necessary. The person should have free, open, repeated expression of conflicts and resentments.

Cluster headaches, like migraines, are associated with changes in the blood vessels of the neck and head, and some specialists consider them migraine variants. They are distinguished from typical migraines by a knifelike, piercing pain around and behind one eye, which is tearing and red, and by a runny nose and a racing heart. The pain is very severe but nonthrobbing, and the onset and cessation are sudden. The headaches tend to occur in clusters of several a day with recurrences every few weeks or more often.

Cluster headaches are much less common than migraines, do not run in families, and affect men much more often than women. Ergotamine tartrate is the most common remedy, but lithium, cortisone, and oxygen are sometimes used. Simply stopping smoking often provides dramatic relief from recurrent attacks.

Sinus headaches can be brought on by sinusitis, colds, or hay fever. See separate discussions of these afflictions.

Food sensitivity headaches can be brought on by chocolate, red wines, ripened cheeses, excessive salt, preservatives, flavor enhancers (such as MSG), and other foodstuffs. Careful observation may be required to determine the culprit.

Alcohol headaches usually occur hours after drinking and are often the main aspect of a hangover. Acetaminophen or aspirin can relieve the pain, but there is a danger of stomach irritation and bleeding, especially with the latter; so take some food, water, or antacid too. Those susceptible to ulcers should not take aspirin (or drink, for that matter).

Smoking headaches can be caused by inhaling cigarette or cigar smoke.

Marijuana headaches can occur shortly after smoking or eating cannabis, especially large amounts, or hours later as a hangover. This is most common with frequent and heavy smokers.

Toxic headaches can be caused by exposure to chemicals such as benzene, gasoline, paints, formaldehyde, and glue.

Caffeine-withdrawal headaches are fairly common to those who normally drink coffee, tea, or colas every day, then suddenly stop. Taking caffeine after the headache starts is often not effective, but aspirin may help. Ease off caffeine rather than quitting "cold turkey."

High blood pressure headaches occur in about 10 percent of those with hypertension, and usually happen in the morning. They may be very severe and resemble a migraine, but migraine medicines should not be used. Antihypertensive drug therapy is usually necessary.

Low blood sugar sometimes causes headaches. See Hypoglycemia.

Bruxism headaches can be caused by excessive clenching and grinding the teeth or excessive gum chewing. Learn to relax and decrease emotional tension.

TMJ headaches. Abnormal temporomandibular joints (where the jaw meets the skull) can cause headaches, neck and shoulder pain, dizziness, and other symptoms. The joint dysfunction may be due to arthritis, injury, habitually clenching the teeth, biting on hard objects, excessive gum chewing or other overuse, or malocclusion (bad bite). TMJ should be considered as a cause of the symptoms if there is pain or clicking noises when the jaw is moved, if the jaw seems to lock or dislocate or has limited movement, or if the teeth are sore or excessively worn.

Many dentists are trained to detect and treat TMJ syndromes. A removable plastic biteplate fitted to the upper teeth and worn for about four months (except when eating or brushing the teeth) often solves the problem. Other remedies include fixing bad teeth, replacing missing teeth, spot grinding of high spots in the bite, braces, and surgical repair of the joints.

Carbon dioxide headaches can be caused by sleeping in an unventilated room with a gas or wood heater on, or with the covers over the head, which some people do in defense against mosquitos.

332 **Dehydration** can cause headaches. Drink lots of water before and during prolonged exercise or exposure to sun or heat, including a sauna bath.

Important: Rarely, a headache is a sign of a tumor, meningitis, stroke, glaucoma, diabetes, or other serious problem. Anyone with a severe headache of unknown origin, or a headache associated with nausea, fever, or other symptoms, or a headache associated with head injury, even days after the injury, should see a physician.

Hearing Loss and Earaches

The ear consists of three compartments: the outer ear with the ear canal leading to the tympanic membrane (eardrum); the middle ear with the three bones of hearing and connected to the throat by the eustachian tube; and the inner ear where mechanical vibrations are converted to nerve impulses. Hearing problems can originate in any of these three parts and can be caused by a variety of factors.

CAUSES AND PREVENTION
Pushing things into the ear is a common cause of outer-ear infection. Common objects for children are pebbles, beads, and pencils; adults prefer toothpicks and earswabs. The ears should be cleaned with a little finger and soapy water. Don't attempt to remove accumulated wax from your ears unless you have been shown how by a nurse or doctor.

Earwax normally works its way out of the ear canal along with dust and bacteria. Occasionally excessive amounts accumulate and interfere with hearing. Earswabs are more likely to impact the earwax against the eardrum than to clean it out. A physician, nurse, or you can remove it with a warm water ear syringe. Using an earwax softener first may help. The syringe and glycerol are available at most drugstores. Keep in mind, though, that earwax helps waterproof and germ-proof your ear canals, and helps keep them warm, thus inhibiting the bony growth of "surfer's ear." Too little earwax probably causes more problems than too much (see below).

Middle-ear infection (viral or bacterial) can come from the throat, nose, or sinuses via the eustachian tube. Vigorous nose blowing or swimming may spread such an infection and should be avoided. Antibiotics are often necessary to clear infection and prevent hearing loss.

Diving (high or deep-water) can cause perforation of the eardrum and infection of the middle ear. If promptly treated, hearing loss can be prevented. Learn to adjust the middle-ear pressure when diving more than about ten feet deep. Many face masks are constructed so that you can hold your nose while blowing out your cheeks with your mouth closed. This forces air into the middle ear to balance the water pressure against the eardrum from the outer ear.

Swimmer's ear, also known as tropical ear or otitis externa, is an inflammation of the skin of the ear canal. The thickened skin narrows the canal, traps water in it, and causes pain, itching, and partial hearing loss. Persons with this problem should wear earplugs or dry their ear canals with a hair dryer or isopropyl alcohol eardrops after swimming.

CAUTION
If the alcohol irritates, stop using it.

Surfer's ear is the growth of bony protrusions into the ear canal as a result of irritation by cold. These growths can block the canal, trap water, promote infection, and cause deafness. Untreated, this condition can require expensive surgery. Use of earplugs whenever exposed to water or wind can conserve earwax, keep the canals warm, and prevent the bony growth. Severe cases may even be reversible if the ears are religiously kept warm with earplugs in the water (except when diving below ten feet) and a hat over the ears out of the water, especially when sleeping. Several months may be required.

    The best earplugs for surfing have tiny holes which allow some sound to enter while keeping water out, and leashes to prevent loss during wipeouts. Ask at a sporting goods store or surf shop. The original brand, Doc's Proplugs, were invented by a Santa Cruz physician with exhaustive experience in the ear problems of surfers; they come in different sizes and work quite well.

Excessive noise is perhaps the greatest threat to hearing, or at least the most widespread. Prolonged exposure apparently harms the inner ear's delicate *organ of Corti*, which converts vibrations to nerve impulses. Loud machinery and loud music are common problems; rock musicians and frequent concert goers often suffer impaired hearing. Many bars and night clubs play music so loud it can only be tolerated by drinking alcohol. Alcohol and barbiturates and have been shown to weaken the ability of the stapedius muscle to contract; marijuana, tranquilizers, and other drugs may do the same. This small muscle in the middle ear is stimulated to contract by loud sounds, and reduces sound transmission to the inner ear. When this safety mechanism is compromised by drugs, the ears are more susceptible to noise damage.

334   **Dietary fat** may affect hearing. The inner ear is highly vascular, well supplied with blood, and has a high metabolic rate. Factors that affect this
supply of blood and nutrients may affect hearing. Some studies have shown
a high correlation of hearing loss with elevated blood fats and cholesterol,
abnormal glucose tolerance, and obesity. Large intake of saturated fats may
cause sludging of the blood, which slows microcirculation. Restriction of
saturated fats and cholesterol and weight loss have been reported helpful in
some cases.

Vitamin A and perhaps the B vitamins appear to be involved in hearing.
Vitamin A is highly concentrated in the inner ear, and deficient animals
develop poor inner-ear circulation and susceptibility to infections. In one
study of 300 patients with hearing loss, 249 showed much improved hearing
after supplements of vitamin A and the B complex.

Other factors that can affect hearing by affecting inner ear circulation or nerve activity are cigarette **smoking, alcohol, hypertension, atherosclerosis,** and numerous **drugs.** The decrease in high-frequency hearing associated with aging may or may not be due to circulatory changes.

It is a good idea to have your hearing tested periodically. **See a
physician** about any ear problems, infections, discharge, buzzing or ringing,
or apparent diminished hearing.

Heart Disease

A variety of anatomical and functional abnormalities cause potentially lethal
disorders of the heart. They may be congenital or due to infections, tumors,
or problems in other organs—but all other forms of heart disease are dwarfed
by *coronary artery disease* (CAD), also (somewhat illogically) called coronary
heart disease (CHD). CAD is the single most common cause of death in the
United States. Most CAD is caused by the deposition of atheromas (fatty,
mineralized plaques) on the insides of the coronary arteries, which feed the
heart muscle. The disease is insidious; it develops over decades until the
arteries are so clogged that severe symptoms, or even death, occur without
warning. CAD is largely preventable (see Atherosclerosis).

Hepatitis

Hepatitis means inflamation of the liver. There are many causes of hepatitis,
including certain poisons and drugs, gallstones, parasites, and bacterial infections, but the term is most often used to indicate viral liver infection, the
most common cause. Only these will be discussed here.

There are three major forms of viral hepatitis: type A, type B, and

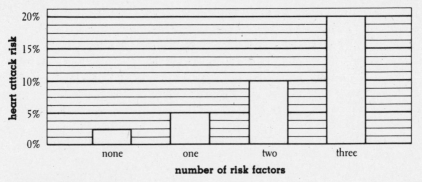

Heart Attack Risk

Heart attack risk as related to number of risk factors in men age 30 to 60. (Though the risk for women is somewhat less, the risk factors are similarly additive.) The risk factors considered here are high blood cholesterol, high blood pressure, and cigarette smoking.

non-A/non-B. The symptoms are similar, but they are caused by distinct viruses (HAV and HBV) and are different diseases. Type A is sometimes called infectious hepatitis and type B serum hepatitis, but these names are misleading and obsolete. Non-A/non-B hepatitis is caused by other, mostly unidentified, viruses.

Hepatitis A

This is the milder, more common form. The infection is very contagious and spreads rapidly where people live in close quarters, share a kitchen, or endure poor sanitary conditions. Prisons, mental hospitals, homes for the retarded, military units, and day-care centers are especially at risk. During the incubation and acute periods, enormous quantities of viruses are excreted with the stool, and invisible traces may contaminate food and water supplies and be passed on by close personal contact. Sexual contact (hetero- or homosexual) can also spread the virus; the infection is common among promiscuous people.

The symptoms begin two to six weeks after exposure. The first ones resemble the flu—muscle aches, headache, eye discomfort in bright light, and low-grade fever. A few days later loss of appetite, malaise, weakness, nausea, and vomiting may occur. At this point the virus is spread throughout the body and the illness resembles the flu. Typically, after about a week of this, the virus invades the liver. The urine turns a brownish color while the stools may become pale. Diarrhea sometimes occurs. Jaundice deepens as malaise and weakness worsen. The right upper abdomen may be swollen and sore due to liver inflammation.

Improvement in all symptoms begins one to two weeks after the onset of jaundice. Full recovery can take several months.

The liver is a very resilient organ capable of completely repairing itself after even the most severe hepatitis A infection. About 99 percent of previously healthy individuals enjoy complete recovery. Death is very rare. One bout of this illness confers lifelong immunity to hepatitis A.

TREATMENT

There is no drug effective against the virus, though this may change in the next few years.

A well-balanced diet with adequate vitamins, minerals, and proteins will speed recovery by providing the nutrients necessary for liver repair. Attractive meals should be served to help stimulate the appetite, which is often poor. There is no proof that any special or extreme diet is helpful, but a moderate to high amount of protein and a moderate to low amount of fat are thought to help.

Absolute bed rest does not seem to speed recovery, but vigorous physical activity should be avoided. The return to normal activities should be gradual.

Alcohol and recreational drugs should be completely avoided and therapeutic drug use minimized.

PREVENTION

Immune globulin injections may be in order if you have been or will be exposed to the virus; ask a physician. For example, if a member of the household or a sex partner comes down with the infection, or if you are going to an area where sanitation is poor and the disease is common, one or more injections could prevent severe illness, even if infection occurs.

Avoid contaminated water for swimming, fishing, and clamming. Heed the warnings of your local health department. Also, do not eat raw shellfish, which often harbor live viruses. Always obey the local laws and codes on sewage disposal. This is very important in preventing contamination of water supplies.

Avoid intimate contact with anyone who has hepatitis.

Infected persons should not handle food, water, or eating and drinking utensils that others use. If possible they should have separate toilet facilities and their clothes should be washed separately. They should keep their hands scrupulously clean, as should close contacts (household members, fellow workers).

Food handlers, especially in institutions and restaurants, should always wash their hands very well before work. If a food handler is diagnosed as having hepatitis A, he or she should be removed from the job (until well) and immune globulin should be considered for fellow employees and possibly patrons.

A vaccine is being developed, but is several years away.

Day-Care Centers and Hepatitis A

The problem of hepatitis A outbreaks in day-care centers is steadily growing.[31] Because infected children of day-care age usually have no symptoms and still wear diapers, which must be changed, the virus is easily spread among the staff and children, then to all their families. If hepatitis occurs in one of these families all the families should be alerted to the possibility of infection, and the staff should take preventive measures focusing on diapered children.

It is very important that the staff, children, and parents wash their hands thoroughly and often. Soiled diapers must be handled carefully and properly disposed of. Surfaces used for diaper changing should be impermeable (but not kitchen tables or counter tops) and should be cleaned and disinfected with household bleach diluted 1:32 (1/2 cup per gallon water) prepared daily and sprayed from spray bottles. Accessories used in diaper changing should also be disinfected each day.

The Center for Disease Control suggests that day-care centers with outbreaks should not be closed and parents should not transfer their children to other centers. But new admissions should be suspended or required to receive immune globulin.

If even one case occurs in a center, immune globulin for all employees and children and their families should be considered.

Hepatitis B

This infection is not quite as common (in the United States) as hepatitis A, is usually more severe, and tends to last longer. The initial symptoms are similar, with a flulike illness for a week or so. Cycles of liver damage and jaundice, with improvement and relapse, can go on for years. The disease is sometimes associated with skin rashes, arthritis, and kidney damage. It is not often fatal in the United States, but it can lead to cirrhosis or cancer of the liver.

Like HAV, HBV can be transmitted through blood, saliva, and feces. An invisibly small speck of blood is enough to infect, so medical technicians and researchers must be extremely careful handling blood and other body

338 fluids. Acupuncture needles can transmit the virus even if they have been soaked in alcohol or ammonium compounds and appear sparkling clean. The sharing of needles by drug users is a common cause of spread of the virus.

A serious problem involving all modes of transmission is that many people, perhaps 1 percent of the United States population, are lifetime *carriers* of the virus without ever getting sick from it. And those who do get sick are "silent" carriers for the six week or longer incubation period.

While hepatitis B is a relatively small problem in the United States, it affects hundreds of millions worldwide.[32] In some countries 20 percent or more of the population are carriers. Some victims never experience illness during years of infection, yet eventually die of liver cancer or cirrhosis. And if they are women, they often pass the infection on to their newborn at birth. In some areas where hepatitis B is common (parts of South America, Western Africa, southern Italy) the newly discovered *delta virus* seems to work in concert with the HBV to cause acute hepatitis and cirrhosis.

TREATMENT
Treatment is essentially the same as for hepatitis A: rest, good nutrition, and avoidance of alcohol and other drugs.

PREVENTION
Hepatitis B is well worth preventing, not only because of the misery it causes itself but because it greatly increases the risk of liver cancer.

Don't inject illicit drugs, especially not with shared needles or syringes.

Dispose of all articles contaminated with blood. It is best not to share razors, toothbrushes, towels, and the like. This is mandatory with infected persons and known carriers.

Avoid sexual intimacies with known carriers of hepatitis B and with sexually promiscuous persons.

In institutions and restaurants heat sterilization of all food-handling implements and careful cleaning of all instruments and surfaces is very important.

Hepatitis B vaccination and immune globulin should be considered for persons belonging to high-risk groups including:

> Health care workers in frequent contact with blood, including dentists and hygienists
>
> Sexual and other close contacts of hepatitis B carriers

Infants born to hepatitis B carrier mothers

Long-term male prison inmates

People from areas where the disease is common

Promiscuous homosexual men

Users of illicit, injectable drugs

Dialysis and hemophilia patients

Institutionalized mentally retarded persons

Unfortunately, very few of those at risk have been vaccinated, in many cases because of fear that the vaccine may cause AIDS since it is derived from the plasma of persons who have been infected with hepatitis, including some who are at risk for AIDS. The hepatitis B vaccine became available about the same time the AIDS epidemic was gaining steam and getting a lot of press coverage. We want to emphasize, then, that the vaccine is highly purified and treated to destroy *all* viruses that might be present; there is *no* chance of contracting AIDS from it.

The main problem with the vaccine is its high cost. Recombinant DNA techniques may lead to a cheaper vaccine not made from plasma. This would lead to much wider—perhaps universal—use. There is even hope of eradication of the virus, as was accomplished with smallpox.

Non-A/Non-B Viral Hepatitis

Several others viruses can cause hepatitis, and these will be collectively called non-A/non-B until further study clarifies their role. Like types A and B, they are transmitted through the oral route, infected blood, or shared needles, and the infection can be as severe as with the type B virus. Thousands of cases each year are associated with blood transfusions. The recent identification of a major non-A/non-B hepatitis virus will result in a safer national blood supply and possibly a vaccine.

Hernia

A hernia is a weakness in the tissue supporting an organ that eventually allows it to protrude. Inguinal hernia is by far the most common, and is much more common in men. It is usually first noticed as a bulge in the groin area. This bulge is a segment of intestine pushing through a weakness in the abdominal wall where, during early development, the testes descended into the scrotum. A variation, femoral hernia, occurs more often in women, but not nearly as often as inguinal hernia.

340

In both cases vigorous straining can force the gut to bulge out through the weakened area. Lifting heavy weights, repeated coughing or sneezing, and straining over stool are all potential precipitating factors. Obesity also increases the pressure on the abdominal wall.

The great danger in hernia is strangulation whereby the blood supply is cut of to the loop of intestine involved. Gangrene can set in and death can occur if the problem is not surgically treated.

TREATMENT

Surgery is almost always the only way to correct a hernia. Trusses are very inconvenient and do nothing to strengthen the weak area or prevent strangulation.

PREVENTION

Keep fit. Especially, keep the abdominal muscles strong.

Don't lift weights you are not fit to lift. Lift weights properly, using leg muscles more than back or abdominal muscles. Carry weights on the shoulders rather than the hip or abdomen.

Avoid constipation and straining while defecating.

Hypertension

Sustained high blood pressure, the "silent killer," is a major cause of death in the United States. One out of five Americans is affected, but only half of them know it and not all of these are being effectively treated. Much progress has been made in recent years in identifying and treating hypertensives, and this is already being reflected in lower stroke and heart disease incidence. But much more remains to be done.

The problem with high blood pressure is that it damages arteries and vital organs like the heart, kidneys, brain, and retina. It is a major factor in about three-fourths of all heart attacks and strokes. The person often feels completely normal until serious harm has been done. Sudden collapse and paralysis due to a stroke (a damaged brain artery) may be the first symptom.

Hypertension is so harmful that blood pressure is the most important factor life insurance companies use to determine life expectancy and premiums. At every age, the higher the blood pressure, the shorter the life expectancy. For example, a thirty-five-year-old man with a moderately elevated pressure of 150/100 is considered to have about a sixteen-year shorter life expectancy than if he had 120/80. The first number, systolic pressure, refers to the pressure (in millimeters of mercury) during heartbeat; the second, diastolic pressure, refers to the pressure between beats.

There is some difference of opinion about the exact definition of high blood pressure. Generally, a diastolic pressure over 90 is cause for concern, especially in younger persons. Systolic pressure is also important, but it is more variable; 150 is slightly high for someone over sixty, but very high for a teenager.

Several readings are usually necessary to be sure the high pressure is sustained and not temporary. It is important that a physician not diagnose a person as hypertensive when he is not, since this could lead to unnecessary drug use, inconvenience, expense, and higher life insurance premiums.

CAUSE[33,34,35]

In very few cases the cause of hypertension can be traced to a drug, an adrenal tumor or other hormone disorder, a congenital pinching of the aorta (the main artery from the heart), abnormal kidney function, or poor circulation to one or both kidneys. But in at least 90 percent of the cases no definite cause can be determined, and the condition is called essential hypertension. Fortunately, some important predisposing factors are well known, and this knowledge makes control of hypertension and prevention of early disability and death possible.

Obesity and inactivity are major factors in hypertension. It has been estimated that men 30 percent overweight have about a sixfold greater incidence of stroke and sudden death. In many cases of hypertension, weight reduction is all that is needed to reduce pressure to normal. Moreover, regular aerobic activity can help normalize hypertension even without weight loss.

Excess salt consumption is often a factor. Sodium is an essential nutrient, but adequate amounts are generally available in natural foods without added salt. In studies of primitive people, those who use salt as a food preserver and as a condiment almost always have significant problems with blood pressure. Neighboring tribes who don't use salt don't have the problem. In parts of Japan where the average consumption of salt is about 30 grams per day, mostly from fermented soy products, almost half the population has hypertension. Not everyone is sensitive to salt, however. It is believed that about 10 percent of the U.S. population is, but there is no way to identify them before hypertension develops.

The intake of salt in the United States is generally 10 to 15 grams per day, about ten times what it needs to be. Much of this is hidden in almost every kind of processed food on the market. Hypertension experts suggest that reduction of salt intake to 2 grams per day starting in infancy could bring this huge public health problem under control in one generation.

Excessive sugar in the diet may act synergistically with excessive salt in promoting hypertension, according to studies on monkeys.

342 **Inadequate potassium** is sometimes a factor in hypertension; it seems to provide some protection against excess sodium intake. When consumption of fresh produce is down and consumption of meat and processed foods is up, hypertension is more likely. The main sources of the mineral are fresh fruits and vegetables, especially bananas, oranges, apples, and tomatoes.

Inadequate calcium and magnesium have been implicated, the former more strongly. The mechanism is not understood, but the effect is strong enough to warrant clinical trials.

Smoking is a factor in hypertension. Other things being equal, smokers are much more likely to develop hypertension than nonsmokers and much more likely to develop the malignant phase of the disease and die than those who don't smoke. Moreover, if a cerebral aneurysm (an abnormal ballooning) is present, the likelihood of rupture is much greater in smokers.

Prolonged stress may contribute to hypertension. Blood pressure normally increases with excitement or alarm, then drops to normal. In some people, each bout of excessive stress pushes blood pressure slightly higher than before, and it eventually remains higher than normal. Some people who lose their jobs experience blood pressure rises which do not drop until they find new work.

Drugs, including estrogens, indomethacin, phenylpropanolamine (the appetite suppressant), amphetamine, and cocaine, provoke hypertension in some users.

Excessive licorice can cause hypertension.

Genetics plays a major role in hypertension. Some people are more susceptible to the risk factors (see above) than others.

TREATMENT
Drugs have been the main treatment since World War II. They have unquestionably helped reduce disability and death. They are relatively innocuous, but they do pose certain hazards (see Chapter 5–2).

Fat loss in obese hypertensives is often the most effective treatment, better than either salt restriction or drugs. See Parts One and Two for tips on exercise and diet.

Exercise can sometimes help reduce blood pressure even if weight does not decrease. Aerobic exercises such as running, swimming, hiking, and biking are the best for all-around fitness.

Salt restriction can be effective in some cases but not others. The first effective treatment for hypertension was Kempner's low-salt rice diet (see High-Starch Diets in Chapter 2–10). Depending on the individual, the restriction may be moderate or strict; the advice of the physician or dietician must be followed.

Polyunsaturates in place of saturated fats in the diet seems to help in some cases. In a study of hypertensive teenagers who were not being treated with drugs, the group that went on a diet rich in corn oil with very little animal fats showed a significant drop in blood pressure compared to the controls, who ate the usual portions of butter, bacon, egg yolks, and whole milk.

Dietary fiber, for unknown reasons, seems to affect blood pressure. A low-fiber diet tends to increase pressure, while a high-fiber diet decreases pressure.

Garlic may help reduce blood pressure.[36] The relatively low incidence of hypertension and heart disease in some Mediterranean countries may be linked to the high consumption of garlic. See Chapter 5–3 for a detailed look at the herb.

Stress control often helps.[37] Yoga, meditation, and biofeedback are all techniques to aid deep relaxation, which helps lower blood pressure. In one study of twenty hypertensives using a yoga relaxation technique and a device that indicates the level of relaxation, sixteen improved greatly, with the average blood pressure dropping from 160/102 to 134/86. Most of the group were able to reduce or eliminate their drugs.

Other studies of those using meditation have also reported significant blood pressure reductions. The specific method used is not as important as applying it faithfully and achieving a deep relaxation one to four times a day. The pressure reduction is not just for the duration of the session; the person's baseline pressure may be reduced over a period of weeks, and stay reduced as long as the sessions continue. It tends to rise as the practice tapers off. See Relaxation and Meditation in Part Six for an effective technique derived from an ancient Tibetan Buddhist meditation.

All the nondrug methods require more willpower than do drug methods. Because of the lack of symptoms, it is often difficult to muster and maintain the willpower to stick to a treatment. Even the drug users have to be reminded and nagged about keeping up the treatment.

If you are determined to use nondrug methods, to stick to a low-salt, low-calorie, high-fiber diet, to exercise, stop smoking, eat garlic, and

344 meditate, or some combination of these, should you avoid or quit drugs and rely completely on the other remedies? In borderline and mild cases, this is probably all right. But in more severe cases, such as when diastolic pressure is consistently above 110, drugs are usually preferable. As the other methods take effect, as weight is lost and the blood pressure drops, the drugs can be gradually reduced. Each individual is different, and whatever works best for him or her is the treatment of choice.

Anyone diagnosed as hypertensive should get a device to measure blood pressure and learn to use it. A doctor or nurse can teach you. Self-monitoring is useful because it involves the person in the treatment and provides more accurate readings than the sporadic office readings, which are so often affected by psychological stress factors.

PREVENTION

About 11 percent of the population between the ages of twelve and twenty-four have hypertension and may eventually suffer strokes, brain damage, or heart disease. While hypertension usually becomes apparent later in life, it often begins in childhood, so preventive measures should start early and involve whole families.

Some experts think all families should have blood-pressure mea-suring devices and record each member's daily fluctuations regardless of the absence of risk factors or signs of high pressure. Use daily much as you would a toothbrush, one popular writer recommends. We think this is going too far. It is fine to have the device and use it periodically, but excessive worry and compulsive record keeping could do more harm than good.

But regular monitoring (once or twice a month) should become a habit if you use birth control pills, are obese or sedentary, smoke, or have a family history of hypertension or heart disease.

Participation, preferably of whole families, in efforts to reduce and eliminate risk factors is much more important than a monitoring device. This means exercising, not smoking, learning to relax, and eating right— avoid excessive salt, sugar, and fat, and get enough potassium, calcium, magnesium, and fiber. A diet with a variety of fruits, vegetables, grains, low-fat dairy products, and lean meat and fish is ideal.

Hypoglycemia

Hypoglycemia is not a disease but an abnormally low level of blood glucose which may be caused by many different factors and diseases. Since the brain and nervous system depend on glucose for proper functioning, the symptoms can include weakness, fatigue, hunger, headache, sleepiness, forgetfulness, and irritability. Because low blood sugar tends to stimulate adrenaline secre-

tion there may also be sweating, trembling, heart palpitations, and anxiety—
and in extreme cases, coma.

CAUSES

Overdose of insulin or diabetes pills

Excess insulin secretion from the pancreatic islet cells due to tumors (rare)

Pituitary abnormalities resulting in inadequate amounts of
adrenocorticotropic hormone (ACTH), thyroid stimulating hormone, or growth hormone (rare)

Liver disease, in which inadequate glucose is stored (as glycogen)
and response to need is sluggish

Liver enzyme defects, such as glycogen storage disease, fructose
intolerance, and other rare hereditary disorders

Many drugs, including alcohol, antihistamines, antidepressants,
salicylates (including aspirin), phenylbutazone, and possibly
marijuana and caffeine

Fasting and starving are obvious causes of low blood sugar—the
stores of glycogen in liver and muscle are depleted in a few
hours, and the conversion of body protein to glucose is not always efficient enough to prevent hypoglycemia

In all these cases, it is necessary to treat the cause of the problem,
not the end results or symptoms.

Reactive Hypoglycemia

This is another form of hypoglycemia, and it may affect more persons than
all the others combined, though surely not as many as some people claim.
After carbohydrates are eaten the pancreatic islet cells overreact and secrete
too much insulin. This causes the blood sugar to plunge, and the person
feels weak, tired, and hungry.

There is disagreement about who and how many people suffer
from this condition. In recent years it has been a fashionable disease to
diagnose and self-diagnose. *Prevention* magazine columnist Carlton Fredericks, the Hypoglycemic Foundation, and others claim that 20 to 50 million
unknowingly suffer from this problem, and that it causes serious depression,
schizophrenia, fatigue, drug addiction, criminal behavior, and sexual impotence. The American Diabetes Association, the Endocrine Society, the

346 American Medical Association, and others say that very few people suffer from reactive hypoglycemia and that the condition rarely contributes to these nervous, mental, and behavioral problems.

The Glucose Tolerance Test (GTT) is often used to detect hypoglycemia. The subject drinks about 100 grams of glucose in water on an empty stomach. Blood glucose, and sometimes insulin and other hormones, are then measured for the next two to six hours. If the blood-glucose level drops to very low levels (below 50 mg per 100 ml blood) and the typical symptoms appear, reactive hypoglycemia is very likely.

The test is not infallible, however, and the results are subject to various interpretations. They may be affected by the level of activity before the test or by fear of the test itself. Moreover, some people experience no symptoms even with very low blood-sugar levels. Others experience symptoms in spite of normal levels, in which case the cause is not hypoglycemia. Anxiety, like hyypoglycemia, can stimulate release of adrenaline, which can cause sweating, fast heart beat, and trembling.

So who should take the test? Some people have severe symptoms suggesting hypoglycemia, and the GTT may be essential in diagnosing the problem, especially if the cause is a tumor or other serious defect. But for millions of people with vague unexplained symptoms who suspect they have hypoglycemia because of what they have read in popular magazines, the GTT is often a waste of time and money. The results are too often equivocal, indicating hypoglycemia to one physician but not to another. In most cases, it makes more sense to simply try the treatment. If it works, stick with it; if not, the problem lies elsewhere.

TREATMENT
The treatment of choice is a change of diet to eliminate rapidly absorbed carbohydrates or avoid eating them alone. If after a breakfast of concentrated sugars (such as fruit juice, toast with jelly or honey, pancakes with syrup) you start to feel weak and hungry long before lunch time, you might suspect reactive hypoglycemia. Try switching to a breakfast with coarse whole grain cereal and little or no added sugar or honey, a piece of fruit instead of the juice, a protein drink with milk, yogurt, peanut butter, and perhaps brewer's yeast and wheat germ. Fish and lean meat are good if you can take the time to prepare them or if you like leftovers. Coffee, tea, colas, and other sources of caffeine and its relatives seem to provoke hypoglycemic reactions in some, so lay off them, too.

If a breakfast of this sort provides you with more stamina and lets you make it to lunch without undue fatigue or hunger, you might well have an oversensitive pancreas and reactive hypoglycemia. You should avoid concentrated sweets and starches as much as possible and have small, frequent meals rather than large ones. Snacks should be nuts, seeds, yogurt, and the like.

Beware the
Hypoglycemia Doctors and ACE

Hypoglycemia is a favorite diagnosis with some physicians because it explains so many symptoms. A few assume that nearly all their patients are hypoglycemic, unless proven otherwise. Some of them, encouraged by very misleading literature from the Hypoglycemic Foundation, give their patients adrenal cortical extract (ACE). ACE is a mixture of adrenal hormones from slaughtered animals and is given on the very dubious theory that all or most hypoglycemia is caused by adrenal insufficiency.

Cortisone from the adrenal glands tends to counter the effects of insulin and raise blood sugar levels. It has the same powerful effects, and the same hazards, as synthetic cortisone. The claims by the Hypoglycemia Foundation that ACE does not inhibit normal pituitary and adrenal function are false. Like all cortisone-type hormones, ACE suppresses the secretion of ACTH by the pituitary, and one's own cortisone production is consequently reduced. This is a natural consequence of the feedback regulation of cortisone output. Used for long periods, ACE can cause serious suppression of the adrenals, making the person dependent on it—and on the physician who dispenses it.

There are no legitimate uses of ACE. The assumptions that nearly all nervous and mental symptoms are due to hypoglycemia and that all hypoglycemia is due to adrenal insufficiency, are completely unwarranted and very dangerous. If a physician suggests ACE injections, we strongly recommend you get a second opinion.

It is ironic that some popular health magazines, such as *Prevention,* which regularly run articles on the dangers of cortisone and other drugs and hormones, have published articles praising ACE as a harmless and useful therapy for hypoglycemics.

Infectious Mononucleosis

See Mononucleosis, below.

Influenza (Flu)

Influenza symptoms such as weakness, loss of appetite, upper respiratory problems, and a feverish feeling often cause it to be confused with the common cold (see Colds). But it is really a different and much more serious disease. Every winter there are outbreaks, frequently epidemics that afflict millions. The vast majority recover fully, but thousands of elderly and

348

chronically ill persons die from the infection or its complications, especially bacterial pneumonia. Moreover, there are occasional pandemics, extremely virulent and deadly outbreaks that result in millions of deaths. The "Spanish flu" of 1918 killed more than a half million in the United States and perhaps 25 million worldwide, more than any other pestilence including the Black Plague epidemics of the Middle Ages. The other major pandemics of this century were the "Asian flu" of 1957 and the "Hong Kong flu" of 1968.[38]

How To Tell a Cold from the Flu

People have widely differing reactions to colds and the flu, and there is no single symptom that distinguishes the two. In general, however, it can be said that colds come on gradually, usually do not cause high fever (except in children), and have localized symptoms such as sneezing and a runny nose. Influenza usually begins with a fever, hits suddenly and severely, and often causes muscle pain, chills, headache, sore and red eyes, flushed skin, and a dry, hacking cough. If there is a local flu outbreak and these symptoms appear, the ailment is probably influenza.

CAUSE

Influenza is caused by three basic types of virus, A, B, and C. They are spread from person to person and by contact with contaminated objects. Type A causes the seasonal outbreaks as well as major pandemics, type B causes smaller outbreaks, and type C is rarely a serious problem.

Once inside a host cell a flu virus commandeers its biochemical machinery and uses it to reproduce itself by the thousands. These break out and infect other cells. Most people easily develop the necessary antibodies, molecules that latch onto the invaders and inactivate them so that a given virus can infect them only once. Unfortunately, influenza viruses have an uncanny ability to change from year to year just enough to confound the immune system. These small changes in structure, known as "drift," are caused by spontaneous mutations and are responsible for the seasonal outbreaks, which are usually limited because lingering immunity to the old form provides partial protection.

When a virus undergoes a large change that results in a completely different protein on its surface, lingering immunity to previous strains no longer helps, and a pandemic results that can afflict hundreds of millions. Such large changes, known as "shifts," are believed to result when two strains of virus infect the same cell and shuffle genes. For example, some scientists believe the Hong Kong flu virus arose when a strain of duck flu virus found its way into a human cell already infected with a human strain. The resulting hybrid struck down about 200,000 Americans and left about 40,000 dead in six weeks.

Wild ducks seem to play an important role in the epidemiology of influenza. The viruses grow rapidly in their intestinal tracts without causing illness, are passed from duck to duck in pond water, and are spread around the world in their feces during migrations. They can then be acquired by humans, pigs, horses, turkeys, and other animals.

TREATMENT

Most people stricken by the flu need only to rest and take lots of fluid to fully recover within a week or so. Vitamin and mineral supplements are advisable if food intake is greatly reduced, but there is no evidence of benefit from megadoses of vitamin C or other nutrients.

Aspirin can help reduce symptoms in adults, but is not recommended for children because of its possible association with the rare but very serious Reye's syndrome which includes vomiting, violent headache, listlessness, irritability, delirium, and disturbed breathing and can lead to coma and death. If such symptoms are seen in a child with or recently recovered from a flulike illness, a physician should be called immediately. The aspirin substitute acetaminophin is safe and effective for reducing flu symptoms in children.

For people in certain high-risk groups influenza can be very serious, and their physicians should be notified so that complications can be watched for. The groups include the elderly, persons with chronic disease, young children, and pregnant women. The antiviral drug amantadine can lessen the severity of the illness if given soon enough, but the side effects often outweigh the benefits.

PREVENTION

Vaccines are strongly recommended every year for certain people, 80 percent of whom never get them. Every spring representatives of the U.S. Center for Disease Control and the Food and Drug Administration and other medical experts meet to determine what flu virus strains to put in the next season's vaccine, based on information from outbreaks all over the world. Many thousands of different flu virus strains are kept on ice in laboratories for this purpose. Those believed to be likely to result in epidemics are inactivated and placed in the vaccine, which stimulates the formation of antibodies to the viruses in those inoculated.

Because the protection provided by the vaccine is transient, immunization of the general population is not feasible. Instead, it is recommended for the following **high risk groups** (in order of priority):

Adults and children with chronic respiratory or cardiovascular disorders

Residents of nursing homes and other chronic-care facilities

Doctors, nurses, and others who have extensive contact with high-risk groups

Otherwise healthy persons over age sixty-five

Adults and children with diabetes, kidney problems, or other chronic disorders

The antiviral drug amantadine is sometimes used to supplement the vaccine.

Avoid close contact with infected persons, including sharing drinks, foods, and eating implements. Avoidance of crowds during the flu season may reduce the chance of infection.

Don't smoke. It increases the likelihood and severity of infection by reducing the effectiveness of the mucus and cilia which normally trap dust and microbes and keep them out of the lungs. Passive exposure to smoke also increases susceptibility, especially in children.

Insomnia

It is estimated that about one-fourth of the adult population of America uses at least one chemical to help them sleep; many others take different measures.

While asleep we are not just in one specific level or stage of consciousness (or unconsciousness). Rather, we move in and out of various stages, including the relaxed awake "alpha state," light sleep, the dream state (with rapid eye movement, muscle twitches, and irregular pulse and blood pressure), and different levels of deep sleep with high-amplitude, slow brain waves and, apparently, complete suspension of consciousness.

We experience each stage several times each night, usually in the order above, including the relaxed awake state. While many people do not remember waking in the night, others seem to remember only the awake stage of the cycle and imagine no others occurred. In one study, insomniacs in a sleep lab were instructed to push a button if they heard the bedside buzzer at night. In spite of failing to respond to the buzzer several times in the night, many subjects insisted they had not slept at all. This and other studies show that some people imagine they sleep much less than they really do.

There is no rigid rule about how much sleep one needs. The average is about eight hours per night. Children, pregnant women, and sick people generally need more than others. Some may need as little as five or six hours, especially healthy older people. The best criterion is how you feel in the morning.

Whatever your daily sleep requirement, it need not be taken all in one session. Some people may function better on five or six hours at night, plus an hour or two in the afternoon. Social inconvenience is the main obstacle, not physiological need.

Illusions aside, sometimes people go for long periods with less sleep, and less restful sleep, than they need physiologically. Prolonged inadequate sleep and dreaming can cause profound psychological and physical disturbances. Sleep is probably necessary for the regeneration of depleted neurotransmitters, without which brain cells cannot communicate properly with each other or with the rest of the body.

Factors that Inhibit Sleep

Mental stress. Don't take your social, business, or other problems to bed with you.

Sedentary life style.

Television at bedtime is overstimulating for some. Commercials are especially irritating. Comedies are the least disturbing for most.

Frustrating sexual stimulation can make for a sleepless night.

Drugs are among the most common causes of insomnia. Stimulants like amphetamines, cocaine, psychedelics, caffeine, and appetite suppressants are obvious. But even supposed sleep aids can disturb natural sleep by suppressing dreams, increasing excitability as they wear off, and creating dependency. Nevertheless, benzodiazepines are sometimes warranted (see Chapter 5–2). They should not be used for more than a few weeks (ten at most), then they should be gradually withdrawn.

Herbs can inhibit sleep and dreaming. Examples are coffee, tea, gotu kola, damiana, yohimbe, desert tea (ephedra, Mormon tea), and large doses of ginseng. Garlic and cayenne pepper can be very stimulating in large amounts and can inhibit sleep. Marijuana may inhibit dreaming, producing less natural, restful sleep.

Factors that Promote Sleep

Regular sleeping habits in a comfortable bed. Regularity helps the mind wind down and turn off as a matter of routine.

352

Exercise during the day or even after dinner can help promote relaxation and sleep. Walking, jogging, yoga, dancing, swimming, bicycle riding, or any activity that works the muscles promotes sleep later. But if it is done too close to bedtime it could be stimulating instead.

Satisfying sexual activity can promote restful sleep.

Autosuggestion and meditation can be very helpful in promoting relaxation and sleep. See Part Six.

Tryptophan, an essential amino acid, apparently helps promote sleep by increasing brain serotonin. Because amino acids compete for absorption into the blood and entry into the brain, it is best to take tryptophan supplements with a high-carbohydrate, low-protein meal or alone near bedtime. Although doses of one or two grams are taken regularly by many people with apparent safety, there is a theoretical possibility that such doses could, over many months, induce a deficiency of other amino acids in those with very low protein intake, especially if the tryptophan is taken with meals.

Chemical sleep aids can help promote relaxation and sleep. They can be useful in occasional cases of extreme anxiety, grief, or pain. Used regularly, they can inhibit rather than promote natural sleep. See Part Five for more details.

Some herbs can promote relaxation and sleep. Like the drugs, they are not recommended for regular use. These are listed approximately in order of decreasing strength: hops, valerian, lady's slipper, passion flower, catnip, skullcap. See Chapter 5–3 for details.

Kidney Disease

There are many diseases that affect the kidneys and interfere with their filtering, purifying, and regulating functions. Since they have a large reserve capacity, the symptoms may be mild until large areas of both kidneys are involved. Then waste accumulates in the blood, causing severe illness with nausea, vomiting, headaches, and anemia. If infection is present there may be painful, burning urination with bloody, brown, or cloudy urine.

In chronic renal failure, calcium and phosphate metabolism are disturbed causing weak bones susceptible to fractures, and (rarely) deposits of calcium and phosphate in soft tissues such as the lung, blood vessels, joints, and the eye.

In severe renal failure, uremia (urine in the blood) may cause convulsions, coma, heart and lung failure, and ultimately death.

CAUSES

Here are some of the major causes of kidney disease and failure.

> Diabetes, which damages small blood vessels in the kidneys
>
> High blood pressure and atherosclerosis, which damage blood vessels in and leading to the kidneys
>
> Urinary tract infections which can spread to the kidneys and cause serious damage (probably less likely than once believed)
>
> Kidney stones, which can damage the kidneys by sheer size or by provoking infection
>
> Bacterial infection such as tuberculosis, which directly damages the kidneys, and streptococcal infection, antibodies to which can turn against the kidneys
>
> Preeclampsia, a complication of pregnancy with hypertension and kidney malfunction
>
> Too much vitamin D, which can cause calcium deposits to form in the kidney
>
> Various drugs including phenacetin (no longer sold in the U.S.) and combinations of aspirin and acetaminophen
>
> Heavy metals such as lead, mercury, gold, and cadmium, as well as insecticides and other chemicals that get into the body through food, water, and air

Unfortunately, in many cases of kidney disease the onset is insidious and the cause is not known.

TREATMENT

Kidney infection must be treated to prevent permanent damage. If it is not completely eradicated it could spread silently and cause severe relapse. Chronic infection can end in destruction of the kidneys and uremia. Therefore it is very important to determine the bacteria involved and clear the infection completely. A patient should not neglect prescribed antibiotics or follow-up examination because the infection seems to be gone.

In some cases large amounts of protein are lost in the urine and must be replaced in the diet. In other cases protein, sodium, potassium, magnesium, water, and some other nutrients must be restricted. The therapeutic diet depends on the type and stage of the disease. Quackery can be deadly here. Expert care is required to lighten the kidneys' load and prevent toxic levels of minerals, protein wastes, and water from accumulating; at the same time, malnutrition and dehydration must be prevented. If protein is restricted, plenty of carbohydrate and fat is recommended to prevent tissue breakdown.

354   Dialysis (blood filtering by a "kidney machine") and kidney transplant are offered to patients with uremia. Potential donors should know that the human kidneys have enormous reserve capacity, and we can live perfectly well with only one (as long as it is healthy, of course).

PREVENTION

Prevent and control hypertension, diabetes, atherosclerosis, and urinary tract infections (see separate discussions of each).

Prevent and control strep throat and skin infections. Children especially should avoid close contact with those with sore throats, boils, or infected cuts or abrasions. If you have a sore throat and relatives or other close contacts have recently had strep throat, or if there is a red skin rash, fever, or pus in the back of the throat, see a physician right away.

Minimize exposure to heavy metals, insecticides, drugs, and toxic chemicals.

Kidney Stones

Kidney stones are common and often very painful. They are most often calcium oxalate precipitates, but phosphate and uric acid stones are also common. They may be the size of a grain of sand or a small fist, and can cause infection, bloody urine, and vomiting. The problem tends to run in families and is often chronic, with recurrences throughout life. Stones are more common in men than women, and are rare in children and blacks. All these stones are dangerous, but the worst are those that block the ureter and cause urine to back up into the kidneys; they are also the most painful. Diagnosis is by urinalysis and X-ray of the kidneys.

CAUSES

There are many causes and precipitating factors. One of the most important is genetic predisposition to high concentrations of calcium, oxalate, or uric acid in the urine. Some people absorb much more than the usual one-third of dietary calcium, or form more than the usual amount of oxalate in metabolism.

Anything that further concentrates these substances can provoke stone formation. Examples are excessive vitamin D, milk, calcium antacids, oxalate-containing foods, and low fluid intake. Prolonged bed rest or immobilization can cause demineralization of the bones and thereby increase the risk of stone formation.

Dietary deficiencies, especially of vitamin B-6, thiamine, and magnesium, encourage stone formation.[39]

High-purine foods (mostly animal meats), acidic urine, and low fluid intake promote uric acid stone formation. Fasting, which mobilizes protein for energy and inhibits uric acid excretion, can do the same.

Infections and anatomic abnormalities of the kidney increase the risk by providing a focus for stone precipitation.

TREATMENT

Surgery may be necessary to remove stones. Newer, less traumatic methods use a tiny stone-breaking jackhammer and ultrasonic devices. Stones should be analyzed so rational measures can be taken, both to eliminate them and to prevent other from forming.

Prevention of Calcium Oxalate Stones

Drink enough fluid to make very dilute urine. This will usually be about two liters a day, more in hot weather.

Take at least 10 mg of vitamin B-6 and 300 mg of magnesium every day. Long-term studies have shown this to be very effective in many cases. Apparently the vitamin B-6 helps reduce oxalate formation, while magnesium helps keep oxalate in solution.

Eat a well-balanced diet with adequate amounts of all the essential nutrients. Avoid excessive vitamin D and calcium-containing antacids. Total vitamin D intake should not exceed about 800 IU per day and total calcium about 2 grams. Half those amounts are adequate for most people, but pregnant women and those susceptible to osteoporosis may need this much.

Avoid, or eat sparingly, foods rich in oxalates such as spinach, dandelion greens, rhubarb, parsely, sweet potatoes, asparagus, cranberries, chocolate, almonds, peanuts, walnuts, pecans, and tea.

Some drugs, including potassium phosphate, potassium citrate, and diuretics, may be prescribed.

Theoretically, too much vitamin C may increase oxalate precipitation. A gram or two per day is not thought to be risky, but larger amounts might be.

Prevention of Uric Acid Stones

Drink lots of water, enough to make very dilute urine. This will usually be about two liters a day, more in hot weather.

Eat a well-balanced diet with adequate amounts of all the essential nutrients. Restrict concentrated purines in the diet—anchovies, sardines, brewer's yeast, organ meats.

356 Keep the urine alkaline. A low protein diet is helpful. Too much vitamin C will acidify the urine.

Allopurinol helps prevent stone formation by reducing uric acid production. Drugs that promote the excretion of uric acid through the urine such as probenecid and sulfinpyrazone must be avoided.

Malaria

Two decades ago malaria was on the decline under the onslaught of insecticides, drugs, and other measures. The optimists once spoke of eradication. But malaria has made a comeback and such hopes have faded. Hundreds of millions of people are stricken each year, mostly in tropical and subtropical areas of Africa, Asia, South America, and the South Pacific. India and other countries have experienced enormous increases in malaria incidence and deaths over the last twenty years. Worldwide, perhaps five million people a year die from the disease and millions are chronically infected. Malaria is rare in the United States, but is of interest because Americans often travel to malarious areas.

The infected person suffers shaking chills, relapsing fever, enlarged spleen, anemia, and prostration. The infection may last for months or years without therapy. Complications can result in kidney failure, shock, pulmonary edema, coma, and death.

CAUSE

The ancient Romans had an inkling of the cause: mal-aria, the "bad air" of the swamps, was responsible. More precisely, as we now know, infected female Anopheles mosquito transmits Plasmodia (a type of protozoan) to humans when it draws blood. The victim may experience slight sickness for about an hour at this time. The protozoa enter the liver cells where they grow for five to sixteen days, depending on the species.

When they are mature, they break out of the liver and enter the blood, causing fever and chills, and find their way into red blood cells. There they grow for two or three days, depending on the species, then break out, again causing fever, and go into more red cells. The infected blood cells become defective and are destroyed when they rupture.

There are several hundred species of Anopheles mosquitos that can transmit the infection to humans. There are at least five species of Plasmodia responsible: *P. falciparium, P. vivax, P. malariae, P. ovale, and P. knowlesi.* Sometimes these parasites are transmitted from cattle, monkeys, or other animals to humans by mosquitos. Transmission also occurs by blood transfusion and by common use of hypodermic syringes among drug addicts.

In falciparium malaria, the most common type, the liver form does not persist. In others it does, which makes effective treatment more difficult. If the liver forms are not killed, they may break out and cause a relapse months, even years, later.

The body fights the infection fairly effectively and death is rarely due directly to infection. Antibodies coat the parasites and prevent their entry into the red cells. Then they are removed from the circulation by special cells in the bone marrow, spleen, and liver. This battle may go on for years.

But complications, such as the damaged red cells clogging up the capillaries, can cause severe damage to vital organs, especially the kidneys, and this can cause death.

TREATMENT

Cinchona bark was used by the Incas for hundreds of years. It contains *quinine*, which is still used today. *Chloroquine*, a close relative, is the drug of choice for most cases, but specific treatments change frequently as the organisms change and new drugs are developed.

Other drugs are used to prevent relapses due to some surviving plasmodia in the liver and red cells. It is especially important that the drugs be used *exactly as prescribed*, since the treatment is based on knowledge of the behavior of the various types of Plasmodia.

There is no other effective treatment. Bed rest and fluids are important. Aspirin may ease discomfort. All serious complications must be dealt with by a physician.

PREVENTION

If you are entering a malarious area, *be prepared*. Use mosquito netting, screens, insecticides, and repellants to avoid contact with mosquitos. N, N-diethyltoluamide or DEET is the best repellant; look for products with it.

To be sure, you may want to take drugs to prevent infection. The choice of medicine will depend on the species in question. Check with a physician or with the Public Health Department for specific recommendations before departure.

Chloroquine is the usual choice, taken for a week or two before entering the area. It must be continued for six weeks after departure. In some cases, fourteen days of primaquine should then be taken to kill the liver forms. Some tourists and other travelers ignore this last phase and are infected weeks or months later.

PREVENTION ON A COMMUNITY LEVEL

Eradication is no longer spoken of; reasonable control is the only hope. The tools include draining and filling mosquito breeding areas, insecticides, daily drug use by large populations, and screening blood donors who have been to malarious areas.

On the bright side, vaccines are being developed and human trials will start soon.

358 Measles (Rubeola)

Measles is a preventable virus disease which usually strikes before adolescence. The first symptoms are like those of influenza, with fever, a dry cough, drowsiness, and loss of appetite, and with tiny white spots on the inner cheeks. Photophobia (light sensitivity and avoidance) and itchy, red eyes are common. There may also be a sore throat.

The rash usually appears on about the fifth day, first on the face then spreading downward, and it lasts up to about a week. The spots start out pink and blotchy and tend to darken and merge into red patches.

Complications can be serious. Encephalitis is rare but may cause permanent brain or nerve damage, or even death. More common are secondary bacterial infections and pneumonia, the major cause of death in measles. Such complications are much more likely in the malnourished or chronically ill.

Measles is highly contagious; the virus is spread in droplets exhaled or coughed out, and on articles that come in contact with nose or throat secretions.

TREATMENT

The person should be isolated from close contact with others, both to avoid spreading the disease and to avoid exposure to bacteria which could cause complications. The room should be well ventilated but comfortably warm.

Plenty of fluids should be taken. Aspirin or acetaminophen and cool sponge baths may ease discomfort.

Reading is not harmful as long as the required light does not cause discomfort.

A physician should be **called** if there is an earache, sore throat, or rapid breathing.

A physician should be **seen right away** if there is vomiting, convulsion, severe lethargy or headache, or bleeding from the nose, mouth, rectum, or into the skin.

PREVENTION

Immunize, preferably at about fifteen months, but later for those who have not had the disease or been vaccinated. Later immunization does not cause adverse side effects as was once feared—large numbers of college students followed for weeks after immunization showed no increase in the incidence of symptoms such as fever, rash, sore throat, or headache. Measles could be eliminated in the United States and possibly the world if people were more diligent about getting their children vaccinated.

Mental and Emotional Disturbances

Mental illness is the most nebulous and controversial class of diseases. Endless arguments have gone on for decades about what is normal, what is sick, and how (and whether) health professionals can help mentally and emotionally disturbed people. The trend is toward increasing demand by the public for treatment. People want professional help for problems they used to handle by themselves or with help from family and friends. Psychotherapy is often seen as a way to perfect oneself mentally and spiritually, a privilege once available only to the rich but now available to the common person, thanks to various forms of health insurance.

Psychotherapy is not for everyone, and some evidence indicates it may not be indicated for most of those who seek it. Studies comparing thousands of patients treated by psychotherapists with untreated controls, persons waiting to get into therapy, and persons given placebo pills (alleged to be new and especially effective) suggest that most of them recover from their emotional or psychoneurotic problems equally fast.

Some people are actually harmed by therapy. They may become addicts, emotionally dependent on the therapist, and unable to let go of the treatment. Or the stress of intense analytic therapy may make their symptoms more severe.

When Psychotherapy Should Be Tried

In spite of its imperfections, there are certainly times when psychotherapy should be tried. While many mild to moderate emotional problems are best dealt with by oneself or with the help of friends and loved ones, the seriously disturbed often do better with professional help. Here are some indications that such help may be called for.

Compulsive behavior such as stealing, gambling, lying, and drug addition

Unexplained fatigue, loss of enthusiasm for life, **sadness,** extreme introversion, decreased libido, vague headaches, waking up hours early and not being able to go back to sleep (get a physical check up first)

Inability to accept one's **sex,** or unhappiness with one's sexual orientation or behavior

360 **Confusion, hallucinations,** or a persistent sense of strangeness that interferes with normal activities

Eating disorders (see Anorexia and Bulimia)

Extreme anxiety and phobias (irrational fears of people, places, or things) with symptoms such as sweating, chest pains, palpitations, trembling, dizziness, fear of dying or going crazy, and nightmares (try eliminating coffee, colas, all other stimulant drinks and pills before seeking help)

Temporary, mild symptoms resembling these should not send you running for the doctor or psychologist. We all get angry, tired, and confused at times. Only persistent, unexplained symptoms are cause for concern.

Is It Your Mind or Your Body?

It is not always obvious whether a problem is mostly physical or mostly mental. You may have physical symptoms with a psychological origin or emotional symptoms with a physical cause. What should you do if you are not sure? If there is any chance that the problem is primarily physical, see a physician; otherwise, consult a psychotherapist. For example, fatigue, decreased libido, and advanced eating disorders call for a thorough checkup and perhaps medical treatment. Problems with sexual orientation or compulsive behavior, on the other hand, usually call for psychotherapy.

Anxiety, phobias, and panic attacks are in the grey zone; they may be purely psychological, or they may have a variety of physical causes including thyroid disorder, heart arrhythmias, menopause, hypoglycemia, temporal lobe epilepsy, and stimulant use or sedative withdrawal. If you have chronic anxiety or experience panic attacks, stop *all* stimulant use and learn to relax (see Relaxation and Meditation in Part Six). If simple measures do not work, you may need professional help. In general, it is a good idea to have a physician rule out physical causes for physical symptoms (trembling, sweating, palpitations) before seeking psychotherapy; but if a phobia is clearcut and the panic attacks limited to certain situations, it is reasonable to try the latter first.

Guide to Finding a Psychotherapist

If you decide you need professional help, unless you have a convincing recommendation from a trusted friend, you may have trouble deciding whom to approach. You can usually find out more about the qualifications, methods, and fees of a carpenter or plumber than a psychotherapist. There are no standard licensing procedures, and in most states the terms psychotherapist and counselor may be used by anyone regardless of training or experience. Therefore, it is important that you ask pertinent questions; if the therapist thinks they are *im*pertinent, take your business elsewhere.

There are important differences between M.D. therapists (psychiatrists) and the non-M.D. variety, many of whom are PH.D psychologists and use the title Doctor. Only psychiatrists can prescribe drugs or hospitalize patients. They therefore tend to treat the more seriously disturbed.

Here is some information about the therapist you should try to get before making an appointment.

Age; you must feel comfortable with the therapist, and age may be important to you in this respect

Type of therapy; while none of the scores of psychotherapy schools has been proven superior to the others, your personal preferences can determine your comfort and your progress

Logistics of scheduling sessions, such as length of wait for treatment, location of meetings, and vacation coverage

Fees and whether they are payable by Medicare, Medicaid, and other insurance

Availability by phone in times of distress

Areas of special interest—or lack of interest—on the part of the therapist

Number of sessions usually required for an evaluation and decision on whether to start therapy

Policy on informing clients of diagnosis and prognosis

Average duration of therapy

Policy on seeing and involving family members

The consumer-activist Health Research Group recommends a contract between the client and therapist worked out over the first meeting or two. This is becoming quite common, and one should not hesitate to suggest it. The contract is not intended to be legally binding but to serve as a tool for clarifying and organizing the goals of the therapy and the obligations of each party, which should be stated as specifically as possible.

If a therapist recommends electroconvulsive therapy (ECT or "shock treatment"), get a second opinion as well as information on the risks and benefits. See Part Five for a look at drugs prescribed by psychiatrists.

362 Can Nutrition Help in Mental Illness?

There is no doubt that good nutrition can be important in preventing and treating serious mental and emotional disturbances. For example, one of the classic symptoms of advanced niacin deficiency is toxic psychosis with confusion and delirium. Hypoglycemia or mild thiamin or folic acid deficiency can cause depression, insomnia, crankiness, and other symptoms of brain dysfunction. Nutrition, then, is a logical consideration.

Some cases of depression appear to be due to a low level of the brain neurotransmitter norepinephrine. The level of this chemical can sometimes be increased by supplements of the amino acid tyrosine. Another amino acid, tryptophan, as well as vitamin B-6, may help relieve depression in women taking birth control pills. Large doses of these supplements should not be taken without the guidance of a physician. Be wary of the endless claims that this or that amino acid or vitamin is a special brain food that can cure depression or other serious problems. The connection between nutrition and psychological problems is tenuous and complex; self-diagnosis and treatment is not likely to succeed.

Can Megavitamin Therapy Help?

"Orthomolecular" or megavitamin treatment is the use of very large supplements (up to 100 times the RDA) of vitamins, especially niacin, vitamin C, vitamin B-6, folic acid, and vitamin E, and sometimes minerals such as zinc. The proponents of this treatment claim substantial, sometimes dramatic, success in schizophrenia.

There is a strong case against the treatment. The claims of success are not substantiated by double-blind studies to rule out the placebo effect. Moreover, since orthomolecular psychiatrists use powerful antipsychotic drugs and electroconvulsive therapy as much as, and sometimes more than, the conventional psychiatrists, it is not possible to credit the vitamins.

There are serious problems with taking excessive amounts of vitamins (see Part Two). There have also been several reports of megadoses of niacin and folic acid exacerbating symptoms in schizophrenics.

Orthomolecular treatment can be extremely expensive, much more so than conventional psychiatry. This is due in part to high charges for nutrition evaluation, often including worthless hair analysis and huge doses of nutritional supplements.

Love, the Most Important Preventive

There are many stories of sudden death upon learning of the death of a spouse or other loved one. Even animals are not immune. Two llamas, Charlie and Josephine, had been inseparable for ten years at the Lollipop Farm Zoo in Rochester, New York. One day Charlie got out of hand and a policeman shot him dead. Josephine sank to her knees besides Charlie's body, placed her head on the wound, and died.

There is some evidence that such sudden death is due to severe heart arrhythmia which leads to ventricular fibrillation, a deadly flutter which fails to pump the blood. The arrhythmia is induced by massive release of adrenalin and noradrenalin in the stressful situation. Death is more likely in those with existing heart or blood vessel disease, but has occurred even in teenagers upon learning of the death of siblings or parents.

Such examples of "death due to a broken heart" are quite rare, but there is growing evidence that friendship, companionship, and lasting love relationships are powerful "medicines" for prevention and healing of emotional and even physical problems. The maintainence of good, close relationships appears to be just as important to health as good diet, physical fitness, and avoidance of smoking and other drug abuse.

Many long-term studies of thousands of people have shown strong correlations between social isolation, disease, and death.[40] Those with underdeveloped social networks, with such elements as marriage, friendships, and group involvements, have much higher death rates than those with many such relationships. Epidemiologists have shown that the death rate of married people is lower than for singles, divorcees, and widows for many major disease, as well as suicide, accidents, and drug addiction. Pregnant women with more developed psychosocial assets such as supportive friendships suffer fewer complications than more isolated women.

How Loneliness Maims and Kills

It promotes self-destructive habits such as alcoholism and other drug abuse.

It increases depression, which predisposes to suicide and accidents.

It increases the stress of life's burdens; friendship and touch are nature's best tranquilizers and stress reducers.

It decreases health surveilance and inhibits recognition of early warning signs. "How are you," is a universal greeting. Couples and friends almost unconsciously monitor each other's health and often encourage healthier living.

364 Child Abuse:

a Crime and a Health Hazard

Each year there are millions of cases of child abuse, and about 5,000 children die at the hands of their parents. Those who survive the batterings and abuse often become violent adults and child abusers themselves. The vast majority of violent criminals were victims of violence in the home. Death and injury due to violence has become so common that the Center for Disease Control has established a Violence Epidemiology Branch.

Richard Restak, M.D., makes a strong case that irrationally hostile, violent behavior has its roots in "love deficiency" in infancy. In general, in societies where infants are handled, caressed, and carried a lot and shown a great deal of affection, the level of violence is much lower than in the societies where the infants are just fed and changed. Rhesus monkeys raised isolated from others, though able to see them, became self-mutilating, cringing, and fearful, then hostile and aggressive. Females raised isolated became indifferent, even brutal, mothers.

One theory is that inadequate early parenting causes permanent defects in pleasure centers of the brain; this results in a life-long heightened sense of emotional pain and loneliness. Those affected have a much greater need for affection and, since they do not usually get it, they have a constant sense of personal deprivation and a low frustration tolerence, which often leads to violence as well as drug abuse, schizophrenia, and other problems. In the case of battered children, who so often become battering parents, we have a psychosocial disease passed on through generations. Therefore, we should follow our best instincts and give our children lots of loving from the first moments of their lives. This will help save them, ourselves, and the rest of society a lot of grief.

Mononucleosis

This contagious disease most commonly affects persons between fifteen and thirty years old. Symptoms usually include enlarged and tender lymph nodes, fever, sore throat, loss of appetite, and weakness. Nausea, jaundice, headache, sore muscles, stiff neck, a fine red rash, coughing, and chest pain may also occur. The spleen may be enlarged and the liver is sometimes affected.

The incubation period is about four to seven weeks. The acute stage usually lasts about one to four weeks. Convalescence may take weeks or months. Some cases are very mild and hardly noticed; others are severely debilitating but serious complications and death are rare.

It has recently become apparent that some people suffer a chronic, recurrent form caused by the same organism but with somewhat different symptoms—mostly headache, paresthesia (numbness and tingling), depression, malaise, and other nervous system manisfestations.

CAUSE

Infectious mononucleosis is caused by the Epstein-Barr virus (EBV), a member of the herpes family, that may be harbored for many months in the throat of a carrier and is apparently spread by kissing, sharing eating and drinking utensils, coughing, or just breathing.

Chronic EBV syndrome is probably caused by reactivation of the latent virus, which is common with herpes virus infections—cold sores, genital herpes, shingles. The EBV is normally held down by the immune system, but pregnancy, aging, other viruses, some drugs, and some kinds of cancer can suppress the immune system enough to reactivate the virus. An alternative theory is that the EBV involved in the chronic syndrome is slightly different from the EBV which causes "mono." In any case, genetic susceptibility may be a factor for some.

TREATMENT

Rest in bed until the fever is gone. Take adequate fluids. Aspirin may relieve discomfort. Return to activity gradually. If the spleen is enlarged, avoid heavy lifting and other actions that put pressure on the abdomen.

PREVENTION

Avoid exposure to persons with mono. This is not always possible because the symptoms may be vague. But if someone has the symptoms mentioned above, avoid kissing and sharing glasses and eating utensils until the problem is diagnosed or gone. Eat well, avoid unnecessary (including recreational) drugs, and keep generally healthy to keep your immune system strong.

Multiple Sclerosis

The nerves of the brain are sheathed in myelin, a white fatlike substance essential to nerve impulse transmission. In multiple sclerosis (MS) the myelin is damaged or destroyed in patches scattered throughout the brain and spinal cord.

The symptoms depend on the exact location and severity of the lesions. They generally include weakness, incoordination, visual problems, bowel and bladder problems, slurred speech, and dizziness. In some cases mental changes include euphoria, mania, and loss of insight.

Onset is usually between twenty and forty years of age. It may be sudden and severe, or insidious with gradual progression of symptoms over weeks or months. In either case, remission and relapse are common. Survival after onset varies from a few weeks to fifty years; thirty years is about average. About a third are able to continue working for twenty years or more.

CAUSE

Genetic susceptibility is apparently one factor, but studies with twins indicate that there must be others.

The measles virus has been a prime suspect. Multiple sclerosis patients sometimes have high levels of measles virus antibodies in the blood and tissue, and sometimes viruslike particles in the brain. The theory is that after the acute measles attack subsides the virus infection persists in the wall of the small intestine. After a long latent period, perhaps twenty years or more, the virus migrates to the central nervous system where it, or the immune reaction to it, damages the myelin. A similar theory has been proposed with the canine distemper virus (CDV) the culprit.

Another theory stresses alleged correlations between MS and vitamin D deficiency, as determined by sun exposure and diet. Large doses are recommended for treatment and prevention. The evidence for this is poor and the treatment can be hazardous.

TREATMENT

Adequate rest and sleep are important. Complications such as bedsores, contractures, spasms, and bladder and kidney infections can usually be prevented with physiotherapy and good nursing care. Excessive heat should be avoided. Psychotherapy may help in rehabilitation. Very strenuous and fatiguing exercise is not beneficial and may be harmful.

ACTH and corticosteroids are sometimes used in acute relapse, but results have not been impressive. These hormones are hazardous and rarely used in long-term therapy. Other drugs sometimes used include isoniazid, procaine, and tolbutamide. There is no evidence they help and they can be hazardous.

As with all serious chronic diseases with unpredictable relapses and remissions, theories and treatments are rife. A healthy skepticism can prevent the needless expense, discomfort, disappointment, and physical harm that can be caused by worthless treatments. Some of the more common unproven treatments are discussed below.

Linoleic acid (from vegetable oils) has been reported to help. Two tablespoons of sunflower seed oil given twice a day was associated with a reduction of the frequency and severity of flare-ups. The effects are not dramatic, but the treatment is inexpensive, convenient, and harmless.

Blood transfusions, vitamin B-12 injections, and other methods have been tried but without convincing success. Plasmapheresis, a kind of filtering of the blood, is an experimental treatment which may prove helpful.

Snake venom products such as PROven, from the deadly krait, cobra, and water moccasin, have been marketed without FDA approval for the treatment of multiple sclerosis and other diseases. The products are very expensive and dangerous, and there is no evidence of benefit.

One treatment in a clinic in Germany, publicized in some health food magazines, is based on a strict diet of raw eggs (sometimes four to six a day), raw milk and butter, raw pork and other meat, and raw fruits, nuts, and vegetables. But absolutely no raw high-fiber greens are allowed. The logic of this escapes us. Such a high intake of animal fats could predispose to cardiovascular disease. Eating raw pork can cause trichinosis.

The Swank treatment, one of the most popular alternative therapies (those unapproved by the Multiple Sclerosis Society), takes the opposite approach. Roy Swank, M.D., PH.D., has been treating MS patients for thirty years. He was impressed by the geographical distribution of the disease, its high incidence in areas of high animal fat consumption, and its correlation with coronary heart disease. While agreeing that genetics seems to play a role, he thinks that saturated fats trigger and exacerbate the disease.

According to Swank, the fats may do their damage partly by decreasing brain circulation. A large dose of cream or other animal fat causes sludging of the blood (rouleau formation) as the red cells stick to each other and to the blood vessel walls. The circulation may remain sluggish for many hours. In one animal study a single large feeding of cream caused a decrease of brain oxygen by 30 percent for seventy-two hours.

With a diet very low in saturated fats, lots of rest, and avoidance of excessive physical and mental stress, Swank's patients have allegedly done quite well. He claims almost all respond favorably, with fewer deaths, shorter and less severe flare-ups, and better recovery between them than is typical in other MS clinics. Most important of all, the earlier the treatment is started, the better the results, and if treatment starts within one year the chance of avoiding disability is 95 percent.

The diet and theory behind it are presented in Dr. Swank's book, *The Multiple Sclerosis Diet Book* (Doubleday, 1977). Basically, total lipid intake is lowered to about 45 grams per day (about one-third the average intake), unsaturated fat is increased to about 35 grams per day (about double the average), and saturated fat is decreased to about 10 grams per day (about one-fifteenth the average). Persons who wish to try this diet should expect scepticism from their physicians because it has not been proven effective in large-scale controlled studies. However, it is harmless and nutritious and provides plenty of variety. The biggest hazard of the diet is probably disappointment and depression if it does not help or seem to help.

PREVENTION

Measles vaccination *might* provide protection; if measles goes the way of smallpox, MS might also. We should know soon because nearly a whole generation has now been immunized in some countries, including the United States.

368 **Vaccination of dogs** for canine distemper virus and control of dog populations *might* provide protection.

Mumps

Mumps is a contagious virus disease which attacks the salivary glands, usually one or both parotids in front of the ears, causing them to swell. Pain, malaise, and fever last from five to seven days. Rare complications include encephalitis (infection of the brain), deafness, kidney disease, pancreatitis (infection of the pancreas), and infection of the ovaries or testicles.

One attack almost always confers lifelong immunity. Subclinical infection (exposure and infection without symptoms), which is very common, also confers durable immunity.

TREATMENT
Rest in bed until the fever and swelling are gone. Adopt a liquid diet and avoid sour foods, including orange juice.

Aspirin, acetaminophen, or codeine may be desirable for severe pain.

See a physician right away if there is lethargy, convulsions, or a stiff neck. Call a physician if there is pain or swelling in the testes, abdominal pain and vomiting, dizziness, or difficulty hearing.

PREVENTION
Mumps vaccine is very effective and safe and is routinely given at fifteen months.

Osteoarthritis

Osteoarthritis is a degenerative joint disease in which the knees, hips, spine, fingers, and toes become tender, stiff, noisy (they creak), and painful, sometimes in response to weather changes. The synovium (lining of the joint) becomes inflamed, the joint space decreases, and (in the fingers) the joint becomes enlarged with little nodes of cartilage and bone. Any number of joints (even just one) may be affected, but osteoarthritis does not affect the wrist, elbow, shoulder, or ankle.

The disorder develops slowly and is rarely serious before the age of fifty. In advanced stages muscle spasms due to the deformities cause substantial pain, and one's walk and grip may become abnormal. Osteoarthritis is very common in people over sixty, though many have mild symptoms. Unlike rheumatoid arthritis, it does not cause systemic (whole-body) illness; the problem is limited to the joints.

CAUSE

Susceptibility to osteoarthritis is inherited, but hormones, stress to the joints, and other factors are important. In women the trait is dominant, while in men it is recessive; men can carry the gene without getting the disease, but they get it if they have two of the genes. Because of this and the influence of hormones, women are affected more often and more severely.

Just how the defective genes cause the inflammation of the synovium and destruction of the joint is not clear, but the results are similar to those of aging or wear-and-tear. The cartilage of the bones of children is bluish-white and perfectly smooth; the synovial membranes lining the joints are pink and unflawed. In the teen years, the membranes begin to thicken, calcify, and roughen. In the twenties, the cartilage becomes opaque, yellow, uneven, rough, and less elastic. The roughness increases with each decade and the surface becomes pockmarked with pits and erosions. The cartilage thins and disintegrates; the exposed bony surfaces rub against each other, break down, and develop abnormal growths and spurs. The joint loses its flexibility, and the surrounding tissues become inflamed and painful.

If we lived long enough we would all develop these problems to some extent. But osteoarthritis is not just a disease of aging or wear-and-tear; the genetic and hormonal factors prove that. Nevertheless, the problems are similar, and osteoarthritis is often accelerated and aggravated by unusual or excessive stress. Basketball, ballet, and many types of hard physical labor can increase the aging of various joints, especially the stress- and weight-bearing joints.

TREATMENT AND PREVENTION

Rest is important, both in prevention and treatment; without it, tissue cannot repair itself.

Anti-inflammatory drugs (not for prevention) relieve the pain and may also slow the degeneration by reducing the synovitis. Aspirin is the most commonly used since it is effective and inexpensive.

Develop and maintain good posture. Slumping increases the stress on vertebral joints. Avoid easy chairs and car seats that make you sit on your tail bone. Use a firm mattress that supports the spine.

Exercise to strengthen the muscles around the joints and thereby decrease the stress on them, but always warm up properly and stay within your capacity. A moderate running program is not likely to be harmful if good shoes and a good surface are used. A variety of moderate exercises for all-round fitness is better than just one but avoid stressing the affected joints.

Eat nutritious foods and watch your weight. Obesity increases the stress on joints and the risk of osteoarthritis. Excessive animal fat in the diet may provoke early onset, perhaps by impairing microcirculation and nutrition of the joint tissue.

Wear proper footwear. You want an adequate cushion for walking on concrete and other hard surfaces. High heels and platform shoes are stressful on various joints and not conducive to good posture.

Surgical treatment to remove bone and cartilage fragments and even replace joints can be very helpful in advanced stages. But the necessity of surgery can be avoided by taking preventive measures early.

Beware of quack remedies, unapproved drugs, exotic herbs, herbal extracts, and all kinds of gadgets. Unscrupulous operators victimize millions of arthritis patients each year. Some of the remedies contain corticosteroids (adrenal cortical hormones), which can provide dramatic temporary relief but are dangerous and have no place in treating osteoarthritis.

Osteoporosis

Osteoporosis is one of the most common, disabling, and costly metabolic diseases; it kills about 50,000 people each year and disables many more. The bones lose mass and become porous, thin, and weak. Vertebrae collapse and fractures occur from simple stresses like sneezing or bumping against a table, or from no apparent stress at all. These breaks are very slow to heal, and the subsequent prolonged bed rest may lead to serious medical problems.

All postmenopausal women, except blacks, are highly susceptible.[41] There is a rapid loss of bone mass in the first few years after menopause, followed by a slower but steady loss thereafter. Women who live to the age of eighty usually lose a third to two-thirds of their entire skeletons and up to six inches of their height. Young women who exercise to excess and lose too much fat, to the point of stopping menstruation, may also develop osteoporosis.

Although men also lose bone mass as they age, the rate of loss is much slower than in women, and osteoporosis is rarely a serious problem, though it may be for men past age seventy. Black men have the densest bones and are the least susceptible.

CAUSE

Bones are metabolically active reservoirs of calcium, which is being constantly removed and replaced depending on the needs of muscles, nerves, and other tissues. The skeleton is constantly undergoing subtle changes to accommodate changes in activities, stresses, and weight distribution and in response to diet, hormones, and drugs.

Bone loss begins in the midthirties and progresses for life, more rapidly in women. Several hormones are involved in bone metabolism, and the changing hormone patterns in aging, especially the decline of estrogen in women, tend to promote bone thinning and weakening.

Lack of activity is a major factor in osteoporosis, and sometimes (as in paraplegia and arthritis) it is the only cause. The osteoblasts (bone-forming cells) must be stressed and strained to function properly. A sedentary life style encourages bone demineralization and weakening.

Calcium absorption decreases with age, and low calcium combined with high phosphorous intake, as in a high-meat, low-milk, low-vegetable diet, encourages demineralization. The development of lactase deficiency (lactose intolerance) may contribute to the problem. High protein intake causes calcium excretion, and this too may add to the problem.

Cortisone treatment can promote osteoporosis by decreasing calcium absorption and blocking the activity of osteoblasts. After several years of high doses of cortisone, loss of bone mass is commonly 30 to 50 percent.

Smoking seems to promote osteoporosis, possibly by increasing bone acidity and thereby the solubility of the bone minerals, and by hastening menopause.

In postmenopausal women, several or all of these factors may be present: decreased estrogen, lack of activity, a diet high in phosphorous and protein and low in calcium, cortisone treatment, and cigarette smoking.

TREATMENT

After decades of research and clinical trials it appears that a truly effective and safe treatment has emerged.[42,43,44] It cannot rebuild bone already lost, so prevention is far preferable, but it can greatly decrease the incidence of fractures and slow further bone loss. The treatment consists of daily estrogen and calcium supplements. Fluoride also seems to help but in large doses may cause side effects.

It has long been know that estrogen is effective in preserving bone, but there has been concern that it might promote cancer of the breast and uterus endometrium and increase the risk of cardiovascular disease. However, it is now clear that the small doses used to treat and prevent osteoporosis substantially decrease the risk of breast cancer. There is still concern about a possible link with uterine cancer, but if small doses of progestin are also given the risk may be decreased. Each case must be decided individual-

372 ly, with the benefits of the therapy weighed against its risks and those of osteoporosis.

In general, estrogen replacement therapy does not have an adverse effect on blood pressure, body fat, blood fats, or other risk factors in cardiovascular disease. In fact, some studies suggest that estrogen replacement therapy greatly decreases the incidence of heart attack in postmenopausal women, perhaps by increasing HDL-cholesterol levels.

Women who cannot take estrogen (those with congestive heart failure or migraine headaches, for example) can be helped with other hormones such as calcitonin or with large doses of calcium.

Whatever therapy a woman is receiving, she should also exercise as much as possible without causing injury and eat a balanced diet with plenty of vegetables and low-fat dairy products and not too much meat. She should also not smoke.

PREVENTION

Prevention of osteoporosis is very important because reversal of the process and rebuilding the bones is difficult. Young women, especially mothers, should anticipate the problem far in advance and avoid the risk factors so they can go into the high-risk postmenopausal years with the densest, healthiest bones possible.

Get adequate calcium (1000 to 1500 mg per day) and not too much phosphorous or protein in your food. Eat low-fat dairy products, soy products, sardines, salmon, beans, leafy greens, and a variety of vegetables. Meat and soda pops are major sources of excess phosphorous. Lacto-vegetarians are generally less susceptible to osteoporosis than omnivores.

If you do not get adequate calcium in your food, take a supplement (pure calcium carbonate is best), preferably at bedtime since bone decalcification peaks in the early morning before rising.

Get adequate vitamin D by being outdoors or taking a supplement of up to 400 units per day. In strong sunlight, about fifteen minutes of head, neck, and arm exposure supplies the RDA. In overcast conditions, longer or more extensive exposure is required.

Calcium and vitamin D supplements can be hazardous so don't overdo it, especially if you have a known tendency to form kidney stones. The total calcium intake from all sources should not exceed about 2 grams per day for most people.

Get plenty of exercise. Many studies have shown that even in advanced age, increased physical activity can decrease or even stop the slow loss of bone mass. But do not exercise so much that your periods stop. This can mimick menopause in effects on the bones.

Prolonged corticosteroid therapy (more than a month) usually calls for extra calcium, vitamins D and C, and protein to prevent or lessen the bone-ravaging effects of the hormones.

Avoid habitual use of aluminum-containing antacids. They inhibit calcium, phosphorous, and fluoride absorption.

Don't smoke.

Postmenopausal women (especially slender, Caucasian smokers) should consider **estrogen** supplements with their physicians; the hormone can very substantially retard bone loss and effectively prevent osteoporosis. The risk of adverse effects is very small, and practically zero if the uterus has been removed.

Peptic Ulcers

A peptic ulcer is an erosion of the mucosa (interior lining) of the stomach or duodenum (upper intestine) caused by excessive stomach acid and decreased resistance of the mucosa to the acid-pepsin juice. It usually causes burning pain which is temporarily relieved by food, drink, or antacid. Stomach ulcers in older people sometimes occur with low acid levels.

Almost a fifth of the U.S. population will have at least one ulcer sometime in their lives, though many will be too minor to cause pain and will go unnoticed.

CAUSES

The causes usually include inherited susceptibility, and chemical and emotional stimulation of excessive acid production. An inborn lack of protection of the stomach or duodeum from its corrosive juice, combined with stimulation by nicotine, alcohol, caffeine, aspirin, or other drugs, leads to an ulcer. Sustained emotional stress—worry, fear, anger, and the like—can contribute to the acid production and sometimes is the main factor; even noise can be a problem. Nutritional deficiencies may predispose to ulcers, though this has not been proven. In some cases there are no identifiable causes.

TREATMENT

A bland diet with lots of milk and cream and almost no fiber was prescribed for many years. But since it is nutritionally poor and there is no good evi-

374 dence that it helps, this treatment has been largely abandoned. It now appears that milk and other high protein foods stimulate excessive stomach acid, which aggravates the problem.

It may be helpful to eat four or five small meals rather than two or three big ones. This avoids too much stomach distension, which increases gastric secretion. However, bedtime snacks should be avoided since they often lead to acid secretion while sleeping and pain hours later in the middle of the night.

Spicy foods such as peppers, mustard, vinegar, and pickles do not cause ulcers but sometimes aggravate them and cause pain. If so, they should be avoided. Otherwise, they are OK.

How you eat may be as important as what you eat. According to some researchers, food that has not been well chewed does not have enough urogastrone, a substance from the salivary glands alleged to protect the intestinal lining of experimental animals from erosion.

Alcohol, caffeine, aspirin, and cigarettes are all known to aggravate ulcers and increase the risk of getting one. Possibly the worst thing a chronic ulcer victim can do is to drink and smoke, then drink coffee to sober up (it doesn't work anyway), then take aspirin to prevent or cure a hangover. This can change a tiny painless ulcer into a large painful one. It can even provoke general gastric bleeding from tiny hemorrhages all over the stomach wall, whether or not there is an ulcer.

Anti-inflammatory drugs used in arthritis can aggravate ulcers, as can reserpine, an antihypertensive. Cortisone and related drugs are also suspect. The use of these drugs must be minimized or eliminated for those with ulcers or prone to them.

Certain nutrients may be especially useful in treating ulcers. Supplementary vitamin A seems to help by stimulating renewal of epithelial cells and increasing the production of protective mucus. Zinc and vitamin E may help, but large doses of these nutrients (more than three times the RDA) should not be used without consulting a physician.[45]

There is no question that severe or prolonged physical, mental, or emotional stress can aggravate, even initiate, ulcers. For example, in wartime bombing raids ulcer incidence skyrockets, even among those not hurt. This is an extreme case, but some households are practically war zones. Many people seem to improve upon hospitalization or otherwise changing environments, removing themselves from the sources of tension and frustration. Relaxation techniques such as meditation and biofeedback are sometimes helpful.[46]

Antacids, best taken between meals and at bedtime, have long been standard medication. They relieve the burning pain and recent studies have shown that they speed healing. Since antacids can be harmful, they should be used with caution and awareness of their side effects (see Chapter 5–1).

The most important drugs for treating ulcers are cimetidine and ranatidine, prescription drugs known as histamine H-2 antagonists, which very effectively reduce stomach acid secretion (see Chapter 5–2). Carbenoxolone, similar to the active ingredient in licorice (see Chapter 5–3), promotes ulcer healing but has not yet been approved in the United States because of questions about its safety.

Simply drinking lots of water or juice, which dilute the stomach acid, can often relieve the pain. Fresh cabbage juice is sometimes recommended by naturopaths and health food magazine writers, who claim it speeds healing. There is no good evidence for this, and cabbage juice can be very peppery and irritating and it might even promote acid production and ulceration.

Soothing herbal teas include camomile, anise, fennel, and flax seed. Some herbs are likely to irritate the stomach lining and should be avoided. These include peppermint, spearmint, and such stimulating herbs as gotu kola (which contains caffeine), desert tea, and damiana.

It is important to remember that healing an ulcer does not always mean permanently curing it. Most ulcers tend to recur. Care and watchfulness are required for life if hemorrhage, surgery, and even removal of the stomach are to be avoided.

See a physician immediately if you have black or bloody stool or vomitus; these may indicate a bleeding ulcer.

Call a physician if you have persistent, severe, or repeated attacks of heartburn or indigestion.

PREVENTION

A **nutritious diet** should help maintain the integrity of the mucosa against the onslaught of acid and pepsin and help to heal any lesions that develop. Studies of animals and humans indicate that vitamin A is especially important in ulcer prevention because of its role in maintaining the healthy functioning of the mucus-producing cells that line the stomach and protect it from digestion by the powerful acid-pepsin juice.

Given the high incidence of ulcers in the general population, and the much higher incidence (about three times) among close relatives of ulcer victims, everyone, especially such relatives, should keep in mind that **alcohol, caffeine** (coffee, tea, colas), **aspirin, cigarettes,** and most **arthritis medications** can provoke and aggravate ulcers.

The claim by some coffee manufacturers that their brands are "acid neutralized" and therefore easier on the stomach is without merit, since the acidity of the coffee is insignificant compared to the stomach acid stimulated by the caffeine and other components. Decaffeinated coffee can be easier on the stomach, but it sometimes stimulates as much acid flow as regular coffee, either by a conditioned reflex association with the flavor or by the action of oils or other substances in the coffee.

Liquid protein supplements with free amino acids stimulate gastric secretion and should be avoided by ulcer-prone persons (and almost everyone else; see Chapter 2–4). Highly concentrated protein foods such as drinks with protein powder, brewer's yeast, and eggs can also promote hyperacidity and ulcers.

Pneumonia

In pneumonia the lungs are inflamed and breathing tends to be difficult; there may be fever, chills, chest pain, coughing, and weakness. It was once the number one cause of death in the United States. Antibiotics have reduced mortality, but it is still a major problem. The very young and those over fifty with other health problems are the most susceptible.

CAUSES
There are at least fifty different causes including bacteria, viruses, fungi, chemical irritants, and allergies. By far the most common causes are pneumococcal bacteria and viruses. Tuberculosis is also a common cause, especially in immigrant populations.

Organisms that can cause pneumonia are usually present in the normal respiratory tract; the development of pneumonia is clearly due to decreased resistance. This can result from malnutrition (often associated with drug addiction and alcoholism), colds, influenza, diabetes, chronic bronchitis, emphysema, chronic exposure to dust and fumes, and cigarette smoking.

A common cause of pneumonia in otherwise healthy young people is a very small bacterium called mycoplasma. The illness is very similar to influenza, but unlike the flu it responds to antibiotics.

TREATMENT
Tests such as sputum culture help determine the cause of the pneumonia. In pneumococcal pneumonia, penicillin is the most effective drug. In other types of infection, and in penicillin allergy, other antibiotics are used.

Bed rest is very important, and sometimes oxygen is necessary. A liquid diet is preferred at first. In a long illness, or when nutrition status is poor, a high-protein diet with vitamin and mineral supplements is advisable.

Viral pneumonia, sometimes called "walking pneumonia," often develops during what seems to be a bad cold. Antibiotics don't help. With adequate rest and good nutrition, it usually runs its course in about two weeks.

PREVENTION
Maintain good general health with good nutrition, exercise, and adequate rest. If your are recovering from an illness or surgery, get adequate rest, avoid crowds, and avoid stresses such as getting cold and wet.

A pneumonia vaccine against thirty-two strains of the pneumococcal bacteria is available and is advisable for persons with lung disease and those who
have had their spleens removed. A flu vaccine is also advisable.

Avoid chronic exposure to fumes, dust, and smoke.

Prostatitis

Only men have a prostate gland, which is located just below the urinary
bladder. It produces seminal fluid, a lubricant, and a nutritive medium for
the sperm.

The most common problem is prostatitis, inflammation and enlargement of the prostate. Most men will have at least one bout in their
lifetime, usually in their later years. In most cases there is no infection, and
the cause of the problem is unknown. But sometimes infection occurs as a
complication of a venereal disease or bladder infection.

Symptoms include difficulty starting urination, dribbling, and decreased force of the stream. This is due to the encroachment by the enlarged
prostate on the urethral tube and obstruction of the flow of urine out of the
bladder. The leftover urine is a fertile breeding ground for bacteria, and it
can back up into the kidneys and promote infection and severe kidney damage.

Usually a physician can detect enlargement of the prostate by pal-
pating it through the rectum. If there are signs of a problem, thorough
examination of the bladder and kidneys may be required.

TREATMENT
Antibiotics are useful in clearing infections. Regular sexual orgasm and exercise such as walking and swimming may help reduce congestion of the
gland.

The prostate is normally very rich in zinc, but men with chronic
bacterial inflammation tend to have less of the element in their prostatic
fluid. It is not clear whether there is a causal connection here, but zinc
supplements of up to 100 mg per day are sometimes given. While this may
help those who are deficient, large doses should not be maintained indefinitely; after a month or so 20 milligrams a day should be sufficient.

Essential fatty acids such as linoleic acid are essential to the synthesis of prostaglandins, the group of powerful hormones first discovered in the
prostate. It has been suggested that inadequate intake of linoleic acid promotes prostate enlargement. If this is true, consumption of whole grains,
nuts, seeds, and vegetable oils might be helpful.

If nothing else works, surgical removal or trimming of the gland
can be done in such a way that sexual response and activity are not affected.
However, the volume of ejaculate is reduced and ejaculation may be retro-

378 grade—that is, the semen may be passed into the bladder to be expelled later with the urine.

PREVENTION

Treat all urinary tract infections until they are completely eradicated; take the *entire course* of prescribed antibiotics no matter how much the symptoms may have subsided.

Avoid prolonged sexual abstinence and prolonged or frequent sexual arousal (intercourse, petting, or masturbation) without ejaculation. Tantric yoga and Karreza sexual practices could be harmful in this regard since they promote prolonged stimulation and intercourse without climax.

Eat a balanced diet with adequate amounts of zinc and unsaturated oils.

Psoriasis

Psoriasis is a common dermatitis with pink or red patches covered with silvery scales. It comes and goes, usually on the knees, elbows, chest, nails, lower back, and scalp. The patches are sharply delineated from normal skin. Itching may occur, especially in the body folds. Arthritis sometimes flares up with it.

Symptoms may appear at any age but usually begin in young adulthood. The problem may last a lifetime or it may clear up completely. There is usually no fever, weight loss, or decline in general health, but in rare cases the condition is so widespread and severe that hospitalization is required. Injury and irritation tend to provoke lesions at the site, and there are often flare-ups during periods of emotional stress.

CAUSE

The skin's DNA synthesis and cell cycle are accelerated and abnormal keratin, the tough protein in nails and hair, is produced, sometimes separating the nails from their beds. The cause is not known, though genetic factors are important and allergies might be involved. It is not an infection, so it is not contagious. However, skin infections can aggravate it.

TREATMENT

There is no real cure, but conscientious treatment can check flare-ups and help keep the skin clear. Most of the treatments work by inhibiting the skin's DNA production and cell proliferation. Psoriasis therapy is as much art as science and will vary with the doctor and the patient. Whatever treatment is used, it is important to keep the skin clean and avoid irritating soaps and skin products. The following treatments are discussed in approximate order of increasing effectiveness—and increasing risk.

Herbalists recommend soaking with a strong decoction of comfrey or goldenseal. Comfrey contains allantoin, which stimulates DNA synthesis and cell proliferation, so its use in psoriasis would seem counterproductive. Nevertheless, there have been reports of its effectiveness in some cases. Goldenseal has not been well studied but it may also be worth trying. Because of the long soaking required, both these remedies would be less convenient than coal tar and steroid ointments for most people.

Emotional stress is clearly capable of provoking psoriasis flare-ups. Most patients and their physicians recognize that tension and worry often exacerbate the condition, and that resolving and avoiding psychic stress can help. It is interesting that this has been recognized at least since the Persian physician, Jasaliq, treated a patient with psychotherapy 1200 years ago.[47].

Topical steroids, cortisone-type drugs in ointments, are probably the most often prescribed psoriasis therapy. The weakest effective concentrations must be used because the steroids can cause skin atrophy and a rebound flare-up of the psoriasis when use is discontinued.

Coal tar lotions, with or without sunlight or ultraviolet light exposure, can help check flare-ups.

Anthralin, an aromatic chemical available in creams and ointments, has been used for psoriasis for nearly a century. Weak concentrations are left on for hours or high concentrations for a few minutes. Caution is necessary to avoid skin irritation. Anthralin should not be used with topical steroids since this can increase the chance of a relapse.

A powerful modern remedy is much like a very ancient one. Thousands of years ago Egyptians treated some skin disorders by eating the seeds of *Ammi majus* and exposing the affected skin to the sun. The plant contains chemicals called *psoralens* which make the skin hypersensitive to ultraviolet light. Today spectacular success is being reported using psoralens and longwave *ultraviolet* light. This is known as *PUVA* therapy, for psoralen with ultraviolet-A. When psoralen ointment is applied to the affected skin or taken orally, the skin is sensitized to the light and its DNA production is slowed. This halts the rapid proliferation and exfoliation of the skin cells.

With topical application the dose can be difficult to control and the drug can cause severe blistering and discoloring of the skin and it can even provoke skin cancer. Oral use is easier to control, less likely to cause skin problems, and very effective when followed by exposure to longwave ultraviolet light. Reports indicate a high rate of success in clearing the skin and keeping it clear with occasional maintenance treatments. However, even oral use can increase the risk of skin cancer and premature skin aging. Therefore, PUVA treatment is worth the risk only in severe cases.

380 **Methotrexate,** a powerful suppressor of cell reproduction used in some cancers, is often effective against stubborn psoriasis. It has serious side effects such as damage to the liver, so its use is limited to the most severe cases.

Corticosteroids taken internally can be effective, but severe worsening may occur upon withdrawal.

Synthetic retinoids, vitamin-A-like chemicals, are proving effective when used alone or in combination with other therapies. Side effects can be severe and the drugs are still experimental.

PREVENTION
There is clearly a genetic component and some chance of transmitting the disorder, but the disease is rarely serious enough to avoid having children.

Those affected might gain some protection from regular sun exposure (without burning) and, to the extent possible, avoiding emotional stress. Skin injury, irritation, and infection should be avoided.

Diets low in calories, proteins, tryptophan, and taurine are apparently of no benefit, though they have been advocated for more than sixty years. However, studies in France indicate that gluten sensitivity might be worth checking for. If it is present, wheat, rye, barley, and oats would have to be eliminated from the diet. The most reliable test involves biopsy of the intestinal villi.

Rabies

Rabies is one of the most ancient, horrible, and fascinating of all diseases. First mentioned in the 23rd century B.C. in the Eshnunna Code, which predates Moses, rabies is a virus disease that attacks the nervous system of all warm-blooded animals, including humans. Symptoms may vary substantially, but they often conform to the description provided by an Italian physician in 1546:

> Once the disease takes hold the patient can neither stand nor lie down: like a madman he flings himself hither and thither, tears his flesh with his hands, and feels intolerable thirst. This is the most distressing symptom, for he so shrinks from water and all liquids that he would rather die than drink or be brought near to water; it is then that they bite other persons, foam at the mouth, their eyes look twisted, and finally they are exhausted and painfully breathe their last.

This fear of water gave rise to the term "hydrophobia," once the common name for rabies.

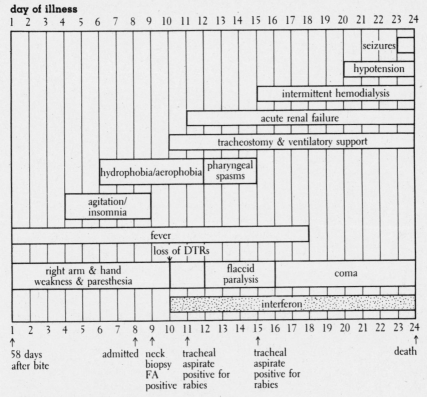

day of illness

DTR - deep tendon reflex   FA - rabies fluorescent antibody

Clinical Course of a Human Rabies Case

The forty-year-old man was bitten on his right hand by his dog while living in
Sonora, Mexico. The animal had been vaccinated, so he discounted the possibility
of rabies. Two months later symptoms began and he returned to Arizona for
treatment. Twenty-four days after that, he died. He had vaccinated the dog
himself, but the vaccine had apparently lost its potency by mishandling. This
illustrates the importance of veterinarians administering the vaccine.

From Center for Disease Control, *Morbidity and Mortality Weekly Report*, 30:538, 1981

Rabies is essentially 100 percent incurable and fatal. Only two or
three persons in the last 4,000 years are believed to have survived the devastating infection, one a woman recently saved by injections of interferon.
Symptoms may not develop for many months after exposure, but once they
appear it is too late for the vaccine to work and there can be very little hope.

CAUSE

Rabies is caused by a virus that enters the blood and concentrates in the
brain. If it simply killed its host quickly, it might perish with is victim instead

382 of being passed on. But the genetic material and protein coat of the virus have evolved a mechanism to ensure that it gets passed on: the virus attacks parts of the brain in a way that makes the animal restless, irritable, and very aggressive. It will then roam for miles, attacking many times without provocation and passing on the virus with is saliva.

The most common sources of human infection are bites and scratches from dogs, cats, rats, bats, squirrels, foxes, raccoons, skunks, mongooses, and various farm animals. There have been a few cases of infection from cornea transplants from persons who had undiagnosed rabies at the time of death.

TREATMENT

Once clinical signs of rabies are evident, the only treatment that offers any hope of survival is interferon, which is apparently responsible for the only certain case of recovery from the disease (subsequent to a bat bite) in its 5,000 year history.[48] However this treatment is extremely costly and not sure to succeed; this is why prevention is so important.

PREVENTION[49]

Only one or two persons per year contracts rabies in the United States, but the cost of this control is eternal vigilance and a lot of money, especially when people fail to take the primary preventive measures.

For example, in Florida a raccoon was taken from the woods and kept as a pet. When it became sick it was taken to a veterinarian, whom it bit. It also bit his assistant. The raccoon was then killed and found to have rabies. The subsequent immunizations, investigations, and counseling cost more than $20,000.

In another case, a dog in California bit three people and was killed when it appeared ill. Tissue tests were positive for rabies. The subsequent investigations and immunizations of dozens of persons exposed to the dog cost more than $100,000.

Thousands of people in the United States, and about a million worldwide, receive rabies immunizations each year because of exposure to rabid or possibly rabid animals. The cost of rabies control, the number of people needing the shots, and the risk to people and their pets could be greatly reduced if people would **strictly follow these preventive guidelines.**

Vaccinate pets and livestock against rabies.

Do not take wild carnivorous mammals (especially skunks, raccoons, bats, and foxes) for pets or try to handle or pet them or get close enough to be scratched or bitten by them.

If you are scratched or bitten by a wild carnivore or an unwanted or stray dog or cat, or even licked on a tiny scratch or abrasion, the wound should be immediately and thoroughly cleaned with soap and water. Call a physician right away. If possible without risking further exposure, the animal should be captured or killed for rabies testing.

Immunization will be required if it is determined that you might have been exposed to rabies. This will include one injection of rabies antibody (passive immunization) and five or six injections of rabies vaccine. This prophylaxis regimen is nearly 100 percent effective and very safe, though there are sometimes side effects. The virus may remain latent for hours or many days, depending on the severity of the wound and the amount of virus left in it; the vaccine will be effective as long as it is administered before dissemination and nervous system infection.

If you are bitten or scratched by a rodent (such as a rat, mouse, chipmunk, squirrel, hamster, or guinea pig), rabbit, hare, or farm animal, clean the wound thoroughly and call a physician. Regional conditions vary, but the chances are that immunization will not be required.

Quarantines must not be evaded. Many islands are completely free of rabies and use quarantine periods of several months for imported dogs, cats, and other susceptible animals to keep the virus out. People who smuggle in animals to avoid the quarantines risk introducing the virus, an irreversible and very costly disaster.

Preexposure prophylaxis is advisable for those at high risk of exposure to rabies; they should receive the vaccine before being bitten, scratched, or otherwise exposed. Candidates include veterinarians and their assistants, biologists and lab workers working with susceptible animals or with the virus itself, spelunkers, trappers, animal control officers, and travelers to areas where rabies is common. This is important because exposure can occur without one's knowledge. For example, cave explorers can inhale the virus from infected bats or even be bitten by bats without feeling it.

Rheumatoid Arthritis

Rheumatoid arthritis (RA) is a systemic (whole body) disease that causes painful inflammation of the joints and severe, permanent damage to them if not properly treated. Most victims are twenty to fifty years old; about 75 percent are women. They often have a fever, lose weight, develop anemia, and have abnormal blood tests such as high sedimentation rate and presence of a "rheumatoid factor."

The pain and stiffness in the joints is usually symmetrical, involving both knees, elbows, ankles, or hands. The disease may progress for many

384 years, but spontaneous remissions do occur and only a minority are severely affected.

CAUSE

RA is still a mystery disease. The most widely accepted theory is that it results from an immune system gone haywire. An initial virus or bacterial infection may be involved, possibly the Epstein-Barr virus which causes infectious mononucleosus or one of the tiny parvoviruses common to cats and dogs. The immune response to the infection somehow turns against the joints and releases chemicals that attack and destroy the cartilage caps at the ends of the bones as well as the synovial membranes that line the joints. The destruction and scarring in and around the joints cause them to be deformed or locked in position.

Obscure allergies, including delayed reaction to a wide variety of common foods, may contribute to arthritic flare-ups in some people. This explains why fasting and monodiets sometimes relieve symptoms. Prolonged stress such as cold, damp weather, and perhaps emotional stress can also be causes. There is some evidence that susceptibility to RA is heredity.

TREATMENT

The goal of therapy is to ease the pain and minimize damage to the joints. About one-fourth to one-third of all RA patients are able to continue essentially all normal activities for life. The chance of being in this group improves with proper care. Details vary with each patient, but in general these are important points.

Get involved in your treatment and care program. Your worst enemies are despair, fear, withdrawal, passivity, and loss of interest in getting better. A positive attitude will help you stick to your care program and minimize joint damage.

Get adequate rest—up to ten or twelve hours a day—to reduce inflammation and slow progression of the disease. But don't get too much rest. Excessive inactivity promotes joint stiffness and bone porosity and weakness.

Exercise your joints to maintain mobility. All the joints should be moved as much as possible without severe pain several times a day. Most yoga exercises are good but only if done gently and with proper warm-up (see Part Six). Don't overexercise the joints; they should not be worked or stressed painfully.

Exercise the muscles to keep strong. If pain is too great for movement, do some muscle-tensing isometric exercises.

Massage, heat, and hydrotherapy can all be helpful. Ideally, every arthritic has access to a skilled physical therapist who can teach useful exercises, proper posture, and procedures. Perhaps even more important, a friend or relative can be taught to help with massage and exercise.

The inflamed joints should be kept straight because they tend to freeze if kept in bent positions. This may call for a very firm mattress and chairs with firm seats and straight backs.

Some people seem to benefit from sleeping in a sleeping bag or wearing thermal underwear to bed. Morning stiffness is reported to be reduced. Stretch gloves may reduce morning stiffness in the hands.

Proper nutrition is very important. Protein intake should be somewhat high to make up for tissue destruction. The constant inflammation and stress dissipate vitamins and sometimes minerals, so supplements are usually advisable. A balanced diet of wholesome foods might reasonably be supplemented with one to two times the RDA of all the vitamins.

It has been suggested that all rheumatoid sufferers should be checked for food allergies. Short fasts or restricted diets may help find the offending foods. However, detection can be difficult because the reaction can be delayed several hours or even days after the offending food is eaten. Moreover, not all experts agree that food allergies are a common cause of RA flare-ups or that it's worth the trouble and risk of malnutrition to test for them.[50]

A warm, dry climate is sometimes beneficial, or seems to be, but one should not expect a miracle cure just by moving.

Aspirin and related drugs are usually a major part of the treatment, not only because they relieve pain but inflammation as well. This may actually slow the process of joint destruction.

Gold salts (oral and injected) are very helpful for some carefully selected patients. Gold is toxic and must be used with great care. Its benefits tend to erode with time.

Cortisone and related drugs are sometimes useful for temporary relief of inflammation, but they do nothing to cure the disease and have very dangerous side effects. They may be used for short periods and in small doses to buy time until a safer remedy is found, but they have no place in long-term therapy. They are sometimes the active ingredients in "miracle cures" available from quacks. This cruel hoax deludes the person into thinking he or she is getting better and it encourages more activity, which can result in serious joint damage.

Other drugs used in severe cases include antimalarials, penicillamine, and methotrexate.

386

Sexual arousal and activity, including fantasy, self-stimulation, petting, oral sex, and intercourse, have been reported to provide several hours of relief from arthritis pain—for 70 percent of one group studied. It is theorized that the release of adrenal steroids (such as cortisone) and endorphins is increased, accounting for the relieve from inflammation and pain.

Some people, including a few physicians, swear by large doses of niacin. Contrary to some claims, this vitamin is toxic. If you decide to try it, read the cautions in Chapter 2–7 and use niacinamide, a somewhat less toxic form.

Several hundred units of vitamin E and up to 150 mg of zinc per day have been reported to reduce joint stiffness and swelling in some patients. Copper supplements and copper bracelets, which may allow absorption through the skin, have also been reported helpful for some, but the placebo effect may be the main factor. Keep in mind that spontaneous remissions, with almost complete disappearance of symptoms, occur very often and may last for months or years. They are completely unpredictable and make it very difficult to evaluate treatments.

Surgery is helpful in many cases. Almost any joint can be improved with silicone spare parts and even complete reconstruction.

PREVENTION

There is no known method of preventing rheumatoid arthritis. If a virus or bacterium is eventually found to be involved, a vaccine would probably be developed. However, for now proper care and treatment can minimize deformity and disability.

Rubella

Rubella, also called German measles, is a viral infection similar to measles (rubeola), but shorter lasting and milder. There are low fever and malaise and in about half the cases a fine rash. Sometime there is pain in the joints or enlarged and tender lymph nodes. The illness itself is rarely more bother than a common cold; almost half the time infection causes no symptoms at all.

The importance of rubella lies in its potential for causing miscarriage and very serious birth defects—cataracts, nerve deafness, mental retardation, heart problems—if a pregnant woman is infected during the first three months of gestation.

TREATMENT

Rest, liquid diet, and cool sponge baths are usually sufficient. Only rarely will fever be high enough to require control with aspirin or acetaminophen. Affected persons should **avoid contact with pregnant women.**

PREVENTION

All children should be vaccinated when they are between one and two years old; the live attenuated virus is very effective and safe. Schools should require evidence of vaccination from all students. If a woman is to be vaccinated, it must be certain that she is not pregnant and will not be for three months. Prior to a planned pregnancy a woman can be tested for immunity to rubella. Some states require the test prior to marriage.

Scoliosis

Scoliosis is lateral (sideways) curvature of the spine, which appears S-shaped from the back.

Mild curvature causes few or no problems; but if it is allowed to progress it can cause degenerative arthritis of the spine, disk disease, severe back pain, sciatica, narrowing of the chest cavity, and difficult breathing. It usually appears between the ages of ten and fifteen and can rapidly worsen during the growth-spurt years. It is often overlooked, though, until it is severe. While common in boys and girls, it tends to be more serious in girls.

CAUSE

The cause is unknown, but the disorder tends to run in families. It is not caused by and should not be confused with poor posture.

TREATMENT

Early detection and treatment are important to prevent the disorder from becoming severe. A brace, worn twenty-four hours a day (except for bathing and such) for three or four years, along with an exercise program can correct the curvature enough to prevent complications. Exercises alone are of little or no benefit. In a few very severe cases surgery is required, followed by a cast for several months.

Some mild curvature gets worse and requires treatment; some does not. It is important that all cases be watched carefully through the adolescent years so treatment can be started as soon as it becomes necessary. If X-rays are used for monitoring, the exposures should be as small and infrequent as possible.

In spite of claims to the contrary, there is no evidence that chiropractic manipulations are an effective and safe treatment for scoliosis. Delay in getting proper treatment can lead to long-term problems.

Early Warning Signs

Parents, physicians, teachers, and school nurses should be alert to these signs in adolescents. If they appear an orthopedist should be consulted.

One shoulder is higher than the other, one arm hangs lower, or one shoulder blade is more prominent.

Hips are tilted or the waistline more indented on one side.

A pronounced curve is seen when tracing the backbone with a finger.

One side of the back is higher than the other when bending forward.

Hemline or pants legs are uneven.

The upper body leans to one side.

Shingles

Shingles, also called herpes zoster, is a rash similar in appearance to chickenpox but with intense, burning pain and sometimes a fever. Any part of the body may be affected, but the trunk and face are the most common sites. In most cases only one side of the body is involved. The rash usually clears up in seven to fourteen days but may last months or even years. Strangely, the pain may outlast the rash.

Shingles is a common disorder; at least half of all persons reaching eighty-five have had it at least once. Contrary to popular belief second attacks can occur, but they are rare. If diagnosis is in doubt, a lesion can be scraped and examined under a microscope for typical "giant" cells.

CAUSE
The chickenpox virus belongs to the herpes family and it behaves much like others in the group: after the illness has subsided, some of the viruses remain in a latent form in the nerve roots near the spinal cord. Many years or decades later, these viruses become active at the nerve roots and travel down the nerves to the skin, where they multiply. The irritation to the nerve and skin causes the pain, itching, and rash that follow the distribution of a peripheral nerve.

TREATMENT
Keep the hands and nails clean and avoid scratching—this helps prevent infection.

Colloidal oatmeal baths (ask a pharmacist) may help relieve itching. Aspirin helps, but in severe cases prescription painkillers may be required.

Consult an ophthalmologist immediately if an eye is affected. Prompt treatment and close follow-up are essential to prevent serious damage and possible blindness.

Cortisone-type drugs do not hasten healing, but they are often prescribed for a short period to prevent the prolonged pain that can occur after the skin has healed.

Discredited treatments which should not be used include X-rays, vasodilator drugs, antibiotics, and gamma globulin.

PREVENTION
A vaccine has been developed which prevents both chickenpox and shingles; it may come into wide use.

Sinusitis

In this very common disorder the sinuses—cavities in the facial bones that normally drain through small opening into the nasal passages—become congested and inflamed due to bacterial infection. In acute sinusitis the pressure build-up from the trapped mucus and pus causes facial pain, headaches, and sometimes tooth pains, especially if the cheekbone sinuses are affected.

In chronic sinusitis there is thickening of the delicate lining of the sinuses, nasal congestion, cough, postnasal drip, and sometimes headache which is made worse by bending over. The infection can spread to the inner ear via the eustachian tubes and to the lungs via the lymphatic system. Chronic sinusitis is often associated with allergies and nasal polyps.

CAUSES
Several different bacteria can cause sinusitis. The infection can be promoted by anything that prevents the normal drainage of mucus from the sinuses, including congestion from a cold, flu, or allergies, and irritation from swimming or diving in chlorinated or salt water. Infection can also be caused by an abscess from the root of an upper tooth penetrating a sinus.

TREATMENT
Acute sinusitis can usually be effectively treated with antibiotics. A chronic condition calls for other remedies since repeated use of the drugs could lead to the development of tolerance by the bacteria. Allergies should be dealt with and irritants avoided. In extreme cases surgical removal of polyps or correction of a deviated septum may be required.

PREVENTION
Treat colds properly. Drink plenty of fluids and get lots of rest. Avoid cigarette and other smoke to prevent irritation, infection, inflammation, and obstruction of the sinuses.

390 **Do not abuse decongestant sprays;** the resulting chronic congestion could aggravate sinusitis (see Chapter 5–1).

Blow your nose gently and without pressing hard to avoid forcing infected mucus further into the sinuses.

Be alert for irritation from swimming in chlorinated or salt water. Use a nose clip if necessary (except in scuba diving).

Eat good food to help maintain healthy resistance.

Spastic Colon

This very common chronic disorder has several other names, including irritable bowel syndrome, nervous indigestion, and mucous colitis. The symptoms typically include abdominal pain, gas, bloating, and diarrhea or constipation. The condition is almost never a serious threat to health, but it can be a major nuisance. Diagnosis must exclude more serious problems.

CAUSE
Chronic GI symptoms can be treated once the causes are known. When there is no apparent cause, just abnormal patterns of intestinal motility sometimes provoked by emotional stress, the condition is called *idiopathic spastic colon* or simply spastic colon. As we learn more about the causes, the category shrinks; it may almost disappear if current theories are substantiated.

For example, many experts believe that most cases are caused by insufficient fiber in the diet, often followed by improper use of laxatives. A vicious cycle is set up and the colon never has a chance to respond normally to good food.

Lactose intolerance is sometimes the real culprit, commonly but not exclusively in nonwhites. It is worth checking for since the simple avoidance of most dairy products and other foods with lactose will clear up the symptoms.

Sorbitol and mannitol can cause symptoms very similar to spastic colon, even in small amounts. Intolerance to these sugar alcohols is much more common than once believed, and may be a major factor.

Food allergies may the cause, especially if there is a history of eczema.

TREATMENT AND PREVENTION OF ATTACKS
Eliminate all sorbitol and mannitol for a couple weeks on a trial basis. If this does not help, try eliminating all lactose. This means avoiding most dairy

products and packaged foods containing the sugar. You may need other sources of protein and calcium (see Part Two).

Develop regular eating and bowel habits. Eat a variety of high-fiber foods and drink sufficient fluids. Don't use laxatives (except bulk type) or enemas. Avoid beans, cabbage, cucumbers, cauliflower, coffee, tea, colas, and other gas-formers and stimulants if they seem to aggravate the problem.

Strep Throat

Most sore throats are caused by virus infections which are self-limiting and generally not a serious problem. But sometimes the throat is infected by streptococcal bacteria, a condition commonly known as strep throat. This is a serious problem which requires treatment because it can lead to kidney disease (glomerulonephritis) or rheumatic fever, a complex disease with skin rashes, joint inflammation, and damage to the heart valves.

Strep throat, which is much more common in children than adults, causes throat pain, fever, chills, muscle aches, swollen lymph glands in the neck, and headache. The infection can be diagnosed using a throat culture. Such cultures are becoming available to the public without a visit to a physician, and they are generally quite accurate.

TREATMENT
See a physician immediately if there is extreme difficulty swallowing, difficult breathing or opening the mouth, or excessive drooling in a young child. Call a physician if there is a temperature over 100°F, pus in the back of the throat, or a rough rash.

When strep throat is confirmed or strongly suspected it is treated with an antibiotic. This clears the infection before complications set in and helps prevent the spread of the infection to others. It is very important to take the entire prescription to insure that the infection is completely cleared. This usually takes at least ten days.

Cold liquids, saltwater gargles, and aspirin or acetaminophen help relieve pain and fever.

Tonsillectomy, surgical removal of the tonsils, is not done as often as in the past because it does not prevent recurrent sore throats or colds as was once believed and because the tonsils may be involved in building immunity. Even greatly enlarged tonsils almost always shrink in time. Only if more than three bouts of strep throat occur each year should tonsillectomy be considered.

PREVENTION
Avoid close contact with persons with sore throats.

If you or a family member has had acute glomerulonephritis or rheumatic fever, preventive use of antibiotics is sometimes prescribed. Be sure your physician is aware of your medical history.

Strokes

Blockage of or damage to an artery that feeds the brain results in damage to the brain—a stroke. Symptoms usually begin with muscle weakness or numbness and progress over the next minutes or hours to visual distortions, loss of speech, or partial paralysis. A severe episode, in which a brain artery hemorrhages or is closed by a clot, may cause serious brain damage, paralysis, and even death.

Early Warning Signs

In many cases there is a history of *transient ischemic attacks (TIAs)*, in which the blood supply to a brain area is cut off for a few seconds, minutes, or hours. The person experiences transient partial paralysis or visual or speaking difficulites. These episodes can be confused with certain forms of epilepsy or migraine and they must be thoroughly evaluated, no matter how brief; proper treatment could prevent a stroke.

CAUSES

Atherosclerosis—fatty blockage of the arteries—is an important factor in the vast majority of cases of cerebral vascular disease (CVD). When brain and neck arteries are severely blocked, blood supply is decreased, and tiny clots can do major damage by plugging arteries.

High blood pressure can lead to a stroke by promoting atherosclerosis, weakening the cerebral artery walls, and causing cerebral hemorrhage.

Osteoarthritis of the neck, with degenerative changes in the spine near the vertebral arteries, can cause compression of the arteries and obstruction of brain circulation.

Heart arrhythmias and heart attacks can lead to strokes by promoting the formation of clots in the heart that can then travel to the brain.

Severe anemia (insufficient red blood cells) limits the oxygen-carrying capacity of the blood, and polycythemia (too many red cells) can impede normal circulation and contribute to CVD.

Cigarette smoking contributes to CVD by accelerating hardening of the arteries and promoting hypertension. Heavy marijuana smoking may have similar effects.

Oral contraceptives increase the risk of CVD in women with a history of hypertension, elevated blood lipids, or smoking.

Isometric exercises and straining while defecating can greatly increase blood pressure, a threat to those with hypertension, CVD, or heart disease.

Chiropractic manipulation of the neck can cause strokes, even in young persons (see Part Six), according to some reports.

TREATMENT
Call a physician immediately if someone experiences symptoms that may indicate a stroke (above). Emergency treatment for a stroke victim depends on the area of the brain affected. In general, the airways must be maintained and adequate oxygen and fluids provided.

Rehabilitation programs (mostly various exercises) can bring gratifying development of remaining functions to compensate for those lost. Success depends mostly on the extent of the damage but partly on emotional factors that determine the patient's enthusiasm and effort. Adequate nutrition must be provided; protein is especially important because of tissue wasting, protein breakdown, and nitrogen excretion.

PREVENTION
Because strokes can be so devastating, prevention is preferable to even the very best treatment. While they remain a major cause of death and debility, the incidence of and mortality from strokes has steadily declined for more than a decade, due largely to attention to the risk factors.

Hypertension, atherosclerosis, osteoarthritis, and diabetes are all risk factors and must be detected, treated, and prevented. Each is discussed separately in this Part.

Don't smoke; see Chapter 5-4.

Avoid birth control pills if you are at risk; see Chapter 3-2.

If you have high blood pressure avoid isometric exercises and straining over stool.

Avoid chiropractic manipulation of the neck.

Call a physician if you have unexplained symptoms resembling a TIA (see above). Depending on the severity of the TIAs, age, blood pressure, and other factors, you may need treatment to prevent a stroke. The most effective medicine so far is aspirin in small daily doses; it helps prevent clots from forming by reducing platelet aggregation. In severe cases surgery may be required to unblock an artery.

Toxic Shock Syndrome

Ever since the late 1970s, whenever a woman having her period suddenly gets sick with a fever, vomiting, diarrhea, dizziness, a headache, aching

394   muscles, peeling hands and feet, and a sunburn-like rash, the immediate (and usually correct) suspect is toxic shock syndrome (TSS). If untreated, blood pressure becomes dangerously low and shock often ensues. There may be damage to the liver, heart, and kidneys. Death is less common now but still happens in about 5 percent of the cases.

TSS is said to be rare because there are approximately ten cases per 100,000 menstruating women per year. The risk is much higher for those who use tampons. These account for the vast majority of cases; but if the same symptoms are seen in anyone with a boil or any kind of infected wound or burn, TSS is to be strongly suspected.

CAUSE

TSS is apparently caused by a powerful toxin produced in lethal amounts by *Staphylococcus aureus* bacteria when they proliferate in large colonies. The disease was rare, or at least unrecognized, until the late 1970s when highly absorbant tampons made of new synthetic materials were heavily promoted and used by millions of women. Their great advantage turned out to be their curse: women can leave the tampons in far longer than was possible in the past, often after inserting them with plastic devices that apparently can produce tiny abrasions in the delicate tissue of the vaginal wall. The warm, moist vagina encourages the rapid growth of the bacteria, which are common and easily introduced with unwashed hands. The abundant "staph" produces the deadly toxin which is absorbed into the blood.

Nonmenstrual cases are similarly caused by the toxin produced by *S. aureus* which have managed to colonize a body orifice or a wound.

TREATMENT

See a doctor now. Early recognition and treatment are important to minimize organ damage and prevent death. At the first signs of fever and either diarrhea or vomiting, a menstruating woman should immediately remove any tampon and see a physician. Hospitalization is required in severe cases. Treatment may include replacing fluids and giving oxygen and antibiotics. Anyone with a skin infection who develops these symptoms should likewise see a physician right away.

PREVENTION

Don't use tampons; this reduces the risk of TSS to near zero. If you must use them, you can minimize the risk by using the less absorbant all-cotton type, using them sparingly and not at night, and changing them every four to six hours. More frequent changing may increase the risk of introducing bacteria.

Wash hands well before inserting tampons. The vaginal area should be kept clean with daily washing.

Do not use tampons for nonmenstrual purposes. (Abnormal discharge should be discussed with a physician.)

Women who have once had TSS are at the greatest risk and should not use tampons without consulting a physician.

Carbuncles, boils, abscesses, and infected wounds and burns should be treated by a physician.

Tuberculosis

Tuberculosis annually afflicts 30 to 40 thousand Americans, and kills perhaps 5 percent of them. Most cases are in urban pockets of poverty, malnutrition, and close quarters with poor ventilation. Contact with immigrants from areas of high incidence is often a factor.

This bacterial infection can affect the bones, joints, skin, the gastrointestinal system, and other organs, but it most often involves only the lungs.

In Western countries the bacteria are almost always contracted by inhalation. Infection via raw milk is common in some areas. The bacteria invade the tissue and cause abcesses, bleeding, and tissue death. Fibrosis and calcification occur in healing.

The early symptoms are usually mild—fatigue, loss of appetite, low fever. Gradually, serious symptoms such as bloody sputum and high fever develop.

CAUSE

The tubercle bacillus, *Mycobacterium tuberculosis*, comes in three types: human, bovine, and avian. All three can infect humans, but the human type is the most common in the United States where pasteurization of milk is the rule. People with active lung infections leave a mist of infective droplets suspended in the air when they cough. Crowded, poorly ventilated living quarters promote the spread of the bacteria. Most of those exposed develop strong immunity right away and never get sick; in others the infection gains a foothold but is walled off, and they don't get sick until months or years later when resistance is low. Malnourished and otherwise weakened persons are more likely to get sick soon after exposure.

TREATMENT

Contagious patients should be isolated and treated in a hospital for a couple weeks, or at home if infection of others can be prevented there. Good nutrition and bed rest in a cheerful, comfortable environment are important.

Drugs are usually very effective. Isoniazid and others are given in various combinations for six months or more. Side effects must be monitored

396 and the drugs adjusted accordingly. (See Chapter 5–2 for more.) Vitamin B-6 supplements, 25 to 50 milligrams per day, are often given with isoniazid.

PREVENTION

Isolation and treatment of those with active TB are the most important preventive measures. Those in contact with contagious patients should wear masks and have regular skin tests or chest X-rays. The patient must cough and spit in ways that do not spread infection.

Testing of all close contacts of active cases should be done as soon as the latter are discovered and again in two or three months. Skin tests determine whether exposure has ever occurred. Recent converters from negative to positive reaction are usually treated with isoniazid for about a year.

Preventive drug treatment seems to be instrumental in keeping down the number of infected persons, but it has been criticized because of the development of resistance in the bacteria and the development of hepatitis and other serious problems in some of those treated.

BCG vaccination may offer some protection against tuberculosis, and serious side effects are rare. It is used only in areas and situations of high incidence or exposure, because it converts negative skin-test reactors to positive reactors by tricking the immune system into acting as though infection has occurred. This prevents early detection by skin test and treatment with isoniazid.

Good nutrition, especially adequate protein, calories, and vitamins A and C, is important in tuberculosis prevention. Malnourished children during growth spurts are very vulnerable.

Given the growing incidence of drug-resistant infection, and the lack of a truly effective vaccine, it is likely that eradication of tuberculosis must await eradication of poverty, overcrowding, and malnutrition.

Ulcerative Colitis

In ulcerative colitis the colon is inflamed, and there may be severe abdominal cramping, pain, and almost constant diarrhea. Tiny lesions on the inner surface of the colon grow, causing the tissue to die. Patches of the mucosa (lining) slough off, leaving large areas denuded and unable to absorb water and minerals.

This loss of fluids, nutrients, and body tissue, along with a loss of appetite, results in malnutrition, anemia, dehydration, weight loss, and debilitation. Arthritis, skin rashs, and liver inflammation may also occur.

Remission and relapse may continue for many years with colon cancer a major risk. But some people have a very mild course and occasionally spontaneous cure takes place.

CAUSE

The cause of ulcerative colitis is not known, but it seems to be an immunological disorder. The favorable response to the elimination of certain foods and the use of corticosteroids, which suppress the immune system, supports this theory.

The removal of milk from the diet helps in about one case in five. It is not clear whether milk proteins, sugar (lactose), or both are involved.

Some researchers think an unidentified infection may be the cause.

TREATMENT

Elimination diets may help determine which foods, if any, provoke flare-ups. Milk and milk products certainly should be considered; grains are also suspect. Foods found to be offensive should be avoided.

Low-fiber, bland diets are almost always prescribed, at least during flare-ups, because of the stimulating effects on the bowel of roughage and spicy foods. But some fruits and vegetables are often well tolerated, especially if cooked. Frequent small meals are usually better than fewer large ones, since they stimulate the bowel less.

It is very important to avoid malnutrition. Sufficient protein, iron, calories, fluids, and electrolytes are critical. This is a challenging problem since the appetite is often poor, and many foods only make matters worse.

Adequate protein, up to 150 grams per day if needed, can be obtained from fish, eggs, lean meat, and tofu. High-protein drinks made from milk, yogurt, kefir, or soymilk with brewer's yeast, wheat germ, and protein powder can help. Of course, sensitivity to any of these ingredients would rule them out.

Additional vitamins and minerals should be in the range of the RDA plus 50 percent, temporarily more in severe malnutrition. (Megadoses are not a good idea—see Part Two.) Iron may have to be given by injection if it causes irritation or cramping when taken by mouth.

Fresh fruit and vegetable juices are excellent sources of vitamins, minerals, and possibly other healing substances. They may have to be finely strained if there is intolerance to their fiber. Remember, though, that delayed hypersensitivity to some chemical components of some foods may be an aggravating factor. With their abundance of complex molecules, fresh juices may do more harm than good.

Attacks of colitis often accompany emotional stress, but the stress may be more an effect than a cause of the problem. Various psychosomatic

398 theories are advocated, and psychoanalysis is often tried, but there is no evidence that it affects the disease, though it may help victims cope with it. The sympathy and understanding of family and friends helps reduce frustration and tension and prevent depression.

Drugs are often necessary in severe cases. The most useful are the corticosteroids (the cortisone group). Many of the serious side effects of these drugs such as weakened bones and diabetes can be avoided if they are given by enema. Properly used, these steroids clearly reduce sickness and death. Atropine, paregoric, and sometimes narcotics are given to control severe diarrhea and cramping. Antibiotics are sometimes beneficial.

Unfortunately, cancer of the colon is common, especially after fifteen years or more of ulcerative colitis. Removal of the colon is curative. A colostomy, or artificial anus, is made through the abdominal wall. There is little disfigurement or interference with normal activities.

PREVENTION

There is no known method of preventing ulcerative colitis. If an infection is involved breast feeding may provide some protection, but this is only speculation.

Prevention of serious complications, including cancer, depends on careful treatment, good diet, and regular examination by a physician.

Urinary Tract Infections

Bacterial infections of the bladder (cystitis) or urethra (urethritis) usually cause painful, difficult, and frequent urination. Typically there is a strong urge to urinate, but only a little comes out and it burns terribly. It may have a strong odor. In severe cases there may be fever, chills, abdominal pain, and bloody urine. Sometimes there are few or no symptoms. These urinary tract infections (UTIs) can spread to the kidneys and cause serious damage, so they must be cleared. There is also evidence that they may cause or promote bladder cancer, but this is not certain.

CAUSE

The most common cause is *Escherichia coli*, bacteria normal to the colon. The most common source of infection is contamination of the urinary opening with fecal bacteria. Women are about ten times as likely as men to contract a UTI because of the proximity of their urethal, vaginal, and anal openings and the shortness of their urethras.

Chlamydia, ultra-tiny bacteria which cause a common venereal disease, also causes some UTIs. Gonorrhea and bacterial prostatitis can also be at fault.

Pregnant women are even more susceptible because the bladder is pressured between the uterus and the pubic bone and it may not empty completely. The stagnant urine is a good breeding medium for bacteria. Hormonal changes may also make the urinary tract more susceptible to infection.

In children recurrent UTIs are often associated with anatomic abnormalities, polyps, or stones that obstruct urine flow. The residual urine provides a medium for bacterial growth.

TREATMENT

Call a doctor right away if urinary symptoms are accompanied by vomiting, fever, chills, bloody urine, or abdominal or back pain. This is very important to prevent kidney infection.

Drink enough fluid to produce lots of very dilute urine. This will probably be at least two liters per day and more in hot weather. This dilutes and flushes out the bacteria.

Cranberry juice is a popular home remedy; it provides organic acids that apparently act as an antiseptic to help keep UTIs in check. However, it may make the burning worse so a little baking soda is often added. Others skip the juice and drink water with baking soda (no more than a half-teaspoon per cup) to ease the pain of urination. Those on sodium-restricted diets should not try this. Vitamin C in large doses is also popular with some, but there is no proof it helps.

Even if home treatment seems to clear the infection, you should get a urinalysis because of the danger of kidney infection. If your symptoms last more than a day call a physician. Antibiotics (mostly sulfa drugs and ampicillin) are usually very effective. In rare cases of extreme susceptibility, perhaps genetic, long courses of antibiotics may be needed. If anatomic abnormalities are responsible, surgery may be necessary.

UTIs tend to recur, so proper treatment must also include preventive measures.

PREVENTION

Keep the vaginal and anal areas clean. Women should clean the anal area by wiping *away* from the vagina; girls should be taught this early.

Don't wear tight pants, noncotton underwear, or anything else that traps heat and moisture in the crotch.

Tampons and diaphragms must be used with care: don't leave the former in too long, and make sure the latter fit right and are clean.

Be careful during love-making: that which touches the anal area should not enter the vagina. The susceptible woman and her partner should bathe

400 thoroughly before making love. Urinating soon after intercourse helps wash out any bacteria that might have been pushed in. Vibrators (and perhaps motorcycles and horse-back riding) may precipitate UTI in some women.

Don't use petroleum jelly. If a lubricant is needed use a sterile, water-soluble product; ask a pharmacist.

Chlamydia in your lover must be cleared up. If he has symptoms or any reason to suspect infection (which may not cause symptoms in him), he should see a physician.

Do not postpone urination when the urge occurs. This may be the single most important pereventive measure for some, especially women. A full bladder accumulates germs and excessive pressure on the bladder wall may damage it and make it more susceptible to infection.

Varicose Veins

Normally, valves in the veins close and open with the ebb and flow of the blood and prevent blood from backing down the legs. But in many women and some men the valves become defective and the blood seeps down through them and pools in the veins. These become distended, push toward the surface, and appear as swollen, stretched, bluish bulges just under the skin.

In the vast majority of cases the problem is cosmetic, not medical. But sometimes there are serious complications, such as inflammation, pain, blood clots, or hemorrhage.

CAUSE
Defective (and sometimes absent) vein valves are genetically determined, but several nongenetic factors can aggravate the condition and accelerate its progression. Being sedentary or standing for long periods encourages the pooling of the blood in the leg veins, while being active helps pump the blood back to the heart. Tight clothes and garments hamper normal venous return. Obesity stresses and stretches the veins. A low-fiber diet tends to cause constipation, straining while defecating, and long sessions on the toilet, which can cause excessive pressure to build up in the leg veins.

Pregnancy can aggravate (but not cause) varicose veins; hormonal changes apparently dilate the veins further, and the pressure on them is increased by the added blood volume of pregnancy and the growth of the fetus.

TREATMENT

If a sore, ulcer, rash, or pain occurs near a varicose vein, a physician should be consulted. In some severe cases the best remedy is to remove the veins; the blood can be returned by the deeper, healthier veins. But this is a last resort. The vast majority of cases can be satisfactorily dealt with and their development slowed by taking some simple measures.

Lose fat if you are obese. Be active. You do not have to become a marathoner; just walk a lot, or swim or bicycle. Use stairs instead of elevators and walk instead of driving if it is feasible. If you have a sedentary or stand-still job, find a way to move and flex your legs at least every hour.

Increase the fiber in your diet by eating plenty of whole grains, fruits, and vegetables. Favor brown rice over white, whole grain bread over white bread, and whole fruits over juices.

Don't wear tight clothes, boots, girdles, or other garments which tend to impede blood flow.

Do wear elastic support stockings during pregnancy or long periods of standing; but avoid those that are tight below the knees.

Elevate your legs above your heart whenever possible.

PREVENTION

Varicose veins are genetically determined but influenced by nongenetic factors. They cannot be prevented, but their progression can be delayed and complications can be prevented by proper treatment.

Vision Loss

Worldwide, the most important causes of vision loss, partial or total, are malnutrition (especially vitamin A deficiency), glaucoma, and infections—especially trachoma, a chronic inflammation due to a strain of *Trachomatis chlamydia*. (For the alert reader who may wonder: yes, close relatives of this organism cause the common sexually transmitted disease known as chlamydia or NGU; see Chapter 3-3.) However, in the United States, the most common causes are cataracts (due to aging and other factors), accidents, glaucoma, and diabetes.

Accident prevention is generally beyond the scope of this book. Suffice it to say that special care, including the use of safety goggles when appropriate, should be taken by carpenters, construction workers, chemists and other lab workers, and those who play tennis, handball, and racketball.

402   Cataracts

The lens is unique—a crystal-clear living tissue floating freely in a fluid (the aqueous humor) without blood or nerve supply. It depends on the fluid for nutrient supply and waste removal. In cataract development the lens gradually (sometimes rapidly) clouds over and vision gets dimmer until it is essentially lost. There is no pain or inflammation, just blurring and dimness. Cataracts usually develop in both eyes simultaneously or nearly so. They can happen at any age but are much more common in older people.

There are many causes and types of cataract, including senile, diabetic, drug-induced, metabolic, traumatic, and radiation-induced. Genetic susceptibility often seems to be a factor.

Senile cataract is by far the most common. Almost everyone's lenses get a little hazy with age. It appears that their vitamin C-dependent respiration and waste-removal systems deteriorate. Vitamin C within the lens, normally ten to twenty times more concentrated than in the rest of the body, decreases with age and drops to near zero in senile cataract.

Oxygen uptake from the aqueous humor depends on high concentration of vitamin C in the lens. As the uptake decreases, the lens metabolism deteriorates, waste builds up, and cloudiness develops. It might appear logical to try vitamin C supplements for senile cataract—increase vitamin C intake, improve lens metabolism, and get rid of the waste. Unfortunately, matters are not so simple and little success has been reported. Apparently the low level of vitamin C in the lens is an effect rather than a cause of deteriorating lens metabolism.

Overall nutrition seems to be much more important than any specific nutrient. In animal studies various combinations of vitamin and amino acid deficiencies lead to cataracts. In malnutrition due to poverty and war, they develop at a younger age. Deficiencies of protein, vitamins A and C, and the B vitamins are especially conducive to early cataract formation.

Diabetes, like malnutrition, encourages early development of senile cataract. Proper nutrition and control of blood sugar help counter this.

TREATMENT

When vision in the better of the two eyes is so poor that daily activities are interfered with, surgical removal of the lens is recommended. In most cases, a permanent plastic lens is then implanted in the eye. It is imperceptible and usually restores vision to near normal.

PREVENTION

Assure adequate nutrition throughout life, especially in later years when activity and nutrient intake tend to decrease. Diabetics should be especially careful about adequate nutrition and control of their blood sugar.

Wear good sunglasses. Senile cataract formation is strongly associated with exposure to ultraviolet radiation. Ophthalmologists recommend sunglasses for all those with high exposure to the sun including farmers, sailors, life-guards, beach lovers, and construction workers. What kind are best? There is a risk (theoretical at press time) that glasses that reduce only visible light may dilate the pupils enough to increase exposure of the lens to ultraviolet radiation. Your best bet is to use only those that are guaranteed (on the label) to stop 100 percent of the ultraviolet.

Some studies of persons on long-term aspirin therapy indicate that the drug may delay the onset and slow the development of senile cataracts. On the basis of preliminary evidence, some ophthalmologists recommend daily aspirin for those over fifty. Don't try this without consulting your physician.

True diabetic cataract is not nearly as common as senile cataract, diabetic retinopathy, or other vision problems caused by diabetes. The lens, unlike most tissues, is not dependent on insulin for its glucose. So when the blood sugar is high, as in diabetes, glucose pours into the lens, where it is converted to sorbitol and fructose. These two sugars cannot penetrate the lens, are trapped inside, and draw in water by osmosis, which causes swelling, changes in refractive power, blurred vision, and eventually clouded vision. Diabetics can decrease their risk by careful control of blood sugar.

Drug-induced cataracts are most often caused by long-term use of moderate to high doses of corticosteroids. The phenothiazines, used to treat serious psychiatric disorders, can also cause cataracts. Always be aware of the hazards of the drugs you use, and use the lowest effective doses. Have your eyes checked frequently if you are taking corticosteroids or phenothiazines for months or years.

Metabolic cataracts are rare. Probably the most common are those that develop in children with galactosemia, a hereditary lack of an enzyme necessary for the metabolism of galactose from milk sugar. The consequent accumulation of galactose-one-phosphate damages various tissues, including the lens. Strict avoidance of milk, milk products, and all other sources of lactose and galactose is necessary. This is important since the cataracts are reversible only in the very early stages.

Galactosemia can usually be prevented by genetic counseling of persons with a family history of the disorder. Otherwise the galactosemic

404 fetus can be treated in the womb; strict avoidance of lactose and galactose by the mother can prevent cataract and other defects in the child.

German measles during the first three months of pregnancy can cause congenital cataract. It can be prevented by vaccination before pregnancy.

Radiation-induced cataract is not common except for the accelerated development of senile cataract caused by sunlight. However, accumulated exposure to excessive X-rays, color television, radar, microwaves, and other radiation may be a factor in some cases.

Glaucoma

The front chamber of the eye is filled with a clear fluid, the aqueous humor, which is constantly secreted into the eye by fluid-producing cells and drained out through tiny canals. In glaucoma the drainage is defective, so fluid accumulates and pressure in the eye builds up. This decreases blood supply to the optic nerve fibers, which are slowly destroyed, resulting in loss of vision starting at the periphery. Sight lost this way can never be recovered, so **early detection and treatment are very important.**

The most common type of glaucoma is the insidious chronic type that usually begins after age thirty-five and tends to run in families. Some signs of early chronic glaucoma are:

> Loss of peripheral vision
> Recurrent blurred or foggy vision
> More rarely, morning headaches, pain around the eyes after watching television, and halos around lights

Unfortunately, there are **usually no symptoms** and no apparent visual defects until damage has been done. This is why regular checks for glaucoma are important.

Acute glaucoma is only about a tenth as common as chronic, but is a significant cause of blindness. A small percentage of people over thirty-five have a narrow space between the iris (the colored diaphragm) and the cornea, which predisposes them to acute glaucoma in which the iris balloons forward and blocks the drainage canal. The rapid buildup of pressure causes blurred or cloudy vision and severe pain. The eye is usually red and there may be nausea, vomiting, and severe headache. **See a physician immediately** if these symptoms occur. Vision will be lost completely and permanently in a day or two without treatment.

In susceptible persons, this sudden canal blockage can be precipitated by anything that dilates the pupils, including:

Prolonged sitting in the dark with open eyes, including watching a movie or television

Careless use of eyedrops or internal medicines which dilate the pupils

A blow to the head

Sudden or sustained emotional stress, which increases circulating epinephrine (adrenalin)

PREVENTION OF BLINDNESS DUE TO GLAUCOMA

Early detection is the best defense against chronic glaucoma. The simple, painless test, **tonometric examination** of intraocular pressure, should be done about every three years after age twenty and perhaps every year after age forty. If there is a family history of glaucoma, tonometric examination is advisable once a year after age twenty (sixteen if black). You don't have to go to an ophthalmologist for this test; the device is inexpensive and simple to use, so your family physician should be able to do it.

If glaucoma is discovered, it is extremely important to follow the ophthalmologist's instructions. Eyedrops are usually used to control the pressure, mostly by increasing the fluid drainage. The drops must be taken as ordered and the eyes should be examined regularly. Other drugs and eyedrops should be avoided without the doctor's approval. When drops are not effective, pills are usually prescribed. In the rare cases where medical therapy is not effective, laser or other surgery may be necessary to reduce the pressure and prevent blindness.

In acute glaucoma, creation of a passage through the iris allows proper drainage to resume and prevents blindness. This is done with a laser beam or simple, quick surgery. Probably the most important measure to prevent acute glaucoma in those predisposed is examination of the anterior chamber angle before instilling drugs into the eyes.

Encouraging reports from Nigeria indicate that some glaucoma can be treated with nutritional methods. It is important to understand that most glaucoma in Nigeria and other developing nations is triggered by years of severe malnutrition and malaria. There is no evidence that glaucoma in affluent nations has a nutritional basis, and those afflicted should not be tempted by articles in health food magazines to switch from their eyedrops or pills to nutritional supplements. Nevertheless, in chronic glaucoma it is important to maintain good general health with proper nutrition, exercise, and rest. Diabetics should aim for optimum control of their blood sugar.

Infant glaucoma can be caused by rubella infection during the first trimester of pregnancy. This is yet another reason for vaccination.

In many people prolonged internal use of corticosteroids, or application to the eye, can lead to increased intraocular pressure and glaucoma.

406 These drugs should be used with great caution under a doctor's supervision.

Marijuana and alcohol both reduce intraocular pressure for several hours, but they are impractical in glaucoma because their use would mean round-the-clock intoxication.

Warts

Warts are slow-growing little bumps than can appear anywhere on the skin and occasionally in the mouth and throat. They usually disappear within a year or two but may recur or spread to other areas. They are more common in children than adults. Most warts are a cosmetic rather than a health problem, but those on the soles of the feet, on the genitals or anus, or on other areas where they may cause pain or irritation, usually require treatment. Ano-genital (venereal) warts may promote cancer of the cervix.

CAUSE

Warts are caused by at least a dozen related viruses. The virus enters the skin through a cut or abrasion, invades a live cell, and takes over its reproductive machinery for its own use. Within a few months a small, smooth bump will be noticeable.

Because they are caused by viruses, warts are contagious. They can be spread on one's own body by scratching or rubbing or to another person by direct or indirect contact. The abrasive surfaces around swimming pools are believed to contribute to the shedding of wart viruses, which can then infect others who walk through the area. Ano-genital warts can be transmitted by sexual contact.

TREATMENT

The immune system controls warts quite well in most people; this is why they do not get very large or spread very far, and eventually disappear. Immunity subsequent to childhood exposure probably explains why warts occur less often in adults. Because of this immunity and the benign nature of most warts, treatment is not usually necessary. If a quicker cure is desirable, consider the following methods.

Warts are believed to be affected by **suggestion**, especially with children, who are generally more suggestible. Such charades as touching the warts with ice and coloring them may speed their resolution.

The only nonprescription wart treatment found effective and safe by an FDA review panel is **salicylic acid**. The area around the wart is protected with petroleum jelly and the wart is painted with the acid. The treatment may be repeated for several weeks if necessary. Read labels or ask a pharmacist for a product with salicylic acid. Ineffective products will be on the market for a long time.

If you want fast results, if you have venereal or plantar warts (on the bottom of your feet) or if you have poor circulation or are a diabetic, see a physician who can remove warts with **liquid nitrogen**. This supercold liquid is held to the wart until it blanches, just a few seconds. It turns black and falls off in a few days. This method is very fast, effective, and painless. It is far preferable to cutting or burning warts out, and is probably even safer than the over-the-counter acid.

If ano-genital warts are treated, they should also be treated in one's **sex partner(s)**.

PREVENTION
Avoid contact with warts; don't scratch, rub, or chew them. Avoid sexual imtimacy with anyone who has veneral warts.

5

Drugs and Health

PART FIVE

Chapter 1   Over-the-Counter Drugs

Chapter 2   Prescription-Only Drugs

Chapter 3   Herbs and Herbalism

Chapter 4   Recreational Drugs

1

Over-the-Counter Drugs

In 1984 the American public spent almost $10 billion on more than 300,000 nonprescription drug products (or OTCs for "over-the-counter" drugs), and medical experts and consumer advocates have long maintained that a great deal of this is unnecessary and unsafe. To find out just how much of this self-medicating is justified, in the 1960s and 1970s the Food and Drug Administration (FDA) established panels of experts (physician specialists, toxicologists, and pharmacists) to review the ingredients that go into the products and determine whether they are safe and effective. This monumental task, which took some twenty years and is the most comprehensive review of its type ever undertaken anywhere, has been completed. The results are very significant for us all.

Only about 700 active ingredients go into the 300,000 proprietary products on the market. Of these, only about 250 have been found to be safe and effective.[1] This is wonderful news to the consumer, who often experiences dizziness, confusion, anxiety, headaches, eye strain, nausea, and other severe symptoms when confronted with hundreds of antacid products, painkillers, allergy remedies, and cold medicines to choose from. By mercifully narrowing our choices, saving us from wasting money on worthless products and protecting us from dangerous ones, and helping us make rational decisions, the FDA review could be worth its weight in growth hormone to the public.

However, its ultimate value is yet to be determined. Two schools of thought have shaped up in the wake of the massive review. The FDA, which is under more pressure from drug companies than from consumers, has been slow in implementing the findings of its expert panels. It appears

411

412 that many worthless drugs will be sold for years to come, though many will eventually be withdrawn. The FDA also continues to allow irrational combinations and, along with the Federal Trade Commission, a great deal of misleading advertising.

A streamlined approach is taken by the modern reformers, led by the Public Citizen Health Reseach Group (HRG), which has taken the FDA to task (and to court) for not consistently implementing the findings of its expert panels.[2] The FDA's rationale for its permissive approach is that the products are widely sold and accepted by the consumers;[3] in other words, they are big business. But they are big business because of vigorous promotion, not proven effectiveness. The FDA seems to forget that the snake oils of the past were popular, and laetrile and other worthless and dangerous products are currently popular with many people. That does not prove they are effective.

The reformist philosophy of OTC drug use can be summed up as follows:

Don't use a drug unless you really need it. In many cases nondrug remedies are safer and more effective.

When you do need a drug, take a single-ingredient generic product proven to be safe and effective for your symptoms. Combinations of active ingredients increase the cost and the risk without increasing the benefit.

Learn to read labels and ignore advertisements. Difficult as the task may appear at first, consumers need to learn the generic names of the products they use, or at least learn to read them and look up their effects, hazards, and proper uses, so their decisions will be based on facts, not on misleading and sometimes fraudulent commercials. If inexpensive, single-ingredient products are not stocked in a store near you, ask a pharmacist to stock them. (See Safe and Effective Ingredients, below.)

Always heed precautions and use the drugs according to instructions on the label or provided by your physician.

Consult your doctor before taking an OTC if you are under a physician's care for any chronic (long-term) health problem or are taking a prescription drug.

Avoid "extra-strength" and most time-released products, and those marketed for specific types of pain. For example, Doan's Pills are marketed for back pain. They contain magnesium salicylate, an aspirin equivalent, and cost about ten times as much as plain aspirin but provide no additional benefits.

In general, with very few exceptions, OTCs should *not* be used for *weight problems, constipation* (except bulk remedies), *nausea, vomiting, "over-indulgence," insomnia, simple nervous tension,* or *hemorrhoids* (except petrolatum and zinc oxide). Some would include diarrhea on this list (see discussion below).

The Health Research Group (HRG) not only wants the FDA to ban substances not proven safe and effective, but it disagrees with the FDA on many specific commercial products because they contain irrational combinations. For example, the FDA rates Alka-Seltzer Blue (the original Alka-Seltzer) as a safe and effective antacid because it contains sodium bicarbonate, but the HRG disagrees because it also contains aspirin, which aggravates hyperacidity and promotes ulcers. Alka-Seltzer has long been marketed as a remedy for "overindulgence." The ads don't specify alcohol hangover, but the implication is there because people rarely get headaches from overindulgence of food. Taking aspirin for an alcohol hangover can be dangerous, especially for anyone prone to ulcers.

The HRG also considers it irrational to combine a safe and effective drug with an unproven or ineffective one. The FDA generally rates a commercial product safe and effective if one of its active ingredients is proven so, even if the others are not effective. The HRG disagrees; why, it argues, should we pay more for unproven benefits and expose ourselves to increased risks?

On the basis of these criteria the reformists recommend against the use of thousands of proprietary products, including most of the heavily advertised and successfully marketed products in the country. In most cases there are more rational, safer, or cheaper alternatives. In the following discussions examples of questionable products are given. Far from being unusual, these are merely the tip of an iceberg too large to include in this volume but clearly outlined for those who wish to avoid it.

The reformist philosophy is most compatible with a preventive approach to health care. If the American public followed these recommendations, its OTC drug bill could be slashed by more than half. Moreover, there would be much less exposure to unnecessary drugs and their hazards, which are especially significant for pregnant and nursing women, the very old, and the very young. Such an approach would not decrease the benefits we derive from OTCs.

It would be impractical to review even a significant fraction of all the proprietary products available. There are not only too many of them, but new ones are often introduced and old ones keep their names while their ingredients are changed. Therefore, we focus on basic principles in the use of the most important *generics*, the active ingredients which are put into the thousands of products. This provides a lasting guide which, combined with careful reading of labels, should make OTC drug use as rational as possible.

The following categories of OTCs are reviewed below: *allergy products, antacids, asthma medicines, cold and cough medicines, diarrhea remedies, diet aids, laxatives, pain-fever-inflammation drugs, sleep aids, and topical products.*

414   Allergy Products

Nonprescription products for allergy relief are mostly for the treatment of allergic rhinitis (hay fever), the runny nose, sneezing, itchy and watery eyes, throat irritation, and cough due to contact with pollens and other allergens. Products for asthma are discussed separately.

The effective OTCs for allergic rhinitis are **antihistamines.** They lower the tissue concentrations of the chemical responsible for the symptoms, *histamine*, and thereby relieve the symptoms. Their most common side effect is drowsiness, which varies widely among people and products. They may also cause dry mouth and occasionally blurred vision, gastrointestinal (GI) distress, and other problems. Try different products until you find one that works and has weak side effects. Antihistamines reputed to cause little drowsiness in most people are **pheniramine, brompheniramine**, and **chlorpheniramine** (note the common suffix *pheniramine*).[4] When using these drugs, do not drive or operate dangerous machinery until you know how you are affected.

Two new antihistamines, terfenadine and astemizole, are likely to be approved soon. They seem to cause drowsiness much less often than the drugs now in use.

Questionable OTCs for allergic rhinitis include **nasal decongestants** and **combination allergy products.** Nasal sprays and drops are good for relieving a stuffy nose during a short cold, but they are not appropriate in hay fever, when the nose is running instead. Moreover, hay fever sufferers usually take remedies for more than three days, and such prolonged use of the sprays often causes rebound congestion and other side effects. Combination allergy pills contain not only antihistamines but nasal decongestants as well, which makes them questionable.

Antacids

Those under a physician's care for peptic ulcers should use antacids only as directed by their doctors. Antacids are also appropriate for *occasional* use to relieve the burning sensation of hyperacidity, commonly called acid indigestion or sour stomach, and for "heartburn," the burning sensation caused by the acidic contents of the stomach rising into the esophagus. Thick, liquid antacids are best for the latter because they coat the esophagus. No one should use antacids regularly or frequently without consulting a physician.

Thousands of antacid products are on the market, but there are only a few active ingredients. They are all effective and safe for occasional use, but some are preferable to others in some circumstances.

Aluminum tends to be constipating, though less so if combined with magnesium.

Calcium carbonate tends to be constipating and is often associated with rebound acidity, which may cause the stomach to become more acid than it was before the product was taken.

Magnesium tends to cause diarrhea, though less so if combined with aluminum.

Sodium bicarbonate products are effective but hazardous to persons who must restrict sodium intake. Baking soda is usually available and generally cheaper than tablets with sodium bicarbonate.

Combination products usually contain aluminum and magnesium, which counter each other's side effects. The balance is not always right for an individual, however, and either constipation or diarrhea may occur.

Simethicone, which makes a few big bubbles out of many small ones, supposedly making them easier to pass, is a questionable ingredient in many antacid products because there is no evidence that it is effective in treating abdominal discomfort after eating. The amount of gas in your GI tract is not associated with the symptoms and expelling the gas will not relieve them. Moreover, simethicone cannot increase the total amount of gas you pass.[5]

Products not to use: any antacid product containing aspirin.

Asthma Medicines

Asthma should not be treated with drugs, even OTCs, without consulting a physician. Prescription drugs are often more effective and sometimes safer.

Theophylline and **ephedrine** are the main ingredients in asthma tablets and elixirs. Theophylline is often the drug of choice for asthma, but its blood level should be studied to determine the proper dose, so self-treatment without consulting a physician is not ideal. Ephedrine is an effective but questionable ingredient because it has many side effects including nervousness, loss of appetite, and insomnia.[6] These combination products often also contain an antihistamine to counter the stimulant effects of the theophylline and ephedrine, but there is no evidence this helps. Theophylline may be designated a prescription-only drug, and ephedrine may be phased out for asthma

416 because there are better products. So OTC asthma pills and elixirs may become a thing of the past.

OTC inhalers for asthma all contain **epinephrine** (adrenaline), which opens the airways to allow breathing. It is generally safe and effective, but short-acting and subject to tolerance. If not used sparingly it may cause nervousness, rapid heartbeat, and other side effects.

Metaproterenol may be changed from a prescription-only drug to an OTC drug. It is not as much a threat as epinephrine to hypertensives and may have fewer side effects. Nevertheless, it can cause nervousness, fast heartbeat, nausea, and other problems.

Questionable products include those with mixtures of active ingredients such as theophylline, ephedrine, and pyrilamine (an antihistamine which many experts believe should not be used for asthma). If more than one drug is needed, they should be taken separately so their doses can be adjusted individually.

Cold and Cough Medicines

There are hundreds of pills and potions marketed as cold remedies; it is an enormous industry. Most of this drug use is unnecessary and undesirable. The heavily advertised multisymptom remedies are particularly irrational. More and more drugs are included in each pill, which always allegedly treats more symptoms than the competition. As of this writing, we're up to twelve symptoms, which can all be treated by one pill. Soon we will be told we have twenty separate symptoms with each cold and more ingredients will be included in the magic pills.

In truth, few people suffer more than one or two symptoms worth taking a drug for, and the shotgun approach of most commercial remedies exposes the users to unnecessary risks for little more than a placebo benefit. The drug industry also does a disservice with its commercials that encourage cold suffers to "keep going" (to school, work, shopping) rather than to rest; this delays recovery and increases the exposure of others to the shedding viruses.

Most people with colds do not develop the long list of symptoms shouted about in the ads for OTC cold remedy cocktails. If you are going to use drugs, it is best to treat individual symptoms with single-ingredient products. This will expose you to only one or two drugs at rational doses rather than several drugs in a fixed ratio.

Stuffy nose can be treated with nose drops or spray containing **oxymetazo-**

line, **xylometazoline,** or **phenylephrine,** and no other active ingredients. Inhalers with **propylhexedrine** or **1-desoxyephedrine** are also effective. There is no need for menthol, eucalyptus, or other aromatic substances which may add to the cost without increasing effectiveness. Sprays with antihistamines (such as pheniramine) are questionable remedies for treating colds since histamine is not responsible for the symptoms. Decongestant sprays should not be used for more than three days; rebound stuffiness and consequent addiction can occur—that is, when the drug wears off the stuffiness is worse than before its use; more is taken, it wears off, and so on.

Runny nose should not be treated with drugs since it helps the body shed the offending virus and correct inflammation. Be careful, though, not to blow your nose hard since this can spread viruses and perhaps bacteria throughout the sinuses and into the eustachian tubes leading to the middle ears.

Productive cough, a cough that brings up mucus, should not be treated with drugs since it helps clear the lungs. The mucus can be thinned by drinking plenty of water and spicy chicken soup.

Dry cough, a cough that does not bring up mucus, can be treated with **dextromethorphan,** which suppresses the cough center of the brain and has few side effects. Look for a product with no other active ingredients, or ask your pharmacist to stock a generic product with dextromethorphan. **Codeine,** an opiate, is available without a prescription in some states. It is an effective cough suppressant but can produce many side effects including nausea, constipation, drowsiness, and dizziness. It is also slightly addicting. Diphenhydramine, an antihistamine, is the active ingredient in some cough medicines, but it has such strong sedative effects that it is also the main ingredient in some sleep aids.

Sore throat due to the common cold can be treated with **aspirin** or **acetaminophen.** These should be swallowed whole, not crushed or chewed in gum because they can irritate the throat, and they do not provide pain relief by contact with the affected tissue. Some sore throat lozenges may sooth and provide temporary relief. Look for **benzocaine, phenol, menthol,** or **hexylresorcinol** in the ingredients. Avoid alcohol-based mouthwashes, which do not affect the cold viruses and can irritate sensitive throat tissue.

Fever, headache, and aching muscles are unusual in the common cold; they may indicate flu or something else. They can be treated with aspirin or acetaminophen, but if they are severe or persistent, consult your physician. See Part Four for details on flu.

Questionable products include all the multisymptom cold and flu remedies

418 such as Alka-Seltzer Plus, Comtrex, Contac, Dristan, Nyquil, Sine-Aid, and Sine-Off, and mouthwashes such as Cepacol and Listerine for sore throat.

In conclusion, the vast majority of colds can be endured with simple measures (mainly rest and fluids) and, if necessary, simple drugs. Few people need more than a single-ingredient nasal spray for stuffy nose; for a sore throat, a throat lozenge, aspirin, or acetaminophen may help. If a dry cough develops, a medicine with dextromethorphan and preferably no other active ingredients can be used.

Diarrhea Remedies

Chronic diarrhea can be caused by many things, including irritable bowel syndrome (spastic colon; see Part Four) and lactose intolerance. These must be treated with medical guidance according to their causes, as must any diarrhea that lasts more than a couple days or is associated with a fever. OTC antidiarrheals are intended for use in *acute diarrhea* (as opposed to chronic diarrhea) due to viral infections of the GI tract, overconsumption of laxative foods and drinks, food poisoning, or reactions to medicines. While the FDA has tentatively approved a few products as safe and effective for acute (simple) diarrhea, critics do not recommend them.

Simple diarrhea, whatever its cause, is almost always self-limiting; it subsides in a day or two without treatment. The simplest remedy is to avoid any foods or drinks suspected of causing or aggravating the problem, drugs not recommended or prescribed by a physician, and most dairy products since the lactose aggravates diarrhea even for those who are not normally lactose intolerant. Water or diluted juice should also be taken to replace lost fluid. At least one glass every three hours is usually advisable. All caffeinated and sugary beverages should be avoided. If diarrhea lasts more than a day, make a mixture of half a teaspoon of salt, half a teaspoon of baking soda, and four tablespoons of sugar in a liter of water. Drink it when thirsty to prevent dehydration.

Polycarbophil (Mitrolan), considered safe and effective by the FDA, is a bulk-forming laxative which is supposedly also effective in consolidating stools and making diarrhea less uncomfortable. It is generally safe since it does not slow down the expulsion of infectious agents and toxins, as truly effective antidiarrheals (such as opiates) can do by practically stopping bowel activity. But it is apparently only marginally effective and has little to recommend it.[7]

Bismuth subsalicylate (Pepto-Bismol) can reduce cramping and frequency of bowel movements in traveler's diarrhea, but large doses (about a cup a day) are required and aspirinlike side effects may occur in some people. There is considerable controversy about whether it is effective in other types of diarrhea, but it does seem to help in some viral cases.

Attapulgite (Rheaban) is supposed to reduce the number of bowel movements, but its effectiveness is in dispute.

Kaolin and **pectin,** as in Kaopectate, are, respectively, a fine white clay and a plant fiber. The FDA has found them both, alone and in combination, ineffective in the treatment of diarrhea. They do not diminish cramping, frequency of bowel movement, or fluid and electrolyte loss. However they do seem to make the stools firmer and thereby decrease discomfort. This may be worthwhile since the treatment is safe.

Questionable products include Donnagel, Donnagel-PG, Kaopectate, Parapectolin, Rheaban.

Diet Aids

All of the drugs available as diet aids (appetite suppressants) are potentially hazardous and of questionable effectiveness. (See Parts One and Two for effective obesity remedies.) Taking pills to treat obesity and control weight has become an American tradition. It took several decades of experience with amphetamine and its relatives for us to admit that they do not work and can be dangerous. But within a few years we embraced **phenylpropanolamine,** (PPA), a newer chemical cousin of amphetamine which is the main ingredient in scores of diet aid products.

PPA is claimed to be an effective and safe appetite suppressant, but it can produce potentially serious side effects including hypertension, heart problems, kidney damage, accelerated pulse, anxiety, restlessness, and other signs of excessive nervous stimulation.[8] These reactions can be aggravated by the caffeine which is added to many of the products. It is no wonder that abuse of these drugs is a common cause of emergency room treatment.

There is only meagre evidence that the drugs help control appetite and no evidence whatsoever that they are a significant aid in the long-term treatment of obesity, the utterly fantastic claims of the dealers notwithstanding. They are explicitly not recommended for persons with heart disease, thyroid disorders, diabetes, or hypertension because of serious potential hazards. However, mass screenings and other surveys indicate that a third or so of those with the latter two disorders, who are among those most likely to be obese, do not know they have them. Given these facts, it is difficult to justify the OTC status and use of these drugs for weight control.

Another important problem with the widespread availability of PPA (practically anyone can buy it in bulk and go into the mail-order diet-pill business), is that it is frequently present in high doses in "look alikes," drugs sold illicitly as amphetamine. They cause thousands of poisonings each year. Common symptoms include severe headache, vomiting, heavy sweating, tremors, and seizures, and hallucinations, delusions, and other psychiatric symptoms. These drugs also lead to suicide attempts and other violence.

Benzocaine is a local anesthetic added to candies and gums to numb your taste buds and thereby decrease your appetite. There is little evidence to support this theory and none at all to support the claims of significant weight reduction.

Questionable products include Ayds, Control, Dexatrim, and Dietac.

Starch blockers are extracts of certain beans that are supposed to block the digestion of starch and thereby allow more eating without weight gain. Studies indicate they do not work. If they did, bacterial action on the undigested starch would be expected to produce fairly severe GI symptoms, especially diarrhea and excessive gas.

Health-food store diet-aids such as spirulina, bee pollen, herbal extracts, glucomannan, and various amino acids are all questionable products; none of them has been shown to work as claimed by their promoters.

Laxatives

Constipation is characterized by infrequent bowel movements or hard stools that are difficult to pass. It can aggravate and promote hemorrhoids and diverticular disease and, if it persists for many years, might be a factor in colon cancer.

Constipation is usually caused by inadequate fiber and fluid intake and insufficient exercise, and by various drugs, including laxatives. But sometimes it is a symptom of a serious problem, and you should consult a physician if there is substantial pain in passing stool, signs of blood (including tarry stools), fever, nausea, weight loss, pencil-thin stools, or no response to simple self-care measures (see Part Four).

It is almost always preferable to treat constipation with high-fiber food, water, and exercise (plain walking is fine) rather than laxatives. However, when traveling, camping, or sailing, it may not be practical to eat the best foods or get enough walking, and laxatives may be a convenient occasional aid. In this event there is only one class of laxatives which is a rational choice. The **bulk laxatives,** which contain methylcellulose, psyllium, and other fibrous plant products, work by absorbing water and creating bulk, just like fiber from food. It is important that they be taken with plenty of water to prevent them from drying and possibly blocking the intestine. Their sodium and sugar content should be checked by those who must restrict sodium or calories.

None of the other types of laxatives works like food and they are all associated with certain risks. Long-term use of **stimulant laxatives** (those with phenolphthalein, senna, disacodyl or danthron), for example, actually dilates the large bowel and decreases its sensitivity to bulk so that it becomes dependent on chemical stimulation for contraction.

Saline laxatives (those with magnesium) are not as good as bulk laxatives, but they do draw water into the colon and can help when bulk laxatives alone don't work. They are safe for occasional use for most people but are hazardous to those with kidney problems or on salt restriction.

Stool softeners (which contain ducosate) and mineral oils are also unnatural and potentially hazardous.

Questionable products include Carter's Little Pills, Correctol, Dulcolax, Ex-Lax, Feen-A-Mint, and Nature's Remedy. Many of the laxatives sold in health food stores are made from stimulant herbs and are among the most hazardous.

Pain-Fever-Inflammation Drugs

In the United States we spend almost $1.5 billion each year on OTCs for headaches, muscle and joint pains, fever, and other miseries. Not counting ibuprofen, which was reclassified as an OTC in 1984, the hundreds of products we choose from have only two active ingredients, **aspirin** (and chemical sisters with equivalent actions) and **acetaminophen.** These two drugs are similar in that they both relieve certain kinds of pain very effectively and they both relieve fever. Their potency is almost identical and the recommended dose is the same, 650 mg every four hours. However, aspirin also relieves inflammation but acetaminophen does not. Their side effects and hazards are also different. Therefore, they cannot be considered equivalents, and rational decisions must be made on which is preferable in given situations.

Aspirin is a popular and effective remedy for common headaches, for pain due to injury and inflammation of muscles and joints, for controlling fever, and for dysmenorrhea and premenstrual syndrome. It has its roots in herbal remedies that contain salicylate. In the 1880s the German pharmacologist Heinrich Dreser converted salicylic acid (SA) to acetyl SA, aspirin, which turned out to be much more potent and less corrosive to the stomach than

SA. (Two decades later he would again add acetyl to an already effective analgesic drug, this time the far more potent morphine. Once again the result was a more potent product, heroin, though the improvement was not nearly as spectacular as with aspirin.)

Side effects of aspirin include ringing in the ears, hyperacidity, and queasy stomach. It is a **serious hazard** and should be avoided by persons who are allergic to salicylates or have ulcers, pregnant women, children under sixteen with suspected viral infections such as flu or chickenpox, and those who take certain prescription drugs. Asthma is sometimes aggravated by the drug. Aspirin generally should not be taken within several hours of drinking alcohol and it should not be taken with acetaminophen.[9] It can promote excessive bleeding, so it should not be used in the days before or after surgery, including tooth extraction, before childbirth and in many other circumstances. These proscriptions include a large percentage of the population, so it is fortunate that there are alternatives to aspirin.

Other salicylates (such as choline and magnesium salicylates) are essentially aspirin equivalents and they have the same effects, uses, and hazards. However, the related drugs salicylamide and salsalate are not considered safe and effective.

Acetaminophen can reduce pain and fever, but since it cannot reduce inflammation its applications are more limited than aspirin's. Its main use is for headache and mild fever. It generally has fewer **side effects** than aspirin, but it can cause nausea. Acute overdose and chronic overuse can cause severe and sometimes fatal liver damage. The toxic dose is lower than for aspirin.

When to use aspirin and when acetaminophen. Aspirin is more effective for pain associated with inflammation, such as in sports-related injuries and arthritis (but not gout!), and in dysmenorrhea, but it should be avoided by those at risk for serious side effects as described above. In these cases acetaminophen may be just as effective and less risky, or it may be somewhat less effective. However, in most headaches acetaminophen is as effective as aspirin and usually preferable because of the lower risk of side effects. Acetaminophen is available in liquid form, which aspirin is not, so it is sometimes useful for young children and persons who cannot swallow pills or other solids.

Are the variations worth the price? Enteric-coated aspirin is designed to dissolve in the intestine rather than the stomach in order to avoid stomach bleeding. Because it is absorbed slowly and less reliably, it was rated ineffective by the FDA panel which reviewed it. Many physicians consider this a mistake since effective blood levels are achieved in many patients, whose stomachs are spared in the process. As long as it affords relief, it would seem to be a good choice for those who must take it often.

Time-released products and capsules are more expensive than regular tablets and there is no added benefit. Aspirin chewing gum is especially not recommended for sore throat because it is irritating and causes a burning sensation in the mouth and throat. There is no reason to buy anything but plain generic or other single-ingredient aspirin or acetaminophen without caffeine, antihistamines, phenacetin, or buffers. Nor is there any reason to buy the costly "extra," "mega," "super," or "arthritis strength" aspirin or acetaminophen; you can just take an extra pill or half a pill of the cheaper and equally effective preparations.

Questionable products include Anacin, Ascriptin, Aspergum, Bayer Time-Release Aspirin, Datril 500, Excedrin, Extra-Strength Tylenol, Goody's Headache Powders, and Vanquish.

Ibuprofen is one of a class of drugs called nonsteroidal anti-inflammatory agents (NSAIDS), which have all been prescription drugs until the reclassification of ibuprofen in 1984. Other NSAIDS may also be changed to OTCs. Some physicians and pharmacists oppose the changes and fear an epidemic of serious side effects from ibuprofen. Persons most at risk appear to be kidney patients, diabetics, those taking diuretics, those with aspirin or ibuprofen sensitivity, and those with ulcers. Ibuprofen is also much more expensive than aspirin and acetaminophen, so if one of the latter drugs works for you, you may as well stick with it. See Painkillers in Chapter 5–2 for more on NSAIDS.

Sleep Aids

The active ingredients of OTC sleep aids are **diphenhydramine, doxylamine,** and **pyrilamine,** all antihistamines that produce drowsiness as a side effect. The use of the drugs is highly controversial, even within the FDA, which approves of the first, dissapproves of the last, and is hedging on the second. It appears that when the FDA found the old ingredients in OTC sleep aids— bromides, scopolamine, and methapyrilene—not safe and effective, it felt obligated to approve something, lest there be no such products. So it rushed to switch prescription antihistamines to OTC status.

These drugs can cause dizziness, dry mouth, blurred vision, confusion, stomach problems, loss of appetite, ringing in the ears, and other side effects. They often produce insomnia and nervousness in children. They are hazardous to people with asthma, glaucoma, prostate enlargement, and other problems, and may interact dangerously with other drugs including

424   sedatives, alcohol, and anticonvulsants. They should not be used by pregnant or lactating women.

The amino acid **tryptophan** is often used as a sleep aid. Since it is marketed as a food supplement, the makers do not have to prove it is safe and effective as a sleep aid. The evidence indicates that it may be effective and is probably safe if used occasionally in moderate amounts. Theoretically, it could cause problems if used excessively.

Questionable products include *all* OTC sleep aids.

See Insomnia in Part Four for better remedies.

Topical Products

The marketplace offers thousands of products that are supposed to make our skin and hair more attractive, make us smell better, and deal with discomfort and disorders of the skin, eyes, ears, genitals, and ano-rectal area. Attempting to decide on a rational basis which, if any, of the products to use can try one's sanity. We cannot review individual products here, except a few for illustrative purposes. But the following comments on the major categories should help improve your health (and attractiveness), save you money, and protect your sanity by narrowing your choices some.

The following categories of products are discussed: *acne products, antiperspirants* and *deodorants, burn products, cosmetics, ear products, eye products, fungus fighters, hair-care products, hemorrhoid medicines, itch remedies, minor-wound products, sting remedies, soaps, sunburn remedies* and *sunscreens, vaginal products,* and *products for warts.*

Acne Products

Acne is a disorder involving oil trapped under clogged pores, and irritation and inflammation provoked by bacteria. (The keys to its control are discussed in Part Four.) Most of the commercial acne products do little good, and many of them can aggravate the problem by clogging the pores. There are some effective products, however; these contain *benzoyl peroxide* in a nonoily base. Look for the simplest, cheapest products with this ingredient and use it carefully and according to instructions on the label.

Antiperspirants and Deodorants

The body odor and body wetness problems have probably been aggravated in recent decades by the increasing use of synthetic fabrics in clothing. Unlike cotton, these newer materials all have a strong tendency to hold moisture in, so skin bacteria proliferate and produce their malodorous gases. The rise of the white-collar class has helped fuel the enormous growth of the antiperspirant and deodorant industry partly because the office workers' pants and shirts must be of the permanent-press, wrinkle-free variety—it is not a law, but a powerful tradition not often bucked. People working in the typical close quarters of modern offices and clad in their several layers of synthetic fabrics would knock each other over with their body odor if they did not do something about it.

That something has been to spray, roll, smear, and bathe on tons of chemicals in hundreds of products. The main ingredients in most current products are perfumes and *aluminum hydroxychloride* (and other aluminum salts), which cause irritation and allergic rashes in some people. The advantage of these products is that by stopping perspiration they not only inhibit odor development but also protect clothes from ugly stains. Deodorant soaps are questionable because the antimicrobials many of them contain are absorbed into the blood and produce photosensitivity in some people; their skin becomes easily burned or irritated when exposed to sunlight.

For those who are allergic to effective commercial products, or who do not like the idea of inhibiting the natural function of perspiring, there is an inexpensive, safe, and effective deodorant, *baking soda*. Simply dissolve about a quarter teaspoon in a quarter cup of warm water and pat it on the offending areas. It will not stop perspiration, so it does not solve the problems of stained clothes. But it is quite effective in reducing body odor, apparently by inhibiting the proliferation of skin bacteria. The wetness problem can be reduced by wearing light cotton clothes and cutting down on coffee and other stimulant drinks which promote sweating.

Burn Products

Suppose you spill hot coffee on yourself, accidently touch a hot motorcycle muffler, or grasp a casserole dish right out of the oven without a potholder. Should you smear grease or butter on it, or run to the drugstore for a remedy? No, you should *quickly apply cold water* to the burned area. Slightly iced water should be applied with a compress, or the area should be soaked, for a half hour to an hour. Ice or ice-cold water could damage the skin.

Sprays and ointments contain local anesthetics which do not promote healing and which can provoke allergic responses. The pain relief is not much more than cold water provides. In short, these are not very useful products.

426 Cosmetics

There are thousands of creams, lotions, foundations, blushes, lipsticks, and brush-ons marketed as beauty aids. The use of these cosmetics is primarily an aesthetic matter, a question of taste which must be decided on by individuals, perhaps with the expert guidance of cosmetologists. There are, however, some health problems associated with cosmetic use, and those who would be beautiful should also be wise—or at least alert to some of the hazards discussed here.

It should be kept in mind that cosmetics are not regulated in the way drugs are. The firms that make cosmetics are not required to register with the FDA or submit their products for approval. But they must declare their ingredients in order of predominance, with the main ingredient listed first. Fragrances need not be named but they must be listed as "fragrance."

Acne is a very common result of the frequent use of cosmetics. Almost all foundations, powders, cold creams, and lotions tend to clog the pores as well as provide acnegenic oils. The stuff can be cleaned off and the pores cleared with an astringent such as rubbing alcohol, but if you put the make-up back on, the pimples will remain. This is an aesthetic judgment which most people would agree with: no make-up is so good that its benefits outweigh acne it might cause. So if a cosmetic aggravates or causes acne, stop using it.

Allergic reactions to cosmetics and hair removers are very common. In fact, the continued application of almost anything to the skin is likely to eventually cause sensitization to the substance and an allergic reaction the next time it is applied—the first or five-hundredth application. Once it does, the substance will always cause a reaction.

Cosmetic manufacturers do extensive testing on all ingredients in order to use those that take the longest to produce sensitization. So-called "hypoallergenic" ingredients are more hype than hypo, since they have not been proven less allergenic than other ingredients. Manufacturers keep complaint files, and when it appears that significant numbers of people are developing allergies to an ingredient it is replaced. This is one reason the formulas for cosmetics are continually changing, though usually imperceptibly and without a name change.

Your best defense against developing allergic reactions to cosmetics is to use them sparingly and infrequently and to change products often. Be alert for reactions (such as little red bumps, a rash, or itching) to anything you put on your skin, and stop using it immediately should any appear.

Irritation is a common side effect of many cosmetics and other skin products. The redness, pain, and itching are caused by the chemical reaction of the substance with the skin, not by an allergic reaction. Aluminum chlorides in antiperspirants, shaving powders, and wax hair-removers are commonly irritating, more so to some people than others. Just about any solvent, such as nail-polish remover and some make-up removers, can be cause irritation and roughness of the skin.

Photosensitization is a common problem with cosmetics and perfumes. Many of the ingredients sensitize the skin to the sun so that relatively brief exposure causes sunburn. Therefore, caution is advised in the use of these products before exposure to the sun.

Ear-Care Products

As explained in Part Four (see Hearing Loss), earwax helps to warm and protect the ear canal. It normally works its way out slowly and should not be removed with bobbypins, cotton swabs, or other probes, which should never be inserted into the ear. The ears should be cleaned with soapy water and the little finger and nothing else. On rare occasions, however, excessive wax does accumulate and needs removing. This is done by squirting warm water into the canal with a rubber syringe made for the purpose. Many drugstores have them.

The task can be made easier, especially if the wax is impacted, by first inserting an ear-wax softening agent. Look for a product with **carbamide peroxide** in glycerin and use it strictly according to instructions. If it irritates do not use it again. Don't get into the habit of removing earwax; most people never have to. If you notice hearing impairment, don't try to treat it yourself; consult a physician.

Ear-canal drying agents, eardrops for use after swimming and bathing, contain rubbing alcohol which mixes with water in the canal and causes it to evaporate more readily. This helps control (prevent and treat) swimmer's ear and "surfer's ear," which are aggravated by wetness. These products sometimes irritate the ear, in which case their use should be stopped. An electric hair dryer is often more effective and less irritating, especially during a flare-up, but also for routine use by persons prone to these ear problems.

CAUTION

If you also use eyedrops, be very careful not to confuse them with your eardrops, which often come in similar bottles. While eyedrops placed in the ear will not cause problems, eardrops placed in the eye will cause excruciating pain for several hours. The alcohol causes the conjunctiva to become

428   very inflamed and frighteningly red. Should you make this mistake, you will know it immediately, so only one eye will be involved. Rinse it copiously for at least ten minutes and consult a physician.

Eye-Care Products

Eyedrops for "soothing tired eyes" and "getting the red out" are among the more questionable OTCs. There is nothing in any eyedrops that can relieve eyestrain or fatigue of the eye muscles, and placing drops in one's eyes is never very soothing. If one frequently has red eyes, an examination is in order. The active ingredients, such as naphazoline and tetrahydrozoline, constrict the superficial blood vessels of the eye and thereby decrease the redness. They are generally harmless, but tolerance to their effect can develop and sensitivity may result, in which the drops cause the eyes to become even redder. The more often the products are used the more likely these reactions are.

  If you use eyedrops and eardrops, read the caution above about not mixing them up. It is best not to store them together to reduce the chance of this happening.

Fungus Fighters

By far the most common fungal diseases are superficial infections of the skin and mucous membranes. (See Fungus Infections in Part Four for details.) A large number of topical agents are available. For the common tinea infections (athlete's foot, jock itch, ringworm), products with **tolnaftate** or **miconazole** are very effective and generally lacking in side effects, though contact with the eyes must be avoided.

Hair-Care Products

Each strand of hair is covered by a cuticle, a protective protein coating. If it is damaged the hair will rapidly fray and become limp and lifeless. As hair grows and ages, the cuticle naturally tends to deteriorate and flake away, leading to split ends. There are factors that promote and hasten this process and factors that delay it. For example, excessive shampooing, blow-drying, bleaching, dying, straightening, habitually pulling (often unconsciously), brushing, backcombing, and teasing can all damage the cuticle. So can hot water, chlorine, brushing while the hair is wet, and over-exposure to the sun. Important systemic (internal) factors that can result in unhealthy hair are poor nutrition, various drugs, and severe illness.

Keeping generally healthy, avoiding the various insults to hair, and keeping it clean with a mild shampoo generally suffice to keep hair healthy and attractive. This would seem to be a simple matter, but there are thousands of products available for cleaning, conditioning, and doing other things to improve hair. Shampoos, dandruff remedies, and conditioners are the most useful and baldness remedies the least. These categories of products are discussed below. Practically all the other products are potentially damaging, and the risks must be weighed against the aesthetic benefits by the owner of the hair.

Baldness remedies, both those taken internally and those rubbed into the scalp, are frauds, in spite of all the testimonials and sophisticated advertisements. There are no lotions, creams, hormones, vitamins, lights, massages, drugs, or other products or procedures that can cure baldness, which is usually due to hormonal changes and heredity. True, there are a handful of prescription-only drugs and hormones that promote hair growth in some circumstances, but they are hazardous substances, and the risks of their use generally far outweigh the potential benefits. In any case, these are not involved in the treatments offered by mail-order firms and baldness "clinics," which offer only cleansers, conditioners, and cosmetics.

Conditioners, which are applied to hair after shampooing, are of several types with different functions. Acid rinses such as dilute lemon juice or vinegar are used to remove any film left by highly alkaline cleansers. They tend to flatten the cuticle and increase sheen, but they are not antistatic and will not prevent "fly-away." Cream rinses are slightly acidic surfactants, substances which coat the hair, flatten the cuticle, add sheen, and neutralize static electric charges, thereby reducing fly-away. Instant and protein conditioners are like cream rinses, but they also contain proteins, fats, oils, waxes, and other ingredients, which lubricate and add luster and body. The protein in particular seems to penetrate the hair shaft and thicken it.

Dandruff products. A certain amount of dandruff (flaking scalp) is normal and can be adequately controlled by washing with a mild shampoo. Hot water and scratching the scalp with a hairbrush can cause irritation and aggravate dandruff. A dilute vinegar rinse seems to help in some cases, probably by serving as a kerotolytic, an agent which loosens up the scaly scalp. Excessive use might irritate the scalp and aggravate the problem, especially if you have dry scalp and hair.

If these simple measures do not work, an OTC dandruff product may be tried, but cautiously and in moderation. The most effective products contain **zinc pyrithione**. Products with **selenium sulfide** are available in low

430 concentrations without a prescription. They often work, but sometimes not for long. Alternating the use of products with these ingredients seems to help in many cases. Use them carefully. If nothing seems to help and you have severe dandruff with large flakes or very oily scalp, you should consult a dermatologist.

Shampoos contain mild detergents which are generally superior to soaps because they clean better, work well in hard water, are less alkaline, and rinse out completely. All the other ingredients in shampoos, the thickeners, colors, fragrances, and so on, are not necessary for cleaning. Conditioners are best used separately after washing.

How often and thoroughly should you shampoo? Usually two to five times a week, depending on how oily and dirty your hair gets. Unless you have acne or severe dandruff which is aggravated by oily hair, it is better to err on the side of less washing. Squeaky clean hair is a sign of excessive shampooing and using water that is too hot. This can damage the hair by weakening and removing the cuticle and promoting dryness and splitting. It cannot, however, make your hair fall out.

The choice of shampoo is mostly a personal and cosmetic matter, not a question of health. However certain health-related points should be kept in mind. Anyone with sensitive skin, frequently lighter-skinned persons, should be alert to signs of irritation and allergic reactions, a good reason to try a different shampoo. In fact, it is a good idea for these people switch shampoos frequently, and always dilute them before applying. Almost all shampoos are only slightly alkaline, and therefore not very harsh, so claims about pH-balance are superfluous.

Hemorrhoid Products

The proper treatment and prevention of hemorrhoids involves walking and other exercise, and adequate fiber and water in the diet. See Part Four for details.

There are no products that promote the healing or resolution of hemorrhoids. Products should be considered only for their temporary relief of acute symptoms.

A wide variety of ingredients go into hemorrhoid products. Astringents are supposed to temporarily relieve itching and burning, counter-irritants distract from the itch and pain, protectants guard against further irritation, and local anesthetics numb the area. Vasoconstrictors are supposed to narrow the swollen blood vessels, atropine and related drugs to inhibit nerve impulses in the area, and vitamins A and D promote healing.

Of all these ingredients the only ones that are undeniably safe and effective are protectants such as petroleum jelly, zinc oxide, cocoa butter, and shark-liver oil, provided they make up at least 50% of the product. All the other ingredients are unproven, irrational, or otherwise inadvisable. Local anesthetics, for example, often sensitize people to novocaine and other anesthetics so that their use in the future would cause an allergic reaction. Atropine agents have no effect on the swollen veins, and there is not the slightest evidence that vitamins applied to the ano-rectal area promotes the healing or resolution of hemorrhoids.

Since we are left with protectants as the only worthwhile ingredients, essentially all the commercial preparations for hemorrhoids are eliminated. There is no reason to buy expensive products with lots of worthless and potentially hazardous ingredients. Preparation H, for example, contains only 3 percent shark-liver oil, which, in any case, is no better than the much less expensive petroleum jelly. As a protectant, lanolin is questionable because many people are allergic to wool products, and it is no better than the cheaper protectants. Therefore, if you feel you must put something on your ano-rectal area for the temporary relief of the symptoms of hemorrhoids, just use petroleum jelly or zinc oxide.

The marketing of Preparation H is instructive, for it shows how millions of people can be persuaded to cough up millions of dollars for a questionable product decade after decade. Using the litany, "It's doctor-recommended," a chant that saturates the airwaves and print media in a continuous and mind-numbing blitz, Whitehall Laboratories has created an enormous and obedient army of faithful users of their product.

But is it not doctor-recommended? Could they lie about that? Well, there are hundreds of thousands of doctors, and you can always find some that will recommend just about any given treatment or product. The question is, how many and which doctors recommend Preparation H? The physician specialists and other experts on the FDA panel which looked into hemorrhoid products included Preparation H among those lacking evidence of safety, effective, or both, so the ads for the product are clearly misleading.

The doctor-recommended bit is so effective that the makers of other hemorrhoid products have taken it up. From the sheer volume of the propaganda one would think doctors are obsessed with hemorrhoids and always recommend some specific medication for them.

Insect Repellants

Insect repellants can help make life livable when mosquitos and gnats threaten to drive you batty. Look for products with **diethyltoluamide** (DEET) or **dimethyl phthalate.** Foams and liquids are better than sprays because they have higher concentrations and are cheaper. Use these products carefully and as sparingly as you can, especially with young children. The active

432 substances can be absorbed through the skin and prolonged use of large amounts can cause neurological symptoms such as anxiety, lethargy, confusion, seizures, and coma.

Thiamin, vitamin B-1, ingested in large doses is sometimes recommended to keep bugs away. Studies have shown that it does not work, so save your money.

Itch Remedies

Colloidal oatmeal is a safe and effective anti-itch remedy, especially useful when large areas of the body are affected. You can soak a limb or your whole body in it. It is available at drug stores; follow the directions on the box. Cornstarch can also be used this way.

Hydrocortisone creams are quite effective. They should be used strictly in accordance with instructions on the label or those of your physician.

Calamine lotion is of marginal and questionable benefit.

Minor Wound Treatments

Minor cuts and scratches can be adequately treated by thorough cleaning with water and perhaps a mild soap. Every particle of dirt or sand must be removed to prevent infection. The wound should be covered with a bandage and kept clean. If pus appears, hot water soaks can be used to promote drainage. There is almost never any reason to apply iodine, alcohol, topical antibiotics, or other liquids or ointments. None of them offers any advantage over thorough cleaning and some of them are painful when applied or capable of producing allergic sensitivity. Therefore, if a minor wound does not seem to be healing after a few days, and especially if an infection seems to be getting worse or spreading to other parts of your skin, consult a physician rather than try to treat it with OTC products.

Sting Remedies

What should you do if stung by a bee, wasp, jellyfish, or other such beastie? There are many folk remedies, including urinating on the area and applying baking soda. A rational remedy is to apply a paste of meat tenderizer, which contains papain, an enzyme that breaks down the protein toxins from the sting. Of course, any stingers or barbs should be removed from the skin.

Some OTC products containing papain for treating stings are now sold in drugstores. Antihistamines like those used for hay fever can help reduce the swelling and itching. See Allergies in Part Four for the dangers of insect stings.

Soaps

In spite of all the claims made for various soaps, very little is really known about how they affect our skin because adequate research is not done. The advertising claims about soaps being mild or gentle are unproven and often completely without foundation. One systematic study of the effects of eighteen popular brands of soap showed that most of the heavily promoted, expensive, supposedly gentle soaps were among the most irritating and likely to produce chapping in sensitive persons.

The only soap in the study which proved to be truly gentle and easy on the skin was Dove, which has large amounts of cold cream. However, Dove has a powerful perfumy odor that many find objectionable, it seems difficult to rinse off completely, and it is expensive for the use one gets from one bar.

Bar soaps can harbor pathogenic bacteria for several hours and theoretically serve as a medium for the spread of disease. Some experts believe they do not belong in public or semipublic bathrooms or large kitchens from which many people are served. However, there is no evidence that they actually do help spread diseases, even in hospitals where germs and bars of soap are everwhere. Nevertheless, the controversy seems to be stimulating a switch to liquid soap dispensers in some institutions and even private homes.

Deodorant soaps are questionable products because they often produce photosensitivity.

Sunburn Products and Sunscreens

Dozens of heavily advertised products for relief of sunburn pain contain benzocaine, a local anesthetic. It provides only marginal relief, probably no more than cold water, and it can provoke allergic reactions. Therefore, none of these products can be recommended. Aspirin (up to two tablets every three hours) is more likely to provide significant relief. It should not be used by those prone to ulcers or hyperacidity.

The best approach, of course, is to prevent sunburn by limiting exposure to the sun and using products with a sunscreen such as PABA or oxybenzone. Look for an SPF (sun-protection factor) of 15 or more in a water-resistant product and apply the product generously for maximum protection. The SPF numbers (2 to 21) are much more important than the

434 specific active ingredients, so choose a product with the protective power you need—a cream, fluid, or gel, depending on convenience, skin type, and possible sensitivity to ingredients.

Vaginal Products

The vagina is normally clean, for it is washed, lubricated, and defended against irritation and infection by its secretions. Any unusual or foul-smelling discharge should be discussed with a physician. The normal though sometimes offensive odor that may develop toward the end of the day is a product of sweat and normal vaginal secretions altered by exposure to oxygen and held by the pubic hair. It is easily controlled with daily washing of the pubic area. All-cotton panties and outer garments are preferable because they allow evaporation of moisture and thereby inhibit bacteria proliferation and odor accumulation. There is no need to use "feminine hygiene sprays," which can cause irritation and allergic reactions. These products can be considered consumer frauds since they have nothing to do with hygiene, which concerns cleanliness and health.

Routine douching is also not necessary, but it is usually not harmful if done properly. Warm water, with or without a little white vinegar, is all that should be used unless a physician advises otherwise. The vagina should *not* be held closed while douching because water may be forced into the cervix and Fallopian tubes and this could cause infection. Also, douching should be avoided during pregnancy and the month after childbirth or abortion, unless a physician recommends it.

Most of the twenty-eight ingredients of vaginal products have not been shown to be safe and effective, and some are deemed definitely not to be: phenol, phenolate sodium, sodium salicylate, sodium salicylic acid phenolate, silica, and talc. They will nevertheless remain available for some time; products containing them should be avoided.

Products for Warts

Warts are caused by viruses and they usually go away by themselves. However, warts on the sole of the foot or the ano-genital area should be treated by a physician. If you want to get rid of a wart elsewhere on the skin, look for a product with **salicylic acid** and use it in strict accordance with the instructions. Products with various vitamins are nothing but placebos. Products with glacial acetic acid are not considered safe and effective.

Liquid nitrogen is probably the best wart-removing tool there is, but it is not generally available to the public. Dry ice, which is solid carbon dioxide, is more readily available and perhaps worth trying. The idea is to hold the cold to the wart until it blanches (turns white) as it freezes. One or **435** two treatments is usually adequate; in a day or so the wart turns almost black and soon falls off. *Be careful not to touch the normal skin.*

Safe and Effective Ingredients

The following is a list of the active ingredients of nonprescription drugs that the Food and Drug Administration, the American Medical Association, and the Health Research Group consider safe and effective when used properly. It is essentially the FDA's list minus those ingredients about which serious questions have been raised by FDA panels and other responsible critics, and those for which nondrug alternatives or a physician's care is almost always preferable—for example, for the treatment of hemorrhoids, skin infections, eye care, and asthma.

In the interests of simplicity, we have not included the many antiperspirants and sunscreens generally considered safe and effective. All the former are aluminum compounds and salts and are best not used in aerosol form. All the latter are rated with an SPF, a sun-protective factor, based on laboratory studies. The use of these products should be stopped if it causes irritation or a rash. The list includes no antimicrobials of the type commonly used in bar soaps for alleged deodorant properties because none has been proven safe and effective; such soaps cannot be recommended.

Note that the ingredients on the list are not effective for purposes other than those listed, **and they are not safe unless used properly.** For example, acetaminophen is effective as an analgesic and antipyretic but not as an antirheumatic, and neither it nor aspirin works as a sleep aid or sedative.

If a product has an active ingredient not listed here, it might be a hazard and a waste of money. Try to find a known safe and effective alternative. For simplicity we have omitted from the names the inactive parts of the chemicals such as hydrochloride, maleate, acetate, nitrate, and phosphate.

INGREDIENT	USES
acetaminophen	internal pain, fever
allantoin	skin protectant
almadrate	antacid
alum	astringent
aluminum (carbonate, others)	antacid
aluminum hydroxide	skin protectant

436

aminoacetic acid (glycine)	antacid
aspirin (and carbaspirin, salicylate)	internal pain, fever, rheumatism
benzocaine	itching; skin, mouth, gum, throat pain; not for toothaches
benzoin compounds	gum protectant
benzoyl peroxide	acne
benzyl alcohol	itching, skin pain
bismuth (carbonate, others)	antacid
bran, dietary	bulk laxative
brompheniramine	antihistamine
butamben picrate	itching, skin pain
calamine	skin protectant
calcium (carbonate, others)	antacid
carbamide peroxide in glycerin	earwax softener, oral wound cleanser
carboxymethylcellulose	bulk laxative
charcoal, activated	absorbent for toxic ingestion
chlorpheniramine	antihistamine
citric acid, citrate	antacid
cocoa butter	skin protectant
cod liver oil	skin protectant
colloidal oatmeal	itching
cornstarch	skin protectant
cyclizine	antiemetic for motion sickness
desoxyephedrine	inhalant decongestant for stuffy nose
dextromethorphan	cough suppressant
dibucaine	itching, skin pain
dihydroxyaluminum	antacid
dimenhydrinate	antiemetic for motion sickness
dimethicone	skin protectant
dimethisoquin	skin protectant, itching, skin pair
doxylamine	antihistamine
dyclonine	itching, skin pain, mouth pain
elm bark	demulcent
ephedrine	inhalant for stuffy nose
fluoride	anticavity rinse, toothpaste
gelatin	demulcent
glycerin	skin protectant, demulcent

haloprogin	antifungal
hemicellulose of psyllium	bulk laxative
hexylresorcinol	mouth, throat pain
hydrocortisone	itching
hydrogen peroxide	wound cleanser
hydroquinone	skin bleach
iodochlorhydroxyquin	antifungal
ipecac and ipecac syrup	emetic for ingestion of certain poisons
juniper tar	itching, skin pain
kaolin	skin protectant
karaya	bulk laxative
lanolin	emollient
lidocaine	skin pain, itching
magaldrate	antacid
magnesium-aluminum-silicate	antacid
magnesium (carbonate, others)	antacid
malt soup extract	bulk laxative
meclizine	antiemetic for motion sickness
menthol	itching; mouth, throat, skin pain
methapyrilene	itching, skin pain
miconazole	antifungal
naphazoline	topical nasal decongestant
nonoxynol 9	contraceptive
octoxynol	contraceptive
oxymetazoline	topical nasal decongestant
pectin	demulcent
petrolatum, white	skin protectant
phenindamine	antihistamine
pheniramine	antihistamine
phenylephrine	topical nasal decongestant
piperonyl butoxide with pyrethrins	kills lice
plantago ovata husks, seeds	bulk laxative
pramoxine	itching, skin pain
propylhexedrine	topical nasal decongestant
pseudoephedrine	topical nasal decongestant
psyllium	bulk laxative
pyrantel pamoate	kills pinworms

438

pyrilamine	antihistamine
racephedrine	topical nasal decongestant
resorcinol	itching
resorcinol with sulfur	acne
salicylic acid	corns, callus, warts, dandruff, seborrheic dermatitis, psoriasis
selenium sulfide	dandruff
shark liver oil	skin protectant
sodium bicarbonate	antacid, skin protectant
starch	skin protectant
sulfur	acne, scabies, dandruff
tartrate, tartaric acid	antacid
tetracaine	itching, skin pain
thonzylamine	antihistamine
tolnaftate	antifungal
tripelennamine	itching
undecylenate	antifungal
urea (2–10%)	itching
xylometazoline	topical nasal decongestant
zinc (oxide, others)	skin protectant
zinc pyrithione	dandruff, seborrheic dermatitis

Stocking Up for a Year

Suppose you wanted to stock up for a year for a large family with members from ages one to eighty who experience a wide range of symptoms treatable with nonprescription drugs. You would not normally have to do this, but it makes an interesting exercise. The task is enormously simplified by using the facts we have presented and ignoring slick advertisements. Rather than puzzle over the claims and counter-claims made for the hundreds of thousands of proprietary products, just get a simple product from each of the categories likely to be important to your family. The following would be a reasonable shopping list, and little would be lost by forgetting all the rest.

acetaminophen or aspirin

an antacid with both magnesium and aluminum

benzocaine
benzoyl peroxide
charcoal, activated
chlorpheniramine, or whichever antihistamine causes the least
    drowsiness
colloidal oatmeal
dextromethorphan
fluoride
hydrocortisone
hydroquinone
ipecac
meclizine
menthol
miconazole or tolnaftate
octoxynol
para-aminobenzoic acid (PABA) (sunscreen)
phenylephrine nasal spray
petrolatum
peperonyl butoxide with pyrethrins
psyllium
pyrantel pamoate
salicylic acid
selenium sulfide

Even this list could be trimmed with little loss to your family's comfort and none to their health. For example, phenylephrine and other nasal sprays might be replaced with spicy soups and steam inhalation; instead of salicylic acid for warts and corns, try to find a physician who uses liquid nitrogen; instead of psillium, eat some fruit; instead of selenium sulfide and other dandruff medicines, use the simple methods outlined earlier. As for meclizine, while it may be helpful in severe cases, most people prefer mild motion sickness to the drowsiness so often caused by this and similar drugs. Benzocaine, menthol, and other skin and oral analgesics are of only marginal benefit, and some people develop allergic reactions to them.

It is clear, then, that of the myriad products available, a dozen or so simple ones will provide your entire family with all the wonders the nonprescription drugs industry has to offer.

440 Examples of Ingredients Considered NOT Safe and Effective

The following ingredients, whatever their benefits, are **definitely not recommended** for the uses given and may indeed be hazardous.

INGREDIENT	USES
acetic acid	warts, corns, calluses
alfalfa	weight control
amino acid combinations	weight control, muscle building, memory enchancement
antipyrene	pain, fever, antirheumatic
benzocaine	hemorrhoids, acne, antifungal, smoking deterent, warts, lice, vaginal douche, boils, psoriasis
boric acid	acne, antifungal, antiseptic, anti-infective, skin healing, vaginal douche, hemorrhoids
caffeine	pain, fever, premenstrual tension
camphor	acne, antimicrobial, hemorrhoids, decongestant, chest rub, boils, warts
capsicum	toothache, smoking deterrent
cresol	psoriasis, antifungal, antimicrobial,
estradiol, estrogen, estrone	hair growth, aphrodesiac, acne
eucalyptol, eucalyptus oil	various cold symptoms, skin problems, smoking deterrent
fructose	weight control, energy, stamina, hangover prevention
homeopathic remedies including "cell salts," organ extracts	variety of ailments
iodine	acne, warts, weight control, toothaches, antiseptic
menthol	hemorrhoids, cough, decongestant, dandruff
mercury	antimicrobial, psoriasis, boils

phenol	wound cleaner, protectant, antiseptic
potassium	digestive problems, colic, weight control, smoking deterrent, sedative, premenstrual tension
pyrilamine	sedative, pain, fever, premenstrual tension
salicylamide	sedative, pain, fever, rheumatism
thymol	acne, cough, dandruff, itching, pain
various vitamins	acne, warts, hair growth, wound healing, sex stimulants, hemorrhoids, weight control

441

2

Prescription-Only Drugs

With Brian Fellmeth, M.D., PH.D

Drugs that are available by prescription only are intended for use supervised by a physician who can determine their need and dose and monitor their effects and side effects. These drugs are generally more potent and more hazardous than nonprescription drugs. They are also more studied, tested, and reviewed, and under greater constraints to be proven effective.[10] To provide the most benefit with the least risk, prescription drugs must be used properly. The following general considerations hold for all prescription drugs; they should be considered an essential part of the discussions of drugs in the following pages.

Don't expect or ask for a drug prescription when you consult a physician. Many health problems are best treated with other therapies; using drugs for them would entail a risk without providing a benefit.

Always inform your physician about your medical history, including all reasons for medical care, all allergies and adverse drug reactions, and *all* drug use, including topical products. You should take the drugs with you and show them to your doctor. All drugs are potentially subject to interactions with other drugs, including antacids, aspirin, birth control pills, medicinal herbs, coffee, tea, colas, marijuana and other recreational drugs, tobacco, and sometimes even food. Heed all precautions from your doctor or pharmacist.

Inform your doctor if you are pregnant or lactating. Many drugs can cause birth defects, subtle neurological damage, small birth weight, kidney damage, and other problems. Taken by the mother, they enter her milk and can cause adverse reactions in the breast-feeding infant.

Keep all appointments with your physician. Many prescription drugs require very careful monitoring of blood levels and effects to determine safety and effectiveness.

Follow your doctor's prescriptions exactly. Take the drugs according to schedule. Know what to do if you forget a dose; in most cases the next dose is *not* increased to make up for the forgotten one, but sometimes it is. If in doubt and you cannot contact your doctor, call and ask a pharmacist.

Be clear on how and when to take the drug. Taking it with lots of water (one or two cups) is usually advisable, but do you take it with meals or between? Are there certain foods and drinks that should be avoided with the drug?

Store your drugs properly. In general, they should be kept in a cool, dry place and *always* out of the reach of children. Refrigerators and bathroom medicine cabinets are not good places. High in a cool bedroom is usually a good spot.

Be sure you understand the side effects the drug may produce and know when to consult your doctor about them. Some are common, mild, and to be expected, while others are serious threats to health. See Guide to the Drug Discussions, below.

Do not suddenly stop taking a prescribed drug without consulting your doctor unless you experience severe side effects. Many drugs need to be decreased gradually and sudden withdrawal can be dangerous. Other drugs, such as antibiotics, may be ineffective if the entire prescription is not taken.

Never take a prescription drug for other than the prescribed purpose; do not keep unused portions of drugs around for later use. *Never* let others "borrow" your drugs.

Remind your doctor that, if it is available, you prefer the least expensive preparation of the prescribed medicine. There is no reason for you to pay for heavily promoted products just because they come to your doctor's mind more readily and are easier to spell than the generic (chemical) equivalents. If you forget to discuss this with your doctor, tell your pharmacist you want the generic equivalent if it is available. This is especially important to persons who must take drugs regularly for long periods. The use of generic

444 products can save some individuals hundreds of dollars a year. These drugs meet exactly the same FDA standards of quality and safety as the brand-name drugs.

Guide to the Drug Discussions

The drugs in this chapter are grouped by function and use except for the cortisone types, which are used in such a wide variety of conditions that they cannot be easily pigeon-holed.

The chemicals listed under each group name are by generic name. They are the active ingredients in the pills (or other preparations), whether sold as generics or under brand names. Because of patents, some drugs are available by brand name only. In time the patents will expire and other companies can then market the drugs under their own brands or simply as generics. To know what you are taking, always ask your doctor to include the generic name on the prescription.

Following the chemical names is a brief discussion of the effects and uses of the drugs. Then we take a look at the side effects, which are usually divided into two categories: the mostly mild and often to be expected, and the potentially very serious. The former are generally tolerable and out-weighed by their benefits; the latter generally represent serious threats to health that may outweigh any benefits and could be worse than the problem being treated. The precautions we mention are not necessarily the only ones; your doctor's advice on these matters must be followed.

It should be understood that the lists of possible side effects are not exhaustive. To include all that have ever been reported would take too much space and not serve any practical purpose, because most of them are very rare. The first listed are the most likely but least important; the more serious ones (such as allergic reactions, liver damage, blood disorders, and kidney toxicity) are rare, and the list should not unduly alarm the users, just alert them to what might happen. In either case, the discussions and precautions are not intended as subsitutes for guidance from your physician, whose advice concerning side effects and hazards should be carefully heeded.

Finally, as with OTCs, prescription drugs are sometimes marketed in forms and combinations which FDA panels, AMA investigators, or other experts have concluded are ineffective, unsafe, or otherwise questionable for the intended uses. Such products often remain on the market for many years because they have been used for so long and are prescribed out of tradition and habit, because they are big business which the FDA is sometimes slow to take on, or because experts disagree on their effectiveness and safety. "Questionable product" here does not necessarily mean the drug is worthless, but

that significant doubt has been raised and that there are probably better 445
alternatives.[11]

NOTE ON DRUG NOMENCLATURE
Brand names of drugs are distinguished by capitalization; generic names are
lower case. At the beginning of a sentence the context will make it clear
which we are referring to.

Antibiotics and Other Anti-Infectives

Antibiotics are chemical weapons evolved by molds, fungi, and bacteria to
fight off parasitic bacteria. By borrowing these weapons we have revolutionized the practice of medicine. Not too long ago hundreds of hospitals were
devoted exclusively to caring for tuberculosis patients and children with
rheumatic fever. Even minor surgery carried a significant risk of uncontrollable infection. Cholera, typhoid fever, syphilis, gonorrhea, diphtheria, bacterial pneumonia, leprosy, bacterial meningitis, and other infections conducted a reign of terror. Now we take for granted that most of these
infections can be completely cleared in a matter of days through the *proper*
use of antibiotics. We emphasize proper because antibiotics are widely mis-
understood and often misused.

Bacteria in general are not our enemies. Only a tiny fraction of
them cause disease; and most of the rest are essential or useful. Our bodies
are covered with and infiltrated by a large variety of bacteria, some of which
protect us against invasion by disease-causing organisms. They defend their
own niche in our bodies by making it inhospitable for the microbial "criminal" element.

Unfortunately, antibiotics often do not distinguish the good bacteria from the bad, and both can be wiped out. This makes the body susceptible to attack by opportunistic microbes that may be resistant to the antibiotic. Antibiotics can cause diarrhea and other gastrointestinal upset, and they
can devastate the normal intestinal flora which synthesizes vitamin K, biotin, and possibly other essential nutrients. Deficiencies of these nutrients can
result. Antibiotics can also provoke severe allergic reactions.

However, **the greatest danger of antibiotic misuse** is not harm to
individual recipients, though this can be serious, but the general disruption
of microbial ecology. A very long time ago, the defensive organisms took the
upper hand by making poisons (antibiotics) against the parasites. Some time
later, some of the parasitic bacteria developed resistance to the poisons, typically by gaining a plasmid, a tiny circular piece of genetic material, with a
resistance factor against the antibiotic. When we first began to use antibiotics

446 for our own defense, very few of the disease-causing bacteria had resistance plasmids. Now many of the susceptible bacteria have been killed off and resistant ones have thrived and passed on their resistance plasmids to other bacteria, even those of different species, by conjugation, a type of sexual union. [12]

Consider a very ill person infected with a billion staphylococcal bacteria. Maybe ten of these have the gene for the enzyme that destroys penicillin. A course of penicillin is given and it kills all of the bacteria except the ten resistant ones. The person gets much better for awhile, but a few days later these ten multiply to a billion again, all of which are immune to penicillin. A second course of penicillin will be useless. Furthermore, this person can now spread his "super germs" and make it far more likely that others will become infected with the resistant strain.

The more frequently antibiotics are used, the faster the resistant strains emerge. After only forty years of antibiotic use, the levels of resistant bacteria have risen dramatically. More than half of the staphylococcal bacteria, including *S. aureus* which causes boils and toxic shock syndrome, have developed resistance to antibiotics that once controlled them. Some strains that cause gonorrhea and meningitis have become resistant, and the first few cases of resistant pneumococcal infections have been reported. Hospitals, where antibiotic use is extensive, are infested with a variety of dangerous, highly resistant bacteria.

Some experts believe that the antibiotic era will end by the year 2000, when all important bacteria may be resistant to all antibiotics. Every time an antibiotic is used, another step toward that disaster is taken. Their inappropriate use is believed to be a major factor in the proliferation of bacteria that resist them. The problem is especially acute in South America and other areas with crowding, poor sanitation, high incidence of infectious disease, and dangerously uncontrolled and often irrational use of antibiotics that are widely available over the counter. In recent decades epidemics of drug-resistant dysentery have killed hundreds of thousands of people in Mexico and Central America.

Another possible factor in the evolution of resistant bacteria is the routine use of antibiotics by the livestock industry. This practice increases the weight of the animals and cuts losses to disease in the short run, but may well be hastening the end of the antibiotic era. Half of all the antibiotics used in the United States are fed to livestock, which develop resistant bacteria in their guts. These bacteria then find their way into the environment and into humans. Congress has directed the FDA to study the problem and make a recommendation.

The potential for disaster is not fully appreciated because, for the most part, we have managed to stay a step ahead of bacteria by switching to different antibiotics or by chemically modifying them to foil the resistant **447** mechanisms. At this writing, there is still at least one effective agent for all classes of disease-causing bacteria, and the more optimistic experts believe we can stay ahead of emergent strains indefinitely. But even they cannot deny it will be costly; pharmaceutical advances do not come cheap.

In any case, the problem has been encouraging more basic research and the development of vaccines, which will be relied on more and more in the future. We already have vaccines for some twenty serious diseases, and another dozen or so are in the works. Most of them are for virus diseases, for which there are no antibiotics.

When Is Antibiotic Use Appropriate?

The decision of when to use an antibiotic is a difficult one that only a good physician can make. Ideally, antibiotics would be used only when bacterial infection has been proved and the type of bacteria has been identified. This is not a practical approach, however, since it is too expensive and often impossible to identify the organism in every instance, and treatment must be started immediately for very sick patients.

Physicians often use antibiotics in a variety of borderline circumstances. Consider the case of people who have had rheumatic fever: though they are free of infection, it is often a good idea for them to take daily antibiotics to prevent a new streptococcal infection which could cause life-threatening heart damage.

Similarly, many surgeons give "protective" antibiotics to surgical patients, and the military has occasionally given antibiotics to men prior to shore leave in VD-infested areas, again to prevent infection rather than to cure it. Others given preventive antibiotics include those with recurrent urinary-tract infections, known exposure to infectious bacteria, and abnormal heart valves, and those severely weakened by chronic illness, cigarette smoking, or immunosuppressant medication.

Antibiotics are commonly given for sore throats pending the outcome of the throat culture. If the culture is negative for streptococcus the medication is stopped. The rationale here is that some sore throats are caused by "strep" or other bacteria, and the antibiotics can prevent progression to serious illness, such as rheumatic fever. Unfortunately, it is impossible to distinguish by examination the treatable bacterial sore throats from the untreatable viral sore throats. A throat culture is required, which takes two to three days to develop. Physicians take age, general health, and medical history into consideration in weighing the risk of giving three days of useless and potentially dangerous drugs to the viral cases versus the three-day delay for giving effective therapy for the bacterial cases.

448   When Is Antibiotic
Use Not Appropriate?

There are some gray areas about which the experts are always debating, but there are also circumstances in which antibiotics are clearly not indicated. For example, unless there is a likely risk of secondary bacterial infection, antibiotics should not be used for viral infections such as colds, flu, some pneumonias, herpes, shingles, measles, rubella, mumps, chickenpox, hepatitis, and most sore throats. Antibiotics are completely useless for these, yet surveys have shown that many physicians, possibly a majority, prescribe them for the common cold and flu, at least occasionally.

Why Take the Whole Prescription?

People are often puzzled when the doctors insists that the entire portion of a prescribed antibiotic be taken, even if the infection clears up after a few days. There are two good reasons for this. When the bacteria population falls below a certain number, the symptoms disappear. If you stop the pills too soon, the survivors can proliferate and put you back where you started—or worse, since many of the survivors may have mutated or picked up resistant plasmids and would be harder to kill.

Second, there should not be old antibiotics in your medicine chest. You should never try to supplement or replace a doctor's prescription with some old antibiotic you may have on hand. Some antibiotics become toxic with time and some combinations negate each others' actions. Clearly then, it is essential to take exactly what is prescribed, no more and no less. If your doctor tells you to stop, throw away any remaining pills you have.

Cephalosporins

cefaclor, cephaloglycin, cephalexin, cephradine (note *cef-*, *ceph-*)

Cephalosporins, about a dozen related drugs, have been gaining in popularity. They originally came from a fungus, *Cephalosporium auremonium*, and were recovered from sewage in Italy around 1950. They are closely related to the penicillins, use the same mechanism to kill bacteria, work against mostly the same types of bacteria as the broad spectrum penicillins, and are inactivated by bacteria that produce cephalosporinase, an enzyme similar to penicillinase. They are especially useful in patients who are mildly allergic to penicillin or have penicillin-resistant infections of the ears, throat, urinary tract, or skin.

Side effects include nausea, vomiting, diarrhea, and stomach pain. If these are severe or persistant, consult your physcian.

More serious side effects, which should be discussed with your physcan, include rash, itching, joint pain, unusual bruising or bleeding, sore mouth, chills, fever, and bloody or tarry stools. Cephalosporins can produce severe allergic reactions and blood disorders. Long-term therapy can promote superinfection, that is, overgrowth of other microbes, especially fungus infections in and around the mouth, vagina, and anus.

Penicillins

ampicillin, cloxacillin, nafcillin, penicillins G and V, others (note *-cillin*)

In 1928, an English scientist named Alexander Fleming noticed that bacteria were dying in culture dishes contaminated with Penicillium mold. Within a decade other scientists had identified and purified the chemical from the mold which had killed the bacteria. Soon afterwards some mortally ill patients were miraculously cured. Chemists have since gone on to produce many modifications of the penicillin molecule that offer various advantages.

Penicillins work by preventing bacteria from constructing the cell walls they need to survive in the human body. Only actively multiplying bacteria are killed. This is because mature, nondividing bacteria already have their walls constructed.

There are three catagories of penicillins: standard, broad spectrum, and penicillinase-resistant. The choice depends on the cause of the infection. Standard penicillins are not as widely effective as in the past due to the emergence of bacterial resistance, but they remain useful against most streptococci, gonococci, pneumococci, meningococci, syphilis, clostridia, anthrax, diphtheria, and listeria bacteria.

The "broad spectrum" penicillins are so named because they kill a wider variety of bacteria such as hemophilus salmonella, proteus, *E. coli*, and shigella, as well as those susceptible to standard penicillins.

The penicillinase-resistant drugs were developed after several species of bacteria foiled penicillin therapy by producing an enzyme, penicillinase, that destroys the antibiotic. Chemists were able to take a step ahead of these bacteria by modifying penicillin in a way that made the enzyme unworkable. Not to be so easily outfoxed, the bacteria are now developing other ways to inactivate even the penicillinase-resistant penicillins. It is important to keep the use of these drugs to a minimum to slow the spread of resistance, so they are generally used only against proven or suspected infection by penicillinase-producing staphylococci.

450

The absorption of penicillin into the blood can be reduced by food and by acidic drinks such as fruit juices. The medicine should be taken a couple of hours before or after meals and *never* with citrus juice.

Side effects include nausea, vomiting, and diarrhea. If these are severe or persistant, consult your physician.

Serious reactions are rare, affecting less than 2 percent of the population. Penicillins are among the safest, least toxic drugs known, but they can be lethal to sensitive persons. All the penicillins are similar, and if you allergic to one, you are allergic to all. The appearance of a rash, itching, difficult breathing, or joint pain should be discussed with your physician; you may require emergency care. If you do have an allergic reaction you will probably have to avoid the drugs for the rest of your life.

Sulfonamides

sulfacetamide, sulfamethoxazole, sulfisoxazole (note *sulf-*)

Sulfonamides, or sulfa drugs, are not made by microorganisms but are by-products of the synthetic dye industry. They were the first drugs used against bacterial infections, representing the dawn of the antibiotic era in 1933. Though once used extensively, they have been largely eclipsed by modern antibiotics and now play a small but still important role. They work by preventing bacteria from making the nutrient folic acid. Human cells are not affected because they get folic acid preformed in the diet and don't have to make it.

Sulfonamides were at one time effective for a very wide variety of infections. However, their frequent use led to rapid development of resistance by many bacteria. For example, gonorrhea, shigellosis (a bacterial dysentery), some bacterial ear infections, and pneumonia once responded dramatically but are now resistant. Many of the bacteria that cause urinary tract infections are still sensitive, and sulfonamides that rapidly concentrate in the urine have been developed. Such agents are ideal for eradicating urinary tract infections, and this is their main role today.

Sulfonamides also see duty in certain types of conjunctivitis, vaginal infections, toxoplasmosis, and in the elimination of the normal bacterial population in the intestinal tract prior to some abdominal surgery. Several sulfonamides are available for topical use, such as protecting burns from infection and treating eye infections.

Side effects of sulfa drugs include headache, tinnitus, dizziness, and GI upset. If these are severe or persistant, consult your physician. The drugs make some people hypersensitive to the sun, so users should be careful about sun exposure until they know how it affects them.

More serious side effects include severe allergic reactions and blood, kidney, and liver problems. If you develop rash, itching, peeling skin, fever, excessive fatigue, easy bruising, or aching joints and muscles, stop taking the drug and consult your physician. Sulfa drugs are dangerous for those who lack the glucose-6-phosphate dehydrogenase (G6PD) enzyme.

Remember that sulfa drugs can be identified by "sulf" in the generic name, and if you are allergic to one you are probably allergic to others, even though they are used for different purposes and in different ways.

Tetracyclines

doxycycline, minocycline, tetracycline (note *-cycline)*

These widely used drugs are made by *Streptomyces* bacteria. They work against a great variety of infectious organisms and are the first choice drugs for brucellosis, psittacosis (parrot fever), nonspecific urethritis (or nongonococcal urethritis, NGU), pelvic infections, mycoplasm pneumonia, rocky mountain spotted fever, tick-bite fever, typhus, and scrub typhus. They are also backup drugs for many other infections when the first choice cannot be used. The mechanism of action involves preventing bacteria from making protein.

Because some foods and nutrients can inactivate tetracyclines, they should not be taken within a couple hours of eating a meal or consuming dairy products or calcium, vitamin C, or iron supplements.

Side effects include gastrointestinal distress and dizziness. If these are severe or persistant, consult your physician. Do not drive or operate hazardous machinery until you know how the drug affects you. Photosensitivity develops in some users, so sun exposure should be minimized until you know how it affects you.

More serious side effects include rash and other allergic reactions, itching or pain of the rectal, genital, or mouth area due to overgrowth of resistant microbes, and unusual bleeding, bruising, or fever due to blood disorders. Consult your physician if any of these occur.

Pregnant and nursing women should avoid tetracyclines because they can discolor and damage the teeth of the fetus or child. For the same reason, young children (under eight) should not be given the drugs unless absolutely necessary.

452   Tuberculosis Drugs

ethambutol, isoniazid, rifampin

Tuberculosis (TB) is a slowly progressing infection by bacteria called mycobacteria. Current therapy is so effective that most victims can be treated on an outpatient basis. Special sanitoriums are obsolete.

Multiple drug therapy is the rule in TB because of frequent development of resistance to a single agent. With expert therapy, the cure rate is about 98 percent. The best agents are ethambutol, isoniazid, rifampin, and streptomycin. The latter is given only by injection. A number of secondary agents are sometimes used. Various combinations of two or three drugs are usually chosen; isoniazid is almost always one of them. Very long courses are needed, between one and two years for many patients, though most are not infectious after four weeks of treatments.

Therapy for TB should probably be supervised by a physician with a lot of experience in this area because it can be difficult. Most states have physicians working with the health department on the problem.

Ethambutol side effects include nausea, vomiting, and loss of appetite. If these are severe or persistant, consult your physician. A more **serious side effect** is inflammation of the optic nerve. If you experience blurred or otherwise impaired vision or eye pain, contact your physician immediately. Rash and other allergic reactions, tingling, weakness and other signs of nerve problems, and joint pains (possibly gout) should be discussed with your physician.

Isoniazid side effects include GI upset, dizziness, and breast enlargement. If these are severe or persistant, consult your physician. More **serious side effects** include vitamin B-6 deficiency, liver damage, and allergic reactions. Consult your physician if you experience clumsiness, tingling or painful extremities, eye pain or vision impairment, unusual fatigue or weakness, or yellowish eyes or skin. Do not drink alcohol during isoniazid therapy; it can increase the risk of liver damage.

Rifampin side effects include GI upset, headache, muscle pain, drowsiness, and dizziness. If these are severe or persistant, consult your physician. Do not drive or operate machinery until you know how the drug affects you. The urine, feces, and other body excretions such as tears may become reddish-orange. This is harmless, though contact lenses may be permanently stained. More **serious side effects** include itching, rash, flulike symptoms, and unusual fatigue, weakness, or bleeding. Contact your physician if any of these occur.

Miscellaneous Anti-Infectives

acyclovir, antifungals, chloramphenicol, erythromycin group, isotretinoin, urinary tract anti-infectives

Acyclovir. This is one of the few drugs that has any antiviral activity and the only one that appears to be gaining wide acceptance. It works by latching onto a viral enzyme essential to the reproducion of the virus' DNA. It is useful in herpes infections in infants and those with immune deficiency, in severe shingles (herpes zoster), and in genital herpes. While the drug is fairly effective against genital herpes, it does little or nothing against oral herpes.[13]

There are topical, oral, and intravenous forms of acyclovir. So far, few side effects have been reported. The biggest problem with inappropriate use appears to be the emergence of acyclovir-resistant strains of herpes viruses, which are potentially lethal to some. Because of this, some physicians feel the drug is used far too much. Another problem is its high cost.

Antifungals (amphotericin B, griseofulvin, ketoconazole) Our resident harmless bacteria provide protection against serious fungal infection, which most commonly strikes in people treated with broad spectrum antibiotics or debilitated by cancer and other diseases. In general, the drugs on the preceding pages are not active against fungi, but special ones are available. Long courses (several weeks) are frequently needed.

The most widely used nontopical agent is **amphotericin B**, which must be given by injection. It may damage the kidneys, so it is used only in widespread and dangerous fungus infections such as coccidiomycosis, blastomycosis, histoplasmosis, and candidiasis. Recipients must be closely watched for numerous toxic effects.

Griseofulvin can be taken orally over long periods for infections of the hair and nails. **Side effects** include headache, GI upset, dry mouth, dizziness, insomnia, and fatigue. If these are severe or persistant, consult your physician. Photosensitivity may also occur, so avoid prolonged sun exposure until you know how it affects you. **More serious side effects** include allergic reactions, blood disorders, and overgrowth of nonsusceptible fungi. Consult your physician if you develop rash, mouth irritation or pain, confusion, tingling or weakness of the extremities, sore throat, or fever. Griseofulvin can decrease the effective of oral contraceptives, so use another method during treatment to avoid *unwanted pregnancy.*

Ketoconazole is a new advance in the treatment of fungus infections, mostly relatively minor ones. It is taken by pill and produces fewer adverse effects than amphotericin B, but often causes nausea and sometimes liver damage, loss of libido, low sperm count, impotence, and breast enlargement in men.

454 **Chloramphenicol** is very powerful against a wide variety of microorganisms, but its use is limited by its hazards. Its rightful place is against very serious infections where the safer agents meet bacterial resistance or are particularly hazardous for the person in question (e.g., because of severe allergy). Incredibly, the drug is sold "over the counter" in some countries.

Streptomyces venezuelae, a bacterium first discovered in South America, was the original source of chloramphenicol. It was first used in the late forties when it dramtically stopped a typhus epidemic in Bolivia. Enthusiastic prescribing followed until the risk of bone-marrow poisoning was exposed several years later. It works by blocking bacterial protein synthesis. Resistance has emerged in several bacterial species, particularly in countries where the drug is heavily used.

Chloramphenicol is capable of revitalizing near-dead victims of typhoid fever in forty-eight hours, and it is the drug of choice in such cases. Unfortunately, typhoid bacteria are becoming resistant in several parts of the world.

The **most serious hazard** of chloramphenicol is the occasional occurrence of irreversible bone-marrow poisoning, which can be lethal. Allergic reactions are rare, but infection by resistant organisms is a risk with this broad-spectrum agent.

Erythromycin and Relatives Erythromycin is derived from *Streptomyces erythreus*, originally isolated from the soil in the Philippines. The mechanism of action involves blockage of bacterial protein synthesis. Erythromycin is perhaps the safest antibiotic used. Allergies are rare and almost always mild.

If erythromycin is so safe, why hasn't it replaced the more dangerous antibiotics? Because it is not very powerful against most bacteria. It is a first-line drug for several infections where it works especially well, such as diphtheria, whooping cough, Legionnaire's disease, and mycoplasma pneumonia. It is a secondary drug for may other infections, particularly when they are mild to moderate, or when allergy to more powerful antibiotics is a problem. This group is the best substitute for penicillin in many streptococcal and pneumococcal infections when penicillin allergy is present.

The most common **side effect** is stomach upset. If it is severe or persistant, consult your physician. **More serious side effects** include rash (rarely) and other allergic reactions. In such cases stop using the drug and consult your physician.

Lincomycin and **clindamycin** are closely related to erythromycin and are active against most of the same bacteria. They are sometimes tried when erythromycin resistance is encountered and may also be used when penicillin allergy is a problem. Because these agents sometimes produce severe colon inflammation, they are reserved for serious infections that do not respond to safer drugs. **Side effects** include mild GI distress. **Serious side**

effects include watery, mucus-laden or pusy diarrhea and painful cramps. Stop using the drug and consult your physician.

Isotretinoin This vitamin A analogue is not exactly an anti-infective, but it is useful in very severe acne.

CAUTION

Isotretinoin is a powerful teratogen; it can cause heart defects, blindness, cleft palate, and other birth defects. Sexually active women should use contraceptives from one month before to one month after using the drug, and they should have a pregnancy test within two weeks of starting therapy. The danger is so great that blood donors must not have taken the drug for several months before giving.

Urinary Tract Anti-Infectives Sulfa drugs are the most important antibiotics for UTIs (see Sulfonamides above). Sulfisoxazole is probably the most used. For those who are allergic to sulfas, some penicillins and tetracyclines are useful. Other antibiotics for UTIs include nitrofurantoin, naldixic acid, oxolinic acid, and methenamine. These drugs are not active throughout the body, just in the kidney and bladder where they are concentrated. This makes them useful for persons who need long-term protection from kidney disease. The rare side effects include vomiting and rashes. Nitrofurantoin can cause anemia in those with glucose-6-phosphate deficiency.

Anticonvulsants

carbamazepine, ethosuximide, methsuximide, phenobarbitol, phenytoin, primidone

An epileptic seizure resembles an electrical storm in the brain which replaces the normal orderly flow of impulses between brain cells. Such storms frequently originate in small, unstable patches of brain matter, such as scars, which can spread their instability through normal brain tissue. Unstable foci can be created by infections, blows to the head, very high fever, damage during brain development, damage during birth, drug or poison intoxication, benign brain tumors, and brain cancer.

The location and origin of the unstable patch determine the pattern of the seizures and greatly influence the choice of drugs, which are sometimes used in combination. One's age, use of other drugs, and sensitivity to side effects are also taken into consideration. How these anticonvulsants work is only vaguely understood. Somehow they stabilize the electrical membranes in the brain, preventing the storms from brewing.

Women taking anticonvulsants should know that there is some suspicion that they can cause birth defects of the heart, brain, and other organs. But seizures themselves may damage the fetus from lack of oxygen, so they must be prevented. Any woman who is taking an anticonvulsant and suspects she may be pregnant should immediately contact her physician.

One should never stop taking anticonvulsants suddenly. They must be slowly withdrawn, or the risk of seizure will be greatly increased.

Carbamazepine is useful in treating some types of seizures as well as facial neuralgia. However, it can produce dangerous side effects, so other drugs are usually tried first. **Side effects** include nausea and vomiting, dizziness, drowsiness, blurred vision, and poor coordination. **Serious side effects** include blood, kidney, and liver disorders, and heart and blood vessel problems. Contact your physician immediately if you develop any severe symptoms or fever, sore throat, skin or eye discoloration, urinary problems, swelling of the extremeties, mouth ulcers, rash, or heart arrhythmias.

Ethosuximide and **methsuximide** are similar drugs both useful in petit mal seizures, in which consciousness is lost for seconds at a time. **Side effects** of these drugs include nausea, vomiting, abdominal pain, loss of appetite, dizziness and drowsiness. There may also be headache, fatigue, and irritability. If the side effects are severe or persistant, discuss them with your physician. **Serious side effects** include rash, joint pain, fever, unusual bleeding or bruising, or other symptoms of allergy or blood disorder. Consult your physician.

Phenobarbitol, a barbiturate, is one of the most effective anticonvulsants and is especially useful in young children because of the low incidence of side effects. For adults it is often combined with other anticonvulsants. **Side effects** include drowsiness and, in children, hyperactivity. Nystagmus (rolling eyeballs) and incoordination should be discussed with your physician.

Phenytoin was discovered in a systematic search for substances that protect animals from experimentally induced seizures and was introduced for human use in 1938. It is very effective and relatively free of major side effects. It works in all seizure disorders except petit mal (absence seizure). Blood levels are periodically checked so that dosage can be regulated at a beneficial yet subtoxic level. **Side effects** include inflammation and bleeding of the gums, nausea, and vomiting. Oral hygiene (brushing and flossing) is important. The urine may be colored pink, red, or brown, but this is of no importance. **Serious side effects** that require medical attention include rash, difficulty in balance and walking, nystagmus (rolling eyeballs), slurred speech, blurred vision, confusion, and jaundice. Viral infections and vaccinations may decrease the metabolism of the drug by the liver, and it may accumu-

late to toxic levels. A reduction of the dose may be necessary and should be   457
discussed with your physician.[14]

Primidone is effective in many forms of epilepsy and is often added to, or
substituted for, phenytoin in cases of resistance to that drug or when its side
effects are intolerable. **Side effects** of primidone include nausea and vomiting, dizziness, and drowsiness. If these are severe or persistant, consult your
physician. **Serious reactions** include rash, joint pain, fever, breathing difficulty, changes in vision, or confusion. If you experience these or any other
symptoms of allergy or nerve toxicity, consult your physician.

Asthma Drugs

bronchodilators, corticosteroids, cromolyn

There are over-the-counter medicines available for asthma prevention, control, and relief (see Chapter 5–1), but results are generally better with prescription drugs and the closer medical supervision that comes with their use.
The three classes of asthma drugs work by different mechanisms and have
different side effects and hazards.

Bronchodilators

albuterol, isoproterenol, metaproterenol, terbutaline, and theophylline and
its relatives (aminophylline, oxtriphylline, dyphylline; note *-phylline*)

Albuterol, isoproterenol, metaproterenol, and **terbutaline** work by stimulating the muscles that dilate the bronchial airways. **Side effects** include nervousness, dry mouth, insomnia, headache, dizziness, nausea, vomiting, fast
heartbeat, and weakness. If these are severe or persistant, consult your physician. **More serious side effects** include chest pain and irregular heartbeat,
which are signs to stop using the drug and consult your physician.

Theophylline and its relatives relax the muscles which constrict the bronchial airways during an asthma attack. They are also used in chronic bronchitis
and other lung disorders. For persons who must use them frequently, a
blood test should be done to determine the proper dosage. Many factors can
affect blood levels including flu, flu vaccine, smoking, high-carbohydrate
diets, high-protein diets, tea, coffee, colas, and charcoal-broiled meat. To
the extent possible these factors should be eliminated or kept constant from
day to day to avoid frequent adjustments of theophylline dosage.

458

Side effects include GI distress (which can be minimized by taking the drug with food), nervousness, insomnia, headache, dizziness, and fast heartbeat. If these are severe or persistant, or if there is a rash, consult your physician. Coffee, tea, colas, and other sources of caffeine and theophylline can increase the side effects.[15] Viral infections and vaccinations might also. Discuss these considerations with your physician if they are relevent.

Corticosteroids

Corticosteroids, hormones produced by the adrenal cortex, are sometimes useful in asthma. There are rarely serious side effects from short-term therapy, but prolonged use is fraught with danger. Since most asthmatics need long-term therapy, corticosteroids are not usually the drugs of choice. However, the hazards are much less if they are taken by inhalant rather than pill. See Cortisone Group below.

Cromolyn

Cromolyn comes as a powder which is inhaled to prevent asthma attacks. It coats the mast cells of the lung and prevents them from releasing the chemicals that cause the constriction of the bronchial airways. It must be used for two to four weeks before its ultimate effect is known. Cromolyn does not work once an attack has started, but it does not interfere with the drugs that do, so when it fails the others can be resorted to.

Side effects include throat irritation, dry mouth and throat, and cough. If these are severe or persistant, consult your physician. **More serious side effects** include rash, difficult breathing or swallowing, tightness in the chest, nausea, vomiting, headache, weakness, and joint and muscle pain. These also require the attention of your physician.

Cancer Chemotherapy

Drugs given for cancer are very carefully supervised and their effects and side effects are monitored frequently. Our purpose here is to provide a broad outline of cancer chemotherapy so patients, their relatives, and the curious will understand the principles involved and what the physicians are trying to accomplish.

In the 1950s when the age of chemotherapy began, the early successes led many to believe that cancer would soon go the way of tuberculosis and smallpox. Thirty years and billions of dollars later, many people are still dying from cancer and the end is not in sight. What happened? Why hasn't the "magic bullet" been found?

First, cancer is a much tougher nut to crack than most infectious diseases. A typical cancer patient may have 10 billion cancer cells. A drug capable of killing 99.9999 percent of these cells would seem very impressive, but it would still leave one million survivors. Furthermore, it is the heartiest and most aggressive of cells that survive the battle with the drug, and the daughters of these super cancer cells will be much more difficult to kill the second time around.

This requirement of near 100 percent kill rate is not needed in the battle against bacterial infectious disease, where the drugs get considerable help from the body's defense system. The antibiotics need only kill 99 percent or so of the bacteria, and the white blood cells would finish off the rest. The anticancer drug gets some, but much less, of this kind of help.

The second difficulty involves finding a drug more poisonous to the disease-causing cells than to the normal ones. This is easy when the former are bacteria, which are biochemically very different from human cells and thus vulnerable to "selective toxicity." But cancer cells are very similar to normal human cells and it is difficult to find chemicals that select them and leave the others alone.

In spite of these tremendous obstacles, considerable progress has been made. Many once deadly cancers have very high (near 100 percent) cure rates with expert chemotherapy. The list grows slowly over the years as new drugs and combinations of drugs are developed and tested. Examples include acute lymphocytic leukemia in children, seminoma (one of the testicular cancers), some types of Hodgkin's lymphoma, and choriocarcinoma in women.

Unfortunately, some cancers respond barely if at all to any chemotherapy. These include choriocarcinoma in men, most lung carcinomas, carcinoma of the pancreas, glioblastoma of the brain, and cancer of the esophagous, stomach, and intestines.

Most cancers fall somewhere between these extremes of nearly 100 percent and near zero cure rates.

Cancer chemotherapy has a poor reputation with the public; most people imagine it an unendurable ordeal. It is true that it can be unpleasant, but most patients have relatively mild side effects, and many lives are saved or prolonged. The fear of chemotherapy keeps cancer victims away from life-saving medication and fills the clinics of quacks and sincere but misguided practitioners of ineffective methods. The promise of quick results without discomfort is tempting, but once prevention has failed, cancer victims have their best shot at survival with a good internist or oncologist.

Current anticancer drugs can be divided into seven categories: alkylating agents (DNA damagers), antibiotics, antimetabolites, hormones, monoclonal antibodies, periwinkle alkaloids, and miscellaneous drugs.

460 Alkylating Agents—DNA Damagers

bisulfan, chlorambucil, cyclophosphamide, dicarbazine, melphalan, semustine, uracil mustard

Nitrogen mustard was the first compound to make the transition from a deadly weapon (used in World War I) to a life-saving therapy. The success of this compound spawned a family of drugs for cancer.

The main characteristic of cancer cells is that they reproduce much faster than most normal cells. This difference allows them to be killed selectively by the alkylating agents. The first thing a cell does before dividing is make an exact copy of its DNA; each daughter cell gets a complete copy of all the genetic material. The alkylating agents stick onto the DNA molecules, making duplication impossible. Thus, the rapidly dividing cancer cells are stopped dead in their tracks; slower growing and nondividing cells will not be hurt severely, since they have enzymes that repair the DNA affected by the alkylating agent.

Normal cells that also grow rapidly will, unfortunately, also be damaged by these medications. These include skin, hair follicles, the lining of the digestive tract, sperm precursors, and the white blood cells. If the dosage is too high, DNA will be damaged beyond enzyme repair and all cells will be poisoned. But the furiously dividing cancer cells are exquisitely sensitive to the DNA damage and they, along with the normal rapid-growers, are poisoned at relatively low dosages.

The results of this selectivity are loss of hair, damage to skin and digestive tract, infertility in men, and a deficiency of white blood cells. Nausea also is frequent. All of these are temporary and the normal cells can recover. By far the most serious of these is the loss of white cells. This leaves the patient vulnerable to infection and reduces whatever anticancer action the body's own white cells are providing. Ironically, these drugs also cause cancer—leukemia to be exact—in a few patients (less than 1 percent). These difficulties represent the price that is often well worth paying to get the tremendously powerful cancer-killing effect.

Antibiotics

adriamycin, actinomycin D, daunomycin, mitharamycin, bleomycin

Antibiotics are best known for ther use against bacterial infections, but some have proved helpful against cancer. They are made by microorganisms to kill other microorganisms, but they have incidental anticancer properties because they inhibit RNA or DNA synthesis. In addition to typical anticancer drug side effects, some of these may damage the heart or lungs. Adriamycin is effective against more different kinds of cancer than any other drug. It would be even more widely used if it did not inexorably damage the heart. The development of related drugs without this toxicity could give us some of our best weapons against cancer.

Antimetabolites

methotrexate, 5-fluorouracil, cytarabine, 6-mercaptopurine, 6-thioguanine

This is a very ingenious class of drugs that have been specifically engineered by biochemists. The molecules are reminiscent of the Trojan horse. Superficially they resemble normal compounds in cellular metabolism, but once inside a cell they end up attacking crucial enzymes, blocking the pathways they have entered and making the production of substances needed by the cells impossible. The pathways blocked are those used to produce the raw materials needed for new DNA synthesis in rapidly reproducing cells. While alkylators prevent DNA duplication by ruining the original copy, the antimetabolites prevent duplication by choking off the supply of new DNA raw materials.

The first antimetabolite to be used successfully was methotrexate. Here is how it works. The vitamin folic acid is needed in several metabolic pathways, including the production of purines, one of the key materials needed to make new DNA. Before the cells can use folic acid, they must convert it to tetrahydrofolic acid. Enzymes that attempt to convert the similar methotrexate are inactivated. With enough methotrexate, the cell soon runs out of enzymes and the supply of tetrahydrofolic acid is cut off. Without it purines cannot be made, DNA cannot be duplicated, and reproduction is impossible. Thus, cells not trying to reproduce will be only mildly affected, but the furiously reproducing cancer cells die of "frustration" (metabolic exhaustion).

Normal cells that reproduce will have the same problem, so methotrexate carries the same side effects as the alkylating agents. These limit the dose that can be tolerated. However, it has been discovered that much higher dosages can be given if tetrahydrofolic acid is given several hours after the methotrexate. This procedure gives a blast of the very thing the depleted normal cells need, just as they get into serious jeopardy; but it's too late for the cancer cells to recover.

462 Hormones

adrenal steroids, estrogen and antagonists, progestins, testosterone

Some cancers are very sensitive to hormones and antihormones. This approach has a great advantage because it provides little toxicity to normal cells. Unfortunately, only a few types of cancer respond, and the response differs with the patient.

Prostate cancer sometimes requires androgenic hormones (such as testosterone) for growth and metastasis (spread). Removal of the testicles, the major source of androgens, is a logical therapy in some cases. Large doses of female hormones—estrogens—are also used. They antagonize androgen activity.

Breast cancer, especially in younger women, is sometimes dependent on estrogens for growth, and the analogous treatment is removal of the ovaries. Antiestrogen compounds such as tamoxifen can also be given to "starve" the cancer of estrogens. Large doses of estrogens paradoxically also slow some breast cancers, especially in older women. The ability of the cancer to respond to hormonal therapy can be predicted by testing the cancer for "estrogen receptors" at the time of removal or biopsy.

Progestins, a second class of female hormones, have been mildly successful in uterine and some ovarian cancers, and thyroid hormone may be beneficial against thyroid cancer.

Adrenal steroid hormones, which inhibit cell division, are used for many cancers. The two most commonly used are prednisone and dexamethasone. There are numerous side effects. (See Cortisone Group, this chapter.)

Monoclonal Antibodies

This is a new and very promising approach to cancer chemotherapy with a potential for much greater selective toxicity. Rather than taking advantage of the higher rate of growth in cancer cells, a property that some normal cells share, monoclonal antibodies (MAs) capitalize on special chemical markers that occur on the cancer cells.

All the cells of the body and of invading organisms are studded with antigens—protein markers—which the immune system uses to identify self from nonself. When the antibodies from our immune system detect a foreign cell, they latch onto it and begin its destruction. Unfortunately, our bodies often do not produce enough antibodies to slow down cancer. But suppose human cancer cells were injected into an animal so that *its* body would also make the antibody, which could then be removed and used in the human.

Better yet, suppose an animal spleen culture were "fed" the cancer cells. The spleen cells would then produce the needed antibody, which would be harvested and injected into the cancer patient. The antibodies, which might have potent anticancer drugs attached, would latch only onto the cancer cells. The cultured spleen cells are cloned from one original cell, hence the name of the product, monoclonal antibodies. It is easy to see why MAS are sometimes called smart bombs and magic bullets. However, we should not be overoptimistic; the smart bombs may yet bomb out against many important cancers.

Monoclonal antibodies have many applications besides cancer treatment. They are used in diagnostic tests (such as for pregnancy and assessing damage after a heart attack), combating transplant rejection, producing interferon, and much more. They represent a quantum leap in biomedical research and their uses are already having profound effects.

Periwinkle Alkaloids

vincristine, vinblastine

These two natural products are extracted from the periwinkle plant, which has a long history of medicinal use. When researchers tried to verify the reputed effectiveness of periwinkle extract for diabetes, they observed depression in the white blood cell count of the diabetic experimental subjects. The extract proved useless for diabetes, but the effect on white blood cell production provided a clue that something in the plant blocked cell division. Chemists eventually discovered that two substances from the plant, vincristine and vinblastine, were inhibiting white cell production, and both proved useful against cancer.

Their mechanism of action is much easier to understand than that of the drugs discussed earlier. When a cell finishes its DNA duplication, it pulls itself apart into two new cells. These periwinkle alkaloids stop this splitting motion; the cell sits ready to divide, but it cannot move. Such a paralyzed cell cannot survive long because is DNA is compacted into strands and cannot send out instructions to maintain the cell.

Side effects are similar to those for alkylating and metabolic blocking agents. Vincristine can also damage the nerves and vinblastine can depress the bone marrow.

Miscellaneous

L-asparaginase is an interesting drug that capitalizes on a unique difference between cancerous and normal cells. It is an enzyme from bacteria that

464 destroys the amino acid asparagine, an essential component for proteins. Without asparagine, cancer cells literally starve to death. Normal cells are different; they can make their own asparagine when L-asparaginase eliminates the supply.

Hydroxyurea also represses DNA reproduction. It is used primarily in leukemia.

Interferon is a protein made by the body in response to viral infections. It stops the multiplication of viruses and has been proven effective against chickenpox and other viral infections. It also seems to block cancer-cell division and multiplication and has been tested with some success against some cancers. There are many kinds of interferon, and a great deal more research is required before its full potential will be known and fulfilled. The substance was once extremely scarce and prohibitively expensive, but, using genetic engineering, scientists now induce bacteria to produce human interferon in large amounts at a more reasonable cost.

Mixed bacterial vaccines are being tested in some cancers. These experimental drugs, derived from bacterial colonies, appear to be directly toxic to tumors and to stimulate the body's production of interferon. The concept comes from the recovery of some patients from apparently terminal cancer after severe bacterial infection with high fever.

Radioactive iodine can be used against some thyroid gland cancers. The cancer cells absorb the "hot" iodine, which then releases its radiation, damaging the DNA in the thyroid cells. Other cells ignore the iodine, so they don't receive as much radiation.

Cardiovascular Drugs

This chapter covers the drugs currently available for the common heart problems: angina pectoris, arrhythmia (irregular heartbeat), and congestive heart failure. These disorders frequently coexist and overlap, and the presence of one often leads to others. Management of these problems, with or without drugs, is difficult and best left to experts—specialists in internal medicine or cardiology. With many of the drugs discussed here, there are thin lines between inadequate, life-saving, and life-threatening doses.

This chapter also includes anticoagulants, antilipemics, and circulation improvers (alleged), but not hypotensive agents, which are discussed separately.

Drugs for Angina

nitrates, beta blockers, calcium channel blockers

Angina pectoris results from insufficient oxygen delivery to the heart muscles, usually caused by atherosclerotic coronary arteries, that is, fatty plaque buildup in the arteries. When the oxygen supply cannot keep up with the heart muscle demands, pain signals are issued. However, the pain is rarely perceived as coming from the heart (under the left nipple). It usually seems to come from under the breast bone, between the shoulder blades, the lower jaw or throat, or the left arm and shoulder, and is characterized by a dull squeezing discomfort. The pain is often felt in the abdomen and mistaken for indigestion. (See Atherosclerosis in Part Four.)

Pain is often brought on by exercise, but attacks may come during eating, subsequent to emotional stress (such as anger or fear), or at random. The pain is usually of short duration (less than ten minutes) and is relieved by rest. The attacks can be quite severe and disabling. While coronary bypass surgery is often the treatment of choice, several drugs can be taken to prevent attacks or relieve attacks in progress. They all work by relaxing the coronary arteries and allowing increased blood flow to the heart muscle, but they do so by different mechanisms and have somewhat different side effects and hazards.

Nitrates

nitroglycerin, isosorbide dinitrate, pentaerythritol tetranitrate

Nitroglycerine, which can be dissolved under the tongue, is used to abort an attack in progress or to prevent an attack when exercise is anticipated, such as before long walks or sexual activity. The protection can be expected to last about thirty minutes. The drug lowers the workload of the heart, decreases its oxygen needs, and perhaps also increases oxygen delivery to heart muscle. It can also be taken in slow-release tablets or in an ointment or patch applied to the skin, through which it is absorbed. There is now some question about whether these preparations deliver an adequate dose of the drug.

Sublingual nitroglycerine works fast, typically bringing relief within two minutes. If the pain persists, a second tablet may be taken. If four or five tablets spaced five minutes apart have failed to stop the pain, or if the pain is far more severe than usual, a trip to a hospital emergency room is recommended. The symptoms may be those of a heart attack.

Nitroglycerine is effective, inexpensive, and safe (there is no danger whatsoever of the tablets exploding; only pure liquid nitroglycerine is explosive). It tends to lose potency unless handled carefully; heat and light

466 destroy it, and the bottle cap must be kept screwed tightly or the drug will vaporize. It must be stored in tinted, airtight containers and not transferred to pill boxes. A fresh supply should be obtained about every four to six months. Potent nitroglycerine causes a mild tingling or burning as it dissolves under the tongue. Tablets that don't do this may have lost some strength.

Side effects include headache, flushing, fast heartbeat, and dizziness, particularly when the drug is first started. These effects often diminish when the body gets used to it. Under some conditions, it can make the angina pain worse. Sitting or lying down often prevents this, as can a lower dose. **More serious side effects** include allergic reactions, especially rash and peeling skin. Consult your physician for any of these.

Other nitrate compounds available for sublingual use include **isosorbide dinitrate** and **pentaerythritol tetranitrate.** These are similar to nitroglycerine in every way except that they don't work as fast, their effects last longer, and they don't require special handling to prevent loss of potency.

Beta blockers
propranolol, metoprolol

The nitrates are designed for intermittent use when an attack has begun or is expected. Another strategy is to take medication continually to, ideally, eliminate all attacks. Propranolol, the oldest of the class, is also a good antihypertensive drug (see Hypertension Drugs), which makes it a good choice when high blood pressure and angina pectoris coexist, as they often do.

Beta blockers prevent the nervous system from stimulating the heart to work harder. Thus, the heart's workload and oxygen needs are kept low. They work best for angina brought on by exercise or stress.

With luck, propranolol will completely eliminate the angina, but it more typically provides reduction in frequency and severity. Nitroglycerine can be continued as needed. In fact, the effects of nitroglycerine and propranolol synergize, and the combination can often control angina that resists both when used alone.

Propranolol is also useful in some cases of migraine headache.

Side effects include dizziness, drowsiness, cold extremities, upset stomach, and loss of appetite. If these are severe or persistant, discuss them with your physician.

More serious side effects, which should be discussed with your physician, include hallucinations, nightmares, and exacerbation of diabetes and heart and respiratory problems. Sudden termination of propranolol can cause a heart attack. If it is to be discontinued, gradual tapering off over a two-week period is safe.

Calcium channel blockers

467

diltiazem, nifedipine, verapamil

These new drugs, also called "calcium blockers," have a variety of effects and are used for angina, hypertension, tachycardia (racing heart), and migraine. Calcium ions (charged atoms) are crucial to the contraction of the smooth muscles of the heart and arteries. These drugs work by blocking the entry of calcium into the muscle cells. In angina they dilate blood vessels so that the heart has less resistance to pump against. They also alter the electrical conduction system of the heart, increase oxygen delivery to the heart muscle, and decrease the strength of the heartbeat.

Calcium blockers are useful when nitrates and beta blockers have failed or cause intolerable side effects (such as severe headaches or asthma). Like beta blockers, they are taken continuously to prevent attacks, and do not work fast enough to abort attacks in progress.

Side effects include dizziness, flushing, swollen extremities, GI upset, constipation, muscle cramps, and headache. If these are severe or persistant, consult your physician.

More serious side effects include aggravation of liver and kidney disease, and slow heartbeat. An unusually low pulse should be reported to your physician right away.

Questionable products for angina include dipyridamole, a vasodilator proven ineffective for angina, and papaverine and ethaverine, both discussed below under circulation improvers.

Antiarrhythmics

disopyramide, procainamide, propranolol, quinidine

Arrhythmias are disturbances in the pattern of the heartbeat. There are many varieties, some harmless and some dangerous. The irregular heartbeats can be classified as very slow, very fast, or early ("skipped beat"). They can be caused by drugs (such as nicotine, caffeine, diet pills, and other stimulants), infections, hypertension, and emotional stress as well as by heart disease. In most cases symtoms such as weakness, fainting, or shortness of breath, rather than the arrhythmias themselves, cause the person to seek medical care. But sometimes the irregular heartbeat is the only symptom. If it occurs often it should be evaluated.

Most antiarrhythmic drugs electrically stabilize the heart, slow it down, and normalize its rhythm. The most important ones are disopyra-

468 mide, procainamide, propranolol, and quinidine. Digitalis drugs also help in arrhythmias but are most commonly used for congestive heart failaure; see below.

Disopyramide is a new drug that is gaining in popularity. It is effective against many of the same arrhythmias and has far fewer adverse side effects. Nevertheless, it is still plagued by **side effects,** such as dry mouth, nausea, vomiting, and diarrhea. If these are severe or persistant, consult your physician. **More serious side effects** include difficult urination, jaundice, hallucinations, depression, and sometimes worsening of the arrhythmia and heart failure. Consult your physician for any of these.

Procainamide slows the heartbeat and improves its rhythm and efficiency. It is used to maintain normal rhythm and prevent fast and early beats. It is very important that it be taken according to schedule, no matter the inconvenience. **Side effects** include GI upset, a bitter taste in the mouth, loss of appetite, weakness, and dizziness. If these are severe or prolonged, contact your physician. **More serious side effects** include development of a serious illness similar to systemic lupus erythematosis. If you experience fever, chills, rash, joint pain, or sore throat, consult your physician.

Propranolol is discussed above under angina drugs.

Quinidine is the oldest drug in the group and is still important. It is closely related to quinine, the antimalaria drug, and comes from the same tree, the South American cinchona. Quinidine was used against malaria in the 19th century. Doctors soon noticed that malaria patients who also had arrhythmias had improved heart function after quinidine use. It is very important that it be taken according to schedule, no matter the inconvenience. **Side effects** include nausea, vomiting, diarrhea, and faintness upon standing. If these are severe or persistant, consult your physician. **More serious side effects** include rash, unusual bleeding or bruising, dizziness, excitement, delirium, and vision and hearing distubances. Contact your physician for any of these. The drug can also cause kidney damage, bone-marrow poisoning, allergic reactions, heart failure, and even worsening of some arrhythmias.

Digitalis Drugs for
Congestive Heart Failure

Congestive heart failure results when the heart does not have enough strength to pump the blood as forcefully as it should. Blood then "backs up" into the lungs and veins. There are many causes including hypertension, heart attack, rheumatic heart disease, chronic severe anemia, severe infections, severe arrhythmias, and congenital heart defects. The treatment strategy is typically to minimize the strain on the weak heart with rest, unload congestive fluids with diuretics and low salt intake, and strengthen the heart with digitalis drugs. (Diuretics are covered in the section on hypertension drugs.)

"Digitalis" refers to a family of drugs that are obtained from plants, principally of the foxglove family. For centuries these substances have been used in a variety of ways including as emetics, rat poisons, arrow poisons, and remedies for many illnesses. Their ability to strengthen the heart was known to the Romans, Egyptians, and ancient Chinese.

The proper dose of digitalis drug must be precisely determined for each patient in order to insure effectiveness and prevent side effects; in large doses they are deadly poisons. The blood levels needed to significantly pep up the heart are not much lower than the fatally toxic levels, and are carefully monitored for safe but effective amounts. Even with expert therapy, about 20 percent of digitalis recipients suffer from toxicity at some point in the treatment.

By far the most widely used digitalis drug is digoxin. It starts to work about one hour after an oral dose and stays in the body about forty-eight hours. If the dose is adequate, it should provide relief from swollen legs and shortness of breath.

Signs of possible digitalis toxicity include nausea, vomiting, abdominal pain, drowsiness, depression, headache, and irregular heartbeat, all reasons for you to consult your physician.

Digitalis poisoning is more likely when potassium concentration in the blood is low. For this reason, potassium-rich foods or supplements are usually taken if diuretics are used. Alternatively, special diuretics that conserve body potassium can be used. Potassium as well as digitalis must be measured periodically to guide dose adjustment.

Anticoagulants

anisindione, dicumarol, phenindione, phenprocoumon, warfarin

Blood clots can form in veins, arteries, and the heart as a result of inflammation, poor circulation, prolonged immobilization, heart-valve disease, or atherosclerosis. These clots are life-threatening and must be treated. Drugs that slow the clotting process are used, but the dose must be precise—large enough to work but small enough to prevent internal bleeding. Careful

470 monitoring and frequent blood tests are usually required. Do not take *any* other drug or alcohol without the explicit approval of your doctor.

Warfarin is the most commonly used anticoagulant, but others are also effective. They all have similar effects and hazards and must be taken exactly as prescribed and on schedule. Vitamin K can decrease their effectiveness, so your diet should be discussed with your physician.

Side effects include rash, hair loss, fever, and GI upset. If these are severe or prolonged contact your doctor. **More serious side effects,** which you should discuss with your physician right away, include nosebleed, gum bleeding, vomiting or spitting blood, unexplained bruises, black or bloody stool or urine, and unusual or persistant headaches, backaches, or other pains. Birth defects are a danger if the drug is taken during pregnancy.

Antilipemics

cholestyramine, clofibrate, niacin

In stubborn cases of excess cholesterol and fats in the blood that do not respond to exercise and diet, certain drugs may be useful.

Cholestyramine is taken as a powder mixed with food. It helps lower blood cholesterol levels. A common and harmless **side effect** is foul-smelling stools with an altered appearance. **More serious side effects,** which should be discussed with your doctor, include constipation, nausea, bloating, and unusual bleeding.

Clofibrate is taken between meals to reduce blood levels of cholesterol and fats. **Side effects** include GI upset, bloating, weight gain, and sore muscles. **More serious side effects** include rash, hair brittleness and loss, headache, dizziness, decreased libido, flulike symptoms, and difficult urination. Contact your physician for any of these. Liver and blood problems can also develop.

Because of the potential for serious side effects, some experts believe that the risks of clofibrate use outweigh the benefits for all but a small minority of patients. Long-term use of the drug has been associated with gallstones, gallbladder inflammation, heart arrhythmias, and angina. Nevertheless, it is clear that for a few properly selected persons, the benefits of lowering the blood cholesterol with clofibrate far outweigh all the risks.

Niacin—nicotinic acid or vitamin B-3—is used in large doses (fifty and more times the RDA) to help control cholesterol and fat levels in the blood. It also dilates blood vessels of the skin, but this is not beneficial. **Side effects** can be significant with large doses of this, the most toxic of the water-soluble vitamins. Flushing, itching, headache, nausea, vomiting, and diarrhea are common. If they are persistant or severe, contact your physician. **More serious hazards** include aggravation of peptic ulcers, diabetes, gout, and liver disease, which it can also cause if given in very large doses.

Circulation Improvers

ergoloid, ethaverine, isoxsuprine, papaverine, tolazoline

The theory behind the use of these drugs is that by relaxing blood vessels these will dilate, and circulation will improve. They are used mostly in cases of poor circulation due to obstruction of blood vessels, such as intermittent claudication (pain and weakness in the legs), angina, and age-related dementia ("senility").

All these drugs can produce a variety of unpleasant and sometimes serious **side effects** including GI distress, headache, dizziness, irregular pulse, chills, weakness, prostration, rash, and jaundice. All side effects should be discussed with one's physician.

All these drugs are questionable products. They have not been proven effective for their intended uses (except tolazoline for some cases of Raynaud's disease) and adverse effects are common, especially liver damage from papaverine (which is derived from opium) and ethaverine. The use of ergoloid for age-related dementia is controversial. There is evidence that it improves brain functions for those with Alzheimer's disease. But its value in other dementias is questionable; good nutrition, exercise, rest, friendship, and meaningful activities are the most effective "medicines" in most of these cases.

Cortisone Group (Corticosteroids)

dexamethasone, hydrocortisone, prednisone, triamcinolone, others

Drugs in this group resemble the hormones cortisone and hydrocortisone produced by the adrenal cortex and enjoy tremendous popularity because

472 they can at least temporarily help in hundreds of problems including rashes, asthma, rheumatoid arthritis, and cancers. Unfortunately, their use is limited by their hazardous nature.

There are several corticosteroids, often called "steroids" for short. The most commonly used are the four listed above. Their effects and hazards are essentially the same, but their potency varies. They have a wide variety of complicated effects on the body, generally favoring metabolism of protein and fat for energy, and conservation of blood sugar (glucose). This is the opposite of insulin. (These steroids should not be confused with anabolic steroids, which have very different effects; they are discussed in Chapter 1–8, Sports and Drugs.)

The release of steroids from the adrenal glands is very carefully regulated by both the brain and the pituitary gland so that just the right amounts are released into the blood from moment to moment. In general, the adrenal gland is stimulated by the pituitary hormone ACTH to put out extra hormone in response to various types of stress. ACTH secretion is inhibited by rising cortisol levels.

Although corticosteroids are used for many disorders, they don't cure anything. They primarily inhibit the body's reaction to disease with no direct effect on the disease itself. In many conditions the main symptoms are caused by the body's overzealous attempts to cope with whatever started the trouble. The goal of corticosteroid therapy is to suppress inappropriate defense mechanisms. For example, in rheumatoid arthritis the drugs decrease the inflammation and pain, in asthma they inhibit the allergic reactions that lead to spasms and mucus production in the bronchial airways, and in rashes they likewise inhibit allergic reaction at fault.

Why they are risky. Using corticosteroids with proper restraint is often difficult. Once an individual has had a taste of what these powerful drugs can do for his discomfort, he naturally wants more. This puts the conscientious physician in a dilemma. He, too, enjoys the relief from suffering but knows the dire consequences of too much of a good thing. Many people, desperate for relief, have abandoned their responsible doctors to seek out unscrupulous or ignorant practitioners willing to provide unlimited supplies of these drugs. Deceptively labeled "herbal" medicines from the Orient and Mexico often contain these steroids and seem to work miracles until the side effects set in.

In severe illness in which constant cortisone administration offers the only hope of control, the drug is often administered every other day. This gives the body a needed day off to recover from the drug. Symptoms may flare up on the off day, but this price is usually worth paying. Morning administration is preferred because it emulates the natural body rhythm. An effort should be made to find the absolute minimum dosage that will do the job. Single dose or short-term administration (less than one week) of even very large doses for some acute illnesses (especially asthma) is generally safe.

After these drugs have been taken for a long period (more than one month), they should never be abruptly stopped when no longer needed because one's own production of corticosteroids has been suppressed by the large external source, and it takes several weeks for normal production to resume.

There are important **nutrient interactions** associated with long-term use of corticosteroids. Requirements for calcium, vitamin D, vitamin C, and potassium are increased. Supplementation of the first three is especially important for children to prevent or minimize growth retardation.

Side effects include stomach upset and pain, euphoria, restlessness, increased appetite, and weight gain. Contact your physician if these are severe or prolonged.

More serious side effects, which may appear after long-term use of large doses and which should be discussed with your physician, include acne and other skin problems, puffy face and extremities, severe stomach pain (possibly ulcers), bloody or black stools, muscle weakness or pains, mood changes, nausea or vomiting, menstrual problems, and bone pain. These drugs can promote dangerous infections (because of compromised defenses), personality changes including psychosis, bone thinning, loss of protein stores, thinned and weakened skin, muscle degeneration, diabetes, aggravation of ulcers, masking of symptoms, and bizarre changes in the shape of the face and body. In children, growth can be severely stunted. Such serious side effects occur only with daily use of high doses for weeks. Short term use of high doses simply mimics the body's own natural response to stress and is quite safe. People taking these drugs should wear a bracelet saying so.

Topical Steroids

Steroids are also available in many creams, gels, and lotions for topical (external) use against skin, ear, and eye disorders and inflammation. The drugs can dissolve through the skin and enter the blood, but with judicious use toxic levels are rarely reached. Topical use is preferable to oral when the primary problem is in the skin.

These creams relieve irritations, eczema, and itching and inflammation due to insect bites, plant contact, and even hemorrhoids. A relatively mild cream, .5 percent hydrocortisone can be bought without a prescription.

474 Depression and Manic-Depression Drugs

Depression is characterized by sadness, low energy, a sluggish feeling, inability to experience pleasure, difficulty sleeping, and appetite changes. The cause is poorly understood, but some cases appear to be associated with low levels of certain brain neurotransmitters.

Manic depression, or bipolar depression, is characterized by wild swings of mood. The manic or "high" phase is energetic and euphoric with increased libido, appetite, and confidence. It gives way to depression with lethargy, apathy, and a feeling of hopelessness. If both components are strong, two separate drugs may be needed, one for each phase, though lithium has been used for both.

There are two families of drugs currently used for depression, tricyclics and monoamine oxidase inhibitors (MAOIs), and only one acceptable drug specific for mania, lithium.

Tricyclic Antidepressants

amitryptaline, desipramine, doxepin, imipramine, nortryptyline

These drugs are generally safer and more effective than the MAOIs (below) and are usually tried first. They were discovered when researchers looking for better tranquilizers noticed that the drugs had no effect on agitated patients but that certain depressed patients showed dramatic improvement. The mechanism of action of this group is poorly understood but involves increasing the effects of the neurotransmitters norepinephrine and serotonin in the brain. The different drugs in this class have very similar effects and hazards, but they differ in effectiveness for concurrent anxiety and in the degree of sedation and other side effects they produce.

These drugs do not produce stimulation or euphoria in normal people. In fact, they have a mild tranquilizing effect. At first the depression may appear worse, and it may take two or three weeks for the antidepressant action begin. It is important not to give up on these drugs too soon. A full five weeks of therapy at adequate dosage is needed before concluding that they are ineffective.

Some newer antidepressants have actions and effects very similar to those of the tricyclics but seem to have less severe side effects. Examples are **amoxapine**, **maprotiline**, and **trazodone**, which is believed to be much safer for depressed persons who also have heart disease.

Side effects include dry mouth, headache, sugar appetite, fatigue, weakness, and faintness upon standing. Diarrhea, vomiting, heartburn, excessive sweating, dizziness, drowsiness, or insomnia may also occur. These are usually mild with proper doses and they tend to decrease later in therapy. If they are severe or persistant, consult your physician.

Serious side effects, for which you should contact your physician, include urinary difficulties, heart arrhythmias, slow pulse, constipation, shakiness, eye pain, rash, itching, sore throat, fever, hallucinations, and discolored eyes or skin.

The hazards are especially great for those with cardiovascular disease, who should use these drugs only under the closest of supervision. Psychosis can be aggravated in some cases.

Questionable products. Tricyclics are sometimes marketed in combination with lithium for manic depression. Tricyclics combined with chlordiazepoxide (see Sleeping Pills and Tranquilizers) are used for those who are anxious as well as depressed. The convenience of these drug cocktails is usually outweighed by the inability to adjust the doses of the drugs independently.

Monoamine Oxidase Inhibitors—MAOIs

isocarboxid, phenelzine, tranylcypromine

MAOIs are sometimes more effective but often more dangerous than the tricyclics. They are usually not used until the tricyclics have proven ineffective.

MAOIs were discovered by accident. In 1950, a new antituberculosis drug, iproniazid, was developed. It soon became obvious that the depressed TB patients receiving the drug had vastly improved in mood and attitude. Iproniazid proved too toxic for either TB or depression, but a close relative, isoniazid, plays a important role in TB to this day. Several similar but less toxic drugs were developed for depression.

The mechanism of action of MAOIs is well understood. MAO is one of the enzymes responsible for the breakdown of amine neurotransmitters in the brain, biochemicals such as norepinephrine which are involved in wakefulness and stimulation. These drugs interfere with this breakdown and thus amplify the stimulant effect of the amines.

Like the tricyclics these drugs need about three weeks of constant administration before the full therapeutic effect blossoms. Similarly, it takes several weeks to wear off after termination.

Tranylcypromine is the flagship MAOI and the most commonly prescribed. **Phenylzine** may be better when anxiety is present. **Isocarboxazid** is the least studied and least used.

Side effects and hazards. Unlike the tricyclics, the MAOIs cause marked stimulation of the brain and autonomic nervous system, much like amphetamines. There is sometimes a therapeutic overshoot, where depression is converted to agitated mania. These amphetaminelike effects tend to occur early in therapy, preceding the true antidepressive effects by several weeks.

An overdose can cause agitation, paranoia, hallucinations, convulsions, hypertension, hypotension, and death. Long-term toxicity involves liver damage, insomnia, mania, confusion, nerve damage, dizzy spells, headaches, sexual malfunctions, suppression of the parasympathetic nervous system (blurred vision, difficult urination, constipation, dry mouth), and fatigue.

MAOIs mix disastrously with many other drugs and even some common foodstuffs. A prudent physician will always allow a ten-day, drug-free washout period between administration of tricyclics and MAOIs. Avoidance of sympathomimetic amines (adrenalinlike drugs, such as amphetamines, cocaine, ephedrine, and isoproterenol) is a must.

Many foods contain tyramine, a sympathomimetic amine, and these must be eliminated from the diet. People are normally unaffected by tryamine because the digestive tract contains vast quantities of MAO that destroy it before it can enter the blood. But MAOI drugs remove this protection. Any aged food with protein may contain tyramine. Examples include aged cheeses (Brie, Camembert, Swiss, sharp cheddar), sausages, liver, some beers, red wine, bananas, avocados, some beans, meat tenderizer, pickled herring, yeast extract, meat extracts, dried fish, and chocolate. (Ask your physician for a more extensive list.) Consumption of these foods while taking MAOIs can cause a hypertensive episode.

Lithium

lithium carbonate

Lithium is a very unusual drug. It is a mineral ion, a member of the same chemical family as sodium and potassium, and is not an organic compound like nearly all other drugs. It has no known role in normal biological systems. Its value in treating mania was discovered completely by accident when a scientist noticed that guinea pigs, receiving lithium for reasons unrelated to behavior modification, became sedate and lethargic. He gave the mineral to manic individuals, and noted dramatic improvement.

Lithium is currently used to stabilize mood in people with cyclical, bipolar (high-low) behavior patterns. Although it is most noted for eliminating the highs of the manic-depressive cycle, it sometimes improves the low (depressive) phase as well. It has even been known to help in some types of pure depression. It produces no behavior modification in normal humans; it is neither a sedative nor euphoriant.

The effects of lithium on brain biochemistry are extremely complex and not well understood. It has been shown to inhibit the release of the brain's own amine stimulants, norepinephrine and serotonin. This helps explain the calming effect, but it is only a small part of the complex lithium story.

Walking the lithium tightrope. Proper lithium therapy is tricky. Side effects are not usually a problem when blood levels are kept in the proper range, but they explode onto the scene as the blood concentration creeps up to toxic levels; toxicity is observed at only four times the minimum beneficial level.

The absorption of lithium from the intestinal tract is nearly always total, but the elimination rate varies with kidney function. High sodium intake speeds elimination and low sodium slows it, so a low sodium diet mandates a low lithium dosage. The same goes for potassium. Sodium and potassium are sometimes administered to speed lithium elimination in over-dosage. Diuretics can also affect lithium levels. It is usually necessary to regularly check lithium blood-levels so that dosage can be precisely adjusted.

Side effects, which may occur even at proper blood levels, include mild tremor of the hands, thirst, frequent urination, nausea, and diarrhea. Fatigue, constipation, coldness of the extremities, and other symptoms of thyroid gland insufficiency may also appear.

Symptoms of toxicity include confusion, tinnitus, weakness, blurred vision, vomiting, diarrhea, excessive thirst and urination, lassitude, slurred speech, and marked tremor. Continued treatment after such symptoms appear can lead to heavy sedation, coma, muscle rigidity, epileptic seizures, and death.

There is some concern that long-term lithium therapy may cause or promote leukemia in a small percentage of users.

Gastrointestinal (GI) Drugs

antispasmodics; drugs for diarrhea, nausea, ulcers

Of the thousands of herbal remedies and other drugs humans have used over

478 the centuries for various ailments, those used to treat (and create, as explained in Chapter 5–3) symptoms of GI (gastrointestinal) ailments have been among the most numerous. Very few of them have stood the test of time and only a handful are now considered safe and effective. By far the most widely used are the ulcer medicines. Antacids are discussed in Chapter 5–1 and histamine antagonists are discussed in this chapter.

Antispasmodics

belladonna alkaloids, belladonna alkaloids with phenobarbitol, clidinium, dicyclomine, propantheline

These drugs are used to treat overactivity and cramping pain of the stomach, intestines, and bladder, most commonly for spastic colon (irritable bowel syndrome) and peptic ulcers. They work by relaxing the muscles of the gastrointestinal tract (or bladder).

Belladonna alkaloids—that is atropine, hyoscyamine, and hyoscine—are powerful anticholinergics, drugs that depress the autonomic nervous system and thereby slow GI and urinary system activity. **Side effects** include blurred vision, dry mouth, constipation, nausea, vomiting, urinary difficulties, dizziness, sensitivity to light, confusion, decreased libido, fatigue, reduced sense of taste, and fast heartbeat. If these are severe or persistent, consult your physician. Reduced sweating increases susceptibility to heatstroke, so greater care in the heat is required. Greater sensitivity to sunlight can be countered by wearing sunglasses. **More serious side effects,** which you should discuss with your physician, include hallucinations and slurred speech from adverse effects on the brain, and rash, sore throat, fever, and yellowish eyes and skin.

Phenobarbitol is added to belladonna alkaloids in some products to reduce any anxiety that might be aggravating the problem. Critics charge that these products are irrational, fixed-ratio combinations which unnecessarily subject too many people to the risks of phenobarbitol, an addicting barbiturate. The need for an antianxiety agent and the required dose are best determined on an individual basis.

Clidinium, dicyclomine, and **propantheline** are synthetic antispasmodics with effects and uses approximately equal to those of the belladonna alkaloids. They are more expensive but cause fewer side effects.

Questionable products include the dozens of mixtures of barbiturates and other sedatives with belladonna alkaloids such as Donnatal, Donphen, and Hybephen.

Diarrhea Drugs

diphenoxylate with atropine, loperamide, opium (as paregoric)

These drugs are used to relieve severe diarrhea in certain situations. They work well but should not be used in mild, short-term diarrhea and should not be used for more than a few days. They also should not be used for young children since they can mask signs of dehydration and cause severe toxic effects and even death.

Diphenoxylate and atropine are combined to relax the intestinal tract. **Side effects** include those discussed above for atropine plus numbness of the extremities and swelling of the gums. If these are severe or prolonged, consult your physician. **More severe side effects** include bloating, constipation, nausea, vomiting, stomach pain, loss of appetite, faintness, pinpoint pupils, shallow breathing, and overexcitement. If these occur, contact your physician.

Loperamide, one of the most widely prescribed antidiarrheals, works by decreasing intestinal motility. **Side effects** are not common, but the drug may cause abdominal discomfort, dry mouth, dizziness, fatigue, and nausea. Consult your physician if these are severe or persistant. In large doses or when taken with alcohol or tranquilizers, loperamide can cause excessive suppression of the central nervous system. Consult your physician immediately if there is vomiting, difficulty breathing, or slow pulse.

Opium, most commonly as paregoric, a combination of opium with anise oil, benzoic acid, glycerin, camphor, and alcohol, is an effective intestinal relaxant and antidiarrheal. **Side effects** include nausea and constipation (it works very well). Consult your physician if these are severe or persistent. **More serious side effects** requiring a doctor's attention include difficult breathing and slow heartbeat. See Chapter 5–4, Heroin and Other Opiates.

Nausea Drugs

hydroxyzine, meclizine, prochlorperazine, trimethobenzamide

Hydroxyzine is an antihistamine which is useful in controlling nausea and

480   vomiting as well as anxiety. **Side effects** include drowsiness and dry mouth.
If these are severe or persistent, consult your physician. **More serious side effects** include rash and shakiness. Contact your physician if these develop.

Meclizine is an antihistamine which is effective in motion sickness and dizziness due to certain disorders. **Side effects** include drowsiness and dry mouth. If these are severe or persistent, consult your physician. **More serious side effects,** which should be discussed with your physician, include blurred vision, loss of appetite, and nervousness.

Prochlorperazine is a phenothiazine antipsychotic drug which is also useful in treating some cases of nausea and vomiting. See the discussion on schizophrenia drugs, this chapter.

Trimethobenzamide is an antihistamine-like drug used only for nausea and vomiting. **Side effects** are similar to those of antihistamines, including meclizine (see above), but there may be some very serious side effects, including severe vomiting, seizures, fever, and sore throat; contact your physician. In general, children should not be given this drug because they are more susceptible to the side effects.

Ulcer Drugs

cimetidine, ranitidine

The antacids that neutralize the excess acid poured out by cells of the stomach lining are discussed in Chapter 5–1. The prescription-only drugs discussed here work not by neuralizing acid but by preventing its secretion.

Cimetidine, the first real breakthrough in ulcer medication, is one of the most widely used drugs in the world, and it has an excellent track record for safety and effectiveness. It belongs to a class of chemicals known as *histamine blockers,* not to be confused with antihistamines, which have different effects. By decreasing the acidity of the stomach contents, it promotes the healing of peptic ulcers. **Side effects,** which are not very common, include headache, dizziness, blurred vision, fatigue, diarrhea, muscle pain, and breast secretion, swelling, and pain. If these are severe or persistant, consult your physician. **More serious side effects** include rash, fever, reduced libido, and confusion, which require your doctor's attention.

Ranitidine, a newer histamine antagonist, is very similar to cimetidine in chemistry and effects. It allegedly produces even fewer side effects than cimetidine, but this may because it has been in wide use for a shorter time. It is much more expensive than cimetidine, but may be worth trying in those who cannot tolerate the side effects of the latter.

Gout Medicines

The development of the current excellent battery of drugs for gout represents one of the major achievements of medicine. Although therapy does not "cure" the disease, there is no reason for anyone to suffer the crippling agony of recurrent gouty arthritis.

The cause of gout is easily understood. When a string is suspended in a concentrated solution of table sugar, sucrose crystals (rock candy) will grow along the string. A similar thing happens in gout, except that the crystals are composed of uric acid, which is produced by the breakdown of nucleic acids; and the "string" consists of the ligaments and membranes of joints. There are two types of antigout drugs: those that relieve the pain and inflammation after they begin; and those for prevention, which act by lowering the uric acid in the blood so the crystals do not precipitate.

Drugs for Acute Attacks of Gout

colchicine, indomethacin, phenylbutazone, oxyphenbutazone, NSAIDS

Drugs for acute attack should be taken only when pain and inflammation of the joint have begun. The temptation to exceed recommended doses to hasten relief from a bad attack is great, but this can be dangerous. If you take drugs for gout, it is important that you understand their proper uses and follow prescriptions exactly. Be sure that your physician clears up any confusion you might have.

Several anti-inflammatory drugs are used in acute gout. Some of the more important ones are discussed below. Cortisonelike steroids are also sometimes used, but the hazards are too great for regular use.

Colchicine is an ancient gout remedy dating back to the time of Christ. Large doses of the seeds of the *Colchium autumnale* plant (known as autumn crocus or meadow saffron) were used to induce violent vomiting and diarrhea. It was thought that the catharsis was the mechanism of relief. We now know that irritation of the digestive tract is an unfortunate side effect of colchicine and has nothing to do with relieving painful gout.

The mechanism of relief involves preventing the body's inflammatory reaction to the uric acid crystals. The pain and swelling are caused by

482 white blood cells "trying" to destroy the crystals. Colchicine enters these white cells and shuts down their attack on the uric acid. Colchicine is very specific for gouty arthritis; it provides virtually no relief from most other types of joint pain. It is sometimes used to prevent gouty attacks, but other drugs (see below) are often preferable.

When used to relieve symptoms, cochicine must be taken at the first sign of pain or it will not be fully effective. It is usually taken every two hours until the pain subsides (usually within a few hours) or side effects appear. Whether used daily to prevent an attack or every two hours to treat one, if a dose is forgotten until it is almost time for the next one, *do not take an extra dose to make up for the one missed.*

The most common **side effects** of colchicine are nausea, stomach pain, vomiting, and diarrhea. These can be avoided by injecting the drug, but this entails other risks. Long-term use may cause skin rashes, tingling and weakness of the hands or feet, and blood disorders with fatigue and unusual bleeding and bruising. *All* side effects of colchicine should be discussed with your physician.

Indomethacin is now preferred over colchicine by most experts, primarily because of the latter's toxicity to the digestive tract. Indomethacin is a more general anti-inflammatory agent that can be used in other forms of arthritis and to bring fever down. Like aspirin, it inhibits prostaglandin synthesis.

Indomethacin is generally less toxic than colchicine for short-term use, but it can be hazardous, especially in long-term use. **Side effects** include headache, dizziness, and gastrointestinal distress. If these are severe or persistent, consult your physician. **More serious side effects** include stomach ulceration and hemorrhage (bloody or tarry stool), visual disturbances, breathing difficulties and other allergic reactions, depression, hallucinations, swelling of the extremities, and anemia due to bone marrow suppression. If you experience these, stop taking the drug and consult your doctor.

Phenylbutazone and oxyphenbutazone are essentially identical to each other and very similar to indomethacin in the mechanism of action, effectiveness, and adverse reactions. Bone marrow suppression and other serious side effects are even more common than with indomethacin, so many physicians avoid prescribing them. Persons using these drugs must be carefully monitored. All side effects should be discussed with your physician.

Nonsteroidal Anti-inflammatory Drugs (NSAIDS) are effective in treating the pain and inflammation of acute gout. See Painkillers for details.

Drugs for Prevention of Gout Attacks

allopurinol, probenecid, sulfinpyrazone

Attacks of gout are effectively prevented by lowering blood uric-acid levels. This can be done in two ways: increase the elimination of uric acid by the kidneys or decrease its production. Probenecid and sulfinpyrazone are eliminators, and allopurinol is an inhibitor of production.

These drugs do not help to relieve an attack once it has begun. Small doses of colchicine or indomethacin are sometimes given with them to protect against their tendency to provoke a gout attack in the first few months of therapy.

Probenecid and sulfinpyrazone inhibit a system in the kidneys that returns uric acid from the urine back into the blood; they thereby allow it to exit with the urine. Probenecid also inhibits the excretion of some antibiotics and thereby increases the potency of a given dose, so it is sometimes given as an adjunct in infectious diseases.

As these drugs lower the uric acid in the blood, they naturally raise its level in the urine. This can lead to a troubling side effect: the formation of uric-acid stones in the urinary tract. This is usually a risk only early in therapy when the large uric-acid burden is being unloaded, and it can be prevented by high fluid intake to dilute the urine during the first few weeks. Six to eight glasses of water or juice each day is the usual recommendation.

Alcohol and aspirin interfere with the actions of these drugs and should be scrupulously avoided. A switch to acetaminophen for common pain and fever relief is usually recommended.

Side effects of sufinpyrazone include nausea, indigestion, gastrointestinal pain, dizziness, tinnitus, and swelling of the hands and feet. If these are severe they should be discussed with your doctor. Uric acid stones may form, so contact your doctor if you have pain in your lower back or painful or bloody urination.

Side effects of probenecid include nausea, vomiting, headaches, and loss of appetite. Uric acid stones may form, so contact your doctor if you have pain in your lower back, or painful or bloody urination.

Allopurinol was engineered by biochemists specifically to slow uric acid production. It inhibits the enzymes that produce uric acid and thereby prevents its concentration in the blood and precipitation in the joints.

Side effects of allopurinol include dizziness, drowsiness, stomach upset, and diarrhea. If these are severe or persistent, discuss them with your physician. Though remarkably safe for the vast majority of people, the appearance of a rash is a warning that you are one of the small minority who

484 may have severe reactions. If you get a rash, stop taking the drug and contact your doctor.

Allopurinol is often given with cancer chemotherapy. As the drugs kill cancer cells, the nucleic acids of the cells are released in large amounts. The drug slows their conversion to uric acid and prevents the build-up of excessive levels.

Hormone-Disorder Drugs

The many functions of our complex biochemical machinery are precisely regulated by tiny amounts of special substances made by various glands. The level of sugar in the blood, the rate at which cells consume oxygen, and the synthesis and breakdown of bone and muscle tissue are all governed by hormones. When these regulators are in short supply or in excess, serious problems can ensue. The most common hormonal problems are diabetes, estrogen insufficiency, and thyroid disorders. The drugs used to treat them are discussed here.

Diabetes Pills

chlorpropramide, glibenclamide, glipizide, glyburide, tolbutamide, tolazamide

These drugs are used in type II diabetes, the maturity-onset type, in which there is usually enough insulin production by the pancreas that shots of the hormone are not necessary. They work by stimulating the release of insulin from the pancreas after a meal and perhaps by increasing the effect of the insulin on its target tissues. However, if diabetic complications develop or if there is a severe injury, burn, or infection, insulin may have to be used instead.

The use of these drugs has been debated for more than a decade. While they do help control blood-sugar levels, there is no evidence that they prolong life. The FDA now requires a warning label which states that the use of oral antidiabetes drugs "has been reported to be associated with increased cardiovascular mortality" but many dispute these conclusions. Still in most cases dietary measures should be the main treatment of maturity-onset diabetes. See Diabetes in Part Four.

Individual reactions to these drugs vary widely; full cooperation with your physician is essential in adjusting the dose to the right level. Many prescription and nonprescription drugs react adversely with diabetes pills, so *all* drugs, including alcohol, should be OK'd by your doctor first. Photosensitivity may result, so be careful about sun exposure until you know how the drug affects you.

All **side effects** are potentially serious and should be reported to your physician at once; the dose may need adjusting or the drug stopped. If you experience excessive hunger, weakness, trembling, sweating, dizziness, or headaches, your blood sugar may have dropped too low. Eat or drink something sweet and call your doctor immediately. If you feel you might faint, have someone drive you to your doctor at once.

Insulin

Insulin, the hormone lacking in diabetes, is essential to the survival of people with type I diabetes and some with severe type II. It must be injected because stomach acid destroys it. The doses must be coordinated with diet and exercise to achieve good control of blood-sugar levels; careful cooperation with your physician is essential. You must know whether your insulin is short- or long-acting and how many units you take with each injection. Ask your doctor what you are supposed to do if you forget a dose.

All **side effects** are potentially serious and should be discussed with your physician. The most common problems are excessive and insufficient doses. The former, as well as excessive exercise, can lead to weakness, hunger, trembling, sweating, dizziness, and headache. The latter can cause thirst, frequent urination, headache, weakness, and dizziness. Either can lead to faintness and loss of consciousness. If you feel you might faint, have someone drive you to your doctor immediately. You should always have with you a necklace, bracelet, or card indicating your name, your doctor's name and phone number, and your insulin dose.

Estrogen

Estrogen is produced by the ovaries and is essential in reproductive functions. It is also involved in growth, bone metabolism, cardiovascular functions, and even mood and behavior. The most common cause of estrogen deficiency is menopause, during which the production of the hormone drops drastically and permanently. This often causes a variety of symptoms such as sweating, hot flashes, and perhaps anxiety, and depression. It also predisposes many women to osteoporosis (see Part Four), a serious disorder. Estrogen replacement therapy is often used to treat and prevent all these problems. The hormone is also used after removal of the ovaries, in some cases of slow maturation, and in some cancers. A vaginal cream is used to prevent thinning of the vaginal lining in menopause.

Estrogen replacement therapy is catching on especially fast for the treatment and prevention of osteoporosis. This is a controversial trend because the hormone may promote uterine cancer in certain circumstances.[16] For women at high risk for the bone disorder and low risk for uterine cancer,

486 the therapy may be appropriate; for others, including those with diabetes, migraine headaches, and heart disease, the risks may be too great. Each case must be decided individually.

Before prescribing estrogen, your physician must have your complete medical history, and you must be frank about all drug use, especially smoking and drinking. You must follow instructions regarding dosage and check-ups.

Side effects include nausea (often relieved by taking the pills with food), bloating, and tenderness of the breasts. Consult your physician if these are severe or persistent. Photosensitivity may occur; be cautious about sun exposure until you know how estrogen affects you.

More serious side effects include puffiness of the extremities, headaches, depression, weight gain, leg cramps, vaginal discharge or bleeding, or tenderness in the calf or groin; call your physician.

Thyroid Drugs

methimazole, propylthiouracil, thyroid hormone

Thyroid hormone regulates the rate of metabolism in almost all the cells of the body. It also helps regulate the metabolism of fats and sugars and is essential for normal growth and maturation. An excess of the hormone due to an overactive thyroid gland (hyperthyroidism) revs up the metabolism too high and results in excitement, tremors, rapid pulse and breathing, increased blood pressure, diarrhea, and weight loss. Growth may be excessive, especially in children, and the eyes may bulge. The cause is unknown, but it tends to be hereditary.

An underactive thyroid (hypothyroidism) does not produce enough hormone. The symptoms are generally the opposite of hyperthyroidism, but in both cases the gland enlarges. Children may not grow properly.

Methimazole and **propylthiouracil** are used in cases of an overactive thyroid gland. They inhibit the release of the hormone into the blood. **Side effects** may include rash, itching, pain in the joints, dizziness, loss of taste, and stomach pain. If these are severe or persistant, call your physician. **More serious side effects** include fever, chills, sore throat, loss of hearing, swollen lymph nodes, unusual bleeding or bruising, jaundice, backache, and swelling of the feet. Consult your physician right away if any of these appear.

Thyroid hormone is used in cases of an underactive thyroid gland. It has all 487 the same effects as the endogenous hormone. **Side effects** are generally due to improper dosage and should always be reported to your physician. They may include rapid pulse, tremor, headache, diarrhea, weight loss, insomnia, excessive sweating, intolerance to heat, and chest pain. The hormone can react adversely with several prescription and nonprescription drugs, so don't take anything else without consulting your physician.

Hypertension Drugs

Nondrug treatments for hypertension often require difficult changes in lifestyle (see Hypertension in Part Four). They can be effective in mild cases (diastolic blood pressure consistently 85–100); but moderate (diastolic 100–120) and severe (diastolic above 120) hypertension often requires drug therapy. Many products are on the market, and most of them do an excellent job, usually with few side effects.

Drugs used to treat hypertension are conveniently divided into **diuretics,** which act primarily on the kidneys, and **antihypertensives,** which act on the nervous system or blood vessels. Therapy usually starts with a mild diuretic. If the response is inadequate, larger doses are used or one of the antihypertensives is added. In severe hypertension, treatment may start with two different kinds of drugs.

Diuretics

benzthiazide, chlorothiazide, cyclothiazide, other thiazides; bumetamide, ethacrynic acid, furosemide, spironolactone, triamterene, amiloride

Diuretics trick the kidneys into producing a greater volume of urine, which unloads fluid and salt from the body.

They also work directly on the walls of the blood vessels to relax them. This usually reduces blood pressure toward safe levels.

Thiazides are the most commonly used diuretics for hypertension. There are many slightly different chemicals, usually with the suffix *-thiazide*. They are relatively safe and have essentially identical actions and hazards, though the dosage varies from product to product.

Side effects include frequent urination (inevitable) and photosensitivity. Be cautious about sun exposure until you know how it affects you. Thiazide diuretics can deplete the body of potassium, sodium, magnesium,

488

and zinc. This leads to fatigue, weakness, and leg cramps. Eating potassium-rich foods (fruits and vegetables and their juices) and taking zinc and magnesium supplements are advisable. The loss of potassium is most serious in patients taking digitalis, which can become more toxic when potassium is low.

Bumetamide, ethacrynic acid, and furosemide are "loop diuretics" (so called because they act on the loop of Henle in the kidney). They are more potent and shorter acting than the thiazides. **Side effects** include frequent urination (inevitable) and nausea and loss of appetite. If the latter two are severe or persistant, consult your physician. **More serious side effects** include dizziness, weakness, and cramps because of fluid loss and electrolyte imbalances. There may be hearing impairment, tinnitus, rash, or jaundice. If so, your physician should be consulted.

Spironolactone, triamterene, and **amiloride** are diuretics that do not deplete potassium. They are used with a thiazide or alone, especially for those with diabetes or gout, which can be aggravated by thiazides. Frequent urination is inevitable. **Serious side effects** include rapid weight gain or puffiness of the hands and feet, and soreness and enlargement of the breasts; consult your physician.

CAUTION

High potassium intake should be curbed by going easy on most fruits and never using salt substitutes with potassium. A regular check of blood potassium is recommended to readjust the dose. Alcohol can increase the side effects of these drugs.

Antihypertensives

One of the jobs of the sympathetic nervous system is to maintain a stable blood pressure as the body's demands for blood fluctuate. Sometimes the sympathetic nerves are overactive. They keep the pressure high by stimulating the muscles in the blood-vessel walls to contract and by increasing the heart rate and strength.

The drugs discussed in this section interfere with the sympathetic nerves, which tend to stimulate the muscles of the blood vessels and counteract their overactivity; or they act directly on the muscle to relax them and dilate the blood vessels. They are used alone or in concert with diuretics.

Clonidine blocks sympathetic outflow from the brain and thereby relaxes blood vessels. It works quickly and is used with a diuretic for moderate to severe hypertension. **Common side effects** include drowsiness, dry mouth, constipation, impotence, and headache. If these are severe or persistent, consult your physician. Do not drive or operate dangerous machinery until you know how the drug affects you. **More serious side effects,** which should be discussed with your physician, include depression, nightmares, insomnia, weight gain, and swelling of the extremities. Sudden withdrawal of this drug can cause dangerous "rebound" hypertension. If it needs to be stopped in severe hypertension, it must be done gradually. Alcohol should be avoided since it makes the side effects worse.

Guanethidine is a very potent drug that prevents the release of neurotransmitters from the nerves. It is usually used only in severe cases and those resistant to milder medication. It is generally used with a diuretic to prevent accumulation of fluids. **Common side effects** include weakness, dizziness, diarrhea, and impotence. If these are severe or persistant, consult your physician. To prevent postural hypotension (faintness upon standing) the user should move gradually from a supine position to allow blood pressure to gradually adjust. **More severe side effects,** which should be discussed with your physician, include fever, chills, sore throat, difficult swallowing, swollen extremities, and sores in the mouth.

Hydralazine acts directly on the blood vessels to relax them. It is usually added to a diuretic and sympathetic blocker when two-drug therapy is not working. **Common side effects** include headache, fast heartbeat, abdominal cramps, ankle swelling, and dizziness. **More serious side effects,** which should be discussed with your physician, include mood changes, nausea, vomiting, loss of appetite, diarrhea and, after prolonged use, fever, weakness, and pain in the joints. A similar drug, **minoxidil,** can cause hair growth, often where it is unwanted.

Methyldopa is another widely used antihypertensive. Its mechanism of action is not clear, but it may affect neurotransmitters used by the sympathetic nerves to raise blood pressure. **Common side effects** include drowsiness, headache, dry mouth, nasal congestion, mild nausea, diarrhea, and postural hypotension. If these are severe or persistant, contact your physician. **More serious side effects,** which should be discussed with your physician, include fever, swollen extremities, depression, impotence, severe gastrointestinal symptoms, and jaundice.

Prazosin relaxes the smooth muscles of the blood vessels. It is inadequate for severe hypertension unless used in combination with other agents. **Side effects** include faintness upon standing, fast heartbeat, headache, nausea, drowsiness, blurred vision, dry mouth, and nasal congestion. The dosage should be built up gradually and the first dose taken at bedtime while lying

490 down since it may cause fainting. **More serious side effects** include swelling of the hands and feet and sexual impotence (very rare with this drug).

Propranolol, metoprolol, and other beta blockers (beta adrenergic blockers) are another class of drugs useful in hypertension as well as several other conditions. They prevent neurotransmitters from affecting the target tissues, and decrease the stress on the heart by slowing it down, reducing the force of contraction, and relaxing the blood vessels. The drugs are also used for cardiac arrhythmia, angina pectoris, post-heart-attack cardiac protection, and migraine headaches. **Side effects** of the beta blockers include dizziness, drowsiness, cold extremities, faintness upon standing, nausea, vomiting, diarrhea, and loss of appetite. Consult your physician if these are severe or persistent. Do not drive or operate heavy machinery until you know how the drug affects you. **Serious side effects,** which should be discussed with your physician, include hallucinations, confusion, nightmares, and exacerbation of heart and respiratory problems.

Reserpine and other rauwolfia alkaloids are the oldest of the antihypertensives. They were first used for hypertension in India in the 1930s, and Western medicine adopted them in the 1950s. The antihypertensive effects are relatively mild, so the drugs are usually inadequate for severe cases. Reserpine is the prototype but there are many others, all very similar. They work by lowering the stores of nerve-cell adrenalin and related substances used by the sympathetic nerves to initiate their actions, both in the brain as well as in the peripheral nerves. **Side effects** include drowsiness, fatigue, stuffy nose, dry mouth, indigestion, red eyes, and dizziness. If these are severe or persistent, contact your physician.

      More serious side effects of reserpine and its relatives, which should be discussed with one's physician, include nightmares, depression, anxiety, weight gain, breast enlargement, menstrual changes, and decreased libido. Anyone with a history of depression should not take these drugs, and if despondency sets in during therapy, the drug must be terminated. Peptic ulcers can be aggravated and diarrhea may occur.

Painkillers

meperidine, NSAIDS, opiates, oxycodone, pentazocine, propoxyphene

Pain, which comes in many forms and has many causes, can often be relieved by drugs. The appropriate one in each case is determined by the cause of the pain and the likelihood of side effects. Aspirin and acetaminophen, discussed in Chapter 5–1, are very effective in most common types of pain but often fall short in severe cases. The more powerful and potentially hazardous drugs are available by prescription only. **491**

Meperidine

Meperidine is a synthetic narcotic almost as potent as morphine. It is especially useful in severe pain due to trauma and childbirth and in supplementing general anesthesia for surgery.

Side effects include nausea, vomiting, drowsiness, fatigue, dizziness, flushing of the face, increased sweating, blurred vision, consipation, dry mouth, difficult urination, mild ankle swelling, and fast heartbeat. If these are severe or persistent, consult your physician.

More serious side effects include very slow heartbeat and difficult or slow breathing. These indicate excessive suppression of the central nervous system. Stop using the drug and consult your physician immediately. Meperidine is addicting and should be used for no longer and in no larger doses than prescribed.

NSAIDS

diflunisal, feldene, fenoprofin, ibuprofen (now available over the counter), indocethacin, naproxen, oxyphenbutazone, phenylbutazone, tolmetin

Nonsteroidal anti-inflammatory drugs (NSAIDS) are most commonly used to treat the swelling, redness, tenderness, pain, and stiffness of arthritis. They are also used in moderate pain due to dental work, surgery, and such.

Side effects include GI distress, drowsiness, dizziness, constipation, headache, dry mouth, insomnia, nervousness, blurred vision, increased sweating, and fast heartbeat. Consult your physician if these are severe or persistent. The nausea and other GI symptoms can be decreased by taking the drugs with food.

More serious side effects include rash, itching, ear ringing, vision or hearing problems, bloody or tarry stools, swelling of the extremities, weakness, fatigue, and difficult breathing. Consult your physician.
Indomethacin, oxyphenbutazone, and phenylbutazone are more likely to produce serious side effects than the others.

492 The Opiates

Heroin, morphine, and codeine are powerful pain killers and sedatives derived from the opium poppy. Morphine has long been the most reliable and potent analgesic available. Heroin is diacetyl morphine, which is converted to morphine in the body. Its effects and hazards are essentially the same as those of morphine. From time to time there is talk of legalizing heroin for terminal cancer, but since it has no advantage over morphine and there is a danger of diversion to the black market, this is not likely.

Heroin and morphine are very addicting; codeine, which tends to cause dysphoria rather than euphoria, only moderately so. It is not nearly as potent a painkiller as morphine, but it is useful in some headaches and other pain and as a cough suppressant.

Side effects include dry mouth, nausea, vomiting, urine retention, constipation, and itching (especially with codeine). If these are severe or persistent, consult your physician. **More serious side effects** can be produced by an overdose, which can cause fatal depression of the respiratory centers of the brain.

Oxycodone

Oxycodone is a synthetic narcotic used to relieve moderate pain due to trauma (such as dislocations, simple fractures), tooth extraction, surgery, childbirth, and other causes. It is combined with aspirin or acetaminophen.

Side effects include nausea, vomiting, drowsiness, dizziness, faintness, flushing of the face, constipation, blurred vision, dry mouth, increased sweating, fatigue, weakness, difficult urination, and fast heartbeat. If these are severe or persistent, call your doctor.

More serious side effects include difficult breathing and slow heartbeat due to excessive suppression of the central nervous system. Consult a physician immediately. Oxycodone is addicting and should not be used longer or in larger doses than prescribed.

Pentazocine

Pentazocine is a synthetic analgesic and mild narcotic used in moderate to severe pain due to many causes, including surgery and childbirth. It has no advantages over other painkillers and causes more adverse reactions.

Side effects include nausea, vomiting, drowsiness, slight euphoria, flushing, itching, constipation, sweating, headache, shakiness, blurred vision, tinnitus, numbness, and difficult urination. If these are severe or persistent, consult your physician.

More serious side effects include allergic reactions such as rash or fever, breathing difficulties, depression, and hallucinations. Consult your physician right away. Pentazocine is addicting and should not be used longer or in larger doses than prescribed.

Propoxyphene

Propoxyphene is a synthetic non-narcotic analgesic used in mild to moderate pain due to headache and other causes. It is often combined with aspirin or acetaminophen. It is heavily promoted and widely used but has no proven superiority over nonprescription pain relievers, and critics say it is not even as good as aspirin or acetaminophen.

Side effects include nausea, vomiting, drowsiness, headache, dizziness, slight euphoria, blurred vision, constipation, stomach pain, weakness, and fatigue. If these are persistent or severe, consult your physician.

More severe side effects include itching or rash due to allergy. If these appear, stop using the drug and consult your physician. An overdose or combination with alcohol or other depressant drugs or antihistamines can cause severe weakness and drowsiness, confusion, and unconsciousness. In extreme cases death may result.

Schizophrenia Drugs

A revolution has taken place in psychiatry; the number of institutionalized patients has plunged in the last thirty years. The once horribly crowded mental hospitals are now usually below capacity and many have closed down. The development of psychotropic drugs is largely responsible for this.

The greatest impact has been on the therapy for depression, manic depression (see Depression and Manic-Depression Drugs, this chapter) and schizophrenia, a common disease that afflicts more than a million people in the United States.

The schizophrenic mind is characterized by irrational thought—a blending of the real with the unreal. The psychotropic drugs, most of which were developed as tranquilizers, seem to numb the mind just enough so that perception and thought can be organized. This is an oversimplification; most

494 general tranquilizers are only slightly helpful. The successful drugs probably have additional specific effects on neurotransmitter imbalances in the brain.

Drugs for schizophrenia do not work miracles. In about 20 percent of the cases they do no good at all. The remainder are by no means cured. The hallucinations and delusions are typically controlled to a point where the individual can function outside the hospital, occasionally hold a job, and cope with moderate stress. But a complete restoration to normal thought and behavior is unusual. Moreover, all of the current medications are plagued by serious side effects.

There are three main classes of schizophrenia drugs: phenothiazines, thioxanthines, and butyrophenones. They are all inappropriate for mild anxiety, tension, and insomnia. With very few exceptions, therapy is restricted to one drug at a time.

Phenothiazines

chlopromazine, prochlorperazine, thioridazine, fluphenazine, trifluoperazine

This is by far the most important and widely used type. The pilot substance, phenothiazine itself, had various medicinal applications in the 1930s. It was later found to prolong and deepen the action of general anesthetics, though it had none of their properties itself. Further study revealed a tremendously diverse and complex constellation of actions on the brain. By 1960 it had become apparent that schizophrenia and closely related disorders responded to treatment with phenothiazines. Chemists then produced many variants, about a dozen of which are effective. The various agents in this class differ in dosage, frequency of administration, relative sedation produced, and tendency to produce the major side effects.

Common side effects, which often subside as the body adjusts to the drug, include dry mouth, drowsiness, blurred vision, constipation, dizziness, racing heart, decreased libido, nasal congestion, menstrual changes, swelling breasts, and difficult urination. Postural hypotension (faintness, dizziness upon standing up) is common but can usually be minimized by getting up gradually. If any of these problems is severe or persistent, discuss it with your physician.

These drugs cause some people to sweat less and overheat more easily, so exposure to excessive heat should be avoided or minimized. Phenothiazines can also promote accidental hypothermia, especially in elderly persons. Some people are sensitized to sunlight by the drugs and may sunburn easily if unprotected.

A more serious side effect is tardive dyskinesia, a syndrome characterized by discomfort, restlessness, spasms, and movement disorders. It generally appears only in those who have taken the drugs for long periods.

Phenothiazines interact with many other drugs unfavorably. A physician should be consulted before any other drugs, including nonprescription drugs, are taken.

Phenothiazines often cause weight gain due to stimulation of the appetite, increased heart rate, cataracts, blurred vision, difficulty with bladder function, and abnormalities with the liver and white blood cells.

Thioxanthines

Two of these are currently used, chlorprothixene and thiothixene. Their actions, side effects, and hazards are nearly the same as for the phenothiazines.

Butyrophenones

Only one is used, halperidol. It is useful for patients with organic dementias and agitation. Its actions, side effects, and hazards are similar to those of the above drugs.

Sleeping Pills and Tranquilizers

barbiturates, benzodiazepines, miscellaneous

These are among the most prescribed drugs in the United States. They are all potentially addicting and should only be used occasionally to help deal with short-term, severe anxiety due to stress such as illness, injury, or death of a loved one; or when tension or insomnia is severe enough to interfere with normal everyday life and nondrug relaxation techniques (exercise, meditation, hobbies, massage) have failed. They are not recommended for regular use in mild anxiety and insomnia.

Barbiturates

amobarbital, butabarbital, pentobarbital, phenobarbital, secobarbital, others (note *-barbital*)

496 Barbital was first made in 1903 and it proved to be a general suppressor of nervous system activity. Chemists have since created thousands of chemical variations of barbital, and about a dozen of these are commonly prescribed today. They differ primarily in the speed and duration of their effects. Most physicians consider them obsolete as tranquilizers and sedatives because there are more effective and safer alternatives, especially the benzodiazepines.

The long-acting group requires a few days to leave the body and includes phenobarbital. The intermediate-acting group leaves the body in about a day and includes amobarbital and butabarbital. The short-acting group lasts about half a day and includes pentobarbital and secobarbital. Several ultra-short-acting barbiturates, lasting less than an hour, are used by injection in hospitals to help induce surgical anesthesia.

Side effects include drowsiness the next day and, less commonly, diarrhea, headache, nausea, vomiting, muscle and joint pain, and slurred speech. If these are severe or persistent, consult your physician.

More serious side effects include rash, sore throat, fever, swelling of the face, jaundice, unusual bruising or bleeding, unusual weakness or fatigue, confusion, slow heartbeat, or difficult breathing. These can be signs of allergic reactions, blood disorders, liver damage, or excessive depression of the brain. Contact your physician.

Barbiturate-induced sleep is of poor quality because the rapid eye movement (REM) stage is suppressed. Moreover, when barbiturates are used frequently, the body becomes resistant, requiring ever higher doses to get the same effect.

Overdose can cause fatal suppression of the respiratory centers of the brain; the comatose victim quietly suffocates. Barbiturates mix disastrously with alcohol, which lowers the lethal dose and must be avoided. Heroin and other narcotics also make a dangerous mix with barbiturates.

Barbiturates are addicting, and withdrawal from high levels is very unpleasant and potentially lethal. They should be used for no longer and in no larger doses than prescribed. Because of the possibility of withdrawal sickness, you should not stop taking them without contacting your physician.

Benzodiazepines

alprazolam, chlordiazepoxide, clorazepate, diazepam, flurazepam, hydroxyzine, halazepam, lorazepam, oxazepam, prazepam, temazepam, triazolam

Benzodiazepines were first synthesized in the 1930s when they were studied for muscle relaxant properties. Researchers noticed that the drugs tamed laboratory animals and thought they might be useful for anxiety in humans. Trials were successful and the drugs have become extremely popular because they are effective and have many advantages over barbiturates, including safety. The longer-acting ones are useful in severe anxiety, while the others are used for insomnia.

The most important advantage over the barbiturates is the low potential for fatal overdose. It takes very large amounts of these drugs (about 100 times the normal dose) to cause real trouble. REM sleep is not blocked, but two other stages of sleep (III and IV) are. This is probably less important, but any drug-induced sleep is undoubtedly inferior to natural sleep because of these pattern distortions.

Resistance to these drugs does develop but much more slowly than with barbiturates. Hangovers are much less likely, and the elimination rates of other drugs are much less affected than with barbiturates. The addiction problem is also less serious except in prolonged use of benzodiazepines.[17]

Side effects of benzodiazepines include excessive sedation, dizziness, weakness, nausea, blurred vision, difficult walking, impaired memory and learning, impaired judgment and coordination, and intestinal upset. If any of these is severe or persistent, contact your physician.

More serious reactions include depression, insomnia, double vision, clumsiness, irritability, weakness, confusion, impaired memory and rash. If any of these develops, consult your physician right away.

Withdrawal from prolonged use of benzodiazepines can be difficult, especially in cases of large doses and especially with the shorter-acting varieties. Symptoms include anxiety, perceptual disturbances, muscle stiffness and twitching, depression, seizures, and psychotic disturbances. If you want to quit taking a benzodiazepine, contact your physician.

Miscellaneous

A diverse collection of chemicals rounds out the sedative/antianxiety group. None of these outperforms the barbiturates and benzodiazepines, and most are distinctly inferior.

Meprobamate resembles the benzodiazepines in actions and adverse effects. Dangerous addiction can occur but fatal overdoses are very rare.

Ethinamate, ethchlorvynol, methyprylon, and glutethimie are all primarily

498   used for insomnia. They share a dangerous addiction and overdose potential and should probably never by used.

Chloral hydrate is the oldest drug in this class, having been used in the 19th century to induce sleep. It is safe in recommended doses but dangerous with alcohol. The potent "mickey finn" is a combination of chloral hydrate with alcohol. The drug has a very unpleasant taste and can irritate the digestive tract. It is physically addicting.

Paraldehyde is another old drug. It has a very strong taste and stays on the breath for several hours, making it a poor choice for daytime sedation. It is most often used for alcohol withdrawal.

Vaccines

In the late 18th century William Jenner discovered that fluid from cowpox sores could immunize people against the deadly smallpox. Since then a great deal has been learned about viruses and bacteria, and vaccines have been developed against several very important infectious diseases. Smallpox has been eradicated, so the vaccine against it is no longer necessary. This is one of the great achievements of scientific medicine and an inspiration for efforts against other deadly diseases.

Vaccination against diphtheria, tetanus, pertussis (whooping cough), polio, mumps, measles, and rubella is routine for infants and children. A chickenpox vaccine is available and may become widely used. Vaccines against hepatitis B, bacterial pneumonia, influenza, yellow fever, cholera, plague, rabies, typhoid fever, typhus, bacterial meningitis, and anthrax are available for high risk groups.[18]

Vaccines are under development for herpes, hepatitis A, cytomegalovirus, malaria, tooth decay, gonorrhea, syphilis, leprosy, infectious mononucleosis, AIDS, and several types of cancer.

A vaccine consists of a dead or modified form of a disease-causing microbe. It works by stimulating the body's production of antibodies to the organism. If the microbe should then enter the body, it is neutralized and removed from the body before it can multiply and cause disease. Vaccines can have an impact far beyond the immediate disease in question. For example, the hepatitis B vaccine is also, in essence, a vaccine against liver cancer, a herpes vaccine might prevent some cervical cancers, and a vaccine against the Epstein-Barr virus should help prevent not only infectious mononucleosis but some kinds of cancer (especially Burkitt's lymphoma) and perhaps rheumatoid arthritis.

Here is the recommended schedule for immunization of normal infants and children.

AGE	VACCINE(S)
2 months	DTP, OP
4 months	DTP, OP
6 months	DTP
15 months	MMR
18 months	DTP, OPV
4-6 years	DTP, OPV
14-16, then every ten years	Td

DTP = diphtheria, tetanus, pertussis

OPV = oral polio vaccine

MMR = measles, mumps, rubella

Td = tetanus and diptheria for adults

Just as there are a few people who believe that the earth is flat and some who doubt the evolution of species, so there are those who do not believe in vaccinations. Until recently the doubts were mostly based on religious beliefs, but the occurrence of polio and other preventable diseases among the Amish and others has prompted a change of heart. Now the opposition to vaccines comes mostly from health cultists and cranks who either doubt that microbes cause disease or believe that doctors and public health officials have conspired with the pharmaceutical industry to foist unnecessary and dangerous drugs on the public.

It is true that some vaccines cause side effects in a small percentage of people. Concern has recently been focused on the pertussis vaccine, which can produce episodes of screaming, convulsions, and brain damage in a very few infants. However, when its use decreases the incidence of the dreadful disease can rise dramatically. Efforts are under way to improve the safety of the vaccine, but in most cases it is already safer to be vaccinated than not. Nevertheless, parents should be told about the possible side effects,

500 and children who have severe reactions should not receive further pertussis vaccine.

No vaccinations are required for persons traveling from the United States to Europe, Canada, Mexico, or the Caribbean. Travelers to other areas should consult their physicians or the nearest Department of Health for specific requirements. The main threats in parts of Africa, Asia, and South America are yellow fever, cholera, and malaria. The latter is preventable by antimalarials but not yet by vaccine. For more on malaria and vaccines against hepatitis B, bacterial pneumonia, influenza, and rabies, see separate discussions in Part Four.

3

Herbs and Herbalism[19]

Plants have been used for therapeutic purposes for thousands of years. The effects of many plants were no doubt discovered by accident when they were tried as food and when they contaminated drinking water. According to an Inca legend, the effectiveness of cinchona bark against malaria was discovered by a malaria victim wandering in the forest after a storm. Delirious with fever, he plunged into a pond into which a cinchona tree had fallen and drank his fill. His fever subsided and he correctly attributed this to the tree.

In other cases the origin of an herb's use is astrological or otherwise superstitious. For example, the anthropocentric "doctrine of signatures," subscribed to by Paracelsus as well as the American Indians and others, held that plants usually provide a clue to their medical uses. Liverleaf is vaguely shaped like a liver and was used in liver ailments; plants yielding milky juices were used to promote lactation; and seneca snakeroot, named for its shape, was used for snake bites.

While usually ineffective for the purported uses, such plants were often found useful for other purposes. Rauwolfia serpentina, an Indian herb first used for snake bites because of the shape of the roots, was found to be an effective sedative, and has been used as a relaxing tea for thousands of years in India. Its active component, reserpine, is now used for hypertension, though not very often. It is more hazardous than was previously believed: reserpine can cause severe depression, sexual dysfunction, and ulcers.

The physiological effects of herbs are due to active chemicals, usually alkaloids, glycosides, oils, gums, and resins. Many of these chemicals have been isolated and purified, but some are still unidentified.[20,21]

502

Alkaloids are complex nitrogen-containing rings, often with powerful physiological activity. Examples are morphine, ergotamine, cocaine, physostigmine, atropine, vincristine, strychnine, and reserpine. There are hundreds of others.

Steroids in plants often resemble human hormonal steroids and may affect hormone functions. Mexican yams are the world's main source of steroids for making birth control pills, cortisone, and other hormones.

Glycosides contain a sugar linked to a nonsugar. The cardiac glycosides (from foxglove, oleander, milkweed) and the cyanogenic glycosides or laetriles (from apricot and peach kernels, and many other sources) are examples.

Plant oils usually contain a mixture of alcohols, ketones, aldehydes, phenols, esters, and ethers. Some are highly germicidal, but usually too insoluble in water to be effective antiseptics in medicine.

In recent decades more and more drugs have been made purely synthetically rather than extracted from plants or made as analogues of plant compounds. Examples include some potent tranquilizers, anesthetics, anticancer drugs, and anti-infectives. More than two-thirds of the prescriptions now filled in the United States are for synthetics. However, more recently, as part of the "back to nature" movement, there has been a definite revival of interest in herbal medicine. This trend is gaining momentum and seems likely to continue for some time.

Much of the available literature on herbal therapies is misleading, false, and dangerous. Most of the popular herbals (as the encyclopedias are called) provide little or no information on the toxicity of many of the herbs they prescribe for dozens of ailments. For example, in *Back to Eden* (written in the 1920s and republished in the 1970s by Beneficial Books) Jethro Kloss says lobelia is completely harmless and "will never hurt anyone." He highly recommends it as the treatment of choice for many major and minor ailments. It is a potent emetic, which is fine with Kloss, who also freely prescribes powerful cathartics. Lobelia can cause death by narcotic-like depression of the brain's respiratory centers.

Kloss recommends mistletoe tea for epilepsy, but it has neurotoxic amines which can cause convulsions, abortion, and other serious problems. He prescribes American mandrake (podophyllum) for intestinal problems, but it is a drastic purgative which can cause nausea, vomiting, and death by gastrointestinal inflammation. He recommends peach kernals for various ailments, but they contain cyanide and were used as a means of execution in ancient Egypt; a handful could do the job. All these and many more poisonous prescriptions and recipes are presented without a word of warning. If this is Eden, we'll take our chances in Hades.

Like *Back to Eden* most herb books, articles, and charts just list all the ailments which each herb has been used for, even if the herb has been found useless for most or all of the old purposes. Some authors add an inconspicuous disclaimer saying they don't necessarily recommend specific herbs for specific conditions, and are just reporting their uses. But many people don't read them and, in any case, the text often seems to make enthusiastic recommendations in spite of the disclaimer. Cures for every conceivable and deadly disease are touted, and the naive reader is easily mislead.

Many people take the dogmatic herbals as gospel. They go out and buy or pick dozens of the recommended herbs (or something resembling them) and use them at every opportunity. Therefore, it would appear irresponsible for publishers of recent editions of such outdated volumes not to warn the readers that the remedies presented are of historical interest only.

Many herbs contain substances which the FDA would ban or allow by prescription only if they were labeled or sold as drugs. While many herbs have important uses, it should be kept in mind that **no physiologically active substance is devoid of some hazard.** Some herbs are extremely dangerous, others moderately so.

It should be obvious that the very potent herbs cannot be practically and safely used in their crude, unassayed form. There is tremendous variation in the concentration of components in different specimens, at different times of the year, and even at different times of the day. For example, the morphine in the opium poppy juice during the early morning can be three times the concentration in the early evening. Without precise knowledge of the amount of active ingredients present, the use of foxglove (digitalis), henbane (atropine), opium (morphine), and many others would be a very risky affair.

An extreme example is the calabar bean, which was long used by some African tribes for trial by ordeal. The person on trial chewed and swallowed the beans. If he vomited it up, he was considered innocent; if not, he died. Calabar bean contains physostigmine, an alkaloid which increases the level of acetyl choline in the body. This can be useful to victims of myaesthenia gravis (a neuromuscular disorder) and often allows them to lead essentially normal lives. But an excess is very toxic and too little is ineffective, so the dose must be exact; the bean simply would not do.

Users should keep in mind that herbs are sometimes accidently contaminated or deliberately adulterated with dangerous substances. In one case a young woman became delirious after drinking burdock root tea which had been contaminated or adulterated with an atropine-containing root or herb. Sometimes ginseng root is adulterated with the dangerous mandrake or other inexpensive roots for higher profits. In fact, a great deal of the so-called ginseng in this country is not ginseng at all (see below).

Another problem for herb users is the presence of tannic acid in hundreds of plants, including scores of those used for medicinal purposes. It apparently acts as an insect repellant and insecticide for the plants. Tannic acid has many uses in industry, textiles, and chemistry. In medicine it can

504

be used topically as an astringent and styptic. It used to be used to check internal bleeding, and plants with a high content were collected for this purpose.

Tannic acid is a weak carcinogen and it apparently interferes with the absorption of some B vitamins and certain drugs, including some pain relievers, tranquilizers, and antihistamines. The extent of the problem is not yet clear, but herb users should be aware of which herbs contain significant amounts of tannic acid. These should probably be avoided when using necessary therapeutic drugs, and if large amounts of an herb are used, B vitamin supplements might be a good idea.

If in doubt about whether an herb has tannic acid, this rule of thumb is probably fairly accurate: if the herb or its tea has an astringent, slightly bitter taste, like black tea which has been steeped too long or too hot, it probably has tannic acid in proportion to this taste. (Tea and coffee have signifiant amounts of tannic acid.) Steeping at lower temperatures for shorter periods decreases the tannic acid in the brew.

A more important problem is the presence in many herbs of pyrrolizidine and other alkaloids which can cause occlusion of the hepatic veins and severe liver disease. There is painful liver enlargement and cirrhosis, sometimes fatal. Such disease is endemic in Jamaica, parts of India, and probably elsewhere. Livestock are often poisoned and they never develop tolerance. In Jamaica about two hundred species of "bush tea" are commonly used and many of them contain the dangerous alkaloids. There is a long time-lag before any symptoms appear, so the victim does not associate them with the plants and continues to drink the bush tea. [22]

Finally, it is important for herb users to understand that herbal medicine has long been an integral part of the purge-and-bleed tradition which held sway for centuries before being largely abandoned as a hazard to humanity. The basic idea in the treatment of practically every disease was that if a sick person is bled and given diuretics, laxatives, diaphoretics (sweat producers), and emetics, the poisons (or demons) would be eliminated by these various routes. Bloodletting has been discarded, but herbalism has largely retained the rest.

The herbals continue to list powerful purgatives and other "eliminators" as useful in a large number of diseases. For example, Kloss recommends a high enema and an emetic for dog bites, snake bites, insect stings, liver disease, kidney stones, gallstones, colitis, cholera, epilepsy, flu, and many other ailments which in reality cannot be helped by such treatment. Kloss's recommendation of the purgative buckthorn for appendicitis could be deadly.

In scientific medicine all this eliminating is considered unnatural and hazardous. Diaphoretics and emetics have practically no use, diuretics are given only for a few specific conditions, and laxatives are very rarely prescribed. The hazard of bleeding is clear enough to most people, but many do not realize that purging and eliminating through various orifices is dangerous since dehydration and depletion of important minerals, vitamins, and electrolytes can occur. Purging is also unpleasant and exhausting.

Our primary purpose here is to put some of the claims for herbs in perspective by examining their chemistry, physiological effects, uses, and hazards. A truly comprehensive guide would include several hundred herbs. Here we limit our discussion to those most commonly used in the Western world.

Consumers should be wary of the many herb extract products on the market. These formulations take an irrational shotgun approach to symptoms. Like the herbals that list all the plants ever used for each symptom, these products contain irrational mixtures of unproven remedies for every ailment under the sun, including impotence, angina, arthritis, liver disease, hypertension, obesity, kidney disease, memory problems, and eczema.

The manufacturers escape government regulation by avoiding drug stores and other large outlets and by tricky wording of the labels and promotional literature. One pamphlet for a nationally distributed line of herbal extracts has a disclaimer in tiny print which says that none of the information is intended to recommend the medicinal use of herbs. Yet the entire text is a catalogue of symptoms and ailments and the herbal extract mixtures best for them. Another way medicinal herb promoters get around the law is to give their products names which strongly hint at their intended uses, but make no explicit claims—LVR for liver problems, ALRG for allergies, GBLAD for gallbladder problems, BP for high blood pressure and RUMART for rheumatism and arthritis, are examples.

CAUTION

Pharmacologically active herbs and herbal extracts should not be taken by persons with chronic illnesses and by pregnant women without the advice of a physician.

Aloes (Aloe vera, Aloe perryi, others)

Aloes are succulent perennials of the lily family with thick, fleshy leaves, usually with spines along their edges. Varieties grow from one to sixty feet high. Aloes have been used since at least the fourth century B.C. when the Greeks cultivated them for medicinal purposes. It is believed that Alexander the Great conquered the island of Socotra for its aloe farms, to assure an abundant supply to treat his soldiers' wounds.

Aloe juice, which is very bitter, contains barbaloin and isobarbaloin, powerful stimulant purgatives which act directly on the colon. Herbalists recommend carminative herbs such as anise and angelica to moderate the violent cramping. The American Pharmaceutical Association recommends against aloe juice or extract as a laxative because the action is too violent. In fact, aloe is no longer even recommended as a horse laxative because it is too powerful and unpredictable. Its action on smooth muscles makes it dangerous for pregnant women. It can also aggravate menstrual cramps.

Aloe juice is often used to speed the healing of cuts, abrasions, sunburn, eczema, and other skin lesions. Proof is lacking that it works, but it is soothing and provides a barrier to dust and dirt if applied thick enough. However, aloe is not an effective sunscreen. It only provides false security, which can contribute to severe sunburn and even solar keratosis, damage to the skin that can lead to cancer.

In recent years some promoters of aloe products have been making outrageous claims in their literature and sales talks. Pyramid-type operations (salesperson-recruiting schemes of questionable legality) promote aloe as a remedy for cancer, diabetes, colitis, asthma, glaucoma, multiple sclerosis, arthritis and many other serious diseases. Aloe has actually been tested by the National Cancer Institute and found worthess against cancer. There is no evidence to support the other claims either.

In conclusion, the use of aloe should be restricted to the skin for minor cuts, scrapes, burns, and sunburn. No one should be diverted from proper treatment of serious diseases or wounds by unproven claims about aloe.

American Hellebore (Vertatrum viride)

This perennial lily was used by the American Indians and pioneers as an analgesic, appetite stimulant, and anticonvulsant. Because of its toxicity, use of the plant declined until its hypotensive effects were discovered in 1950. Since then its alkaloids (especially germine) have sometimes been used in hypertension, especially in combination with reserpine, but its major use is as an insecticide.

WARNING

All parts of the plant are highly toxic and potentially lethal. Symptoms include impaired vision, abdominal pains, nausea, retching, violent vomiting, diarrhea, headache, dizziness, weakness, tremors, convulsions, and loss of consciousness.

Angelica (Angelica archangelica)

All parts of this perennial herbaceous plant are strongly aromatic; since ancient times they have been used as a perfume and to flavor wines and liquors such as vermouth and Chartreuse. It has long been used in perfumes, soaps, and incense.

Angelica has also been used as a carminative, sedative, vulnerary, diaphoretic, and expectorant. The main active component is angelic acid, a mild sedative, diuretic, and antiseptic.

WARNING
The fresh root is deadly; it was frequently used to commit suicide in some Canadian tribes.

Anise (Pimpinella anisum)

This small, white-flowered, umbelliferous annual contains anethol which provides its strong, pleasant odor and which is used to flavor drinks, soups, cakes, and other foods.

Anise oil is said to be good for hard, dry coughs, and is incorporated into lozenges. Mixed with wine, it is said to be beneficial for bronchitis, asthma, and other repiratory problems. It has not been proven effective as claimed.

Autumn Crocus
(Colchium autumnale)

This short perennial lily has been used for thousands of years for gout, rheumatism, arthritis, and other painful ailments. It contains colchicine, which is still a mainstay for gout.

Black Cohosh (Cimicifuga racemosa)

This tall herbaceous annual, also known as squaw root, was a major medicinal herb to the American Indians, who used the very bitter root to relieve arthritis pain, and as a sedative, astringent, emmenagogue, and expectorant.
    The root contains tannic acid, cimicifugin (a bitter astringent), and salicylic acid. The latter can aggravate peptic ulcers and provoke gastric bleeding, so caution is in order.

Bloodroot (Sanguinarias canadensis)

The American Indians used this small perennial, also known as tumeric, as an emetic, cathartic, and antiseptic. It contains the poisonous alkaloid sanguinarine as well as dangerous alkaloids related to those in belladonna.

Blue Cohosh (Caulophyllum thalictroides)

Also known as squaw root, this small perennial with yellow-green flowers and dark blue fruit was much used by American Indians. It contains methycylisine, an alkaloid, and caulosaponin, a saponin, which elevate blood pressure and stimulate respiration and smooth muscle contractility. Caulosaponin also constricts coronary arteries and may be hazardous to those with atherosclerosis or angina. Self-treatment with this herb to promote menstruation or hasten childbirth can be risky.

Boneset (Eupatorium perfoliatum)

This perennial herb was used by American Indians who introduced it to settlers. An infusion of the leaves is used as a stimulant, febrifuge, laxative, and diaphoretic. It is foul-tasting and can cause nausea and vomiting. It does not heal bones; the name comes from its use against dengue, a viral infection also called bonebreak fever. There is nothing of value in it, and its current revival is irrational. It should be avoided, unless you enjoy sweating and vomiting. [23]

Buchu (Barosma betulina)

This small shrub grows mainly in the southwest part of South Africa. The leaves and twigs are used to make a unique-tasting, pleasant tea. The taste is strong and vaguely mintlike. The Hottentots use the plant to make a body perfume.

Besides the aromatic volatile oils, buchu contains diosphenol, an antiseptic. Strong infusions have been used in bladder infections and kidney stones. Potential hazards of long-term use are not known.

Buckthorn (Rhamnus frangula)

Also known as black alder dogwood, the bark and berries of the buckthorn are used as a purgative, diuretic, and emetic. Herbalists recommend it for constipation, rheumatism, gout, and intestinal parasites. Jethro Kloss calls it an effective remedy for appendicitis, but this is a very dangerous recommendation.

WARNING

Buckthorn can cause very severe diarrhea and has not been proven effective for any disease or dysfunction. It should never be used in the presence of abdominal pain if the appendix has not been removed. Use of buckthorn during appendicitis can cause appendix rupture, peritonitis, and death.

Burdock (Arctium lappa)

The dried root of this short biennial is the most common burdock product. Burdock root tea, a favorite on several continents, has a sweet, earthy flavor. The leaves are slightly bitter. Japanese and other Orientals eat the fresh roots after boiling or frying.

Burdock contains inulin, mucilage, lappin (a glycoside), resins, oils, and tannic acid. Atropine has been found in at least one batch of commercial burdock root tea, which caused at least two cases of atropine poisoning. The poison was probably due to contamination, but the possibility that burdock has some atropine at some time in its life cycle has not been ruled out.

Burdock has been used as an alterative, diuretic, diaphoretic, and blood purifier, and a decoction for boils, ulcers, bruises, eczema, and other problems. It has significant nutritive value (carbohydrate, minerals, possibly vitamins) but no proven pharmacologic action.

Calamus (Acorus calamus)

Also known as sweet flag and sweet root, calamus root is recommended by herbalists to control fevers, colic, dyspepsia, and other symptoms. It is also used externally for burns and sores. Calamus contains carcinogenic substances and is banned by the FDA as a food or food additive. Nevertheless, it is still sold in some herb stores.

Camomile, Common
(Anthemis nobilis)

This is a low-growing, perennial creeper with tufts of leaves and flowers about a foot high. It has a strong, pleasant scent of apples, but the taste is slightly bitter.

The flowers are used for an infusion which is used as a mild sedative and for soothing an upset stomach. Camomile contains volatile oils (which dissipate if boiled or not covered while steeping), angelic acid (a mild sedative), and small amounts of tannic acid.

German camomile (*Matricuria chamomilla*), a more potent herb, is much used in Europe as a digestive aid, antispasmodic for menstrual cramps, and anti-inflammatory for the skin and mucous membranes.

Catnip (Nepeta cataria)

This relative of the mints has a perennial root and leafy stems. Its characteristic odor drives cats wild, especially if the plant has been bruised. Cats will attack and destroy the plant, and consume substantial amounts of the leaf. Rats, on the contrary, are reported to fear it, and won't eat it even if hungry.

Catnip contains nepetalactone, an aromatic chemical that sets cats off and is apparently responsible for its physiological effects. Catnip tea has long been used as a carminative, diaphoretic, and antispasmotic in stomach upset, fever, headache, and other ailments. The herb is infused, not boiled. More than a few swallows a day may produce nausea.

Cayenne (Capsicum minimum)

The fruit of this perennial tropical shrub contains capsicin and capsaicin, powerful rubefacients (local blood supply stimulants). Cayenne, also known as chili pepper, is a favorite carminative and appetite stimulant, considered useful in sluggish digestion. It has also been used as a stimulant, diaphoretic, and antiseptic.

There is evidence that cayenne is a mild adrenocortical stimulant which causes an increase in circulating cortisol and cortisone; this may account for claims that it is a stimulant. Cayenne may also increase fibrinolytic activity and thereby provide a measure of protection against thrombosis (blood clot formation).

512 Chinese Herbs

Hundreds of herbs are used in Chinese medicine and they are gradually being tested for effectiveness and safety by the Chinese and others using modern scientific methods. Many of them show promise and their use may become widespread. However, aside from ginseng, ma huang (desert tea), and a few others, Chinese herbs are still almost unknown in the West. Therefore, our discussion will focus on an important hazard associated with so-called Chinese herbal remedies in pill form.

Herbal remedies, both as whole herbs and as herbal extracts and mixtures, have been imported from Hong Kong, Taiwan, Singapore, and elsewhere in the Orient for decades with no particular hazards reported. However, since the early 1970s many cases of sickness and some deaths have been associated with the pills, many of which turn out to contain various powerful drugs such as phenylbutazone, aminopyrine, diuretics, tranquilizers, cortisone-type drugs, antibiotics, and common painkillers. It appears that some manufacturers have been cashing in on the American fascination with and preference for "organic" remedies by marketing shotgun mixtures of drugs as herbal remedies.[24]

These drugs are smuggled into the United States and sold in health food stores, specialty shops, by mail, and through other outlets. Typically, a few dozen pills are packaged in a cellophane bag or glass bottle and labeling or illustrations may suggest the pills help in arthritis and similar conditions. The pills have been found to contain not only the powerful and hazardous drugs but animal bones, horns, and shells, toxic heavy metals, insect parts, and rodent droppings.

Coltsfoot (Tussilago farfara)

The leaves and flowers of this small perennial herb have been used since ancient times for coughs and colds. "Tussilago" means cough dispeller, and this is what Galen, Pliny, and others recommended it for.

A thick decoction is drunk to soothe the mucus membranes and loosens mucus. The abundant mucilage and phytosterols (high molecular weight alcohols) are probably responsible for the beneficial effects. Smoking the herb or boiling it and inhaling the vapors is ineffective because the active components are destroyed.

Coltsfoot has been found to contain the pyrrolizidine alkaloid senkirkine, which has been shown to cause liver cancer in rats. It can no longer be considered safe.

Comfrey (Symphytum officinale)

The roots and leaves have been used for thousands of years as a vulnerary for all kinds of external wounds and internal ulcers. Comfrey contains large amounts of mucilage, which makes it an effective demulcent. More importantly, it contains allantoin, a reported stimulant of cell proliferation and growth. During World War I it was observed that maggot-infested wounds tended to heal faster than clean ones, and maggot therapy for open wounds became widespread. In 1935 allantoin from the maggots was reported to be responsible for the speedy healing, but more recent studies throw doubt on its efficacy.

Herbalists recommend a freshly crushed leaf as a poultice for abscesses, ulcers, and other open wounds. Sipping an infusion of the leaf or root is recommended to speed the healing of peptic ulcers.

Comfrey also contains vitamins A and C, as well as calcium, potassium, and other minerals. The tender young leaves are often used in salads and are a good source of protein. Reports of vitamin B-12 in comfrey are probably mistaken and due to traces of soil in the samples tested (bacteria in the soil produce the vitamin).

CAUTION
Reports indicate that comfrey may contain small amounts of pyrrolizidine alkaloids which are known to cause liver cancer in large amounts.[25] Internal use of comfrey should be avoided. External use is safe.

Desert Tea
(Ephedra vulgaris, E. sinica)

Also known as Mormon tea, ephedra, and ma huang (the Chinese name), this little twiggy bush has been used for at least 5,000 years by the Chinese

514   for colds, coughs, headaches, and other problems. An infusion of the twigs is drunk. It contains some tannic acid but tastes good if not boiled or steeped too long.

The active components are ephedrine and pseudo-ephedrine, potent adrenalin analogues, stimulants, and bronchial dilators widely used for asthma, hay fever, and emphysema. Tolerance develops in a few days and for further effect use of the herb or drug should be suspended for about a week. Some studies suggest that the American variety is devoid of active components.

CAUTION

An overdose may cause nervousness, insomnia, headache, heart palpitations, and nausea. Asthma is best treated with the guidance of a physician.

Devil's Claw
(Harpagophytum procumbens)

This is a tuberous annual which grows in the deserts of southern Africa. It blossoms with a large thorny seedpod that clings tenaciously to whatever might touch it, sometimes inflicting severe wounds—hence the name. The secondary tubers growing off the long, slender roots are used by natives and European settlers for many kinds of pains and disorders.

Devil's claw is now being heavily promoted as an arthritis remedy. Teas, tablets, and liquid extracts are sold in herb shops, health food stores, and chiropractors' offices, and by mail. The active ingredient, called harpagosid, is said to work by stimulating the digestive system, cleansing the blood, and strengthening the endocrine system.

CAUTION

While preliminary studies indicate an anti-inflammatory effect, too little research has been done to determine whether devil's claw is effective and safe. It can cause uterine contractions and may be hazardous in pregnancy. Devil's claw can reportedly reduce the insulin requirement in diabetes, so persons with the disorder should not use the herb without careful medical supervision.

Elder
(Sambucus mexicana, S. canadensis, S. nigra)

This large tree, also called wild elderberry, is indigenous to the western United States. The berries are almost black when ripe; they are juicy and apparently safe to eat, especially if cooked.

The bark, root, leaves, flowers, and young buds have long been used as laxative, diuretic, alterative, diaphoretic, expectorant, and emetic. The flowers go into elder flower water, which is used for skin blemishes. The active components appear to be the alkaloid sambucine, a purgative resin, and eldrin. Valeric acid is largely responsible for the aroma.

CAUTION
All parts of the elder trees, except the ripe berries, contain a glycoside which can produce hydrocyanic acid and cause cyanide poisoning. Large animals, including pigs, cattle, and sheep, have been killed by eating various parts of the tree. The berries are alleged to contain tyrosine, a nonessential amino acid which reacts dangerously with MAO inhibitors, and should not be consumed by persons taking these antidepressant drugs.

Elecampane (Inula helenium)

Appropriately known as wild sunflower, elecampane is one of the largest flowering herbaceous plants. Only the roots are used; they are unearthed in the fall, cut up, and dried.

Elecampane is used mainly as an expectorant, antiseptic, and tonic for colds, coughs, chronic bronchitis, and other respiratory problems. Up to half the dry weight of the root is inulin, a carbohydrate consisting of chains of fructose. As the root is chewed, it becomes aromatic and slightly bitter. It also contains helenin, a tasteless and odorless antiseptic, and alantcamphor, a pepperminty component perhaps responsible for the reported mucus-loosening effect.

516 Eucalyptus
(E. globulus, E. polybractea, others)

The new leaves of older branches, and their oils, are used to make a tea or vapor bath. It is used as an expectorant, mild stimulant, and antiseptic. The oil contains a terpene, a cymene, and a resin. It is a common ingredient in cough drops and syrups, but has never been proven effective.

CAUTION
Repeated large doses can irritate the kidneys, depress the respiratory center of the brain, and cause death by asphyxia.

Fenugreek
(Trigonella foenum-graecum)

The seeds of this annual herb were used by ancient Egyptians, Greeks, and Romans as a medicine, food, and spice. They contain large amounts of mucilage and the tea is said to make a good emollient for stomach and intestinal inflammation.

A good source of nutrients, fenugreek seeds contain proteins, choline, lecithin, iron, and trace minerals. Sprouted seeds are also used as a food.

Fenugreek has long been reputed to stimulate lactation and increase breast size even in nonlactating women. This has not been proven, but the seed does contain diosgenin, a steroidal sapogenin used in the commercial preparation of progestin (synthetic progesterone). Given this potential hormonal activity, it would be prudent to use fenugreek in moderation.

Flax, or Linseed
(Linum usitatissimum)

The crushed seeds contain large amounts of mucilage and make a good emollient, demulcent, and poultice. They have long been used for colds, coughs, and external and internal ulcers.

Foxglove (Digitalis purpurea)

The leaves of this little herb have been used for hundreds of years to make a heart-strengthening tea. Foxglove contains four important glycosides, three of which are cardiac stimulants. The most potent, digitoxin, is extremely poisonous and cumulative in its action. These glycosides are still mainstays in the treatment of congestive heart failure.

WARNING
Foxglove is a deadly poison; do not attempt to use it.

Garlic (Allium sativum)

Of all the herbal panaceas used and promoted over the centuries, garlic probably fulfills the most promises. This fascinating member of the lily family has been used since ancient times when Hippocrates, Galen, and others recommended it for various ailments. It is still widely used in herbal medicine and even more commonly as a food and condiment.

Unfortunately, scientific research on the pharmacology of garlic is in its infancy, so it is difficult to come to firm conclusions regarding its effects. But some good studies have been done, some of the active components have been isolated, and we can come to some tentative conclusions.

Allyn is an odorless, sulfur-containing amino acid in garlic. In the presence of the enzyme allinase, it breaks down to the highly reactive and odorous allicin. The mixing of allyn with allinase produces allicin, which accounts for the generation of odor during chopping.

Cooking easily destroys the allinase, but allyn is still slowly converted to allicin in the body. It is not yet clear just which of the many effects of garlic are due to allyn and its metabolites. Other active constituents are yet to be isolated and identified, but garlic may contain important prostaglandin-like substances which affect blood pressure.

Garlic for Cardiovascular Health This is perhaps the most active and most important area of research on garlic. Several studies have shown effects which would tend to prevent atherosclerosis and are generally regarded as favorable to circulatory health. In one experiment a group of healthy young volunteers ate large amounts of butter on bread with a meal. As expected, their serum cholesterol levels shot up within three hours. But if the juice of

518 large amounts (two ounces) of raw or boiled garlic was added to the same meal, the serum cholesterol rose much less.[26]

In another study six young men took two cloves a day for three weeks and otherwise maintained their same diets. After only three weeks their LDL-cholesterol levels had dropped signifiantly.[27]

People with advanced atherosclerosis need a high fibrinolytic (clot dissolving) activity in the blood to prevent the formation of small clots (thrombi) which could lodge in an already narrow artery of the heart or brain and cause a heart attack or stroke. In one group of heart attack survivors, 60 grams of garlic (about twenty cloves) every day increased fibrinolytic activity 100 percent in three weeks. This is a lot of garlic, but no bleeding tendency or other side effects were noticed.[28]

In another study, ten healthy adults ate lots of garlic for three months. Their fibrinolytic activity gradually increased. When they stopped the garlic, it decreased.

Other studies have shown dramatic protection of rabbits on very high cholesterol diets, which normally produce atherosclerotic plaques in their arteries. With garlic added, there is less of an increase in serum cholesterol and fats, as well as increased fibrinolytic activity and reduced plaque development in the aorta.

Garlic seems to decrease sludging of the blood, which is generally increased by fats in the diet. This is the tendency of red blood cells to clump and stack, which reduces oxygen delivery and waste removal. There is also some evidence that garlic can help prevent heart disease by lowering blood pressure, apparently by dilating arterioles.

Garlic for Other Purposes Some bacteria and fungi are inhibited or killed by garlic juice, at least in the test tube, and possibly in humans. Albert Schweitzer is said to have used it with some success against typhus and cholera. Some people insist that garlic prevents traveler's diarrhea.

Some herbalists recommend that crushed garlic or garlic juice be spread on athlete's foot, a fungus infection, once a day. It is left on for about thirty minutes, then washed off. But the potent fresh juice can be very irritating and painful to the raw skin, and it could aggravate the condition. A better remedy, tolnaftate, is effective, yet very mild and nonirritating.

For the same reason, garlic juice is not recommended for minor cuts and scratches, in spite of the fact it was used in World War I as an antiseptic. It can burn and blister the skin. Topical antiseptics generally aren't necessary for minor wounds anyway.

Garlic is widely used to treat and prevent colds, influenza, and bronchitis. Soups and teas with garlic, ginger, and cayenne pepper help loosen mucus, clear the airways and sinuses, and ease breathing. Some claim the garlic helps prevent secondary bacterial infections. This has not been proven, but deserves investigation.

During flu epidemics, the Soviet government encourages the public to use garlic to stay healthy. There is no evidence that it has antivirus activity, but few studies have been done.

Garlic may increase the absorption of dietary thiamin. This may account for the low incidence of beriberi in areas where thiamin intake is small but garlic is eaten every day.

There have been a few reports of garlic inhibiting cancer development in mice, but their signifiance for humans is not clear.

Nutritionally, garlic is a good source of selenium and perhaps other trace minerals. It is also considered an aid to digestion, especially of protein. It stimulates stomach acid secretion and possibly pepsin.

Garlic has long been used to control gastrointestinal worms in humans and animals. Pinworms, tapeworms, and roundworms are apparently vulnerable to the allicin or other component.

Garlic is a diuretic and sweat promoter, perhaps about as potent as coffee. And like coffee, garlic is a stimulant. Some laborers and carpenters take garlic powder in capsules, instead of coffee or amphetamines, to increase speed and stamina.

That it is a general stimulant may be responsible for the aphrodisiac effect claimed by some. It is interesting that many Buddhist, Hindu, and yoga sects prohibit even small amounts of garlic, on the ground that it stimulates sexual appetite.

Garlic-sliver suppositories are sometimes recommended by naturopaths for hemorrhoids, but this can be irritating and painful and reportedly can induce a fever.

Some writers claim garlic is useful in both diabetes and hypoglycemia. This is highly unlikely, though it may have effects on blood sugar worth investigating.

So much for the wonders of garlic. At the very least, it is worthy of much more study. Considering its numerous effects, it could have a dozen or more pharmacologically active and useful substances. It may be premature to recommend daily garlic for cardiovascular health, since more studies are needed, but the potential benefits are signifiant and the hazards small.

The Hazards of Garlic Excessive consumption of garlic can burn the mouth, irritate the stomach, and cause hyperacidity, "heartburn," indigestion, and diarrhea. It might aggravate ulcers in some people, but this has not been established.

The combination of large doses of garlic with aspirin or anticoagulants could theoretically cause bleeding problems. No such cases have been reported, but caution is advised.

Finally, the odor of the breath and the body must be considered. It is said that vampires fear only three things, the sun, the Holy Cross, and garlic. Small particles can lodge between the teeth, and as the allyn is con-

520 verted to allicin over the next few hours, the strong odor is released. Furthermore, the aromatic metabolites of allicin are thrown off by the lungs, imparting an odor to the breath from which most people shrink. Body odor is affected by garlic metabolites, such as hydrogen sulfide and acreolein, released in the sweat.

Little can be done about these odors, but rinsing the mouth and chewing parsley help a little. Kyolic is an aged garlic extract almost free of odor, but it is quite expensive. Perhaps if everyone ate a little garlic, the smell would not bother anyone. This seems to be the situation in Italy, Spain, and some other countries.

Gentian (Gentiana lutea)

The very bitter root of this three-foot-high herb is a favorite of herbalists for treating liver diseases and as a febrifuge, emmenagogue, anthelmintic, antiseptic, and appetite stimulant. It is considered a general tonic of special value in treating exhaustion from chronic disease and in all cases of general debility. Herablists like to combine it with purgatives to moderate their debilitating effects.

So far, the only proven effects of gentian are a slight anti-inflammatory effect and an increase in salivary and gastric activity, probably due to bitter glycosides. It is the main ingredient in Angostura Bitters and is especially popular in Europe as a flavoring for alcoholic beverages. It may also be effective against some worms and microbes. Its use in liver disease appears to be without foundation; nor is there evidence of a stimulant or "tonic" effect.

Ginseng
(Panax quinquefolius, P. ginseng, others)

For thousands of years ginseng root has been considered an effective tonic, rejuvenator, and vitalizer. It is said to work subtly to improve hormonal and nervous functions, mood, memory, sexual response, and resistance to disease.

The earliest use of ginseng was probably as a food. The root is usually substantial enough to be nourishing and it contains starch, sugars, vitamins, and minerals. Use as a food would naturally have led to discovery of its pharmacological properties.

The name of this short perennial is derived from the Chinese for "essence of man." Until recently, the closer the shape of the root resembled a person, the higher the price it commanded. This superstition is probably of prehistoric origin.

Is It Really Ginseng? A major problem with ginseng has been the lack of agreement on exactly what it is. Some experts and ginseng entrepreneurs believe the whole Araliaceae (Ginseng) family can legitimately be called ginseng. This includes about 900 different plants in seventy genera, such as Panax, Acanthopanax, Aralia, Oplopanax, and Kalopanax. There is wild and cultivated, sun-dried and dryer-dried, bulk root, powder, solution, tincture, chewing gum, candy, soda pop, tea bags, and even cigarettes of ginseng whole root, rhizome, root bark, and root peelings of various species from China, Korea, Japan, and North America. This enormous variability and the inadequate or nonexistent labelling make it almost impossible for the average consumer to know what a product contains and how pharmacologically active it is. Even the concentrated extracts have no standardized assay label.

Other experts think only certain species of the genus *Panax* should be called ginseng. The only universally accepted and unquestioned ginseng species are *Panax quinquefolius* (American ginseng), *P. ginseng* (Oriental ginseng), and several varieties of *P. pseudo-ginseng* of Asia. The purists are opposed to the marketing of *Acanthopanax senticosus* (eleuthero or "Siberian ginseng") and others as ginseng, but they are fighting a losing battle. Even wild rhubarb (*Rumex hymenosepalus*), which belongs to the buckwheat family, has been called wild red American ginseng or desert ginseng. Such marketing ploys further confuse matters and deceive consumers.

What Does Ginseng Really Do? In spite of ginseng's ancient reputation as a panacea, there are serious doubts about its alleged health benefits. There is no doubt that real ginsengs (the ones listed above) contain active glycosides; some of them mimic cortisone, some mimic estrogen, and some are central nervous system stimulants. The pleasant stimulation and mood elevation can give an ill person a psychological boost and it is speculated that the actions of the hormonelike glycosides may help the body adapt to the stress of illness.

However, it should not be surprising that regular heavy consumption of the potent substances in ginseng can lead to adverse effects. These include hypertension, nervousness, insomnia, headaches, diarrhea, and rashes. Sudden withdrawal can provoke a hypotensive (low blood pressure) crisis. These effects mimic cortisone overdose. There is also concern about the estrogen activity in ginseng, which can cause swollen and painful breasts and possibly decreased libido in men and women, and menstrual irregularities in women.[29]

522

Ginger (Zingiber officinale)

Ginger root conains a variety of volatile oils and alcohols and a soft acrid resin. It stimulates saliva and gastric juice secretion and other digestive functions, and is considered useful in flatulence, dyspepsia, and diarrhea. Ginger tea is also said to promote menstruation, and to loosen mucus in colds and other respiratory ailments. Pregnant women should limit their use of ginger.

Goldenseal (Hydrastis canadensis)

A perennial that grows about a foot in height, goldenseal has a rootstock marked with seal-like depressions where the annual stems have fallen away.

Goldenseal root infusions have long been used by American Indian tribes as a vulnerary, eyewash, mouthwash, insect repellent, and for other purposes. Herbalists recommend it for acne, eczema, sinus and nasal inflammation, poor appetite, indigestion, nausea, worms, constipation, hemorrhoids, peptic ulcers, uterine congestion during menstruation, morning sickness during pregnancy, and all conditions involving inflamed or ulcerated mucous membranes or skin.

The active components are the alkaloids hydrastine and berberine. Hydrastine is closely related to papaverine and other minor opium alkaloids. Studies show that it tends to depress smooth muscle tone, casting doubt on its utility as an emmenagogue. It has been used as an internal astringent, and is an ingredient in commercial eyedrops. Berberine is a yellow, bitter alkaloid with effects and uses similar to those of hydrastine.

CAUTION
Large doses may cause diarrhea, convulsions, abortion, and hypertension. Prolonged use may lead to the accumulation of the alkaloids, which can cause digestive dysfunctions and other toxic symptoms. Internal use should be avoided by pregnant women and persons with hypertension.

Henbane (Hyoscyamus niger)

This is an annual herbaceous plant of the nightshade family. Like belladonna and other relatives, henbane contains atropine and scopalamine, which depress the parasympathetic nervous system. Henbane has long been used as an antispasmodic, antisecretory, and sedative.

WARNING
An overdose can cause death by respiratory depression. Do not attempt to use henbane.

Hops (Humulus lupulus)

The female fruit pistils (hop cones) have been used for many centuries as a sedative, pain reliever, sex depressant, poultice, and bitter preservative for beer. Hops tea is made by steeping about a tablespoon of the herb in a pint of hot water for about ten minutes. The taste is very bitter.

     Hops contains lupulon, a bitter antibiotic, and lupulin, a bitter sedative related to THC, the active component of marijuana. Hops are sometimes stuffed into pillows to calm the nerves and promote sleep. It is not clear whether lupulin is actually absorbed this way or if the placebo effect is at work.

CAUTION
Hops tea is strongly sedative, and it may decrease libido. A hangover of drowsiness may occur.

Juniper (Juniper communis)

Juniper berry tea is used as a urinary antiseptic and diuretic. It contains a variety of oils and tannin.

CAUTION
Juniper can irritate the gastrointestinal tract and possibly injure the kidneys. There are safer antiseptics and diuretics.

Lady's Slipper (Cyripedium pubescens)

Also known as American valerian, the dried root of this aromatic perennial orchid was a favorite of the American Indians and pioneers. An infusion was used for anxiety and insomnia, and as an antispasmodic. The active components are unknown, but this mild sedative is apparently safe for use in moderation.

Lavender (Lavandula vera)

The aromatic flowers of this small shrub are used in a tea to allay nausea and as a stimulant. The volatile oils and alcohols are used in the perfume industry.

CAUTION
An excess of the tea may cause cramping and colic. An excess of the oil can cause convulsions and death.

Licorice (Glycyrrhiza glabra)

The root of this perennial herb contains up to 20 percent glycyrrhizin, a glycoside fifty times as sweet as sucrose. Licorice root tea is an old favorite and the extract is a common ingredient in cough drops and syrups as a flavoring, demulcent, mild expectorant, and mild anti-inflammatory.

Licorice root also contains carbenoxolone, which promotes ulcer healing. Licorice extract helps heal ulcers, but the treatment is not practical in most cases because of the danger of edema, increased blood pressure, and abnormal heart activity due to sodium retention and potassium depletion. Kidney damage may also occur.

CAUTION
Licorice root, candy, and extract should be avoided by those with heart problems, hypertension, obesity, kidney problems, or a difficult pregnancy. As little as two or three ounces of candy a day is potentially harmful. Children should be discouraged from heavy consumption.

Lily of the Valley (Convallaria majalis)

Also called May lily, herbalists recommend a tea of the root for heart disorders and neurological problems.

WARNING
Lily of the valley contains covallatoxin and other toxic cardiac glycosides which can cause heart dysfunction and death.

Lobelia (Lobelia inflata)

Also known as Indian tobacco and wild tobacco, the seeds, leaves, and bark of this short, erect annual are used by herbalists as an expectorant, a diaphoretic, a respiratory stimulant in asthma, and an emetic. Lobeline and lobelic acid are the active components.

WARNING
Lobelia is poisonous, with effects similar to those of nicotine, including nausea, vomiting, profuse sweating, low body temperature, rapid and feeble pulse, coma, and death.

Mandrake (Atropa mandragora)

The large parsniplike roots were used by the ancients as an anodyne, sedative, anticonvulsant, and anesthetic for surgery. The fresh root is a powerful emetic and purgative.

WARNING
The atropine-like alkaloids in mandrake can cause severe poisoning and death. Do not attempt to use this plant.

526 Mayapple (Podophyllum pelatum)

Also known as American mandrake, American Indians and pioneers used the root as a purgative, liver stimulant, and bile stimulant. The resin was used to clear warts. The active components are podophyllotoxin and podophylloresin, both powerful purgatives.

WARNING
Mayapple leaves are a deadly poison. The root is a drastic purgative even in moderate doses. Large doses may cause nausea, vomiting, and fatal inflammation of the gastrointestinal tract. As little as one-third of a gram can be fatal. Even leaving podophyllum ointment on a venereal wart can be lethal.

Mistletoes
(Viscum flavescens and V. album)

These are American and European mistletoe, respectively, evergreen parasites of deciduous trees. Herbalists and Indians used the tea or powdered leaves as a nervine, antispasmodic, anticonvulsant, and sedative for epilepsy, delirium, hysteria, neuralgia, and other nerve-related ailments. Mendocino County (California) tribes used large doses to induce abortion. Mistletoes contain various toxic amines under study for possible anticancer activity.

WARNING
Mistletoes contain the toxic amines tyramine and phenylethylamine, and may cause miscarriage, convulsions, shock, and cardiac arrest. Some actions are similar to those of cobra venom.

Mullein (Verbascum thapsus)

The leaves and flowers of this herb are an old favorite for treating colds, coughs, asthma, and other respiratory ailments. An infusion is taken as tea once or twice a day. A mullein vapor bath is reputed to help clear the airways. It is considered a demulcent and expectorant and a weak astringent.

The active components are mucilage, soponins, a gum, hesperidin and other flavonoids, and a little tannin. Only the mucilage is abundant enough to have a significant effect.

Myrrh
(Balsamodendron myrrh, others)

The gum myrrh tree is a bush that grows on the dry and barren Red Sea coast. The resin of the stems has been used since biblical times as an antiseptic and mouthwash for sores and ulcers, as an expectorant and emmenagogue, and as a tonic in dyspepsia to increase appetite and gastric juice secretion. The oil of myrrh is said to be a useful styptic for canker sores.

Nux Vomica (Strychnos nux-vomica)

The dried seed of the nux tree was widely used in old herbal medicine and is still used by some herbalists and homeopaths. The main uses were as an appetite stimulant and general tonic.

WARNING
Nux vomica is the original source of strychnine, a deadly nerve poison. It is worthless except as a rat poison.

Oleander (Nerium indicum)

Some herbalists recommend oleander leaf tea for congestive heart failure on the basis of its diuretic action and the presence of cardiac glycosides (similar in action to digitalis) such as oleandrin. This is a serious mistake; a single leaf can kill an adult.

WARNING
Oleander is a deadly poison. Many deaths have occurred when used as a tea and when consumed accidently, such as when the sticks are used to roast hot

528 dogs, marshmallows, and other foods. If ingestion is suspected induce vomiting with a finger down the throat or warm salt water. See a physician right away.

Orris Root
(Iridis germanica, I. versicolor, others)

Also known as blueflag, this beautiful ornamental iris has been used as a purgative since ancient times. The juice of the fresh root is a powerful cathartic and was used to promote dehydration in congestive heart failure and other ailments.

CAUTION
Orris root is a powerful purgative and can cause severe cramping and diarrhea.

Passion Flower (Passiflora incarnata)

This is a deciduous perennial vine with flesh-colored flowers. An infusion of the dried herb (leaves and stems, not flowers) is used as a sedative, antispasmodic, and anodyne.

While passion flower is generally considered a sedative and is used as an ingredient (considered not safe and effective by the FDA) in some commercial sleep aids, it may also contain hallucinatory harmine alkaloids during part of the year, and some people report a stimulant effect.

Pennyroyal (Mentha pulegium)

This species of mint was used by the ancients as a flea repellent, digestive stimulant, emmenagogue, and expectorant. It has a powerful but basically pleasant taste. An infusion of the leaves makes a tea recommended to help loosen phlegm in bronchitis, asthma, coughs, and colds. Crushed leaves rubbed on the skin help repel insects. Some people hang sprigs in every room to keep the bugs out.

CAUTION

Pennyroyal should not be used by pregnant women. Oil of pennyroyal should not be taken internally. It has caused death (by kidney and liver damage) in women using it to induce abortion.

Peppermint (Mentha piperita)

Peppermint leaf tea is a tasty, refreshing drink, hot or cold, but is not likely to be of much help in insanity, cholera, heart disease, or any of the other serious diseases some herbalists claim it can cure. It may, however, have value as an antispasmodic to relieve gastrointestinal and gallbladder pain. It is also useful to disguise the taste of bitter medicines.

Peppermint oil's highly penetrating, burning, camphorecious smell and taste improve with age, even for ten to fifteen years. The main components of peppermint tea and oil are menthol, methyl acetate, isovalerate, and jasmone. It also has small amounts of tannic acid.

Periwinkle
(Vinca major, V. minor, V. rosea)

A tropical and subtropical perennial that grows about two and a half feet high, periwinkle is often cultivated as an ornamental. The bitter, astringent leaves have long been used around the world as an emetic, purgative, diaphoretic, gargle for sore throat, eyewash, and treatment for diabetes.

Periwinkle's real importance was discovered by scientists in the 1950s while testing the leaf tea on animals for hypoglycemic (blood-sugar lowering) effects. None was found and periwinkle's use in diabetes could not be supported, but leukopenia (decreased white blood cells) was noticed in the animals. It was decided to try the herb on leukemic mice. The effect was profound: the active components, vincristine and vinblastine, were found to arrest mitosis in metaphase, stopping cell division, and they became widely used in cancer. They are still among the most effective anticancer drugs and are often used in combination with other drugs.

The roots contain few of these anticancer elements but do have high concentrations of reserpine, more even than *Rauwolfia serpentina* (Indian snakeroot).

WARNING
Periwinkle may cause nausea, vomiting, diarrhea, constipation, hair loss, muscle pain, malaise, leukopenia, thrombophlebitis, and liver and kidney damage. Neurological symptoms may last for months after stopping prolonged use.

Pleurisy Root (Asclepias tuberosa)

The root of this deciduous perennial is an old American Indian favorite for respiratory problems. It is used as an expectorant and antispasmodic. The active components are glycosides and several resins.

CAUTION
Large doses may cause vomiting and diarrhea.

Pokeweed (Phytolacca americana)

This perennial grows to about nine feet with white to pink flowers, clusters of dark purple berries, and extensive gnarled roots. It has been used as an antirheumatic, emetic, and purgative. Externally, it has been used as an ointment for scabies, tinea (athlete's foot), and acne. Pokeweed contains the alkaloid phytolaccine, phytolaccic acid, resins, and tannic acid. The fresh young leaves are used as a salad green, but this is a risky business.

WARNING
All parts of the pokeweed plant are toxic and may cause diarrhea, nausea, vomiting, dizziness, and headache. The root is the most poisonous part of the plant, but other parts are also toxic, especially in mature and older plants. Even experienced users have been poisoned by the leaves.[30]

Red Clover (Trifolium pratense)

An infusion of the flowers makes a pleasant tea, but it cannot cure cancer, leprosy, syphilis, or any of the other serious diseases Jason Winters, Jethro Kloss, and other herbalists claim it is effective against. No serious side effects have been reported. Red clover seems to have little or no pharmacologic activity.

Rue (Ruta graveolens)

The leaves and flowers of this herb have been used for thousands of years, especially for gastrointestinal cramps, spasms, headaches, anxiety, and painful menstruation, and as a poultice for joint pain. The herb is either chewed or steeped in hot water for drinking, but never boiled.

The active components include xanthotoxin and various alkaloids which apparently have some antispasmodic activity and may act as a mild sedative. Long term or excessive use should be considered potentially hazardous.

Sage (Salvia officinalis)

This is a perennial herb with grayish-green leaves much used in cooking and herbal medicine. An infusion is considered a mild sedative, expectorant, and antispasmodic. A more concentrated solution is used as a gargle for sore throat and as a mouthwash. When used in cooking sage slows bacterial growth and rancidity.

The active components include camphor, various alcohols, flavonoids, a resin, and an estrogen analogue. It also contains thujone, a nerve toxin.

CAUTION
Sage has a reputation among herbalists for quelling "excessive sexual desires." The estrogen analogue may be an effective libido depressant. Prolonged or heavy use may cause nerve damage. Moderation is recommended.

532

Sarsaparilla, Jamaican (Smilax ornata)

The powdered root or fluid extract of the root is used as a diuretic, diaphoretic, alterative, eyewash, and carminative. Active components include several saponins and glycosides. Herbalists recommend it in rheumatism, gout, fevers, and venereal disease in infants, but there is no evidence of effectiveness. Little is known about possible adverse effects from excessive use. Caution is advised.

Sassafras (Sassafras albidum)

The bark and root of the sassafras tree are used as a flavoring, carminative, diaphoretic, alterative, and diuretic. The active components are glycosides and saponins. It is generally used as a decoction, about an ounce of bark to a quart of water.

Sassafras oil contains nerve toxins and safrole, a phenolic ether long used to flavor root beer, confections, and drugs. But in 1960 safrole was found to have carcinogenic activity and it is no longer used as a flavoring. Nevertheless, sassafras is still available in many herb stores.

CAUTION

Sassafras contains a known carcinogen and various toxins. The tannins present can greatly decrease the absorption of therapeutic drugs.

Saw Palmetto
(Serenoa repens, S. serrulata)

This small fan palm, also called sabal, grows in sandy soil across the American south, especially in Texas and Florida, where it is grown commercially. Its ripe berries were once used as a diuretic and a treatment for enlarged prostate, but decades of use have proved it ineffective for the latter purpose. The herb has recently been resurrected as a stimulant to breast enlargement, sperm production, and libido. Estrogenlike components called sitosterols are said to be responsible for the effects, but this is impossible because estrogen, while it may enlarge breasts, would likely decrease sperm production and libido.

In any case, it has been established that the berries contain far too little estrogenic activity to have any effect whatsoever. Saw palmetto berries have no therapeutic value. Claims to the contrary are simply part of modern, commercial herbal mythology.

Scullcap (Scutellaria lateriflora)

This deciduous perennial is a an alleged sedative, long used by herbalists for insomnia, anxiety, narcotic withdrawal sickness, neuralgia, and "undue sexual desire." Scullcap contains several glycosides and some tannin, but very little pharmacologic activity. It is apparently more a placebo than anything else.

Senna (Cassia acutifolia)

The dried leaves and pods of this small shrub were used by ancient Arab physicians as a purgative and anthelmintic. It is still used by modern herbalists, often combined with cloves, ginger, or licorice to disguise the nauseating taste. The active component, cathartic acid, works by local irritation of the colon.

CAUTION
May cause vomiting, cramping, and severe diarrhea.

Slippery Elm (Ulmus fulva)

Also known as red elm, this large, common deciduous tree has been a favorite of herbalists since the American Indians taught the pioneers how to use it. The dried inner bark contains large amounts of mucilage and starch, and is an effective demulcent and emollient. It is soothing in coughs and sore throats and is well tolerated as a food when nothing else is, such as in severe ulcers, spastic colon, and food allergies. It is sometimes used as a baby food flavored with cinnamon, nutmeg, and other spices. It is added to some throat lozenges as a demulcent, and is very helpful for those with dry mouth due to disease or medication.

Snakeroot, Indian
(Rauwolfia serpentina)

The dried root of this deciduous perennial herb has been used for several thousand years in India as a tranquilizer and sedative. It is usually used to make a tea, but is sometimes chewed or smoked. The active component, reserpine, is used in medicine as a tranquilizer and hypotensive agent.

WARNING

May cause depression, sexual dysfunction, ulcers, and breast cancer.

Tansy (Tanacetum vulgare)

The leaves and flowers of this herb have been used by herbalists as an emmenagogue, digestive tonic, and anthelmintic. It contains tanacetin, tannic acid, and thujone, a brain poison. Extracts used for flavoring are (or should be) free of the toxins.

CAUTION

Tansy may cause convulsions and abortion. Fatal poisonings have occurred.

Tonka bean (Dipteryx odorata)

Also known as Mexican coumarin, the bean of this tall tree of the pea family smells very much like the bean of the much more expensive vanilla, another native of Mexico. Tonka bean extract was used for many years as a flavoring in chocolate products, but it was banned in 1954 when it was found to cause damage to the liver and other organs of rats. Now the bean and its extract are being passed off as vanilla to tourists in Mexico. To be on the safe side, buy only whole beans, not liquid extracts. Vanilla beans are long and thin like a pencil and have small, round seeds. The whole pod is ground up and used. Tonka beans are oval, about 3 by 5 inches and contain one large seed.

Uva-Ursi (Arctostaphylos uva-ursi)

Also known as bearberry, this small evergreen shrub is related to the common manzanita (A. glauca) shrub.

A tea of the leaves is used as a diuretic and urinary antiseptic. The berries are not used.

The active components are the glycoside arbutin, which is a diuretic and urinary antiseptic, and gallic and tannic acids, which are powerful astringents. The herb is worthless in diabetes, kidney disease, and gonorrhea, Jethro Kloss and other herbalists to the contrary.

CAUTION

The tannic acid content is so high that uva-ursi is sometimes used for tanning leather.

Valerian (Valeriana officinalis)

This tall perennial herb with white or red flowers was also known as all-heal since Galen, who held it in high esteem as a sedative, anodyne, and antispasmodic. Not to be confused with American valerian (lady's slipper), valerian was much used in Britain in World War II to help decrease the stress caused by nighttime bombing raids on the cities.

Active components include the alkaloids valerianine and chatinine. The powerful, sweetish odor is due to valerianic acid. Commercial preparations and even home-made teas are often without effect because the sedative components are easily deactivated by prolonged healing or storage.

CAUTION

May cause excessive sedation, stupor, hangover.

Wintergreen (Gaultheria procumbens)

This small, creeping, aromatic, evergreen shrub was a favorite of the American Indians and is still widely used. The leaf contains methyl salicylate and

536

is used to make a tea for pain relief, especially for headache, neuralgia, and arthritis. Oil of wintergreen is sometimes applied topically for aching joints. Though sometimes effective, it may cause severe irritation and allergic reaction. The synthetic oil of wintergreen with methyl salicylate is less likely to provoke an allergic reaction. Wintergreen is also used as a flavoring agent.

CAUTION
Oil of wintergreen has caused death by gastric hemorrhage and should not be taken internally. The tea can cause gastric bleeding and should be used in moderation (and not at all by those with ulcers).

Wormwood (Artemisia absinthium)

This short perennial herb has been used since ancient times to expel worms. All parts of wormwood are very bitter. The infamous alcoholic drink, absinthe, was made from wormwood along with anise, licorice, peppermint, and other flavoring herbs. It was first used as a digestive aid, but its toxicity has caused it to be banned in most countries. It causes brain damage which results in "absinthe epilepsy." Vincent van Gogh, who cut off his ear and mailed it to a friend and later killed himself, is believed by some to have been a wormwood addict.

Wormwood contains thujone (a nerve toxin), aromatic oils, and various bitter compounds.

WARNING
Wormwood can cause brain damage and is not useful for any purpose.

Yellow Dock (Rumex crispus)

This is a perennial herb that grows to about five feet and has yellow to green flowers. The American Indians and pioneers used the roots and leaves for cuts, sores, external ulcers, and various skin diseases. Herbalists now use the root as a digestive aid and mild laxative.

CAUTION
Yellow dock contains chrysarobin, which can cause kidney damage and gastroenteritis if used excessively.

Yerba Santa (Eriodyction glutinosum)

The bitter leaves of this herb were very much used by all the tribes of Mendocino County, California. The tea is said to be an effective expectorant in colds, bronchitis, and other respiratory problems. It contains a bitter resin, a volatile oil, and tannic acid, and it should be used in moderation.

Yucca
(Yucca aloifolia, Y. brevifolia, others)

Several species of the genus Yucca grow wild and are cultivated in North America. Some are attractive and useful in landscaping, but their use as a medicine is very recent. Common yuccas—such as dagger plant, Joshua tree, our-Lord's-candle, and soapweed—all contain numerous saponins, which have been much studied as possible starting materials for the synthesis of cortisone and other steroids. Better sources have been found, but yuccas have not faded from the scene.

Not a traditional herbal remedy, the commercial boom for yuccas started in 1975 after an article titled "Yucca Plant Saponins in the Management of Arthritis" was published in the *Journal of Applied Nutrition*. The article concluded that a "saponin extract of the desert yucca plant" was a safe and effective remedy for various types of arthritis.

Unfortunately, the study was deficient in many ways: it did not distinguish between rheumatoid arthiritis and osteoarthritis; other medications were continued and not controlled for; the results reported were based on subjective responses, not physical evidence; neither the species of yucca nor the part of the plant used was specified; the method of preparation of the product tested was not described; and there was no evidence that the different batches used were the same. It is no wonder that many nutritionists consider the journal's standards of publication to be well below par.

The claims made for yucca are based on pseudoscience, not science. We suggest that you save your money and not let yourself be diverted from proper treatment; irreversible joint damage could result.

4

Recreational Drugs

Since prehistoric times people have been eating, drinking, smoking, snorting, and taking rectally various plant potions and brews not for therapeutic purposes but for group ritual, inspiration, insight, stimulation, sedation, and pleasure. Here we discuss some of the most commonly used and abused nontherapeutic drugs. The focus is on the physiological effects, health hazards, and means of combating abuse.[31]

Alcohol

Ethyl alcohol (ethanol) was independently discovered many times by accidental fermentation of fruit juices and grains. In some cultures alcoholic beverages have been used for thousands of years as a palliative or sedative in illness, a crude anesthetic for bone setting or surgery, and a tasty, fairly nutritious drink. Some wines and beers have substantial amounts of iron, chromium, and other essential minerals. They also provide calories from the carbohydrates they contain as well as from the alcohol itself.

But the most important use of alcohol is as a psychoactive drug. In small amounts it commonly reduces inhibitions and promotes social interactions. There is usually an easing of worry and anxiety and a feeling of elation. But as the blood level of alcohol increases there is, progressively, incoordination, slowing of the reflexes, slurring of speech, dizziness, impairment of memory and judgment, lack of self-control, confusion, inability to walk, loss of bladder control, vomiting, loss of consciousness, coma, and death. Drinking can also cause a hangover the next day with a throbbing headache, dizziness, nausea, stomach upset, and thirst.

538

Best Bets
To Prevent and Treat a Hangover

Eat before drinking and sip slowly; don't gulp. The faster you drink and the more you drink, the more likely you are to experience a hangover.

Drink water or juice to replace fluid lost in alcohol-stimulated urination.

Red wines, dark beers, and whiskeys are believed to be more likely to cause a hangover than light spirits (vodka, gin) and light beers and wine, but this theory has not been proven.

If you do wake up with a hangover, drink some water or juice slowly; try an alternating hot-cold shower and have a small breakfast. Aspirin may relieve your headache, but it is not recommended if you have an upset stomach or are prone to ulcers. Acetaminophen is widely considered the best medicine for a hangover headache.

Alcohol Abuse

Alcohol abuse is an enormous health problem in the United States and dozens of other countries. The cost in lives, limbs, and property is staggering. In brief summary, alcohol addiction and other alcohol abuse cause the following serious problems.

More than 25,000 deaths a year (in the U.S.) and far more injuries are caused by drinking drivers, whether drunk or not. The combination of increased self-confidence, poor judgment, and impaired reflexes is deadly. Studies have shown that even one drink can significantly impair driving ability. Two drinks can impair ability by about one-third. The National Safety Council recommends that a person **wait one hour for every drink consumed before driving.** Coffee does not speed alcohol metabolism and sobering up.

Brain damage and premature senility are common in alcoholics. The damage is so severe that the brains of long-term alcoholics are unfit for use in anatomy classes. Some experts believe alcohol causes sludging of the blood with sticky red cells adhering to each other and clogging brain capillaries. The nearby brain cells are deprived of oxygen and nutrients and they die. It may be that every episode of moderate to heavy drinking causes the death of hundreds or thousands of irreplaceable brain cells. This has not been proven, but serious intellectual impairment seems to be at least as common as liver damage, even in young drinkers. Since almost half of America's teen-

540 Blood Alcohol Levels

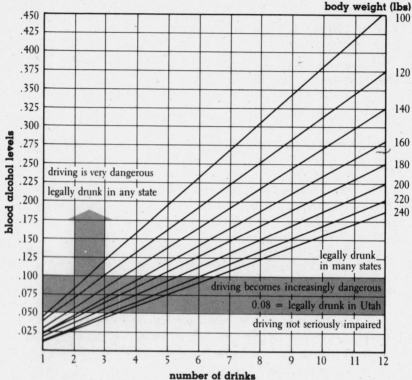

body weight (lbs)

1 drink = 1 oz of 100 proof liquor or 12 oz of beer

Adapted from Kenneth L. Jones, Louis W. Shainberg, and Curtis O. Byer, *Drugs and Alcohol*, New York, Harper & Row, 1973.

agers become confirmed drinkers by age twenty, the magnitude of the problem is clearly significant. Death and brain damage can also be caused by mixing alcohol with other drugs, especially sedatives, tranquilizers, and narcotics.

Birth defects, the "fetal alcohol syndrome," can be caused by drinking during pregnancy. The syndrome includes small body, head, eyes, and ears; failure to thrive; heart and kidney defects; brain damage and intellectual impairment; and poorly developed limbs, fingers, and genitals. It is estimated that in the United States several thousand infants, perhaps 1 percent of those exposed to alcohol in the womb, are born each year with some or all the defects. There is disagreement about how much alcohol can produce the syndrome, but it is clear that alcoholism is much riskier than occasional binge drinking. While it has not been proven that light drinking (the equivalent of less than two beers a day) causes defects, some authorities neverthe-less recommend abstention from all alcohol from conception through lactation.

Malnutrition is often caused by heavy drinking. Some alcoholics get half of their total calories from alcohol itself and most of the rest from the protein- and vitamin-poor carbohydrate of the drinks. Besides replacing nutrient-rich foods and contributing to obesity, alcohol increases the requirement, while reducing the intake, of protein, thiamin, folic acid, magnesium, potassium, zinc, and possibly vitamin C, calcium, vitamin A, and other nutrients.

Liver disease, including fatty liver, alcoholic hepatitis, and often-fatal liver cirrhosis, are notorious results of alcoholism.

Homicide, suicide, child beating, and other violent crimes are often asso-ciated with drinking.

Heart disease and heart failure are common in alcoholism, not just because of malnutrition but because of direct poisoning of the heart muscles, and abnormal function that does not respond to nutritional therapy unless al-cohol is withdrawn.

Skeletal muscle poisoning also occurs and may cause general weakness, muscle tenderness, cramping, and chemical evidence in the urine of muscle breakdown. This, of course, makes it more difficult to lose fat if you are obese or to stay fit if you are not.

Cancer of the mouth, esophagous, pancreas, and possibly breast are promot-ed by alcohol. The cancer risks of smoking are increased by drinking.

Sexual impotence is frequent among alcoholic men apparently because of direct damage to the nerves of the penis and brain, and because of liver damage that results in lower testosterone and higher estrogen levels.

Are Alcoholics Born or Made?

Some studies indicate an inherited tendency to become alcoholic. Men raised by foster parents are much more likely to become alcoholics if their natural fathers are. And identical twins raised by different foster parents tend to have similar drinking habits. However, there is no clear familial pattern and apparently no one is immune to alcohol abuse and addiction. Social, psychological, and environmental factors which tend to encourage alcohol abuse include the following factors.

Easy availability of alcohol and social encouragement to drink, including heavy advertising, parental example, and peer pressure, promote drinking. In countries like France where even children drink wine alcoholism is a monumental problem.

Family problems and other emotional stresses often trigger excessive drinking and alcoholism.

Ignorance of the dangers of alcohol can lead to its abuse. Since most Americans do drink, all youngsters should be made aware of all the hazards involved long before they start drinking.

Malnutrition may promote alcohol abuse. Some studies suggest that rats deficient in one or more B vitamins chose dilute alcohol rather than water, whereas rats on adequate diets chose pure water. However, there is no evidence of this in humans.

Treatment of Alcoholism

Treatment is essential or the alcoholic will likely end up in a mental hospital, a jail, or an early grave. The following are useful methods. Their success is strongly dependent on an acknowledgment of the problem and a determination to solve it.

Good nutrition, including lots of protein and vitamin and mineral supplementation, is essential to minimizing the damage done to the liver, brain, and muscles by alcohol. It may even decrease the urge to drink somewhat.

Alcoholics Anonymous, with nearly 30,000 local groups of helpful ex-problem drinkers, has helped millions of alcoholics go on the wagon for long periods, even for life. The approach is based on group support, self-understanding, and religious (nondenominational) faith. Most cities have chapters (check your phone directory).

Aversion therapy is often resorted to by those not helped by Alcoholics Anonymous or other approaches. An injection of emetine, which causes severe nausea, is given and the person is handed his favorite drink to carefully smell and swish around in the mouth. At the height of the sensual pleasure and anticipation of the eminent intoxication, there is a wave of nausea and dizziness. This reprogramming process is repeated several times over a few days. When successful, the person experiences physical and emotional discomfort at the thought of taking a drink. The effect wears off with time, but may last long enough for the alcoholic to turn his life around.

Antabuse (disulfiram), originally developed as a remedy for intestinal worms, is a more severe form of aversion therapy. The drug interferes with the normal metabolism of alcohol, so if alcohol is taken, acetaldehyde accumulates and causes violent vomiting, chest pain, headache, and other symptoms. This punishment can be effective, but it carries a risk of death if the impulse to drink is succumbed to. The drug should be avoided by persons with thyroid, liver, or kidney problems or diabetes.

Alcoholism Warning Signs (from Early to Late)

Do you drink because of fatigue, worry, depression, or disappointment, or to increase your self-confidence and lose your shyness?

Do you drink after quarrels or friction with friends or family?

Do you occasionally pass out or have memory blackouts?

Is your drinking increasing? Do you lie about this, and get annoyed and defensive when family or friends ask about your drinking?

Do you often drink alone? Are you losing interest in your family and friends?

Do you drink almost continuously for days at a time?

Do you get drunk on important occasions for which you should be sober?

Do you get the shakes in the morning and try to chase them away with a drink?

If your answer is "yes" to one or more of these questions, you may have a problem and should reconsider your drinking habits and seek help.

Amphetamine Group

Amphetamine, which is chemically similar to adrenalin, was first synthesized in 1887, but not recognized as pharmacologically active unitl 1927 when its hypertensive, bronchial dilating, and central stimulating effects were noticed. It was soon found to be useful in narcolepsy, and has since been used for barbiturate poisoning, weight control, depression, and hyperactivity, though with questionable and highly controversial long-term results in the last three applications. There is no evidence that it helps in weight control and it is likely to make depression worse. Variations of ampheta-

544 mine, such as methamphetamine, methylphenidate (Ritalin), and phenmetrazine (Preludin), are very similar in their effects and controversial applications.

One aspect of these drugs that is not controversial is that they are potent stimulants to the sympathetic and central nervous systems and euphoriants with effects similar to cocaine, but longer-lasting. They produce in most people wakefulness, alertness, elevation of mood, increased self-confidence, and increased physical activity. They were used in World War II by the armed forces of America, Britian, Germany, and Japan, and have been popular with millions of truck drivers, students, dieters, businessmen, and athlets.

However, it is also undeniable that, as with cocaine, tolerance to amphetamines develops rapidly, and the dose tends to increase, often until the person must take large amounts just to feel normally alert and awake. Withdrawal or reduction of the dose causes depression, lethargy, increased appetite, constipation, and other symptoms. Even with a constant dose these symptoms may set in.

The extreme of amphetamine abuse is reached by the "speed freaks" who inject methamphetamine intravenously in large doses several times a day. They usually start at about 20 mg in one shot a day and rapidly progress to several hundred milligrams several times a day, sometimes for many days without sleeping. One young man is reported to have shot up 15,000 mg in a twenty-four-hour period. This dose would kill someone without a profound tolerance. Amphetamines, however, rarely cause death directly; the expression "speed kills" comes from overdosing with barbiturates in order to "crash" for a day or two after speeding.

During prolonged "speed runs" the user often develops symptoms indistinguishable from cocaine psychosis with all kinds of illusions including intense paranoia; violence may be done in perceived self-defense. Moreover, after months of amphetamine use the intellect may become severely disorganized and imcompetent. Though he can hardly take care of himself, the speed addict keeps shooting or swallowing his drug for fear of the profound depression that is inevitable should he stop. The intellectual impairment and depression may persist for several months after withdrawal. However, a surprising degree of recovery usually appears within a year of stopping the drug.

WARNING
Even moderate use can cause insomnia, irritability, mood swings, habituation, and a tendency to increase the dose and the frequency of use.

Belladonna
(Atropa belladonna)

Also known as deadly nightshade, the leaves and roots of this perennial herb are taken in very small amounts as an antispasmodic and pain reliever, and in dangerously large amounts to produce a strange and frightening intoxication with vivid hallucinations. Belladonna has been used for thousands of years by sorcerers and medicine men in Europe and Asia.

The active components are atropine and scopolamine, potent parasympathetic and central nervous system depressants.

WARNING

Belladonna is extremely toxic; even a small dose can be fatal. Extremely vivid and realistic hallucinations may provoke psychotic reactions. It is also conducive to serious accidents, such as walking into traffic and out of windows. Not described as pleasant by those who survive it. (See Chapter 5–3, above.)

Betel Nut

The large seed of the Asian betel-nut palm tree is wrapped in the leaf of the betel pepper bush and sprinkled with burnt lime, catechu gum, and spices. This concoction is sucked on for several hours for a stimulant effect similar to that of strong coffee or desert tea. It is popular in the South Pacific and often encountered by travelers; but its effects are not so spectacular that importing or smuggling into the United States is likely to flourish. Betel nut is used mostly by young adults as a social drug; it seems to facilitate communication and socializing much as coffee does in the United States. The active component is arecoline, a volatile oil with stimulant effects similar to caffeine.

CAUTION

An overdose can cause dizziness, nausea, vomiting, diarrhea, agitation, heart palpitations, and convulsions. The lime erodes the teeth and gums, and the catechu gum stains them red. Prolonged, regular use is reputed to decrease libido and has been associated with the development of oral cancer. Arecoline is strongly suspected as the responsible carcinogen.

546 Broom

Also known as Scotch broom, this herb is common in parks and gardens. While it is not as popular as in the premarijuana days, youngsters are still tempted to try it after they hear about it or read books in "head shops." The blossoms are aged in a sealed jar for about ten days, then dried and smoked. The effect is strongly sedative and lasts about two to six hours, depending on the dose.

WARNING

Broom flowers are extremely toxic when ingested orally. Cytisine, the active component, resembles nicotine in its actions and may cause nausea, vomiting, racing heart, dizziness, convulsions, and respiratory paralysis leading to death. Call a physician if any drug or herb use leads to severe symptoms.

Caffeine Group

According to legend, the first coffee lover was an Ethiopian goatherd who noticed that his goats stayed awake all night if they ate the berries of the *Coffea arabica* tree. He tried them and passed along the practice. By about 1500 A.D. coffee was popular all over the Islamic world and making inroads into Europe. It created a prolonged scandal almost as great as the contemporary controversy about cannabis use, and many people called for its prohibition for health reasons. J.S. Bach composed the amusing *Coffee Cantata* about a father and daughter tusseling over her coffee habit. In the late 1600s Italian priests asked Pope Clement VIII to ban the brew, which they saw as a Satanic plot perpetrated by the Muslims. He replied that the drink was too delicious to leave to the infidels, and cheated Satan by baptizing coffee.

Coffee, of course, is not the only source of caffeine, and caffeine is not the only stimulant in its class, the xanthines. Other sources of these alkaloids (caffeine, theophylline, and theobromine) are tea, cola drinks, mate (a small evergreen tree of South America), guarana, kola nuts, gotu kola herb tea, chocolate, and over-the-counter stimulants and pain relievers. The xanthines are the most widely used drugs in the United States. The typical American starts on hot chocolate as an infant, soon graduates to colas, and continues on coffee, tea, and caffeine pills for life.

The Effects and Hazards of Xanthines[32]   547

The main effect of caffeine and its relatives is to stimulate the central nervous system and the heart, relax the bronchial airways, and act as a diuretic. It is the central stimulation, the apparently greater energy level, relief from drowsiness, and clarity of mind, that keeps people coming back for more.

Caffeine periodically comes under fire whenever a study is released showing it to be harmful to this or that part of the body. The study is debated, doubted, and usually forgotten, but the evidence continues to grow and now there is increasing pressure for health-warning labels and removal of caffeine from colas. The following is a brief summary of the case against caffeine (which applies to some extent to its relatives).

Caffeine tends to aggravate ulcers by stimulating secretion of gastric acid. Most ulcer victims are familiar with the intense burning sensation they get in their stomachs after drinking coffee, tea, or colas. Some studies suggest that coffee drinkers are more likely to develop ulcers than nondrinkers, but part of the blame may lie with the oils and other components of coffee rather than caffeine.

Caffeine can cause anxiety, insomnia, "restless legs," irritability, dizziness, and other symptoms of excessive nervous stimulation.[33] Some people go through years of suffering with these problems and even go to psychiatrists for help, without ever suspecting the true cause of their misery. When the caffeine is withdrawn the symptoms often disappear within a day or two.

Malnutrition can be a problem. Caffeine, tannic acid, and other components of coffee and tea appear to cause the excretion of signifiant amounts of thiamin and other B-vitamins. Combined with a borderline intake, this could contribute to the development of a deficiency syndrome as described in Chapter 2–7 under Thiamin. Heavy coffee and tea consumption can also reduce the absorption of iron, calcium, and possibly other minerals. Women should be especially wary of this and avoid xanthine consumption just before and for about two hours after meals. Otherwise, supplements may be in order.

Diarrhea and other gastrointestinal disturbances can be caused by caffeine and its relatives. If you have unexplained chronic diarrhea, stop all xanthine intake, as well as sorbitol and mannitol. The xanthines can also cause pruritis ani; if your anus itches mysteriously, try stopping your consumption of caffeine and related substances.

548

Cancer of the bladder has been linked to coffee consumption, but studies which control for cigarette smoking, a more likely cause of bladder cancer, exonerate coffee and caffeine. Coffee, especially decaffeinated coffee, has been linked to cancer of the pancreas, but the largest and most thorough studies refute this.

Benign breast lumps may be promoted by xanthines. This has not been proven and many experts remain skeptical, but sometimes the lumps seem to resolve upon withdrawal of all xanthines.

Cardiovascular health may be affected. Some studies suggest that heavy caffeine consumption increases cholesterol levels, provokes heart palpitations, and aggravates hypertension, all of which increase the risk of heart disease. But no studies have shown a definite association of heart disease with caffeine consumption.

Caffeine is addicting—the most socially acceptable addicting drug in the West. Sudden withdrawal often causes headache, lethargy, depression, irritability, and constipation.

Birth defects. Studies have shown that caffeine in very large doses can cause cleft palate, missing toes and fingers, and other birth defects in animals. Until epidemiological studies determine whether there is a hazard to humans, the Center for Science in the Public Interest wants a warning label on cans and packages of tea and coffee—"Warning to pregnant women: Consuming coffee or tea may cause birth defects or other reproductive problems." Most studies suggest that if there is a hazard to the fetus it is only at the very highest levels of consumption, and even then the hazard is slight. Nevertheless, moderation is in order for pregnant women.

Conclusions. The evidence that coffee and other sources of xanthines are serious health hazards is not overwhelming, but it is strong enough to warrant caution and moderation in their use. The heavy marketing to children of "soft drinks" that contain caffeine is especially objectionable. It is added to the drinks not as a flavoring agent but simply as a drug, and it is the only drug marketed so freely.

Cocaine

Cocaine is the big scandal drug of the 1980s; movie stars, athletes, and other celebrities are in the news almost daily because of their involvement with it. Each year thousands of users seek help for their cocaine habits, thousands end up in emergency rooms because of adverse reactions, and hundreds die after snorting or injecting the drug.[34] Cocaine is relatively new to American culture and many people start using it without any knowledge of what it is and does.

History[35]

The coca plant, *Erythroxylon coca*, is an evergreen shrub that grows in western South America, especially Bolivia and Peru. (There is also *E. novogranatense*, but the two varieties are much the same; our discussion refers to both.) It has been used at least since 500 A.D. and possibly much earlier; this is known from Indian mummies buried with coca leaves and ancient pottery showing the cheek bulge typical of a coca chewer.

Coca very likely sustained early travelers across the Andes. The leaves contain substantial calories, protein, calcium, iron, and several vitamins, and they can easily keep a person alive for weeks. For many centuries the Indians have chewed coca leaf with alkaline ashes from burned shells, limestone, or plants. The alkali seems to improve the flavor and may increase the potency.

During the Inca rule coca plantations were a state monopoly and use was restricted to the highest classes, with some exceptions for soldiers going into battle and workers on important projects. Coca was believed to be of divine origin, and indiscriminate use was considered a sacrilege. It may also have been used as an anesthetic for skull trepanation (making a hole to release evil spirits).

As the Incan empire declined during the 15th century, coca use became less restricted. By the time Francisco Pizarro arrived in Cuzco, completing his conquest of Peru, coca was no longer a symbol of status. The Spanish conquerors had mixed attitudes: the missionaries at first opposed coca as idolatry and a barrier to conversion; but the government found it essential for recruiting workers for the mines, farms, and forests. The Spanish also came to recognize the role of coca in Indian folk medicine—it was used to treat chronic pain and a variety of ailments. Eventually the church grew plantations of coca to sell to the workers or use as a wage. The Spanish came to control most of the coca and used it to manipulate and exploit the Indians.

Spanish physicians began to use coca for rheumatism, toothaches, colds, asthma, and other disorders. In the 18th century physician Antonio Julian advocated coca chewing for the Spanish working class for health and productivity. He also urged that coffee and tea be replaced by coca, not only in Spain but in all of Europe. He argued that this would help Spain's balance of trade since coffee and tea were imported, while Spain held almost all of the coca in the world. But coca leaf never caught on in Europe, probably

550 because of the deterioration of the leaves during the long sea voyage and because the plant was not suited to cultivation in Europe.

In the 1880s researchers at the University of Gottingen isolated the most potent of several alkaloids in coca and named it cocaine. Shortly thereafter, Italian neurologist Dr. Paolo Mantegazza studied the effects of coca on himself and reported his findings in "On the Hygienic and Medicinal Virtues of Coca." Besides describing the physiological effects, he wrote of the "deeply joyful and intensely alive" feelings, and flying through thousands of worlds, each more splendid than the preceding. God is unjust, he wrote, because he did not make man capable of sustaining the effects of coca for a lifetime.

Dr. Freud and Cocaine

Mantegazza's report strongly influenced Sigmund Freud. He decided to try it on patients with heart disease, "nervous exhaustion," and morphine withdrawal sickness. Freud's friend and colleague, Ernst von Fleischl-Marxow, had become addicted to morphine using it for pain from the stump of an amputated thumb.

Freud tried cocaine on himself and was very impressed with the increased capacity for work and the improved mood he experienced. In 1884 he wrote "On Coca," his famous paper which extolled the virtues of cocaine. He agreed with Mantegassa's observations and concluded that moderate use was "more likely to promote health than impair it." He suggested therapeutic use of cocaine for digestive disorders, cachexia (wasting), morphine addiction, alcoholism, asthma, and sexual impotence; and use as a local anesthetic.

Only the latter has survived medicine's test of time. Freud participated in the first application of cocaine as a local anesthetic for eye surgery; the patient was his own father. In surgery for glaucoma the patient's cooperation is needed, so general anesthesia cannot be used. The cocaine worked well and is still used for this purpose.

However, Freud's other experiment with cocaine was a disaster. His morphine-addict friend, Fleischl, rapidly progressed to large intravenous doses of cocaine and deteriorated fast. He had paranoid hallucinations similar to those of alcoholic delirium tremens with snakes crawling over him and insects under his skin. It was said that he had gone from being the first morphine addict in Europe to be cured by cocaine, to being the first cocaine addict in Europe.

Other users were reporting similar problems. Within three years of introducing what he thought would be a major advance in medicine, Freud found himself widely accused of irresponsibility and recklessness, and charged with unleashing the third scourge on humanity (after alcohol and opiates).

Freud had also contended that there seemed to be no lethal dose for humans, and that the toxic dose was very high. Shortly after this one of his patients died from an overdose Freud had prescribed. By 1900 scores of severe poisonings and dozens of deaths had been reported. European enthusiasm for cocaine waned.

In America William S. Halsted, the "father of modern surgery," developed a technique using cocaine as a neural block to produce regional anesthesia. He reported such use in over a thousand operations. However, Halsted and some of his assistants, apparently not aware of the problems being reported in Europe, experimented with cocaine and became heavily dependent on it. In an ironic reversal of Freud's suggested use, Halsted used morphine to ease the misery of cocaine withdrawal and he became addicted to morphine. He died thirty-five years later and still an addict in 1922.

The late 1800s saw a great proliferation of products that contained cocaine: patent medicines, tonics, soft drinks, ointments, suppositories, wines, cigarettes. They were advertised as effective in just about every disease. One was Coca-Cola, originally marketed as a medicine for headache, melancholy, and many other problems. In 1903 cocaine was removed from the formula and it was advertised as just a soft drink.

In 1914 the Harrison Narcotics Act removed most cocaine from the open market. Since 1970 it has been classified as a schedule II drug, which includes drugs with recognized medical uses but with high abuse potential. (Schedule I includes heroin, with no recognized medical uses and high addiction potential.)

Only one U.S. company is licensed to import coca leaves. It produces all of the 500 or so kilograms used in medicine as well as the decocainized extract used to flavor soft drinks.

Pharmacology and Physiology

There are at least a dozen alkaloids in coca. The most powerful of them is cocaine. Others may also have significant effects, but few of them have been studied. Cocaine probably affects neurotransmitters in the brain. The peak effect comes about fifteen to twenty minutes after snorting it into the nostrils; it lasts about an hour.

Oral doses are at least as potent as snorted but take about an extra hour to work. There is a wide variation of physiological effects in different people, but heart rate and blood pressure usually increase and appetite usually decreases. Cocaine is rapidly metabolized to ecgonine and other inactive products and excreted in the urine.

Initial euphoria is almost universally reported, and this is undoubtedly the reason for the drug's popularity. Negative effects include restlessness, irritability, depression, anxiety, and paranoia. These, including eu-

552 phoria, are also common in amphetamine use. In fact, subjects familiar with both cocaine and amphetamine cannot distinguish between them except that cocaine has a shorter action.

Illicit Cocaine

Illicit "coke" reaches the United States as flake or rock crystals, 80 to 95 percent pure. Down the line it is adulterated ("stepped on") with one or more of the following.

> Mannitol, lactose, and glucose—these are harmless additives.
>
> Lidocaine and procaine—these are bitter and numbing like cocaine, and commonly used as deceptive additives; serious allergic reactions may occur.
>
> Caffeine and amphetamine—these add inexpensive zip to diluted coke.
>
> Yohimbe extract—this is often sold as "incense," popular with dealers for diluting cocaine because of its bitter taste, white crystals, and mild stimulation (see separate discussion, this chapter).
>
> Quinine—this is rarely used; allergic reactions may cause death.
>
> Heroin—this takes some of the edge off the coke without affecting the euphoria; the combination is known as a "speedball."

In spite of dilution, illicit cocaine is quite potent, usually 30 to 70 percent.

Hazards of Cocaine

Sudden death may occur by direct suppression of respiratory centers in the brain and cardiovascular collapse. Dozens of cases have been reported, including both medical and illicit use. Snorting, injection, free-basing (inhaling cocaine vapors from a special pipe), and topical application have all been implicated. Injection is the most dangerous since it delivers a large dose to the brain all at once; moreover, it entails other risks such as hepatitis and AIDS.

Cocaine psychosis, which is similar to paranoid schizophrenia, may occur during heavy use (not as a withdrawal symptom). "Cocaine bugs," similar to Fleischl's insects under the skin, may be so real to the victim that the skin may be injured by attempts to remove them. There may also be insomnia, anorexia, seizures, irritability, and headaches.

Nasal membranes may become chronically inflamed and ulcerated, and the tissue may die and slough off. The nasal septum may become perforated. The destruction of the mucus lining may increase the cancer risk to smokers by increasing contact of carcinogens with live tissue.

Addiction is a real possibility. Monkeys, rats, and other animals given un-limited access to cocaine will self-administer it until they die, often ignoring food and water. In humans the withdrawal symptoms are not, as with opi-ates, a flulike sickness. The main problem is mild to severe depression, probably due to temporary depletion of the brain's neurotransmitters. If use continues at a given level of intake, the pleasure diminishes, so in most cases the dose is steadily increased. If it is stopped, even for half a day, the person feels lethargic and dysphoric. Heavy users often wake up during the night feeling depressed and do some coke to chase the blues and return to sleep.

Hypertension, heart attack, and intracranial bleeding have been associated with cocaine use. Persons at risk for heart attack or stroke and those with high blood pressure or blood clotting disorders should be especially wary of using cocaine.

Cocaine and Sex

Cocaine is often hyped as a wonderful aphrodesiac, but the truth is less glamorous. Applied to the vaginal mucosa, coke is well absorbed. Applied to the penis, it tends to delay ejaculation by its numbing action. This prolongs intercourse and, some say, intensifies orgasm. But long-term use by any method of administration can result in a dramatic reduction of libido. More-over, even novice users are likely to experience decreased sex drive for hours after a dose. For those who progress to injecting the drug, the orgasmic rush of the injection often replaces sex.

Conclusion

Cocaine in the coca plant probably discourages animal consumption because of its bitter taste. By a chemical accident of nature it also stimulates pleasure centers and systems in the human brain. In so doing it disrupts normal brain chemistry and depletes vital brain chemicals, often causing depression, anxi-ety, paranoid delusions, and other symptoms. The sum total of the suffering is ultimately greater than the pleasure for most people who use the drug on a regular basis—or so it appears from the testimony of thousands of users and

554 ex-users who seek help. Most regular users wish they had never seen cocaine and they eventually resolve to quit, with varying degrees of success.

How To Kick Cocaine

Write down all the reasons you want to quit using the drug—the irritability, anxiety, depression, insomnia, nasal destruction, nose bleeds, run-down health, and risk of getting convulsions or even a heart attack or stroke. Contemplate all the things you could do with the money and time you would save. Resolve firmly to refuse the drug if it is offered and to never seek it or buy it—even if you have to change the company you keep. If you cannot quit at once or within a week of tapering off, you should seek help. Call Alcoholic Anonymous, Narcotics Anonymous, a local drug treatment program, or 800–COCAINE, the national hot line.

Datura
(Datura inoxia, D. stramonium, others)

Also known as thornapple, devil's weed, and jimson weed, the flowers, seeds, leaves, stems, and roots of this annual herb contain atropine, scopolamine, and other tropanes. It resembles belladonna and other members of the potato (Solanaceae) family in this. Small amounts of the leaves, seeds, and stems are smoked for asthma relief; more for intoxication. The roots are crushed and soaked in water for several hours; then the water is drunk. The plant was commonly used by American Indians as an anesthetic, antispasmodic, sedative, and magic potion for divination and puberty rites.

The whole plant exudes a heavy "narcotic" odor, especially the bruised leaves. The flowers smell sweet and can produce stupor by prolonged inhalation. Yaque Indians say that eating or smoking the flowers produces insanity. Vivid hallucinations and forceful delusions make this a very dangerous drug. The potent seeds are a hazard to children especially, since they are sweetish when half ripe. Children have died after chewing on them.

WARNING
Datura is a very dangerous plant, capable of causing headache, stupor, delirium, amnesia, prolonged psychotic reaction, unconsciousness, and death.

DMT Group

For many centuries various South American tribes have used the bark and seeds of the trees *Virola calophylla, Psychotria viridis,* and others to prepare a powerful hallucinogenic snuff. The active components are N, N-dimethy-tryptamine (DMT) and 5-methoxy-DMT (MEO-DMT). Various relatives (DPT, DET, DBT, and others) have similar effects.

DMT and its cousins are generally inactive if eaten and must be smoked or injected. The effectiveness of snuffs and drinks made by Indians apparently depends on proper mixture of the drug with harmine- and harma-line-containing drinks made from yage, *Banisteriopsis caapi;* or the presence (in the DMT plants) of monoamine oxidase inhibitors which allow the DMT to be absorbed before it is destroyed by intestinal enzymes.

The effect of DMT (usually smoked on parsely or marijuana) is explosively hallucinogenic with colorful, swirling, vibrating visions. A single dose usually lasts a half hour to two hours, depending on the method of administration and the dose. This shortness of action made DMT popular for a time in the late sixties and early seventies. But tolerance develops, the dose increases, and side effects—headaches, lethargy, memory lapses, confusion —increase.

CAUTION

The potency, imprecision of the dose, and suddenness of onset makes over-dosing easy and common. There may be serious and long-lasting psychotic reactions. One young man said that after taking "a few good hits" of DMT, he "left this world" and for almost two years he "could not tell the difference between a parking meter and a person."

Heroin and Other Opiates

Opium is the dried juice of the capsule of the opium poppy *Papaver somniferum* and it contains **morphine** and **codeine**. Morphine is a very powerful and addicting painkiller and narcotic; codeine is a weaker painkiller and not nearly as addicting. Opium is swallowed or smoked; morphine is snorted or injected under the skin, into a muscle, or into a vein; and codeine is swal-

556 lowed as a pill or liquid. All the opiates act directly on the central nervous system to produce pain relief, sedation, constipation, pupil constriction, and sometimes euphoria or dysphoria, nausea, and dizziness. Very large overdoses can cause death by respiratory depression.

Heroin, diacetylmorphine, is made by heating morphine with acetic acid. It was developed in Germany at the turn of the century as a "heroic" or super-aspirin, hence the name. It was used for many aches, pains, and ailments and for treating morphine addiction. It took about twenty years of over-the-counter sales and widespread use for it to be generally recognized that heroin has essentially the same effects and hazards as morphine, to which it is converted in the body.

Opiates in Early America[36]

During the 1800s opium was imported into the United States as well as grown commercially in New England, California, Arizona, and some southern states. Morphine became widely available from many sources, all legal. Physicians, drugstores, grocery stores, and mail-order companies provided pure products as well as hundreds of patent medicines containing opiates. They were used for all kinds of aches and pains, diarrhea, coughs, "women's troubles," and even colic and teething pain in infants.

Morphine was often used to treat alcoholism, which usually meant converting an alcoholic to a morphine addict—which was preferable because morphine was cheaper and less harmful to the mind and body. Compared to the loud, foul-mouthed, often violent drunkard, the morphine addict was a model citizen. And while the alcoholic often suffered from ulcers, gastritis, malnutrition, liver disease, mental deterioration, and heart trouble, the morphine addict suffered little more than constipation and decreased libido.

In 1914 Congress passed the Harrison Narcotics Act, which effectively eliminated all legal supplies of morphine to addicts, who then typically switched to the still-legal heroin. When this loophole was closed in 1924 a new era began. Opiate addicts all over the country were no longer able to get their drugs from the corner drugstore, quietly take them when they felt the need, continue their occupations, and lead almost normal lives. Many older people who had been addicted for decades subsequent to opiate use for medical purposes suffered enormously from the withdrawal sickness, especially when it was imposed on pain from arthritis and other causes. In the following years addicts concentrated in cities where they could "score," usually with adulterated, contaminated, expensive heroin which was usually injected intravenously for economy.

The Nature of Heroin Addiction[37]

During the last century and the first part of this, most opiate addiction occurred subsequent to the often misguided use of opiates to relieve the symptoms of various major and minor ailments and injuries. In recent decades addiction due to medical uses has been rare, and most heroin users start taking the drug as a tranquilizer to relieve anxiety and tension, or a "high" to relieve boredom.

A very few users (perhaps 3 percent) experience intense pleasure from the first dose and they rapidly become addicted. Another small minority take heroin once or twice a week for many months or years without becoming addicted. The vast majority of addicts start off as occasional users, gradually increase the frequency, and become addicted months after their first dose.

While many addicts who mainline heroin (inject it into a vein) experience a rush of warmth in the abdomen which they perceive as pleasant, **the basis of addiction is not pleasure but pain.** The addict must take the drug three or four times every day to prevent the very distressful **withdrawal sickness,** which typically includes yawning, hot and cold flashes, profuse sweating, watering eyes and nose, abdominal cramps, nausea, vomiting, diarrhea, muscle and joint aches and pains, and severe anxiety.

After an addict kicks the habit he is likely to suffer from a **postaddiction syndrome** consisting of anxiety, depression, poor tolerance for major and minor stresses (loud noises, heat, cold, annoyances, and inconveniences), and a craving for the drug. If he relapses and returns to the drug he is generally not motivated by a hedonistic love of pleasure but by a desperate attempt to feel normal. The postaddiction syndrome varies in severity, comes and goes in waves, and can last many months, which helps explain why relapse is so common.

Health Hazards of Heroin Addiction

The health hazards of opiate addiction depend on social circumstances, especially whether or not the drug is legally available. When it is, it can be taken regularly for many years with surprisingly mild effects on health. For example, Dr. William S. Halsted, "the father of modern surgery," became addicted to morphine at age thirty-four, subsequent to using it to cure his cocaine addiction. He remained healthy, vigorous, active, renowed for his skill, and still addicted until his death at seventy.

There have been many like Halsted and they apparently suffer little more than constipation, decreased libido, and constricted pupils which

558

makes it hard to see in the dark. While constipation can promote hemorrhoids and possibly other problems, there is no evidence of the kind of malnutrition, brain damage, mental deterioration, and psychosis often seen in alcoholics.

The effects on women may include cessation of ovulation and, if they do get pregnant, complications such as toxemia, hemorrhage, and prematurity. It is not clear whether these effects are due to the drug or the stress and malnutrition that accompany addiction when the drug is expensive and hard to get.

The typical heroin addict who uses illicit, expensive, adulterated heroin is at risk for a host of serious health problems, including hepatitis, AIDS, and other infections; kidney failure; malnutrition and all its consequences; and violent injury, even murder and suicide.

In recent years illicit laboratories have produced and marketed so-called synthetic heroin. The drug is actually a potent analogue of meperidine (Demerol), the synthetic narcotic and painkiller. The products often contain a contaminant, methylphenyltetrahydropyridine (MPTP) that can cause irreversible brain damage leading to Parkinsonism, a syndrome characterized by resting tremor, rigidity, difficult moving, flexed posture, and loss of postural reflexes. The condition is permanent, though temporary relief can be obtained by treatment with L-dopa or bromocriptine, drugs used to treat Parkinson's disease.

The effects of the chemical appear to be cumulative and may not appear for months or years. Since the "synthetic heroin" has been used by many people, we may face an epidemic of Parkinsonism in the near future.

Death from
So-called "Heroin Overdose"[38]

Since the 1960s there has been an epidemic of sudden deaths associated with the injection of heroin. Many thousands of addicts have dropped dead immediately after mainlining, sometimes before getting the needle out of their arms. These deaths have been attributed to heroin overdose, but this is questionable for a number of reasons. Very large overdoses can be tolerated by addicts without even causing sickness and dealers are not likely to carelessly provide many times the dose an addict pays for. Moreover, in most cases autopsies have not proven the deaths to be a result of heroin overdose.

More likely causes of heroin-associated sudden death include adverse reaction to quinine or other adulterants, and a synergistic action of heroin with another drug, such as barbiturates or alcohol. It is well known that an ordinary dose of an opiate can kill a person who has been drinking.

If an addict cannot procure a fix when he needs it, he will often turn to alcohol, barbiturates, and other drugs for the interim. When he finally "scores" and shoots up, he may have large amounts of the other drug in his system and the combination may prove lethal. Janis Joplin is assumed to have died of a heroin overdose, but her constant companion, a bottle of Southern Comfort, may have been half the culprit. Persons who have not yet managed to kick heroin (or morphine or synthetic narcotics such as Demerol) should remain absolute teetotalers until they are no longer using the drug.

The Treatment of Heroin Addiction

Experience with several decades of heroin addiction has not led to a cure, but current therapy controls the problem much more effectively and humanely than before. Even when opiates were legal and widely used, addiction to them was viewed with alarm; few people wanted to become or remain addicted. Physicians and addicts tried various means of quitting the drugs, including gradual withdrawal with carefully tapered doses, going cold-turkey, taking hot or cold baths, and taking belladonna, strychnine, naloxone (an opiate antagonist), and other drugs. Whatever was tried, even if the addicts got past withdrawal sickness and stayed clean for weeks, the vast majority returned to the morphine or heroin within a few months, driven by the postaddiction syndrome.

Since the 1960s the most successful programs for kicking heroin have involved daily oral doses of the drug methadone, a synthetic narcotic developed by opium-poor Germany during World War II. Methadone substantially reduces withdrawal sickness, so is very useful in detoxification—substitution of methadone for heroin, followed by gradual withdrawal from methadone over a week or two.

Methadone maintainence programs help the addicts who can get past heroin withdrawal but always end up back on the needle within a few months. Methadone quiets the postaddiction syndrome and blocks the effects of heroin should the addict take it. As long as he stays on methadone he can lead an essentially normal life. Many thousands of heroin addicts who would otherwise be busy stealing and "fencing" all day to support their habits have been freed by methadone programs to hold jobs, go to school, and otherwise function in society.

Side effects of methadone include constipation and slightly decreased libido, but the effects are generally weaker than with heroin. A large dose can kill a child and, like all drugs, methadone should be kept out of the reach of children.

560 Kava Kava (Piper methysticum)

The roots and lower stems of this tall perenial shrub, also called *ava*, have been used in Polynesia and the South Pacific for hundreds of years as a sedative, headache remedy, local anesthetic, diuretic, and ritual intoxicant. The traditional method of preparation is for the material to be chewed, spit into a bowl, and mixed with coconut milk; the bowl is then passed around so all might savor its contents. Modern users chop the root, mix it with water, oil, and lecithin, and blend it all in a food mixer. The bitter mixture is then drunk, usually rapidly and with the nose closed.

The active components are methysticin and other unusual aromatic compounds known as pyrones. Some people experience up to a half hour of mild stimulation before the relaxing effects take over. Some say the drug induces dreams and some say it inhibits them; it probably does neither.

Popular books and magazines have claimed awa is an aphrodesiac, "the love drug of the South Pacific," according to one article. "The fun-loving islanders discovered the plant could turn any social occasion into a Pacific love-in," the writer claimed. This is completely false; the drug does nothing for the libido and, although it may decrease inhibitions as much as any mild sedative, Polynesian scholars scoff at the idea that South Pacific islanders need a dis-inhibitor or use kava kava for sexual purposes.

WARNING

Excessive intake can cause death by respiratory depression. Used as a local anesthetic, kava kava can be very irritating to the skin, much like pepper. Frequent internal use may cause habituation, jaundice, rashes, diarrhea, loss of appetite, emaciation, and disturbances of vision.

Ketamine

Synthesized in 1962 by Parke-Davis laboratories as a PCP substitute, ketamine is a general anesthetic which, in smaller doses, may produce a sense of dissociation from the body, floating, flying, dying, or regressing in time. It is very similar to PCP in chemical structure and effects (see below) and is capable of causing smilar problems, such as psychotic reactions, depression, panic, paranoia, dependence, and loss of contact with reality.

Marijuana

The hemp plant, *Cannabis sativa,* has been used by humans since the dawn of history. Stone Age Chinese used the fibrous weed to make fabrics for clothing, bedding, mats, nets, and the like. Before long, hemp was found useful for making ropes and sails, and it became important to all seafaring people. Just when its psychoactivity was discovered is unknown, but it was clearly a very long time ago. There is evidence of cannabis use as an anesthetic, a medicine, an aid in magic, and a sacred giver of joy from at least a thousand years B.C. in China, Persia, and India.

In a documentary film by anthropologist Jean Paul Hallet, Congo Pygmies claim to have been smoking marijuana since the earliest days of their existence, several thousand years ago. If this is true, the Pygmies were the only early users who smoked the drug. In all the areas of Asia and Africa where it was used, it was taken orally in an enormous variety of ways—raw, baked, cooked with food, mixed with honey and nuts into a candy—but it was never smoked.

The whole idea of smoking was practically unknown in the Old World, and even after it was introduced from the New World, cannabis users swallowed pellets or tinctures of hashish. These preparations (imported from Islamic nations) became common in pharmacies in the West, but the drug was only used by a few until smoking it became popular. Ironically, North America, which gave the world tobacco, is one of the few places where cannabis is almost always smoked pure. In most of Asia and Africa, hashish is usually mixed with tobacco, the New World smoke.

The stems of the cannabis plant are used for fiber and the leaves, and especially the flowers, for psychoactivity. The plants are generally grown for one purpose or the other. The flowers can be made larger (and the drug yield much higher) by culling the males and other tricks; the crop requires careful tending. Cannabis allowed to grow tall and wild has excellent fiber but only small flowers and little psychoactivity. It is called hemp, while cannabis grown for the flowers is called marijuana.

Marijuana and the Body[39]

The psychoactive constituent of marijuana is tetrahydracannabinol, THC. When it is smoked the THC vaporizes and is inhaled. From the lungs it is absorbed into the blood, which takes it to all areas of the body.

THC is lipophilic ("loves fat"), so it tends to concentrate in cell membranes and lipid-rich tissue such as fat, the brain, sex glands, adrenal glands, and the kidneys. It is metabolized, especially in the liver, and is eventually excreted, mostly in the feces and urine. A single dose may remain

562 in the tissue for ten days or more, mostly in a slightly altered, nonpsychoactive form. Regular smokers may build up large tissue deposits. In this sense, THC is more like DDT than alcohol, amphetamines, caffeine, or psychedelics, which are all rapidly excreted from the body.

There is considerable loss of THC in smoking, at least 50 percent. Some is destroyed by the heat, some is exhaled, and some disappears with the uninhaled side stream of smoke. If a "joint" has 10 mg of THC in it, 1 to 5 mg will get into the blood. This would be about the size of a grain of salt and only a fraction of this would go to the brain, so we're talking about a very potent substance.

Can Marijuana Kill?

When marijuana is eaten the THC is absorbed into the blood as the marijuana is digested, a half hour to three hours later. Smoking is usually preferred because the effects are felt within a few minutes, making dose control easier, and it is believed to be more potent than eating it. However, specially prepared marijuana (cooked in oil to render the THC more assimilable), eaten on an empty stomach, may deliver a larger dose than smoking. Very rarely, fatalities have happened in India when children, probably hungry, ate large amounts of hashish, most likely on empty stomachs, assuring rapid and complete absorption of the THC.

Although death from smoking canabis is practically unheard of, there is a report of a young French soldier who tried to commit suicide by smoking hashish. He was in a coma for four days and almost died. It is estimated he had smoked about 90 grams (three ounces) with 5 percent THC, or 4500 milligrams, over several hours. Common fare in the U.S. is a joint with about 10 mg (500 milligrams of marijuana with 2 percent THC), much less than 1 percent of a near-lethal dose.

However, some marijuana preprations may rival very potent hashish. For example, the empty seed pods of sinsemilla marijuana (nonfertilized female flower tops) may have up to 10 percent THC. As domestic growers refine the art, and as experimenters and entrepreneurs develop ever more potent oils, we may begin to see fatal overdoses. Five grams of a potent hashish oil could be lethal. This amount could fit into about five large gelatin capsules.[40]

Among regular users the daily dose of THC varies enormously. A once-a-day smoker might get 1 to 10 mg a day. A very heavy user might smoke 10 grams of hashish per day and get 500 mg. Because THC is lipophilic and persistant, dose and total intake over months and years are all-important in considering the effects and potential hazards of marijuana use.

One regular user's daily intake of THC may be several hundred times another's, especially if he is using hashish oil, which may contain 10 to 80 percent. The dose delivered by one "toke" of oil can be fifty times the dose delivered by ordinary leaf marijuana.

To complicate matters, there are at least thirty-five other substances in marijuana which have varying biological effects, but are not psychoactive. They are closely related to THC, having the same nucleus, and are classified as cannabinoids.

Should Women Smoke Marijuana?

Animal studies and a few clinical observations of women marijuana smokers indicate that heavy marijuana use may inhibit normal pituitary hormone production and thereby cause changes in the menstrual cycle, including anovulation and missed periods.[41]

There are also indications that the chemicals in marijuana may inhibit DNA and protein synthesis in cells, and thereby directly interfere with maturation of the ovum or with fetal development. However, the National Institute of Drug Abuse studied pregnant rats using doses 10 to 100 times the effective human dose. At those levels, which few women reach, marijuana did not seem to have deleterious effects on the fetus or mother. Such studies, plus the lack of evidence of severe birth defects in humans associated with cannabis use, indicate that a pregnant woman would have to smoke the most potent cannabis from dawn to dusk to risk a thalidomide-type tragedy.

This doesn't settle the matter, though, because it only considers gross malformations induced by large doses. Could not more subtle harm be done by smaller doses? When we think of drug-induced birth defects we tend to think of children without arms or legs, or other severe defects. But this is only the extreme end of the spectrum of malformations. It's one thing to see whether a newborn rabbit, rat, monkey, or human has all is limbs and seems normal and healthy, but it's quite another to detect mild to moderate brain defects which could impair learning. Since THC is known to cross the placenta, it is not surprising that there have been reports of low birth weight and symptoms similar to the fetal alcohol syndrome in infants exposed to THC in the womb, and it should not be surprising if subtle learning deficits also occur in some of these children.

Clearly, marijuana is no exception to the general rule to avoid drugs during pregnancy and before. Nor should a woman smoke marijuana if she is breast feeding, unless she wants to feed a regular dose of THC and its metabolites to her infant and risk permanent endocrine and brain changes.

Marijuana and Cancer

Marijuana smoke contains known carcinogens and has much the same effects on cultured lung tissue as tobacco smoke—it induces cancerous

564 changes.[42] A major group of carcinogens in tobacco and other kinds of smoke are the polynuclear aromatic hydrocarbons (PAHs). Marijuana smoke contains more than 150 PAHs, some in larger amounts than in tobacco smoke. The total tar content is about two to three times higher in marijuana than tobacco smoke.

The habit of mixing cannabis with tobacco, popular around the world but not yet in the United States, may be more hazardous than smoking only one or the other. Studies suggest that smoke from a mixture causes more cellular abnormalities than from tobacco alone. Burning the two together may produce different, more potent carcinogens than those present in either one alone. Or the simultaneous presence of components of both types of smoke from smoking one, then the other, may harm the lung cells more than one alone.

Although definitive epidemiological studies have not yet been done, it seems clear from the evidence that smoking marijuana entails a risk of developing lung cancer. If one also smokes cigarettes, the risk is certainly greater. Paradoxically, there is also evidence that marijuana may inhibit some kinds of cancer and may be useful in other ways in cancer treatment (see below).

Marijuana and the Respiratory System

As might be expected, inhaling the hot oil and resin vapors and ashes of burning marijuana or hashish can cause respiratory problems. The list of reported symptoms includes bronchitis, sinusitis, asthma, increased nasal secretions and irritations, nasal stuffiness, frequent colds, sore throat, abnormal cells lining the respiratory tract, increased bronchopulmonary markings (on X-ray), loss of cilia, and chronic inflammation.

The vital capacity of the lungs is often reduced, sometimes by almost half in very heavy smokers. This results in a much lower capacity for exercise, and at rest the blood of smokers is poorly oxygenated compared to the nonsmokers. After exercise the smoker's blood is more acid, again indicating poor oxygenation.

These problems are generally in proportion to the amount of cannabis habitually smoked. In some cases of very heavy smoking for weeks or months, the smoker is disabled by severe symptoms. They usually subside after smoking stops, but emphysema may develop in some and this can be a lifelong disabling condition.

Marijuana and the Circulatory System

Cannabis always makes the heart beat faster. How is unknown, but this is one of the few very predictable actions of the drug. It could present a hazard to those prone to heart disease.

In one study of patients with angina pectoris (heart pain when exercising), after smoking one joint they could exercise only half as long as they normally could without heart pain. Marijuana apparently decreases oxygen delivery to the heart muscle. Other muscles may be similarly weakened.

Blood shot eyes is another predictable effect of cannabis. It occurs whether the drug is eaten or smoked, so it is caused by a pharmacologic effect on the blood vessels or nervous system, not by smoke irritation of the eyes.

Cannabis sometimes lowers blood pressure or induces postural hypotension, so that sudden standing up causes a person to black out or become dizzy.

Marijuana and Sex

Hashish endows its users with superhuman sexual stamina according to "The Fabulous Feats of the Futtering Freebooter," and other old Arab tales.[43] There are similar praises of cannabis as a great aphrodesiac in India and China, and many in the West agree with this sentiment.

On the other hand, scientists and physicians including Dr. William Masters, the pioneer sex researcher, report that marijuana causes decreased testosterone in the blood, lowered sperm count, and decreased sex drive, as has been reported for chlorpromazine, methadone, morphine, alcohol, and other drugs. These results are especially significant because lowered testosterone levels might affect normal development at puberty, and more and more youngsters are smoking marijuana now.

Some researchers have failed to find a difference in testosterone levels between users and nonusers. Evidently if there is an effect it is not universal or very large. But even a small decrease in the hormone might push a man with a mildly low sperm count to the point of infertility.

In our own informal survey, several women reported that marijuana causes them to dry up, making intercourse difficult in spite of strong desire. Others said they lost their passion after smoking because they felt paranoid, strange, or inhibited; some men said similar things. Moreover, some women said they felt their lovers became less passionate after they started smoking marijuana regularly.

However, many of those we asked said that marijuana enhanced their pleasure in bed, allowed them to forget everything else, and made their pleasure seem to last longer. One man said, after his first sexual experience while on marijuana, "Our ecstasy went from peak to peak and our orgasms seemed to last for several minutes."

These testimonials don't prove cannabis is an aphrodesiac. The enhanced enjoyment may be more a matter of relaxed inhibitions and sug-

566 gestibility, much as with alcohol. Moreover, contrasting with the stories of increased libido, it is said that many Hindu holy men, the Saddhus and other celebates use cannabis to help them renounce all worldly pleasures, including sexual urges.

The notions that cannabis is an enhancer of sexual urges and pleasures and that it destroys the libido are not necessarily contradictory. Evidence from animal and human studies points to initial stimulation and decreased inhibitions, which enhance sexual response, followed by a long-term depression which diminishes libido. The effects of marijuana on the brain seem to fit the pattern of initial stimulation followed by long-term depression.

It is interesting that the attitude of the cultural rebels of the 1960s and early 1970s that helped propel the wave of marijuana popularity likewise seems to fit the pattern of initial stimulation followed by long-term depression. For example, in the 1960s the counterculture press never said a bad thing about marijuana, which was the badge of rebellion and widely considered completely harmless, even a psychic vitamin of sorts. *High Times* magazine and similar publications carried centerfolds of high-quality cannabis flower tops and railed against anyone who suggested that the weed was something less than a 20th century panacea. Little by little, however, negative comments seeped in until in 1984 the magazine suggested a ban on the *hash bud*, a voluntary refusal to buy or smoke the most potent preparation of marijuana, the mature seedless female flowers of *Cannabis indica*. (This is a stabilized variant of *C. sativa*, not a separate species.)

Marijuana, Mind, and Brain

The millions of neurons of the brain communicate with each other by means of chemicals called neurotransmitters, which travel across the gaps between the cells. Like most psychoactive chemicals, THC affects the neurotransmitters—norepinephrine, serotonin, acetylcholine—in different parts of the brain in various ways. These changes lead to changes in the brain's electrical activity and in consciousness.

Monkey studies by Dr. Heath and other researchers at Tulane have shown that THC is highly concentrated in the limbic system of the brain.[44] And, in probably the only study ever done on the effects of marijuana using electrodes inside a human brain, Heath recorded large changes in the septal region of the limbic system associated with rushes of euphoria after the subject smoked marijuana. The monkey studies have been more publicized because they have been said to prove that marijuana causes irreversible brain damage after six months of daily doses. However, the doses were much larger than those most people use; the smoke was delivered directly into the monkeys' nasopharynx by a respirometer; and the large doses were started all at once rather than gradually increased over weeks or months, which is the typical human experience.

In spite of the flaws of the experiment, it is interesting that some of the brain regions apparently most affected by THC are the structures of the limbic system. These areas are involved with emotions, instincts, fear, anger, appetite, motivation, pleasure, biological rhythms, and sexual behavior. It is tempting to attribute some effects of the drug to stimulation or depression of these areas by effects on neurotransmitters since euphoria, sexual stimulation, heightened orgasms, hunger, altered time sense, fear (panic or paranoia), and emotional "rushes" are familiar to marijuana users.

The limbic system, however, is not the only area of the brain affected. THC also tends to concentrate in the frontal cortex, sensory relay areas, the visual cortex, and the cerebellar cortex. This could explain some sensory and motor changes. Marijuana has been reported to increase total sleeping time, increase napping, and reduce rapid eye movement (REM) sleep (dreaming).

The decrease in dreaming may be related to marijuana's inhibition of memory. Both may be caused by THC's interference with nucleic acid and protein synthesis in the brain, processes believed to be essential steps in memory formation. It has been shown that rat brain slices kept alive in physiological solutions make less nucleic acids and protein after THC has been added.

Mental Changes

There seems to be a remarkable agreement between subjective reports and objective psychological testing results. Over a hundred years ago, in the classic The Hashish Eater, Fitz Ludlow wrote, "Now for the first time I experienced the vast change which Hashish makes in all measurements of time. The first word of my reply occupied a period sufficient for the action of a drama; the last left me in complete ignorance of any point far enough back in the past to date the commencement of the sentence. Its enunciation might have occupied years."

Similarly, a report from Stanford University, "Marijuana and Temporal Disintegration," says that THC causes a disintegration of sequential thought, related to impairment of immediate memory, and associated with disorganized speech and thinking." One of the subjects in this study said, "I can't follow what I'm saying....I can't remember what I just said or what I want to say...because there are just so many thoughts that are broken in time, one chunk there and one chunk here."[45]

The effects are often perceived as pleasant, but this isn't always the case. Ludlow stated that on some occasions after eating hashish he would

568 suffer visions of death, rooms closing in on him, and faces mocking him, and he would feel himself burning up.

Modern smokers also sometimes suffer acute panic reactions and request medical help. The victim often feels he has been poisoned and is dying or losing his mind. His heart beats very fast and he becomes agitated, tearful, confused, and sometimes paranoid. Ludlow wrote, "Suspicion of all things and persons is characteristic of the hashish delirium." The person may be unable to understand what others are saying and unable to speak coherently. In very rare cases he may have delusions and hallucinations and suffer amnesia. He may remember nothing of his actions over a period of many hours, as often happens in an alcoholic blackout. Sometimes depression is the dominant mood and it may linger for many days.

Long-term Hazards of Marijuana

More important than occasional freakouts, which are usually due to overdosing, is the possibility of subtle harm caused by changes in brain chemistry after months or years of heavy smoking. Such long-term adverse effects can include lethargy, difficulty in thinking and speaking, confusion, apathy, loss of motivation, forgetfulness, irritability, suspiciousness, deterioration of time sense, flat affect (emotional dullness), headaches, depression, feelings of unreality, difficulty concentrating, decreased libido, negligence to details, and loss of sense of purpose.

These changes make optimal functioning impossible. The person may become withdrawn, asocial, and unable to relate to others or perform adequately in his work. Such people often seek medical help on their own or are persuaded to by concerned relatives or friends. Dozens of cases are described in the medical literature. If the person can be induced to stop smoking cannabis, the symptoms tend to subside over a period of weeks—alertness returns, thinking improves, and energy levels increase. But how easy is it for a heavy user to abstain or drastically cut down once he is motivated to do so? This brings us to the question of addiction.

Cannabinolism—Marijuana Addiction

According to the 1972 report of the National Commission on Marijuana and Drug Abuse (the Shafer Commission), "Cannabis does not lead to physical dependence." Yet Fitz Ludlow lamented his enslavement to hashish and describes the agony he suffered in his efforts to free himself, which he finally did after several years of regular use. Was his dependence imaginary or a literary invention for dramatic effect? Was he mimicking Thomas DeQuincy (*Confessions of an Opium Eater*) or did the commission miss something?

Taber's *Cyclopedic Medical Dictionary* defines addiction as "en-slavement to some habit, especially the drug habit." The drugs universally recognized as addicting, such as heroin, morphine, and Demerol induce brain chemical changes which make the addict sick, or at least extremely uncomfortable, if the drug is withdrawn. The symptoms are generally the opposite of the effects of the drugs. The chemistry overpowers the will, so even if the person has full insight into his plight, he finds it impossible to resist the drug, and he tends to increase the dose because tolerance develops.

Psychoactivity, tolerance, and withdrawal symptoms are the main features of addicting drugs. In the case of marijuana there is no question about the psychoactivity. Nor is there any question that tolerance develops. All animals tested with THC rapidly develop profound tolerance to its ef-fects. Within a month of starting the drug, birds, rats, dogs, and monkeys require several times the original dose for the same physiological and behav-ioral changes to occur. Very heavy smokers may smoke 10 grams of potent hashish a day and function normally (though not necessarily optimally), while one-twentieth that amount would incapacitate a novice smoker for several hours.

More evidence of physical tolerance comes from a study of the metabolism of THC in long-term marijuana users compared to nonusers. Radioactively labeled THC (0.5 mg) given intravenously to the users disap-peared from the blood with a half-life of about one day compared to more than two days for the nonusers. As with all drugs to which tolerance devel-ops, the body quickly increases its ability to destroy THC, mostly by increasing certain liver enzymes.

The last criterion of addiction is the withdrawal syndrome. Such symptoms have been detected in monkeys given THC for two weeks, starting twelve hours after the last dose and lasting five days. They consist of loss of appetite, yawning, piloerection, irritability, hair-pulling, tremors, twitches, and photophobia. Two of the six monkeys in this study learned to self-inject and kept themselves free of withdrawal symptoms this way.

In humans the situation is similar. Withdrawal symptoms are re-ported to include decreased appetite, insomnia, restlessness, anxiety, gastric hyperacidity, irritability, seclusiveness, excessive perspiration, increased libi-do, and, of course, a craving for the drug. The symptoms may last for several days. The craving can last for months but is especially strong in the first month.

Therefore, while it is true that cannabis withdrawal does not cause extreme sickness as seen in opiate and barbiturate withdrawal, it is mistaken to assume that the insomina, anxiety, poor appetite, and so on do not have a physical basis just because they are not life-threatening. Since the reported withdrawal symptoms seem to be generally the opposite of the effects of the drug, and since THC affects neurotransmitters, it seems likely that some com-

570 pensatory, homeostatic brain chemistry changes occur in the regular user, and that these changes are the physical basis of the withdrawal syndrome and addiction.

This is not to say that everyone who uses cannabis becomes addicted to it, just that the possibility exists. Some people are more prone to addiction than others and, just as some people can drink a glass of wine or beer every day without becoming alcoholics, so some people remain light cannabis smokers without becoming addicted. Others, possibly for genetic reasons, may be more prone to cannabis addiction and should completely avoid the drug, just as alcoholics must avoid alcohol or risk ruining their lives.

"Cannabinolism" is the most logical term for addiction to cannabis products. *Cannabinol* is short for *tetrahydracannabinol* and *cannabinolism* and *cannabinolic* are perfectly analogous to *alcoholism* and *alcoholic*. None of the other terms commonly used is adequate. *Pothead*, for example, would seem to apply only to the users of crude marijuana, not hashish or other cannabis products; it is also harsh and derogatory sounding. "Hashaholic" may have a nice ring to it, but it grates on one's sense of logic; it is a nonsense word.

As marijuana use increases in this country we may see the emergence of specialists in THC addiction and special counseling services and clinics for the cannabinolic. These clinics would likely draw on the techniques used in tobacco, alcohol, and narcotic addiction clinics—individual counseling, group therapy, exercise, aversion therapy, and so on. There is already a group called Potsmokers Anonymous in some cities.

Marijuana as Medicine

For many centuries marijuana has been used as an analgesic, a sedative, and a euphoriant. Now modern medicine is taking marijuana seriously. A few people have special permits to smoke marijuana obtained from government sources to treat glaucoma, a disease of excess pressure in the eyeballs which can destroy vision if not controlled. THC reduces the pressure to normal, apparently by inhibiting the synthesis of the prostaglandin PGE-2, a hormone involved in increasing ocular pressure.

Effects on prostaglandins may also account for THC's antipyretic and anti-inflammatory effects, which may be as effective as aspirin in fever and pain. However, it is not nearly as effective as opiates for the relief of severe pain.

THC has some bronchial dilator activity and it may be useful in asthma. Oral preparations would be a must, though; smoking is no way to deal with any respiratory problem.

Some cases of hypertension might yield to THC, but the dose required is quite high and is not practical for everyday use.

THC has been found to retard the growth of Lewis lung adenocarcinoma implanted in mice, but it has been found ineffective against other cancers. Nevertheless, it may find wide use in cancer for its remarkable effects against nausea and vomiting when patients are being treated with drugs for cancer. Its appetite-stimulating effect may also help in cancer and other ailments. Eating it would, of course, be much preferable to smoking it, and obligatory in cancer and other diseases of the lung.

Physicians who want to use marijuana as a drug must apply for an Investigational Drug permit from the FDA. For more information, write to: Medical Reclassification Project, NORML, 2317 M Street, N.W., Washington, D.C.

Conclusions

On the positive side we have several medical uses of cannabis and, for some, pleasant emotional and mental stimulation. These are subjective and we leave their descriptions to the poets. Such benefits must be weighed by the individual against the hazards of using the drug.

All medicines and psychoactive drugs, all herbs and chemicals used to speed healing, relieve symptoms, give pleasure, or induce visions are two-edged swords. **No physiologically active herb or chemical is without hazards.** Marijuana, whether taken to induce pleasure or relieve pain, is no exception. The question never should have been, Is marijuana harmful? but, At what level and frequency of use is marijuana harmful and what are the hazards?

Certainly, pregnant and possibly pregnant women should abstain from using cannabis in any form. So should couples planning on having a child and women nursing a child.

For most people the main hazards are to the lungs (when smoked) and the mind, especially memory and motivation. Long-term heavy use can result in damaged lungs and consequent decreased fitness, as well as loss of mental sharpness. Tolerance develops, doses increase and often the bad trips come to outweigh the good. Ludlow said, "The ecstasy became daily more and more flecked with shadows of an immeasurable pain."

It appears that the areas of the brain stimulated by marijuana, giving rise to pleasure, heightened awareness, and positive sexual and emotional expression, are ultimately suppressed, as if partly "burned-out." "Clogged-up" may be more accurate, since there is a return towards normal when a long-term abuser quits. The severity and persistance of the changes depend on the amount of THC consumed. A very little harm can go a long way if repeated daily for years. What is insignificant for a day may become very significant after a few hundred or few thousand days.

572

Regular smokers should remember that half of a given dose is still in the blood one or two days later. Cannabis is extremely "greasy" and hard to wash out. Although individuals vary, daily smoking is likely to start the process of accumulation of cannabinoids in the body. The daily or almost-daily user should watch for the following **signs of incipient cannabinolism.**

Lethargy, decreased motivation, activity, stamina, and libido

Forgetfulness, losing things

Decreased dreaming and dream recall

Coughing, sore throat, chest pains, being easily winded

Tolerance, as indicated by smoking more and more for the same effect

Harm to many individuals adds up to harm to society. Individuals claim a right to pursuit of happiness, while society claims a right to self defense and defense of the young. Each has a case. The users of cannabis should keep in mind that THC, the agent of their delight (or horror), is an extremely potent chemical whose harmlessness is a myth. Society should realize that education is its best defense and that criminalizing the user plays into the hands of the myth-makers, since the hazards of cannabis are subtle, long-term, and not always obvious to the user, especially the novice.

How To Quit Smoking Cannabis

Make a list of all the reasons you want to quit—the low energy level, poor memory, wasted money and time, harm to the lungs, and so on. Concentrate on these and resolve to avoid the drug. Develop good eating and exercise habits so you'll feel good, and get involved in physical and intellectual hobbies that keep you constructively busy. If you cannot quit on your own, get in touch with Alcoholics Anonymous, Narcotics Anonymous, Potsmokers Anonymous, or another treatment program.

Morning Glory (Ipomoea violacea)

Several varieties of this common ornamental of the bindweed family have substantial amounts of lysergic acid and other substances related to LSD, especially in the seeds. One to two hundred seeds are ground thoroughly, soaked in water, and strained; the liquid is drunk. The experience is mildly LSD-like and it lasts about eight to twelve hours.

Another bindweed, ololuique (Rivea corymbosa), has been used since pre-Columbus times in areas of Mexico. It has similar components and effects.

CAUTION

Morning glory seeds may cause stomach pain, nausea, and vomiting. They are often treated with poisons to retard spoilage and discourage use by thrill seekers. Especially not recommended for pregnant women or those with a history of liver disease or emotional instability.

Muscaria (Amanita muscaria)

Also known as fly agaric, muscaria is one of the most spectacular plants in the forest. The large mushrooms have red caps with white flakes and grow in clusters in temperate zone forests around the world. Muscaria has been used as a vision inducer for centuries in some places. In *The Sacred Mushroom and the Cross* (Doubleday, 1970) author John Allegro makes a case that Christianity evolved from a muscaria-eating fertility cult. Most Christian theologians and historians reject this theory, but there is no doubt muscaria has been involved in religious cults for many centuries.

The main active component, the alkaloid muscimole, is generally considered inferior to psilocybin and mescaline, with more severe side effects and weaker psychedelic effects. Another muscaria alkaloid, ibotenic acid, causes lethargy and flushing of the skin. The various alkaloids are clearly poisonous, and the mushroom has been used as an insecticide; hence the name, fly agaric.

The common pattern after ingestion is nausea, sometimes with vomiting, dizziness, muscle spasms, loss of equilibrium, numbness in the limbs, and a half-sleep stupor with or without visions and increased sensitivity to sounds for about two hours. This is followed by a feeling of well-being or elation, largely relief at the end of the sickness, sometimes with sensory changes and hallucinations for three or four hours.

Most of the muscimole is passed unchanged in the urine. Some traditional users recycle the muscimole by drinking the urine.

CAUTION

Amanita muscaria is closely related to several extremely toxic amanitas, including A. *verna*, A. *phalloides* (the white angel of death), and others. Posi-

574 tive identification of muscaria is absolutely essential. Even then, users risk severely unpleasant sickness, delirium, coma, amnesia, headache, and prolonged confusion. One small to medium mushroom is usually enough to cause symptoms. Few people care to repeat the experience.

Nitrous Oxide

Also known as laughing gas, nitrous oxide was used for fun for at least fifty years before it was used as an anesthetic for simple surgery and childbirth. It was synthesized in 1776 by the English chemist Humphrey Davy, who exposed nitrous peroxide to iron and got nitrous oxide. Davy soon had a swarm of intellectual gay spirits gathered about him for purposes of experimenting and enjoying. Among the luminaries who partook of the gas with Davy were Peter Roget of *Roget's Thesaurus* and the poet Samuel T. Coleridge. To this day laughing gas has been a popular recreational drug, sometimes the main attraction at parties. The usual source is theft from a hospital or restaurant (the aerosol is used for whipping cream).

The effect is generally described as a floating, numb, cool sensation with pleasant tingling, and giddy hilarity. It only lasts about three to five minutes and has little perceivable after effect.

CAUTION
Prolonged inhalation without added oxygen can cause anoxia, brain damage, and death. Frequent use may cause peripheral nerve damage, abnormal sensations, and concentration and memory impairment.

Nutmeg
(Myristica fragrans)

The ground seed of this tropical evergreen tree is a popular spice. It is also sometimes consumed in large amounts (10 to 20 grams) in capsules, mixed with applesauce, or in a drink for its psychoactive effects.

The typical nutmeg "high" includes up to an hour of nausea, followed by a detached, somewhat drunk and silly feeling, with a dry mouth and throat, bloodshot eyes, incoordination, and incoherent speech. Sedation, stupor, and deep sleep usually follow. The total experience lasts about twelve to forty-eight hours, depending on the dose. Prolonged stupor and sleep is the dominant effect. Few people care to repeat the experience.

The active components include myristicin and other volatile oils, which apparently act synergistically to produce the effects. Safrole, the volatile oil which is also present in sassafras and other plants, is a major flavor component, but it is not clear whether it is involved in the psychoactivity.

CAUTION

Safrole is a liver toxin, and should not be consumed frequently or in large amounts.

PCP

Phencyclidine, or PCP, is a synthetic drug patented in 1963 for surgical use as an analgesic and anesthetic that does not depress respiration or heart function. It was withdrawn for use in humans in 1965 because of serious after effects such as confusion, disorientation, agitation, and delirium. It is now marketed as an animal tranquilizer and anesthetic. Ketamine is similar in chemistry, effects, and hazards, and most of what we say about PCP applies to ketamine; the latter is, however, not as easy to synthesize in illegal laboratories and not as widely available.

PCP is easy to make and is sold on the black market as "angel dust," "hog," or (mixed with LSD) as "mescaline" or "psilocybin." This latter has been a very common hoax since the late 1960s. PCP is usually smoked with marijuana or parsley, though it is also snorted up the nostrils, taken by pill, or injected. The dose is 5 mg or more. Tolerance develops and the dose tends to increase with continued use.

The desired effects are a sense of sensory deprivation, isolation, floating, and numbness, sometimes with visions, vivid "dreams," and a sense of separation from the body. The effects last about two to five hours, depending on dose and tolerance. Residual effects and a hangover may include depression, lethargy, irritability, anxiety, and confusion.

PCP abuse is one of the most serious drug problems in the United States. Severe adverse reactions send several thousand young Americans to emergency rooms every year and cause at least a hundred deaths. There is no generally agreed-on antidote to PCP. Minor tranquilizers are sometimes given, but their effectiveness is doubted, and they may actually interfere with the metabolism and excretion of the PCP. Nor does reassurance, or talking a person down, seem to help as it often does with marijuana and LSD overdose.

576

Regular use can cause depression, lethargy, memory and concentration impairment, decreased libido, and other problems. Tolerance and dependence can develop; there may be withdrawal symptoms. Impairment of reflexes and judgment may cause serious accidents.

Overdose is common and may be followed by a psychotic reaction with mania, severe anxiety, severe depression, catatonia, confusion, delusions, paranoia, and violent behavior. There may also be physical symptoms such as nystagmus (involuntary eye rolling), high blood pressure, vomiting, drooling, heavy sweating, loss of bowel and bladder control, and slurred speech. Coma and death are also possible. Psychotic reactions may last days or weeks, with complete amnesia of having taken the drug.

Psychedelic Drugs

Practically everything about these drugs is controversial, though probably less so than in the 1960s when they were at their peak of popularity and notoriety, and their mere mention excited intense fascination or fear. Even the term "psychedelic" is disputed. It was coined by psychiatrist Humphry Osmond from the Greek for "mind revealing" or "mind manifesting" as an alternative to the misleading "hallucinogenic" and "psychotomimetic."

"Hallucination" generally refers to a vivid, convincing perception of sights or sounds with no objective reality such as delirium tremens, "cocaine bugs," the imaginary companions and demons of some psychotics, and the full-blown delusional state induced by an overdose of the deadly nightshade alkaloids. A good example of the latter is Carlos Castaneda turning into a crow after having a smoke of Don Juan's "magic mixture" of nightshades and mushrooms, as described in his book, A *Separate Reality*. Psychedelic visions, on the other hand, are usually limited to altered colors, shapes, and motion, and rarely involve convincing perception of nonexisting objects, situations, or events.

"Psychotomimetic" is misleading because it implies that these drugs mimic psychosis, which they do not, although some of their effects may resemble some symptoms of schizophrenia.[46]

"Psychedelic" is considered misleading by some because, they say, it implies that these drugs are mind expanders, and that nonusers have unexpanded, underdeveloped minds. Here we use the term with recognition that one person's tool for mind expansion, revelation, and ecstasy may be another person's trigger for psychotic withdrawal, paranoia, and misery.

LSD (lysergic acid diethylamide), mescaline, psilocybin, and psilo-cin are the basic or prototype psychedelics. Some would include DMT and a dozen or so methoxylated amphetamines such as MDA and DOM, also known as "STP." DMT is a close chemical relative of psilocybin and has some similar effects but is much shorter acting. (See separate discussion, this chapter.) MDA, DOM, and the rest are chemical hybrids of amphetamine and mescaline, and their effects are generally a similar hybrid.

THC (tetrahydracannabinol), the active component of marijuana, is often listed as a psychedelic, but this is misleading, since its chemistry and effects are very different from the true psychedelics. (See separate discussion of marijuana, this chapter.)

Harmala alkaloids (from yage and other plants) are considered psychedelics by some, but they are substantially different from the classic four, which are generally stimulants, while the harmalas are sedatives.

Here our discussion is limited to LSD, psilocybin, psilocin, and mescaline, which are chemically similar and produce essentially identical effects; cross tolerance between them occurs. They differ greatly in potency, however. The usual doses (which produce equivalent effects) are .1 mg LSD, 10 mg psilocybin or psilocin, and 300 mg mescaline.

What the Psychedelics Do

These drugs produce dramatic changes in perception, mood, emotion, and thinking, without producing (at moderate doses) major physiological changes, delirium, amnesia, or addiction. This has been their primary appeal and accounts for the fact that, far more than all other drugs combined, psychedelics have attracted poets, philosophers, artists, scientists, mystics, and other soul-searching persons as well as thrill seekers. Compelling accounts of the effects of the drugs have been written by Aldous and Laura Huxley, Alan Watts, Anaïs Nin, Humphry Osmond, Weir Mitchell, and many others. Artists and musicians have also given expression to psychedelic inspiration.

The written descriptions are not of euphoria as with cocaine or amphetamines, but of complex perceptual and emotional changes and a sense of wonder, awe, and sometimes terror. Aldous Huxley theorized that the normal filtering mechanisms of the brain are suspended by the drugs, so the person consciously experiences a great deal more of the sensory data and random brain activity than normally. Our filters are necessary to our survival since without them we cannot focus our attention adequately or remember and reason well, because an excess of sensory data is distracting.

But, Huxley reasoned, why not suspend those filters periodically so that we might have a taste of the infinite? This he did regularly until he died. On the day he knew he would finally succumb to the cancer he had fought for so long (November 22, 1963, the day JFK was shot), he asked for and received an LSD injection from his wife, Laura. This was probably its first use in an effort to "die with dignity."

LSD has been used with some reported success (and some failures) as an adjunct to psychotherapy, in alcoholism, and in criminal rehabilitation. It has also been used to ease pain and psychic trauma in terminal cancer patients. However, severe government restrictions have almost eliminated all therapeutic use. Some animal studies continue, but by far the greatest use of these drugs in the United States is illicit.

Psychedelics and the Brain

The billions of neurons in the brain and throughout the nervous system communicate by releasing specific chemical signals (neurotransmitters) across the gaps (synapses) of their junctions. Some areas of the brain depend primarily on the neurotransmitter acetylcholine while others depend on serotonin (5-hydroxytryptamine), norepinephrine, or other substances.

Different psychoactive substances affect different neurotransmitters by increasing or decreasing their release across the synapses, or their uptake by the receiving neurons. In spite of thousands of chemical and animal studies on the psychedelics, especially LSD, about all that can be said so far is that these drugs seem to affect the neurotransmitters serotonin, dopamine, and norepinephrine in various areas of the brain and nervous system.[47]

The Hazards of the Psychedelics

Death by overdose has never been reported except in animals. However, an accidental dose of 20 mg of LSD mistaken for cocaine caused internal bleeding, hypertension, and coma. This is about 200 times the usual dose and is probably close to lethal. It would be difficult to ingest enough mushrooms or peyote to receive lethal doses of psilocybin or mescaline, but large doses of the purified chemicals could probably be fatal.

Death and maiming by accident are real possibilities when psychedelics are taken carelessly, frivolously, and in unsuitable environments. People have walked out of windows and into moving traffic while their perceptions and judgment were distorted or overwhelmed by the onslaught of sensory and emotional data.

Death by suicide during or soon after a psychedelic drug experience has been reported in a few cases of LSD therapy, but the overall incidence of such suicides is no higher than the rate among non-LSD-users undergoing therapy.

Suicides reported among illicit users are complicated by the simultaneous use of other drugs and preexisting emotional problems. Fear of insanity and profound depression after a trip may provoke suicide. Probably the best known case is that of Frank Olson, who was slipped LSD in a drink by the head of MKULTRA, the CIA's mind-control project. Olson had a psychotic breakdown and, two weeks later, killed himself by jumping out of a tenth-story window. His lack of preparation for the experience and his consequent belief that he was insane probably played a large role in his suicide. Slipping people LSD should legally be considered similar to rape, assault, or even attempted murder.

The bad trip can be caused by an overdose, poor preparation, poor setting, mixture with other drugs, or individual susceptibility. It is dominated by fear, anxiety, remorse, paranoia, and above all a sense that one will never be normal again, that insanity and misery will prevail for life, even that the universe itself is inherently evil and hellish. Such reactions usually fade within a day or two, and the person's return to normal is almost as fast and remarkable as his descent into hell had been.

A trusted companion, friend, loved one, or health professional can greatly ease the suffering and reduce the risk of self-harm by repeated assurances that all the changes are illusory and temporary and that everything will be all right in a few hours. It only makes things worse to react with alarm, take drastic therapeutic measures, or reprimand the person.

Chlorpromazine and other tranquilizers often help, possibly by directly inhibiting the drug activity in the brain. Niacin in large doses (up to about a half-gram) may also decrease the effects of the drug and hasten return to normal, but this has not been proven. Coffee and other stimulants should not be taken since they tend to increase anxiety.

Flashbacks are transient recurrences of the perceptual and emotional changes experienced while on a psychedelic. They are most likely during emotional stress, fatigue, and above all marijuana intoxication. They last a few seconds to a few minutes; some enjoy the flashbacks, but some find them frightening.

Brain damage from long-term use has been sought but not found, though very heavy users (several hundred trips) sometimes do suspiciously poorly on some nonverbal abstraction tests. Frequent users tend to be eccentric, unable to hold a job, childlike, passive, and given to magical thinking, but these characteristics are often due, at least in part, to preexisting personality traits and cultural factors.

Precipitation of psychosis by chronic psychedelic use in vulnerable persons has been reported by at least one psychiatrist. His data indicate that hospital-

580 ized schizophrenics who used psychedelics became psychotic at a younger age than those who did not. But critics say too much varied drug use was involved to pin the blame on psychedelics. Some psychiatrists conclude that psychedelic use is often an attempt, usually unsuccessful, to treat one's emotional problems, and that abuse is a symptom, not a cause, of psychosis.

Psychedelics tend to create cults. The charismatic person who takes a psychedelic and comes to believe he has seen or become God easily gathers a flock of unsettled young people made more suggestible by psychedelic use. Such communities and cults were very common in the 1960s and early 1970s. Steve Gaskin's Farm in Tennessee, still thriving, is the bright side of this coin; Charles Manson's murderous cult is the dark side. Many ancient religions and cultures were inspired and heavily influenced by psychedelics. The 3,000-year-old culture of the peyote-using Huicholes of Mexico and the Mazatecas who worship (and ingest) the Sacred Mushroom (psilocybe) are prime examples.

Genetic damage, birth defects, and cancer are apparently not caused by psychedelics, in spite of early fears. At least a hundred studies on animals and humans have shown no excess of these problems in users over nonusers. However, it is still considered prudent for pregnant women to avoid these and all unnecessary drugs.

LSD-25, lysergic acid diethylamide, the 25th in the lysergic acid series, was synthesized in 1938 at Sandoz Laboratories in Switzerland and put aside for lack of interesting effects on animals. But five years later, on April 16, 1943, Dr. Albert Hofman, one of the discoverers, made a few milligrams and accidently ingested or absorbed through his skin a tiny amount, probably about 50 to 75 *micro*grams. He had to interrupt his work and go home. When he lay down he sank into a semiconscious state with fantastic kaleidoscopic visions which lasted about two hours.

Suspecting the LSD, a few days later he took what he thought was a very small dose, 250 micrograms. He expected a mild taste of the previous experience to confirm his suspicion, but got a jolt about three times as great as the first.

Gradually researchers started to work with it the chemical. By 1965 at least 100,000 psychiatric patients and volunteers, including many psychologists, psychiatrists, and other health professionals, had taken LSD. Many of these people effectively proselytized and got their spouses, friends, and collegues to take it. Hofman himself, his wife, and some friends continued to take LSD for many years in the manner of Aldous Huxley, reverently and infrequently.

In the late sixties, with the Vietnam War and social unrest raging, the mass proselytizers like Tim Leary inspired millions to take it, and illicit

LSD use soon dwarfed authorized and discrete use. This is still the case, probably more so than ever.

LSD as it comes from the illicit labs is usually pure, but the "tabbers" who buy it wholesale and make pills ("tabs") often add PCP, a cheaper chemical, and call the product "psilocybin" or "mescaline." Elaborate, ever-changing hoaxes are perpetrated, involving food dyes, chocolate, dried rose hips (to simulate peyote), and other tricks. The doses are quite variable and almost always less than what is stated; "200 mikes" is likely to be about 50 micrograms.

In February 1968, Tim Leary, speaking to a large crowd of cheering Berkeley (California) teenagers, said that "dope dealers are the real campus heroes," and he praised Orange Sunshine (a particularly potent formulation of LSD) as the purest and best "acid" (LSD) available. In the same breath he said the happiest, holiest people he knew took LSD once a week. We can only guess how many bad trips, suicides, and psychotic reactions were precipitated by this talk and the scores of others he gave in those days.

All this has had a profound impact on the use of psychedelics. Leary promoted multidrug use and blatant hedonism. He linked smoking cannabis with taking psychedelics, something that had not been done before. Most of the traditional psychedelic users take their sacraments alone and consider other drugs harmful. Aldous Huxley had earlier (in *Doors of Perception*) put smoking marijuana in a class with drinking alcohol, a relaxing but sometimes unhealthy pastime and the antithesis of a psychedelic experience.

Mescaline is the active component of peyote. Black market products include sliced and dried peyote "buttons" and, rarely, purified mescaline sulfate. Most so-called mescaline sold in tablets and capsules is LSD or PCP or both.

Mescaline is relatively weak and the effective dose is large, nearly a third of a gram, which would be about 3,000 LSD doses. It is very bitter and causes nausea and vomiting for an hour or so. The effects last about six to ten hours.

Peyote, an even stronger emetic than pure mescaline, contains other alkaloids, some of which are toxic. Strychnine is abundant in the hairy tufts on the cactus and these are removed. Peyote has been used for hundreds of years by the Huicholes and other American Indians, especially members of the Native American Church, for whom it is legal. Some young users abuse it and seem to suffer some degree of personality disintegration, much as LSD abusers do. However, moderate use by Church members, no more than once every few months, seems to have socially beneficial effects, somewhat like group therapy, but with rituals and chemically induced suggestibility.

Psilocybin and psilocin are the active components of several species of *Paneolus* and *Psilocybe* mushrooms which grow in many areas of the world

582

and have been used for centuries. Because they are so perishable they are rarely sold on the black market. Almost all illicit "psilocybin" is really LSD or PCP. Psilocybin and psilocin are very powerful drugs with effects comparable to those of LSD, so it is rather astonishing that growing kits, including viable spores, are sold openly and legally through the U.S. mail. Full-page color ads have been running in *High Times* and other magazines for many years, so the enterprise must be very successful. There are apparently no plans to outlaw the spores, so psilocybin and psilocin will remain by far the most potent (gram for gram) of all recreational drugs available legally and without a prescription.

Tobacco

Tobacco use, especially cigarette smoking, is recognized by experts to be the single greatest cause of preventable illness, incapacitation, and death in the United States and many other countries. Almost 400,000 Americans die each year from smoking.[48] The growing recognition of the wide array of health problems caused by tobacco and the astronomical cost of treating them has led to a significant antitobacco movement. Its activities have helped reduce the percentage of people who smoke, but we still have a very long way to go.

History

We can only guess who the first tobacco smoker was and what prompted him or her to inhale the smoke of this large-leafed member of the *Solanaceae* (nightshade, potato) family. Perhaps it was a shaman (medicine man) using the abundant smoke from the burning plant for ritual purposes. By accidently inhaling small amounts regularly he could have become addicted without even knowing it, then learned to roll a dried leaf up so he could conveniently take it everywhere and smoke whenever the urge arose.

Others would have been impressed with the streams and clouds of smoke. They might have believed it was the source of his power, so imitated him. Whole populations could have become addicted this way. In any case, Columbus and other early visitors to America were amazed at the "smoke drinking" habit of the natives. Many sailors who tried it enjoyed it and became addicted. To assure their supply, they took tobacco leaves and seeds back to Europe and around the world.

Tobacco conquered Europe and Africa rapidly. By 1614 there were about 7,000 tobacco shops in London alone. The demand was so high that the dried leaf was worth its weight in silver. It was lamented that many young noblemen's estates were scattered to nothing "for the drinking of smoke," and "lost through their noses." Poor people squandered their bread money and harmed their nations' balance of trade. Naive natives traded valuable land, herds of cattle, and precious stones for a few weeks' supply of the leaf.[49]

Even the Catholic missionaries in the Americas became nicotine addicts. Efforts by the Church to prevent the use of tobacco by the public and the clergy failed. When smoking in church was banned, tobacco snuff was used.

Draconian efforts to stem the tobacco tide failed in many countries. The Sultan Murad IV banned tobacco smoking in Constantinople in 1633. Offenders were hung, beheaded, chopped up, or tortured and maimed to death. Still, people smoked. Eventually Turkish tobacco became world famous. The Czar of Russia outlawed smoking in 1634 under penalties of fines, nostril slitting, and severe beatings. Today the Soviet government insures that the masses get their daily nicotine fix—and it gets the profits.

The Japanese were introduced to tobacco by the very first Europeans to land in their islands, Portuguese seamen on board a Chinese pirate vessel which took refuge from a storm in a Japanese harbor in about 1542. The Portuguese taught the Japanese how to smoke; within a few years the habit had become widespread. In the early 1600s tobacco smoking and cultivation were outlawed. Increasingly severe penalties, including the confiscation of all property and jail terms, were enacted. Still the habit spread. Eventually most of the military and feudal aristocracy became addicted; the laws were rescinded in 1625.

To this day, no country that has once accepted tobacco has later given it up, even in the most dire circumstances such as war and epidemic heart and lung disease associated with smoking.

Nicotine Addiction

The rapid and tenacious spread of the smoking habit around the world, in spite of the initial sickness it causes and the lack of any strongly pleasureable effects, is evidence of the power of the chemical addiction. No one should feel inferior or weak-willed because of failure to quit. Some of the finest minds of the world have been hooked for life.

As early as age thirty-eight, Sigmund Freud was warned by his doctor to reduce his twenty-cigar-a-day habit or risk continued heart arrhythmias and possibly serious heart disease. Freud stopped once for seven weeks but suffered depression and "severe affection of the heart, worse than I had when smoking." He renewed the habit. Later he quit again, this time for fourteen months. According to his friend and fellow psychoanalyst Dr. Ernest Jones, "the torture was beyond human power to bear." He struggled

584 unsuccessfully against the habit for another twenty years, in spite of his own concern that the habit interfered with his psychoanalytic studies and caused increasing heart pain, "tobacco angina," whenever he smoked.

At age sixty-seven, Freud noticed cancerous sores on his palate and jaw. For the next sixteen years of his life he went through thirty-three operations, during which most of his jaw was removed. He was often in severe pain and unable to speak, eat, or work. His doctors blamed his cigars, but he continued to smoke; he died of cancer at the age of eighty-three. It seems plausible that Freud's unsuccessful struggle against his tobacco habit helped to inspire his theory of Thanatos, the opposite of Eros, the subconscious longing for the grave.

There have been thousands, perhaps millions, like Freud: victims of tobacco-induced angina but unable to quit smoking; lung cancer and stroke victims puffing away on their way home from the hospital; emphysema patients reaching alternately for their oxygen masks and their cigarettes until the bitter end.

Heroin addicts often say that kicking tobacco is more difficult than kicking heroin. Part of the problem is that the withdrawal symptoms can last for many months before subsiding. They include extreme anxiety, voracious and uncontrollable appetite with weight gain, depression, irritability, intellectual impairment, drowsiness, lethargy, insomnia, dizziness, and heart palpitations.

Many studies have shown that the addicting substance in tobacco is nicotine, an alkaloid which is well absorbed by lung and mouth, acts as a sympathetic and parasympathetic nervous system stimulant, and liberates norepinephrine from its stores, causing sharp vasoconstriction and increased blood pressure. It also enters the brain and produces changes perceived as stimulating or relaxing, depending on the person's needs at the moment. It is very short acting; the typical addict takes tobacco smoke or snuff continuously throughout the day. If the nicotine concentration is lowered, more cigarettes are smoked. If he is given nicotine (without his knowledge) by intravenous drip, he unconsciously smokes less.[50]

Nicotine is actually a deadly poison. The amount in one cigarette, if all absorbed at once, could cause death by respiratory paralysis. It has been used as an insecticide. The body recognizes it as a poison and tries to cough or vomit it out the first few times but tolerance develops, the immediately unpleasant side effects subside, and the dose is increased. The youngster who gags on his first few puffs but persists is soon a full-fledged addict. It has been estimated that 70 percent of those who smoke more than one cigarette during adolescence will continue smoking for the next forty years. Few if any other drugs can claim such potent addicting power. Even in wartime conditions with near-starvation rations, addicts will often trade their little food for tobacco.

America's Favorite Poison

The tobacco habit is the largest single cause of disease and premature death in the United States. It is also enormously costly. The lifetime cost of the tobacco alone can top $50,000 (including interest if the money were saved instead) for one person. The cost of medical care for the many health problems caused by smoking can be even greater. Then there is the cost of fires, insurance, and lost work time. This drain on resources can greatly decrease an individual's, a family's, or a nation's standard of living. The total cost to Americans is $50 billion to $100 billion, not counting subsidies to tobacco farmers.

Below is a brief summary of the problems of smoking. The degree of risk is associated with the number of cigarettes smoked, their tar and nicotine content, and the depth of inhalation. Some of the risks also apply, but usually to a lesser degree, to cigar and pipe smoking and, to a far less extent, to chronic exposure to smokefilled air.

Atherosclerosis and heart attack. By promoting hardening of the arteries, weakening heart muscle, increasing the clotting rate (platelet clumping), causing wild, irregular beating, and reducing the oxygen-carrying capacity of the blood, smoking increases the rate of heart attack by about three-fold. The excess of deaths from heart disease due to smoking is much greater even than the excess of deaths from lung cancer due to smoking. The risk is greatly increased by the presence of other factors such as high cholesterol levels and the use of birth control pills. The generalized atherosclerosis promoted by smoking can also impair memory and causing hearing loss.

Hypertension and strokes. High blood pressure can be aggravated by smoking. This and the increased atherosclerosis increase the risk of a stroke. Women who both smoke and use birth control pills are especially at risk. Malignant hypertension is much more likely to develop in persons with high blood pressure who smoke than in those who don't. Once this phase develops, it is more likely to be lethal in smokers.

Peripheral vascular disease is promoted by cigarette smoking. The legs are commonly affected by intermittent claudication, muscle pains from exercise due to poor circulation. Diabetics are especially vulnerable because the smoking increases the blood vessel damage done by the disease. Buerger's disease, with inflammation, scarring, and clot formation in blood vessels of the leg occurs in a few people, mostly young Jewish men with unusual sensitivity to tobacco.

Emphysema. Tobacco smoke with its tars coats the alveoli (air sacs) of the

586 lungs causing them to lose their normal elasticity. The alveoli eventually disintegrate into nonfunctional scar tissue worthless for breathing. The damage is irreversible and the victim becomes a cripple for life. Smoking is by far the most important single cause of emphysema.

Lung cancer. Tobacco smoke is full of proven carcinogens and cocarcinogens that coat the lungs of smokers. It is not surprising that smoking is by far the most important cause of lung cancer, one of the leading causes of cancer deaths. Women, who once rarely got lung cancer, have come a long way and now die of the disease with increasing frequency. One reason the cancer is so deadly is that there are often no symptoms or X-ray signs until it has spread to other organs.

Mouth cancer. Carcinogenic chemicals from tobacco smoke enter the cells of the lining of the mouth and tongue. Years of exposure leads to yellowish-white, leathery plaques (leukoplakia) which frequently become cancerous.

Cancer of the larynx is six times as frequent in smokers as in nonsmokers. Detected early (watch for persistent hoarseness without pain), it can be cured by X-ray treatment or removal of the larynx. An artificial voicebox may be necessary for speech. Almost 90 percent of these cancers could be prevented if no one smoked.

Chronic bronchitis is a frequent consequence of cigarette smoking. The respiratory mucosal cells produce extra mucus in response to the irritating smoke particles and chemicals. There is frequent coughing and shortness of breath, and recurring respiratory infections. Smokers and children frequently exposed to cigarette smoke are more susceptible to colds and influenza.

Cancer of the uterine cervix is strongly associated with cigarette smoking, especially if the habit was taken up in the early teens or sooner. The cause is apparently the smoke carcinogens carried to the uterine epithelium by the circulation. Many young and middle-aged women die or are rendered sterile by surgery. The total of tobacco-related deaths due to cervical and lung cancers in women exceeds the total of tobacco-related deaths due to lung cancer in men.

Bladder cancer is more frequent among smokers because the carcinogens from the smoke are in the urine and in continuous contact with the bladder cells for years and decades.

Kidney, esophageal, and pancreatic cancer risks are also greatly increased by smoking.

Peptic ulcers are aggravated and sometimes caused by smoking; the nicotine increases inflammation and retards healing of the lesions.

Burns. About a third of all fatalities and serious injuries from burns are caused by fires associated with smoking.

Sinusitis is much more frequent in smokers and in persons living with smokers. The headache and sinus pain are caused by chronic inflammation of the mucus membranes of the sinuses.

Dental and gum disease is greatly increased in smokers, who have about twice the nonsmokers' chance of becoming toothless before age sixty. This is largely due to the contribution made to plaque formation by the tobacco tars.

Osteoporosis. Smoking may promote osteoporosis, a crippling bone disease, by increasing calcium removal from the bones. This is especially hazardous to postmenopausal women.

A weakened esophageal sphincter can be caused by smoking. This can lead to reflux of stomach contents and consequent "heartburn."

Vitamin C deficiency. Cigarette smoking decreases vitamin C absorption and increases the requirement.

Low birth weight, stillbirths, and serious maternal bleeding are much more likely if the mother smokes during pregnancy. This is because the nicotine and carbon monoxide decrease the supply of blood, oxygen, and nutrients to the fetus. Malformations, such as cleft palate, may also be more likely.

Infant and child health can be adversely affected by tobacco components ingested in the breast milk of smoking mothers or inhaled in the air. Bronchitis and pneumonia are more common in infants with smoking mothers. Infants are very sensitive to cigarette smoke and can develop aversions to foods they associate with the nausea from nicotine.

Mouth odor and stained teeth due to smoking are significant aesthetic turn-offs. Smoking also deadens the taste buds and decreases the pleasure of eating.

Decreased libido among smokers has been noted by several researchers. This may be due to the decreased testosterone production, which tends to increase within a week or two of quitting.

588
What About Low-Tar, Low-Nicotine, and Filtered Cigarettes?

Cigarettes with lower levels of harmful substances have been developed by changes in growing and curing methods and by the use of various kinds of filter tips. These low-yield cigarettes are apparently slightly less dangerous to the lungs and larynx, but there is no evidence that they do less damage to the cardiovascular system than regular cigarettes.[51] This is to be expected since filters generally do not lower the level of carbon monoxide, which does the most harm to the blood vessels and heart. Anyway, smokers tend to inhale deeper and faster when they switch to a low-nicotine brand. In a sense low-yield cigarettes are the most dangerous because they are generally milder tasting and make it much easier for novices and youngsters to start the habit.

What About Chewing Tobacco and Snuff?

Early American Indians not only smoked rolled tobacco leaves; a few of them preferred to sniff powdered tobacco through tubes. Many Europeans preferred this more discrete method of getting a dose of nicotine. At some point someone decided to suck rather than sniff the tobacco. Chewing tobacco, which usually has sugar and other additives, is now much more popular than snuff but still far less so than cigarettes. Smokers enjoy the clouds of smoke and the ritual of smoking.

Smokeless tobacco has certain health advantages over the smoking varieties since it does not produce the dangerous gases (carbon monoxide, hydrogen cyanide, and nitrogen oxides) that are so harmful to the lungs and circulatory system. However, in most users there is abrasion of the teeth and recession of the gums which can lead to or aggravate **dental and gum disease**. Even more important, nearly 5 percent of habitual user develop **cancers** in their mouths, often in the area where the tobacco is held.[52] This causes almost 10,000 deaths a year in the United States. Moreover, the nicotine in smokeless tobacco can aggravate **ulcers** and **hypertension** and provoke **heart arrhythmias**.

How To Stop Smoking

Not everyone finds quitting as difficult as Freud did. Millions of Americans have quit smoking for long periods. Some eventually return to smoking, but many stay free of the habit for life. Success depends on a number of factors, including the level of addiction (how much smoking for how long), the motivation to quit, and the use of effective quitting techniques.

We can't affect anyone's level of addiction, but the above discussion should provide some motivation to quit. Here we briefly discuss some of the methods that have been used successfully by others. No one of them can be guaranteed to work for everyone. It has been said that there are as many stop-smoking methods as there are ex-smokers. And some people do not need any particular method or technique; with motivation and willpower they simply quit. If this has not worked for you, some of the following suggestions might help.

Work up to quitting for a few days. When you smoke, concentrate on the harshness and the stench. Visualize the hundreds of harmful chemicals coating your mouth, throat, and lungs, and damaging your arteries, heart, and brain. When you are not smoking, imagine yourself an ex-smoker with clean-smelling breath and clothes and a clear brain. Visualize your lungs pink, clean, and healthy; your heart unhurried by nicotine and unencumbered by carbon monoxide; and your arteries clear and wide open. Imagine yourself declining offered cigarettes. It is important to recognize that you are not giving up or losing anything; you are gaining health, money, and time.

Learn stress-reducing deep relaxation techniques such as autosuggestion and meditation (see Part Six). The visualizations above are especially effective if practiced during relaxation. During the withdrawal period, application of stress-reduction methods helps minimize the anxiety and other symptoms.

Start a regular exercise program. This will counter the withdrawal symptoms by making you feel generally better physically and mentally, helping you to relax and sleep better, and building your self-confidence. It will also help prevent fat gain, which is a problem in about a third of those who quit smoking.

Recruit at least one supporter, preferably an ex-smoker, who will accept your commitment to quit, check on your progress, and lend encouragement when you need it. Your local American Cancer Society can provide you with names of ex-smokers who volunteer for this role.

When the urge to smoke is strong, invoke the negative imagery of "rotted" lungs and clogged-up arteries. Make the image vivid so you emotionally feel it. Within a few minutes the urge should subside. Now invoke the positive image as a "reward" for holding out. When the urge to buy cigarettes hits you, think of how much it costs and what important or fun things you could buy instead.

590

Improve your diet. Smokers tend to have lower levels of vitamin C and sometimes other nutrients. Supplements may be helpful if the diet has been poor. A tablespoon or two of brewer's yeast or wheat germ or a vitamin B pill can assure your jangled nerves a plentiful supply of the vitamins they need most on a regular basis.

Use oral substitutes if necessary. Carrots, cucumbers, celery, chewing gum, cinnamon sticks, ginger root, and toothpicks are favorites. (Caution: toothpicks are the most commonly choked-on items in America.) If you do gain weight, don't use this as an excuse to resume smoking. You would have to gain about a hundred pounds to equal the damage to your health done by tobacco.

Avoid alcohol and caffeine since these tend to increase the urge to smoke. Avoid other sedatives and stimulants, since they tend to cloud the mind and weaken resolve. In some cases, however, the anxiety is so severe that tranquilizers may be useful in getting through the first few days. Small amounts of herbal sedatives such as valerian and skullcap may help (see Chapter 5-3).

Get plenty of rest and sleep. Chronic fatigue weakens the resolve and willpower.

Break up the patterns in your life associated with smoking. If you normally smoke after eating, take a walk or bike ride instead. If you are used to smoking while you watch television, floss your teeth instead. For the first few days keep as busy as you can. Spend time in areas where smoking is prohibited. Go camping without any cigarettes.

If you are tapering off, postpone lighting each day's first cigarette for an hour. Don't empty your ashtrays; this will remind you how unpleasant smoking is, and how much you smoke. Set a schedule and stick to it. For the last week before you quit, smoke about four to six cigarettes a day. When you light up concentrate on the negative imagery developed earlier.

Many smokers find that reducing their frequency below ten to fifteen cigarettes a day is especially difficult. It may be necessary to stay at this level for several weeks before cutting down to less and quitting. If you find you can't stick with very low levels, don't give up and return to your previous level. Rather, return to your tapering rate of about half a pack a day and stay there until you feel stronger, less stressed, and more motivated to quit.

Chemical aids are of limited benefit. Bantron contains lobeline, a chemical analogue of nicotine which theoretically reduces withdrawal symptoms but seems more a placebo. Some products contain silver acetate, copper sulfate, or other chemicals which leave a bad taste in the mouth when a cigarette is smoked. None of them can boast of very significant success.

Nicotine gum, available by prescription only, is apparently quite helpful in reducing withdrawal symptoms and helping people quit smoking.[53] It satisfies the craving without the carbon monoxide, cyanide, tars, and other toxins supplied by cigarettes. It doesn't even cause gum and dental problems like chewing tobacco does. If you have not been able to quit smoking, ask your doctor about nicotine gum. If you do get a prescription, use the gum strictly according to instructions and keep it out of the reach of children. It is usually not recommended for persons with peptic ulcers or cardiovascular disease or for pregnant or nursing women. The gum works best when one is also enrolled in a stop-smoking program. It costs about $2 to $5 a month and usually must be taken for ten to twenty weeks.

Formal group programs can be very helpful. Some are free and some charge up to $450 with a money-back guarantee. The American Cancer Society, Seventh Day Adventist Church, and some hospitals offer regular group sessions. Stop-smoking programs on the job have been proving quite successful and are an ideal way to improve employee health and reduce absenteeism and health care costs.

Rapid smoking is a technique we would advise against for most people. Two cigarettes are smoked in rapid succession, puffing fast to increase the heat. You inhale deeply and recall the nausea you felt the first time you smoked.

CAUTION

This rapid smoking technique, which is used in some stop-smoking clinics, can be hazardous. Because the carbon monoxide combines with hemoglobin, there is a drastic reduction of oxygen available to the heart and brain, yet the nicotine speeds up the heart. Therefore, this method should not be used by persons with known or suspected atherosclerosis or heart disease.

Let's Save Our Children

The initial motivation for an individual youngster to start smoking is probably similar to the motivation for our hypothetical early smokers who imitated shamans. Children associate the clouds and streams of smoke with adulthood, authority, and power. If cigarette smoke were invisible, or if nicotine addicts took pills instead of smoking, the fascination would not exist. Movies and cigarette commercials further enhance the appeal with their grossly misleading association of smoking with beauty, love, machismo, sex, fun, and health.

592

The power of these lures is so great that adolescents gladly suffer nausea and other symptoms to achieve the perceived status of the smoker. The prospect of heart disease or lung cancer forty or even twenty years down the road seems infinitely remote to teenagers. But a three-pronged approach could eventually reduce the number of youngsters who take up smoking.

Parents can set a good example by not smoking, not allowing smoking in the house, and encouraging a healthy life style with involvement in sports, good nutrition and so on. This is more likely to be effective than prohibiting children from smoking, which might produce the forbidden-fruit syndrome.

Legislatures and communities can further restrict smoking in public buildings, the sale of cigarettes to children, and advertising.

Schools can "inoculate" students against smoking at an early age. Some such programs have greatly reduced the number of students who take up smoking in subsequent years. Kindergarten to seventh grade appears to be the best time to present the facts of smoking, develop an awareness of the absurd and misleading nature of cigarette ads, and provide assertiveness training and effective counters to peer pressure to smoke.

The government should stop subsidizing tobacco growers, and a hefty federal tax should be levied to force cigarette manufacturers and smokers to pay a fair share for the health facilities smokers use so much more than nonsmokers.

For information on the rights of nonsmokers in public areas and work places, contact ASH (Action on Smoking and Health). (See Appendix B.)

Yohimbe
(Corynanthe yohimbe)

The commonly available inner bark of this tropical West African tree is steeped for several minutes and drunk. It is a stimulant and alleged aphrodesiac. The main active component is the alkaloid yohimbine, which resembles LSD in chemical structure but not in effects. It is mainly a mild mental stimulant, but large doses can cause profuse sweating, anxiety, nervousness, and insomnia.

Preliminary clinical studies show that yohimbine belongs to a class of drugs known as alpha blockers, which dilate skin capillaries, and suggest that the drug may be useful in the treatment of impotence due to diabetes. Studies are under way. Yohimbine is also reported to be a monoamine oxidase inhibitor, which means it might be hazardous if mixed with nasal de-congestants or foods containing Tyramine, such as liver, wines, and cheeses.

A crystalline extract of yohimbe containing large amounts of yohimbine is sold ostensibly as incense but commonly used as a cocaine substitute or aldulterant. The white crystals resemble cocaine in appearance and taste (bitter) but not in effects or cost. Snorting yohimbe extract alone or mixed with cocaine can be hazardous, especially to persons with abnormal blood pressure, heart problems, or kidney or liver disease.

6

Controversial Alternatives

PART SIX

Acupuncture and Acupressure
Chelation Therapy
Chiropractic
Colonic Lavage
DMSO
Gerovital, the "Anti-Aging Wonder Drug"
Hair Analysis
Hanging Upside Down
Homeopathy and Cell Salts
Hypnosis and Autosuggestion
Iridology
Jason Winters' Herbal Tea
Laetrile
Laugh Therapy
Mendelsohn's "Heresy"—A Reply
Muscle Response Testing
Naturopathy
Pangamic Acid ("Vitamin B-15")
Pearson/Shaw Longevity Theory
Psychic Surgery
Rebirthing
Relaxation/Meditation
Snake Venom
"Tanning" Pills
Yoga for Health

Introduction

Over the last twenty years or so the medical profession and its methods have come under heavy critical attacks from within and without its ranks. There is unhappiness with the cost of medical care, its often impersonal nature, and its failure to produce expected miracles, and with abuses such as unnecessary surgery and excessive drug prescription. This has encouraged the revival of old methods and folk remedies, as well as the development of new alternatives.

Some of these methods would discard the baby with the bathwater. Rather than improve the science and humanity of medicine, they would throw it all out and start over with their own premises and principles. Other alternative systems seek only to contribute a method and not overthrow anything. In either case the proponents may be sincere or they may be cynical con artists out to make a buck.

While some of the methods are useful, practical, and inexpensive, others are money-making scams. A quack remedy is one which is based not on facts but on pseudoscientific false claims deliberately cooked up to defraud people of money. Bogus cancer and arthritis treatments alone cost Americans $7 billion each year. Mail-order companies and clinics, especially along the U.S.-Mexican border, dispense worthless, dangerous, and costly treatments to millions. We should all understand and keep in mind that, contrary to common belief, neither the government nor the private sector, including the medical profession, protects us from charlatans and sincere but misguided zealots. It is our responsibility to learn the truth and protect ourselves.

While Federal laws prohibit mail fraud and all states have laws regulating health professionals and forbidding the practice of medicine without a license, these laws are easily circumvented. Incredible as it may seem, most states do not have criminal sanctions against the promotion of quack remedies. The FDA, which has the broadest authority to control quackery, devotes less than one-thousandth of 1 percent of its budget to that purpose. Neither it nor the Postal Service has the manpower to pursue any but the most flagrant lawbreakers, and they are frequently stymied in the courts by the lawyers of wealthy operators who keep raking in vast profits while their cases are litigated. Even if the quacks are finally shut down, they usually start a new racket in a new area.

The nation's magazines and newspapers participate in health scams by running hundreds of millions of dollars worth of false and misleading ads for bust developers, wrinkle removers, aphrodisiacs, weight reducers, penis enlargers, baldness remedies, and various quack remedies for arthritis and other problems. Most people assume that postal regulations and responsible media managers assure the integrity of commercials. It just is not so. The

Quackery A huge growth industry that dwarfs its competition

cancer quackery $5 billion	arthritis quackery $2 billion	anti-aging quackery $2 billion	other quackery $1 billion

$10 billion   This total does not include money spent on books, articles, and para-
phernalia for worthless and dangerous weight-loss diets; megavitamins,
and other unnecessary supplements; unnecessary use of OTC drugs
stimulated by false and misleading ads; and chiropractic treatments for
a wide range of ailments for which there is no evidence of effectiveness.
If these were included, the total would be much higher.

Bona Fide Expenditures

Rx $1.4 billion	OTC $1.2 billion

$2.6 billion   spent on approved drugs for arthritis

$1 billion   cancer research

$.5 billion   heart disease research

$80 million   arthritis research

$76 million   total American Cancer Society budget for public education, patient services,
community services

3.9 million   total combined anti-quackery budgets of FDA, FTC, Postal Service

Source: See Appendix B

postal inspectors simply cannot keep up with the flood of health promotions, and the ad editors are loathe to cut dubious but profitable ads. Even some of the nation's most respected and widely read periodicals have continued to run misleading ads from promoters already in trouble with the Postal Service or other government agency for fraudulent practices. Newspapers all over the country run misleading ads and puff pieces (interviews and cheery articles) for local chiropractors, naturopaths, acupuncturists, and other practitioners who advertise in their pages.

Books are perhaps even less subject to any compulsion to be accurate and truthful. Although civil redress is sometimes possible where false information has led to bodily harm, there is no law that prevents mistaken theories from being printed. Since there is usually no way to legally prove someone lied rather than simply held a mistaken belief, lies can also be published. This is as it should be in a free society; but the price we must pay is eternal vigilance and skepticism. So, *caveat emptor:* let the buyer beware. The information in this chapter should help you make rational decisions.

Acupuncture and Acupressure

There are several distinct systems of diagnosis and healing derived from the ancient Chinese practice of acupuncture. In the United States these systems are semisanctioned. Neither Medicare nor Medicaid honors claims for acupuncture treatment, but some health insurance companies will pay if an M.D. performs it. Most states allow only M.D.s, but some license traditional acupuncturists to practice with physicians and a handful let them practice on their own. For information on the status and regulation of acupuncture in your state, call your state board of regulatory agencies or your local medical society.

Traditional Acupuncture[1]

Traditional acupuncture is practiced mostly by non-M.D.s and is considered archaic by many who use modern methods. The theories and practices have been handed down largely unchanged from ancient Taoist China. The basic theory is that the human organs are subject to disease when there are imbalances in the chi (ki), or energy flow, which has two components: yin and yang, or feminine and masculine.

Balance between these forces can be restored by stimulating, with extremely fine needles, certain specific points (there are several hundred) located along fourteen major meridians running the length of the body.

Each point corresponds to an organ and its functions. The needles are inserted a millimeter or so deep and twirled to move the chi into or out of different organs as deemed necessary. They may then be left in for several minutes. In a variation called moxabustion, small piles of moxa, the leaves of the Chinese wormwood tree, are burned at the ends of the needles or directly on the acupuncture points.

The points to be stimulated depend on the symptoms, the season and weather, the patient's sex, the time of day, and above all the results of taking the pulse at the wrist. This takes several minutes to a couple hours since it is believed that each wrist has six pulses corresponding to six different organs, and each pulse has about twenty-five qualities. So some 300 distinct characteristics in a patient's pulse must be studied and judged to make a diagnosis and commence treatment. The master pulse readers can supposedly detect illnesses long before there are any symptoms and cure them with acupuncture treatments.

To obtain the desired effects on the organs, that is, to increase or decrease the yin or yang to the liver, lungs, heart, or other organ, the needles are inserted rapidly or slowly, twirled clockwise or counterclockwise, used hot or cold, left in for longer or shorter periods, and removed rapidly or slowly. Using these methods acupuncturists can supposedly cure just about any disease, ailment, or symptom one might suffer including infections like malaria, cholera, measles, and pneumonia as well as heart disease, ulcers, kidney diseases, epilepsy, visual disorders, and hundreds of others.

Does It Work?

There are several good reasons to be skeptical of traditional acupuncture and its claims. The system was developed in China more than 4,000 years ago, long before there was any real understanding of human physiology and anatomy or even physics and chemistry. Bodies were not dissected and studied, and each organ was either yin or yang and likened to one of the "basic five elements": water, metal, earth, fire, or wood. The network of meridians and points, claimed by the traditionalists to function independently of the nervous and circulatory systems, has never been proven to exist. The concept of twelve pulses for twelve organs is perhaps the most difficult to accept.

Acupuncturists speak of moving yin and yang energies along the meridians to and from yin and yang organs, guided by scores of superstitious sounding principles such as the spleen is the center of thought, the liver produces tears, and the kidneys are the seat of willpower and fear. But there are serious disagreements among the different schools; anywhere from 35 to 900 points are claimed to exist, and the existence of some meridians is in dispute.

Given all this, skepticism is the natural reaction. Moreover, there is no hard evidence, in the form of careful clinical studies which control for the power of suggestion, that disease processes can be slowed by acupuncture. Nevertheless, there appears to be a basis in fact for at least some of the claims. The core of apparent truth is pain relief. If it relieves the pain while the body heals itself, it will get credit for a cure. This analgesic claim is discussed further under Modern Acupuncture (below).

What Are the Hazards?

Students of traditional acupuncture are warned that a slightly misplaced needle can cause more harm than the disease they are trying to cure by moving the chi the wrong way or by damaging a blood vessel or nerve. The needles used in the old days were more like slender knives and did carry severe risks. But most of the needles used now are hardly larger than a human hair and carry only a small risk of causing injury. There is, of course, a risk of contracting hepatitis and other infections from improperly sterilized needles.

After each use acupuncture needles should be physically cleaned, then sterilized in a steam autoclave of at least 121°C for at least fifteen minutes. Chemical disinfectants are not adequate.

But surely the **greatest hazard** of relying on a traditional acupuncturist is the danger of **suppressing pain without a diagnosis** of the cause. Unless and until it is clearly proven that acupuncture can help cure diseases, it should be considered as a reliever of symptoms, somewhat like aspirin. We all know better than to take aspirin to, say, relieve a toothache without getting a dentist to clean out the infection and repair the tooth. It is similarly unwise to rely on an acupuncturist without consulting a medical doctor to determine the cause of the problem.

Modern Acupuncture

In the 1970s Western interest in acupuncture was given a tremendous boost by the American-Chinese rapprochement, which fostered cultural, scientific, and medical exchanges. American politicians, journalists, and other visitors were treated to remarkable demonstrations of acupuncture anesthesia for brain, abdominal, and other major surgery with the patient completely conscious, speaking, and sometimes eating. Enthusiasts predicted a revolution in anesthesiology, with acupuncture replacing chemicals.

As is turned out, the patients in the staged surgery had been very carefully chosen on the basis of various criteria, including, no doubt, a desire to make a political gesture supporting the correctness of the ideas of Chairman Mao, who had long given strong official support to traditional

Chinese medicine. The patients were generally strong and healthy, and the required surgery was not of the most traumatic variety. Moreover, many of them were given tranquilizers before the surgery.

In post-Mao China only a small minority of patients requiring major surgery receive acupuncture anesthesia. Chemical anesthetics such as ether, nitrous oxide, and sodium pentathol are considered simpler, faster, and much more reliable. Moreover, when acupuncture is used the majority of patients experience some pain and discomfort, which can be seen in the faces of some of the patients in the staged operations. Another consideration is that most people would not want to be awake while their innards were being worked on. Who would want to hear the crunching or sawing of their bones and the discussion of the operation as it proceeds? Or see their blood and parts of organs being removed?

Nevertheless, the interest stimulated has led to laboratory and clinical studies by competent scientists in the United States, the People's Republic of China, and other countries, and to a clearer view of acupuncture's efficacy as an analgesic in myriad chronic-pain syndromes, in spite of its inappropriateness in most cases for surgery. Modern acupuncture research has radically altered the theories and practices of the art. Not all the studies have been duplicated or the conclusions verified, but the picture emerging seems to explain a lot and provides a basis for further study.

The most significant of the modern studies purport to link acupuncture to brain neurotransmitters such as serotonin and acetylcholine, as well as endorphins and enkephalins, extremely potent brain hormones which relieve pain. Chinese scientists claim their experiments show that acupuncture stimulates the release of endorphins. For example, the drug naloxone, which blocks the effects of opiates and endorphins by occupying the receptor sites for these chemicals in the caudate nucleus of the brain, apparently also blocks acupuncture analgesia. If verified, experiments like this will help put acupuncture on a solid scientific footing.[2]

Important studies in the West have shown that many major acupuncture points coincide with the points where the nerves enter the muscles and that needling some points activates muscle pressure and stretch receptors, sending impulses along afferent (sensory) nerves to the brain where they interfere with and overwhelm incoming pain impulses.

In the West most modern acupuncturists are medical doctors who have abandoned the fanciful ancient theories, the meridians, and most of the acupuncture points themselves. Many fewer points are used and the doctors, instead of twirling the needles, usually send tiny electrical currents through them. The treatments are apparently of significant benefit in certain types of chronic pain. But the results are usually not immediate or dramatic and treatment sometimes continues daily for months. So one must not entertain hopes of a miracle.

Traditional Acupressure

Traditional acupressure, also known as reflexology, *do-in*, or *shiatsu*, is almost identical to traditional acupuncture except that the points are stimulated by hand rather than with needles. Using the thumbs and fingers, the reflexologist rubs, massages, slaps, and applies prolonged deep pressure to specific points in order to alleviate specific symptoms.

Books, articles, and advertisements about reflexology make rather fantastic claims about curing and preventing all manner of minor and serious ailments. Such claims have never been scientifically studied, much less proven, so skepticism is in order, and we would not recommend the treatment for anyone with persistant pain or other symptoms without first consulting a physician to determine the cause.

Nevertheless, reflexology treatments can be very pleasant and relaxing, and there are no potentially contaminated needles to worry about. If pain and discomfort are relieved at a moderate cost and without sidetracking a person from adequate medical care, a useful service is being performed. It should also be noted, however, that acupressure treatments are sometimes painful; this depends on the practitioner and the particular methods used.

Modern Acupressure

Modern acupressure was developed by Dr. Howard Kurland, Professor of Psychiatry at Northwestern University Medical School. He describes the system, which he calls auto-acupressure because it is a do-it-yourself technique, in his book, *Quick Headache Relief Without Drugs* (William Morrow, 1981).

Kurland's simple system has nothing to do with mystical meridians or channeling chi into yin and yang organs. Nor is it about preventing or curing diseases, and Kurland cautions persons with persistant headaches, or fever with a headache, to consult a physician.

In Kurland's system the dozen or so points used are loci where sizable nerves are close to the surface and responsive to direct pressure. The idea is to stimulate impulses in the nerve which will travel to the brain and interfere with the pain impulses. Pressure is applied with a thumbnail which has been rounded to prevent penetration of the skin.

The following is a brief discussion of how to use some of the points. As far as we know, proper studies have not been done and there is no proof of efficacy, so the system should be considered experimental. But many people claim to have been helped, and the procedures cost nothing and are so simple and harmless that they seem worth trying.

604

When attempting to locate the points, keep in mind the sensation of hitting your ulnar nerve ("funny bone") at the elbow. It is a combination of pain, numbness, and tingling. This is similar to what you feel when you have found a point. According to Kurland, the points are more sensitive and easier to find when one has a headache.

Use the smooth, trimmed nails of the thumbs, bent at right angles, to locate and put pressure on the points. Do not be afraid to dig in and press hard, even if it hurts a little (but not so hard that the skin breaks).

Here are some details on the three pairs of points that seem to be the most responsive. Practice locating them beforehand so you can quickly apply pressure next time you feel a headache developing. Kurland recommends always treating both points of each pair and treating the hand points before the head points. The following three all come in pairs.

Hand point one is between the base of the thumb and index finger. When the thumb and finger are held together the point is on the back of the hand on the peak of the fleshy mound formed by the triangular web of flesh. When you locate this tender spot press down and in with the thumbnail while pressing up with the fingers on the palm side. Press hard for up to about thirty seconds.

Head point one is a finger's breath from the bony ridge at the outer corner of the eye. It is not as far back as the hollow of the temple. Both points of the pair should be simultaneously stimulated. Clasp your hands in front of your face with your fingers interlocked and bend your thumbs at right angles. Bring the thumbs to the points and hold your head in a caliper-like grip. Press the points hard and maintain a steady or rhythmic on-and-off pressure for at least fifteen seconds.

Head point two is in the back of the neck, right under and against the base of the skull in a small muscular groove about halfway between the center groove of the back of the neck and the mastoid bone just behind the ear. To stimulate the pair simultaneously, clasp your fingers together behind your head (or on top) and push your bent thumbnails hard inward against the base of the skull.

The Strange Case of EAV

Electroacupuncture according to Voll (EAV), named by Dr. Reinhold Voll of West Germany after himself, makes some of the most astonishing claims in the annals of alternative medicine. Either EAV will revolutionize medicine (as is supporters promise it will) and win Voll a Nobel prize, or it will go down in history as one of the strangest, yet most sophisticated, health hoaxes ever dreamed up. We wouldn't bet on the former.

In several textbooks, most of which sell for $50 or more, and in articles, especially in the *American Journal of Acupuncture*, Voll presents his findings and theories. EAV is based on traditional acupuncture with its meridians and points, but there are many modifications. Voll uses a galvanometer to measure the voltage between hundreds of points, primarily for purposes of diagnosis. Treatment consists of traditional needling, diet, homeopathic remedies, and surgery.

Using his machine, Voll claims to be able to pinpoint the site of a lesion in an organ, such as the precise location of a peptic ulcer. The diagnoses and reported causes are often utterly fantastic. Arthritis, diabetes, heart disease, and other ailments can be traced to childhood vaccinations and, according to some followers, even to tuberculosis, venereal disease, or other infection in one of your ancestors several generations ago.

Voll assures us his techniques can immediately and precisely determine the cause of any disease without reference to any other tests or to the patient's history or medical records. Among the most common causes of serious diseases such as cancer and kidney disease, as well as less severe problems like bed-wetting and grouchiness, are "focated" (electrically imbalanced) teeth, tonsils, and sinuses. Hence the frequent resort to surgery.

Voll and his followers do not bother with controlled studies and experiments to prove their contentions. The truth of EAV is taken for granted, and the wild assertions are dogmatically presented as obvious facts. Real science proceeds cautiously and logically. We suggest that you do not take seriously any diagnosis or suggested treatment, especially surgery, derived from the technique. You might lose healthy teeth or tonsils for no good reason.

Chelation Therapy

The drug EDTA (ethylene diamine tetraacetic acid, or edetic acid) is a chelating agent, that is, it attaches itself to some metals and minerals and takes them out of the body when it is excreted in the urine. It is injected intravenously in cases of poisoning with lead, cadmium, and other toxic metals, and in iron overdose. In these uses there is always a danger of kidney damage which can lead to death.

In recent years a few physicians have taken to injecting EDTA to treat coronary artery disease, angina, and other manisfestations of atherosclerosis, as well as varicose veins, arthritis, multiple sclerosis, and many other problems. The theory is that the drug breaks up atheromas (calcium-cholesterol plaques in the arteries) and causes the material to be excreted in

606 the urine. Each treatment takes several hours and the patients are generally hospitalized for a week or two, though some physicians treat them in their offices. The cost is high, from $200 to $2500 per week, and is generally not covered by any insurance. The usual course is twenty to fifty treatments, but some people are treated hundreds of times.[3]

The problem with the theory is that if EDTA removes calcium from the blood, hormones will cause the mineral to be released from the bones. There is no evidence that the mineral is removed from atheromas or that atherosclerosis can be cleared as the proponents claim. Moreover, the treatment can be dangerous.

Hazards of Chelation Therapy

The Food and Drug Administration has not approved the use of EDTA for atherosclerosis or other chronic diseases and considers such treatment **extremely hazardous**.[4] The American Heart Association also disapproves of the treatment. Potentially serious side effects include kidney damage and failure, bone marrow damage, irregular heart rhythm, hemolytic anemia, and severe phlebitis (inflammation of the vein EDTA enters). Other reported side effects include nausea, vomiting, muscle spasms, headaches, loss of appetite, malaise, and aching joints. Since the treatment removes body calcium, the mineral is leached from the bones (not from atheromas), which can promote osteoporosis.

Another danger is that people can be diverted from surgery or balloon catheter treatment which are safer and of proven benefit in properly selected patients.

Chelation therapy has been the subject of much litigation. Patients who have been harmed by it have sued for damages and the FDA has prosecuted physicians for advertising the treatment. While the FDA cannot prevent a physician from using a drug in an untested, unproven way once it has been approved for one use, it *can* prohibit mislabeling of drugs. Advertising the use of EDTA for the treatment of atherosclerosis and other chronic diseases is considered mislabeling, and this has been the basis of prosecution.[5]

Chiropractic

For almost a century chiropractors have claimed they can cure diseases, including most of the serious and deadly diseases known to humans, by manipulation of the spine. For just as long medical science has said these claims are false and that the whole theory behind chiropractic is absurd, but chiropractic has flourished. The issues involved can be better understood if we start from the beginning.

History of Chiropractic[6,7]

Daniel David Palmer was born in Ontario, Canada, in 1845 and as a young adult he settled in Davenport, Iowa. For a few years he worked as a grocer, but his heart was elsewhere; he was fascinated by the psychic and medical cults popular in his day.

In 1886 he set up a "magnetic healing" studio and practiced the art of personal magnetism for nine years. During this time he was convinced that there was one cause of all disease, and he became obsessed with finding that cause.

In 1895 Palmer's theory gelled. It had been common practice to apply leeches, hot irons, and other irritants to the spine for various ailments. Palmer tried a certain type of manipulation of the spine. Based on two cases, one of deafness and one of heart disease which, he claimed, responded to spinal manipulation, Palmer concluded that "subluxated (displaced) vertebrae are the cause of 95 percent of all disease." The misaligned vertebral bone, he explained, presses against a nerve, pulling it taut, creating heat in it, and altering nerve impulses through it. Organs innervated by the nerve become diseased.

The cure is to push the misaligned bone back into place. He called his discovery "chiropractic" from the Greek, "done by hand." This is still the chiropractic theory today.

At first Palmer tried to keep his discovery a secret, but he changed his mind and in late 1895 set up the Palmer School of Chiropractic in Davenport. The three-month course cost $450, and the only admission requirement was ability to pay. Advertisements assured students that lack of previous education need not be a barrier to becoming a professional with a high income.

By 1902 the school's influence was spreading nationwide, thanks largely to Palmer's aggressive twenty-year-old son, "BJ." In 1906 the father went to jail for practicing medicine without a license. When he was released BJ bought him out of the business for about $2,000.

Shortly thereafter, when BJ published the world's first book on chiropractic, Daniel claimed his son had stolen the work from him. Daniel later set up a rival chiropractic college in Davenport, but it failed and he left town. BJ's school continued to thrive. The course was increased to nine months and a correspondence course was made available. Graduates received a Doctor of Chiropractic degree and BJ became a multimillionaire. Such success was naturally widely imitated. Hundreds of chiropractic schools, including some mail-order diploma mills, set up business. Rather than fight them, Palmer sold them adjustment tables and other paraphernalia.

Although BJ always said he agreed with his father that chiropractic

608

would cure all diseases, when he was sick he went to see medical doctors in Davenport. He lived to be seventy-nine. When he died of colon cancer in 1961, his son David Daniel took over the business.

David toned down the flamboyant image of the Palmer School, renamed it the Palmer College of Chiropractic, and worked hard to improve chiropractic's professional image. He took BJ's books off the school library shelves; the new image was to be modern and scientific.

Chiropractic colleges now have four-year courses leading to the Doctor of Chiropractic, the D.C. Chiropractic is licensed in all fifty states and its services are reimbursable through Medicare, Medicaid, and most private health insurance plans. Its educational system has been officially sanctioned by the United States Office of Education since 1974.

Chiropractic
Theory and Practice Today[8,9,10]

There are really two types of chiropractor today. One of Palmer's early converts, Willard Carver, set up a chiropractic school in Oklahoma City. While he agreed with the central importance of spinal alignment, he advocated that chiropractors should also use nutrition, physiotherapy, and a few other methods as adjuncts. This mixed philosophy was rejected by the Palmers, who retained the "straight" approach, that spinal manipulation is fundamental to the treatment of all disease, and chiropractors should concern themselves only with this.

The schism still prevails; some schools teach one, some the other. Both types of school thrive, though the mixers are clearly in the majority. Each has its own association: the International Chiropractic Association for the straights, and the American Chiropractic Association for the mixers. Chiropractic colleges are associated with either one or the other.

Chiropractors vary considerably in their beliefs and practices. The more modern ones, even the straights, admit the importance of nutrition and the necessity of vaccinations and other medical procedures. The straights generally see themselves as specialists of the spine, and usually refrain from performing other manipulations, massage, or physiotherapy.

The mixers, on the other hand, often use diets, physiotherapy, acupuncture, colonic lavage, iridology, and much more. Still, the basic theory of both schools remains the same: for maximum health and longevity, and for the specific treatment of almost all disorders and diseases, the spine must be properly manipulated to remove pressure on nerves where they exit from the spine on their way to the various organs.

One newspaper ad, which most chiropractors would probably agree with, said that vertebral subluxations kill millions of people every year. The problem, they say, is that our vertebrae are constantly being slightly displaced by normal activities as well as unusual stresses and they often get locked into dislocations and thereby impinge on the nerves. This causes pain at the site and illness in the organs served by the affected nerves. Heart disease, diabetes, ulcers, allergies, eye trouble, acne, appendicitis, kidney disease, and many other serious ailments can result, they say.

While other treatments may be helpful, their benefit is optimized by spinal adjustment which keeps the nerves unencumbered and the body's own resistance to disease at a maximum. Some chiropractors speak of a "spinal tune-up" in this sense. There appears to be general agreement among chiropractors that just about everybody, no matter how healthy, can benefit from regular spinal adjustments.

Whatever symptoms a person has, the chiropractor analyzes the spine, then manipulates accordingly. The analysis is done by feeling with the fingers and taking X-rays. Usually a series of treatments is done, sometimes once or twice a week for a year or longer, with periodic X-rays.

The Chiropractic Manipulation

The adjustment is usually done with the person lying face down. The chiropractor places his hands over the vertebrae to be adjusted and gives a sudden heavy downward thrust ("dynamic thrust") on the spine. This may be repeated several times at each site believed to be affected, usually until a characteristic cracking sound is heard. For the cervical vertebrae (the neck), the person may stand or lie on his back. The head is rotated to either side, then jerked suddenly to one side until a snap is heard, then to the other side.

Let's consider what this does. Most of the vertebrae are joined to ribs by synovial joints, fluid-filled joints which can be popped, similar to knuckle popping. The sound is due to gases rushing out of solution in the synovial fluid to fill the vacuum created by enlarging the joint space. When the pull on the joint is released, the gases slowly return to solution. This is why you have to wait several minutes before you can pop a joint a second time.

Chiropractors generally consider the popping sound as an indication that a beneficial adjustment has taken place. But there seems to be confusion among chiropractors concerning what joints are dislocated and need adjustment. Whatever the theoretical details, the point of the manipulation seems to be to produce lots of popping, and this is accomplished by the characteristic sudden, vigorous manipulation.

610 Problems with
Chiropractic Theory and Practice

The major flaw in chiropractic theory, obvious to any anatomy student with a cadaver or good illustration, is that the openings through which the nerves leave the spine are very large with plenty of room to spare. If Palmer had had a cadaver to examine, it is hard to imagine his coming up with the same theory. There must be some difficult moments in chiropractic anatomy classes when instructors try to demonstrate how the nerves are pinched or in any way pressured or impinged upon by the ring of bone and ligament without major trauma such as a fractured vertebra or prolapsed disc.

Another problem with the theory is that many important nerves leave the central nervous system not through the spine but through openings in the skull or sacrum. These openings are solid rings of bone, completely beyond the chiropractor's reach. The nerves serve all the facial structures, the heart, stomach, liver lungs, intestines, prostate, bladder, uterus, and other important organs which chiropractors claim are diseased by pinched nerves.

Chiropractors insist that deadly subluxations are common, but they provide no proof. Where are the autopsy reports showing the cause of death to be, say, kidney disease due to subluxation at thoracic nine? Where, for that matter, are the autopsy reports that demonstrate the existence of subluxations impinging on nerves at all? A 1973 study on fresh cadavers could not detect impingements on nerves even when the spines were forced into extremely abnormal positions using great pressure.[10]

After ninety years we are still lacking proof that chiropractic subluxations can cause any disease or even a backache. Nine decades should be long enough for any science to prove its contentions. One of the persistant criticisms of chiropractic has been that it spends millions on promotion and peanuts on research. From the very beginning Palmer's theory has been accepted as gospel and little effort has been made to test it.

Thousands of chiropractors attend courses on attracting clients and getting them to return. Many use charts which show the spine and diseases supposedly caused by subluxations at each level, as well as impressive rates of success chiropractic has with each condition. One practice booster, Clinic Masters, claims over 10 percent of all American and Canadian chiropractors as members. The chiropractor pays about $10,000 and agrees not to divulge any elements of the system to other chiropractors. The method apparently works; Clinic Masters brags that many of its clients earn more than $300,000 per year. Using mass-production techniques, some chiropractors see several hundred clients a day.

Does Chiropractic Work?

There is no evidence that chiropractic works in the systemic diseases it is claimed effective against, nor are there theoretical reasons why it should. The whole edifice of chiropractic pathology is based on the 100-year-old wild guess of a person completely untrained in the sciences of physiology, anatomy, and medicine. It makes no sense to manipulate the spine as a treatment for allergies, heart disease, visual problems, cancer, or any of the scores of disorders chiropractors have been known to treat.

A good deal of the reported benefit of chiropractic is surely due to the placebo effect. Most ailments go away by themselves in time, and whatever treatment one might be taking is easily perceived as the cure. If an authoritative person in a white coat and surrounded by impressive charts and machines expresses concern and seems to know what he is doing, whatever he does has about one chance in three of making the person feel better for awhile. This is why scientific physicians don't advertise with personal testimonials as chiropractors often do. Any treatment whatsoever can elicit this kind of "evidence."

Nevertheless, it appears that manipulative therapy by chiropractors can be helpful in some types of pain. One study of dozens of persons with low back pain compared results of treatment by chiropractic manipulation with treatment by soft-tissue massage. The manipulated patients were more likely to report immediate relief after the first treatment. A few weeks after treatment there was no difference between the two groups, but to the sufferers even a few days of freedom from pain can be important.[11]

Should you see a chiropractor for back pain? The problem here is that back pain can be caused by kidney disease, spinal arthritis, tumors, gallbladder disease, problems of the uterus and ovaries, and many other things chiropractors are not trained to diagnose or treat. It would seem that any back pain worth seeing an expert about is worth seeing a physician about. In the likely event that simple back strain (pulled muscle or ligament) is the problem, rest is needed, not "adjustment." Even if manipulation is the treatment of choice, it is best to consult a physiatrist, an M.D. who specializes in back pain and other muscle and joint problems. These physicians also use ultrasound, cold, heat, and exercise in a rational way, and they are trained to diagnose serious internal disorders.

The Dangers of Chiropractic

While popping one's knuckles seems to be harmless, popping spinal joints is something else. The trauma can tear ligaments, bruise blood vessels, and

612 fracture the vertebrae, that is, break backs and necks. Many people have been seriously injured, crippled, and killed by chiropractic manipulations.

Vigorous rotation of the neck can distort and narrow the vertebral artery feeding the brain and thereby cause strokes. In March 1980, at the Fifth Joint Meeting on Stroke and Cerebral Circulation, fifteen cases of stroke induced by chiropractic rotation of the neck were reported by two physicians. When the 300-odd doctors present were surveyed, about 100 of them said they had seen at least one such case.[12] In one physician's survey of thirty-eight cases he knew of, the average age was thirty-seven years, very young for stroke victims. Many of these victims died.

Chiropractic manipulation of the back when there is a prolapsed or ruptured disk can make the injury worse. Healing requires rest, gentle treatment, and avoidence of strain. Manipulation of the chiropractic type is too rough.

The incidence of serious injury due to chiropractic adjustments is difficult to estimate since chiropractic journals and reports don't keep track. But if, as suggested by the survey of neurologists (above), a third of all neurologists have seen strokes, induced by chiropractic, the incidence of all such injuries must be significant.

In addition to direct injury, harm may be done by misleading people and diverting them from adequate treatment. Many chiropractors insist that their role is that of primary physician, the family doctor who refers people to M.D.s only when they believe it is necessary. Their title "Doctor" misleads people into thinking they have diagnostic and therapeutic skills equal to physicians. People have died from appendicitis, diabetes, cancer, and various infectious diseases after being diverted from medical treatment by chiropractors. Chiropractors have convinced parents that their children needed spinal adjustments rather than drugs or surgery, and the children have died from uncontrolled epileptic seisures or rapidly growing tumors.

In spite of such disasters, ad campaigns for chiropractic continue to imply that it is superior to medicine because it can treat problems without drugs. Chiropractic journal articles and pamphlets recommend treatment for children with infectious diseases, digestive problems, respiratory illnesses, heart problems, and other serious disorders. Childrens' diseases are often acute and proper diagnosis and rapid treatment can be lifesaving. Yet chiropractors X-ray and treat children and decide whether to refer them to an M.D. Ads in local papers all over the country claim that chiropractic "care" is beneficial for children only a few days old and much more so later when their spines allegedly get thrown out of kilter during minor bumps and tumbles.

In an experiment done by *Consumer Reports* magazine (see notes 6 and 7 in References) a perfectly healthy four-year-old girl was taken to five chiropractors for a check-up. Each one found different problems needing treatment, such as a "pinched nerve to the stomach and gall bladder," shoulder blades "out of place," "twisted pelvis," "elevated hip," "short left leg," and "spinal misalignments which will cause headaches and nervousness later." The recommended treatment, of course, was invariably regular chiropractic manipulation for prolonged periods.

In an experiment of our own, we had a young woman with a lipoma (a benign fatty tumor) on her shoulder consult a chiropractor. Sure enough, he told her he could clear it with spinal manipulations. She was to come to his office for a treatment twice a week at a cost of $15 per treatment. He could not say how long it would take to cure her. She had it removed by a physician for less than $50.

Sometimes chiropractic tragedy is a combination of diversion from adequate treatment and manipulation doing harm. One young woman went to a chiropractor because of pain in the back and abdomen. After his powerful manipulations she hemorrhaged from the vagina and bled to death. If she had gone to a physician, her tubal pregnancy would have been recognized and she would have been treated very gently and saved by surgery.

Much more common than such serious injury is a simple sore back for a few days or weeks due to slight injury to the spinal ligaments.

Chiropractors Love Gadgets

An interesting characteristic of chiropractic is its dependence upon mechanical and electronic gadgets that don't really do anything. Its history is a history of thermeters, the Detoxacolon, radionic vibrators, the Micro-Dynameter (which supposedly diagnoses vitamin requirements), radioclast devices, and the neurocalimeter.

These instruments are shiny technological placebo machines. Some are actually gutless; that is, they have little if any real electronics behind the facade of dials, meters, and switches. The Neurocalimeter is a meter in a wooden frame housing with a protruding electrode, supposedly to help locate subluxations. When BJ first came out with this $30 device he leased it to chiropractors for $2200 for ten years, $600 payable in advance.

The chiropractor's gadgets have come and gone. Their appeal is in their contribution to the placebo effect. In one ingenious twist which avoids the legal hassles of promoting gadgets, chiropractor Mark Grinims and coauthor Walter Fischman promote the concept of "muscle response testing" (see separate discussion in this section), which some chiropractors and naturopaths have adopted. In recent years chiropractors have opted for less external gadgetry and more internal gadgetry, that is, megavitamins and other nutrient formulas, herbal extracts, homeopathic remedies, cell salts, and the like. Manufacturers of these unproven remedies advertise heavily in chiropractic journals.

614 X-Radiation, the Chiropractor's Toy

One device that was born almost simultaneously with chiropractic and remains central to the theory and practice today is the X-ray machine. Taking full spine X-rays before, during, and after a series of treatments is a common practice. Physicians never use the broad-field X-rays and in major hospitals and clinics fewer than 5 percent of all patients are X-rayed at all. But almost all chiropractic clients are X-rayed, often with doses hundreds of times those delivered by chest X-rays.

The purpose of the X-rays is not always what it seems. One chiropractic text says all clients should be X-rayed because it promotes confidence, procures business, attracts a better class of patients, and helps to eliminate the so-called starvation period many practitioners go through.

Radiologists, the medical specialists in the uses and dangers of X-radiation, usually study at least three years beyond the M.D. before being certified as specialists. Yet chiropractors with very much less training set themselves up as experts and dose their clients with unnecessary and hazardous radiation.

Subluxation or Imagination?

In a sense, the chiropractic X-ray is never what it seems. It is supposed to demonstrate a pathological state, but all it usually demonstrates are minor, normal variations in spinal structure and slight movements or shifts from perfectly straight posture just before the picture is taken. These variations that chiropractors call subluxations are generally judged normal by radiologists.

Even chiropractors are not sure which variations to call subluxations. According to *Consumer Reports*, when chiropractic was included in the health plan for the National Association of Letter Carriers, the Association received claims for treatment of cancer, heart disease, mental retardation, infections, and many other disorders. When in 1964 the chiropractors were asked to justify their claims by sending X-ray evidence, hundreds of X-rays were sent, all supposedly showing subluxations. But chiropractic officials reviewing them were unable to agree where the subluxations were.

When challenged to present "before and after" X-rays demonstrating subluxations and their resolution, one chiropractic college official replied that chiropractors do not claim to be able to read specific subluxations from an X-ray. But if that is the case, why take X-rays at all?

Moreover, if that is the case, why did Congress include chiropractic under Medicare with the stipulation that payments for treatment would be made only if subluxations are demonstrated by X-rays to exist? Our legislators should have made chiropractic prove the objective existence and significance of subluxations before passing this law, which encourages more X-ray dosing.

Millions of X-rays are taken annually by chiropractors, many of them the type which irradiates the eye lens, the thyroid gland, bone marrow, and reproductive organs, and increases the risk of cataracts, thyroid cancer, leukemia, and genetic damage to future offspring. *Consumer Reports* concluded that all such radiation is unwarranted because it serves no scientifically valid purpose and is hazardous.

Chiropractic and the Law

Chiropractic has been sanctioned by all the state legislatures and accredited by the U.S. Office of Education. Doesn't this mean it has been determined to be a valid system of healing? Not at all. The sanctioning by the states is strictly political, not scientific, and simply proves that decades of intense lobbying can get results.

As for the accreditation by the Commissioner of Education, the Office legal counsel made this remarkable statement: "The Commissioner is not called upon to express his opinion as to the legitimacy or social usefulness of the field of training of the agency seeking listing."[13] In other words, the Office only checks such things as the presence of a permanent campus, the total hours spent learning the discipline, bookkeeping practices, and so on. The validity of what is taught is not examined or challenged. By this logic a College of Voodoo could be accredited if the paperwork were in order. So the public is on its own in judging the merits of chiropractic.

Anyone who goes to a chiropractor should keep this legal situation in mind: chiropractic seems to be succeeding in gaining recognition as a distinct profession, not subject to the standards of, or review by, the medical profession. For example, an appelate court in Virginia sustained a trial judge's refusal to admit testimony by an orthopedic surgeon in a malpractice suit against a chiropractor. The court held that since medicine and chiropractic are distinct professions with their own standards, the orthopedist was not competent to decide whether a chiropractor had exercised proper skill. Only another chiropractor could make such judgments. This means that if a chiropractor harms you and you want to recover damages, you may have to find a chiropractor who will testify on your behalf. This could prove exceedingly difficult.

Conclusions

Current laws protect the chiropractors rather than the public and allow them to practice medicine with very limited qualifications. They are even less

616   restricted in their range of practice than M.D.s. Psychiartrists, radiologists, neurologists, and other specialists study and train for years before diagnosing and prescribing, yet chiropractors offer treatments in many specialties without training in any of them. They do this on the basis of the disproven claim that practically all diseases can be caused or promoted by subluxations.

The lack of protection for children and for future generations is grossly negligent on the part of our legislators. Given the power of the chiropractic lobby, the success of its propoganda campaign, and its near entrenchment as a "separate but equal" healing system, the present situation is not likely to change soon. As long as chiropractors make unsubstantiated claims and offer unproven remedies with little regard to their hazards, responsible health professionals will remain skeptical. Peace between physicians and chiropractors might come if the latter would limit their concern to certain muscle and joint problems and give up their ancient dogma, but such limitation would decrease the pool of potential clients, so chiropractic is not likely to limit itself.

If you think a chiropractor might help alleviate a stubborn back problem or sciatica (pain down the back of the leg due to an inflamed sciatic nerve), try to do your business with one who is not deluded about the powers of his art. Avoid chiropractors who use gadgets and X-rays and claim to be able to diagnose or cure systemic diseases (those of the blood and internal organs). Be wary of those who try to sell you herbal extracts, "glandulars," megavitamins, or other dubious nostrums.

Colonic Lavage

Giving enemas for just about every disease has long been a favorite practice with herbalists, naturopaths, and others. The idea is that accumulated fecal wastes produce toxins that enter the blood and cause all kinds of disorders. Like remedial bleeding, enemas have been largely abandoned. Centuries of use have not revealed any benefit, except in preparation for abdominal surgery and in cases of severe impacted constipation such as that seen in morphine addiction. The hazard is significant, for the colon may become distended and therefore unresponsive to the normal stimulation provided by dietary bulk. The more enemas are used, the worse constipation gets.

Oddly enough, enemas are now making a comeback. "Colon therapy" centers have recently opened in many U.S. cities. They run large, often misleading, newspaper and magazine ads and distribute pamphlets in health food stores. Colonic lavage with the added gimmick of oxygenated water can, we are assured, relieve colds, flu, fatigue, headaches, insomnia, loss of memory, depression, irritability, nausea, poor circulation, weak heart, obesity, sexual dysfunction, and even insanity and shock. The skin glows and the person looks years younger. Some people, we are told, have lost twenty-five pounds just by getting the colon cleaned.

These "colon clinics" are usually run by lay persons but often have an associated physician who takes X-rays of referred clients. One typical ad shows barium X-rays of diseased or distorted colons, and says that such photos are definitely advisable for anyone who has ever suffered from headache, depression, irritability, weakness, fatigue, or low sex drive. Obviously, this includes everyone. These examinations deliver more radiation than any other type, except for the upper GI exams and chiropractic broad-field exams. The dose is fifty to eighty times the dose for an X-ray of the chest or whole mouth and is an unnecessary hazard to health.

This same ad says that the therapy removes tapeworms and other parasites, claimed to be present in 90 percent of us. But when we called this clinic and asked whether they routinely check for parasites in the stool, they said no, and could not give any estimate of how many people are relieved of parasites by their treatment. The parasite ploy is a clever scare tactic. Very few people in the United States have intestinal parasites, and those who do are not likely to be helped by enemas.

The treatment usually costs $25 to $40, excluding X-rays. Most clients sign up for a series costing up to several hundred dollars.

We were told that a series of treatments strengthens the intestinal muscles and improves their tone. This is false, of course; it is well known that repeated enemas can distend the colon and thereby cause chronic constipation.

The therapeutic claims made for colon lavage are completely without supporting evidence. If you do need an enema, $25 is far too much to pay for one; see Part Four for better and cheaper constipation remedies.

CAUTION

The enema machines are not always properly designed or properly cleaned. Microbes from one person's intestines may contaminate a machine, then enter the intestines of many others. One outbreak of amebiasis in Colorado was traced to a chiropractor's enema machine. Ten of the victims required surgery. Seven died.[14]

Some naturopaths and herbalists recommend coffee enemas. This is dangerous because the coffee leaches potassium and other elements from the body. The resulting electrolytic imbalance can cause heart dysfunction and failure. Deaths have been reported. The large dose of caffeine delivered this way can cause anxiety and promote diarrhea and dehydration.

---

618 DMSO

Dimethyl sulfoxide, or DMSO, is a simple organic chemical with some remarkable properties that make it potentially useful in medicine. It is a clear, colorless, highly polar, and hydroscopic liquid that dissolves many substances and has been used as an industrial solvent for decades. DMSO can penetrate intact skin and carry other chemicals with it, and animal studies show it has anti-inflammatory, analgesic, vasodilatory, and other properties.[15]

By late 1965 at least 100,000 persons had been treated by physicians with DMSO which was reported effective in many varying conditions, including injuries and inflammation of muscles and connective tissues, arthritis, gout, viral and bacterial infections, skin parasites, burns, wound healing, scleroderma (a connective tissue disorder which first affects the skin, then internal organs), interstitial cystitis (a bladder disorder), and even mental and emotional problems. However, DMSO was found to cause changes in the lenses of dogs, pigs, and rabbits, so all clinical studies were stopped. For about fifteen years very few studies were done, but in 1980 the FDA revoked the restrictions on clinical testing because no evidence had been found of harm to the human eye, even after prolonged use of the drug.[16]

However, the FDA and the National Academy of Sciences reviewed the thousands of scientific articles on DMSO and concluded that the evidence was adequate to approve the drug only for interstitial cystitis, but that further study was warranted because there were strong indications that DMSO might be effective in several other disorders and types of injury. Studies are being carried out and the drug may eventually be approved for scleroderma, sprains, various types of arthritis, and possibly strokes.

Over-the-Counter DMSO

DMSO is cheap and easy to make and get, and an enormous market for it has been created by media attention to its potential applications. Several states have even legalized the drug for human use under certain conditions, and some state medical societies have urged its approval for more uses. It is not surprising that entrepreneurs have capitalized on the situation by bottling DMSO and marketing it to the public for considerable profit.

The preparations generally available are Rimso-50, a 50 percent solution for direct instillation into the urinary bladder for treating interstitial cystitis, a 90 percent gel for veterinary use in reducing swelling due to trauma, and a 99 percent industrial degreaser with 1 percent unknown impurities. The latter is the one usually sold to the public in health food stores, beauty palors, novelty and gift shops, flea markets, and by mail. People rub it in and inject it without much concern about the contaminants or possible side effects.

Adverse Effects and Hazards

Common side effects of topical DMSO application include burning, itching, local and generalized dermatitis, and an unpleasant oysterlike odor of the breath, clothes, and furniture.

Potential hazards are presented by the unknown impurities, even if "guaranteed pure," and possible kidney and eye damage after prolonged use of large amounts. Such application has not been adequately tested on humans, although small amounts of pharmaceutical-grade DMSO appears to be safe. Another serious problem is that some people are diverted from proper and effective treatment by quacks making outrageous claims about curing cancer and other serious diseases with DMSO.

In conclusion, of the three types of DMSO preparation on the market, one, the diluted Rimso-50, is too weak to be useful in the strains, sprains, and arthritis most people use the chemical for, and the other two do not fit the high standards of purity, effectiveness, and safety for human use. If the usual remedies for these disorders are not effective and you want to try DMSO, rather than using an unproven, impure product try to find a physician who is licensed to do clinical testing with pure preparations.

It should be kept in mind that hundreds of drugs have been trumpeted as cure-alls in much the same way DMSO has been, and in most cases few of the promises have been fulfilled. DMSO is an amazing substance and it is slowly but surely finding its place in the healing arts. With proper care its place will be found with a minimum of casualties. Until its role is more clearly defined, **caution is in order.**

Gerovital, The "Anti-Aging Wonder Drug"

Procaine, a synthetic chemical related to cocaine, was first used in medicine in 1905 and has played a vital role ever since. It is an excellent local anesthetic, especially useful in dentistry, and anyone who has ever had a tooth drilled and filled or pulled has most likely experienced its powerful numbing effect.

620

But some people think procaine (also called novocaine) is much more than a numbing agent. In the 1920s and 1930s Dr. Ferdinand Huneke of Germany experimented with procaine injections in hundreds of patients with various serious diseases and severe pain syndromes. He claimed remarkable results, but other physicians could not duplicate his successes and many denounced him as a quack.

In the 1950s a Romanian physician, Dr. Anna Aslan, started using procaine injections mostly in older people with chronic diseases. She claimed spectacular successes not only in the treatment of ulcers, arthritis, hypertension, and other specific ailments but in actually retarding and reversing aging. She said that procaine, or GH3 as she called her procaine solutions, was a vitamin, in spite of the fact that it does not occur in nature and is purely synthetic. The scientific community was sceptical of Aslan's claims, but the world press quickly spread the word and now thousands of people every year flock to her spa-like clinic with hopes of rejuvenation and healing. The drug is also available in some other European countries and in one U.S. state, Nevada.

In the 1960s American supporters of Dr. Aslan formed a company to import procaine from Romania and sell it under the brand name Gerovital. They applied to the FDA for permission to test the drug as an antidepressant in the elderly. The FDA said okay, but only if they would also test it on young people since they get depressed, too, and only if the name were changed since "Gerovital" implies an anti-aging effect, which has not been proven and which the company did not want to test. The application was eventually withdrawn.

The Gerovital promoters then did an end-run around the FDA, just as the laetrile (phony cancer cure) promoters had. They lobbied very hard to legalize the drug in one state, so the feds would not have jurisdiction. It worked. Both Gerovital and laetrile are now available in Nevada, whose legislators apparently feel the drugs are good tourist attractions. In other states Gerovital is sold through "clubs" and "foundations" which do more or less constant battle with the FDA.

Sophisticated Gerovital propaganda frequently claim that scientific studies have proven its value. But the nearly 300 reports of Dr. Aslan and others who have studied the effects of Gerovital on their patients were reviewed and evaluated by the National Institute on Aging.[17] This review was highly critical of the poor scientific methods used by the Gerovital proponents and concluded that the evidence for anti-aging effects was unconvincing. The authors concede that the drug may have a slight antidepressant effect but maintain that even this has not been proven.

The hazards of Gerovital are more to your bank account than your health, but some people develop life-threatening allergies and some are diverted from effective treatment.

Hair Analysis   621

Since the mid-1970s certain companies have used hair analysis to determine nutritional status. These are mail-order services promoted mostly through health magazines. The client sends in a couple locks of hair and gets back a computerized list of the minerals found in the hair along with recommendations for supplements to correct imbalances. Vitamin supplements may be recommended even though hair has no vitamins.

Some companies run ads claiming or implying that mineral imbalances, which they allegedly can diagnose, can cause a long list of serious diseases and symptoms. People with arthritis, migraine headaches, and other ailments send in their hair and get a prescription for supplements, usually a lot of them, all of which happen to be available from the very same company. Sometimes more expensive tests are recommended. Altogether, hundreds of dollars can be spent by one person.

Does It Work?

The only real value of hair analysis is as a preliminary examination to detect toxic heavy metals such as lead, cadmium, arsenic, and mercury. The results are not definitive; they must by confirmed by blood and urine tests.

The results of hair analysis, the diagnoses, statements of nutritional status, and recommendations, should not be taken seriously for the following reasons.

Hair consists primarily of protein. The small amounts of minerals present are of unknown significance and have never been proven to be related to body levels of minerals, vitamins, or other nutrients. The amount of a given mineral in one's hair does not provide reliable information about the amount in the blood or tissues or about one's needs.

The mineral content of hair can be affected by its color; the season of the year; contact with shampoos, sprays, dyes, and other products; and the sex, race, and age of the subject.

The reliability of laboratory techniques is highly questionable. In one investigation, samples, including duplicates, were sent to three different labs. The results varied from lab to lab and from sample to sample from the same person. One company says its recommendations are based on careful analysis of each individual's hair, yet recommends practically the same fifteen or so supplements in the same amounts to everyone. It also suggests periodic tests to update the programs.

622 Hanging Upside Down

Inversion therapy was developed in the sixties as a method of traction or spinal decompression. Since then it has become a fitness fad and hot commercial item. Full-page ads in major magazines and newspapers across the country have convinced millions that hanging upside down will make them healthier and more attractive.

One ad shows a paunchy man under the headline, "Your Chest Doesn't Belong On Your Stomach." It goes on to say that uncontrolled gravity can move your chest downward, cause your whole body to droop, and make you a little shorter each day. The answer to the gravity problem is to build a Gravity Body using the revolutionary Gravity Guiding System of exercising upside down with the help of Gravity Boots, Inversion Bars, and Gravity Guiders (like a vertical stretcher for hanging upside down). The capitalization refers to trade marks or patent registrations. (Yes, even Gravity Body is a trade mark.)

Is Inversion Hazardous?

Many people who believe in the system will hang for ten to twenty minutes once or more daily and do various exercises and weight lifting while inverted. The question naturally arises whether such unnatural activity might be harmful. One osteopathic physician who took daily hanging sessions noticed they made him dizzy afterward. Then he found that hanging made his blood pressure zoom from 125/85 to 210/165. He decided to study the effects of inversion in a systematic way with volunteers.

In Dr. Klatz' study twenty healthy college students were inverted for three minutes. Measurements of their blood pressure, pulse rate, central retinal arterial pressure, and intraocular pressure were taken during inversion and within one minute after. The results were striking. All these pressures increased dramatically, much more so than in normal exercise, and this was after only three minutes of simple inversion without simultaneous exercise.[18]

CAUTION
The results of the study provide clear warning that the fad could be dangerous to persons with hypertension, glaucoma, congestive heart failure, and other disorders, as well as persons on anticoagulant, aspirin, or platelet inhibition therapy. Since elderly people are most at risk for these conditions and for having a stroke, it would seem irresponsible to encourge them to use inversion systems; yet some ads do just that.

Nor is there any good reason for young, healthy people to hang upside down; none of the supposed benefits has been proven, and they do not make much theoretical sense. Humans are designed to be upright most of the time and, although some are considered slothlike, there is no evidence they or anyone else can be helped by hanging upside down, any more than we would expect sloths to benefit from being forced to stand upright.

It should be noted that hanging upside down can sometimes relieve back pain due to disc problems. But it is no better than traction, while it is riskier and more uncomfortable.

Homeopathy and Cell Salts

Homeopathy is a system developed in the early 1800s by Samuel Hahnemann, a German physician. The basic principle is expressed in the homeopathic law, *similia similibus curentur,* "like cures like." Hahnemann made this conclusion after a single experiment with cinchona bark, which contains quinine and was known to cure "intermittent fever," that is, malaria. He took the drug when he was well and it produced palpitations, a rapid hard pulse, prostration, flushing, and thirst, symptoms which he believed very similar to those of malaria. He generalized from this and asserted that if a substance given to a healthy person causes certain symptoms, small amounts of the substance will cure a person sick with those symptoms.[19]

Another major premise of the Hahnemann's doctrine was that two diseases cannot coexist and one will always drive out the other. He believed that a drug-induced disease will drive out a preexisting disease if the two are similar. The entire edifice of homeopathy was then constructed by claims of similarities between various poisons and diseases.

For example, suppose a person is experiencing delirium, hallucinations, dilated pupils, and wild, insane behavior. The proper remedy is a little belladonna, large doses of which cause these symptoms in normal persons. Or if signs of kidney or liver disease or anemia occur, the proper remedy is a little arsenic, which can produce these problems in healthy persons.

One of the homeopath's favorite remedies is ground *nux vomica* seeds. It is used to relieve nervous fatigue and irritability, since in larger doses it produces these symptoms. It contains strychnine, which in large enough doses can cause convulsions and death.

There are hundreds of remedies for hundreds of symptoms, and the homeopathic student has a hard time learning them all because, in reality, disease symptoms are rarely the same as reactions to toxic chemicals. To complicate matters further, some homeopathic texts emphasize that the whole person must be treated, not just the symptoms, which are merely

624 superficial and often misleading signs of deeper disease. This leads to efforts to treat personality types regardless of the disease or symptoms.[20]

One bizarre aspect of this is that personality types are equated with toxic symptoms of various chemicals. Thus, homeopaths speak of the "belladonna," who is a violent character prone to "turmoil in the brain," and the "arsenicum," who is a "covetous, malicious money-maker with green, putrid excretions," according to one text. The remedies for these characters are, of course, belladonna and arsenic.

The question naturally occurs, how far does the homeopathic law go? Do they treat, say, lead poisoning with more lead? Incredibly, the answer is yes. Bee stings are treated with more bee venom, mercury poisoning with more mercury, and so on for any kind of poisoning, be it benzene, alcohol, heroin, streptococcus, or atomic radiation.

A currently popular modification of homeopathy involves so-called **tissue salts** or **cell salts.** These are mostly very small amounts of common salts of magnesium, phosphorous, sodium, chloride, and potassium mixed with lactose in tiny pills. But they may also include lead, arsenic, and boron, which some practitioners consider essential elements. The pills are not labeled or spoken of as, say, sodium chloride, magnesium phosphate, or potassium sulphate. Rather, they are respectively, *natrum muriaticum, magnesia phosphorica*, and *kali sulphuricum*. This helps disguise the fact that the substances are common minerals, available in much larger amounts in common foods. Also, the official-looking Latin labels enhance the placebo effect.

Another popular product similar to homeopathic remedies and cell salts, and often sold by the same companies, is the so-called **glandular pill.** Tiny amounts (usually 1 to 30 mg) of dried beef adrenal gland, kidney, brain, spleen, thymus, heart, ovaries, testicles, and other organs are packed into pills. These homeopathic doses are supposed to revitalize one's own corresponding organs. There is no evidence to support this belief, which is reminiscent of the most primitive notions about the workings of the human body.

A curious feature of homeopathy, including tissue salts, is the idea that the remedies must be prepared by a process called trituration, which involves many hours or days of dry crushing and diluting with lactose. Some say this is absolutely essential to the assimilation and activity of the remedy, but some homeopathic remedies are now water-diluted.

An even stranger feature is the assertion that the smaller the dose, the greater the potency and effect. For example, if someone has symptoms resembling arsenic poisoning, the homeopath or assistant dilutes some arsenic in lactose, takes a small amount of the mixture and dilutes it with more lactose, and so on, dozens or hundreds of times. The remedy is supposed to become more potent with each dilution. For very severe cases, dilution continues even after it is mathematically impossible that a single atom of arsenic remains, and the remedy continues to get more potent! This resembles alchemy more than anything else.

Obviously, the homeopath must be careful not to dilute the remedy too many times or the treatment will be dangerous. So if someone has lead poisoning, the homeopath must be sure to give a large enough dose of lead or the treatment will be dangerously strong.

If the logic of all this escapes you, you are not alone. Homeopathy is surely one of the most irrational pseudosciences ever devised and is completely contrary to common sense. The theory was thoroughly demolished in 1842 by Oliver Wendell Holmes in his essay, "Homeopathy and Its Kindred Delusions," and has been further refuted many times since. Perhaps the strongest evidence that its founder was slightly addled is Hahnemann's own textbook, published in 1828, in which he attributes most chronic diseases to the improper treatment of scabies infection by establishment physicians.

Yet, there was a small grain of truth to the early homeopath's claims of success. Many disorders clear themselves and many more respond to placebos. Only a minority of problems really require intervention. By simply encouraging the patient and not poisoning him, the early homeopath often got better results than his colleagues. For while he was often treating with insignificantly small doses of poisons, the more conventional physicians were usually treating with larger doses of arsenic, mercury, calomel, and other toxic drugs.

Nevertheless, we would be very hesitant to accept any diagnosis or advice deriving from such an irrational system. And the proliferation of poisons in home medicine cabinets is disturbing, even if the doses are small.

Hypnosis and Autosuggestion

Hypnosis has a curious and colorful history. Its roots are more in magic and religion than science, but its modern advocates consider it a branch of psychology and it seems to be gaining favor with physicians and dentists. Power to heal by "laying on the hands" was attributed to divine intervention until the 17th century when a German scholar, Athanasius Kircher, proposed that "animal magnetism," a natural force, was involved.

In the 18th century Franz Mesmer, a Viennese physician, expanded on this idea. A student of astrology, he believed planets affected humans by their magnetism. Why not, he reasoned, use magnetic lodestone to harmonize and balance the disturbed animal magnetism of sick humans? He tried making passes and gestures over the affected parts of patients. Lo and behold, it worked in some people. Others apparently had a mysterious force which resisted the magnets. Those who were helped always went into shaking, screaming fits, went limp, and were "cured."

All this was too much for the conservative medical establishment,

626 which threw him and his magnets out of Vienna. He then went to Paris under the patronage of Marie Antoinette and his healing clinic became the rage among the wealthy French. He worked in an atmosphere of mysticism with dim lights, exotic perfumes, and soft music. He wore a long silk robe, carried an iron wand, and claimed miraculous cures.

Imitators set up business all over France. Naturally the French medical profession reacted much as the Austrians had. In 1784 a commission, which included Benjamin Franklin (in France seeking foreign aid), was convened. It concluded that all the affects of "mesmerism" were due to the subject's imagination. Franklin said there was no evidence of a "Mesmeric ability."

Mesmer was also charged by the press with using his skills to seduce women. The notion that hypnotists can and might do this still colors popular imagination. Later one of Mesmer's disciples, the Marquis de Puysegur, discovered he could induce a "trance" without the magnets or convulsions. He retained the vital fluids theory and made passes with his hands over the subjects to transfer the animal magnetism from his fingertips. This sedate procedure was more acceptible to the medical profession and by the early 19th century Mesmerists, many respectable physicians, were practicing all over Europe. But in 1837 the French Academy of Medicine proclaimed that animal magnetism did not exist and that all mesmeric cures were due entirely to suggestion.

At about the same time the English physician James Braid found he could elicit all the same responses without magnets or passes with the hands. Instead, he used concentration on a bright object. The subject would go limp without convulsing first and seemed to be in a type of sleep. Braid coined the words *hypnosis* and *hypnotism* from the Greek for sleep. Later, when he better understood the phenomenon, he tried to change the word to "mono-ideaism," but failed. So unfortunately we seem to be stuck with "hypnosis" and all the false notions that go with it. Braid made a good case for hypnosis in surgery and it might have gained wide application if chloroform had not come into general use about then. Instead, spiritualists took up hypnosis and scientists and physicians largely lost interest.

Still, the famous French neurologist Jean Charcot worked with it and so did Sigmund Freud, who studied hypnosis at the Nancy School of Hypnotism. This work helped him develop his theories of psychogenic illness and psychoanalysis and the technique of free association. He found the latter tool more reliable for getting at the subconscious than hypnosis, which he eventually dropped.

Since then, interest in hypnosis for medical purposes has waxed and waned, but its basic form has remained the same. The Frenchman Hippolite Bernheim, one of Freud's teachers at Nancy, eventually concluded that the "hypnotic sleep trance" did not exist and attributed all the effects to suggestion and imagination. But by then the stereotype of the hypnotized subject slumping forward and "going under" at the command of the hypnotist was firmly fixed in the popular and professional imagination and has remained so to this day.

In 1958 the American Medical Association put its stamp of approval on hypnosis in the healing arts for intractable pain, neurotic fears, nail biting, insomnia, and other problems. At the same time, the AMA spokesmen warned the public that the "hypnotic trance" can be dangerous and only qualified persons (doctors and psychologists) should attempt it. This position has reinforced such popular misconceptions as the subject cannot hear anyone but the hypnotist, is unaware of his surroundings, and will follow the orders of the operator (unless they "conflict with his morals").

Hypnosis as Witchcraft

It appears that widespread ignorance of the nature of hypnosis has sometimes led to abridgment of civil liberties and even a touch of social hysteria. A legal case in England in the early 1950s illustrates this. An American stage hypnotist, Ralph Slater, was sued by a young woman he had hypnotized. With Dr. Van Pelt, a medical hypnotist, as her expert witness, she accused Slater of mental damages, and won. In a throwback to the days of burning witches, Slater was not permitted to face the jury lest he hypnotize them.

In response to the case, a law was passed forbidding public displays of hypnotism. Fortunately, the verdict was later reversed and the law rescinded.

Another example of loss of civil liberties is the abduction and detention of adult members of religious sects for "deprogramming." The justification is often that the "victim" has been brainwashed or hypnotized. In one case a lower court in New York went along with the prosecuter's charges of "mind control" against leaders of a Hare Krishna group, even though their "victims" were adults and had clearly joined of their own free will. This comes very close to the witchcraft of old. Suggestion and conditioning undoubtedly play a large role in religious practices, but they are not effective against a person's will. Fortunately, the New York Supreme Court threw the case out with stern reprimands against those who would abridge freedom of speech and religion.

Absurd notions about hypnosis still prevail. In the United States, hypnosis displays and experiments are banned from network television on the grounds that the viewers might "go under," do dangerous things, and not come out of the "trance."

The American Society of Clinical Hypnosis called for a ban on hypnosis except by people with medical or psychological qualifications. Many states now have such laws, which is very curious, since it has never been shown that the "hypnotic trance" is a specific state or condition.

628   Neither electroencephalogram nor polygraph nor sophisticated psychological tests have ever proven that the effects of hypnosis are any different from the effects on a child when his mother kisses his bruised arm, rubs it, and says "now the hurt is gone." (Arrest that woman!)

Kreskin, the remarkable mentalist and hypnotist, confesses that after nineteen years and many thousands of hypnotized subjects, he finally broke through his self-delusion and realized that he had never entranced anyone and that all his success was due to suggestion and imagination. He now does shows with the same hilarious effects and crazy behavior in his subjects without any efforts of entrancement, utilizing only suggestion.[21]

Kreskin has publicly offered $100,000 to anyone who can prove the existence of a hypnotic trance. We doubt it will ever be collected. Still, the myth will prevail. The hypnotists want to believe they have a unique, almost supernatural, power like the marvelous Svengali or Mesmer, which sets them apart from ordinary people. The myth is a money maker for those who perpetuate it, including some psychologists, dentists, doctors, entertainers, and, above all, writers of fiction. Hypnosis is a favorite theme in fiction, especially mysteries and children's cartoons.

Hypnosis as Mono-Ideaism

We do not intend to minimize or belittle the fascinating and powerful phenomenon—only to clarify and properly label it. Suggestion is no minor matter; it is the basis of voodoo, shamanism, and the "royal healing touch" of kings of old. A voodoo curse can apparently cause a believer to worry himself sick to death; the medicine man can help muster the will to live and get better.

Everyone is naturally suggestible; this seems necessary for social life from romantic love to persuasion of all kinds. Complete absorption in a book, film, or play requires suggestibility and imagination. The sweating palms, racing heart, or sexual arousal are real. So is the laughter of the "hypnotized" subject who is told he is watching a very funny movie. In either case, there is profound concentration (Braid's mono-ideaism) on the matter or object at hand and relative oblivion to the world outside, but there is no "hypnotic trance."

This is not just academic. Demystification of the phenomenon makes it more accessible to everyone. As we shall see, submitting to the services of a professional hypnotist may actually inhibit creative use of self-hypnosis, more properly called **autosuggestion,** an oversimplification but far more accurate.

The subconscious mind is vulnerable to suggestion and will accept and incorporate ideas and information from the conscious mind and from external sources. Simple examples of suggestion and unconscious mental processes at work are yawning with others, beating time to music, panicking with a crowd, tranquility in group meditation or prayer, and blushing at the question, "Why are you blushing?"

Another example is waking up at a specific time without an alarm. Many people have this ability and some are amazed at the precision and consistency of their internal clocks. All they do is take ten seconds to affirm, preferably aloud at first, that they will awaken at the chosen time.

Another example is forgetting a name or fact and trying to remember it. If you concentrate a few seconds, then stop, a while later it often pops into your mind when you're not thinking about it. It helps to calmly affirm, "I will remember so-and-so in a few minutes," and then think about something else.

Many creative geniuses do their best work subconsciously. Goethe, Coleridge, and others have dreamed great poems. Isaac Newton sometimes awoke with new formulas to write down. Mozart's dreams composed some of his best work. And Kekule, the master chemist who could not figure out the structure of benzene in months of conscious effort, was presented with its ring structure in a dream. This opened up a whole new branch of organic chemistry.

Using Autosuggestion

Perhaps the most important use of autosuggestion is an as aid to relaxation and stress reduction. Here is a five-minute mental exercise similar to Kreskin's which helps induce a state of deep relaxation and suggestibility.

Sit or lie comfortably with eyes closed. Imagine a very relaxing, restful experience, perhaps lying on a deserted beach watching the clouds go by. Picture it and feel yourself in it.

Count from 30 to 0 very slowly. Don't concentrate intensely; if you loose count, let it go. Repeat to yourself, "relax" or "rest" with every breath. If practiced twice a day for a few weeks, the ability to relax at will develops and the visualizing and counting becomes unnecessary. Relaxation becomes a conditioned response.

In this relaxed state, autosuggestion is facilitated, distractions are minimized, and concentration is enhanced. Now is the time to imagine yourself successfully answering all the questions on an upcoming exam, finding the lost wallet, or being repulsed by tempting junk food.

For stopping smoking, try visualizing a mirror with a reflection of you smoking and getting sick from it. Then smash the mirror and replace it with one showing you not smoking, clean and healthy. The impression should be reinforced by daily application.

630

In using autosuggestion for general self-improvement, stress the positive. Visualize and feel yourself as you want to be and do it with some emotional involvement, not just words or vague thoughts. See yourself in the job you want or finishing the upcoming marathon. Some people scoff at such positive thinking, but self-esteem is generally recognized as one of the most important indicators of mental health, and autosuggestion is a good way to promote it.

Suggestion and autosuggestion have proven useful in Raynaud's syndrome, in which cold causes decreased circulation and cyanosis (cellular strangulation) in the fingers. The person imagines the arteries open and blood rushing through them. Whirling the affected arm in a vertical plane forces blood into the fingers and provides some relief. After this is done a few times, merely imagining whirling the arm may help the next time.

The situation with migraine headaches is almost the same. Whirling the arm helps in some cases; imagining this may help in later attacks. Alternatively, imagining the hands very warm and the head very cold also helps reduce the throbbing pain in the head by reducing blood flow.

Other applications include psoriasis, sexual dysfunction, asthma, urinary incontinence, insomnia, muscle spasms, neurotic fears, and practically any disorder which is made worse by emotional stress or which may be affected by conscious influence on the autonomic nervous system. Suggestion also helps minimize pain in dentistry, childbirth, and minor surgery.

Don't Get Hooked on a Hypnotist

In most medical and general applications it is important not to have a lot of sessions with a conventional medical hypnotist to the exclusion of autosuggestion, for this tends to foster passive dependence and inhibit development of effective autosuggestion. One landmark study in experimental hypnosis concluded that self-hypnosis in naive (new) subjects was significantly impaired by as little as two previous sessions with a conventional hypnotist, one who relied on the power and control myth.[22]

Most medical hypnotists usually do give at least lip service to self-hypnosis, but they often speak of "eventually" teaching the person the technique, and this comes after many sessions, often by phone for months. By the time "eventually" arrives the person is hooked on the hypnotist.

If you think a medical hypnotist can help you, try to find one who will teach you autosuggestion right away. He or she can use the first person while illustrating the process, rather than giving directions in the second person ("I feel relaxed..." rather than "You feel...").

CAUTION:
Don't use autosuggestion for long-term alleviation of pain of an unknown origin or cause.

The Placebo Effect

No discussion of suggestion is complete without a word on the placebo effect, which is so persuasive and powerful that all studies of new treatments must take it into account. One survey of studies on more than one thousand patients given inert pills shows they are effective about a third of the time in a wide variety of conditions, including wound pain, angina pectoris, headache, nausea, anxiety, and cold symptoms. Some people even experience toxic side effects from placebos if told they might.

This is why it was so easy for the snake-oil peddlers of the past to get lots of honest people to swear the product worked, and the placebo effect allows modern quacks to peddle their nostrums and procedures with great success. And this is why the double-blind study, in which neither the patient nor the physician knows who is getting the active ingredient and who is getting the placebo, is usually the only way to control for suggestion and determine whether the effects of a drug are pharmacological or psychological. The placebo effect is further evidence of the enormous power of suggestion regardless of a "trance."

Iridology

Iridology is a system of health analysis and diagnosis based on examination of the irises of the eyes. According to the theory, the iris reflects the state of the organs and limbs in a precise way that can be read by trained iridologists. Iridology charts show the different parts of the body represented by the segments of the iris. Abnormal spots, lines, and colors develop when the corresponding organs are disturbed, we are told.

Examination of blown-up color photos of the iris is said to reveal drug deposits and diseases in organs, hereditary weaknesses, healing processes, and subconscious tensions. Even a person's life expectancy can be determined. In fact, it is so powerful a method that one pair of photos furnish more accurate and detailed information than a series of blood tests, X-rays, or biopsies, and can be useful in very early diagnosis. So they say.

Naturally, such claims can be very appealing. Who wants to give flesh and blood for tests, be exposed to X-rays, or pay for these procedures?

632

Typical Iridology Chart

Each segment of the iris
is said to be connected
to an organ or function.
Specks, spots, and
"abnormal" colors
indicate abnormal
function or
weakness of
the organ.

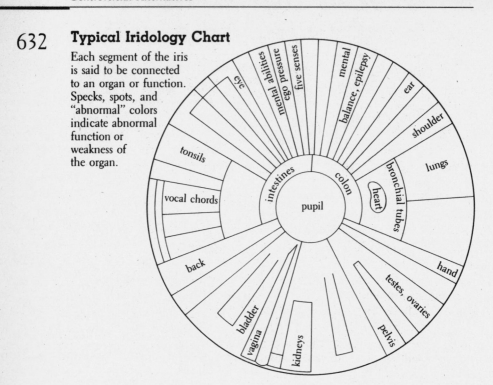

Iridologists (mostly chiropractors and naturopaths) find sympathetic listeners
(and clients) when they claim medical science unfairly ignores their technique and keeps it out of the medical schools.

Does It Work?

Medical science, of course, does not ignore the eyes for signs of illness, and
recognizes that jaundice, dilated pupils, bloodshot eyes, red spots, mineral
deposits, and other changes can result from systemic disease. The iris is
known to be affected in some cases of tuberculosis, diabetes, atherosclerosis,
Crohn's disease, and other disorders. But these changes are not always seen
with these disorders, nor are they confined to specific segments of the iris.
Moreover, there is no anatomic or other evidence that certain parts of the iris
are associated with certain organs.

　　　Theoretical discussion and argument could go on forever. The best
way to determine the truth of the matter is to put the method to a test. This
was done in a well-controlled study involving kidney disease, carried out by

researchers at the University of California and Veterans' Medical Center in San Diego.[23]

Three practicing southern California iridologists, including the world-renowned author of a popular text on the subject, participated in the study. Twenty-four patients with severe kidney disease, twenty-four with moderate kidney disease, and ninety-five controls who had no kidney problems had photos taken of both eyes. The camera used belonged to one of the iridologits, and the slides were presented to them in their offices, at their leisure, and with the option of discarding any slides they thought unsatisfactory. They were asked to give an estimate of kidney function based on the photos.

The results were very interesting. Not one of the iridologists could predict the presence or absence of kidney disease with any accuracy. The best score had only a 2.5 percent predictive value. That is, of those in the general population identified as having kidney disease by this iridologist, only 2.5 percent really will. And others with serious kidney disease will be told their kidneys are fine.

This contrasts with the established methods, which can correctly assess kidney function 95 percent of the time with one blood test (creatinine level), and the remaining cases with one or two subsequent tests.

Iridologists apparently do not have as much confidence in their method as they used to. Instead of stating with certainty that this or that disease is present, they usually make vague diagnoses, such as "you have a weakness in your liver," or colon, adrenal glands, or other organs. They then prescribe expensive vitamins and other supplements, which they sell, to prevent the weakness from developing into disease.

Iridologists also have the strange idea that only blue eyes are normal. Green and brown eyes are really blue eyes polluted with toxins and waste. If you were born with nonblue eyes it is because your mother passed on her pollution and toxins to you. If you follow your iridologist's advice your eyes will gradually turn blue.

In conclusion, since even the master practitioners cannot come close to correctly assessing kidney function, doubt is thrown on the whole system; why should we believe the iridologist any more than a palm reader? Serious psychological harm can be done when a person is told he has a disease which he doesn't have. Even more serious physical harm can be done when a person is assured he does not have a disease when, in fact, he does.

Jason Winters' Herbal Tea

Jason Winters believes he has found an effective treatment (and prevention) for cancer. It is an herbal tea, a combination of three ingredients which is taken several times a day. It sells for $30 to $80 a pound.

Of course, there are no claims on the label about curing cancer or any other condition. If there were the FDA would seize the products. The claims are made in speeches and in Jason Winters' book, *Killing Cancer*, which is invariably stacked right next to the bags of tea. It tells the story of Winters' struggle with cancer of the throat, his treatment with radiation, his physicians' conviction that he would die, and his search for a cure.

He went to Mexico and tried laetrile, which he says works for many people but which failed in his case. Then he obtained various herbs that were considered folk remedies for cancer. They are chaparral from the American southwest, red clover from England, and "herbaline" from China. He tried them separately with no apparent effects, but upon finishing his first cup of the combination tea, he claims, he could feel it working. Within one month the tumor was gone.

The tea does not cure anything, he says. It just "purifies the blood" so the body's immune system can do its job. He claims that more than a hundred thousand cancer victims are enjoying the same results he got using the tea, and many others are getting relief from arthritis, hypertension, and other problems. He accepts the contention of the laetrile proponents that doctors and medical researchers are not interested in a real cure for cancer because that would endanger their livelihoods.

Many people find Jason Winters' story persuasive, and they regularly drink his tea—so many that sales generate at least 20 million dollars each year. They don't drink it for the taste; it is vile tasting and can cause nausea and dizziness. They take it because they believe it is effective against cancer. The obvious danger here is that an unknown percentage of these buyers do have cancer and are relying on the unproven treatment; this could cost them their lives. Valuable time could be lost before a person seeks or accepts help with effective methods.

But does not Jason Winters' case prove the tea works? Or is Winters a cynical quack who is making millions from a lie? Let's consider the facts. Winters underwent such intensive cobalt radiation therapy that the right side of his face turned black and his hair fell out. Only after this did he start using herbs. It seems he experienced an excellent, if somewhat delayed, response to the radiotherapy. He might just as well have been trying any treatment at the time he first noticed an improvement, and that treatment would have gotten credit for the cure. The euphoria induced by feeling stronger, feeling less pain, and knowing he was going to live could instill a powerful belief in the concurrent treatment. The same thing could have happened if the healing was simply a spontaneous remission, which can happen in many types of cancer.

Does It Work?

Some of Winters' assertions are clearly absurd. Are we really to believe, for example, that our physicians would prefer to see us (and their own families) not recover from cancer because a genuine cancer cure would threaten their livelihoods? And that medical researchers are not striving for the Nobel Prize in medicine but are busy covering up cures for cancer and other diseases so they can stay in business? It is a paranoid theory and obviously contrary to the facts. It may have taken hold when Winters had poor relations with his own physicians. He says he was given a premature death sentence and that the doctors were resentful at his long survival and refusal to give up hope.

Among the thousands of possibilities tested by the National Cancer Institute are herbal folk remedies. Chaparral, for example, has been tested and found ineffective. Nor is there any evidence for the other ingredients. Winters is secretive about the "herbaline" or "special spice" listed on some labels. It may be from the chrysanthemum flower, which is often used in the Orient, though not as a cancer cure. There is no evidence that it has any anticancer activity.

This secretiveness would be understandable if the ingredient were a soft-drink flavoring. But it is supposed to be a vital ingredient in a spectacular cancer cure, and it is being kept secret apparently for commercial purposes—this from the man who accuses the medical profession of covering up or ignoring cancer cures for monetary purposes.

In scientific medicine, important developments are made available to scientists around the world for testing and, when proven, are made available to the public without secrets. If Jason Winters really has a cancer cure he should prove it works and share it with researchers so they can verify his claims. One month's income from the tea would be enough to do extensive animal testing and studies of people who have taken it. We challenge Mr. Winters to fully disclose the ingredients of his tea, sponsor scientific studies of its effects, and stop making claims until the results are in.

We recommend that the public not buy the tea until proper studies are completed.

Laetrile

Laetrile is a trade name for a synthetic variant of amygdalin, a cyanide-containing chemical called a cyanogenic glycoside, naturally present in the kernals of apricot pits, apple seeds, bitter almonds, and some other stone fruits and nuts. Promoters consider the two substances essentially identical; so Laetrile and laetrile can be used interchangeably. Proponents of laetrile

636

for cancer prevention and therapy also call it "vitamin B-17." They claim that cancer is actually a vitamin deficiency disease, and that amygdalin is to cancer what vitamin C is to scurvy or thiamin is to beriberi. The cyanide, they say, is harmless to healthy tissue but deadly to cancer cells. They rail against other forms of cancer therapy such as surgery, radiation and chemotherapy, as "cutting, burning, and poisoning."[24,25,26]

Laetrile, they say, is a safe, nontoxic, effective cancer treatment which is being suppressed by government and orthodox medicine for the sake of perpetuating the profits of the cancer research and treatment industries. Only the dedicated, selfless labor of distinguished researchers and doctors keeps laetrile available. Many thousands have accepted these claims, and laetrile has become a billion-dollar-a-year industry.

It would be wonderful if these claims were true, for it would be just a matter of time before cancer would be as rare as scurvy. This would be the medical advance of the century. Unfortunately, some hard facts stand in the way of the golden age of freedom from cancer.

The Evidence Against Laetrile

At least twenty studies conducted at Sloan Kettering Memorial Institute, the University of California, Yale, and other prestigious institutes have failed to detect any beneficial effects of laetrile on cancers. In a massive effort to document some benefit to the nearly 100,000 Americans who have taken laetrile, the National Cancer Institute surveyed almost a half million physicians and other health professionals and pro-laetrile groups. Only six cases of possible improvement could be found. A controlled study on cancer patients at the Mayo Clinic showed cyanide poisoning and no anticancer effect.[27]

In spite of the overwhelming evidence, the myth persists that laetrile can cure cancer. All too often people are seduced into forgoing life-saving surgery, chemotherapy, or radiation. In his book, *Healing: A Doctor in Search of a Miracle*, Dr. William Nolen tells of Mary, a thirty-five-year-old mother of three who had early, treatable cancer of the cervix. But radiation and surgery frightened her, and when she heard that laetrile could cure cancer, she decided to try it. If it didn't work, she reasoned, she could go back for standard therapy.

Neither her husband nor Dr. Nolen could dissuade her. She spent about $1,000 per month for the treatment. By the sixth month she was bleeding every day and losing strength. She went back to Dr. Nolen and requested surgery, but by then the cancer had spread throughout the pelvis. She died a month later. There have been thousands of such cases.

Laetrile (Amygdalin)

Enzymatic action here releases the deadly cyanide, which can poison all organs of the body.

Laetrile Is Toxic

Laetrile is potentially deadly. Many cases of severe sickness and death from cyanide poisoning have been reported; cyanide blocks normal metabolism in every cell of the body.[28] This chemical strangulation is so efficient that "cyanosis" is synonymous with the bluish color of an area of the body deprived of oxygen.

The claim that the cyanide in laetrile is no more toxic than the cyanide in vitamin B-12 is absurd. Actually, cobalamine (vitamin B-12) in nature does not contain cyanide, which is metabolically worthless in any biological system. In some pharmaceutical preparations, cyanide is added to cobalamine as a stabilizer, but the daily intake is less than one-millionth that taken by persons using laetrile. Hydroxocobalamine (vitamin B-12 without the cyanide) in huge doses can be used to prevent or treat cyanide poisoning due to laetrile by "soaking up" the cyanide as it is released.

The concentrated form of laetrile is not the only danger; apricot kernals have also caused extreme illness and some deaths. When a kernal is crushed by blending or chewing, the amygdalin comes in contact with beta-glucosidase, the enzyme in the kernal that releases the toxic free cyanide. As little as fifteen well-crushed kernals can be lethal. One laetrile promoter, June DeSpain, author of *The Little Cyanide Cookbook*, fell into a coma and almost died from acute cyanide poisoning after following one of her own

638 recipes. She had eaten about twenty-five kernals. Her book is still on the market.

A case reported in *California Morbidity* illustrates the typical symptoms of amygdalin poisoning: "A man and his wife purchased a two-pound bag of apricot kernals at a local health food store. They soaked some thirty of them with dried apricots in distilled water overnight and the following day pureed the ingredients in a blender. The resulting concoction was bitter and took some effort to swallow.

"About an hour after drinking the mixture, the wife complained of abdominal discomfort, tachycardia (racing heart), and feeling strange. She drank some water and vomited. Within minutes of his wife's onset, the husband became symptomatic also and complained of headache, light-headedness, tachycardia, a generally strange sensation, and impaired vision as if looking through frosted glass. He felt impending doom.

"They were rushed to the emergency room of a nearby hospital. Vomiting was successfully induced, and after several hours of observation they were released. For the next three days the husband complained of insomnia and tinnitus (ringing in the ears). The wife had diarrhea which abated in one day. Both recovered fully."

Notice that this small dose of only about twenty-five kernals each made them very sick and might have killed them had they not been treated. Other reported symptoms include generalized weakness, dizziness, flushing, heavy perspiration, low blood pressure, itching, hemorrhage into the GI tract, coughing, and fever.

The lethal dose for children can be remarkably small. In June 1977 an eleven-month-old girl in Attica, New York, ate five tablets of her father's laetrile. It killed her.

ANTIDOTE

If amygdalin ingestion is suspected, induce vomiting with warm salt water or a finger down the throat. Call a physician or ambulance immediately. Speed is essential.

Chronic cyanide poisoning by repeated sublethal doses can also be very serious. Known symptoms include hypothyroidism, goiter, weakness, fatigue, insomnia, increased susceptibility to bacterial infections, weight loss, cataracts, and serious neurological damage including mental retardation, blindness, and nerve deafness. Thousands of Africans are affected by these conditions because of amygdalin in the diet, largely from cassava (manioc) root, a staple in some diets. Laetrile proponents ignore this, and the fact that these Africans are not protected from cancer by their diets.

Proponents often couple laetrile with a diet of fruits and vegetables as part of a "holistic approach" to cancer prevention and therapy. Ironically, it is precisely these foods that have large amounts of the cyanide-releasing enzyme, beta-glucosidase. Eating peaches, mushrooms, lettuce, carrots, almonds, bean sprouts, or other normally excellent, nutritious foods with laetrile greatly increases the risk of cyanide poisoning. The toll taken on the body can only hurt the chances of combating the disease and delay of proper treatment can be fatal.

Even more ironically, **laetrile may cause cancer.** It is mutagenic (damages DNA) and gives a positive Ames test, which makes it highly suspect as a carcinogen.[29]

Laetrile promoters are not "distinguished, respected researchers and physicians working for the good of humanity," as they claim. Ernst Krebs, Jr., the originator of the swindle and a convicted criminal, flunked out of medical school but calls himself "Doctor" on the basis of an honorary doctorate from the American Christian College in Tulsa, Oklahoma, which had no science department and no legal power to grant the degree. In spite of his testimony that he had never made money from laetrile, many thousands of dollars were found hidden in his San Francisco mansion during probationary searches.

Andrew McNaughton, owner and co-owner of several laetrile factories, is no scientist at all but a convicted criminal once found guilty of stock fraud. In 1963 the McNaughton Foundation, a laetrile propaganda machine, received $300,000 from Joseph (Joe Bayonne) Zicarelli, a *caporegime* in the New York-New Jersey Mafia. Much of this money no doubt financed the wave of propaganda that swept the U.S. in the 1960s. The Mafia's share of the subsequent profits is not known.

John Richardson, M.D., is a criminally convicted and defrocked physician. According to the U.S. attorney who prosecuted him, Richardson's take was almost 3 million dollars in his short career in the laetrile dispensing business. At least one of his patients died from cyanide poisoning. Survivors of other dead patients of his have filed lawsuits against him.

Laetrile promoter Dr. David Rubin of Israel was Medical Director of the "Israel Medical Research Foundation," which has never done clinical research and is now out of business. All forty-five patients he treated with laetrile in 1976 and 1977 were dead in 1978.

Harold Manner of Loyola University, another "star" of the cult, accepted money from the laetrile industry for a study claiming regression of mouse mammary tumors by laetrile, vitamin A, and digestive enzymes, all recommended for human cancers in his cult book, *The Death of Cancer.* The study was scientifically worthless and the treatment extremely dangerous for humans. Manner has admitted to being a consultant to profitable laetrile industries and has traveled widely to promote the chemical.

Many other promoters have had brushes with the law for various kinds of fraud and other criminal activities, but the penalties have been light and the rewards great. The public has been duped, and millions of dollars are still being made, so the grisly game goes on. It seems likely that thousands more will die prematurely from cyanide poisoning and untreated cancer before this, one of the most destructive and lucrative health frauds ever perpetrated, is ended.

The Laetrile
Movement as a Cyanide Cult

It has been pointed out that the laetrile movement has all the markings of a cult, complete with irrational beliefs and rituals, paranoid delusions, and venerated leaders (usually made wealthy by their activities), and it bears a striking resemblance to another cyanide cult, that of Jim Jones's People's Temple, 900-odd members of which perished by cyanide in the jungles of Guyana. The final toll of the laetrile cult could be 100 times that before it is over.

Chad Green is the most famous victim of the cult. Persuaded by sophisticated propaganda that laetrile could cure his leukemia, his parents whisked him off to the Del Mar Clinic in Tijuana in spite of a court order that the child continue treatment at Massachusetts General Hospital. Leukemia once meant certain death, but many are now being saved, and Chad had a chance with chemotherapy.

In Mexico, Dr. Contreras, multimillionaire cancer quack and owner of a laetrile factory, kept Chad on chemotherapy (as well as laetrile), obviously fearful of the adverse publicity that would follow if he were to die. But eventually the chemotherapy was stopped and the laetrile continued. Eight weeks later he did die. In the weeks before his death his serum cyanide level was .22 micrograms per milliliter, very close to the fatal .29 level in the Attica girl. In an unusual and suspicious move, Chad's body was quickly embalmed. This prevented any possible detection of cyanide poisoning of his vital organs.[30]

There followed an ironic spectacle, with Chad's parents and Contreras blaming each other for discontinuing the drugs that might have saved him, and finally announcing that Chad had died of stress from homesickness caused by the authorities who made it necessary for them to flee to Mexico for "proper" treatment. This is described in *New Age* in an article by P.B. Chowka titled "Chad Green, A Matter of Life, Death, and Freedom." This article is a good example of the persistence of myth in the face of a mountain of reality, of an almost religious faith in a deified substance. Although Chowka knows and reports most of the essential facts of the case, he somehow fails to draw the only logical conclusion, that laetrile failed, as it always has, and that the treatment probably hastened Chad's death.

With an exercise in doublethink right out of *1984* (or *The People's* **641** *Temple)*, Chowka makes laetrile proponents the heroes in a struggle for life and freedom. This two-part cover article gave the laetrile cult (and, no doubt, *New Age's* circulation) a boost when it should have suffered a black eye if not a knockout punch. When we repeatedly asked Chowka and the magazine's medical editor, Rick Ingrasci, M.D., whether they knew of any cases of laetrile curing leukemia or any other cancer, they did not reply.

In a repeat performance after actor Steve McQueen's death, *New Age* continued its alliance with the laetrile cult with a worshipping article on Dr. William D. Kelly, the dentist who treated the actor with his phony "metabolic therapy," which includes laetrile, fasting, coffee enemas, and other worthless and dangerous nostrums. While *New Age* and *The Los Angeles Free Press* have been especially cozy with the cult, the press in general has been remarkably soft on laetrile, considering the magnitude of the hoax and the harm it does.

Laugh Therapy

Three hundred years ago it was observed that "the arrival of a good clown exercises more beneficial influence upon the health of a town than twenty asses laden with drugs." In early America the Ojibway Indians used doctor-clowns called *windigokan* to help heal the sick.

More recently, writer-publisher Norman Cousins helped popularize the concept of laugh therapy with accounts of his successful battle against a serious immunologic disease of uncertain diagnosis.[31] He had nodules and "gravel" under his skin, fever, prostration, and almost constant pain. One specialist guessed he had one chance in 500 to recover.

Cousins was endowed with a powerful will to live and resolved to take an active part in his treatment. He was convinced that the pain killers and sleep aids he had been taking were harmful and would inhibit his recovery. His treatment would consist of large doses of vitamin C (essential in collagen synthesis), and "love, hope, faith, laughter, and confidence."

The most difficult of these to "administer" was laughter; he was flat on his back with an aching spine and joints aflame. Using humor books and films of *Candid Camera* and other comedies, he found that ten minutes of laugher was good for immediate pain relief and two hours of pain-free sleep without drugs. His sedimentation rate (a biochemical index of the disease activity) steadily improved and he eventually recovered.

Cousins has refrained from making spectacular claims for his methods, but others have not. In truth, we don't know how "miraculous" his recovery was. Such rare diseases are very unpredictable, even for the experts. It is entirely possible that the specialist was wrong and that Cousins was destined to recover, or at least had a 50-50 chance.

But surely we can accept his testimony that laughter helped him sleep and eased his pain. And surely this helped reduce the stress level and increase the odds of recovery. Laughter can be considered a form of physical as well as mental therapy. A good laugh vibrates the whole body and exercises the diaphragm, abdomen, heart, lungs, and chest muscles. Laughter relieves tension and anxiety and may even stimulate the release of endorphins, powerful painkillers produced in the brain. It is not surprising that some hospitals and nursing homes are adding laughter to their medicine bags.

Mendelsohn's "Heresy"— A Reply

Robert S. Mendelsohn, M.D., who teaches preventive medicine at the University of Illinois School of Medicine, believes that the greatest hazard to your health is your doctor. In his popular book, *Confessions of a Medical Heretic* (Contemporary Books, 1979), he describes the physicians of America as the Devil's Priests carrying out Holy War on the Family. Ninety percent of Modern Medicine, including the Devil's Priests and the Temples of Doom (hospitals), could disappear from the face of the earth and our health would not suffer. In fact, we would all be better off because the god of the Church of Modern Medicine is Death itself.

To stay healthy, Mendelsohn says, you must avoid hospitals ("one of the most dangerous places on earth") and doctors like the plagues that they are. They will addict you to worthless and dangerous drugs, slice you up for no good reason, dose you with dangerous X-rays, infect you with deadly germs, and rob you blind while doing you in. Modern Medicine tortures all citizens with its four Holy Waters: immunization, fluoridated water, intravenous fluids, and silver nitrate (eyedrops that prevent gonorrhea in the newborn). It also unfairly suppresses unorthodox methods such as chiropractic, homeopathy, laetrile, and muscle response testing.

Dr. Mendelsohn's suggested solution is nothing less than the total elimination of Modern Medicine and its replacement with the New Medicine and New Doctors, who will be trained at his New Medical School. The New Doctor will be truly prevention oriented, so hospitals will not be needed. Babies will be born at home and the fields of obstetrics, gynecology, and pediatrics will disappear. Modern cancer therapy, with its irrational use of drugs, surgery, and radiation, will vanish, as will psychiatry and internal medicine. The New Doctor will be a generalist, not a specialist, and will help educate and motivate people about good health habits.

While we wait for this revolution to take place we must do all we can to save ourselves and our children from the modern-medicine monster.

This includes fighting fluoridation, keeping our kids out of school to save them from immunization, having our babies at home, and generally distrusting doctors. We spoke with several practicing physicians about Mendelsohn's book. The following is a composite of their reactions.

The book has the spirit of a teenage beach-blanket horror movie. It panders to irrational fears and is "medexploitation" at its worst. It is not surprising that, instead of providing scientific references to support his many fantastic claims, Mendelsohn says the ideas are based on "common sense" and that he has not ignored unorthodox sources of medical information such as *Prevention* magazine and *The National Enquirer.*

Mendelsohn's grasp of medical science seems to be woefully inadequate for an associate professor of preventive medicine and he does a great disservice to the public with his inflammatory rhetoric and many false claims. For example, the benefits of fluoride and vaccines are extremely well documented around the world and strongly supported by the World Health Organization and the world medical community. Only a tiny minority of horror mongers, who have no good data to support their claims, question their value. Mendelsohn also opposes routine screening for a variety of disorders. But it is clear to all who look at the facts that tests for colon, breast, and other cancers save many lives; screening for glaucoma helps prevent blindness; blood pressure checks help prevent strokes; cholesterol checks help prevent heart disease. Clearly, many types of screening are valuable public health tools.

Mendelsohn does much of his hatchet work on straw men he sets up. For example, he praises breast feeding as the greatest of preventive medicines and rails against modern medicine for forcing bottles on mothers and their kids. Pediatricians are especially guilty because they know the bottle-fed children will get sick more often and this generates more business. But the American Academy of Pediatrics, that Temple of Gore, has long encouraged breast feeding, which has increased steadily now for almost three decades. Mendelsohn says modern medicine labels persons interested in nutrition as faddists, freaks, and quacks. In reality, the American Heart, Dental, and Diabetes Associations and several other Sacred Academies of Modern Medicine have advocated good nutrition for many years.

The reason for Dr. Mendelsohn's vendetta against the medical profession is not clear. Perhaps he feels he was slighted and denied his proper place by the powers that be in medicine. In any case, his vision is rather paranoid: the whole profession is rotten except Dr. Mendelsohn; other doctors are greedy scoundrels who don't care about their patients' health; the entire system must be leveled to the ground and a new one constructed based on Mendelsohn's principles.

No one claims that modern medicine is infallible or modern physicians perfect. There are still too many cases of misdiagnosis, overtreatment, irrational drug use, excessive testing, and impersonal care, but they are not

644 nearly as common as Mendelsohn implies. Moreover, many of these problems are not entirely the fault of physicians but are partly due to unrealistic expectations in a lawsuit-happy society.

We agree with Mendelsohn that we should all develop healthy habits to minimize our chances of needing medical care. But what should you do if you get sick or hurt anyway? You won't find any practical suggestions in Mendelsohn's book. We suggest that instead of letting him seduce you into terminal paranoia, you use *this* book to educate yourself; in particular, use the guide to consulting a physician in Part Seven. Unless, like Dr. Mendelsohn, you prefer to check *The National Enquirer* for better ideas.

Muscle Response Testing

In their book *MRT* (Marek, 1979), chiropractor Mark Grinims and acupuncturist/herbalist Walter Fischman describe a system that, they promise, will determine exactly your requirements of all the nutrients without blood tests or dietary analysis, and determine what foods, cosmetics, fabrics, and chemicals you are allergic to without your eating, touching, or inhaling the substances. Diseases can also be diagnosed, even in babies and animals, with the revolutionary system of "muscle response testing" (MRT).

The essence of MRT is this: a subject to be tested stands erect with one arm relaxed and the other held straight out with the palm down. The tester presses down on the subject's wrist for a second or two and gauges the resistance to his pressure. Now a finger of the subject's relaxed hand is stuck into a bottle of aspirin (for example) so it is in contact with the tablets. The extended arm immediately weakens, we are told, because aspirin is a poison and the body's "aura" somehow senses this.

Elaborate and time-consuming modifications of this procedure are used to determine your need for dozens of nutrients. Basically, you hold the vitamin or mineral in question in the free hand while the strength of the other arm is checked. You keep adding pills until your arm suddenly weakens. Subtract a pill or two, and that is how much you should take. Unfortunately, we are not told how often we are supposed to take the determined dose. Perhaps we are supposed to keep taking pills until the arm suddenly gets stronger. Or maybe once a day or once a week. Only the authors know for sure.

The series of tests for nutrients can take several hours a day for many weeks. We are told to retest at least every two months, since our requirements supposedly change often. As if this were not enough, the procedure should also be done for a long list of suspected allergens which could be causing many vague but serious problems without our knowledge.

There is not a shred of evidence that muscles can be affected by substances in the magical manner Grinims and Fischman claim. They certainly don't present any. The subjective sense of resistance is no measurement. Even if it were, or if a scale were used for accurate measurement, there are many variables that can affect muscle strength from moment to moment, including the subject's knowledge of the substance being tested.

If you decide to try this system, you should do the tests "blind" so your prejudices don't color the results. Have the tester periodically place a placebo, toxin, or powerful drug, instead of a vitamin, in your hand without your knowledge. This is also a good method for checking practitioners, to see if their "auras" can distinguish between aspirin and vitamin C, as yours is supposed to. We think you will quickly see this silliness for what it is, a monumental waste of time.

MRT is a branch of "applied kinesiology," which is not related to the legitimate study of muscle physiology and action known as kinesiology, but is one of the latest "healing miracles" used by self-styled naturopaths and taught by unaccredited schools, such as the Biokinesiology Institute in Oregon. A favorite diagnosis of biokinesiologists is skull bone "faults," which supposedly alter cerebrospinal fluid pressure and thereby induce various allergies. It is a nonsensical theory with no basis in physiological fact, but it is discussed seriously on television talk shows and accepted by many clients as reasonable and true.

Naturopathy

Naturopathic medicine, sometimes called biological medicine, is recognized as a legitimate healing art in several countries, and in some of the United States. Superficially, its basic tenets appear sensible and reasonable: the role of the physician is to help the patient's body heal itself with a minimum of "unnatural" intervention, especially drugs. Most naturopaths say they are eclectic physicians and use a wide variety of diverse methods to achieve their ends.

In practice, however, naturopathy leaves much to be desired. Paavo Airola, probably the best known member of the International Naturopathic Association, is somewhat of a guru. His popular books provide some useful information on exercises, massages, and baths. Unfortunately, however, much of what he advocates is nonsensical, and some of it is dangerous. Here is a brief summary of some of the fallacies gleaned from his book, *How To Get Well* (Health Plus, 1974), considered a definitive classic among his followers. Most of these concepts are discussed in detail elsewhere in this book.

Fasting and taking enemas are supposed to be highly beneficial for a great many ailments and symptoms such as acne, jaundice, Parkinsonism, multi-

646   ple sclerosis, and alcoholism. All these applications are irrational and potentially harmful, but the last is particularly ill-advised. Most alcoholics are
already moderately to severely malnourished and they often suffer from liver
disease. Fasting, especially for the two weeks Airola advocates, can seriously
complicate the problem. The three enemas per day he recommends can
adversely affect normal bowel function.

Megadoses of many vitamins are recommended for most conditions. The
irrationality and hazardousness of this are discussed in Part Two. Massive
doses of vitamin A (up to 150,000 units) are recommended for psoriasis and
acne without any warning of the hazards in pregnancy. There is no evidence
it helps.

Adrenal cortical extract (ACE) is recommended for hypoglycemia. This is
senseless and very dangerous.

Constipation is said to be a major cause of eczema and many other skin
conditions. This is nonsense.

Pangamic acid, or so-called vitamin B-15, a poisonous nonvitamin, is recommended for angina, emphysema, and epilepsy.

Laetrile, or so-called vitamin B-17, a poisonous nonvitamin, is recommended for cancer.

Diabetics must (!) (his emphasis) be on a strict lacto-vegetarian alkaline diet
with plenty of fruit. This is nonsense. Diabetics can do very well eating
generous amounts of fish and lean meat.
    Eating certain cactus pads (Tuna, Nopal) is supposed to be good
treatment for diabetes because of their "natural, organic" insulin content.
There is no such thing as nonorganic insulin. And insulin cannot be absorbed through the digestive system; it must be injected.

Raw skim milk and raw egg yolks are recommended for jaundice, a symptom most often caused by liver disease but with other possible causes. There
is no conceivable justification for this prescription. Raw eggs are recommended for multiple sclerosis. There is no possible benefit from this.

Salads should not be eaten before protein foods because they supposedly
prevent full digestion of the protein by using up the stomach's hydrochloric
acid. In reality, leafy greens and other common salad ingredients have very
little ability to neutralize acid, and the bulk they provide tends to stimulate
acid release. If they could effectively neutralize acid, they could be useful in
the treatment of peptic ulcers, which they are not except to the extent that

they provide vitamin A, zinc, and other nutrients involved in wound healing.

Brewer's yeast is supposed to have the highest quality protein. In fact, its protein is of rather poor quality, ranking far below that of milk, eggs, fish, meat, and even some legumes and grains.

Magnesium is recommended for diarrhea. While it is a good idea to provide some mineral supplements during extended bouts of diarrhea, magnesium is a well-known laxative, and its use can aggravate the problem.

Garlic suppositories are recommended for hemorrhoids. This can cause severe irritation and pain, and there is no evidence it helps. Garlic supposito- ries have been used by prisoners to produce a fever in order to gain admit- tance to a hospital.

Gerovital, which is nothing but procaine and a few vitamins, is recom- mended for impotence and to slow aging. This is a hoax which originated in Rumania decades ago. Licorice, false unicorn, and elder are also supposed to slow aging. This is a superstition of ancient origin with no basis in fact.

Halva (a sesame seed and honey candy) and fertile eggs are said to be special virility foods. More hogwash.

      Naturopaths often use such discredited methods as iridology, homeopathy, and hair analysis. While usually harmless in themselves, these can be expensive and can lead to mistaken diagnosis and worthless treat- ments.

What Is Natural about Naturopathy?

Naturopaths often criticize scientific medicine as being "unnatural," and pose as spokesmen for "natural healing." They are especially shrill in their condemnation of modern pharmacology. While the use of drugs by physi- cians is sometimes irrational and dangerous, it is fair to ask why it is more natural to use such poisons as laetrile, pangamic acid, dangerous herbs, enemas, procaine injections, ACE, or megavitamin doses.

Pangamic Acid ("Vitamin B-15")

"Vitamin B-15" is the ultimate wonder-vitamin, surpassing even "vitamin B-17" (laetrile). According to its purveyors, it prevents and cures heart dis-

648 ease, cancer, asthma, arthritis, diabetes, eczema, neuritis, hangovers, emphysema, poisoning, headaches, mental retardation, insomnia, and premature aging.

The only problem is, there is no general agreement on what "vitamin B-15" is, and the products on the market vary enormously. The Ernst Krebses, Sr. and Jr., first used the term as a trade-name for a substance they isolated from apricot pits and called "pangamic acid" in their patent application. (Krebs, Jr., also gave amygdalin, first isolated from apricot pits in 1830, the name *laetrile,* and later called it "vitamin B-17.")

The application for a patent made wild snake-oil-type claims without the slightest evidence. They did not report basic chemical information on their isolation method or even a melting point. Years later they used the term "pangamic acid" for gluconodimethyl glycine, which is lab-synthesized and has not been proven to exist in nature, or to be available, absorbable, or necessary in the diet. Later still, they promoted a synthetic mixture of three other chemicals as "vitamin B-15."

The usually reliable Merck Index was apparently taken in by the game. The 8th edition (1968) identifies pangamic acid as a mixture of glycine, gluconate, and diisopropylamine dichloroacetate. The latter is a chlorinated hydrocarbon and possible carcinogen. The 9th edition (1978) says "vitamin B-15" is methylethyl amino acetate. The editors now say they were deceived into listing the product, and future editions will delete "panagamic acid" and "vitamin B-15."

There are about fifty products on the market labeled B-15 or pangamic acid. Here is a partial list, with brief discussions, of the substances found in these products. Apparently all the products (including the Russian) are synthetic, and each contains one or more of the following chemicals.[32]

Gluconodimethyl glycine is an unstable ester with neuromuscular blocking activity and hypotensive effects in animals, and effects on humans similar to those of DMG.

Dimethyl glycine (DMG) is a product of choline metabolism naturally found in meat. It reacts with nitrites in saliva to form dimethylnitrosamine, a potent carcinogen, and nitrososarcosine, a weak carcinogen. The concentrated pill form is more likely to induce cancer than the same amount in meat since the latter is chemically bound and diluted by other substances. DMG is sometimes sold as such, with no mention of pangamic acid or "vitamin B-15," but the claims are the same: it can provide pep and stamina and cure and prevent many serious diseases.

Gluconic acid, sodium gluconate, and **calcium gluconate** are essentially inert in humans, though sodium gluconate can be a source of excessive sodium in the diet.

Glycine is a nonessential amino acid made in the body from other amino acids and from choline. It has no remarkable effects or hazards associated with it.

Diisopropylamine lowers blood pressure and body temperature. Large doses may cause death by cyanosis and respiratory failure.

Diisopropylglycine is related to the above and probably has similar effects. It has no known role in normal metabolism.

Diisopropylammonium dichloroacetate is related to the above two and is probably similar in effects, with the added danger of carcinogenesis from the dichloroacetate.

Dichloroacetic acid is a chlorinated hydrocarbon which easily forms free radicals, causes mutations in bacteria, and is a suspected carcinogen. It interferes with metabolism in the liver, causes sedation and increased uric-acid levels in diabetics, and may promote oxalic acid kidney stones. In animals and humans it may produce leg paralysis, nerve degeneration, testicular degeneration, and widespread nerve damage.

As anyone can see, the Food and Drug Administration had no choice but to reject the vitamin claim. Far from being an essential nutrient or miracle drug, it is not even an identifiable substance, and the mixtures that go by the "B-15" label are potentially toxic.

The Russian Studies

But what about the Russian reports? many will protest. A fat volume of papers from Moscow, *Vitamin B-15 Properties, Functions and Uses*, is distributed by the McNaughton Foundation (which is also involved in laetrile promotion), mostly through health food stores. At a glance, the papers appear impressive, espcially to the scientifically naive and the careless reader. At least the Russian "B-15" is one substance, laboratory-made gluconodimethyl glycine. But the papers are not convincing evidence for claims about "vitamin B-15" for several reasons.

They provide no data at all on the basic biochemical and physiological effects, or on absorption, excretion, metabolism, or blood and urine levels, without which no valid claims for the chemical can be made.

They provide no evidence that the chemical is a required nutrient or even that it occurs in nature.

Few of the studies used controls to account for placebo effects or the effects of concurrent therapies, such as diet, activity, rest, and other drugs. The positive reports mostly involve very small groups of patients and little hard clinical data is presented.

650   Many of the Russian discussions uncritically parrot the Krebs's claims rather than checking them, and quote the Krebs as if they had established scientific fact, when in reality they invented a clever money-making scheme and their papers are scientifically worthless.

The John Birch-Moscow Alliance

It is very ironic that the deficient work done in Russia is used to support the claims made by the pangamic-acid-laetrile complex, which consists mostly of avid rightwingers who normally scoff at any and all Russian claims as propaganda. But this particular propaganda suits their purposes, so they use it as "evidence." The late Congressman Larry McDonald of Georgia, for example, who perished in the Korean airliner downed by the Soviets in 1984, was a John Bircher and a strong supporter of prolaetrile legislation. In cities all over the country the best place to find laetrile and pangamic acid propaganda is in John Birch Society book stores.

We should not be surprised at inept science coming out of the Soviet Union. Stalin wiped out a whole generation of Soviet biologists and imposed Lysenkoism (Soviet Lamarkism). Science was politicized in a life-and-death way and the effects remain today. Although conditions are not as severe as before, the biological and medical sciences in the Soviet Union are naive by Western standards, and Soviet scientists are pressured to produce positive-sounding results, the kind which indicate progress, provide handy placebos for the masses, and please the Party bosses. The surprise is the alliance between John Birchers and communists. But then, greed has always made strange bedfellows.

The "B-15" issue illustrates how easy it is to fool the public, which has literally swallowed the hoax whole and now spends millions on the worthless, hazardous chemicals. While the law prohibits the lies from appearing on the labels, the First Amendment protects the right to lie in books, pamphlets, and vitamin charts. As it now stands, it is fairly easy for anyone to proclaim any worthless chemical a vitamin. If the lies are big enough and the public guillible enough, millions can be made.

The Pearson/Shaw Longevity Theory

Durk Pearson and Sandy Shaw, neither of whom is a physician or medical researcher, present their theory of aging and longevity in their book, *Life*

Extension—A Practical Scientific Approach (Warner Books, 1983). The thesis is that there is now a fountain of youth which can greatly improve the length and quality of life for everyone who cares to dip into it. Brain power can be increased; cardiovascular disease, cancer, arthritis, and other diseases can be prevented; and smoking, drinking, and breathing polluted air can be made safer. Skin aging can be slowed and even reversed and sexual capacity and athletic prowess increased. We can combat baldness, prevent hangovers, and even develop our muscles without exercise.

What magical substances flow from this fountain to produce the miracles? They are certain vitamins, amino acids, minerals, food preservatives, and prescription drugs. What they almost all have in common is a chemical property; they are antioxidants, substances that tend to retard oxidation reactions in the body. The recommended doses are enormous—in the megavitamin range for the nutrients and far in excess of the usual doses for the drugs.

The theory is that the antioxidants protect cells from the ravaging effects of highly reactive chemicals, known as free radicals and peroxides, which create abnormal chemical bonds in various tissues. These abnormal bonds cause brittleness in arteries and lung tissue, wrinkling and spotting of the skin, nerve and brain damage, and other symptoms of aging. By flooding the body with antioxidants this damage can be greatly reduced and aging retarded, even reversed.

The authors say their book is a "practical how-to-do-it-yourself book on life extension." They make the obligatory disclaimers and say that we are all biochemically distinct, so each person must experiment and explore to find the formula best for him- or herself. But they do not begin to provide the information necessary to choose between, say, 100 and 1,000 units of vitamin E, or 5 and 50 milligrams of Hydergine. So most people will just mimic the formula they use, even though they say the formula is strictly experimental and recommended only for themselves. (If it's good enough for these experts, it's good enough for me, most people will reason.)

Nearly 100 of the book's 800 pages are devoted to a tirade against the Food and Drug Administration and other government agencies for their restrictive policies on nutritional supplements and new drugs. And while the authors concede that anecdotal case histories are scientifically worthless, they devote more than fifty pages to them.

In practical terms, the impact of the book is to further increase the use of nutritional supplements and create a demand for routine use of certain prescription drugs. So let's look at the components of the formula, the theories and evidence for their use, and the potential consequences.

Vitamins A, most of the Bs, C, and E are taken in daily doses up to 600 times the RDA. (The Recommend Dietary Allowances are determined by scientists working with the National Research Council, not by the Food

652 and Drug Administration as erroneously stated by the authors. See Vitamins in Part Two). While these vitamins are, by definition, required in the diet to maintain health, the evidence they rely on to support the megadoses is very poor. They often refer to old, poorly designed, already refuted studies and anecdotes from the likes of the Shute brothers of vitamin E fame and convicted quack Kurt Donsbach, for whose diploma mill Pearson and Shaw used to write pamphlets.

The authors scarcely mention and seriously underestimate the hazards of taking such huge doses of supplements. They either fail to mention or make light of such side effects as reduced thyroid hormone in the blood, fatigue, headaches, and low blood sugar from too much vitamin E; and nausea, stomach bleeding, headaches, liver damage, and abnormal heart metabolism from too much niacin.

The amino acids in their formula include arginine, ornithine, cysteine, tryptophan, and sometimes phenylalanine and tyrosine. As with most of the vitamins, the main reason for the first three amino acids is their antioxidation properties. The main reason for the latter three is to normalize brain metabolism and neurotransmitter function in order to promote normal sleep, prevent depression, and provide stamina and enthusiasm in work and play. Several of these amino acids are also claimed to promote the release of growth hormone which stimulates the immune system and so helps combat infections, cancer, and even atherosclerosis. No references to support this claim are given, and there is no evidence that we know of to support it.

The minerals zinc and selenium are also taken in large daily doses, again because they are antioxidants and therefore supposedly anti-aging and antidisease. BHT and other antioxidant food preservatives are taken in much larger amounts than those available in foods. The market for BHT created by the authors has led many health food stores to supply the chemical. This is ironic because not long ago one of the main reasons for going to a health food store was to avoid preservatives. Many of the packaged foods were, and still are, emblazoned with the slogan, "No preservatives." It is also dangerous; doses of BHT smaller than those recommended by the authors have been shown to be toxic to the liver of animals, and some countries have banned even the very small amounts used in foods to prevent rancidity. An overdose of BHA or BHT can apparently be lethal; about one gram will kill a rabbit. Their plan calls for 2 grams a day.

The antioxidant prescription drugs Hydergine, Deaner, bromocryptine, and L-Dopa, and the prescription hormones vasopressin and thyroid extract are taken to improve memory and learning, stimulate the immune system, and scavenge free radicals to slow aging.

Is It Scientific?

If you are skeptical of panaceas, you will have doubts about Pearson and Shaw's claims and recommendations. The antioxidant substances are presented as the cure-all and prevent-all for humanity. No discussion is given to the possible consequences of all this antioxidant power flooding our bodies, but it is oxidation within the cells that provides the energy to drive bodily functions. Why must we assume that the body's own mechanisms for balancing these two forces are incompetent? Might not an overdose of anti-oxidants cause the body to slow down its own production or interfere with the vital function of normal cells? Is the thyroid extract in the formula necessary to combat the excess of antioxidants?

Pearson (thirty-seven years old) claims to be in a chair or water bed 85 percent of the time and to excercise only thirty seconds a day with a pair of dumbbells, yet to be more muscular than he was as a teenager. This he attributes to his use of the nutrients that purportedly release growth hormone. But when one looks at the near-nude photograph of him flexing, with the caption, "It took me a total of about 30 minutes of exercise (over 2 months) to build these muscles," the inevitable reaction is, "What muscles?" He not only does not resemble a trained athlete with only 13 percent body fat (as he claims), but there is no "before" picture and nothing to compare with.

The authors claim to have the skin of people in their early twenties (Shaw is also thirty-seven). This is supposedly due to the antioxidants in their formula, and is proven by a skin pinch test on the back of the hand. The skin, shown in photos of Pearson's hand, supposedly snaps back in place hardly more slowly than a teenager's. They make no mention of the many variables than can affect such a test, such as muscle tension, sun damage, and hereditary factors. They give no comparison data or even anecdotal evidence to support their claims of having younger skin due to antioxidant intake. They claim to have witnessed age spots gradually disappear from an elderly man's skin after he started taking Deaner. But in just the case where photos might have been of real value, there are none.

They claim that men and women who cannot reach orgasm often respond to large doses of niacin, which can cause a flush resembling the flush of orgasm. This is apparently pure speculation, since they cite no studies and provide no evidence. They do allow, though, that they often ingest niacin before sex; however, many people find artificial flushing extremely uncomfortable and often accompanied by nausea and stomach bleeding. Liver damage and other health problems can result from long-term use in large doses.

They claim, on the flimsiest anecdotal evidence, that BHT is an effective antiherpes medicine. They say they recommended it to several people and, lo and behold, their herpes subsided in a week. But herpes sores

654 always go away and no remedy can be proclaimed effective without carefully controlled double-blind studies.

There is no evidence whatsoever, and no references are cited by them, to support their claim that large doses of such vitamins as E and C and other antioxidant nutrients can maintain sexual capacity into older age and increase a depressed sex drive.

They claim to have reduced their sleeping times by an hour a day using Deaner. But with all they are taking, how do they know what is responsible? They say BHT reduces sleeping time and prevents alcoholic hangovers, but cite no studies.

They give no support for the questionable claims that the amino acid phenylalanine is twice as effective as the antidepressant drug imipramine; that antioxidant vitamins can lower serum cholesterol (many studies refute this), regress atherosclerotic plaques, and increase stamina; that vitamin-containing creams can increase hair growth in balding men; that 20 to 25 percent of male impotence is due to excessive prolactin; that old rats can be made to swim like young rats if given the right antioxidants; that raw pineapple and papaya applied to the skin can make it look younger; or that "chelation therapy" (which has caused deaths due to kidney damage) can help in atherosclerosis.

Is It Practical?

Clearly, the book is not as scientific as its title claims, but what about the claim of being practical? How practical would it be for you to obtain and swallow all the pills and powders? Can you afford it? The daily cost would be in the neighborhood of $30 to $60, depending on how well you shop for sales and bulk discounts.

Then there is the cost of regular visits to a physician to get the necessary prescriptions plus the cost of the extensive lab work which, the authors emphasize, is absolutely essential. Including these costs, the total cost of the program appears to be well over $10,000 per year. Estimates by other critics range as high as $39,000 per year.

Can you even talk your physician into prescribing for you powerful drugs with potentially serious side effects in large doses when you do not exhibit the usual indications for using the drugs? Their Hydergine dose, for example, is 40 milligrams a day, seven to ten times the usual dose for therapy in age-related forgetfulness—for which, incidently, the drug has not been proven effective.

Is it practical to monitor effects and side effects, as the authors say we must, when taking so many different chemicals that, no doubt, have complex interactions with each other? How would we know what substance or combination of substances was having what effect?

The fact that the book hardly lives up to is claim of being practical and scientific will not likely affect its sales. Everyone yearns for a fountain of youth, and many people will buy the book and try the chemicals out of hope and curiosity. Pearson and Shaw will be able to buy all the things they say (in the afterword) they hope to buy with the book's proceeds: lots of scientific instruments, computers, fine art, sports cars, and a Cessna 185 light plane. But the really big beneficiaries of the book's message will be the megavitamin industry and Sandoz Pharmaceuticals, the main maker of Hydergine, bromocryptine, and vasopressin.

It should be added that Sandoz has denounced the book and the proposed uses of the drugs. Perhaps the company would consider donating the profits generated by the book to the fight against quackery. Their statisticians could make a reasonable estimate.

Psychic Surgery

One evening in the mid-1970s, "The Decade of Cults," an auditorium full of medical, premedical, and other students in the San Francisco area sat in awed silence as a speaker showed slides and then a film of what appeared to be a medical miracle. In the film a woman with inoperable spinal tumors lies on her stomach, fully conscious. The "surgeon" holds his hands just above the flesh of her lower back, then he kneads the flesh with his fingers. Suddenly, there is blood as his fingers seem to sink into the flesh. They quickly withdraw with stringy bits of bloody material said to be tumors. The wound seems to spontaneously close as the assistants sponge up the blood and the patient has felt no pain.

More patients are shown undergoing "surgery," mostly for various tumors but also for heart disease and other disorders. The pattern is always the same, from the kneading to the appearance of blood to the pulling out of tissue to the mopping up. Some of the patients are interviewed and they all say they feel better.

These patients had flown from the United States to the Philippines in a chartered jet liner and paid up to several thousand dollars each for a series of these psychic surgery treatments. The genius at work, who explains his talent in terms of mental power and cosmic vibrations, is Tony Agpaoa, ex-magician and one of the wealthiest men in the Philippines. Many of his imitators have also done very well for themselves.

The reactions of the students in the auditorium was a sign of the times. Only one person questioned the presentation, which was well received. Several students expressed a desire to drop out of medical school to study with Tony. They had witnessed a miracle and were ripe for conversion. Few recognized the sleight of hand, the subtle pressing down of the flesh to create a little pool to hold the blood which was easily sneaked in,

656 probably in capsules in the cotton, and the palming of bits of animal tissue.

Tony has been exposed many times. A newspaper reporter once grabbed a piece of tissue he had supposedly pulled out of a patient and ran off with it. A laboratory analyzed it and concluded it was chicken gut. Author-physician William Nolen thoroughly debunked psychic surgery in his book *Healing, a Doctor in Search of a Miracle*, in which he reports on his trip to the Philippines to watch Tony operate, and his follow-up of Tony's patients.

The exposés have not put much of a dent in Tony's operation. The power of suggestion, the placebo effect, is no doubt the basis of whatever success, or seeming success, Tony achieves. It is not out of courtesy that mirrors are usually set up so the patients can view the whole gory process; all that blood and guts can have a powerful impact on the mind.

There are now psychic surgeons in the United States treating people for every imaginable illness, mostly serious. The placebo benefits of the treatment may be substantial, but they are only temporary and cannot alter the course of serious diseases. The morality of charging hundreds or thousands of dollars for a short-lived relief of pain and false hope of cure is highly questionable, especially when people are diverted from treatments which might save their lives.

Rebirthing

Birth trauma is much worse than anyone imagines, according to Leonard Orr, self-styled miracle healer and inventor of the "rebirthing" system of attaining health, happiness, and riches. It causes not only neuroses and psychoses, but also sleep (a symbolic return to the womb), disease, and death itself (the permanent return to the womb). If only we could do it over and be born without pain and fear, we could escape and this. And we could always be awake instead of wasting all that time sleeping.

Fortunately for humanity, in 1974 Orr discovered a method of inducing a rebirth experience, which is now available to all who can afford it. It can, Orr claims, cure cancer, diabetes, and other deadly diseases. Details on the moment of discovery are sketchy, but Orr is believed to have been in his bathtub with a mask and snorkel on when he saw the light.

In the original version of rebirthing, after thorough indoctrination of the impending miracle, the rebirthee floats face down in a hot tub with a snorkel in his mouth and a rebirther at his side supporting the hips and providing guidance, which consists almost entirely of urgings to hyperventilate. "Breathe deeper, keep breathing, faster, deeper," go the exhortations.

The subject often blacks out for a few seconds. When he comes to, the exhortations to hyperventilate continue. This goes on for fifteen to forty-five minutes. Then the rebirthee is pulled out of the water and lies down, sometimes unconscious, while the rebirther plays loving midwife-mother-father. Many subjects repeat the experience several times until they have the right experience—or give up trying.

The blacking out is said to be caused by "plugging into" the anesthetic used in the subject's birth and is taken as confirmation that a return to the womb has been achieved. Strangely, no effort is made to determine whether an anesthetic was used in the birth of the subjects. However, our own interviews determined that the blacking out occurs regardless of method of birth or drug use.

More recently, Orr has discovered that the hyperventilation and presence of the rebirther are the important factors, not the flotation in warm water. So the tubs have been largely dispensed with, and now the subject simply relaxes and hyperventilates with coaching by the rebirther. This has reduced the cost, since overhead for the hot tubs can be considerable. The fee is now about $25 to $60 per session (up to about an hour).

But what is one paying for, the coaching in hyperventilation? No, the fee covers the presence of the rebirther who, at the moment of rebirth, "telepathically absorbs the psychic garbage stirred up, and disposes of it," according to Orr. Without the trained, bona fide, certified rebirther in the room, all the effort would be wasted.

The Hazards of Rebirthing

All this would be too absurd to even discuss if it were not for the facts that Orr has used nationwide advertising to get thousands to pay to be "reborn," and that prolonged hyperventilation, especially in a hot tub, can be danger-ous. The blacking out has nothing to do with anesthetics but is caused by reduction of blood flow to the brain. Excessive heat causes the peripheral blood vessels to dilate. This leaves less blood for the brain and by itself can cause fainting.

Hyperventilation also decreases blood and oxygen supply to the brain. The arteries dilate in response to carbon dioxide in the blood and contract in its absence. This controls the brain blood supply. Hyperventila-tion throws off carbon dioxide, the blood levels drop, and the brain arteries contract. Loss of consciousness can result.

(The oxygen level of the blood is not increased by hyperventilation because the oxygen is carried by hemoglobin, which is saturated by normal breathing. Carbon dioxide is carried mostly in solution, and can be increased by holding the breath and decreased by hyperventilating.)

Regaining full consciousness and strength after a rebirthing session can take two or three hours. During this time, a mild to ferocious headache may develop. Orr, of course, attributes this to the mythical anesthetic. In reality, it is more likely due to the starvation of the brain for oxygen and the

658

rebound rush of blood to the brain when the torture is finally ended. Such stress on the arteries and normal metabolism of the brain could be very harmful, especially to those with high blood pressure or atherosclerotic cerebral arteries.

Relaxation/Meditation

A widely accepted theory is that for some people, perhaps most, life in modern civilization with such stresses as noise, driving in traffic, and long-term worry about money and family problems tends to promote a chronic state of low-level fear with changes similar to those in the "fight or flight" mechanism. The physiological changes such as increased adrenal hormones, pulse, and blood pressure are generally adverse when the person is not fighting or fleeing but just sitting. If sustained during most waking hours, these changes can be harmful.

If we learn to relax and consciously practice relaxation on a daily basis, we can reduce the stress on our minds and bodies and thereby live happier, healthier, and longer lives. More specifically, regular relaxation can help in hypertension, insomnia, tension headaches, and other disorders aggravated by psychological stress. Other reported benefits include reduced irritability, depression, and shyness; less use of tranquilizers and other psychoactive drugs; and improved emotional stability, psychological stamina, social interaction, and creativity. [33]

Meditation and the Relaxation Reflex

Relaxation is a measurable physiological state in which breathing and heart rate slow and the metabolic rate decreases. Everyone relaxes just before and during sleep, but it is useful to be able to relax at will and without necessarily getting sleepy. For those who have trouble relaxing, simple exercises may help develop the relaxation reflex.

For example, close your eyes, be still, and imagine yourself, as vividly as possible, floating in a clear pool, serene and totally comfortable. Take five deep breaths and go limp, melting into the bed or chair. Now with every exhalation repeat to yourself, "Relax." If you practice this twice a day for a few weeks, you will develop the ability to relax at will, and the impact of stress can be reduced without even lying or sitting but merely *wishing* to relax.

Meditation is deep relaxation with mental alertness and no sleepiness. Many studies done on meditation clearly show rapid physiological changes toward deep relaxation while alert consciousness is maintained. The metabolic rate is decreased by as much as 20 percent below normal consciousness, as it is during sleep. Oxygen consumption and carbon dioxide production go down, cardiac output decreases by up to a third, and respiratory rate decreases by up to a half.

We have all experienced sweaty palms in a tense situation with real or imagined danger. Skin resistance, an indication of the dryness of the skin, is considered a measure of relaxation and reduction of anxiety. Meditation can promote a rapid and large increase in skin resistance. Blood lactate is produced in the muscles by anaerobic (non-oxygen-using) metabolism. It normally falls during rest and increases during activity and anxiety, possibly due to muscle tension; during meditation it drops rapidly. Meditation usually does not change blood pressure but may promote a significant reduction in hypertensives.

How To Meditate

Transcendental Meditation (TM), the trade name of one effective approach, is the most studied method because there are so many people who use it. Other approaches are equally effective. Meditation does not require intense concentration and is easily learned. Here is the essence of the TM method.

Sit in a comfortable position with eyes closed. Pick a simple, relaxing sound and imagine it. The mantrum "aum," drawn out to a low-pitch hum, is an example. Ignore distracting thoughts as they arise; let them fade out or fly away. Maintain the sound and experience it freely for five to fifteen minutes twice a day.

Another effective method is this visually oriented derivative of an ancient Tibetan Buddhist meditation.

Sit comfortably with eyes closed, and visualize a flower, preferably a real one you have seen with four to eight petals. See it against a solid-color background, preferably a relaxing color like blue, green, or white. Count five inhalations while you hold the image. Now let the flower disappear, one petal with each exhalation until only the solid color remains. Maintain this for five to twenty minutes, ignoring other thoughts, not trying to stop them, but letting them glide by.

Snake Venom

Snakes have an ambiguous role in medicine. For centuries they have been symbols of healing used in official seals of medical groups, and their body parts and venoms have been used as medicines in various disorders. Yet

660 these have not been effective drugs, and "snake oil" has become a synonym for quack remedy.

In recent years snake venoms have made a comeback in the form of PROven, a mixture of venoms from several snakes. The product was conceived by William Haast, the owner of the Miami Serpentarium. Haast, not a physician or trained medical researcher, supplied the venom to a local doctor, who quietly provided it to his patients for arthritis, multiple sclerosis, and other disorders. They were generally given twenty shots in his clinic, then provided with enough venom for another 200 self-injections.[34]

This might have gone on indefinitely had not a shipment of 1,000 krait snakes from China been lost en route to Miami. This led to stories in the press and on CBS's "60 Minutes" about the clinic. It also led to an FDA investigation, which showed that PROven was being produced in violation of almost every aspect of the Good Manufacturing Practices regulations, and was being sold for medical use in violation of laws that require drugs to be tested and licensed before marketing.

Rather than shut the operation down and impose fines, the FDA tried to help Mr. Haast correct his manufacturing methods and begin proper studies. It held special workshops for him, his assistant, and his doctor friend with experts in arthritis, neurology, and venom research. Even the National Multiple Sclerosis Society got involved with a commitment to help carry out clinical trials of PROven if proper preparation, standardization, and animal tests were done first. Unproven PROven would get its day in scientific court.

Unfortunately, when the FDA's Bureau of Biologics and other experts analyzed PROven, it was found to contain the venom of water moccasins and other snakes as well as the reported cobras and kraits. The former is a powerful anticoagulant (and apparently less expensive), while the latter two are neurotoxins. Haast had also falsified records and mislabeled batches of his product in order to mislead the FDA. Caught red-handed, Haast continued to sell PROven for up to $100 a vial. Some paid thousands altogether.

In September 1980 the FDA asked Mr. Haast to stop selling PROven until he met manufacturing regulations, properly labeled and tested the product, and obtained the necessary licenses. He disregarded the request, and it took four more months to get a court injunction forbidding the continued manufacture and sale of the product.

Effects and Hazards of Snake Venom

In sufficient doses snake venoms, especially the three types used in PROven, can be lethal. A typical dose can kill various laboratory animals; some users have died, possibly because of the drug. Others have reported dizziness, headaches, visual disturbances, and other symptoms consistent with snake poisoning.

Whether or not PROven ever returns to the market, the case is of 661
interest because there have been other snake venom products in the past
(Cobroxin and Nyloxin, for example) and there will be more in the future.
We hold snakes in awe, we revere and fear them, and this makes snake
venom a powerful placebo, especially for disorders highly subject to spontaneous remissions. Most MS and arthritis patients, for example, experience
somewhat dramatic improvement now and then. If they happen to be taking
a drug they believe is powerful around the time they start to feel better,
nothing on earth will convince them the drug was not responsible, or keep
them from paying.

"Tanning" Pills

Suppose you could take a pill and develop a beautiful glowing tan all over
your body without spending a minute lying in the hot sun or standing in a
tanning booth. There are products that promise this, and they have been
entering the United States from Canada and Europe since the early 1980s.

These "tanning" pills generally contain two ingredients, beta-carotene and canthaxanthin. Beta-carotene is a yellow-orange pigment which
gives peaches, apricots, carrots, and many other fruits and vegetables their
color. It is slowly converted to vitamin A in the body. Canthaxanthin, the
main ingredient in most of these products, is a red-orange pigment that also
occurs in some plants as well as brine shrimp and other marine life. Flamin-
gos and other water birds get their pink hue from eating the colored marine
life.

So it is with humans, too. If you drink enough carrot juice you
will start to turn a bit orange after a few weeks. And if you take "tanning"
pills, which are more accurately called dyeing pills, you will gradually take
on an orange tint. The dye accumulates in the skin, fat, blood, and certain
organs. The blood plasma becomes bright orange and the stools brick-red.
Even the sweat contains the dye.

The pills are generally taken in large doses for a couple of weeks,
then in smaller maintainence doses when the desired color is achieved. The
cost to maintain the color is about $25 to $40 per month (1984).

Both beta-carotene and canthaxanthin are approved by the FDA as
dyes for foods such as soups, fruit drinks, salad dressings, catsup, and margarine. But the doses in the "tanning" pills are twenty to thirty times the
amount ingested in an average diet. The effects of such large doses have not
been thoroughly tested, so the FDA has not approved the dyes for "tanning"
purposes and considers the sale for such use illegal. Some shipments of the
pills into the United States have been intercepted, but the products can still
be obtained.

Beta-carotene in large doses is also approved as a prescription drug

662 for people with a rare inherited disorder of the skin called erythropoietic protoporphyria (EPP). Exposure to the visible radiation of the sun causes their skin to burn, itch, and sometimes ulcerate. The carotene in the skin blocks much of the visible light and protects against the photosensitivity. But it does not block the ultraviolet radiation, so does not protect against sunburn or skin cancer.

Problems with "Tanning" Pills

Persons who wish to take these products in spite of their expense and unproven safety should consider these facts:

> The color obtained is not a tan and does not look much like one; it is too orange.
>
> Some people experience drying and itching of the skin. In one young man the pills caused severe itching and welts over his entire body. These symptoms lasted for several days.
>
> There have been cases of chemical hepatitis with severe nausea, diarrhea, and stomach cramps associated with the tablets.
>
> Nausea, cramps, and diarrhea are vey common side effects of taking large doses of beta-carotene for EPP.
>
> Pregnant women should not take the dye tablets since the chemicals may harm the fetus.

Yoga for Health

There are many systems and methods that go by the name *yoga*, which means "union" in Sanskrit. The ultimate goal is usually described as union with God, attainment of Nirvana, or the dispelling of ignorance. The intermediate goals are control over the emotions and the rambling mind, and conditioning and improvement of the body. We will discuss only the intermediate goals.

The methods generally include good nutrition (lactovegetarian), good hygiene, and avoidance of intoxicants, along with the practice of mantras (meditation), pranayamas (breathing exercises), and asanas (exercises and postures).

The meditation practices of yoga are similar to the methods discussed under Relaxation/Meditation and Hypnosis and Autosuggestion, and they have the same potential as tools in controlling high blood pressure, tension and migraine headaches, insomnia, and other stress-related disorders. Here we discuss some of the more interesting and useful pranayamas and asanas, which are excellent preliminaries to meditation and autosuggestion. They are also good methods of strengthening, stimulating, and limbering muscles and ligaments, and improving breathing habits and respiratory efficiency.

All the exercises should be done with great care not to injure muscles or connective tissue by excessive stress and strain. Too rapid, vigorous, or prolonged stretching, twisting, or rotating, especially without adequate conditioning and warm-up, can tear muscles and ligaments. Overzealous bellows-breathing or holding the breath can cause dizziness and headaches.

Yoga classes can be very helpful for learning exercises, but some teachers don't allow for individual capacities and needs and often run the classes like military drills, with everyone in unison. If you join a class, do only the exercises you feel comfortable with, and go at your own pace. The same goes for those discussed here. All but the mildest exercises should be avoided for about two hours after a meal.

Diaphragmatic breathing. This is usually the first topic of discussion in a yoga class, since it is a requirement in the exercises and in meditation. It is the natural, normal way to breathe, but is often replaced by a shallow chest breathing due to sedentary habits and other factors. Yogis have long maintained that diaphragmatic breathing exercises help control asthma and other respiratory problems. The American Academy of Pediatrics concurs, and prescribes similar exercises for asthmatic children.

To practice diaphragmatic breathing, lie on your back or sit up straight. Keeping the chest flat and the shoulders and collarbone still, inhale by lowering the diaphragm as far as it can go and swelling the abdomen. Exhale completely by contracting the abdomen and raising the diaphragm all the way. Repeat ten times sowly. Exhalation should take about twice as long as inhalation. Estimate seconds or count heart beats.

In normal breathing, there is no reason to restrict chest movement. In a proper complete breath, the lowering of the diaphragm (abdominal swelling) is closely followed by chest expansion, then simultaneous contraction of abdomen and chest. The point of the exercise above is to emphasize the more efficient diaphragmatic component, which often gets slighted.

Bellows breathing. Sit up straight. Concentrate only on exhalation; inhalation will come automatically. With the diaphragm and abdominal muscles only, exhale sharply (sudden and shallow) and relax. Repeat in rapid succession twenty-five times in about ten seconds. Then rest. Repeat several times. This is the only pranayama in which inhalation is longer than exhalation, and it is an excellent exercise for the abdominal muscles.

Abdominal contraction. Stand with your hands just above your slightly bent knees. Completely empty the lungs with a strong expiration. Now pull the

664 navel in and up as far as you can. Relax and repeat in rapid succession while holding your breath. This strengthens the abdominal muscles which aid in breathing, urinating, defecating, and supporting and protecting internal organs.

The Bow. Lie face down. Bend your legs up and grasp your ankles. Inhale deeply. Lift your head and chest and pull your legs up, arching your back into a bow. Rock back and forth. Exhale and relax. Repeat several times. Do the exercise slowly and carefully. If you have back problems, consult your therapist before doing the bow.

Some teachers, especially those of the kundalini yoga school, emphasize simultaneous practice of asanas and pranayamas. For example, while holding the bow pose, ten to twenty rounds of bellows breathing is done and the last breath is held for several seconds before relaxation. Kundalini yoga classes are often very strenuous and special care must be taken to avoid injury.

Yoga and sex. Tantric yoga, or one branch of it, utilizes sexuality as a tool on the path to enlightenment. Intercourse is preceded by an elaborate mystical ritual and is characterized by prolonged sexual union with minimal movement and no orgasm. Whatever the benefits to the spirit may be, frequent Tantric intercourse could promote prostatitis.

Consulting a Physician

PART SEVEN

Chapter 1   When To Consult a Physician

Chapter 2   Choosing a Physician or Health
Care Plan

1

When To Consult a Physician

edical care professionals and facilities are both overutilized and underutilized. That is, people often go to an emergency room when they should go to a doctor's office, they go to a doctor's office when home treatment would suffice, and they ignore symptoms that should be medically evaluated. This section is intended to answer these questions: When should I go for a checkup? When should an ambulance be called? When should someone be driven to a doctor's office or hospital? What symptoms require medical attention?

Health Monitoring Through Life

Hardly any physicians suggest routine annual physicals for the general population anymore, but periodic screening for certain problems is strongly recommended. Here is a brief summary, which applies to apparently healthy people only. All ages are approximate.

All ages: Regular dental checkup and cleaning every six months to about age 12 and at least every year after that. (See Part Four, Dental and Gum Disease, for daily care.)

Ages 7–11: Screen for the risk factors associated with coronary heart disease (CHD), including blood pressure, cholesterol levels, fitness, and family history of CHD, diabetes, and smoking.

668 **Ages 17–25:** At least one complete medical history and physical examination including blood pressure and cholesterol checks, eating habits and nutrition status, and tests for sexually transmitted diseases if sexually active. Men should learn to check their testes for signs of cancer and do the check every month for life (see Cancer in Part Four). Women should have a Pap smear within a year or two of beginning sexual intercourse. Everyone should have at least one tonometric exam for glaucoma before age twenty-five, more if there is a family history of the problem.

All adults: Blood pressure check annually. Blood cholesterol check every year or two or as advised by physician. Glaucoma check annually or as advised by physician.

Ages 30–35: Complete physical and medical history. Women should learn to do a breast self-exam (see Cancer in Part Four) and do the check every month for life. They should also have a Pap smear at about these ages or more often as advised by physician.

Ages 40–60: Periodic check for prostate cancer. Complete physical, including checks for colo-rectal cancer, and medical history every two to five years for men and women. Colo-rectal tests more often for those at high risk (see Cancer in Part Four).

Ages 60–75: Complete physical exam and medical history every year or two.

Ages 75 and over: Complete physical exam and medical history every year.

Women should have a mammogram every year after age 50. Earlier screening may be indicated for high-risk women. Postmenopausal women at high risk for osteoporosis (see Part Four) should consult a physician about estrogen replacement.

Common Emergencies

In some situations medical care is needed right away and the people present must think straight and act quickly. They must decide whether to call an ambulance, drive the patient, or call a cab, and whether the patient should go to a hospital or doctor's office. Generally speaking, if the patient has a personal physician who can be quickly reached by phone he or she should be consulted before making a move. If a decision must be made without a physician, keep in mind that ambulances are expensive and often not as fast as a car which is already on the scene, but they come with experienced medics and drivers. A car is usually the fastest way to get a patient to a doctor but should not be used if movement might cause further harm, if the available car is unsafe, or if the available driver is intoxicated. Taxicabs should also be considered if they are readily available.

An ambulance should be called when there is a severe back or neck injury or compound fracture (with a bone protruding from the skin) which could be aggravated by inexperienced hands. In such injuries time is not as important as careful handling. An ambulance should also be called if resuscitation, say from drowning or smoke inhalation, is required. An ambulance should also be called in any of the emergencies below if other safe and fast transportation is not available. Many areas of the U.S. have a toll-free number—911—for all emergencies including medical, police, and fire. Use it; it works beautifully.

Bleeding which is severe and cannot be stopped by direct pressure must be dealt with quickly. The patient should be driven to a doctor's office if one is nearby and open, or to an emergency room.

Breathing trouble that is severe even at rest requires immediate medical attention. The person's physician should be called. If he or she cannot be reached the patient should be driven to a hospital.

Broken bones and knocked-out teeth usually require medical attention. In the case of a simple fracture of anything but the back or neck, the patient should be driven to a hospital. The injury can be splinted with almost any straight piece of wood or plastic or just heavily taped, but this is unnecessary if medical care is minutes away. If an adult tooth is broken or knocked out, it should be wrapped in a clean cloth and taken immediately to a dentist with the patient.

Burns which are obviously severe, especially on the hands or face, require immediate medical attention. The patient should be driven to a hospital and his or her physician called.

Choking on food or another item can lead to suffocation and death. If medical personnel are more than a minute or so away, the Heimlich maneuver should be applied. Stand behind the person and bring your hands together at the base of the sternum (just under the diaphragm). Give a sharp thrust in and up; the idea is to force the diaphragm up to force air out of the lungs which will propel the object out of the windpipe. Someone else there should try to contact a physician in case the object won't come out.

If an infant or small child is choking, place it across your lap with

670 head and arms hanging down. Using the heel of your hand, give several thumps between the shoulderblades.

Labor at an unexpected time is an emergency. The woman's physician should be called and she should be driven to a hospital.

Shock is a serious disturbance of blood circulation that can follow injury, hemorrhage, poisoning, adverse drug reaction, heart attack, and other conditions. The skin is pale, the pulse and breathing are rapid and weak, blood pressure is very low, and thirst may be extreme. The patient should be kept warm and lying down with the head slightly lower than the body and driven to a hospital as soon as possible.

Stupor or disorientation, as indicated by extreme confusion, drowsiness, or near-unconsciousness, requires immediate medical attention. The person should be driven to a hospital right away.

Unconsciousness requires immediate medical attention. The patient should be driven to a hospital right away.

Symptoms Requiring Medical Care

To determine whether given symptoms should be evaluated by a physician the following three aspects of the symptoms should be considered: **severity, duration, and direction**. Are the symptoms mild or very severe, how long have they lasted, and are they getting worse or better? Symptoms that are mild, short-lasting, or improving can be watched for a while. Those that are very severe, long-lasting, or getting worse often require medical attention. More specific guidelines are provided below, symptom by symptom; the list is alphabetical.

"See a physician now" means get to a doctor right away, preferably the patient's own physician who is more likely to be familiar with the problem. If possible, the doctor should be called first to avoid a trip to a hospital when the doctor's office would suffice or vice versa.

"Call a physician" means discuss the problem with the doctor or a trained assistant (often a nurse) to make an appointment is recommended.

Abdominal Pain

Abdominal pain is most often caused by gas, hyperacidity, and intestinal viral infections, but it can also be caused by appendicitis, ectopic pregnancy, tumors, and other serious problems. If you are unsure of the source or cause of the pain, avoid all food, sip water, relax, and see what direction the symptoms take.

See a physician now if:

> The pain is extremely severe or associated with vaginal discharge or bleeding
>
> Stool or vomitus is very dark or bloody

Call a physician if:

> You are pregnant or possibly pregnant
>
> There is vomiting, severe diarrhea, prolonged constipation, painful urination, or fever

Abrasions

See Cuts, Abrasions, Punctures, and Animal Bites.

Animal Bites

See Cuts, Abrasions, Punctures, and Animal Bites.

Back Pain

The most common type of back pain is an ache in the lower back, and it can usually be prevented or treated with simple measures. See Backaches in Part Four. Sometimes, however, back pain is a symptom of kidney disease, pelvic infections, tumors, osteoporosis, or other serious problem.

See a physician now if there is also:

> Very dark or bloody stools or vomitus
>
> Severe abdominal pain

Call a physician if there is also:

> Urinary difficulty, fever, or sore throat
>
> Severe menstrual pain or heavy vaginal bleeding

672 Bites

See Insect, Spider, and Jellyfish Stings and Bites.

Blood in the Urine

This is often due to overexercise. If it happens once on such an occasion and there are no other symptoms, don't worry about it. Otherwise, consult a physician; there could be a kidney or bladder problem.

Bone and Connective Tissue Injuries

Sprains, strains, and other injuries due to stress and trauma are discussed in detail in Chapter 1–7, Common Sports Injuries, but they also happen in a wide variety of accidents such as falling off ladders or down steps, slipping on wet sidewalks or in bathtubs, and car and cycle accidents. In most cases self-care measures are sufficient, but sometimes a physician should be consulted.

See a physician now if:

> A fracture is obvious or likely; if it involves the thigh, pelvis, back, or neck call an ambulance.
>
> A limb is crooked, cold, numb, or blue
>
> A suspected fracture is accompanied by heavy sweating, dizziness, or other severe symptoms
>
> A joint (knee, ankle, wrist, elbow, or shoulder) is deformed, moving abnormally, or in severe pain

Call a physician if:

> An injury involves severe bruising and pain, but a fracture is uncertain
>
> Pain from an injury lasts more than a few days and severely limits use of the affect part

Breathing Problems, Chest Pains, and Palpitations

Breathing problems and chest pains are often due to anxiety, gas, and colds, but they can also be indications of a wide variety of serious health problems, including asthma, emphysema, bronchitis, and heart disease. Palpitations (racing, pounding heart) not associated with other symptoms is not necessarily abnormal and is not an emergency.

See a physician now if:

> An infant has breathing difficulties
>
> The symptoms are associated with an insect sting or drug use (including aspirin, antibiotics, many others)
>
> There is severe chest pain or a sensation of crushing pressure around the breastbone, either arm, or the jaw
>
> There is breathing difficulty, except controllable asthma, at rest or in association with chest pain or palpitations (resting pulse more than 120 beats per minute)
>
> There is irregular pulse, dizziness, or profuse sweating

Call a physician if:

> Known asthma is unusually active and difficult to control
>
> There is breathing difficulty after slight exertion or while sleeping
>
> Chest pain or palpitations (resting pulse more than 120 beats per minute) continue or recur for several days

Burns

First-degree burns are superficial and minor. A moderate sunburn and a tongue burn from too-hot food or drink are examples. *Second-degree burns*, such as a severe sunburn or a burn from a motorcycle muffler or stove, cause blistering, splitting, and peeling of the skin. *Third-degree burns* char and destroy the skin, including the nerves (so pain is minimal), and can lead to severe fluid loss, infection, and scarring. All burns should be immediately treated with cool water (not ice) to minimize tissue injury.

674   **See a physician now if a burn is:**

> Obviously very severe, yet relatively painless (third degree)
>
> Very painful and extensive, with blistering or splitting of the skin (second degree)
>
> Very painful and on the hands or face

Call a physician if:

> A burn or severe sunburn does not heal in a few days or has pus

Cancer Early Warning Signs

Everyone should be familiar with the early warning signs of cancer. See Cancer in Part Four for details. The following is a brief summary.

Call a physician if:

> There is unusual bleeding or discharge between periods or after menopause
>
> The monthly breast self-examination shows unusual signs
>
> A cough or hoarseness lasts more than about ten days or blood is coughed up
>
> There is rectal bleeding or if there are large changes in bowel habits unexplained by dietary changes
>
> Urinary difficulties in a man are persistant or associated with pain in the pelvis or back
>
> A monthly testicular self-examination reveals a lump or enlargement
>
> There is persistent difficulty swallowing or a lump in the throat
>
> Stomach pains or digestive difficulties last more than a couple weeks
>
> A lump, white spot, or scaly area persists on the lip or mouth
>
> Swollen lymph glands last more than three weeks
>
> A mole or wart bleeds or changes in color or shape
>
> You experience persistant fatigue, weight loss, mild fever, nausea, or repeated infections

Chest Pains

See Breathing Problems, Chest Pains, and Palpitations.

Constipation

Constipation can usually be cured with proper diet, adequate fluid intake, and exercise. See Constipation in Part Four.

Call a physician if:

>Stools are persistently pencil-thin
>
>There is also significant weight loss

Convulsions, Seizures

Seizures, when the body goes rigid and limbs and head jerk rhythmically, can be caused by very high fever, especially in children, and by epilepsy. Medical evaluation is usually required.

Call a physician if:

>A seizure occurs
>
>Call *now* if the patient is an infant or the seizure is the patient's first ever

Cough and Hoarseness

Most coughs are caused by smoking and viral infections which can usually be treated with simple home remedies, but some coughs require medical attention.

See a physician now if:

>Coughing starts suddenly in a child and may be due to choking on a piece of food or other small object
>
>There is also excessive drooling or difficult breathing in a young child

Call a physician if:

>Coughing occurs in an infant less than three months old

676

A cough in an infant or young child sounds like a seal's bark and is associated with rapid or difficult breathing which is not relieved by breathing steam

A cough produces chest pain or a thick, foul-smelling mucus

A cough lasts more than a week or is associated with a fever for five days

Hoarseness lasts a week in a child or a month in an adult

Cuts, Abrasions, Punctures, and Animal Bites

Minor wounds can be treated with thorough cleaning with soap and water. Simple puncture wounds, such as a needle prick to the finger or stepping on a tack, should be allowed to bleed freely to clean them. All wounds should be kept scrupulously clean until they are completely healed. Bandages can hold the edges of a wound together, help keep dirt out, hasten healing, and minimize scarring.

See a physician now if the wound:

Is very severe with bleeding that cannot be stopped with pressure, edges that cannot be held together by a bandage, or the possibility of nerve damage as indicated by numbness or inability to move the affected part normally

Is difficult to clean or remove the glass, metal, or other culprit from

Is a deep puncture of the head, neck, or trunk

Is a puncture of the eyes or genitals

Call a physician if:

The wound develps pronounced inflammation (redness and swelling) or pus

You have not had four or more tetanus shots in your life or one in the last ten years

You are bitten or scratched (no matter how small the wound) by any wild or domestic mammal and you don't know if it has had rabies vaccination

Diarrhea, Nausea, and Vomiting

Minor viral infections of the gastrointestinal tract are the most common causes of diarrhea, nausea, and vomiting. Food-borne diseases of various kinds also cause these symptoms (see Chapter 2–15). Sometimes the symptoms are serious and require medical attention.

See a physician now if:

> Stool or vomitus is very dark or bloody
>
> There is severe abdominal pain, stiff neck, or headache
>
> There is confusion or extreme lethargy in a young child

Call a physician if:

> Medication is being taken—it may be the cause or it may be rendered ineffective by the symptoms
>
> There are signs of dehydration (thirst, intensely yellow urine, dry mouth, inelastic skin), diabetes, pregnancy, urinary problems, or a recent head injury
>
> There is no improvement within three days

Dizziness and Fainting

There are several innocuous reasons for faintness and vertigo (dizziness, visual field spinning or lurching). Sometimes one need only recover from the flu, a cold, or alcohol or other drug intoxication, or not stand up too quickly to recover from the symptoms, but sometimes medical attention is required.

See a physician now if:

> The symptoms are related to drug use (medicines, alcohol, cocaine, or any other)
>
> There is loss of consciousness

Call a physician if:

> Vertigo is severe

678 Ear and Hearing Problems

Common causes of ear pain, stuffiness, and itching, and hearing problems are allergies, colds, swimmer's ear, surfer's ear, and unusual wax accumulation. The problems can usually be cleared up with simple home treatments, but sometimes medical care is necessary.

Call a physician if:

> There is hearing loss or ear pain unexplained by excessive wax accumulation, a cold, or allergy
>
> There is itching, pain, or redness of the ear opening and canal lasting more than five days
>
> There is ear pain followed by a white or yellowish discharge
>
> There are signs of ear or hearing problems in an infant or child, such as rubbing and pulling an ear and trying to scratch the ear canal; lack of reaction to sounds in an infant; and babbling without word formation after one year of age

Eye and Vision Problems

Except for minor allergic itching and easily removable foreign objects, most eye and vision problems should be evaluated and treated by a family physician, ophthalmologist, or optometrist.

See a physician now if there is:

> An injury to the eye, such as a cut or puncture, or a blow that affects vision or causes severe pain
>
> Something in the eye that remains after flushing the eye with water
>
> A solvent, acid, or other chemical gets into the eye and causes pain or severe irritation which persists after copious flushing with water
>
> Sudden vision loss in one or both eyes or the appearance of halos around lights
>
> Inflammation of an eye in conjunction with a cold sore or genital herpes

Call an ophthalmologist if there is:

>   Eye pain, itching, or discharge that is severe or persists longer
>   than two days
>
>   Visual loss or visual defects that seem to be progressing
>
>   A discharge that resembles pus
>
>   Inflammation of the tear ducts

Fainting

See Dizziness and Fainting

Fatigue and Weakness

Fatigue is most commonly caused by insufficient rest, boredom, mild
depression, and abuse of alcohol, marijuana, caffeine, and other drugs, but
it can also be a sign of an illness that requires medical attention.

Call a physician if:

>   A child appears unusually tired or lethargic for several days with-
>   out apparent cause such as a cold or excessive stress
>
>   Weakness is constant and limited to one area of the body
>
>   There is also excessive hunger, thirst, or urination, decreased
>   libido, poor wound healing, or significant weight loss
>
>   You are over forty and fat
>
>   There is also sadness or insomnia for more than two or three
>   weeks

Fever

The normal resting body temperature is about 98.6°F (37°C), but it can be
almost a Fahrenheit degree lower or higher without being a sign of illness.
Eating and excitement can raise the temperature and exercise can increase it
to about 103°F. (A higher temperature associated with exercise may be a sign
of impending heat stroke; see below.) A fever is a resting temperature above
100°F, except in ovulating women.

   The most common causes of fever are viral and bacterial infections
such as measles, chickenpox, flu, and strep throat. A fever helps the body

680 fight off the infection, so unless it causes significant discomfort there is no reason to treat it. If relief is needed, a cool sponge bath and aspirin or acetaminophen are usually effective. Drink water and take at least a little food or juice. Clothing and bedding should be all-cotton to absorb sweat. Do not bundle the patient up.

See a physician now if the temperature is above:

> 100°F in an infant less than four months old
>
> 100°F and there is also a stiff neck, seizures, rapid breathing, or confusion
>
> 104°F in spite of sponge baths and aspirin or acetaminophen

Call a physician if a fever:

> Persists for more than three days
>
> Persists for more than one day in an infant between four and twelve months of age
>
> Is associated with a rash or hives
>
> Is associated with drug use (licit or illicit)
>
> Is associated with other symptoms that might need medical attention such as an earache, abdominal pain, or a rash

Frostbite

Mild and superficial frostbite, with numbness, whiteness, and a waxy appearance, can be treated with general warming and warm water (not more than 108°F) or gentle pressure with warm hands. *Do not rub, expose to high temperature (such as an oven or open fire), or apply ointments, lotions, or medicines of any kind.*

See a physician now if:

> The frostbite is so severe that the underlying tissues are frozen hard and do not give when the area is gently pressed. Wrap the affected area in a blanket to protect it from bruising, keep it elevated if possible, and get the person to a hospital.

Call a physician if:

> Mild frostbite becomes painful, blue, or swollen as the area warms up.

Headaches

Most headaches can be treated with the simple measures discussed in Part Four, but sometimes medical evaluation and treatment are necessary.

See a physician now if:

> There are also visual problems, fever, or stiff neck
>
> A severe headache comes on suddenly and is unlike any previous one

Call a physician if:

> Headaches have persisted for three days or longer
>
> Frequent headaches are worse in the morning
>
> A headache is associated with a head injury

Head Injuries

Head injuries that involve or put pressure on the brain or cranial nerves require immediate medical attention.

See a physician now if there is:

> Unconsciousness, seizure, stupor, any visual change, or lack of memory of the injury
>
> Persistant vomiting (one or two episodes are usually not serious)
>
> Irregular breathing or heartbeat
>
> Bleeding or other fluid from the nose, eyes, ears, or mouth
>
> Blackness around the eyes or ears

"Heartburn" and Hyperacidity

Excessive acid production and inadequate protection by the gastric mucus are the most common causes of a burning sensation in the stomach and beneath the breast bone. Hiatus hernia, an anatomical defect which allows stomach acid reflux into the esophagus, can also be the culprit. The symptoms can usually be treated with simple measures such as not reclining after eating, avoiding tight clothing, drinking lots of water, taking antacids (occasionally), and avoiding alcohol, cigarettes, aspirin, and caffeine.

See a physician now if:

> There is very dark or bloody stool or vomitus

Call a physician if:

> Pain is severe and seems to involve the back
>
> Pain lasts more than three days

Heatstroke

Heatstroke is a syndrome associated with overexercise and is most likely in a hot environment and when water intake has been inadequate. A body temperature above 104°F and climbing is approaching the danger zone and must be treated to prevent convulsions, brain damage, and death. The patient should be immersed in cool water or wrapped in wet cloth until he or she is driven to a hospital or an ambulance arrives.

See a physician now if:

> Heavy exercise or work is associated with extreme fatigue, confusion, headache, dizziness, racing pulse, and hot, dry skin

Hoarseness

See Cough and Hoarseness.

Hyperacidity

See "Heartburn" and Hyperacidity.

Insect, Spider, and Jellyfish Stings and Bites

Most of these can be treated by removing any remaining stinger and applying a paste of meat tenderizer followed by ice. However, some cases require medical attention.

See a physician now if:

> This or a previous sting has led to signs of allergic response such as difficult breathing, fainting, abdominal pain, hives, or a rash
>
> The culprit was a black widow or brown recluse spider

Call a physician if:

> The wound is very inflamed and painful or has pus

Jaundice

The skin and white of the eyes can be tinged yellow or orange by excessive intake of carrot and other vegetable juice, possibly papaya and other fruit juices, and beta-carotene and canthaxanthin, natural chemicals which are used as food dyes, and "tanning" pills (see Part Six). True jaundice, however, is caused by an accumulation of bilirubin (a product of the breakdown of normal red blood cells) in the blood and can be a sign of hepatitis, cancer, blood disease, or other serious problems.

Call a physician if:

> The whites of the eyes, the skin, or the sweat is yellowish

Joint Inflammation and Pain

The most common types of arthritis are gouty arthritis, osteoarthritis, and rheumatoid arthritis, which are discussed in Part Four. Once arthritis is diagnosed it can usually be treated at home.

Call a physician if:

> There is very severe pain, swelling, or inability to use a joint
>
> There is also a fever
>
> The problem is chronic and sometimes associated with a general feeling of sickness or weakness

Menstrual Problems

Most menstrual problems can be dealt with by simple home measures (see Chapter 3–5), but sometimes medical evaluation is necessary.

684 *Call a physician if:*

Bleeding is heavy for several consecutive periods

Pain is very severe and does not respond to simple treatments

Premenstrual syndrome (see Chapter 3–5) includes severe depression, anxiety, or suicidal impulses

Mental and Emotional Problems

Minor mental and emotional problems are best dealt with with the help of family and friends, but sometimes professional attention is required. Details are discussed in Part Four under Mental and Emotional Problems.

Call a physician or qualified psychologist if you experience:

Suicidal or homicidal urges

Unexplained fatigue associated with sadness, headaches, decreased libido, or insomnia

Extreme anxiety, phobias, hallucinations, confusion, or temper tantrums

Symptoms of an eating disorder, such as being repulsed by food or eating compulsively

Mouth Sores

There are several kinds of sores that can occur in and around the mouth. The most common are canker sores and oral herpes. Canker sores are painful little ulcers with a yellowish border and surrounded by a red zone. They may be precipitated by some toothpastes and foods and last up to a week. Time is usually the only cure. Herpes infections (see Part Four) usually do not require medical attention, but it may be useful for the consideration of treatment with acyclovir and for counseling on symptomatic treatment and avoiding the spread of the virus. Some other kinds of mouth sores definitely require medical attention.

Call a physician if you:

Have painful, recurrent mouth sores and are not sure what they are

Have white patches on the roof of your mouth

Developed mouth sores after starting a medication

Have a persistent, painless sore or lump anywhere in or around the mouth

Nasal Discharges and Bleeding

Nasal discharges are almost alway due to colds or allergies and can be treated with simple home remedies and nonprescription drugs (see Parts Four and Five). Nosebleeds are usually due to excessive nose blowing, a blow to the nose, and habitual nose picking (especially in children). These almost always stop by themselves, but it may require ten to fifteen minutes of pressure on the nose. The person should sit upright. Applying ice may help.

Call a physician if:

The discharge is thick and foul-smelling or from one nostril only

The discharge is clear or bloody and began after a head injury

Nosebleeds are frequent and unexplained

Nosebleeds are caused by snorting drugs

Nausea

See Diarrhea, Nausea, and Vomiting.

Palpitations

See Breathing Problems, Chest Pains, and Palpitations.

Poisoning

In any case of suspected poisoning a physician should be called or seen immediately. If one cannot be reached, call the local poison center.

If an ingested substance is known to be a drug or poisonous plant (such as aspirin, iron, apricot kernals, toxic mushroom, or oleander) induce vomiting with a finger down the throat or warm salty water (about one-half

686 teaspoon per cup) or two to four teaspoons of syrup (not extract) of ipecac and *call a physician*.

If the material is a caustic substance such as battery acid, bleach, drain cleaner, furniture polish, or gasoline, *give milk and call a physician*.

PREVENTING POISONINGS

Keep all drugs, nutritional supplements, skin and hair products, and household chemicals out of the reach of young children. Keep only those household chemicals you really need and use, and get rid of old containers. Use all dangerous chemicals with proper protective clothing, safety glasses, and utmost care.

Punctures

See Cuts, Abrasions, Punctures, and Animal Bites.

Seizures

See Convulsions, Seizures.

Sexually Transmitted Diseases

Most STDs can be prevented by simple measures (see Chapter 3–3), but once one is contracted it must be medically evaluated.

Call a physician if:

> You had sexual contact with a person with a suspected STD
>
> You have a sore or wart on your genitals
>
> There is a thick discharge from the penis or pain and swelling of the testicles
>
> There is a vaginal discharge associated with abdominal pain
>
> Vaginal discharge occurs in a prepuberty girl

Skin and Hair Problems

Most skin and hair problems can be prevented or treated by the simple measures discussed in Chapter 5–1, Nonprescription Drugs, and in Part

Four under Acne, Boils, and other specific problems. Sometimes, however, a physician should be consulted.

See a physician now if:

> Hives or itching are associated with rapid or difficult breathing or dizziness, or occur subsequent to drug use
>
> A rash suspected of being measles, rubella, or chickenpox is associated with rapid or difficult breathing, stiff neck, severe lethargy or headaches, convulsions, vomiting, or bleeding from the mouth, nose, rectum, or under the skin
>
> A fine, rough rash occurs on the trunk and extremities, and there is a fever (this could be scarlet fever, a strep infection that can cause heart and kidney problems)

Call a physician if:

> *Acne* is very severe, painful, emotionally disturbing, and unresponsive to home treatment
>
> A *boil* is on the face, is associated with a fever, has a streak extending from it, or is unusually large and painful
>
> *Contact dermatitis* or *eczema* is very severe, widespread, persistent, or shows signs of infection such as much weeping and crusting
>
> *Dandruff* is very severe and unresponsive to home treatments for several weeks
>
> *Hair loss* is associated with an abnormal scalp condition
>
> *Hives* occur in association with the use of a medicine or other drug, a fever, breathing difficulties, or very severe and prolonged itching
>
> An *infant rash* has blisters, is more severe in skin creases, or is outside the diaper-covered area
>
> A *mole* or *wart* has changed color or shape or it bleeds, or a new mole appears
>
> A *patch* of discoloration and roughness associated with frequent sunburn persists
>
> A *wart* appears on the genitals or bottom of the foot, or interferes with normal functions

688 Sore Throat

Most sore throats are caused by minor viral infections which can be treated with simple home measures. Sometimes, however, they are caused by bacteria and may require treatment, usually antibiotics.

See a physician now if there is:

> Severe difficulty swallowing or breathing
>
> Excessive drooling in a child or infant

Call a physician if:

> There is fever, rash, or pus in the throat
>
> A sore throat follows exposure to someone known to have strep throat

Stings

See Insect, Spider, and Jellyfish Stings and Bites.

Swollen Lymph or Salivary Glands

Swelling of the salivary glands (below and in front of the ears) is caused by mumps, for which home treatment is usually adequate (see Part Four). Swelling of the lymph glands is a sign of a localized infection, such as a boil, infected wound, ear infection, or sore throat. More general illness such as mononucleosis and rubella may also cause swollen lymph glands.

Call a physician if:

> There is head or face infection
>
> Lymph glands are tender or inflamed
>
> Swelling lasts more than three weeks

Tooth and Gum Problems 689

Toothaches and bleeding gums can be prevented by proper oral hygiene and nutrition, including fluoride. When they do occur they should be treated by a dentist.

Call a dentist if:

> You have a toothache
>
> Your gums bleed, unless it is slight and occasional
>
> You injure a tooth; if a mature, healthy tooth is knocked out, rinse it well and reinsert it—or wrap it in a clean cloth—and go to a dentist immediately

Urinary Problems

A burning sensation, unusually frequent urination, and dribbling or weak urination can be signs of serious problems.

Call a physician if burning lasts more than a day, or if there is also:

> Fever, vomiting, back pain, or bloody urine
>
> An unusual vaginal discharge and abdominal pain
>
> An unusual penile discharge
>
> Pregnancy or possible pregnancy

Vaginal Discharge or Bleeding

Vaginal discharges and bleeding are usually normal, but they can be signs of a variety of problems that require medical treatment.

See a physician now if:

> There is heavy bleeding and pain during pregnancy or possible pregnancy

Call a physician if:

> A discharge is associated with abdominal pain

690

A discharge is associated with vaginitis and persists longer than about two weeks

A prepuberty girl experiences a discharge

A sexually transmitted disease is suspected

There is heavy bleeding between periods

There is frequent bleeding between periods

There is bleeding after menopause

Vision Problems

See Eye and Vision Problems.

Vomiting

See Diarrhea, Nausea, and Vomiting.

Weakness

See Fatigue and Weakness.

2

Choosing a Physician or Health Care Plan

hen you need medical care, routine health surveillance, or simple advice, how do you decide whom to consult? And how will you pay for the services? Should you pay as you go? Or should you get some kind of health insurance that would cover most of your expenses if you need care? The answers to these questions depend on your general health, your family situation, your financial situation, and your personal philosophy.

Choosing a Health Care Plan

When shopping for health care insurance it's a good idea to find out what the various plans are in your area and call for their promotional literature. When you've read it, ask them to clear up any questions you might have. Then, considering your needs, list the advantages and disadvantages of each. How large is your family? How often do you need medical care? Do you have a long-standing relation with a physician you want to stay with? Do you foresee a need for prenatal and maternity care? Would you use preventive services such as classes in nutrition and exercise?

Before making your decision and starting payments, carefully consider the costs, if any, of such services as office visits, surgery, X-ray, laboratory tests, hospital services, drugs, and emergency care. Be sure you under-

692

stand the restrictions on coverage for preexisting conditions. Don't wait until you get sick to join a plan and expect to get full coverage.

You should also ask around about the hospitals and doctors. Discuss them with experienced friends and neighbors. Take notes on what people say about hospital food, nursing care, and doctors. In short, educate yourself on the available health services and use them intelligently. Should you get sick, be aware of the benefits and risks of the treatment options. Rather than passively following "doctor's orders," take an active role in any treatment program you might enter so you and your doctor will be partners in the effort.

Choosing a Physician

You may prefer to stay with one doctor for many years, and your choice of a health care plan may be secondary to this preference. The doctor might have taken care of family members in a caring and competent manner, or perhaps he was strongly recommended by several good friends. You may, on the other hand, be new to an area and want a personal physician for checkups and occasional care for minor problems. We can only give general advice on making this personal decision. It is important that you be comfortable with your physician so you will be completely open and frank. If sex, age, or ethnic background matters to you, take it into consideration before you make an appointment. These are emotional and philosophic issues, not medical ones, and no generalizations can be made.

There are, however, a few guidelines to keep in mind in order to protect yourself from incompetents, quacks, and unlicensed practitioners. The information needed can be obtained from your local medical society or state library.

Physicians educated in the United States are generally better trained than those from abroad. American medical schools are better equipped and have better staffs than most others. This is not to say that doctors from Mexico, Italy, and England are incompetent; most of them do fine work. But on the whole those from American schools have an edge in diagnostic and treatment skills.

Look for *board certification* of any specialists you consult. This indicates that the physician took several years of advanced training in surgery, internal medicine, pediatrics, obstetrics, psychiatry, radiology, or another area of medicine, and passed a comprehensive examination designed by the most experienced and competent doctors in the field. *Board eligibility* indicates that the physician has taken the training in the specialty and is eleigible to take the test but has not done so yet. Most such doctors know their stuff, but some have not mastered their art and will never become board certified. Unless you have a strong recommendation from a knowledgeable and trusted source, avoid the merely board-eligible specialist.

If you need a specialist, how do you select one? Your best bet is usually to ask a trusted, reputable family physician or other doctor whom he or she would go to or send his or her family to.

Should you see a solo practitioner or one associated with a group? There are many competent soloists, but your best bet is usually with a physician associated with a group with a good reputation. Such doctors tend to communicate with and teach each other more. They have conferences, discuss cases, and review the work of their peers.

Keep in mind that a good doctor is not only well educated and has plenty of experience, but is a good listener and teacher. The doctor's primary role is to inform the client or patient about the anatomy and physiology of the problem at hand and the risks and benefits of the alternatives available. If you feel that your doctor does not really listen and understand, and that he or she leaves you in the dark and doesn't explain things clearly, you may want to shop around.

References

Note on the references: We make no pretense that this book is as thoroughly documented as an academic text for health professionals covering the same ground would be; that would take thousands of references. Nevertheless, we refer to a couple hundred important sources. Those included are excellent in themselves and, in most cases, they provide many more references to reputable sources of further information. References are more likely to be included if the information is relatively new, important, or controversial, and likely to stimulate interest in more reading. So while our documentation is not exhaustive, it certainly points the way for the serious student.

Most of the papers listed here have more than one author. In the interest of space, we name only the first. For books all authors are named.

PART ONE
Exercise and Fitness

1. Holloszy, J. O. Physiological Consequences of the Biochemical Adaptations to Endurance Exercise. *Annals New York Academy of Sciences*, 301:440, 1977.

See also: Nikkila, E. A. Lipoprotein Lipase Activity in Adipose Tissue and Skeletal Muscle of Runners. *Metabolism*, 27:1661, 1978.

2. Hirsch, J. Cell Lipid Content and Cell Number in Obese and Non-obese Human Adipose Tissue. *Journal of Clinical Investigation*, 45:1023, 1966.

3. Van Itallie, T. B. Obesity: Adverse Effects on Health and Longevity. *American Journal of Clinical Nutrition* 32:2723, 1979.

4. Johnson, W. R. and Buskirk, E. R. (editors). *Science and Medicine of Exercise and Sport*. Harper & Row, 1974.

5. Huttunen, J. K. Effect of Moderate Physical Exercise on Serum Lipoproteins. *Circulation*, 60:1220, 1979.

6. Brown, R. S. The Prescription of Exercise for Depression. *The Physician and Sportsmedicine*, December 1978.

7. Bortz, W. M. Disuse and Aging. *Journal of the American Medical Association*, 248:1203, 1982.

8. Groom, D. Cardiovascular Observations on Tarahumara Indian Runners—the Modern Spartans. *American Heart Journal*, 81:304, 1971.

See also: Martin, R. P. Blood Chemistry and Lipid Profiles of Elite Distance Runners. *Annals New York Academy of Sciences* 301:346, 1977.

9. Bonen, A. Athletic Menstrual Cycle Irregularity. *The Physician and Sportsmedicine*, 12(8):78, 1984.

See also: Caldwell, F. Light-Boned and Lean Athletes. *The Physician and Sportsmedicine*, 12(9):139, 1984.

10. Cooper, K. M. *The Aerobics Way*. Bantam, 1977.

11. National Fitness Test. *American Health*, May 1984.

12. Nicholson, J. P. Carboxyhemoglobin Levels in New York City Runners. *The Physician and Sportsmedicine*, 11(3):134, 1983.

696

13. Cann, C. E. Decreased Spinal Mineral Content in Amenorrheic Women. *Journal of the American Medical Association*, 251:626, 1984.

14. Clement, D. B. Iron Status and Sports Performance. *Sports Medicine*, 1:65, 1984.

15. Keller, K. Preexercise Snacks May Decrease Exercise Performance. *The Physician and Sportsmedicine*, 12(4):89, 1984.

16. Dimsdale, J. E. Postexercise Peril. *Journal of the American Medical Association*, 251:630, 1984.

17. Siscovick, D. S. The Incidence of Primary Cardiac Arrest During Vigorous Exercises. *New England Journal of Medicine*, 311:874, 1984.

18. Gledhill, N. The Ergogenic Effect of Blood Doping. *The Physician and Sportsmedicine*, 11(9):87, 1983.

19. Strauss, R. H. Side Effects of Anabolic Steroids in Weight-trained Men. *The Physician and Sportsmedicine*, 11(12):87, 1983.

PART TWO
Nutrition Science and Mythology

1. *Recommended Dietary Allowance, Ninth Edition*. National Academy of Sciences, 1980.

2. *Dietary Goals for the United States*. U.S. Government Printing Office, 1977.

3. Ibid.

4. Goodhart, R. S. and Shils, M. E. (editors). *Modern Nutrition in Health and Disease*. Lea and Febiger, 1973.

5. Ibid.

6. Anand, C. R. Effect of Protein Intake on Calcium Balance of Young Men Given 500 mg Calcium Daily. *Journal of Nutrition*, 104:695, 1974.

7. Roughage in the Diet. *Medical World News*, September 6, 1974.

8. Robertson, J. The Effect of Raw Carrot on Serum Lipids and Colon Function. *American Journal of Clinical Nutrition*, 32:1902, 1979.

9. Blackburn, H. Diet and Atherosclerosis: Epidemiologic Evidence and Public Health Implications. *Preventive Medicine*, 12:2, 1983.

10. Serum Vitamin and Provitamin A Levels and the Risk of Cancer. *Nutrition Reviews*, 42:214, 1984.

11. Bernhardt, I. B. Hypervitaminosis A and Congenital Renal Anomalies in a Human Infant. *Obstetrics and Gynecology*, 43:750, 1974. *See also* reference 1.

12. Lonsdale, D. Red Cell Transketolase as an Indicator of Nutritional Deficiency. *American Journal of Clinical Nutrition*, 33:205, 1980.

13. Niacin and Myocardial Metabolism. *Nutrition Reviews*, 31:80, 1973.

14. Schaumburg H., et al. Sensory Neuropathy from Pyridoxine Abuse. *New England Journal of Medicine*, 309:445, 1983.
   See also letter on the subject in vol. 311, no. 15, 1984.

15. Cottrell, J. E. Prevention of Nitroprusside-induced Cyanide Toxicity with Hydroxocobalamin. *New England Journal of Medicine*, 298:809, 1978.

16. Schrauzer, G. N. Ascorbic Acid Abuse. *International Journal of Vitamin and Nutrition Research*, 43:201, 1973.

17. Butterworth, C. E. Improvement in Cervical Dysplasia Associated with Folic Acid in Users of Oral Contraceptives. *American Journal of Clinical Nutrition*, 35:73, 1982.

18. Hodges, R. E. The Effect of Stress on Ascorbic Acid Metabolism in Man. *Nutrition Today*, Spring 1970.

19. Pelletier, O. Smoking and Vitamin C Levels in Humans. *American Journal of Clinical Nutrition,* 21:1259, 1968.

20. Udomratn, T. Effects of Ascorbic Acid on G6PD-Deficient Erythrocytes. *Blood,* 49:471, 1977.

21. *See* reference 16.

22. *See* reference 16.

23. Seelig, M. S. Vitamin D and Cardiovascular, Renal and Brain Damage in Infancy and Childhood. *Annals New York Academy of Sciences,* 147:537, 1969.

24. Witting, L. A. Dietary Levels of Vitamin E and Polyunsaturated Fatty Acid and Plasma Vitamin E. *American Journal of Clinical Nutrition,* 28:571, 1975.

25. Lawrence, J. D. Effects of Alpha-Tocopherol on Swimming Endurance. *American Journal of Clinical Nutrition,* 28:205, 1975.

26. Cohen, H. M. Effects of Vitamin E: Good and Bad. *New England Journal of Medicine,* 289:980, 1973.

See also letters on the subject in *New England Journal of Medicine,* 290:579, 1974.

27. Recker, R. R. Effect of Estrogens and Calcium Carbonate on Bone Loss in Postmenopausal Women. *Annals of Internal Medicine,* 87:649, 1977.

28. Taylor, F. Iodine—Going from Hypo to Hyper. *FDA Consumer,* April 1981.

29. Dallman, P. R. Prevalence and Causes of Anemia in the U.S. *American Journal of Clinical Nutrition,* 39:437, 1984.

30. Zinc Toxicity. *Medical Letter,* 20:58, 1978.

31. Selenium Intoxication. *Morbidity and Mortality Weekly Report,* 33:157, 1984.

32. Folin, A. On Starvation and Obesity with Special Reference to Acidosis. *Journal of Biological Chemistry,* 21:183, 1915.

33. A Critique of Low-Carbohydrate Ketogenic Weight Reduction Regimens. *Journal of the American Medical Association,* 224:1415, 1973.

34. Johnson, E. Effects of Level of Protein Intake on Urinary and Fecal Calcium and Calcium Retention in Young Adult Males. *Journal of Nutrition,* 100:1425, 1970.

35. *See* reference 4.

36. *See* reference 1.

37. Sacks, F. M. Plasma Lipids and Lipoproteins in Vegetarians and Controls. *New England Journal of Medicine,* 292:1148, 1975.

38. Kempner, W. Treatment of Heart and Kidney Disease and of Hypertensive and Arteriosclerotic Vascular Disease with the Rice Diet. *Annals of Internal Medicine,* 31:821, 1949.

39. Miller, R. W. EMS: Fraudulent Flab Remover. *FDA Consumer,* May 1983.

40. Larkin, T. Bee Pollen as a Health Food. *FDA Consumer,* April 1984.

41. Offenbacher, E. G. Beneficial Effect of Chromium-rich Yeast on Glucose Tolerance and Blood Lipids in Elderly Subjects. *Diabetes,* 29:919, 1980.

See also Podell, R. N. Chromium Supplementation: Can it Improve Glucose and Cholesterol Metabolism? *Postgraduate Medicine,* 74:136, 1983.

42. Potter, M. E. Unpasturized Milk—The Hazards of a Health Fetish. *Journal of the American Medical Association,* 252:2048, 1984.

43. The most important source of information on food additives is the Federal Register. Consumer-oriented articles can be found in *FDA Consumer.*

698

44. Elder, D. M. A New or Old Chinese Restaurant Syndrome? *British Medical Journal*, 285:1205, 1982.

45. Good sources for information on food-borne diseases include *FDA Consumer, Morbidity and Mortality Weekly Report*, and various medical journals, and *The Merck Manual* and various medical texts.

46. Good sources for information on health and the environment include the following journals:

American Journal of Public Health; Archives of Environmental Health; Environmental Research, Food and Chemical Toxicology; Journal of Toxicology and Environmental Health.

PART THREE

Healthy Sex and Reproduction

1. Masters, W. H. and Johnson, V. E. *Human Sexual Response.* Little, Brown, 1970.

2. Masters, W. H. and Johnson, V. E. *Human Sexual Inadequacy.* Little, Brown, 1970.

See also: Annon, J. S. *The Behavioral Treatment of Sexual Problems.* Enabling System, 1974.

Other good sources of information on sexual dysfunctions and their treatment include these journals: *The Journal of Sex Research; Medical Aspects of Human Sexuality; The American Journal of Psychiatry;* and *The Journal of Reproductive Medicine.*

3. Frequent articles in the journal *Medical Aspects of Human Sexuality.*

Good review article: Watts, R. The Physiological Interrelationships Between Depression, Drugs, and Sexuality. *Nursing Forum*, 17:168, 1978.

4. Cooke, C. W. and Dworkin, S. *The Ms. Guide to A Women's Health.* Anchor Press, 1979.

5. Nofziger, M. A. *Cooperative Method of Natural Birth Control.* The Book Publishing Company, 1976.

See also: Fertility Awareness: Four Metholds of Natural Family Planning. *Journal of Obstetrics, Gynecology and Neonatal Nursing*, 6:9, 1977.

6. Major sources include the journals *Contraception* and *Fertility and Sterility.*

7. Senanayake, P. and Kramer, D. G. Contraception and the Etiology of Pelvic Inflammatory Disease: New Perspectives. *American Journal of Obstetrics and Gynecology*, 138:852, 1980.

8. Major sources include the journals: *American Journal of Public Health, Cutis, Journal of Infectious Diseases, Journal of Medical Microbiology.*

9. Good review article: Birth Defects, *Medical World News*. Sept. 12, 1983. *See also* the journals: *Teratology, Early Human Development, Pediatric Research,* and *Journal of Pediatrics.*

10. Good review articles: Pregnancy's Special Problems—A Four-Article Symposium. *Postgraduate Medicine*, 75:135, 1984.

11. Major sources include the journals: *American Journal of Obstetrics and Gynecology, Obstetrics and Gynecology, Clinical Obstetrics and Gynecology,* and *International Journal of Gynaecology and Obstetrics.*

PART FOUR

Common Disorders—A Preventive Approach

1. Michaelsson, G. Effects of Oral Zinc and Vitamin A in Acne. *Archives of Dermatology*, 113:13, 1977.

2. Prevention of AIDS: Report of Inter-Agency Recommendations. *Morbidity and Mortality Weekly Report*, 32:101, 1983.

3. Gallo R. C. The Virus-Cancer Story. *Hospital Practice*, June 1983.

4. Aledort, L. M. AIDS: An Update. *Hospital Practice*, September 1983.

5. Goodhart, R. S. and Shils, M. E. *Modern Nutrition in Health and Disease*. Lea and Febiger, 1974.

6. Schmidt, G. Mechanisms and Possible Causes of Alzheimer's Disease. *Postgraduate Medicine*, 73:206, 1983.

7. Bartus, R. T. The Cholinergic Hypothesis of Geriatric Memory Dysfunction. *Science*, 217:408, 1982.

8. Goudamit, J. Evidence For and Against the Transmissibility of Alzheimer's Disease. *Neurology*, 30:945, 1980.

9. Eating Disorders: the Price of a Society's Desire to be Thin? *Medical World News*, July 1984.

10. Levenkron, S. *The Best Little Girl in the World*. Contemporary Books, 1978.
    See also: Palmer, R. L. *Anorexia Nervosa—A Guide for Sufferers and their Families*. Penguin, 1982.
    And: Bruch, H. *The Golden Cage: The Enigma of Anorexia Nervosa*. Harvard University Press, 1978.

11. Kannel, W. B. Preventive Cardiology. *Medical Practice Today*, 61:74, 1977.

12. Hay, D. R. Coronary Artery Disease Prevention and Control. *New Zealand Medical Journal*, May 11, 1983.

13. The Lipid Research Clinics Coronary Primary Prevention Trial Results. *Journal of the American Medical Association*, 251:351, 1984.

14. Morrison, L. M. Serum Cholesterol Reduction with Lecithin. *Geriatrics*, January 1958.
    See also: Simons, L. A. Treatment of Hypercholesterolaemia with Oral Lecithin. *Australian and New Zealand Journal of Medicine*, 7:262, 1977.

15. Goldberg, A. P. Soybean Protein Independently Lowers Plasma Cholesterol Levels in Primary Hypercholesterolemia. *Atherosclerosis*, 43:355, 1982.

16. Sidney, S. Cholesterol, Cancer, and Public Health Policy. *The American Journal of Medicine*, 75:494, 1983.

17. Wynder, E. L. The Dietary Environment and Cancer. *Journal of the American Dietetic Association*, 71:385, 1977.

18. Ames, B. N. Dietary Carcinogens and Anticarcinogens. *Science*, 221:1256, 1983.

19. Winick, M. (editor) *Nutrition and Cancer*. John Wiley and Sons, 1977.

20. Whelan E. *Preventing Cancer*. Norton, 1977.

21. Hartley, H. L. Meeting Report, National Conference on Nutrition and Cancer. *Nutrition Today*, September/October 1978.

22. Aurelian, L. Viruses and Gynecologic Cancers. *Cancer*, 48:455, 1981.

23. Lynch, J. J. *The Broken Heart: the Medical Consequences of Loneliness*. Basic Books, 1979.

24. Lillienfeld, A. M. *Cancer in the United States*. Harvard University Press, 1970.

25. Sheiham, A. Is There a Scientific Basis for Six-monthly Dental Examinations? *Lancet*, 1:442, 1977.

26. Anderson, J. W. High-carbohydrate, High-fiber Diets for Insulin-treated Men with Diabetes. *American Journal of Clinical Nutrition*, 32:2312, 1979.

27. Linos, D. A. Cholecystectomy and Carcinoma of the Colon. *Lancet*, August 22, 1981. *(See also* related article in the September 12 issue.)

28. Kritchevsky, D. Influence of Vegetable Protein on Gallstone Formation in Hamsters. *American Journal of Clinical Nutrition*, 32:2174, 1979.

700

29. Dalessio, D. J. Conditioned Adaptation-Relaxation Reflex in Migraine Therapy. *Journal of the American Medical Association*, 242:2102, 1979.

30. Podell, R. N. Is Migraine a Manifestation of Food Allergy? *Postgraduate Medicine*, 75:221, 1984.

31. Hadler, S. C. Hepatitis A in daycare centers. *New England Journal of Medicine*, 302:1222, 1980.

32. Beasley, R. P. Prevention of Perinatally Transmitted Hepatitis B Virus Infections with Hepatitis B Immune Globulin and Hepatitis B Vaccine. *Lancet*, November 12, 1983.

33. Beeson, P. B. and McDermott, W. (editors) *Textbook of Medicine*. W. B. Saunders, 1975.

34. *The Merck Manual, Fourteenth Edition*. Merck, 1982.

35. Isles, C. Effect of Weight Loss without Salt Restriction on the Reduction of Blood Pressure in Overweight Hypertensive Patients. *New England Journal of Medicine*, 298:44, 1978.

36. Banerjee, A. K. Effect of Aqueous Extract of Garlic on Arterial Blood Pressure of Normotensive and Hypertensive Rats. *Artery*, 2:369, 1976.

37. Agras, W. S. Relaxation Therapy in Hypertension. *Hospital Practice*, May 1983.

38. Larkin, T. Flu/Cold—Never the Strain Shall Meet. *FDA Consumer*, September 1983. (This article had some erroneous figures. See corrections in the February 1984 issue.)

39. Gershoff, S. N. Effect of Daily MgO and Vitamin B-6 Administration to Patients with Recurring Calcium Oxalate Kidney Stones. *American Journal of Clinical Nutrition*, 20:393, 1967.

40. Lynch J. J. *The Broken Heart: The Medical Consequences of Loneliness*. Basic Books, 1979.

41. Osteoporosis: A Three-Article Symposium. *Postgraduate Medicine*, 75:117, 1984.

42. Ibid.

43. Medical Staff Conference on Osteoporosis. *Western Journal of Medicine*, 139:204, 1983.

44. Horsman, A. The Effect of Estrogen Dose on Postmenopausal Bone Loss. *New England Journal of Medicine*, 309:1405, 1983.

45. Frommer, D. J. The Healing of Gastric Ulcers by Zinc Sulfate. *Medical Journal of Australia*, 2:293, 1975. *See also:* Kangas, J. A. Effects of Vitamin E on the Development of Stress-Induced Gastric Ulceration in the Rat. *American Journal of Clinical Nutrition*, 25:864, 1976.

46. Wolcott, D. L. Serum Gastrin in the Family Environment in Duodenal Ulcer Disease. *Psychosomatic Medicine*, 43:501, 1981.

47. Shafii, M. Exploratory Psychotherapy in the Treatment of Psoriasis 1200 Years Ago. *Archives of General Psychiatry*, 36:1242, 1979.

48. Human Interferon Cures a Case of Suspected Rabies. *Medical World News*, February 4, 1980.

49. Practices Advisory Committee. Rabies Prevention. *Morbidity and Mortality Weekly Report*, 29:265, 1980.

50. Little, C. H. Platelet Serotonin Release in Rheumatoid Arthritis: A Study of Food-intolerant Patients. *Lancet*, 2:297, 1983.

PART FIVE

Drugs and Health

1. Kaufman, J. and the Public Citizen Health Research Group. *Over-the-Counter Pills that Don't Work*. Pantheon, 1983.

2. Ibid.

3. Progress Report: The OTC Drug Review. *FDA Consumer*, February 1979.

4. West, S. A Review of Antihistamines and the Common Cold. *Pediatrics*, 56: 100, 1975.

5. 47 Federal Register 454–86, January 5, 1982.

6. Ephedrine. *Medical Letter*, 24:83, 1982.

7. Calcium Polycarbophil (Mitrolan). *Medical Letter*, 23:52, 1981.

8. Horowitz, J. D. Hypertensive Responses Induced by Phenylpropanolamine in anorectic and decongestant preparations. *Lancet*, 1:60, 1980.

See also Swenson, R. D. Acute Renal Failure and Rhabdomyolysis after Ingestion of PPA-containing Diet Pills. *Journal of the American Medical Association*, 248:1216, 1982.

9. Panel Urges FDA to Reconsider OTC Status of Combination Analgesics. *Medical World News*, March 26, 1984.

10. For detailed information on therapeutic drugs see the latest editions of *The Merck Manual*, *AMA Drug Evaluations*, *Physicians' Desk Reference*, and *The Pharmacological Basis of Therapeutics* by L. S. Goodman and A. Gilman.

See also The Lancet, The New England Journal of Medicine, The Journal of the American Medical Association, FDA Drug Bulletin, the Medical Letter, and other medical journals.

11. See reference 10.

See also Wolfe, S. M., Coley, C. M., and the Health Research Group. Pills that Don't Work. *Public Citizen's Health Research Group*, 1980.

12. Lappe, M. *Germs that Won't Die: Medical Consequences of the Misuse of Antibiotics*. Doubleday, 1982.

See also: Lowbury, E. J. L. and Ayliffe, G. A. J. *Drug Resistance in Antimicrobial Therapy*. Charles C. Thomas, 1974.

13. Nilsen, A. E. Efficacy of Oral Acyclovir in the Treatment of Initial and Recurrent Genital Herpes. *Lancet*, 2:571, 1982.

14. Levine, M. Toxic Reaction to Phenytoin following a Viral Infection. *Canadian Medical Association Journal*, 128:1270, 1983.

15. Combining Coffee, Theophylline May Increase Risk of CNS Side Effects among Asthmatics. *Medical World News*, December 12, 1983.

16. Smith, D. C. Association of Exogenous Estrogen and Endometrial Carcinoma. *New England Journal of Medicine*, 293:1164, 1975.

17. Mellinger, G. D. Prevalence and Correlates of the Long-term Regular Use of Anxiolytics. *Journal of the American Medical Association*, 251:375, 1984.

See also, Tyrer, P. J. Benzodiazepines on Trial. *British Medical Journal*, 288:1101, 1984.

18. The best source for current information on vaccines is the Center for Disease Control publication, *Morbidity and Mortality Weekly Report*.

19. Good sources of information on herbal medicines include: *The U.S. Pharmacopeia and National Formulary* (old editions good for historical perspective), The British Pharmacopeia; Martindale, *The Extra Pharmacopeia*, Pharmaceutical Press, 1982; *The Merck Index*; Grieve, M., *A Modern Herbal*, Dover, 1971.

20. Lewis, W. H. and Elvin-Lewis, M. P. F. *Medical Botany—Plants Affecting Man's Health*. John Wiley, 1977.

21. Thomson, W. A. R. *Medicines From The Earth*. Alfred Van Der Marck Editions, 1978.

702

22. Editorial. Liver Injury, Drugs, and Popular Poisons. *British Medical Journal*, 1:574, 1979.

23. Tyler, V. E. *The Honest Herbal.* George F. Stickly, 1981.

24. Samula, E. Of Pills that Pack Too Much Punch. *FDA Consumer*, February 1984.

25. Hirono, I. Carcinogenic Activity of *Symphytum officinale*. *Journal of The National Cancer Institute*, 61:865, 1978

26. Jain, R. C. *American Journal of Clinical Nutrition*, September 1977.

27. Jain, R. C. Effect of Garlic on Serum Lipids, Coagulability and Fibrinolytic Activity of Blood. *Atherosclerosis*, 29:1380, 1978.

28. Bordia, A. Effects of Essential Oil of Garlic on Serum Fibrinolytic Activity in Patients with Coronary Heart Disease. *Atherosclerosis*, 28:155, 1977.

29. Siegel, R. K. Ginseng Abuse Syndrome. *Journal of the American Medical Association*, 241:1614, 1979.

30. Plant Poisonings—New Jersey. *Morbidity and Mortality Weekly Report*, 30:65, 1981.

31. Good general sources of information on recreational drugs include: Brecher, E. M., *Consumer Union Report on Licit and Illicit Drugs*, Little, Brown, 1972; Goodman, L. S. and Gilman, A. *The Pharmacologic Basis of Therapeutics*. *Sixth Edition.* MacMillan, 1980.

32. *See* Brecher and Goodman and Gilman, reference 31.

33. Greden, J. F. Anxiety or Caffeinism: A diagnostic Dilemma. *American Journal of Psychiatry*, 131:1089, 1974.

34. Updates in recent issues of *Morbidity and Mortality Weekly Report, Journal of the American Medical Association*, and other journals.

35. *Cocaine* (Monograph Series 13). National Institute of Drug Abuse Research, 1977.

36. Latimer, D. and Goldberg, J. *Flowers in the Blood*. Franklin Watts, 1981.

37. Brecher, L. M. *Consumer Union Report on Licit and Illicit Drugs*. Little, Brown, 1972.

38. Stimmel, B. *Heroin Dependency*. Stratton, 1975.

39. There are thousands of reports on the effects of marijuana. Two of the best collections of papers are: Tinklenberg, J. R. (editor). *Marijuana and Health Hazards*. Academic Press, 1975; and *Cannabis and Health Hazards. Proceedings of an ARF/WHO Scientific Meeting*. Addiction Research Foundation, 1983. *See also: Marijuana and Health*. Annual Report to the US Congress from the Department on Health and Human Services.

40. Starks, M. *Marijuana Potency*. And/Or Press, 1977.

41. The Surgeon General's Warning on Marijuana. *Morbidity and Mortality Weekly Report*, 31:428, 1982.

42. Leuchtenberger, C. Effects of Marijuana and Tobacco Smoke on DNA and Chromosomal Complement in Human Lung Explants. *Nature*, 242:403, 1973.

43. Edwardes, A. and Masters, R. *The Cradle of Erotic*. The Julian Press, 1963.

44. Heath, R. Effects of Marijuana on EEG in Humans. *Archives General Psychiatry*, 26:577, 1972.

45. Melges, C. Marijuana and Temporal Disintegration. *Science*, 168:1118, 1970.

46. Grinspoon, L. and Bakalar, J. B. *Psychedelic Drugs Reconsidered*. Basic Books, 1979.

47. Ibid.

48. Tobacco Consumption. *Morbidity and Mortality Weekly Report*, 33:322, 1984.

49. Brecher, E. M. *Consumer Union Report on Licit and Illicit Drugs*. Little, Brown, 1972.

50. Lucchesi, B. R. The Role of Nicotine as a Determinant of Cigarette Smoking in Man. *Clinical Pharmacology and Therapeutics*, 8:791, 1967.

51. Lenfant, C. Are Low-Yield Cigarettes Really Safer? *New England Journal of Medicine*, 309:181, 1983.

52. Effects of Smokeless Tobacco on the Oral Cavity. *Dental Abstracts*, May 1983.

53. What Role for the New Nicotine Gum? *Patient Care*, June 15, 1984.

PART SIX

Controversial Alternatives

1. O'Connor, J. and Bensky, D. (translators, editors). *Acupuncture—A Comprehensive Text*. Eastland Press. 1981.
    See also: Mann, F. *Acupuncture*. Random House, 1972.

2. Ulett, G. A. Acupuncture Treatments for Pain Relief. *Journal of the American Medical Association*, 245:768, 1981.

3. Walker, M. *The Chelation Answer*. Cancer Control Society, 1982.
    See also: Gutting, R. D. *Chelation Therapy*. Textbook Publications, 1979.

4. Chelation Therapy. *Journal of the American Medical Association*, 250:672, 1983.
    See also letter on chelation therapy in same volume, p. 2926.

5. Couric, J. M. Chelation Therapy Overdone. *FDA Consumer*, March 1982.

6. Chiropractors—Healers or Quacks? Part 1: The 80-year War with Science. *Consumer Reports*, September 1975.

7. Chiropractors—Healers or Quacks? Part 2: How Chiropractors Can Help—or Harm. *Consumer Reports*, October 1975.

8. Barrett, S. B. Chiropractors—Knocking at Your Door? *Family Physician*, May 1980.

9. Ballantine, H. T., Jr. Federal Recognition of Chiropractic: A Double Standard. *Annals of Internal Medicine*, 82:712, 1975.

10. The Research Status of Spinal Manipulative Therapy. NINCOS Monograph No. 15. U.S. Department of Health, Education, and Welfare, 1975.

11. Hoehler, F. K. Spinal Manipulation for Low Back Pain. *Journal of the American Medical Association*, 245:1835, 1981.

12. Chiropractors Urged to Consider Stroke Risk. *Medical World News*, March 17, 1980.

13. *See* reference 9.

14. Amebiasis Associated with Colonic Irrigation. *Morbidity and Mortality Weekly Report*, 30:101, 1981.

15. Leake, C. C. (editor). Biological Actions of DMSO. *Annals New York Academy of Sciences*, vol. 141, 1967.

16. Dimethyl Sulfoxide: Controversy and Current Status. Report by Council on Scientific Affairs. *Journal of the American Medical Association*, 248:1369, 1982.

17. Ostfeld, A. The Systemic Use of Procaine in the Treatment of the Elderly: A Review. *Journal of the American Geriatrics Society*, 25:1, 1977.

18. The Gravity of Defying Gravity. *Hospital Practice*, September 1983.

704

19. Pizer, H. *Guide to the New Medicine*. William Morrow, 1982.

20. Puddephatt, N. *The Homeopathic Materia Medica—How it Should Be Studied*. Health Sciences Press, 1972. *See also*: Smith, T. *Homoeopathic Medicine*. Thorsons, 1982.

21. Kreskin. *The Amazing World of Kreskin*. Random House, 1973.

22. Ruch, J. C. Self-Hypnosis. *Journal of Clinical and Experimental Hypnosis*, October 1975.

23. Simon, A. An Evaluation of Iridology. *Journal of the American Medical Association*, 242:1385, 1979.

24. Kittler, G. D. *Control for Cancer*. Warner, 1963.

25. The Laetriles-Nitrilosides in the Prevention and Control of Cancer. Published by The Committee for Freedom of Choice in Cancer Therapy, undated.

26. Griffin, G. E. World without Cancer—the Story of Vitamin B-17 (two volumes). *American Media*, 1974.

27. Moertel, C. G. A Clinical Trial of Amygdalin (Laetrile) in the Treatment of Human Cancer. *New England Journal of Medicine*, 306:201, 1982.

28. Herbert, V. Laetrile—the Cult of Cyanide. *American Journal of Clinical Nutrition*, 32:1121, 1979.

29. Fenselau, C. S. Mandelonitrile Beta-glucuronide: Synthesis and Characterization. *Science*, 198:625, 1977.

30. Pathologist Tells of Strange Tijuana Autopsy of Chad Green. *Medical World News*, November 12, 1979.

31. Cousins, N. Anatomy of an Illness (as Perceived by the Patient.) *New England Journal of Medicine*, 295:1458, 1976.

32. Herbert, V. Pangamic Acid ("Vitamin B-15"). *American Journal of Clinical Nutrition*, 32:1534, 1979.

33. Wallace, R. K. The Physiology of Meditation. *Scientific American*, 226:84, 1972.

34. Hecht, A. Snake Venom. *FDA Consumer*, September 1981.

Glossary

adrenalin epinephrine

aerobic oxygen using

AIDS acquired immune deficiency syndrome

alterative a substance that allegedly normalizes body functions without dramatic physiological effects

alveoli plural of alveolus; these are the tiny air sacs in the lungs from which oxygen enters the blood

amenorrhea lack of menstrual periods

amino acid an organic acid, usually containing nitrogen, that can combine with other amino acids to form proteins

amniocentesis puncturing the amniotic sac (in which the fetus develops) with a needle and syringe, usually to study the chemical and chromosomal content of the amniotic fluid

anaerobic non-oxygen-using

analgesic pain reliever

anaphylactic shock collapse after exposure to an allergen

anemia reduced oxygen-carrying capacity due to fewer red blood cells, or less hemoglobin in them, or both

angina pectoris a crushing pain in the chest often due to atherosclerosis of the coronary arteries

anodyne pain reliever

anovulation lack of ovum (egg) production

anthelmintic a medicine to expel parasitic worms

antibody a protein made in response to the presence in the body of an antigen (foreign substance) such as a virus or bacterium

antioxidant a substance that inhibits oxidation; some are made by the body to inhibit the destructive actions of chemicals called free radicals; some (such as vitamins C and E) are nutrients; some (such as BHA and BHT) are food additives

antispasmodic an agent that relieves spasms

aorta the major trunk of the system of arteries that feed blood from the heart to the tissues; it arises from the left ventricle

apnea cessation of breathing, usually temporary; may be due to a variety of diseases, but may also occur in apparently healthy people in deep sleep

arrythmia irregular heart beat

astringent a constricting agent, such as tannic acid, alum, or zinc oxide, that checks bleeding and secretions

atheroma an area of thickening and fatty degeneration of an artery

atherosclerosis a condition of deteriorating arteries due to atheromas

atrophy wasting and shrinking due to disease, malnutrition, or lack of use

BHA butylated hydroxyanisole, an antioxidant used as a food preservative

BHT butylated hydroxytoluene, an antioxidant used as a food preservative

biofeedback the use of electronic devices that amplify body electricity and vibrations in order to exert control over subtle autonomic processes such as blood flow

blood purifier seems to mean different things to different herbalists; often refers

706

to an antibiotic action, in particular for the treatment of veneral disease

brucellosis a disease caused by three species of Brucella bacteria; common in cattle and other farm animals; known as undulant fever in humans, among whom it is not common

bulimia pathological overeating, often followed by intentional vomiting

bursa a connective tissue sac that serves as a cushion between muscles and other tissues

cachexia malnutrition and wasting

calorie a measure of the chemical energy provided by food; one gram of carbohydrate or protein provides about four calories, while one gram of fat provides about nine calories

carcinogen a substance that causes cancer

cardiovascular referring to the heart and blood vessels

carminative a substance that allegedly removes or expels gas from the GI tract

catabolism metabolic breakdown

cholesterol a fatty substance present in animal tissue such as egg yolk, fat, blood, and muscle; used by the body to make sex and adrenal cortical hormones, bile acids, and nerve tissue; excessive amount in the blood is associated with an increased risk of atherosclerosis and heart disease

chondromalacia softness of any cartilage

CMER in reference to treatment of connective tissue injuries: cooling, motion (very careful), elevation, rest

cocarcinogen a substance that promotes the action of a carcinogen

coenzyme a substance necessary for the action of an enzyme; many vitamins are coenzymes

colon the large intestine

comedo blackhead; darkened oil plug in oil duct; can lead to pimple

conjunctiva mucous membrane that lines eyeballs and inner eyelids

coronary arteries the arteries that feed oxygenated blood to the heart muscle

corticosteroid cortisone or similar hormone made by the adrenal cortex

cystitis bladder inflammation

decoction the liquid obtained by boiling vegetable matter

demulcent a soothing, softening agent for the skin or mucous membranes

diaphoretic a substance that promotes perspiration

disc short for intervertebral disc, the connective tissue that separates one vertebra from the next

diuretic a substance that promotes urination

DMSO dimethyl sulfoxide, a powerful solvent

DNA deoxyribonucleic acid in a cell nucleus, the chain of nucleotides (complexes of nitrogenous base, sugar, and phosphate) arranged in a double helix that carries all the genetic information for an organism

Down's syndrome commonly called mongolism; a chromosomal defect (trisomy 21, an extra #21 chromosome) that results in congenital defects such as dwarfism, mental retardation, and a deformed head

duodenum the upper part of the intestine into which the stomach empties

ECG electrocardiogram for electrical monitoring of the heart

edema swelling of a part or area of the body

embolism obstruction of a blood vessel by a blood clot, air, fat, or other substance

emetic a substance that promotes vomiting

emmenagogue a substance that allegedly promotes menstruation

emollient a soothing, softening agent used on the skin

endometriosis a disorder in which endometrial tissue (uterine lining) somehow gets into the abdominal cavity and to other areas of the body; this tissue responds to monthly hormone changes, and their cyclic swelling and bleeding can cause severe pain

endorphin a morphinelike substance produced by the brain

enzyme a protein that promotes a certain chemical reaction such as the breakdown of protein to amino acids in the GI tract and the building of proteins from amino acids inside cells

epinephrine a hormone produced by the adrenal medulla that stimulates the heart, relaxes the bronchioles, and prepares the body to "fight or flee"

episiotomy cutting the perineum (the area between the anus and vulva) during labor to facilitate delivery and avoid tearing

epithelium the outer layer of cells of skin and mucous membranes

estrogen a principle hormone produced by the ovaries and responsible for secondary sexual characteristics; smaller amounts are produced by the adrenal cortex, so men also have some

expectorant helps expel mucus from the respiratory tract

Fallopian tubes the two tubes that carry the eggs from the ovaries to the uterus

fascia membranous connective tissue that surrounds muscles or binds skin to underlying tissue

fat a combination of glycerol with fatty acids such as stearic acid, palmitic acid, or oleic acid; one gram yields nine calories

febrifuge fever reducer

fiber those components of plant foods that are not digestible, such as

cellulose; they attract normal bacterial colonies, absorb water, and give bulk to the stool, promoting normal bowel function

galactose the least sweet of the monosaccharides (six-carbon sugars); one-half the lactose molecule

gene a unit of heredity in the nucleus of a cell; a section of DNA

GI gastrointestinal

gingivitis inflammation of the gums

glucose a monosaccharide (six-carbon sugar); one-half the sucrose and lactose molecules; the most important carbohydrate in the body

glycerol (or glycerine) a three-carbon portion of all fat molecules, usually comprising less than 10 percent of the total weight of the fat; by itself it is a clear, syrupy liquid used as an emollient and solvent

glycogen "animal starch"; glucose combined in long chains for storage in the liver and muscles

glycoside a substance derived from plants and made by chemical combination of a sugar and nonsugar; many (such as digitoxin) are pharmacologically active

granuloma a granular growth or nodule

Hansen's disease a chronic disease, also called leprosy, caused by *Mycobacterium leprae*, bacteria discovered by Norwegian physician Gerhard Hansen in 1871. It causes skin and nerve damage, muscle weakness, and sometimes damage to internal organs. Treatment with sulfone drugs is usually effective. Isolation is no longer considered necessary, but children, who are more susceptible, should not have contact with leprosy patients. The vast majority of people exposed to the bacteria quickly develop resistance. Only a small minority is susceptible to the disease. There are only a few thousand cases in the United States, but at least 15 million worldwide, only 5 percent of whom are being treated.

hermaphroditism the presence of both male and female sex organs in one person

histamine a substance in the body that has a variety of effects, usually after tissue is injured or stressed

hormone a regulatory substance produced by the pituitary, thyroid, adrenal, or other gland that travels through the blood to target organs where it has powerful effects

hyperacidity excessive acid in the stomach which can cause pain and eventually ulceration

hypertension high blood pressure; not the same as mental tension or stess, though these may aggravate the problem

hyperventilation excessive breathing, usually unconscious, that can result in excessively low carbon dioxide levels in the blood and a variety of symptoms

hypoglycemia low blood sugar

hysterectomy removal of the uterus

immunity the condition of having resistance to harmful organisms or toxins due to previous exposure to them or vaccination against them

inflammation heat, redness, swelling, and pain subsequent to trauma, infection, allergic reactions, or other stress or injury to tissue

infusion the liquid obtained by steeping vegetable matter in hot but not boiling water

insulin a hormone from the beta-cells of the pancreas that promotes the entry of glucose into muscle, fat, and certain other cells

interferon an antiviral protein made by some cells; there are several types, some of which show promise against certain cancers and virus infections

ischemia death of cells and tissue due to insufficient blood supply

isometric exercise one in which the muscles are held in the contracted position for extended periods rather than alternately relaxed and contracted as in dynamic exercise

IU international units

IUD intrauterine device for birth control

jaundice yellowing of the skin and eyes, usually due to liver dysfunction

ketones acetone and other products of incomplete fat metabolism

lactase the enzyme that catalyzes the breakdown of lactose to galactose and glucose

leprosy Hansen's disease

leucocyte white blood cell

libido sex drive

ligament strong, fibrous connective tissue that (in most cases) attaches bone to bone (see *tendon*)

lipid fat; oil

lipoprotein a complex of protein and fat in one molecule

LSD lysergic acid diethylamide-25, a powerful and dangerous psychedelic drug

macrophage wandering or stationary cell that surrounds and destroys foreign matter

mastectomy removal or radical reduction of a breast

MECE in reference to treatment of connective tissue injuries: movement, ethyl chloride, and elevation

metabolism the chemical reactions that take place in each cell and provide the energy and material for all the cell's functions

metastasis the spread, via the blood or lymph, of cancerous cells from one part of the body to another

mucilage a gelatinous, sometimes gummy substance that makes some herbs useful as a demulcent; sometimes extracted from plants for use in preparing drugs

myelin a fatty substance, composed of several lipids, present in the myelin sheath that surrounds many nerves and some brain cells

myocardial infarction death of an area of heart muscle due to the cessation of blood flow to the area; commonly known as a heart attack

neoplasm new and abnormal tissue growth; may be benign or malignant (cancerous)

neuron nerve cell

neurotransmitter a chemical that travels across the synapse, the junction between two nerve cells, and communicates impulses; examples include norepinephrine, serotonin, and acetylcholine

norepinephrine a neurotransmitter that functions mostly in the sympathetic nervous system

oncologist cancer specialist

osteomalacia softening or weakening of the bones, usually due to deficiency of calcium or vitamin D

osteoporosis weak, demineralized bones

ovulation the release of an egg from an ovary; it occurs about once a month in most fertile women

oxidize to cause a substance to chemically combine with oxygen

palpate to examine by feeling with the hands

palpitation a rapid, irregular, or excessively forceful heartbeat

Pap test (or Pap smear) short for Papanicolaou test, an examination of the cells of the cervix and vagina for precancerous and cancerous abnormalities

paragoric an oral opium compound used to treat diarrhea

parasympathetic nervous system the branch of the autonomic nervous system that tends to slow the heart, constrict the pupils, and promote digestive and sexual functions

Parkinsonism symptoms of Parkinson's disease, a chronic nervous disorder characterized by a fine tremor, muscle weakness, rigidity, a peculiar gait, and lack of facial expression

peristalsis intestinal motility, which keeps contents moving along

pH a measure of acidity; a lower pH indicates higher acidity

photosensitivity a condition, promoted by contact with certain chemicals and intake of certain drugs, of hypersensitivity to sunlight, which can cause hives and other skin problems

PKU phenylketonuria, a genetic disorder of amino acid metabolism; can cause brain damage if not controlled by diet

placebo a therapeutic substance, agent, or procedure that works (or seems to work) by suggestion, not by consistent physical effects on the body

platelets tiny discs in the blood that are involved in blood coagulation and clot formation

polyunsaturated fats fats, mostly from plants, with double bonds and room for more hydrogen; these tend to be liquid at room temperature and are called oils

progesterone a principle hormone produced by the corpus luteum (the part of the ovary that the egg vacated); responsible for the proliferation of the uterine endometrium in the second half of the menstrual cycle

progestin any of a large number of synthetic substances that resemble progesterone

prostate a gland in men that wraps around the neck of the bladder and produces a thin fluid that forms part of the semen

prostatectomy removal of part or all of the prostate gland

protein a complex chain of amino acids in a specific sequence which depends on function; examples are digestive and cellular enzymes, structural proteins in bones, muscle proteins, and enzymes

psychogenic derived from the mind

pyruvate an intermediate product in the breakdown of glucose to carbon dioxide and water

Raynaud's disease and the related Raynaud's syndrome; afflicted persons are highly sensitive to cold, which causes tingling, numbness, paleness followed by redness, swelling, and pain in exposed hands

RDA recommended dietary allowance, an estimate of human needs determined by the Food and Nutrition Board of the National Research Council

retinopathy abnormality of the retina

Reye's syndrome a severe childhood disease, often associated with viral infections; causes fever, lethargy, agitation, seizures, and other neurological symptoms

rheumatism pain, stiffness, and swelling in muscles, joints, and connective tissue due to one type of arthritis or another, overuse, or injury

RICE in reference to treatment of connective tissue injuries: rest, ice, compression, elevation

RNA ribonucleic acid, similar to DNA; the several types serve mainly to mediate DNA's instructions to the cell's biochemical machinery

saponin one of several bitter glycosides widely distributed in plants, especially roots; foams when shaken in water; can cause diarrhea, vomiting, and other toxic effects

saturated fat a fat with no double bond and no capacity to accept more hydrogen; such fats tend to be solid at room temperature and are mostly from animal sources such as meat, whole milk, butter, and eggs

sciatica pain that occurs along the path of the sciatic nerve (down the buttock and back of the leg); sometimes caused by a prolapsed intervertebral disc in the lower back

sebaceous oil producing

SIDS sudden infant death syndrome

sorbitol a sugar-alcohol made from glucose; in diabetics it accumulates in peripheral nerves, the lens, and certain other tissues which it gradually damages (the source of the sorbitol inside cells is glucose, not dietary sorbitol; the main problem with the latter is that it causes gas, cramping, and diarrhea in some people)

spermicide chemical that kills sperm

steroid this broad term includes a large number of chemicals with a certain four-ring structure, including vitamin D, cortisone, testosterone, estrogen, and bile acids; since the effects and functions of the steroids vary widely, the steroids in question should be specified

stress the physiological effects of a stressor, an extreme stimulus or situation such as cold, heat, noise, confinement, pain; also, the stressor itself

sympathetic nervous system the branch of the autonomic nervous system that tends to promote motor and mental excitation and is responsible for the "fight or flight" mechanism, which includes faster heartbeat, dilated pupils, and digestive and sexual inhibition

synapse the junction between two neurons (nerve cells) across which chemical messengers carry nerve impulses

syncope fainting

Syndenham's chorea abnormal twitching, especially of the face and extremities, due to a neurological defect

synovial pertaining to synovia, the lubricating fluid in some joints and between some muscles and connective tissues

tachycardia racing heart

tendon fibrous connective tissue that attaches muscle to bone (see *ligament*)

testosterone the principle hormone produced by the testes; also produced in smaller amounts by the adrenal cortex, so women also have some

tetanus an acute infectious disease caused by the toxin produced by *Clostridium tetani*, a bacterium that can infect wounds which have little or no exposure to oxygen

tinnitus ringing in the ears

toxoplasmosis a disease caused by infection with *Toxoplasma gondii*, a protozoan

ultraviolet radiation invisible electromagnetic energy out of the range of human vision on the violet (short wave) side of the spectrum; excessive exposure is associated with skin cancer and cataracts

uric acid a product of DNA and RNA breakdown; a normal blood component, though excessive levels can lead to gout

vaginismus abnormal spasms of the muscles around the vagina; may interfere with coitus

vapor bath inhaling the vapors from boiled plant material

vegan strict vegetarian; consumes no meat, eggs, milk, or any other animal products

vulnerary a substance that promotes wound healing

xerosis drying

Suffixes

   -ectomy removal

   -itis inflammation

   -osis a process, infection, or parasitic invasion

Appendix A

Recommended Daily Dietary Allowances (RDAs)[a]

Protein Age in years		Weight (kg)	Weight (lb)	Height (cm)	Height (in)	Protein (g)
Infants	0.0–0.5	6	13	60	24	2.0/kg
	0.5–1.0	9	20	71	28	2.2/kg
Children	1–3	13	29	90	35	23
	4–6	20	44	112	44	30
	7–10	28	62	132	52	34
Males	11–14	45	99	157	62	45
	15–18	66	145	176	69	56
	19–22	70	154	177	70	56
	23–50	70	154	178	70	56
	51+	70	154	178	70	56
Females	11–14	46	101	157	62	46
	15–18	55	120	163	64	46
	19–22	55	120	163	64	44
	23–50	55	120	163	64	44
	51+	55	120	163	64	44
Pregnant						+30
Lactating						+20

Fat-Soluble Vitamins Age in years		Vitamin A (μg RE)[b]	Vitamin D (μg)[c]	Vitamin E (mg α-TE)[d]
Infants	0.0–0.5	420	10	3
	0.5–1.0	400	10	4
Children	1–3	400	10	5
	4–6	500	10	6
	7–10	700	10	7
Males	11–14	1000	10	8
	15–18	1000	10	10
	19–22	1000	7.5	10
	23–50	1000	5	10
	51+	1000	5	10
Females		800	10	8
	15–18	800	10	8
	19–22	800	7.5	8
	23–50	800	5	8
	51+	800	5	8
Pregnant		+200	+5	+2
Lactating		+400	+5	+3

[a]The allowances are intended to provide for individual variations among most normal persons as they live in the United States under usual environmental stresses. Diets should be based on a variety of common foods in order to provide other nutrients for which human requirements have been less well defined.

[b]Retinol equivalents. 1 retinol equivalent = 1 μg retinol or 6 μg β carotene.

[c]As cholecalciferol. 10 μg cholecalciferol = 400 IU of vitamin D.

[d]α-tocopherol equivalents. 1 mg d-α-TE.

[e]1 NE (niacin equivalent) is equal to 1 mg of niacin or 60 mg of dietary tryptophan.

712

Water-Soluble Vitamins Age in years		Vitamin C (mg)	Thiamin (mg)	Riboflavin (mg)	Niacin (mg NE)ᵉ	Vitamin B-6 (mg)	Folacin (μg)	Vitamin B-12 (μg)
Infants	0.0–0.5	35	0.3	0.4	6	0.3	30	0.5
	0.5–1.0	35	0.5	0.6	8	0.6	45	1.5
Children	1–3	45	0.7	0.8	9	0.9	100	2.0
	4–6	45	0.9	1.0	11	1.3	200	2.5
	7–10	45	1.2	1.4	16	1.6	300	3.0
Males	11–14	50	1.4	1.6	18	1.8	400	3.0
	15–18	60	1.4	1.7	18	2.0	400	3.0
	19–22	60	1.5	1.7	19	2.2	400	3.0
	23–50	60	1.4	1.6	18	2.2	400	3.0
	51+	60	1.2	1.4	16	2.2	400	3.0
Females	11–14	50	1.1	1.3	15	1.8	400	3.0
	15–18	60	1.1	1.3	14	2.0	400	3.0
	19–22	60	1.1	1.3	14	2.0	400	3.0
	23–50	60	1.0	1.2	13	2.0	400	3.0
	51+	60	1.0	1.2	13	2.0	400	3.0
Pregnant		+20	+0.4	+0.3	+2	+0.6	+400	+1.0
Lactating		+40	+0.5	+0.5	+5	+0.5	+100	+1.0

Minerals Age in years		Calcium (mg)	Phosphorus (mg)	Magnesium (mg)	Iron (mg)	Zinc (mg)	Iodine (μg)
Infants	0.0–0.5	360	240	50	10	3	40
	0.5–1.0	540	360	70	15	5	50
Children	1–3	800	800	150	15	10	70
	4–6	800	800	200	10	10	90
	7–10	800	800	250	10	10	120
Males	11–14	1200	1200	350	18	15	150
	15–18	1200	1200	400	18	15	150
	19–22	800	800	350	10	15	150
	23–50	800	800	350	10	15	150
	51+	800	800	350	10	15	150
Females	11–14	1200	1200	300	18	15	150
	15–18	1200	1200	300	18	15	150
	19–22	800	800	300	18	15	150
	23–50	800	800	300	18	15	150
	51+	800	800	300	10	15	150
Pregnant		+400	+400	+150	f	+5	+25
Lactating		+400	+400	+150	f	+10	+50

ᶠThe increased requirement during pregnancy cannot be met by the iron content of habitual American diets nor by the existing iron stores of many women; therefore the use of 30–60 mg of supplemental iron is recommended. Iron needs during lactation are not substantially different from those of nonpregnant women, but continued supplementation of the mother for 2–3 months per parturition is advisable in order to replenish stores depleted by pregnancy.

Source: FOOD AND NUTRITION BOARD, NATIONAL ACADEMY OF SCIENCES NATIONAL RESEARCH COUNCIL. Revised 1980.

Appendix B

Nutritive Values of Common Foods

VALUES FOR EDIBLE PART OF FOODS

FOOD, APPROXIMATE HOUSEHOLD MEASURES AND MARKET UNITS

Food, approximate household measures and market units			Water	Food energy	Pro-tein	Fat	Carbo-hydrate	Cal-cium	Phos-phorus	Iron	Sodium	Potas-sium	Vitamin A value	Thia-min	Ribo-flavin	Niacin	Ascor-bic acid
		Grams	Percent	Calo-ries	Grams	Grams	Grams	Milli-grams	Milli-grams	Milli-grams	Milli-grams	Milli-grams	Interna-tional units	Milli-grams	Milli-grams	Milli-grams	Milli-grams
ALMONDS:																	
Dried:																	
In shell (refuse: shells, 60%):																	
Cup	1 cup	78	4.7	187	5.8	16.9	6.1	73	157	1.5	1	241	0	.07	.29	1.1	Trace
Pound (yields 6.4 oz., approx. 1¼ cups, shelled whole nuts).	1 lb	454	4.7	1,085	33.7	98.3	35.4	424	914	8.5	7	1,402	0	.44	1.67	6.3	Trace
10 nuts	10 nuts	25	4.7	60	1.9	5.4	2.0	23	50	.5	Trace	77	0	.02	.09	.4	Trace

Source: Nutritive Value of American Foods Agriculture Handbook No. 456

FOOD, APPROXIMATE HOUSEHOLD MEASURES AND MARKET UNITS

VALUES FOR EDIBLE PART OF FOODS

			Water	Food energy	Pro-tein	Fat	Carbo-hydrate	Cal-cium	Phos-phorus	Iron	Sodium	Potas-sium	Vitamin A value	Thia-min	Ribo-flavin	Niacin	Ascor-bic acid
		Grams	Percent	Calo-ries	Grams	Grams	Grams	Milli-grams	Milli-grams	Milli-grams	Milli-grams	Milli-grams	Interna-tional units	Milli-grams	Milli-grams	Milli-grams	Milli-grams
Shelled:																	
Whole	1 cup	142	4.7	849	26.4	77.0	27.7	332	716	6.7	6	1,098	0	.34	1.31	5.0	Trace
Pound (yield from approx. 2½ lb., in shell)	1 lb	454	4.7	2,713	84.4	245.9	88.5	1,061	2,286	21.3	18	3,506	0	1.09	4.17	15.9	Trace
Roasted (in oil), salted:																	
Cup (approx. 120 nuts)	1 cup	157	4.7	984	29.2	90.6	30.6	369	791	7.4	311	1,214	0	.08	1.44	5.5	0
Pound	1 lb	454	.7	2,844	84.4	261.7	88.5	1,066	2,286	21.3	898	3,506	0	.23	4.17	15.9	0
APPLES:																	
Raw, commercial varieties:																	
Fruit, 3-in. diam. (approx. 2½ per pound)	1 apple	180	84.4	96	.3	1.0	24.0	12	17	.5	2	182	150	.05	.03	.2	7
Pound	1 lb	454	84.4	263	.9	2.7	65.8	32	45	1.4	5	499	410	.14	.09	.5	18
APRICOTS:																	
Raw:																	
Pound	1 lb	454	85.3	217	4.3	.9	54.6	72	98	2.1	4	1,198	11,510	.18	.17	2.6	43
Dried, sulfured	1 lb	454	25.0	1,179	22.7	2.3	301.6	304	490	24.9	118	4,441	49,440	.05	.78	15.0	54
Medium	10 halves	35	25.0	91	1.8	.2	23.3	23	38	1.9	9	343	3,820	Trace	.06	1.2	4
APRICOT NECTAR, CANNED OR BOTTLED (APPROX. 40% FRUIT):	1 cup	251	84.6	143	.8	.3	36.6	23	30	.5	Trace	379	2,380	.03	.03	.5	8
ARTICHOKES, GLOBE OR FRENCH, COOKED (BOILED), DRAINED																	
Bud or globe	1 bud, medium	300	86.5	—	3.4	.2	11.9	61	83	1.3	36	361	180	.08	.05	.8	10

Food	Measure	Grams	Water %	Food energy	Protein	Fat	Carbohydrate	Calcium	Phosphorus	Iron			Vitamin A				Ascorbic
ASPARAGUS:																	
Raw spears (green):																	
Pound	1 lb	454	91.7	118	11.3	.9	22.7	100	281	4.5	9	1,261	4,080	.82	.91	6.8	150
Cooked spears (green) (boiled), drained:																	
Medium, ½-in. diam. at base	4 spears	60	93.6	12	1.3	.1	2.2	13	30	.4	1	110	540	.10	.11	.8	16
Pound	1 lb	454	93.6	91	10.0	.9	16.3	95	227	2.7	5	830	4,080	.73	.82	6.4	118
AVOCADO:																	
All commercial varieties:																	
Whole fruit (refuse: seed and skin, 25%); wt., 10⅓ oz.	1 avocado	302	74.0	378	4.8	37.1	14.3	23	95	1.4	9	1,368	660	0.25	0.45	8.6	82
BACON, CURED:																	
Cooked (broiled or fried), drained:																	
Slab, yield from 1 lb., raw	4.8 oz	136	8.1	807	35.8	70.7	4.3	19	305	4.5	1,389	321	(0)	.69	.46	7.1	—
Slice, thick (approx. 12 slices per pound, raw)	2 slices	24	8.1	143	6.4	12.5	.8	3	54	.8	245	57	(0)	.12	.08	1.2	—
Slice, thin (approx. 28 slices per pound, raw)	2 slices	10	8.1	61	2.7	5.2	.3	1	22	.3	102	24	(0)	.05	.03	.5	—
BANANAS:																	
Raw:																	
Medium	1 banana	175	75.7	101	1.3	.2	26.4	10	31	.8	1	440	230	.06	.07	.8	12
	1 lb	454	75.7	386	5.0	.9	100.7	36	118	3.2	5	1,678	860	.23	.27	3.2	45
Red	1 banana	193	74.4	118	1.6	.3	30.7	13	24	1.0	1	485	520	.07	.05	.8	(13)
	1 lb	454	74.4	408	5.4	.9	106.1	45	82	3.6	5	1,678	1,810	.23	.18	2.7	(45)
Dehydrated or banana flakes:	1 cup	100	3	340	4.4	.8	88.6	32	104	2.8	4	1,477	760	.18	.24	2.8	7
BASS, STRIPED, OVENFRIED:	16⅝ oz	480	60.8	941	103.2	40.8	32.2	—	—	—	—	—	—	—	—	—	—
Yield from 1 lb., raw fillets	1 fillet	200	60.8	892	43.0	17.0	13.4	—	—	—	—	—	—	—	—	—	—
BEANS, COMMON, MATURE SEEDS, DRY:																	
White:																	
Cooked, Great Northern or navy (no residual cooking liquid):																	
Great Northern	1 cup	180	69.0	212	14.0	1.1	38.2	90	266	4.9	13	749	0	.25	.13	1.3	0
Pea (navy)	1 cup	190	69.0	224	14.8	1.1	40.3	95	281	5.1	13	790	0	.27	.13	1.3	0

FOOD, APPROXIMATE HOUSEHOLD MEASURES AND MARKET UNITS

VALUES FOR EDIBLE PART OF FOODS

Food, household measure		Grams	Water Percent	Food energy Calories	Protein Grams	Fat Grams	Carbohydrate Grams	Calcium Milligrams	Phosphorus Milligrams	Iron Milligrams	Sodium Milligrams	Potassium Milligrams	Vitamin A value International units	Thiamin Milligrams	Riboflavin Milligrams	Niacin Milligrams	Ascorbic acid Milligrams
Pound	1 lb	454	69.0	535	35.4	2.7	96.2	227	671	12.2	32	1,887	0	.64	.32	3.2	0
Canned, solids and liquids:																	
Cup	1 cup	255	68.5	306	16.1	1.3	58.7	173	309	5.1	862	683	150	.18	.10	1.5	5
Pound	1 lb	454	68.5	544	28.6	2.3	104.3	308	549	9.1	1,533	1,216	270	.32	.18	2.7	9
Red, kidney:																	
Cooked (no residual cooking liquid):																	
Cup	1 cup	185	69.0	218	14.4	.9	39.6	70	259	4.4	6	629	10	.20	.11	1.3	—
Pound	1 lb	454	69.0	535	35.4	2.3	97.1	172	635	10.9	14	1,542	30	.50	.27	3.2	—
Canned, solids and liquid:																	
Cup	1 cup	255	76.0	230	14.5	1.0	41.8	74	278	4.6	8	673	10	.13	.10	1.5	—
Pound	1 lb	454	76.0	408	25.9	1.8	74.4	132	494	8.2	14	1,198	20	.23	.18	2.7	—
BEANS, SNAP:																	
Green:																	
Cooked (boiled), drained	1 cup	125	92.4	31	2.0	.3	6.8	63	46	.8	5	189	680	.09	.11	.6	15
	1 lb	454	92.4	113	7.3	.9	24.5	227	168	2.7	18	685	2,450	.32	.41	2.3	54
BEEF, TRIMMED TO RETAIL BASIS:																	
Boneless chuck and chuck cuts:																	
Cooked (braised or stewed), drained (81% lean, 19% fat):																	
Yield from 1 lb. raw beef (item 218)	10.7 oz	304	49.4	994	79.0	72.7	0	33	426	10.0	138	632	130	.15	.61	12.2	—

	Measure	Grams															
Cup, chopped or diced pieces (not packed)	1 cup	140	49.4	458	36.4	33.5	0	15	196	4.6	64	291	60	.07	.28	5.6	—
T-bone steak, choice grade:																	
Cooked (broiled):																	
Lean with fat (56% lean, 44% fat):																	
Yield from 1 lb., raw beef with bone	10.4 oz	295	36.4	1,395	57.5	127.4	0	24	490	7.7	141	644	220	.17	.47	12.1	—
Lean, trimmed of separable fat:																	
Yield from 1 lb., raw beef with bone	5.8 oz	165	57.9	368	50.2	17.0	0	20	401	6.1	123	562	30	.13	.38	9.7	—
Ground beef:																	
Lean with 10% fat:																	
Cooked:																	
Yield from 1 lb., raw ground beef	12 oz	340	60.0	745	93.2	38.4	0	41	782	11.9	228	1,044	70	.32	.78	20.4	—
Patty	1 (3 oz)	85	60.0	186	23.3	9.6	0	10	196	3.0	57	261	20	.08	.20	5.1	—
Lean with 21% fat:																	
Cooked:																	
Yield from 1 lb., raw ground beef	11½ oz	326	54.2	932	78.9	66.2	0	36	632	10.4	193	884	120	.28	.68	17.6	—
Patty	1 (2.9 oz)	82	54.2	235	19.8	16.6	0	9	159	2.6	49	221	30	.07	.17	4.4	—
BEETS, COMMON, RED:																	
Cooked (boiled), drained, peeled:																	
Diced or sliced	1 cup	170	90.9	54	1.9	.2	12.2	24	39	.9	73	354	30	.05	.07	.5	10
Pound (approx. 2⅔ cups diced or sliced)	1 lb	454	90.9	145	5.0	.5	32.7	64	104	2.3	195	943	90	.14	.18	1.4	27
BLUEBERRIES:																	
Raw	1 cup	145	83.2	90	1.0	.7	22.2	22	19	1.5	1	117	150	(.04)	(.09)	(.7)	20
	1 lb	454	83.2	281	3.2	2.3	69.4	68	59	4.5	5	367	450	(.14)	(.27)	(2.3)	64
BRAZIL NUTS:																	
In shell (refuse: shells, 52%):	1 lb	454	4.6	1,424	31.1	145.6	23.7	405	1,509	7.4	2	1,557	Trace	2.09	.26	3.5	—
Shelled	1 cup	140	4.6	916	20.0	93.7	15.3	260	970	4.8	1	1,001	Trace	1.34	.17	2.2	—
	1 lb	454	4.6	2,967	64.9	303.5	49.4	844	3,143	15.4	5	3,243	Trace	4.35	.54	7.3	—
	1 oz. or 6–8 kernels	28	4.6	185	4.1	19.0	3.1	53	196	1.0	Trace	203	Trace	.27	.03	.5	—

Food, Approximate Household Measures and Market Units		Water	Food energy	Protein	Fat	Carbohydrate	Calcium	Phosphorus	Iron	Sodium	Potassium	Vitamin A value	Thiamin	Riboflavin	Niacin	Ascorbic acid
	Grams	Percent	Calories	Grams	Grams	Grams	Milligrams	Milligrams	Milligrams	Milligrams	Milligrams	International units	Milligrams	Milligrams	Milligrams	Milligrams
BREAD:																
White, enriched	1 loaf or 1 lb	454	35.6	1,225	39.5	14.5	229.1	381	440	11.3	2,300	476	Trace	1.13	.95	10.9	Trace
Whole-wheat	1 loaf or 1 lb	454	36.4	1,102	47.6	13.6	216.4	449	1,034	13.6	2,390	1,238	Trace	1.17	.54	12.7	Trace
BROCCOLI, STALKS (HEAD OR BUD CLUSTERS, STEM AND LEAVES):																
Raw	1 lb	454	89.1	145	16.3	1.4	26.8	467	354	5.0	68	1,733	11,340	.45	1.04	4.1	513
Cooked (boiled), drained:																
Stalks, cut into ½-in. pieces	1 cup	155	91.3	40	4.8	.5	7.0	136	96	1.2	16	414	3,880	.14	.31	1.2	140
Stalks, whole or cut	1 lb	454	91.3	118	14.1	1.4	20.4	399	281	3.6	45	1,211	11,340	.41	.91	3.6	408
BRUSSELS SPROUTS:																
Raw	1 lb	454	85.2	204	22.2	1.8	37.6	163	363	6.8	64	1,769	2,490	.45	.73	4.1	463
Cooked (boiled), drained	1 cup	155	88.2	56	6.5	.6	9.9	50	112	1.7	16	423	810	.12	.22	1.2	135
	1 lb	454	88.2	163	19.1	1.8	29.0	145	327	5.0	45	1,238	2,360	.36	.64	3.6	395
CABBAGE:																
Common varieties																
Raw:																
Shredded finely or chopped	1 cup	90	92.4	22	1.2	.2	4.9	44	26	.4	18	210	120	.05	.05	.3	42
Cooked (boiled until tender), drained	1 lb	454	92.4	109	5.9	.9	24.5	222	132	1.8	91	1,057	590	.23	.23	1.4	213
	1 cup	145	93.9	29	1.6	.3	6.2	64	29	.4	20	236	190	.06	.06	.4	48
CARROTS:																
Raw:	1 carrot 3 oz.	81	88.2	30	.8	.1	7.0	27	26	.5	34	246	7,930	.04	.04	.4	6

Food	Measure																
Grated or shredded	1 cup	110	88.2	46	1.2	.2	10.7	41	40	.8	52	375	12,100	.07	.06	.7	9
	1 lb	454	88.2	191	5.0	.9	44.0	168	163	3.2	213	1,547	49,900	.27	.23	2.7	36
Cooked (boiled), drained: Sliced	1 cup	155	91.2	48	1.4	.3	11.0	51	48	.9	51	344	16,280	.08	.08	.8	9
	1 lb	454	91.2	141	4.1	.9	32.2	150	141	2.7	150	1,007	47,630	.23	.23	2.8	27
CAULIFLOWER: Raw: Sliced	1 cup	85	91.0	23	2.3	.2	4.4	21	48	.9	11	251	50	.09	.09	.6	66
	1 lb	454	91.0	122	12.2	.9	23.6	113	254	5.0	59	1,338	270	.50	.45	3.2	354
Cooked (boiled), drained: Cup	1 cup	125	92.8	28	2.9	.3	5.1	26	53	.9	11	258	80	.11	.10	.8	69
	1 lb	454	92.8	100	10.4	.9	18.6	95	191	3.2	41	934	270	.41	.36	2.7	249
CELERY, GREEN: Raw: Chopped or diced pieces	1 cup	120	94.1	20	1.1	.1	4.7	47	34	.4	151	409	320	.04	.04	.4	11
	1 lb	454	94.1	77	4.1	.5	17.7	177	127	1.4	572	1,547	1,220	.14	.14	1.4	41
Cooked: Diced pieces	1 cup	150	95.3	21	1.2	.2	4.7	47	33	.3	132	359	390	.03	.05	.5	9
	1 lb	454	95.3	64	3.6	.5	14.1	141	100	.9	399	1,084	1,180	.09	.14	1.4	27
CHARD, SWISS: Raw	1 lb	454	91.1	113	10.9	1.4	20.9	399	177	14.5	667	2,495	29,480	.27	.77	2.8	145
Cooked (boiled), drained: Leaves	1 cup	175	93.7	32	3.2	.4	5.8	128	42	3.2	151	562	9,450	.07	.19	.7	28
	1 lb	454	93.7	82	8.2	.9	15.0	331	109	8.2	390	1,456	24,490	.18	.50	1.8	73
NATURAL CHEESES: Blue or Roquefort type:	1 lb	454	40	1,669	97.5	138.3	9.1	1,429	1,538	(2.3)	—	—	(5,620)	.14	2.77	5.4	(0)
	1 oz	28	40	104	6.1	8.6	.6	89	96	(.1)	—	—	(350)	.01	.17	.3	(0)
Brick:	1 lb	454	41.0	1,678	100.7	138.3	8.6	3,311	2,064	(4.1)	—	—	(5,620)	—	2.04	.5	(0)
	1 oz	28	41.0	105	6.3	8.6	.5	207	129	(.3)	—	—	(350)	—	.18	Trace	(0)
Cheddar (domestic type):	1 lb	454	37	1,805	113.4	146.1	9.5	3,402	2,168	4.5	3,175	372	(5,940)	.14	2.09	.5	(0)
	1 oz	28	37	113	7.1	9.1	.6	213	136	.3	198	23	(370)	.01	.13	Trace	(0)
Cottage cheese (cottage cheese dry curd with creaming mixture; 4.2% milk fat), large or small curd: Packed	1 cup	245	78.3	260	33.3	10.3	7.1	230	372	.7	561	208	(420)	.07	.61	.2	(0)
	1 lb	454	78.3	481	61.7	19.1	13.2	426	689	1.4	1,039	386	(770)	.14	1.13	.5	(O)
	1 oz	28	78.3	30	3.9	1.2	.8	27	43	.1	65	24	(50)	.01	.07	Trace	(0)

FOOD, APPROXIMATE HOUSEHOLD MEASURES AND MARKET UNITS

VALUES FOR EDIBLE PART OF FOODS

Food	Unit	Grams	Water Percent	Food energy Calories	Protein Grams	Fat Grams	Carbohydrate Grams	Calcium Milligrams	Phosphorus Milligrams	Iron Milligrams	Sodium Milligrams	Potassium Milligrams	Vitamin A value International units	Thiamin Milligrams	Riboflavin Milligrams	Niacin Milligrams	Ascorbic acid Milligrams
Cottage cheese dry curd (without creaming mixture; 0.3% milk fat): Packed	1 cup	200	79.0	172	34.0	.6	5.4	180	350	.8	580	144	(20)	.06	.56	(.2)	(0)
	1 lb	454	79.0	390	77.1	1.4	12.2	408	794	1.8	1,315	327	(50)	.14	1.27	(.5)	(0)
	1 oz	28	79.0	24	4.8	.1	.8	26	50	.1	82	20	(Trace)	.01	.08	(Trace)	(0)
Parmesan: Grated: Packed	1 cup	140	17	654	59.8	43.1	4.9	1,893	1,296	.7	1,218	248	(1,760)	.03	1.22	.3	(0)
	1 tbsp	5	17	23	2.1	1.5	.2	68	46	Trace	44	9	(60)	Trace	.04	Trace	(0)
	1 lb	454	17	2,118	193.7	139.7	15.9	6,133	4,200	2.3	3,946	803	(5,720)	.09	3.95	.9	(0)
	1 oz	28	17	132	12.1	8.7	1.0	383	263	.1	247	50	(360)	.01	.25	.1	(0)
Swiss (domestic)	1 lb	454	39	1,678	124.7	127.0	7.7	4,196	2,554	4.1	3,221	472	(5,170)	.05	(1.81)	(.5)	(0)
	1 oz	28	39	105	7.8	7.9	.5	262	160	.3	201	29	(320)	Trace	(.11)	(Trace)	(0)
CHERRIES: Raw: Sweet: Whole	10 cherries	75	80.4	47	.9	.2	11.7	15	13	.3	1	129	70	.03	.04	.3	7
Pound	1 lb	454	80.4	286	5.3	1.2	71.0	90	78	1.6	8	780	450	.20	.24	1.6	41
CHESTNUTS: Fresh: In shell	1 lb	454	52.5	713	10.7	5.5	154.7	99	323	6.2	22	1,668	—	.81	.81	2.2	—
Shelled	10 nuts	90	52.5	141	2.1	1.1	30.7	20	64	1.2	4	331	—	.16	.16	.4	—
	1 lb	454	52.5	880	13.2	6.8	191.0	122	399	7.7	27	2,059	—	1.00	1.00	2.7	—

CHICKEN, COOKED:
All classes, roasted:

Food	Measure	Grams	Water (%)	Calories	Protein (g)	Fat (g)	Carb. (g)	Calcium (mg)	Phosphorus (mg)	Iron (mg)	Sodium (mg)	Potassium (mg)	Vit. A (I.U.)	Thiamine (mg)	Riboflavin (mg)	Niacin (mg)	Ascorbic acid (mg)
Light meat without skin: Chopped or diced	1 cup	140	63.8	232	44.2	4.8	0	15	371	1.8	90	575	80	.06	.14	16.2	—
	1 lb	454	63.8	753	143.3	15.4	0	50	1,202	5.9	290	1,864	270	.18	.45	52.6	—
	2 pieces	50	63.8	83	15.8	1.7	0	6	133	.7	32	206	30	.02	.05	5.8	—
Dark meat without skin: Chopped or diced	1 cup	140	64.4	246	39.2	8.8	0	18	321	2.4	120	449	210	.10	.32	7.8	—
	1 lb	454	64.4	798	127.0	28.6	0	59	1,039	7.7	390	1,456	680	.32	1.04	25.4	—
	4 pieces	40	64.4	70	11.2	2.5	0	5	92	.7	34	128	60	.03	.09	2.2	—
Broilers, ready-to-cook, broiled, flesh only: Yield from 1 lb., ready-to-cook broilers	7.1 oz	201	71.0	273	47.8	7.6	0	18	404	3.4	133	551	180	.10	.38	17.7	—
Fryers, ready-to-cook, fried: Flesh, skin, giblets: Yield from 1 lb., ready-to-cook fryers	8 oz	227	53.3	565	69.7	26.8	6.6	30	577	5.2	34	217	1,860	.16	1.29	20.7	—
Light meat without skin	2 pieces	50	59.5	99	16.1	3.1	.6	6	140	.7	35	132	30	.03	.13	6.5	—
Dark meat without skin	4 pieces	40	57.5	88	12.2	3.7	.6	6	94	.7	—	—	50	.03	.18	2.7	—
cut-up parts:	½ breast	94	58.4	160	25.7	5.1	1.2	9	218	1.3	—	—	70	.04	.17	11.6	—
	1 drumstick	56	55.0	88	12.2	3.8	.4	6	89	.9	—	—	50	.03	.15	2.7	—
	1 thigh	65	55.8	122	15.0	5.9	1.3	7	121	1.2	—	—	100	.03	.25	3.5	—
	1 wing	50	52.6	82	8.8	4.5	.8	3	72	.6	—	—	80	.02	.08	2.1	—
COCONUT MEAT: Fresh: Shredded or packed	1 cup	130	50.9	450	4.6	45.9	12.2	17	124	2.2	30	333	0	.07	.03	.7	4
	1 lb	454	50.9	1,569	15.9	160.1	42.6	59	431	7.7	104	1,161	0	.23	.09	2.3	14
Dried, unsweetened (desiccated)	1 lb	454	3.5	3,003	32.7	294.4	104.3	118	848	15.0	—	2,667	0	.27	.18	2.7	0
COD: Cooked (broiled), with butter or margarine: Fillet, 5 in. long, 2½ in. wide, ⅞ in. thick	1 fillet	65	64.6	111	18.5	3.4	0	20	178	.7	72	265	120	.05	.07	2.0	—
CORN, SWEET: Cooked (boiled), drained: Kernels, cut off cob before cooking	1 cup	165	76.5	137	5.3	1.7	31.0	5	147	1.0	Trace	272	660	.18	.17	2.1	12
	1 lb	454	76.5	376	14.5	4.5	85.3	14	404	2.7	Trace	748	1,810	.50	.45	5.9	32

FOOD, APPROXIMATE HOUSEHOLD MEASURES AND MARKET UNITS

VALUES FOR EDIBLE PART OF FOODS

Food	Measure	Grams	Water Percent	Food energy Calories	Protein Grams	Fat Grams	Carbohydrate Grams	Calcium Milligrams	Phosphorus Milligrams	Iron Milligrams	Sodium Milligrams	Potassium Milligrams	Vitamin A value International units	Thiamin Milligrams	Riboflavin Milligrams	Niacin Milligrams	Ascorbic acid Milligrams
Kernels, cooked on cob (refuse: cob, 45%): Ear, 5 in. long, 1¾-in. diam	1 ear	140	74.1	70	2.5	.8	16.2	2	69	.5	Trace	151	310	.09	.08	1.1	7
	1 lb	454	74.1	227	8.2	2.5	52.4	7	222	1.5	Trace	489	1,000	.30	.25	3.5	22
CRESS, GARDEN: Raw	1 lb	454	89.4	145	11.8	3.2	24.9	367	345	5.9	64	2,749	42,180	.36	1.18	4.5	313
Cooked (boiled), drained	1 cup	135	92.5	31	2.6	.8	5.1	82	65	1.1	11	477	10,400	.08	.22	1.1	46
	1 lb	454	92.5	104	8.6	2.7	17.2	277	218	3.6	36	1,601	34,930	.27	.73	3.6	154
CUCUMBERS, RAW: Not pared: Sliced	1 cup	105	95.1	16	.9	.1	3.6	26	28	1.2	6	168	260	.03	.04	.2	12
	1 lb	454	95.1	68	4.1	.5	15.4	113	122	5.0	27	726	1,130	.14	.18	.9	50
Pared: Sliced	1 cup	140	95.7	20	.8	.1	4.5	24	25	.4	8	224	Trace	.04	.06	.3	15
	1 lb	454	95.7	64	2.7	.5	14.5	77	82	1.4	27	726	Trace	.14	.18	.9	50
DATES, MOISTURIZED OR HYDRATED: With pits (refuse: pits, 18%)	10 dates	92	22.5	219	1.8	.4	58.3	47	50	2.4	1	518	40	.07	.08	1.8	0
	1 lb	454	22.5	1,081	8.7	2.0	287.7	233	249	11.8	4	2,557	200	.36	.39	8.7	0
Without pits:	1 lb	454	22.5	1,243	10.0	2.3	330.7	268	286	13.6	5	2,939	230	.41	.45	10.0	0
	10 dates	80	22.5	219	1.8	.4	58.3	47	50	2.4	1	518	40	.07	.08	1.8	0

	Measure																
EGGS: Chicken:																	
Medium	1 egg	50	73.7	72	5.7	5.1	.4	24	90	1.0	54	57	520	.05	.13	Trace	0
Medium	1 white	29	87.6	15	3.2	Trace	.2	3	4	Trace	42	40	0	Trace	.08	Trace	0
EGGPLANT, COOKED (BOILED), DRAINED:																	
Cup, diced	1 cup	200	94.3	38	2.0	.4	8.2	22	42	1.2	2	300	20	.10	.08	1.0	6
	1 lb	454	94.3	86	4.5	.9	18.6	50	95	2.7	5	680	50	.23	.18	2.3	14
FARINA: Enriched: Regular (about 15 min. cooking time):																	
Cooked	1 cup	245	89.5	103	3.2	.2	21.3	10	29	—	353	22	(0)	.10	.07	1.0	(0)
Quick cooking (about 2–5 min. cooking time): Cooked	1 cup	245	89.0	105	3.2	.2	21.8	147	162	—	466	25	(0)	.12	.07	1.0	(0)
Instant cooking (about ½ min. cooking time): Cooked	1 cup	245	85.9	135	4.2	.2	27.9	189	147	—	461	32	(0)	.17	.10	1.2	(0)
Unenriched, regular (about 15 min. cooking time): Cooked	1 cup	245	89.5	103	3.2	.2	21.3	10	29	.5	353	22	(0)	.02	.02	.2	(0)
FIGS: Raw: Medium, 2¼-in. diam. (approx. 9 per pound)	1 fig	50	77.5	40	.6	.2	10.2	18	11	.3	1	97	40	.03	.03	.2	1
FILBERTS (HAZELNUTS): In shell (refuse: shells, 54%): Pound (yields approx. 7⅓ oz., shelled nuts)	1 lb	454	5.8	1,323	26.3	130.2	34.9	436	703	7.1	4	1,469	—	.96	—	1.9	Trace
	10 nuts	30	5.8	87	1.7	8.6	2.3	29	47	.5	Trace	97	—	.06	—	.1	Trace
Shelled: Whole	1 cup	135	5.8	856	17.0	84.2	22.5	282	455	4.6	3	950	—	.62	—	1.2	Trace
Pound (yield from approx. 2¼ lb., in shell)	1 lb	454	5.8	2,876	57.2	283.0	75.8	948	1,529	15.4	9	3,193	—	2.09	—	4.1	Trace
FLOUNDER, BAKED WITH BUTTER OR MARGARINE: Fillet, 8¼ in. long, 2¾ in. wide, ¼ in. thick	1 fillet	100	58.1	202	30.0	8.2	0	23	344	1.4	237	587	—	.07	.08	2.5	2

FOOD, APPROXIMATE HOUSEHOLD MEASURES AND MARKET UNITS

Food, approximate household measures and market units		Water	Food energy	Protein	Fat	Carbohydrate	Calcium	Phosphorus	Iron	Sodium	Potassium	Vitamin A value	Thiamin	Riboflavin	Niacin	Ascorbic acid
	Grams	Percent	Calories	Grams	Grams	Grams	Milligrams	Milligrams	Milligrams	Milligrams	Milligrams	International units	Milligrams	Milligrams	Milligrams	Milligrams
GRAPEFRUIT																
All varieties:																
3½-in. diam. 1 grapefruit	400	88.4	80	1.0	.2	20.8	31	31	.8	2	265	160	.08	.04	.4	74
Juice 1 cup	246	90.0	96	1.2	.2	22.6	22	37	.5	2	399	200	.10	.05	.5	93
GRAPES:																
Raw:																
American type (slip skin) as Concord, Delaware, whole (refuse: seeds and skins, 34%):																
10 grapes	40	81.6	18	.3	.3	4.1	4	3	.1	1	42	30	(.01)	(.01)	(.1)	1
1 cup	153	81.6	70	1.3	1.0	15.9	16	12	.4	3	160	100	(.05)	(.03)	(.3)	4
1 lb	454	81.6	207	3.9	3.0	47.0	48	36	1.2	9	473	300	(.15)	(.09)	(.9)	12
European type (adherent skin) as Thompson Seedless																
Whole:																
Seedless types 10 grapes	50	81.4	34	.3	.2	8.7	6	10	.2	2	87	(50)	.03	.02	.2	2
1 cup	160	81.4	107	1.0	.5	27.7	19	32	.6	5	277	(160)	.08	.05	.5	6
Seeded types (refuse: seeds, 5%) 10 grapes	60	81.4	38	.3	.2	9.9	7	11	.2	2	90	(60)	.03	.02	.2	2
1 cup	160	81.4	102	.9	.5	26.3	18	30	.6	5	263	(150)	.08	.05	.5	6
GRAPEJUICE:																
Canned or bottled: 1 cup	253	82.9	167	.5	Trace	42.0	28	30	.8	5	293	—	.10	.05	.5	Trace

Table columns (left to right): measure, weight (g), water, food energy, protein, fat, carbohydrate, calcium, phosphorus, iron, sodium, potassium, vitamin A, thiamine, riboflavin, niacin, ascorbic acid.

Food	Measure																
HALIBUT, ATLANTIC AND PACIFIC, BROILED WITH BUTTER OR MARGARINE: Yield from 1 lb., raw fillets	12⅝ oz	365	66.6	624	92.0	25.6	0	58	905	2.9	489	1,916	2,480	0.18	0.26	30.3	—
KALE, LEAVES WITHOUT STEMS, MIDRIBS: Raw	1 lb	454	82.7	240	(27.2)	(3.6)	40.8	1,129	422	12.2	(340)	(1,715)	45,360	.73	1.18	9.5	844
Cooked (boiled), drained	1 cup	110	87.8	43	(5.0)	(.8)	6.7	206	64	1.8	(47)	(243)	9,130	.11	.20	1.8	102
LENTILS, MATURE SEEDS, DRY: Cooked	1 cup	200	72.0	212	15.6	Trace	38.6	50	238	4.2	—	498	40	0.14	0.12	1.2	0
LETTUCE, RAW: Butterhead varieties such as Boston types and Bibb: Chopped or shredded pieces	1 cup	55	95.1	8	.7	.1	1.4	19	14	1.1	5	145	530	.03	.03	.2	4
	1 lb	454	95.1	64	5.4	.9	11.3	159	118	9.1	41	1,198	4,400	.27	.27	1.4	36
Crisphead varieties such as Iceberg, Chopped or shredded pieces	1 cup	55	95.5	7	.5	.1	1.6	11	12	.3	5	96	180	.03	.03	.2	8
	1 lb	454	95.5	59	4.1	.5	13.2	91	100	2.8	41	794	1,500	.27	.27	1.4	27
Looseleaf or bunching varieties such as Grand Rapids, Salad Bowl, Simpson: Chopped or shredded pieces	1 cup	55	94.0	10	.7	.2	1.9	37	14	.8	5	145	1,050	.03	.04	.2	10
	1 lb	454	94.0	82	5.9	1.4	15.9	308	118	6.4	41	1,198	8,620	.23	.86	1.8	82
LOBSTER, NORTHERN, COOKED:	1 lb	454	76.8	431	84.8	6.8	1.4	295	871	3.6	953	816	—	.45	.32	—	—
MACKEREL, ATLANTIC, BROILED WITH BUTTER OR MARGARINE: Yield from 1 lb., raw fillets	12⅝ oz	365	61.6	861	79.6	57.7	0	22	1,022	4.4	—	—	(1,930)	0.55	0.99	27.7	—

FOOD, APPROXIMATE HOUSEHOLD MEASURES AND MARKET UNITS

Food		Water	Food energy	Protein	Fat	Carbohydrate	Calcium	Phosphorus	Iron	Sodium	Potassium	Vitamin A value	Thiamin	Riboflavin	Niacin	Ascorbic acid
		Grams	Percent	Calories	Grams	Grams	Grams	Milligrams	Milligrams	Milligrams	Milligrams	Milligrams	International units	Milligrams	Milligrams	Milligrams	Milligrams
MANGOS, RAW: Whole (refuse: seeds and skin, 33%)	1 fruit	300	81.7	152	1.6	.9	38.8	23	30	.9	16	437	11,000	.12	.12	2.5	81
Pound	1 lb	454	81.7	299	3.2	1.8	76.2	45	59	1.8	32	857	21,770	.28	.23	5.0	159
MILK, COW: Whole, 3.5% fat	1 qt	976	87.4	634	34.2	34.2	47.8	1,152	908	0.4	488	1,405	1,410	0.29	1.66	1.0	10
	1 cup	244	87.4	159	8.5	8.5	12.0	288	227	.1	122	351	350	.07	.41	.2	2
Skim	1 quart	980	90.5	353	35.3	1.0	50.0	1,186	931	.4	510	1,421	40	.34	1.76	.7	10
	1 cup	245	90.5	88	8.8	.2	12.5	296	233	.1	127	355	10	.09	.44	.2	2
MUSHROOMS: *Agaricus campestris,* cultivated commercially, raw: Cup, slices, chopped or diced pieces	1 cup	70	90.4	20	1.9	.2	3.1	4	81	.6	11	290	Trace	.07	.32	2.9	2
Pound	1 lb	454	90.4	127	12.2	1.4	20.0	27	526	3.6	68	1,878	Trace	.45	2.09	19.1	14
MUSKMELONS: Cantaloups, Whole, 5-in. diam.; wt., approx. 2⅓ lb.	1 melon	1,060	91.2	159	3.7	.5	39.8	74	85	2.1	64	1,330	18,020	.21	.16	3.2	175
Pound	1 lb	454	91.2	136	3.2	.5	34.0	64	73	1.8	54	1,139	15,420	.18	.14	2.7	150
OATMEAL OR ROLLED OATS: Cooked	1 cup	240	86.5	132	4.8	2.4	23.3	22	137	1.4	523	146	(0)	.19	.05	.2	(0)

	Measure	Grams	Water (%)	Food energy (cal.)	Protein (g)	Fat (g)	Carbohydrate (g)	Calcium (mg)	Phosphorus (mg)	Iron (mg)	Sodium (mg)	Potassium (mg)	Vit. A (I.U.)	Thiamine (mg)	Riboflavin (mg)	Niacin (mg)	Ascorbic acid (mg)
OLIVES, PICKLED; CANNED OR BOTTLED:																	
Green:																	
Whole (refuse: pits, 16%):	10 olives	46	78.2	45	.5	4.9	.5	24	7	.6	926	21	120	—	Trace	—	—
Large, pitted	1 lb	454	78.2	526	6.4	57.6	5.9	277	77	7.3	10,886	249	1,360	—	Trace	—	—
Ripe:																	
Mission:																	
Whole (refuse: pits, 14%):	10 olives	46	73.0	73	.5	8.0	1.3	42	7	.7	297	11	30	Trace	Trace	—	—
Large, pitted	1 lb	454	73.0	835	5.4	91.2	14.5	481	77	7.7	3,402	122	320	Trace	Trace	—	—
ONIONS, MATURE (DRY):																	
Raw:																	
Chopped	1 cup	170	89.1	65	2.6	.2	14.8	46	61	.9	17	267	70	0.05	0.07	0.3	17
	1 lb	454	89.1	172	6.8	.5	39.5	122	163	2.3	45	712	180	.14	.18	.9	45
Cooked (boiled), drained:																	
Cup, whole or sliced	1 cup	210	91.8	61	2.5	.2	13.7	50	61	.8	15	231	80	.06	.06	.4	15
ORANGES, RAW:																	
All commercial varieties:																	
Whole fruit, 2½ in. diam.	1 orange	180	86.0	64	1.3	.3	16.0	54	26	.5	1	263	260	.13	.05	.5	(66)
Juice	1 cup	248	88.3	112	1.7	.5	25.8	27	42	.5	2	496	500	.22	.07	1.0	124
PAPAYAS, RAW:																	
Whole, medium fruit	1 papaya or 1 lb.	454	88.7	119	1.8	.3	30.4	61	49	.9	9	711	5,320	.12	.12	.9	170
PARSLEY,																	
Chopped	1 tbsp	3.5	85.1	2	.1	Trace	.3	7	2	.2	2	25	300	Trace	.01	Trace	6
PEACHES:																	
Raw:																	
Fruit, 2½-in. diam. (aprox. 4 per pound)	1 peach	115	89.1	38	.6	.1	9.7	9	19	.5	1	202	1,330	.02	.05	1.0	7
	1 lb	454	89.1	150	2.4	.4	38.3	36	75	2.0	4	797	5,250	.08	.20	3.9	28
PEANUTS:																	
Roasted in shell, whole																	
Pounds (yields approx. 10.7 oz., shelled nuts)	1 lb	454	1.8	1,769	79.6	148.0	62.6	219	1,237	6.7	15	2,130	—	.97	.40	52.0	0
Jumbo	10 nuts	27	1.8	105	4.7	8.8	3.7	13	74	.4	1	127	—	.06	.02	3.1	0
Shelled, chopped form:	1 cup	144	1.8	838	37.7	70.1	29.7	104	586	3.2	7	1,009	—	.46	.19	24.6	0
Roasted, salted	1 cup	144	1.6	842	37.4	71.7	27.1	107	577	3.0	602	971	—	.46	.19	24.8	0
	1 lb	454	1.6	2,654	117.9	225.9	85.3	336	1,819	9.5	1,896	3,057	—	1.45	.59	78.0	0

FOOD, APPROXIMATE HOUSEHOLD MEASURES AND MARKET UNITS

		Water	Food energy	Pro-tein	Fat	Carbo-hydrate	Cal-cium	Phos-phorus	Iron	Sodium	Potas-sium	Vitamin A value	Thia-min	Ribo-flavin	Niacin	Ascor-bic acid
	Grams	Percent	Calo-ries	Grams	Grams	Grams	Milli-grams	Milli-grams	Milli-grams	Milli-grams	Milli-grams	Interna-tional units	Milli-grams	Milli-grams	Milli-grams	Milli-grams
PEANUT BUTTER MADE WITH MODERATE AMOUNTS OF ADDED FAT, NUTRITIVE SWEETENER, SALT																
1 tbsp	16	1.7	94	4.0	8.1	3.0	9	61	.3	97	100	—	.02	.02	2.4	0
PEARS: Raw, (approx. 2½ per pound)																
1 pear	180	83.2	100	1.1	.7	25.1	13	18	.5	3	213	30	.03	.07	.2	7
1 lb	454	83.2	277	3.2	1.8	69.4	36	50	1.4	9	590	90	.09	.18	.5	18
PEAS, GREEN, IMMATURE: Cooked (boiled), drained																
1 cup	160	81.5	114	8.6	.6	19.4	37	158	2.9	2	314	860	.45	.18	3.7	32
PEAS, MATURE SEEDS, DRY Cooked																
1 cup	200	70.0	230	16.0	0.6	41.6	22	178	3.4	26	592	80	0.30	0.18	1.8	—
PECANS: In shell (refuse: shells, 47%): Pound (yields approx. 8.5 oz., shelled nuts)																
1 lb	454	3.4	1,652	22.1	171.2	35.1	175	695	5.8	Trace	1,450	310	2.07	.31	2.2	5
Shelled: Pound (yield from approx. 1.9 lb., in shell)																
1 lb	454	3.4	3,116	41.7	323.0	66.2	331	1,311	10.9	Trace	2,735	590	3.90	.59	4.1	9
PEPPERS, SWEET, GARDEN VARIETIES: Immature, green: Raw: Chopped or diced																
1 cup	150	93.4	33	1.8	.3	7.2	14	33	1.1	20	320	630	.12	.12	.8	192
1 lb	454	93.4	100	5.4	.9	21.8	41	100	3.2	59	966	1,910	.36	.36	2.3	581

Food	Measure															
Cooked: Boiled, drained: Strips	1 cup	135	94.7	24	1.4	.3	5.1	12	22	.7	12	201	570	.08	.09	.6	130
Mature, red, raw: Chopped or diced	1 cup	150	90.7	47	2.1	.5	10.7	20	45	.9	—	—	6,680	(.12)	(.12)	(.8)	306
Mature, red, raw: Chopped or diced	1 lb	454	90.7	141	6.4	1.4	32.2	59	136	2.7	—	—	20,190	(.36)	(.36)	(2.3)	925
PINEAPPLE: Raw: Cup, diced pieces	1 cup	155	85.3	81	.6	.3	21.2	26	12	.8	2	226	110	.14	.05	.3	26
Pound (approx. 3 cups, diced pieces or 5½ slices)	1 lb	454	85.3	236	1.8	.9	62.1	77	36	2.3	5	662	320	.41	.14	.9	77
PISTACHIONUTS: In shell (refuse: shells; 50%)	1 lb	454	5.3	1,347	43.8	121.8	43.1	297	1,134	16.6	—	2,204	520	1.52	—	3.2	0
Shelled	1 lb	454	5.3	2,694	87.5	243.6	86.2	594	2,268	33.1	—	4,409	1,040	3.04	—	6.4	0
PLUMS: Raw: Damson: Whole (refuse: pits and clinging pulp, 9%): Fruit, 1-in. diam	10 plums	110	81.1	66	.5	Trace	17.8	18	17	.5	2	299	(300)	.08	.08	.5	—
Damson: Whole: Fruit, 1-in. diam	1 lb	454	81.1	272	2.1	Trace	73.5	74	70	2.1	8	1,284	(1,240)	.83	.12	2.1	—
Prune type: Whole (refuse: pits, 6%): Fruit, 1½-in. diam.	1 plum	30	78.7	21	.2	.1	5.6	3	5	.1	Trace	48	80	.01	.01	.1	1
Prune type: Whole: Fruit, 1½-in. diam.	1 lb	454	78.7	320	3.4	.9	84.0	51	77	2.1	4	725	1,280	.18	.18	2.1	17
POPCORN: Popped: Plain, large kernel	1 cup	6	4.0	23	.8	.3	4.6	(1)	(17)	(.2)	(Trace)	—	—	—	(.01)	(.1)	(0)
Oil and salt added, large kernel	1 cup	9	3.1	41	.9	2.0	5.3	1	19	.2	175	—	—	—	.01	.2	0
PORK, FRESH, RETAIL CUTS: Ham: Cooked (baked or roasted): Lean with fat (74% lean, 26% fat): Yield from 1 lb., raw ham with bone and skin	9.2 oz	262	45.5	980	60.3	80.2	0	26	618	7.9	148	675	(0)	1.84	.60	12.1	—

FOOD, APPROXIMATE HOUSEHOLD MEASURES AND MARKET UNITS

FOOD, APPROXIMATE HOUSEHOLD MEASURES AND MARKET UNITS			Water	Food energy	Protein	Fat	Carbohydrate	Calcium	Phosphorus	Iron	Sodium	Potassium	Vitamin A value	Thiamin	Riboflavin	Niacin	Ascorbic acid
		Grams	Percent	Calories	Grams	Grams	Grams	Milligrams	Milligrams	Milligrams	Milligrams	Milligrams	International units	Milligrams	Milligrams	Milligrams	Milligrams
Yield from 1 lb., raw ham without bone and skin	10.9 oz	308	45.5	1,152	70.8	94.2	0	31	727	9.2	178	793	(0)	1.57	.71	14.2	—
Cup (not packed): Chopped or diced: 1 cup		140	45.5	524	82.2	42.8	0	14	880	4.2	79	361	(0)	.71	.82	6.4	—
2 pieces or 3 oz		85	45.5	318	19.6	26.0	0	9	201	2.6	48	220	(0)	.43	.20	3.9	—
Lean, trimmed of separable fat: Yield from 1 lb., raw ham with bone and skin	6.8 oz	194	58.9	421	57.6	19.4	0	25	598	7.4	141	645	(0)	1.24	.56	11.1	—
Yield from 1 lb., raw ham with bone and skin	8.1 oz	228	58.9	495	67.7	22.8	0	30	702	8.7	166	758	(0)	1.46	.66	13.0	—
Cup (not packed): Chopped or diced 1 cup		140	58.9	304	41.6	14.0	0	18	431	5.3	102	466	(0)	.90	.41	8.0	—
2 pieces or 3 oz		85	58.8	184	25.2	8.5	0	11	262	3.2	62	282	(0)	.54	.25	4.8	—
Loin and loin chops: Cooked: Lean with fat: Baked or roasted loin roast (80% lean, 20% fat): Yield from 1 lb., raw loin with bone	8.6 oz	244	45.8	883	59.8	69.5	0	27	625	7.8	147	670	(0)	2.24	.63	13.7	—
Yield from 1 lb., raw loin without bone	10.9 oz	308	45.8	1,115	75.5	87.8	0	34	788	9.9	185	846	(0)	2.83	0.80	17.2	—

Cup, chopped or diced pieces (not packed)	1 cup	140	45.8	507	34.3	39.9	0	15	358	4.5	84	384	(0)	1.29	.36	7.8	—
	1 piece or 3 oz	85	45.8	308	20.8	24.2	0	9	218	2.7	51	233	(0)	.78	.22	4.8	—
Lean, trimmed of separable fat: Baked or roasted loin roast:																	
Yield from 1 lb., raw loin with bone	6.9 oz	195	55.0	495	57.3	27.7	0	25	605	7.4	140	642	(0)	2.11	.60	12.7	—
Yield from 1 lb., raw loin without bone	8.7 oz	247	55.0	627	72.6	35.1	0	32	766	9.4	178	813	(0)	2.67	.77	16.1	—
Cup, chopped or diced pieces (not packed)	1 cup	140	55.0	356	41.2	19.9	0	18	434	5.3	101	461	(0)	1.51	.43	9.1	—
	1 piece or 3 oz	85	55.0	216	25.0	12.1	0	11	264	3.2	61	280	(0)	.92	.26	5.5	—
PORK, CURED: Light cure, commercial: Ham: Baked or roasted: Lean with fat (84% lean, 16% fat):																	
Yield from 1 lb., unbaked ham with bone and skin	11.3 oz	320	53.6	925	66.9	70.7	0	29	550	8.3	2,395	749	(0)	1.50	.58	11.5	—
Yield from 1 lb., unbaked ham without bone and skin	13.1 oz	372	53.6	1,075	77.7	82.2	0	33	640	9.7	2,782	870	(0)	1.75	.67	13.4	—
Chopped or diced	1 cup	140	53.6	405	29.3	30.9	0	13	241	3.6	1,049	328	(0)	.66	.25	5.0	—
	2 pieces or 3 oz	85	53.6	246	17.8	18.8	0	8	146	2.2	637	199	(0)	.40	.15	3.1	—
Lean, trimmed of separable fat: Yield from 1 lb., unbaked ham with bone and skin	8.7 oz	246	61.9	460	62.2	21.6	0	27	492	7.9	2,227	697	(0)	1.43	.57	11.1	—

Food, Approximate Household Measures and Market Units		Water	Food energy	Protein	Fat	Carbohydrate	Calcium	Phosphorus	Iron	Sodium	Potassium	Vitamin A value	Thiamin	Riboflavin	Niacin	Ascorbic acid
	Grams	Percent Calories	Grams	Grams	Grams	Milligrams	Milligrams	Milligrams	Milligrams	Milligrams	International units	Milligrams	Milligrams	Milligrams	Milligrams
Yield from 1 lb., unbaked ham without bone and skin																
10.2 oz	288	61.9	539	72.9	25.3	0	32	576	9.2	2,610	816	(0)	1.67	.66	13.0	—
1 cup	140	61.9	262	35.4	12.3	0	15	280	4.5	1,267	396	(0)	.81	.32	6.3	—
2 pieces or 3 oz	85	61.9	159	21.5	7.5	0	9	170	2.7	770	241	(0)	.49	.20	3.8	—
POTATOES: Baked in skin (refuse: skins and adhering potato, 23%): Potato, long type, 2⅓-in. diam., 4¾ in. long																
1 potato	202	75.1	145	4.0	.2	32.8	14	101	1.1	6	782	Trace	.15	.07	2.7	31
1 lb	454	75.1	325	9.1	.3	73.7	31	227	2.4	14	1,757	Trace	.34	.15	6.1	69
French fried: Length, over 2 in. to 3½ in																
10 strips	50	44.7	137	2.2	6.6	18.0	8	56	.7	3	427	Trace	.07	.04	1.6	11
RAISINS, NATURAL (UNBLEACHED), SEEDLESS TYPE: Uncooked: Package, net wt., 15 oz. (approx. 3 cups)																
1 pkg	425	18.0	1,228	10.6	.9	329.0	264	429	14.9	115	3,243	90	.47	.34	2.1	4
1 tbsp	9	18.0	26	.2	Trace	7.0	6	9	.3	2	69	Trace	.01	.01	Trace	Trace

Food	Measure																
RICE: Brown: Cooked, long grain: Cup: Hot rice	1 cup	195	70.3	232	4.9	1.2	49.7	23	142	1.0	550	137	(0)	.18	.04	2.7	(0)
White Enriched: Cooked (moist, soft stage), long grain: Hot rice	1 cup	205	72.6	223	4.1	.2	49.6	21	57	1.8	767	57	(0)	.23	.02	2.1	(0)
Parboiled, long grain, regular: Cooked: Hot rice	1 cup	175	73.4	186	3.7	.2	40.8	33	100	1.4	627	75	(0)	.19	.02	2.1	(0)
Unenriched: Cooked (moist, soft stage), long grain: Hot rice	1 cup	205	72.6	223	4.1	.2	49.6	21	57	.4	767	57	(0)	.04	.02	.8	(0)
SESAME SEEDS, DRY, HULLED, DECORTICATED:	1 cup	150	5.5	873	27.3	80.1	26.4	165	888	3.6	—	—	—	.27	.20	8.1	0
	1 tbsp	8	5.5	47	1.5	4.3	1.4	9	47	.2	—	—	—	.01	.01	.4	0
SHRIMP: Medium, approx. 2½ in. long	10 shrimp	32	70.4	37	7.7	.4	.2	37	84	1.0	—	39	20	Trace	.01	.6	—
	1 lb	454	70.4	526	109.8	5.0	3.2	522	1,193	14.1	—	553	270	0.05	.14	8.2	—
SOYBEANS: Mature seeds, dry: Cooked	1 cup	180	71.0	234	19.8	10.3	19.4	131	322	4.9	4	972	50	.38	.16	1.1	0
SOYBEAN CURD (TOFU): Piece (2½ × 2¾ × 1 in.)	1 piece	120	84.8	86	9.4	5.0	2.9	154	151	2.3	8	50	0	.07	.04	.1	0
	1 lb	454	84.8	327	35.4	19.1	10.9	581	572	8.6	32	191	0	.27	.14	.5	0
SPINACH: Raw: (chopped spinach)	1 cup	55	90.7	14	1.8	.2	2.4	51	28	1.7	39	259	4,460	.06	.11	.8	28
	1 lb	454	90.7	118	14.5	1.4	19.5	422	231	14.1	322	2,182	86,740	.45	.91	2.7	281
Cooked (boiled), drained: Cup, leaves	1 cup	180	92.0	41	5.4	.5	6.5	167	68	4.0	90	583	14,580	.13	.25	.9	50
STRAWBERRIES: Raw	1 cup	149	89.9	55	1.0	.7	12.5	31	31	1.5	1	244	90	.04	.10	.9	88
	1 lb	454	89.9	168	3.2	2.3	38.1	95	95	4.5	5	744	270	.14	.32	2.7	268

FOOD, APPROXIMATE HOUSEHOLD MEASURES AND MARKET UNITS

VALUES FOR EDIBLE PART OF FOODS

FOOD, APPROXIMATE HOUSEHOLD MEASURES AND MARKET UNITS			Water	Food energy	Protein	Fat	Carbohydrate	Calcium	Phosphorus	Iron	Sodium	Potassium	Vitamin A value	Thiamin	Riboflavin	Niacin	Ascorbic acid
		Grams	Percent	Calories	Grams	Grams	Grams	Milligrams	Milligrams	Milligrams	Milligrams	Milligrams	International units	Milligrams	Milligrams	Milligrams	Milligrams
SUNFLOWER SEED KERNELS, DRY:																	
In hull (refuse: hulls, 46%):																	
Pound (yields approx. 1⅔ cups hulled seeds)	1 lb	454	4.8	1,371	58.8	115.8	48.7	294	2,050	17.4	73	2,253	120	4.80	.56	13.2	—
Cup (yields approx. ⅓ cup hulled seeds)	1 cup	85	4.8	257	11.0	21.7	9.1	55	384	3.3	14	422	20	.90	.11	2.5	—
Hulled:	1 lb	454	4.8	2,540	108.9	214.6	90.3	544	3,797	32.2	136	4,173	230	8.89	1.04	24.5	—
	1 cup	145	4.8	812	34.8	68.6	28.9	174	1,214	10.3	44	1,334	70	2.84	.33	7.8	—
SWEETPOTATOES:																	
Cooked,																	
Baked in skin (refuse: skin, 22%):																	
Potato, 5 in. long 2-in. diam.	1 potato	146	63.7	161	2.4	.6	37.0	46	66	1.0	14	342	9,230	.10	.08	.8	25
	1 lb	454	63.7	499	7.4	1.8	115.0	142	205	3.2	42	1,061	28,660	.32	.25	2.5	78
SWORDFISH, BROILED WITH BUTTER OR MARGARINE																	
Yield from 1 lb., raw	10.1 oz	305	64.6	499	80.3	17.2	0	77	788	3.7	—	—	5,880	.11	.14	31.3	—
TANGERINES, Medium	1 tangerine	116	87	39	.7	.2	10.0	34	15	.3	2	108	360	.05	.02	.1	27
TOMATOES, RIPE:																	
Raw	1 tomato, 7 oz	200	93.5	40	2.0	.4	8.6	24	49	.9	5	444	1,640	.11	.07	1.3	42
	1 lb	454	93.5	91	4.5	.8	19.4	54	111	2.1	12	1,007	3,720	.25	.17	2.9	95

	Measure	Grams															
TUNA:																	
Canned:																	
In oil:																	
Solids and liquid:																	
7 oz	1 can	198	52.6	570	47.9	40.6	0	12	582	2.2	1,584	596	180	.08	.18	20.0	—
	1 lb	454	52.6	1,306	109.8	93.0	0	27	1,334	5.0	3,629	1,365	410	.18	.41	45.8	—
Drained solids:																	
6 oz	1 can	169	60.6	333	48.7	13.9	0	(14)	395	3.2	—	—	140	.08	.20	20.1	—
	1 lb	454	60.6	894	130.6	37.2	0	(36)	1,061	8.6	—	—	360	.23	.54	54.0	—
In water:																	
Solids and liquid: 7 oz	1 can	198	70.0	251	55.4	1.6	0	32	376	3.2	81	552	—	—	.20	26.3	—
	1 lb	454	70.0	576	127.0	3.6	0	73	862	7.3	186	1,266	—	—	.45	60.3	—
TURKEY, COOKED:																	
All classes, roasted:																	
Flesh only:																	
(not packed):																	
Chopped or diced	1 cup	140	61.2	266	44.1	8.5	0	11	351	2.5	182	514	—	.07	.25	10.8	
Light meat without skin:																	
Chopped or diced	1 cup	140	62.1	246	46.1	5.5	0	—	—	1.7	115	575	—	.07	.20	15.5	
Piece,	3 oz	85	62.1	150	28.0	3.3	0	—	—	1.0	70	349	—	.04	.12	9.4	
Dark meat without skin:																	
Chopped or diced	1 cup	140	60.5	284	42.0	11.0	0	—	—	3.2	139	557	—	.06	.32	5.9	
Piece,	3 oz	85	60.5	173	25.5	7.1	0	—	—	2.0	84	338	—	.03	.20	3.6	
WALNUTS:																	
Black:																	
In shell (refuse: shells, 78%), 1 lb (yields approx. 3½ oz., shelled nuts)	1 lb	454	3.1	627	20.5	59.2	14.8	Trace	569	6.0	3	459	300	.22	.11	.7	—
Shelled:																	
Chopped or broken kernels:																	
Cup	1 cup	125	3.1	785	25.6	74.1	18.5	Trace	713	7.5	4	575	380	.28	.14	.9	—
Pound (yield from approx. 4½ lb., in shell)	1 lb	454	3.1	2,849	93.0	269.0	67.1	Trace	2,586	27.2	14	2,087	1,360	1.00	.50	3.2	—
	1 oz	28	3.1	178	5.8	16.8	4.2	Trace	162	1.7	1	130	90	.06	.03	.2	—

FOOD, APPROXIMATE HOUSEHOLD MEASURES AND MARKET UNITS

Food, Approximate Household Measures and Market Units		Water		Food energy	Protein	Fat	Carbohydrate	Calcium	Phosphorus	Iron	Sodium	Potassium	Vitamin A value	Thiamin	Riboflavin	Niacin	Ascorbic acid
		Grams	Percent	Calories	Grams	Grams	Grams	Milligrams	Milligrams	Milligrams	Milligrams	Milligrams	International units	Milligrams	Milligrams	Milligrams	Milligrams
Persian or English:																	
In shell (refuse: shells, 55%):																	
Pound (yields approx. 7.2 oz., shelled nuts)	1 lb	454	3.5	1,329	30.2	130.6	32.2	202	776	6.3	4	918	60	.67	.27	1.8	4
10 large nuts (aprox. 1-5/16-in. diam.)	10 nuts	110	3.5	322	7.3	31.7	7.8	49	188	1.5	1	223	10	.16	.06	.4	1
Shelled:																	
Halves, 1 cup (approx. 50)	1 cup	100	3.5	651	14.8	64.0	15.8	99	380	3.1	2	450	30	.33	.13	.9	2
Pound (yield from approx. 2¼ lb., in shell)	1 lb	454	3.5	2,953	67.1	290.3	71.7	449	1,724	14.1	9	2,041	140	1.50	.59	4.1	9
Ounce (approx. 14 halves)	1 oz	28	3.5	185	4.2	18.1	4.5	28	108	.9	1	128	10	.09	.04	.3	1
WATERCRESS, LEAVES INCLUDING STEMS, RAW:																	
Chopped, finely	1 cup	125	93.3	24	2.8	.4	3.8	189	68	2.1	65	353	6,130	.10	.20	1.1	99
WATERMELON, RAW:	1 lb	454	92.6	118	2.3	.9	29.0	32	45	2.3	5	454	2,680	.14	.14	.9	32

Appendix C

Health Information, Counseling, and Referral Services

The following organizations provide a variety of publications and services for little or no charge. Before writing or calling, check your phone directory for local chapters. If you do write, enclose a stamped, self-addressed envelope.

AA World Services, Inc. (Alcoholics Anonymous)
P.O. Box 459, Grand Central Station
New York, NY 10017
(212) 686-1100

Action on Smoking and Health
2013 H St., N.W.
Washington, DC 20006
(202) 659-4310
(Specializes in the rights of nonsmokers)

Al-Anon Family Group Headquarters, Inc.
1 Park Avenue
New York, NY 10016
(212) 683-1771

Alcohol and Drug Problems Association of America
400 N. Capitol Street
Washington, DC 20002
(202) 737-4340

Alcohol, Drug Abuse, and Mental Health Administration
5600 Fishers Lane
Rockville, MD 20857
(301) 443-3783

Alliance for Information and Referral Services
P.O. Box 10705
Phoenix, AZ 85064
(602) 263-8856
(Contact the Alliance if you don't have a local Information and Referral Services office.)

Alternatives to Abortion, International
Hillcrest Hotel, Suite 511
Toledo, OH 43699
(419) 248-4471

Alzheimer's Disease Association
360 N. Michigan Ave., Suite 1102
Chicago, IL 60601

American Academy of Allergy and Immunology
611 E. Wells St.
Milwaukee, WI 53202
(414) 272-6071

740

American Academy of Child Psychiatry
1424 Sixteenth St., N.W.
Washington, DC 20009
(202) 462-3754

American Academy of Pediatrics
1801 Hinman Ave.
Evanston, IL 60611
(312) 787-5518

American Association of Retired
Persons
1909 K St., N.W.
Washington, DC 20049
(202) 872-4700

American Association of Sex
Educators, Counselors, and
Therapists
200 N St., N.W.
Washington, DC 20001
(202) 296-7205

American Brittle Bone Society, Inc.
1415 E. Marlton Pike, Suite 113
Cherry Hill, NJ 08034
(609) 829-6212

American Cancer Society
777 Third Ave.
New York, NY 10017
(212) 371-2900

American College of Radiology
20 North Wacker Dr.
Chicago, IL 60606
(312) 236-4963

American Council of the Blind
1211 Connecticut Ave., N.W., Suite
506
Washington, DC 20006
(202) 833-1251

American Dental Association
Bureau of Dental Health Education
211 E. Chicago Ave.
Chicago, IL 60611
(312) 440-2500

American Diabetes Association
2 Park Avenue
New York, NY 10016
(212) 683-7444

The American Dietetic Association
430 N. Michigan Ave.
Chicago, IL 60611
(312) 280-5000

The American Fertility Society
2131 Magnolia Ave. #201
Birmingham, AL 35256
(205) 251-9764

American Foundation for the Blind,
Inc.
15 W. 16th St.
New York, NY 10023
(212) 620-2000

American Group Psychotherapy
Association
1995 Broadway, 14th Floor
New York, NY 10023
(212) 787-2618

American Health Foundation
320 E. 43rd St.
New York, NY 10017
(212) 953-1900

American Heart Association
7320 Greenville Ave.
Dallas, TX 75231
(214) 750-5300

American Lung Association
1740 Broadway
New York, NY 10019
(212) 245-8000

American Medical Association
535 N. Dearborn St.
Chicago, IL 60610
(312) 751-6000

American Parkinson Disease
Association
116 John St.
New York, NY 10038
(212) 732-9550

American Podiatry Association
20 Chevy Chase Circle, N.W.
Washington, DC 20015
(202) 537-4900

American Psychiatric Association
1400 K St., N.W.
Washington, DC 20005
(202) 682-6000

Art Hazards Information Center
Center for Occupational Hazards, Inc.
5 Beekman St.
New York, NY 10038
(212) 227-6231

Arthritis Foundation
1314 Spring St., N.W.
Atlanta, GA 30309
(404) 872-7100

Association for Children with Learning
  Disabilities
5244 Clarwin
Pittsburgh, PA 15234
(412) 931-7400

Association for Voluntary Sterilization,
  Inc.
Public Information
122 E. 42nd St.
New York, NY 10168
(212) 573-8322

Better Hearing Institute
1430 K St., N.W., Suite 600
Washington, DC 20005
(202) 638-7577

Braille Institute of America
741 N. Vermont Ave.
Los Angeles, CA 90029
(213) 663-1111

Centers for Disease Control
1600 Clifton Road, N.E.
Atlanta, GA 30333
(404) 329-3311

Child Welfare League of America
67 Irving Place
New York, NY 10003
(212) 254-7410

Choice
15th and Cherry Streets
Philadelphia, PA 19102
(215) 567-2904

Committee to Combat Huntington's
  Disease, Inc.
250 W. 57th St.
New York, NY 10019
(212) 757-0443

Cystic Fibrosis Foundation
3384 Peachtree Rd., N.E.
Atlanta, GA 30326
(404) 233-2195

Department of Health and Human
  Services
200 Independence Ave., S.W.
Washington, DC 20201
(202) 245-6296

Environmental Defense Fund
1525 Eighteenth St., N.W.
Washington, DC 20036
(202) 387-3500

Epilepsy Foundation of America
4351 Garden City Dr.
Landover, MD 20785
(301) 459-3700

Federation of the Handicapped, Inc.
211 W. 14th St.
New York, NY 10011
(212) 242-9050

Fight for Sight, Inc.
139 E. 57th St.
New York, NY 10019
(212) 751-1118

Food and Drug Administration
5600 Fishers Lane
Rockville, MD 20857
(301) 443-3380
*(For local consumer affairs office, see tele-
phone directory in federal government
listing.)*

Health Resources Administration
5600 Fishers Lane
Rockville, MD 20857
(301) 443-2086 (cont'd)

742

Information and Referral Services
(Check your local phone directory. Trained specialists will refer you to the resources that meet your needs. This is perhaps your most important resource. If your area does not have this service, see Alliance for Information and Referral Services.)

Institute of Rehabilitation Medicine
New York University Medical Center
400 E. 34th St.
New York, NY 10016
(212) 340-7300

International Association of Pacemaker Patients
272 Boulevard, N.E.
Atlanta, GA 30312
(404) 523-0826

International Glaucoma Congress
211 E. Chicago Ave.
Chicago, IL 60611
(312) 787-3335

Juvenile Diabetes Foundation
23 E. 26th St.
New York, NY 10010
(212) 889-7575

La Leche League International, Inc.
9616 Minneapolis
Franklin Park, IL 60131
(312) 455-7730
(These people help with breast-feeding problems. Check your phone directory for a local chapter.)

Leukemia Society of America, Inc.
Education Department
800 Second Ave.
New York, NY 10017
(212) 573-8484

Library of Congress

National Library Service for the Blind and Physically Handicapped
Washington, DC 20542
(202) 882-5500

Medic-Alert Foundation International
2323 Colorado Ave.
Turlock, CA 95380
(209) 632-2371

Muscular Dystrophy Association
810 Seventh Ave.
New York, NY 10019
(212) 586-0808

The Myasthenia Gravis Foundation, Inc.
15 E. 26th St.
New York, NY 10010
(212) 889-8157

Narcotic Educational Foundation of America
5055 Sunset Blvd.
Los Angeles, CA 90027
(213) 663-5171

National Abortion Federation
110 E. 59th St., Suite 1011
New York, NY 10022
(212) 688-8516

National Abortion Rights Action League (NARAL)
1424 K St., N.W.
Washington, DC 20005
(202) 347-7774

National Anorexic Aid Society, Inc.
550 S. Cleveland Ave.
Columbus, OH 43229
(614) 895-2009

National Association for Retarded Citizens
P.O. Box 6109, Avenue E East
Arlington, TX 76011
(For local chapters see phone directory.)

National Association for Sickle Cell Disease
3460 Wilshire Blvd.
Los Angeles, CA 90010
(213) 731-1166

National Association for Visually
Handicapped
305 E. 24th St., 17–C
New York, NY 10010
(212) 889-3141

National Association of the Deaf
814 Thayer Ave.
Silver Spring, MD 20910
(301) 587-1788

National Association to Aid Fat
Americans
P.O. Box 43
Bellerose, NY 11426
(516) 352-3120

National Cancer Institute
9000 Rockville Pike
Bethesda, MD 20205
(301) 496-5737

National Committee for the
Prevention of Child Abuse
332 S. Michigan Ave.
Chicago, IL 60604
(312) 663-3520

National Committee on the Treatment
of Intractable Pain
P.O. Box 34571
Washington, DC 20034
(301) 983-1710

National Congress of Organizations of
the Physically Handicapped
6106 N. 30th St.
Arlington, VA 22207
(703) 532-4960

National Council on Alcoholism, Inc.
733 Third Ave.
New York, NY 10017
(212) 986-4433

National Federation of the Blind
1800 Johnson St.
Baltimore, MD 21223
(301) 659-9314

National Foundation for Asthma
P.O. Box 50304
Tucson, AZ 85703
(602) 624-7481

National Foundation for Ileitis and
Colitis, Inc.
295 Madison Avenue
New York, NY 10017
(212) 685-3440

National Foundation March of Dimes
1275 Mamaroneck Ave.
White Plains, NY 10602
(914) 428-7100

National Genetics Foundation
555 W. 57th St.
New York, NY 10019
(212) 586-5800

National Geriatrics Society
212 W. Wisconsin Ave. Centre Bldg.,
3rd Floor
Milwaukee, WI 53202
(414) 272-4130

National Handicapped Sports and
Recreation Association
10085 W. 18th Ave.
Denver, CO 80222
(303) 232-4575

National Heart, Lung, and Blood
Institute
5600 Rockville Pike
Bethesda, MD 20205
(301) 496-2411

National Hospice Organization
1901 North Fort Myer Dr., #402
Arlington, VA 22209
(703) 243-5900

National Huntington's Disease
Association
1182 Broadway
New York, NY 10018
(212) 684-2781

National Institute of Allergy and
Infectious Diseases
9000 Rockville Pike
Bethesda, MD 20205
(301) 496-1521

National Institute of Arthritis,
Metabolism, and Digestive Diseases
9000 Rockville Pike
Bethesda, MD 20205
(301) 496-5741

744

National Institute of Dental Research
9000 Rockville Pike
Bethesda, MD 20205
(301) 496-6621

National Institute of Mental Health
5600 Fishers Lane
Rockville, MD 20857
(301) 443-3877

National Institute on Aging
5600 Rockville Pike
Bethesda, MD 20205
(301) 496-5345

**National Institute on Alcohol Abuse
and Alcoholism**
5600 Fishers Lane
Rockville, MD 20857
(301) 443-4373

National Institute on Drug Abuse
5600 Fishers Lane
Rockville, MD 20857
(301) 443-6487

National Institutes of Health
9000 Rockville Pike
Bethesda, MD 20205
(301) 496-4000

National Kidney Foundation
2 Park Avenue
New York, NY 10016
(212) 889-2210

National Leukemia Association
Roosevelt Field, Lower Concourse
Garden City, NY 11530
(516) 741-1190

National Midwives Association
P.O. Box 163
Princeton, NJ 08540
(609) 799-1942

National Migraine Foundation
5252 N. Western Ave.
Chicago, IL 60625
(312) 878-7715

National Multiple Sclerosis Society
205 E. 42nd St.
New York, NY 10017
(212) 986-3240

National Organization for Women
425 13th St., N.W., Suite 1001
Washington, DC 20004
(202) 347-2279

**National Rehabilitation Information
Center (NARIC)**
4407 8th St., N.E.
Washington, DC 20017
(202) 635-5826

National Self-Help Clearing House
Graduate School University Center
33 W. 42nd St.
New York, NY 10036
(212) 840-7606

National Society for Autistic Children
1234 Massachusetts Ave., N.W., Suite
1017
Washington, DC 20005
(202) 783-0125

**National Society for the Prevention of
Blindness**
79 Madison Avenue
New York, NY 10016
(212) 684-3505

National SIDS Foundation
8240 Professional Pl., #205
Landover, MD 20785
(202) 459-3388
Toll free: (800) 221-SIDS

**National Wheelchair Athletic
Association**
40–24 62nd St.
Woodside, NY 11377
(212) 424-2929

Neurotics Anonymous
3636 16th St., N.W.
Washington, DC 20010
(202) 628-4379

**Occupational Safety and Health
Administration**
Department of Labor
200 Constitution Ave., N.W.
Washington, DC 20210
(202) 523-8017
(For regional office see phone directory.)

Office of Cancer Communications
National Cancer Institute
9000 Rockville Pike
Bethesda, MD 20205
(301) 496-4000

Parent Information Center
Coordinating Council for Handicapped
  Children
220 S. State St.
Chicago, IL 60604
(312) 939-3513

Parents Anonymous
22330 Hawthorne Blvd., Suite 208
Torrance, CA 90505
(213) 371-3501
(This group helps abusive parents. For local chapters see phone directory.)

Parkinson's Disease Foundation
Columbia University Medical Center
650 W. 168th St.
New York, NY 10032
(212) 923-4700

**Planned Parenthood Federation of
  America, Inc.**
810 Seventh Ave.
New York, NY 10019
(212) 541-7800

**Public Citizens' Health Research
  Group**
Dept. P
2000 P St., N.W., Suite 708
Washington, DC 20036
(202) 872-0320

Recording for the Blind
215 E. 58th St.
New York, NY 10022
(212) 751-0860

Scoliosis Research Society
444 N. Michigan Ave.
Chicago, IL 60611
(312) 822-0970

**Sex Information and Education
  Council of the U.S. (SIECUS)**
80 Fifth Ave.
New York, NY 10011
(212) 929-2300

The SLE Foundation of America, Inc.
95 Madison Avenue
New York, NY 10016
(212) 685-4118

Society for the Right to Die, Inc.
250 W. 57th St.
New York, NY 10019
(212) 246-6973

Spina Bifida Association of America
343 S. Dearborn St., Room 319
Chicago, IL 60604
(312) 663-1562

**Take Off Pounds Sensibly Club, Inc.
  (TOPS)**
P.O. Box 07489
Milwaukee, WI 53207
(414) 482-4620

**United Cerebral Palsy Associations,
  Inc.**
66 E. 34th St.
New York, NY 10016
(212) 481-6300

United Parkinson Foundation
220 S. State St.
Chicago, IL 60604
(312) 922-9734

United Stroke Program, Inc.
522 S. Sepulveda Blvd., Suite 101
Los Angeles, CA 90040
(213) 475-2714

**U.S. Consumer Product Safety
  Commission**
1111 18th St., N.W.
Washington, DC 20207
(202) 634-7740

Voice, Inc.
P.O. Box 3724
Grand Junction, CO 81502
(203) 241-2746
(Incest prevention and referrals to support groups for victims.)

Appendix D

QUACKERY
A $10 BILLION SCANDAL

A REPORT

BY

THE CHAIRMAN

OF THE

SUBCOMMITTEE ON HEALTH AND

LONG-TERM CARE

OF THE

SELECT COMMITTEE ON AGING

HOUSE OF REPRESENTATIVES

NINETY-EIGHTH CONGRESS

SECOND SESSION

MAY 31, 1984

Comm. Pub. No. 98–435

U.S. GOVERNMENT PRINTING OFFICE
WASHINGTON : 1984

Contents

Preface

Introduction

    I. Scope of the problem

    II. Committee and Subcommittee activities

    III. Arthritis and quackery

        A. Questionable drugs and serums said to cure arthritis

        B. Questionable dietary cures for arthritis

        C. Other questionable cures for arthritis

    IV. Cancer and quackery

        A. Historical cancer cures of questionable worth

        B. Questionable drugs and serums used in treatment of cancer

        C. Questionable dietary cures for cancer

    V. Anti-Aging cures and quackery

    VI. Witchcraft and spiritual healing

    VII. Curealls and other curious cures

    VIII. Paper promises

    IX. Devices

        A. Historical quack devices

        B. Quack devices said to "cure" arthritis

        C. Recent quack devices said to cure cancer

        D. Quack devices said to reverse the aging process

        E. Other questionable devices

    X. Clinics—Organized quackery

        A. Domestic clinics

        B. International clinics

    XI. Foundations

    XII. Enforcement efforts—Agencies responsible for combating quackery

        A. The Food and Drug Administration

        B. The Federal Trade Commission

        C. The U.S. Postal Service

        D. The Department of Justice

        E. State enforcement activities

        F. County and local governmental efforts to control health frauds

        G. Private efforts to control quackery

    XIII. Summary and conclusions

    XIV. Suggestions for reform

Appendixes

Appendix I. Questionnaire on consumer fraud efforts

Appendix II. Sample of questionnaires sent to the Council of Better Business Bureaus, Action Line Reporters, the National Arthritis Foundation, and the American Medical Association

Appendix III. Sample of an ad the subcommittee responded to

Appendix IV. Sample of a medical opinion received by the subcommittee concerning expert analysis of a questionable product

Appendix V. Sample of questionnaire submitted by the subcommittee to the Kushi Foundation

Appendix VI. Listing of books reviewed by the committee in the course of its review

Appendix VII. List of the basic standards in philanthropy provided by the National Charities Information Bureau

[Note: This is the table of contents of the actual Report, not of the excerpt we have included here.]

Introduction

The persons who seek the aid of health professionals are very honest and sincere in their wish to get rid of their complaints . . . there is nothing people will not do, there is nothing they have not done, to recover their health and save their lives. They have submitted to be half-drowned in water, half-cooked with gases, to be buried up to their chins in earth, to be seared with hot irons like slaves, to be crimped with knives, like codfish, to have needles thrust into their flesh, and bonfires kindled on their skin, to swallow all sorts of abominations, and to pay for all this, as if to be singed and scaled were a costly privilege, as if blisters were a blessing and leeches were a luxury.

Oliver Wendell Holmes

In 1978, the House Select Committee on Aging initiated a series of investigations and hearings into the panoply of frauds against the elderly. The Committee conducted more than 12 hearings on this subject, reviewing business frauds, pension frauds, medicare frauds, land frauds, insurance frauds, quackery, and health frauds directed at the elderly.

The Committee found the elderly were being targeted and systematically bilked by conmen and crooks. The elderly, which at that time accounted for 11 percent of our population, were found to account for more than 30 percent of the number of fraud victims in this country.

The Committee found the elderly were particularly vulnerable to quackery and health frauds perpetrated through the mail. The Committee received testimony indicating more than 60% of those victimized by health frauds perpetrated through the mail were elderly.

Because of the prevalence of these frauds and the particular vulnerability of the elderly to health frauds, Chairman Claude Pepper directed the Committee staff to conduct a detailed review of this problem. This report represents the findings of that inquiry.

This project began in the fall of 1980 under the sponsorship of the full Committee when Congressman Pepper was chairman. The work was continued and concluded by the Subcommittee on Health and Long-Term Care under Chairman Pepper's direction.

Summary and
Conclusions

In order that this complex subject can be presented with maximum clarity to the general public, this summary and conclusion section is presented in question and answer form. Obviously, the answers to the questions reflect the facts and conclusions found in the body of this report.

What is medical quackery as defined in this report?

Quackery as used in this report refers to the promotion of medical remedies known to be false or which are unproven for a profit, usually by means of false representations that they will "cure" or aid in the cure of various diseases and problems.

How did the Committee on Aging come to investigate the problem?

Between 1978 and 1982, the Committee conducted a dozen hearings on various frauds perpetrated against the elderly. The Committee learned that senior citizens make up 11 percent of the population but more than 30 percent of the victims of crime. Fraud is the most significant category of non-violent crime. The Committee sent questionnaires over the signature of Chairman Claude Pepper to all State Attorneys General, Departments of Consumer Affairs, District Attorneys, selected Police Chiefs and United States Attorneys. The responses were unanimous that health care frauds represent the single most important kind of fraud perpetrated against the elderly.

If health care fraud was the single most important kind of fraud perpetrated against the elderly, what are other problems?

The Committee learned that senior citizens are increasingly victimized in business opportunity frauds, questionable land sales, pension frauds, and through the sale of questionable insurance policies in supplementation of Medicare.

Is health care fraud limited to the elderly?

No. It affects all age groups. Americans of all ages have health care problems and out of hope, desperation or because they simply do not know any better, they often turn to unproven remedies. It should be emphasized however, that senior citizens by a wide margin are the number one victims of health fraud. Seniors make up 11 percent of the population but 60 percent of the victims of health care frauds.

Why are the elderly particularly vulnerable?

Senior citizens are vulnerable because they have very real health care problems. They are sick three times as often and three times as long as the younger population and their per capita medical bills are three times as high. These medical bills hit at a time when having retired, they have less than one-half of the income of their younger counterparts. Senior citizens are afraid of being ill and helpless. They are afraid of "going on welfare." They want to continue to pay their own way as independent, productive members of society. They do not want to become a burden on their families. Yet another reason is that seniors were raised in a more trusting, less cynical era. And then too, they are likely to have tried all manner of remedies in the search for help for their chronic medical problems. The average senior who lives to be 75 will have . . . four major disabilities. Finally, it should be stated that many seniors are lonely and welcome a friendly face at the door or a friendly voice on the telephone. It is sometimes easy to win their confidence and therefore defraud them. As one convicted confidence man told the Committee in 1980, "The elderly are particularly vulnerable. They make easy marks for the con man."

How long did the investigation take and what was its purpose?

The Committee's investigation took place over four years. It is the most comprehensive investigation of medical quackery and related health care frauds ever undertaken. The purpose of the investigation was to document the scope of the problem as well as what was being done about it and what should be done to deal with it. Another purpose was to give the public the best judgments of modern medical science about the effectiveness of various claimed remedies and to expose those who systematically seek to profit out of the pain of others.

Does that mean that the Committee condemns each unproven remedy mentioned in this report?

No. Many of the so-called "cures" listed in this report have been proven false. Others are so ludicrous that commonsense indicates they cannot be of much value. Others have a scintilla of credibility. It may be that the next major breakthrough in medical science is listed in this report, although that is highly doubtful. What the Committee is saying is that a cure or remedy, before it can be proclaimed as such, must be proven to be so through the established procedures of the scientific method. There must be unbiased, scientific evidence that a remedy is helpful and that it does not provide harm or untoward side effects before society can allow its widespread use by the general public.

Does this report and this investigation relate to home remedies used by individuals?

No. In the privacy of their homes Americans can and do try a host of unproven remedies. In many cases they believe such remedies help them. It is not within the scope of this report to condemn this practice. Nor is it within the scope of this report to limit what individuals can say about the purported remedy. The American public enjoys freedom of speech and is free to advocate whatever cause it likes, either through speeches or in writing books, pamphlets and articles. If and when individuals began to charge money for such writings or advice, with knowledge that the advice is false, then society should begin to become concerned. The old Consti-

754 tutional adage applies. It is said one's freedom to swing one's arm stops where another's nose begins.

If the practices of individuals are not the central focus of this investigation, what is?

The central focus of this report is on the profiteers who promote medical remedies known to be false or which are unproven for a profit generally through the mechanism of false representations that the product or therapy will "cure" or aid in the cure of various ailments. In short, the central concern of this report is people who deliberately seek to defraud the public and particularly the elderly. These promoters are sometimes individuals, sometimes major corporations or informal partnerships of several people who conspire to defraud the public often through the U.S. mails.

What steps did the Committee undertake in its investigation?

In addition to its questionnaires to local, state and national law enforcement officials, the Committee staff interviewed selected law enforcement officers and reviewed case files which they shared with the Committee. The Committee contacted the American Cancer Society and reviewed its files. Similarly, the American Medical Society agreed to let the Committee review its files of questionable medical remedies. The Arthritis Foundation also cooperated fully and all of its files were reviewed.

The Committee secured the cooperation of three institutes in the National Institutes of Health. Dr. Robert Butler, then Director of the National Institute of Aging, was particularly helpful. Dr. Jane Henney of the National Cancer Institute helped guide the Committee staff through its files. Similarly, the Committee received assistance from the National Institute on Arthritis, Kidney and Digestive Diseases.

The National Library of Medicine was asked for a print-out of all relevent articles related to unproven remedies. The Library of Congress provided all the information it had available in the form of articles in the press or books on the topic of medical quackery going back 30 years.

The Federal Trade Commission was contacted and it agreed to let the Committee staff review all its closed files and to give a summary of its ongoing cases. . . . By the same token, the Committee received the full cooperation of the U.S. Postal Service. The Committee staff reviewed all files relating to medical quackery in possession of that agency for the last 20 years.

The Committee contacted senior citizens directly and also through their national organizations. The Committee next assembled a list of the nation's most preeminent experts in the science of medicine. The list of these scientists is carried in Chairman Pepper's foreword to this report. These experts agreed to advise the Committee in its investigation and to evaluate various products and therapies.

Next, in cooperation with investigators detailed to the Committee by the U.S. Postal Service, the Department of Health and Human Services and the Federal Trade Commission, the Committee staff searched through advertisements appearing in over 100 major magazines and newspapers. Literally thousands of ads were evaluated and a number were answered, meaning that the offered products and cures were purchased. These products were then sent for analysis by the cooperating medical experts enlisted by the Committee. These products were evaluated in light of the representations made about them.

Finally, the Committee conducted six hearings specifically on the subject of medical quackery and mail frauds perpetrated against the elderly.

The massive evidence which was assembled forms the factual basis for this report.

What was the Committee's primary conclusion?

The Committee concluded that medical quackery is a massive problem. It is growing at an alarming rate. In 1965, at hearings by the U.S. Senate Special Committee on Aging, it was estimated as costing the nation $1 billion a year. Today the Committee estimates conservatively that it costs the nation more than $10 billion. Phony cancer cures constitute the largest share of such frauds, accounting for $4 to $5 billion a year. Questionable arthritis cures now cost the nation $2 billion a year and anti-aging remedies probably meet or exceed that total. It is important to add that these are only the costs associated with quackery. For example, with respect to arthritis, the total direct and indirect cost to the nation is estimated at $25 billion a year. These amounts dwarf amounts spent for legitimate research. For example, only $80 million was spent for research in arthritis in fiscal 1984.

In short, the size of the problem is massive and it is growing. . . . Moreover, enforcement efforts at the local, state or national level to prevent such frauds are almost non-existent. Only the U.S. Postal Service which is greatly overworked and undermanned has anything like a reasonable enforcement effort underway. The result is not only that millions of dollars are lost but that thousands of people every year suffer needless injury and death.

What are some examples of the questionable arthritis remedies discovered by the Committee?

It is a long list. First there are questionable drugs. Some promoters tout cocaine and novacaine as cures. Others push shots or pills made from the male or female sex hormones. Bee venom, snake venom, and ant venom has been touted. Then there are various diets and so-called food cures. Some promote green-lipped mussel extract; other say avoid potatoes and tomatoes; honey and vinegar is a favorite.

Various plants and herbs such as poke root, aloe vera, wolf herb, yucca, alfalfa, ginseng and rattlebox are put forward as cures, most often in the form of tea. Evidence is that not only are they not helpful, they may cause great harm as well.

Water has been put forward as a cure by some people. Sometimes it is salt water, mineral water, water allegedly from Lourdes or water altered with chemicals. It can be consumed by mouth, taken by injection, sprayed with a nozzle on various parts of the body. There is virtually no end to the permutations. However, it is not a cure in any form.

There are radiation "cures" where promoters have charged good money to lower sufferers down into uranium mines to be exposed to supposedly healing radon gas. Federal authorities stepped in to stop the practice. Vitamins and minerals are pushed as a cure as are copper bracelets.

The report notes that flu vaccines are not a cure, nor are light, acupressure, blood treatments, tonics, elixirs or thousands of different kinds of pills. Some supposed cures such as mud packs, cow manure poultices and so-called "moon dust" which is really just sand are ridiculous on their face.

756   *What are some examples of questionable cancer cures?*

Despite what some promoters would have one believe, eating grapes is not a cure for cancer, nor is ingesting ground up diamonds in powder form. Mistletoe, the juice from Easter lilies, ground up horse warts in a sour milk suspension, goat serum (made from goat intestines), Jojoba oil, serum made from human fecal matter, and asparagus oil have not been proven to cure cancer. Other questionable remedies include carrot juice, celery juice, coffee enemas, marijuana, mold, olive oil, snake meat, snake oil, sunflower seeds, and the Zen macrobiotic diet.

What are some examples of questionable "youth cures" identified by the Committee?

Phony "youth cures" constitute the fastest growing and maybe the most profitable of questionable medical remedies. One promoter was making over $110,-000 a day according to Postal Authorities is sales on phony diet pills. Another promoter made some $13 million on a phony hair restoring nostrum in about 9 months. There was the "instant face lift" which turned out to be nothing more than one page of facial exercises. Other kinds of products include products to soften the skin, to "make the person feel young again," to remove brown spots and cellulite. Of course, there is no product that will work in this way any more than there is a product known to medical science that retards baldness or helps grow hair back on a bald scalp. Other products offered "unrenewed energy." They consisted of herbs and pills which had no pharmacological effect or which contained caffeine equivalent to drinking several cups of coffee. Other remedies in this area offered to "end hot flashes" to heal the prostate with a vinegar preparation or by sitting on a hot light bulb. Still others promised to increase sexual potency. What these products have in common is that they do not work and that they are purely and simply a ripoff.

What about witchcraft, psychic healing, and spiritual healing?

Some promoters advertise in tabloids and magazines that they can cure arthritis, cancer and other maladies through witchcraft or voodoo. For example, in arthritis, one remedy is to split a frog, fry it in lard, and rub it on the affected part. Another voodoo remedy is to combine tobacco, salt and kerosene and rub it on the arthritic joint.

Psychic healers also promise cures either in person or over the telephone. Some of these promoters claim that they can perform surgery without a knife—that is without opening an incision. Similarly, the tabloids are full of ads from so-called spiritual healers usually called Madame Zelda or Sister Sarah or the like. They promise cures over the telephone once they have received the sufferer's money. Such healers appear to take on the mantle of legitimate religion but generally have no such affiliation. The Committee could find no scientific evidence that any of these methods were effective.

What are other examples of cures found in this report?

The report contains numerous examples of phony cures which did not fall into its three main subheadings: arthritis, cancer and youth cures. Some examples include the "natural birth control," which turned out to be advice to insert a lemon wedge in the vagina prior to sex. Another promoter claimed coffee enemas was the answer to gallstones. A "guaranteed herpes cure" turned out to be one mimeographed sheet of paper with advice on diet. In answer to an ad to improve eyesight without surgery, the Committee investigators received an elaborate kit including a phonograph record with advice to look directly into the sun and to exercise the eye muscles. An ad on how to be rid of warts brought one printed page advising shouting incantations at the moon—but only during the first quarter moon, never before or after. A hemorrhoid cure turned out to be advice to use vinegar on a cotton swab. The guaranteed psoriasis cure turned out to be a typewritten diet and the "former astronauts" formula for improved intelligence was essentially a multivitamin.

What about books that promote unproven remedies—isn't that free speech?

No. There is nothing wrong with publishing a book telling the world that chewing on old socks cured you of arthritis. That is free speech. When you start making representations about the book which are false and charging for the book, then it becomes a different matter, particularly if the advice you offer can result some way in public harm. In short, there is nothing wrong with writing the book. But claiming that you have the only cure to arthritis and charging $30 for the book can be fraud. Even so, it is *the advertising* and not your book that will be the forces of concern.

More and more promoters are turning to books and typewritten articles as the solution they offer to those who answer the ads they have placed in periodicals. The reason for this, according to postal experts, is that such promoters want to hide behind the protections of the First Amendment to the Constitution which guarantees free speech.

What are some of the examples of questionable devices which the Committee identified?

There are items as common as an ordinary vibrator which was received in response to an ad promising arthritis cure and as rare as the radon generator which supposedly generates radon gas for the same purpose. The spectrochrome is an example of a product alleged to be effective for a host of ills including cancer and arthritis. It is essentially a metal box with a 1000-watt light bulb in its center. Different colored filters are pulled in front of the light depending what malady one wants to cure. One further catch is that the moon has to be full and the patient nude and facing north for this therapy to work. The virllium tube cost $300. It is a piece of brass tubing about two inches long with a trace of barium chloride in its center. The solorama board which was supposed to aid in arthritis is in essence a hot pad made out of rigid plastic which one puts between the mattress and box springs. The acu-dot was a small round plastic bandage with a tiny piece of plastic in its center which was supposed to be applied to the skin at pressure points. The FDA pulled these products off the market because they were found to be ineffective.

Are there clinics which specialize in questionable or unproven remedies?

Yes. There are hundreds of clinics in the United States and Mexico which specialize in unproven remedies. Some clinics offer only "bootleg" remedies, others offer them in conjunction with legitimate and more conservative medical practice. Some clinics are run by well-educated practitioners and some by outright charlatans. It is very difficult to generalize except in one thing: this is big business. Millions of dollars every day are taken in by these clinics. The operation of some of them have been investigated and exposed. Many flout the law. Still others operate in the absence

758

of state law. Since the states have primary responsibility for regulating medical practice, there is little that the Federal government can do except in the case of drugs or products or advertising which is distributed in interstate commerce. These clinics, at least the ones in the United States, deserve closer scrutiny by the FDA. There seems little that can be done about the Mexican or other foreign clinics except through pressure on their governments.

What about foundations?

There are some enterprises that have been organized as non-profit, protected . . . corporations which are little more than fronts for promoters who are purveyors of fraudulent health care schemes. Of course, there are legitimate foundations and therein lies the problem. How does the public know the difference? How does the public know that a foundation with the word "cancer" in its name might be set up for a nefarious rather than a noble purpose? Then there is the question of accountability for public funds. What is done with the money that is taken in by these promoters? The U.S. Postal Service has brought legal action against several phony Foundations which were serving as fronts by which the public was being defrauded.

What about the government agencies which are supposed to police these kinds of frauds? Are they doing a good job?

In a word, no. The Food and Drug Administration is the agency with primary authority and yet it spends less than .001 percent of its total budget to combat medical quackery. To be precise, it spends $1.8 million out of a total of $362 million. This compares rather poorly with the estimated $10 billion quackery problem. The former FDA Commissioner, Arthur Hull Hayes Jr. excused this by saying the FDA was "simply overmatched . . . there are too many quacks, too skillful and the quick change of address and the product name for the cumbersome FDA."

The FTC has a budget of $66.9 million and says it has 14 people assigned to investigate medical quackery in the context of false claims and advertising. As noted, their efforts are imperceptible.

The FBI and the U.S. Department of Justice have shown no interest in health care frauds and in general there has been a decrease of emphasis on white collar fraud in the past two years.

The U.S. Postal Service is the one exception. It has a special unit called the Inspection Service which yearly handles over 200,000 complaints. In 1982, 5 people within the section were assigned to medical quackery and they investigated 79 cases, some 58 of which were referred to the Justice Department for prosecution. In addition the Service filed 54 false representation (civil) actions, 28 of which resulted in false representation, consent orders and the remainder were pending.

There is little emphasis on fighting medical quackery at the local level even though both State Attorneys General and District Attorneys identified it as the number one kind of fraud perpetrated against the elderly. What this means in general is that fraud ranks low on their list as compared to violent crimes. Frauds against the elderly ranked lower yet, and health care frauds ranked still lower.

What about private efforts to control fraud?

The Arthritis Foundation has done a commendable job in this respect. Credit should be given in particular to Mr. Charles Bennett. The American Cancer

Society has had a historical interest which seems to have waned somewhat in recent years. The American Medical Association had an excellent unit headed by Mr. Oliver Fields which was disbanded a few years ago under threat of an antitrust law suit filed by other health care providers who claim a share to the title "doctor."

What can be done about the problem?

First, there must be greater public awareness. This is one of the primary objectives of this report. Second, the states, which have the primary authority for enforcing criminal laws, must devote more of their resources to the problem. As noted in this report, two-thirds of the states do not even have adequate laws on their books to allow them to deal with the massive problem of health care frauds.

Third, the Federal government must increase its enforcement efforts. The U.S. Postal Service needs more inspectors in general and more of them assigned to medical quackery. The Postal Service also needs authority to issue investigative demands. The Service is handicapped at the present time and cannot get access to the books and records of promoters making the prosecution of fraud cases difficult indeed. The Federal Trade Commission once again must begin its efforts to monitor deceptive advertising in some serious way. The Food and Drug Administration has had a proud history but current efforts resemble indifference and neglect. The FDA is the best equipped agency in terms of resources and legal powers. It must make better use of these efforts to bring some of these promoters to the bar of justice and protect the general public and particularly the aged.

Criminal penalties for those who defraud the elderly under Federal mail order statutes are low and must be increased to allow for inflation if for no other reason. The current penalties ($1,000 fines in some instances) pose no real deterrent to those who can make $110,000 a day or $13 million in 9 months of operation.

It is clear that there must be greater allocation of public dollars for legitimate research in arthritis and cancer and diseases of the aged. Legislation recently passed by the House of Representatives as introduced by Chairman Pepper and Congressman [Henry A.] Waxman to create a separate National Institute of Arthritis should be enacted. Arthritis is too important and has too great an effect on the nation as a whole to be buried with a host of other medical problems and diseases. It deserves its own institute.

Finally, it is clear that some type of public clearinghouse is needed so that the public can call and learn whether a proposed remedy is legitimate. At the same time, Congress needs to establish a mechanism for the impartial testing of unproven remedies. The present system of relying upon major drug companies to come before the FDA and champion various new drugs which they think may have therapeutic effect is somewhat restrictive and inefficient. The FDA itself does not test potential drugs. There is good argument that some Government agency should do this directly instead of trusting to others who clearly have vested interests. If the FDA is not the entity which should do so, then there should be some other, perhaps under the jurisdiction of the National Science Foundation. Congress could then refer unproven remedies to such an entity for fair and objective trials the results of which would be definitive. This kind of agency would be an adjunct and not a substitute for the existing system.

Index

Abdominal pain, 15, 670
Abrasions, 676
Abravanel, Dr. Elliot D., 131
Acetaminophen, 417, 422
Acetylcholine, 135, 146, 578
Achilles' tendons, 44, 47
Acid indigestion. See Hyperacidity
Acne, 248–50, 424, 426
Acquired immune deficiency
  syndrome (AIDS), 250–52,
  296, 339
  cause, 251
  prevention, 252
  risk groups, 251
  treatment, 251
Acromion, 40
ACS, 300
ACTH, 472
Acupressure, 603
Acupuncture, 598
Acyclovir, 453
Additives, see Food additives
Adrenal cortical extract (ACE),
  347
Adrenal gland, 472
Aerobic exercise. See Exercise,
  aerobic
Aerobics, dancing, 25–26
Aging, and exercise, 11
Agpaoa, Tony, 655
AHA. See American Heart Association
AIDS. See Acquired immune
  deficiency syndrome
Airola, Paavo, 645
Albuterol, 51
Alcohol, 142, 496, 538
  abuse, 539
  and cancer, 291
  and pregnancy, 219
  and Vitamin C, 90
Alcholics, 87, 541
Alcoholics Anonymous, 138,
  542
Alcoholism, 81, 556
  aversion therapy, 542
  treatment, 542
  warning signs, 543

Alkaloids, 502
Alkylating agents, 460
All-heal. See Valerian
Allegro, John, 573
Allergic reactions, cosmetics,
  426
Allergy, 252
  insect stings, 258
  products, 414
Aloes, 505
Alpha-I antitrypsin, 321, 322
Alphafetoprotein, 222
Aluminum, 415
  chlorides, 427
  hydroxychloride, 425
Alzheimer's disease, 259–62
  causes, 259
  prevention, 261
  treatment, 261
AMA, see American Medical
  Association
Amanita muscaria, 573
Amblyopia, 85
Amenorrhea, 17, 30, 236
American Academy of Pediatrics, 643, 663
American Cancer Institute, 63
American Cancer Society, 63,
  287
American Chiropractic Association, 608
American Dental Association
  (ADA), 63, 315
American Diabetes Association,
  63, 345
American Heart Association, 63,
  126, 606
American Journal of Acupuncture, 605
American Medical Association,
  346, 444, 627
American Society of Clinical
  Hypnosis, 627
Amino acid, 5, 59, 60, 68ff.,
  83, 88, 135
  supplements, 71
Amniocentesis, 222
Amphetamine, 50, 552, 543
  and cancer, 291

Amygdalin. See Laetrile
Anabolic steroids, and cancer,
  291
Anaerobic metabolism. See Metabolism,
  anaerobic
Androgens, 51
Anemia, 30, 68
  acquired hemolytic, 265
  aplastic, 264
  folate-deficiency, 264
  hemolytic, 91
  iron-deficiency, 262
  macrocytic, 85
  pernicious, 263
  sickle-cell, 265
Angelica, 507
Angina pectoris, 465
Angioplasty, 273
Animal bites, 676
Anise, 507
Ano-genital warts, 209
Anorexia nervosa, 266
Anovulation, 17
Antacids, 414
Antiarrhythmics, 467
Antibiotics, 51, 445, 460
Anticoagulants, 469
Anticonvulsants, 86, 455
Antidepressants, 39
  tricyclic, 474
Antifungals, 453
Antihistamines, 39, 256, 414
  effect of Vitamin C, 90
Antihypertensives, 488
Anti-infectives, miscellaneous,
  453
Antilipemics, 470
Antimetabolites, 461
Antioxidants, 651
Antiperspirant, 424
Antispasmodics, 478
Appendicitis, 269
Appetite suppressants, 141, 419
Apricot kernals, 142
Arm hang. See National Fitness
  Test
Arrythmia, 29, 33, 363, 467
Arteries, coronary, 29

Arthritis, 40, 683
rheumatoid. See Rheumat-
oid Arthritis
Artificial sweetners, 129
Ascaris worms, 166
Ascorbic acid. See Vitamin C
Aslan, Dr. Anna, 620
Aspirin, 279, 349, 385, 403,
413, 415, 417, 421, 433
and impingement syndrome,
40
and Vitamin C, 90
Asthma
attacks, 16
cause, 270
from milk, 61
medicines, 415, 457
preventing attacks, 271
prevention, 273
questionable products, 416
treatment, 271
Atheroma, 273; *illus.* 274
Atherosclerosis, 3, 23, 53, 75,
91, 392, 517, 585
causes, 273
prevention, 279–80
risk factors, 275; *chart*, 274
Athlete's foot, 325, 428
Atkins' Diet Revolution, 63
Atkins, Robert, M.D., 115, 121
Atropine, 39
Attapulgite, 419
Autosuggestion, 628–30

Back pain, 671
Back to Eden, 306, 502
Backaches, 280
causes, 281
exercises, *illus*. 282–83
prevention, 284
treatment, 281
Bacteria, 445
drug resistant, 446
role in health, 446
Baking soda, 425
Baldness, 429
Banting, William, 113
Barbiturates, 495
Bearberry. See Uva-ursi
Bee pollen, 142
Belladonna, 478, 545, 623
Bennett, Iva, 123
Benzocaine, 420, 433
Benzodiazepines, 496
Benzoyl peroxide, 249, 424
Berger, Dr. Stuart, 135
Beriberi, 81
Bernheim, Hippolite, 626
Beta blockers, 466
Betel nut, 545
Beverly Hills Diet, the, 130
BHA, 290
BHT, 290
Bio-Diet, the, 130
Biofeedback, 329
Bioflavinoids, 97
Biotin, 87

Birth control, 192ff.
condoms, 192
diaphragms, 193
fertility awareness, 194
intrauterine devices (IUDs),
198
morning-after methods, 200
oral contraceptives ("the
pill"), 202–208
spermicidal barriers, 200
sterilization, 201
Birth defects, 386, 540, 548
prevention, 217–22
Bismuth subsalicylate, 163, 418
Bites, 676, 682
Black cohosh, 508
Blacking out, 677
Bladder, cancer, 586
Bleeding, 669
nasal, 685
Blindness, night, 79
see also Vision loss
Bloating, from lactose, 73
Blood, 7
clots, 469
doping, 51
flow, 7
packing, 51
sugar, 7, 73
in the urine, 672
Bloodroot, 508
Blue cohosh, 508
Body-contour creams, 140
Body-Type Diet, the, 130
Body types, 131
Boils (furuncles), 284–86
Bones, 32
broken, 669
surgery, 672
Boneset, 509
Bottle feeding, 226
Botulism, 162
Braid, James, 626
Brain damage, 540
Bran, 143
Breakfast cereals. See Cereals,
breakfast
Breast cancer, 231
self-examination, 299
Breast feeding, 225–27, 253,
273
Breast, sagging and pain, 25
Breasts, lumpy, 234
Breathing problems, 15, 39,
669, 673
Brewer's yeast, 69, 82, 144
Bromides, 423
Bronchitis, 286
chronic, 586
Bronchodilators, 457
Broom, 546
Buchu, 509
Buckthorn, 509
Buerger's disease, 585
Bulimia, 268
Burdock, 510
Burns, 425, 669, 673
Bursitis, 39

Butter, 65
Butyrophenones, 495

Cadmium, 109
Caesarean section, 228
Caffeine, 51, 546, 552
Calabar bean, 503
Calamine lotion, 432
Calamus, 510
Calcium, 102–103, 118
channel blockers, 467
in ideal diet, 64
and osteoporosis, 371–72
Calcium carbonate, 103, 414
Calculus, 308
*California Diet and Exercise
Program, the*, 127
California Morbidity, 638
Calories
illus., average amount
burned, 27
and exercise, 30
in fat, 77
from sugar, 74
Calories Don't Count, 115
Camomile, 510
Campylobacter, 162
Canadian Health and Welfare
Ministry, 316
Cancer, 78, 287–301, 529
basal-cell, 295
of the bladder, 548
breast, 462
of the cervix, 296
chemotherapy, 458–64
diet factors, 287
drugs that promote, 291–92
early warning signs, 298–
301, 674
fat, 287, 288
of the larynx, 586
of the lung, 586
and marijuana, 563
melanoma, 295
miscellaneous factors, 298
of the mouth, 586
obesity, 288
occupational hazards, 292
pancreatic, 586
prevention, 289, 298ff.
prostate, 462
psychological factors, 297
and sex, 296
skin, 295
squamous-cell, 295
and the sun, 295
of the uterine cervix, 586
Cannabinolism, 568, 572
Cannabis sativa. See Marijuana
Carbamide peroxide, 427
Carbenoxolone, 524
"Carbo" loading. See Carbohydrate, loading
Carbohydrate, 59, 65, 72ff., 77,
83, 117, 118, 123
loading, 31
Carbuncle, 285
Cardiovascular drugs, 464–71

Cardiovascular problems,
  and exercise, 33
Caries, 307
Carob, 145
Cartier, Jacques, 57
Carver, Willard, 608
Castaneda, Carlos, 576
Catabolism, and Vitamin C, 91
Cataracts, 402
Catnip, 511
Cayenne, 511
Cell metabolism, *chart*, 6
Cell salts. See Homeopathy
Cellulite, 140
Cellulose, 75
Center for Disease Control, 337,
  364
Cephalosporins, 448
Cereals, breakfast, 143
Cerebral vascular disease (CVD),
  392
Cervical dysplasia, 86
Cervical erosion, 231
Cervical intraepithelial neoplasia
  (CIN), 232
Cervicitis, 233
Chaparral, 634, 635
Charcot, Jean, 626
Cheese, 60
Chelation therapy, 605
Chemonucleosis, 284
Chemotherapy, cancer, 458ff.
Chest pain, 15, 38, 673, 675
Chi, 598
Chickenpox, 301–302
Child abuse, 364
Childbirth, 229
Chinese herbs, 512
Chiropractic, 606ff.
  danger, 611
  gadgets, 613
  history, 607
  and the law, 615
  manipulation, 609
  problems, 610
  subluxations, 609, 610, 614
  theory and practice, 608
  X-rays, 614
Chlamydia, 209, 398
Chloral hydrate, 498
Chloramphenicol, 454
Chloride, 107–108
Chlorpromazine, 579
Choking, 669
Cholecalciferol. See Vitamin D
Cholera, 162
Cholescystokinin (CCK), 130
Cholesterol, 10, 38, 53, 65, 75,
  78, 82, 115, 147, 275, 280
Choline, 86–87, 146, 422
  deficiency, 87
  sources, 87
  supplements, 87
Chondromalacia, 40
Chowka, P.B., 640–41
Chromium, 109
Chromosomes, defects,
  217

Cigarettes, filter, 588.
  See also Tobacco
Cinchona bark, 501
Circulation, 471
Circumcision, 230, 297
Citrus fruit, 60
Clinitest, 91
Clonidine, 488
Clostridium, 162
CMER, 38, 41, 42, 44
Cobalamine, 637.
  See also Vitamin B-12
Coca plant, 549
Cocaine, 548, 619
  addiction, 553
  effects, 551
  hazards, 552
  history, 549
  how to kick cocaine, 554
  illicit, 552
  pharmacology and physiolo-
    gy, 551
  and sex, 553
  and sports, 51
Cocoa butter, 431
Codeine, 417, 492
Coffee, 51, 539, 546
Colas, 51
Colchicine, 508
Cold and cough medicines, 416
Cold sores, 305
Colds, 302–305
Colitis. See Ulcerative colitis
Collagen, 88
Colloidal oatmeal, 432
Colon, 45
  therapy, 616
Colonic lavage, 616
Coltsfoot, 512
Comedos, 248
Comfrey, 513
*Complete Scarsdale Medical
  Diet, the,* 120
Condoms, 192
Congestive heart failure, 464,
  468
Constipation, 3, 306, 420, 675
Controversial alternatives, 598ff.
Convulsions, 675
Copper, 103
Coronary artery disease (CAD),
  33, 276, 334
  and exercise, 9
Coronary heart disease (CHD),
  334
Coronary occlusion, 10
Corticosteroids, 256, 458.
  See also Cortisone group
Cortisone group (corticosteroids),
  471
  nutrient interactions with,
    473
Cortisone, 43, 46, 51, 52, 385
Cosmetics, 248, 426
Cough, 675
Cough medicines. See Cold and
  cough medicines
Cousins, Norman, 641

Cramps, 45
  heat, 39
  from lactose, 73
  from milk, 61
  muscle, 33, 41ff.
  stomach, 33
Crocus, autumn, 507
Cromolyn, 458
  sodium, 51
Curl-ups. See National Fitness
  Test
Cuts, 676
Cyanide, 85, 502, 637
  poisoning, 143
Cyst, ovarian, 239
Cystitis, 398
Cytomegalovirus (CMV), 212
Cytotoxic testing, for allergy,
  255

Dancing, aerobic, 25–26
Dandruff, 429
Danthron, 421
Datura, 554
Davis, Adelle, 99ff., 144
Davy, Humphrey, 574
Day-care centers and hepatitis,
  337
Deep-knee-bend, 41
DEET. See Diethyltoluamide
Dehydration, 29
Dehydrocholesterol, 93
Demerol, 558
Dental and gum disease, 307–
  317, 587
  causes, 307
  early warning signs, 309
  and nutrition, 311
  prevention, 311
  problems, 689
  treatment, 310
Dentist, choosing a, 314
Deodorants, 424
Deoxyribonucleic acid. See
  DNA
Depression, 474
Dermatitis
  atopic, 257
  contact, 257
  psoriasis, 378
Desert tea, 513
DeSpain, June, 637
Devil's claw, 514
Dextromethorphan, 417
Diabetes, 9, 276, 317–320
  adult-onset, 115
  coma, 318
  pills, 318, 484
  prevention, 320
  recommended diet, 319
  Type I, 317
  Type II, 10, 317
  vision loss, 402
Diabetics, 75, 144
  and Vitamin C, 91
Dialysis, 354
Diaphragms, 193

Diarrhea, 547, 677
  acute, 418
  drugs, 479
  from lactose, 73
  from milk, 61
  remedies, 418
Diet
  aids, 419
  average American, 113
  near-zero carbohydrate, 115
  pills, 120
Diet for a Small Planet, 70
Diet sodas. See Sodas, diet
Diet Workshop, the, 139
Dietary Allowances. See Recommended Dietary Allowances
Dietary Goals for the U.S., 62–
  63, 128, 287
Diethylstilbestrol (DES), 200, 231
  and cancer, 29
Diethyltoluamide, 431
Diets, 111ff.
  high-fat, 78
  high-fat, low carbohydrate,
    113–17
  high-fiber, 75
  high-protein, low-carbohy-
    drate, 117–22
  high-starch, low-fat, 123–28
  macrobiotic, 63
  miscellaneous, 128–36
  prudent, 123
  recommended for diabetes,
    319
  table of comparisons, 114
Digestion, 68
Digitalis, 468, 517.
  See also Foxglove
Digitoxin, 517
Dimethyl glycine (DMG), 145
Dimethyl phthalate, 431
Diphenhydramine, 417, 423
Disacodyl, 421
Discs, vertebral, 280
  prolapsed, 284
Diuretics, 39, 487
Diverticular disease, 320–21
Dizziness, 15, 39, 677
DMG. See Dimethyl glycine
DMSO (dimethyl sulfoxide),
  212, 618
DMT, 555
DNA, 84, 85, 143
"Doctrine of signatures," 501
*Doctor's Quick Weight Loss
  Diet, the*, 121
Donsbach, Kurt, 652
Dopamine, 135
Double sugars, 73
Down's syndrome (mongolism), 217
Doxycycline, 162, 423
Dr. Atkins Diet Revolution, 115
Dreser, Heinrich, 421
"Drinking man's diet," 117
Drug allergies, 256
Drug ingredients
  basic list for home use, 438
    –39

Drug ingredients (cont'd)
  safe, 435; *table, 435–38*
  unsafe, 440; *table, 440–41*
Drug substitutes, 439
Drugs, 218
  and hypertension, 342
  nomenclature, 444–45
  and pregnancy, 218
  prescription only, 442ff.
  proper use, 442–43
  psychedelic, 52
  recreational, 538ff.
  and sex, 190–91
  synthetic, 502
Drugs, nonprescription. See
  "Over-the-counter" drugs
Ducosate, 421
Dufty, William, 74
duPont Diet, 115
Dynamic exercise, 8
Dysmenorrhea, 236

E. coli. See *Escherichia coli*,
  162
Ear care, 427
  problems, 427, 678
Earache, 678.
  See Hearing loss and ear-
    ache
Early warning signs, of cancer,
  298–301
Eber's Papyrus, 79
ECG. See Electrocardiogram
Eclampsia, 220
Eczema (atopic dermatitis), 239,
  256
  from milk, 61
Edelstein, Dr. Barbara F., 119
Edelstein's Women's Diet, 119
Edema, 68
EDTA, ethylene diamine tetraa-
  cetic acid, 606
Eggs, 60, 65
Ehret, Arnold, 133
Ejaculation
  incompetence, 182–83
  premature, 181
Elder, 515
Elecampane, 515
Electrical muscle stimulators
  (EMS), 140–41
Electroacupuncture according to
  Voll (EAV), 604
Electrocardiogram, 39
Emergencies, medical, 668
Emotional problems, 684
Emphysema, 321–22, 585
EMS. See Electrical muscle
  stimulators
Endocrine Society, the, 345
Endometrial hyperplasia, 233
Endometriosis, 233
Endometrium, 235
Endorphins, 602
Enemas, 616, 645
Environmental Protection
  Agency (EPA), 169, 294
Enzyme, 5

Enzymes, fat-burning, 11
EPA. See Environmental Pro-
  tection Agency
Ephedrine, 52, 415
Epilepsy, 323–24
Epinephrine, 33, 256, 416
Epstein-Barr virus (EBV), 365
Erythromycin and relatives, 454
Erythropoietic protoporphyria
  (EPP), 662
Escherichia coli, 162, 398
Estrogen, 17, 202, 235, 485
  deficiency, 25
Ethinamate, 497
Ethyl chloride, 33
Ethylene dibromide (EDB), 168
Eucalyptus, 516
*Everything You've Always Want-
  ed To Know About Energy,
  But Were Too Weak To Ask*,
  119
Exercise
  aerobic, 7, 14, 24, 26, 322
  and aging, 11
  beneficial effects, 9
  capacity, 15
  cooling down, 33, 38
  dynamic, 8, 23
  general principles, 32
  hazards, 32
  and heat, 39
  and illness, 16
  illustrations, 35–37
  importance of, 113
  injuries, 32
  isometric, 8, 23, 41
  for pleasure, 23
  risk factors, 38
  suits, 42
  stretching, 25
  warming up, 25, 33, 38
Exhaustion, heat, 39
Eye problems, 678.
  See also Vision loss

Fainting, 677
Fascia, 43
Fasciitis. See Plantar fasciitis
Fasting, 132, 645
Fat, 17, 59, 65, 77ff.
  allowance, *table, 66–67*
  deficiency, 77
  maximum for health, 17
  measuring, 17
  polyunsaturated, 275
  saturated, 77, 147, 275
  from sugar, 74
  unsaturated, 77
Fatigue, 679
  heat, 39
Fatness, 4ff.
Fatty acids, 116
FDA. See Food and Drug Ad-
  ministration
Female, masculinazation, 53
Female problems, 231ff.
Fenugreek, 516
Ferritin, 30

764

Fertility
  awareness, 194–98
  problems, 241
  rhythm method, 194
  temperature method, 197
Fever, drugs. See Pain-fever-in-
  flammation drugs
Fever, 679
Fibers, 60, 75, 290
  excess, 76
  supplements, 76
Fibrinolysis, 10
Fibroid tumor, 234
Fischman, Walter, 613, 644
Fish, 60, 70
  oils, 145
  worms, 165
Fitness, 4ff.
Fixx, Jim, 15
Flax, 516
Flu. See Influenza
Fluoride, 104, 309, 311, 315–
  317
Fluorides and Human Health
  (WHO report), 315
Fly agaric. See Muscaria
Folacin, 85–86
Folic acid. See Folacin
Food additives, (alphabetical
  list), 151ff.
Food allergies, 255
Food and Drug Administration
  (FDA), 141, 170, 349, 406,
  412, 444, 503, 571, 606,
  618, 649, 651
Food and Nutrition Board, Na-
  tional Research Council
  (NRC), 59
Food "poisoning," 161ff.
Food, processing, 60
Foods, high-fat, 78
Formula diets
  problems, 121
Four Food Group System, 60–
  61, 63
Foxglove, 517
Fracture, 669
Fractures, stress, 45–46
Fredericks, Carlton, 345
French Academy of Medicine,
  626
Freud, Sigmund, 189, 550,
  583, 626
Friedman, Meyer, 279
Frostbite, 680
Fructose, 72, 146
Fungus, 428
  infections, 325–26
"Funny bone." See Ulnar nerve

GABA, 135
Galactose, 73
Galactosemia, 218, 403
Gallbladder, 9
Gallstones, 326–27
Garlic, 279, 343, 517
  uses, 517
  hazards, 519

Gas, from milk, 61, 73
Gastrointestinal (GI) drugs, 477
Gentian, 520
German measles, 404.
  See also Rubella
Gerovital, 619
Ginger, 521
Gingivitis, 308
Ginseng, 520
Glands, swollen, 688
Glandular pill, 624
Glandulars, 146
Glaucoma, 404
Glucomannan, 146
Glucose, 5, 73, 83, 552
  metabolism, 52
  tolerance, 10
Glucose Tolerance Test (GTT),
  346
Glucose 6-phosphate dehydroge-
  nase (G6-PD), 91
Glycogen, 5, 31, 75
Glycoside, 524
  cardiac, 502
Goiter, 104
Goldenseal, 521
Gonorrhea, 210
Gout, 327–28
  medicines, 481
Grains, 60
GRAS (Generally regarded as
  safe), FDA list, 151
Green, Chad, 640
Grinims, Mark, 613, 644
Guanethidine, 489
Guerro, Dr. Luis A., 130
Gum disease. See Dental and
  gum disease
G6-PD. See Glucose 6-phos-
  phate dehydrogenase

Haast, William, 660
Hahnemann, Samuel, 623
Hair analysis, 110, 621
Hair care, 428
  problems, 686
Halsted, William S., 551, 557
Hanging upside down (inversion
  therapy), 622
Hangover, 539
"Happy foods," 135
Harrison Narcotics Act, 551,
  556
Hart, Fred J., 315
Hashish, 562
Hashish Eater, the, 567
Hay fever, 253, 414
Hayden, Naura, 119
Hayden's High-Protein Diet,
  119
Headaches, 39, 328–32, 681
  migraine, 329
  sinus, 330
  tension, 328
*Healing: A Doctor in Search of
  a Miracle*, 636
Health care plan, 691
Health Research Group, 361

Hearing loss and earache, 332–
  34, 678
Heart, effects of exercise on, 9
Heart attack, 33, 273, 585
  and exercise, 9, 38
  and overexercise, 15
Heart disease, 9, 23, 38, 53, 541
  ischemic, 91.
  See also Atherosclerosis
"Heartburn," 681
Heat
  cramps, 39
  and exercise, 39
  exhaustion, 39
  fatigue, 39
  stress, 39
  stroke, 29, 682
  syncope, 39
Hegsted, D. M., 62
Hellebore, American, 506
Hemicellulose, 75
Hemoglobin, 30, 88
Hemophilia, 218
Hemorrhoids, 3, 430
Hemp, 561
Henbane, 503, 521
Hepatitis, 334–39
  chemical, 53
  and day-care centers, 337
  non-A/non-B, 339
  Type A, 164, 335
  Type B, 296, 337
Herbs
  Chinese, 512
  extracts, 505
  medicinal, 501ff.
Hermaphroditism, 217
Hernia, 339–40
Heroin, 492, 496, 552, 555ff.
  addiction, 557
  hazards, 557
  history, 556
  overdose, 558
  synthetic, 558
Herpes simplex virus type 1
  (HSV-1), 305
Herpes, 210, 250
  genital, 00
  labial, 305
  oral, 00
Herpes zoster. See Shingles
Hesperidin, 97
Hexylresorcinol, 417
High blood pressure, 10, 23, 38,
  275, 392.
  See also Hypertension
Hiking, 25
Hill climbing, 25
Hippocrates, 9
Histamine blockers, 480
Histidine, 69
Hives, 254
Hoarseness, 675
Hodgkin's disease, 250
Hofman, Albert, 580
Holiday, 115
Holmes, Oliver Wendell, 625
Homeopathy, 623

Homosexuals, 213
Honey, 146
Hops, 522
Hormones, 33, 462
    adrenal, 52, 88
    human-growth, 52
    sex, 52
Human chorionic gonadotropin
    (HCG), 215
Humerus, 40, 48
Huxley, Aldous, 577–78
Huxley, Laura, 577–78
Hydralazine, 489
Hydrocortisone, 432
Hydroxocobalamine, 85
Hydroxyurea, 464
Hyperacidity, 71, 414, 681
Hyperglycemia, 317, 318
Hyperlipidemia, type II, 276
Hypermenorrhea, 236
Hypertension, 3, 9, 30, 91, 275,
    340, 585
    causes, 341
    drugs, 487
    prevention, 344
    treatment, 342
Hyperventilation, 657
Hypnosis, 625
Hypoglycemia, 344–47
Hypoglycemic Foundation, the,
    345, 347
Hypothyroidism, 279
Hysterectomy, 189, 234

Ibuprofen, 421, 423
Ice cream, 60
Ice massage, 46
Ideal diet, 63–64, 65
Immunization. See Vaccines
Immunosuppressants, and can-
    cer, 291
Impingement syndrome, 39ff.
Impotence, erective, 179–81
Inbreeding, 221
Incest, 221
Indigestion, 32
Infancy, over-feeding, 7
Infant rash, 687
Infants, nutrition, 225ff.
Infection, protozoal, 163
Infectious mononucleosis. See
    Mononucleosis
Inflammation, drugs. See Pain-
    fever-inflammation drugs
Inflammation, joint, 683
Influenza, 347–50
Injury
    head, 681
    jogging, 25
    kneecap, 40
    running, 25
    in sports, 32ff.
Inositol, 98
Insect repellants, 431
Insomnia, 350–52
Insulin, 91, 485
    response, 75
    shock, 91

Intercourse
    during pregnancy, 228
    painful, 179
Interferon, 464
International Chiropractic As-
    sociation, 608
Intrauterine device (IUD), 198–
    99
    problems, 199
Intrinsic factor. See Vitamin
    B-12
Iodine, 104–105, 464
Iridology, 631; *chart*, 603
Iron, 30, 88, 105–106
Ischemic heart disease, 91
Isoleucine, 69
Isometrics, 8, 41
Isotretinoin, 455
IUD. See Intrauterine device

Jason Winters Herbal Tea. See
    Winters, Jason
Jaundice, 683
Jenner, William, 498
Jock itch, 428
Jogging, 24
    women and, 25
John Birch Society, 650
Jolliffe, Norman, M.D., 123
Jones, Dr. Ernest, 583
Jones, Jim, 640
Jumping jacks, 24
Jumping rope, 24
Juniper, 522

Kaolin, 419
Kaposi's sarcoma, 250
Kava kava, 560
Kelly, Dr. William D., 641
Kempner, Dr. Walter, 123, 125
Kempner Rice Diet, 123
Ketamine, 560, 575
Ketones, 115
Ketosis, 115, 317
Keyes, Dr. Paul, 310
Kidney disease, 352–54
Kidney stones, 91, 354–56
Killing Cancer, 634
Kircher, Athanasius, 625
Kloss, Jethro, 306, 502, 509,
    531, 535
Knee injuries, 40ff.
    treatment, 41
Krebs, Ernst, Jr., 639
Krebses, Ernst, Jr. and Sr., 648
Kreskin, 628
Kurland, Dr. Howard, 603
Kushi, Michio, 123

L-asparaginase, 462
L-dopa, 84
La Costa Spa Diet, 123
Labial herpes. See Herpes, labi-
    al
Labor, childbirth, 670
Lactase, 73
    deficiency, 150
Lactation, 203

Lactic acid, 5
Lactose, 73, 552
    intolerance, 150, 390, 418
Lady's slipper, 524
Laetrile, 85, 142, 635
    molecular diagram, 637
Lanolin, 431
Laparoscopy, 233
Lappe, Frances, 70
Last Chance Diet, the, 122
Laugh therapy, 641
Lavender, 524
Laxatives, 420
LDL. See Lipoproteins
Leary, Tim, 580
Lecithin, 146, 278
Legumes, 60
Leucine, 69
Leucocytes, 91
Licorice, 524
Lidocaine, 552
*Life Extension—A Practical Sci-
    entific Approach*, 651
Ligaments, 32
    rupture, 33
Light-headedness, 15
Lignin, 75
Lily of the valley, 525
Lind, James, 57
Linn, Robert, D.O., 122
Linoleic acid, 77–78
Linseed, 516
Lipoproteins, 10
Liquid amino acid diet, 122
Lithium, 476
Little Cyanide Cookbook, the,
    637
Live Longer Now, 125
Liver, 147
    disease, 541
Lobelia, 502, 525
Loneliness, 363
Longevity Center, 126
Los Angeles Free Press, 641
Love, and mental illness, 363
Low-back pain. See Backaches
LSD (lysergic acid diethyla-
    mide), 52, 575, 580
Ludlow, Fitz, 567
Lung cancer, 586
Lysine, 69

Macrobiotics, 123
    diets, 63, 123
Macrocytic anemia, 85
Mafia, 639
Magnesium, 31, 106, 415
    salicylates, 422
Mail fraud, 597
Malaria, 356, 501
Male climacteric, 187
Malnutrition, 401, 547
Maltose, 73
Mammography, 299
Mandrake, 502, 525
Manganese, 109
Manic-depression, 474
Manner, Harold, 639

Mannitol, 552
Mantegazza, Dr. Paolo, 550
Margarine, 147
Marijuana, 561ff.
    addiction, 568
    and the body, 561
    and cancer, 563, 291
    and circulation, 564
    dangers, 562
    effects on mind and brain,
        566
    hazards, 567–68
    history, 561
    how to quit smoking canna-
        bis, 572
    as medicine, 570
    mental changes, 567
    and pregnancy, 563
    and respiratory problems,
        564
    and sex, 565
    withdrawal symptoms, 569
    and women, 563
Massachusetts General Hospital,
    640
Mastectomy, 189
Masters, Dr. William, 565
Mayapple, 526
Mayo Clinic, 636
Mazel, Judy, 128
McDonald, Larry, 650
McDougall, John, M.D., 127
*McDougall Plan for Super
    Health and Lifelong Weight
    Loss, the,* 127
McGovern Committee. See Se-
    lect Committee on Nutrition
    and Human Needs
McNaughton Foundation, 639,
    649
Measles
    vaccination, 368.
    See also Rubella
Meat, 60
    in ideal diet, 65
Mebendazole, 166
MECE, 33
"Medical Heretic," 642
Medical Reclassification Project,
    571
Meditation. See Relaxation/
    Meditation
Megavitamins, 82, 362.
    See also Vitamins, mega-
        doses
Menaquinone. See Vitamin K
Mendelsohn, Robert S., M.D.,
    642
Menopause, 187
Menstruation
    irregularity, 235
    problems, 235ff., 683
Mental and emotional distur-
    bances, 3, 359–64
Mental illness, 359
Mental problems, 684
Mental retardation, prevention,
    217

Menthol, 417
Meperidine, 491, 558
Meprobamate, 497
Merck Index, 648
Mescaline, 52, 575, 581
Mesmer, Franz, 625
Metabolic block, 218
Metabolism, 5ff., 118
    anaerobic, 5, 15, 31
    carbohydrate, 88
    glucose, 52
Metaproterenol, 416
Methadone, 559
Methapyrilene, 423
Methionine, 69
Methylcellulose, 420
Methyldopa, 489
Methylphenidate (Ritalin), 50
Metropolitan Life Insurance
    Company, tables of desirable
    weights, 112
Miconazole, 428
Midwife. See Nurse-midwife
Milk, 60, 69
    allergies from, 61
    and cataracts, 403
    certified, 148
    intolerance, 45, 61
    raw, 147, 163
Milk sugar. See Lactose
Minerals, 59, 102ff.
    trace, 58
Minipill, 203
Miscarriage, 217, 386
Miscellaneous diets, 128–136
Mistletoe, 526
Mitrolan, 418
Molecular diseases, 217
Moles, 295
Molybdenum, 109
Mongolism. See Down's syn-
    drome
Mono-ideaism, 628–30
Monoclonal antibodies, 462
Monoamine oxidase inhibitors
    (MAOIs), 475
Mononucleosis, 364–65
Morning glory, 572
Morphine, 492, 503, 555
Mouth sores, 684
MPTP, 558
MRT. See Muscle response test-
    ing
*Mucusless Diet and Healing
    System, the,* 133
Mullein, 526
Multiple sclerosis (MS), 365
Multiple Sclerosis Diet Book,
    367
Multiple Sclerosis Society, 367
Mumps, 367
Muscaria, 573
Muscle response testing (MRT),
    644
Muscles, 32
    cell, 5
    cramps, 33, 41 ff.
    fibers, 52

Muscles (cont'd)
    protein, 5
    spasms, 38
    strain, 42
    wasting, 68
Mushrooms, 581
Mycotoxins, 163
Myelin, 84
Myocardial infarction (MI), 273
Myoinositol, 98
Myrrh, 527

Nancy School of Hypnotism,
    626
Naphazoline, 428
Nasal congestion, from milk, 61
Nasal discharges, 685
National Academy of Sciences,
    618
National Cancer Institute, 287,
    316, 506, 635, 636
National Commission on
    Marijuana and Drug Abuse
    (Shafer Commission), 568
National Enquirer, the, 643,
    644
National Fitness Test
    exercises, 20
    table of scores, 21
National Health Federation
    (NHF), 315
National Institute of Drug
    Abuse, 563
National Institute on Aging, 620
National Multiple Sclerosis So-
    ciety, 660
National Research Council
    (NRC), 59
Native American Church, 581
Naturopathy, 645
Nausea, 39, 677
    drugs, 479
Net protein utilization (NPU), 69
Neurotransmitters, 86, 135,
    578, 602
New Age, 640
New York City Health Depart-
    ment Diet, the, 123
NGU. See Nongonococcal ure-
    thritis
Niacin, 82, 471.
    See also Vitamin B-3
Nickel, 109
Niclosamide, 166
Nicotine. See Tobacco
Nicotine addiction, 583
Night blindness, 79
Nitrates and nitrites, 90, 288,
    465
Nitrogen, retention, 118
Nitroglycerine, 465
Nitrosamines, 90
Nitrous oxide, 574
"No pain, no gain," 15
Nolen, William, Dr., 636
"Non-Glue Food" Diet, 117
Nongonoccal urethritis (NGU),
    209

Nonspecific bacterial vaginitis, 213, 240
Nonsteroidal anti-inflammatory agents (NSAIDS), 422, 491
for gout, 482
Norepinephrine, 33, 135, 578
Novocaine, 619
NPU. See Net protein utilization
NSAIDS. See Nonsteroidal anti-inflammatory agents
Nuclear radiation, and cancer, 293
Nurse-midwife, 215
Nutmeg, 574
Nutrients, 57, 59
Nutrition, 57ff.
and cancer, 289–90
and dental disease, 311
infants, 225ff.
and mental illness, 362
Nutritive value of common foods, *table*, 715–38
Nuts, 60
Nux vomica, 527, 623

Obesity, 7, 38, 78, 276, 288, 341
behavior control approach, 137
early prevention, 139
Occupational Safety and Health Administration (OSHA), 292
Oleander, 527
Oleomargarine. See Margarine
Opiates, 492
Opium, 479, 503, 555
Opsin, 79
Oral contraceptives, 202–208, 392
bonus benefits, 204
side effects, hazards, 204–207
when not to use, 207–208
Orgasm, 176
Orr, Leonard, 656
Orris root, 528
OSHA. See Occupational Safety and Health Administration
Oshawa, George, 123
Osteoarthritis, 368–70
Osteomalacia, 92
Osteoporosis, 3, 10, 17, 239, 370–73, 485, 587
Ovarian cysts, 239
"Over-the-counter" drugs (OTCs), 411ff.
Overeaters Anonymous, 139
Overexercise, dangers, 15
Ovulation, 197
Oxalic acid, 91
Oxybenzone, 433
Oxycodone, 492
Oxygen, maximum-consumption test, 18

PABA. See Para-aminobenzoic acid
Pain, 15
chest, 15, 38

Pain (cont'd)
muscle, 33
stomach, 15
Pain-fever-inflammation drugs, 421
Painkillers, 490
Palmer, BJ, 607
Palmer College of Chiropractic, 608
Palmer, Daniel David, 607, 608
Palmer School of Chiropractic, 607
Palpitations, 673
Pangamic acid, 145, 646, 647
Russian studies, 649
Pantothenic acid, 88
Pap smear, 216, 668
Para-aminobenzoic acid (PABA), 97, 433
Paracelsus, 501
Paraldehyde, 498
Parasites, 161ff.
Parathyroid hormone, 102
Parkinsonism, 84
Passion flower, 528
Passwater, Richard A., 95, 100
Patella, 40
Pauling, Dr. Linus, 92
PCP, 575
Peach kernals, 502
Pearson, Durk, 650
Pearson/Shaw Longevity Theory, 650
Pectin, 75, 82, 147, 419
Pelvic inflammatory disease (PID), 210
Penicillin, 209, 210, 376, 446, 449
Pennington, Dr. Alfred, 115
Pennyroyal, 528
Pentazocine, 492
People's Temple, the, 640, 641
Peppermint, 529
Peptic ulcers, 373–76, 587
cautions, 375
and diet, 375
Pepto Bismol, 163, 418
Periodontal disease, 308
Peripheral vascular disease, 585
Peristalsis, 45
Peritonitis, 269
Periwinkle, 529
alkaloids, 462
Pesticides, 170
Petroleum jelly, 431
Peyote, 52, 581
Phenobarbitol, 456, 478
Phenol, 417
Phenolphthalein, 421
Phenothiazines, 39, 494
Phenylalanine, 69, 135
Phenylketonuria (PKU), 218
Phenylpropanolamine (PPA), 419
Phospholipids, 86
Phosphorous, 106–107
Photosensitivity, 427, 486
Phylloquinone. See Vitamin K
Physical examination, 667–68

Physician, choosing a, 692
"The Pill," see Oral contraceptives
Piperazine, 166
Plant oils, 502
Plantar fasciitis, 43
Plaque, 308, 311
Pleurisy root, 530
PMS. See Premenstrual Syndrome,
Pneumocystis carinii pneumonia (PCP), 250
Pneumonia, 376–77
Podophyllum, 502
Poison oak and ivy, 257
Poisoning, 685
Pokeweed, 530
Pollution, 166–71
air, 24, 167
and cancer, 294
food, 170
water, 168
Polycarbophil, 418
Polynuclear aromatic hydrocarbons (PAHs), 564
Polyps, 239
Polysugars, 74
Polyunsaturated fats. See Fat, polyunsaturated
Poor person's weight gym, 37
Pope Clement VIII, 546
Postmenopausal estrogens, and cancer, 291
Potassium, 30, 107
Potassium chloride, 99
Poultry, 60
Prazosin, 489
Pregnancy,
and alcohol, 219
critical period, 219
and drugs, 218
disorders, 222
etopic (tubal), 199
exercise during, 228
infections during, 220
intercourse during, 228
and marijuana, 563
septic,
toxemia, 220
X-rays during, 220
Premenstrual syndrome (PMS), 238
Prenatal care, 215–17
Preorgasmia, 177–78
Preparation H, 431
Prevention, 95, 345, 643
Priapism, 183
Primadone, 457
Pritikin, Nathan, 125
Pritikin Program, the, 125
Procaine, 552, 619
Produce, in ideal diet, 64
Progesterone, 235
Progestogen, 202
"Prolinn," 122
Propanolol, 466
Propoxyphene, 493
Propranolol, 490

Prostaglandins, 77, 377
Prostate gland, 377
Prostatectomy, 189
Prostatitis, 377–78
Protein, 59, 65, 68ff., 77, 83, 117
  deficiency, 68
  excessive, 70
  in ideal diet, 64
  quality, 69
  requirements, 30
  RDA, 68
  source, 68
  supplements, 30, 70–71
  synthesis, 79
Prudent Diet, the, 123
Prudent diets, 123
Psilocin, 577, 581
Psilocybin, 575, 577, 581
Psilocybin mushroom, 52
Psoralens, 379
Psoriasis, 378–80
Psychedelic drugs, 52, 576
  and the brain, 578
  hazards, 578
  what they do, 577
Psychic surgery, 655
Psychotherapy, 359
  electroconvulsive therapy, 361
  finding a therapist, 360
Psyllium, 420
Public Citizen Health Research Group (HRG), 412
Pulse, 18
  Five-Minute Rule, 14
  Five-minute test, 18
  measuring, 14
  pulse reduction test, 18
  recovery rate, 18
  resting, 9
  resting pulse test, 18
  Ten-Minute Rule, 14
  Twelve-minute test, 18
Punctures, 676
Push-ups. See National Fitness Test
PUVA therapy, 379
Puysegur, Marquis de, 626
Pyridoxine, see Vitamin B-6
Pyrilamin, 423
Pyrrolizidine, 504
Pyruvate, 5

Quackery, 597–99
  chart, 598
  Pepper Report, 747
Questionable products
  for asthma, 416
  for colds, 417
  for diarrhea, 419
  diet aids, 420
  laxatives, 421
  for pain, fever, inflammation, 423
  sleep aids, 424
Quick Headache Relief Without Drugs 603
Quinine, 357, 552

Rabies,
  chart, 381
  immunization, 383
Rapid eye movement (REM) sleep, 350, 496
RAST test (radioallergosorbant technique), 253
RDA. See Recommended Dietary Allowances
Rebirthing, 656
Recommended Dietary Allowances (RDA), 59ff.; *chart, 712–13*
Red clover, 531
Red elm. See Slippery elm
Red 3, food coloring, 104
Redbook, 123
Reducing gimmicks, 140–41
Reflexology, 603
Reich, Wilhelm, 189
Relaxacisor, 141
Relaxation/Meditation, 658
Reserpine, 490, 501
Restak, Richard, M.D., 364
Retinol. See Vitamin A
Rh disease, 220
Rheaban, 419
Rheumatoid arthritis (RA), 383–86
  and nutrition, 385
Rhinitis, 414
Rhodopsin, 79
Riboflavin, 82.
  See also Vitamin B-2
RICE, 33
Richardson, John, M.D., 639
Rickets, 92
Ringworm, 428
Ritalin. See Methylphenidate
RNA, 143
Rosenman, Ray, 279
Roughage, 75
Rubella, 386–87
Rubin, Dr. David, 639
Rue, 531
Runner's knee, 40
Running, in place, 24
Rutin, 97

Saccharin, 288
Sacred Mushroom and the Cross, the, 573
"Sad foods," 135
Safrole, 575
Sage, 531
Salicylic acid, 434
Salmonella, 147, 161, 163
Salt, 125
  and sweating, 29
Sarsaparilla, 532
Sassafras, 532
Saturated fats. See Fat, saturated
Saw palmetto, 532
Scarsdale Diet, the, 120
Schizophrenia, drugs for, 493
Sciatica, 281
Scoliosis, 387–88

Scopolamine, 423
Scotch broom, 546
Scullcap, 533
Scurvy, 89, 92
SDA. See Specific dynamic action, 120
Seizures, 675
Select Committee on Nutrition and Human Needs (the McGovern Committee), 62
Selenium sulfide, 429
Self-hypnosis. See Autosuggestion
Separate Reality, a, 576
Senna, 421, 533
Serotonin, 135, 352, 578
75 percent rule, 13, 38
Sex,
  aids, 184–85
  and cancer, 296
  after childbirth, 186
  after diabetes, 188
  and drugs, 190–91
  dysfunctions, 177
  education, 175
  frequency, 186
  and the heart patient, 188
  during hospitalization, 189
  in illness, 188
  in later life, 187
  during menstruation, 185
  and mental illness, 189
  during pregnancy, 185
  and sports, 186
  therapy, 183–84
Sexercises, 184
Sexual response, 176–77
Sexually transmitted diseases (STDs), 209ff, 686
  prevention, 214
Shafer Commission. See National Commission on Marijuana and Drug Abuse
Shampoos, 430
Shark-liver oil, 431
Shaw, Sandy, 650
Shigella, 162
Shin splints, 43–44
Shingles, 388–89
Shock, 670
Shock, insulin, 91
Shock treatment. See Psychotherapy, elecroconvulsive therapy
Sickle-cell anemia, 91, 218, 265
Side stitches, 33
SIDS. See Sudden infant death syndrome
Silicon, 109
Silver nitrate, 210
Simethicone, 415
Simon, Martha, 123
Simple sugars, 72–73
Sinsemilla, 562
Sinuses, 389–90
  headache, 330
Sit and reach. See National Fitness Test
Skiing, cross-country, 24

Skin cancer. See Cancer, skin
   problems, 686
   resistance, 659
Skunk lily, 146
Slater, Ralph, 627
Sleep, 350ff.
   aids, 423, 495
   factors that inhibit, 351
   factors that promote, 352
Sleeping pills. See Sleep, aids
Slippery elm, 533
Sloan Kettering Memorial Insti-
   tute, 636
Smallpox, 498
Smokers, 168
Smoking, 38, 275
   and cancer, 291
   how to stop, 588
   and hypertension, 342
   and stroke, 392
   and Vitamin C, 90
Snake venom, 659
Snakeroot, 529, 534
Soaps, 433
Sodas, diet, 145
Sodium bicarbonate, 415
Sodium, 107–108
Solar elastosis, 296
Sorbinil, 319
Sore throat, 417, 688
Southampton Diet, the, 135
Soy protein, 278
Spasms, muscle, 38
Spastic colon, 390–91
"Special" foods, 142ff.
Specific dynamic action (SDA),
   117
"Speed," 52, 544
Spermicidal cream, 193
Spirulina, 148
Sports, injuries, 32ff.
Sprains, 38, 44–45, 672
   knee, 40
Sprouts, 148
Squaw root. See Black cohosh,
   Blue cohosh
Stanford University, marijuana
   study, 567
Staphylococcal bacteria, 446
Staphylococcus aureus, 162
Starch
   blockers, 141, 420
   in ideal diet, 64
STDs. See Sexually transmitted
   diseases
Step test, the. See National Fit-
   ness Test
Sterilization, 201–202
Steroids, 51, 52, 472, 473, 502
Stillbirths, 587
Stillman, Dr. Irwin M., 121
Stillman diet, the, 118, 121
Stimulants, 39
Stings, 682
   insect, 258
   remedies, 432
Stitches, 45
Stomach cramps, 33

Stomach pain. See Abdominal
   pain
Stomachache. See Abdominal
   pain
Strains, 38, 672
   muscle, 33
Strep throat, 391
Stress, emotional, 11, 279
Stress, fractures, 45–46
Stress, of tissues, 32
Stress test, 39
Stretching, 25, 33
Strokes, 91, 392–93, 585
   early warning signs, 392
   risk factors, 393
Stuart, S. L., 122
Stupor, 670
Sucrose, 73
Sudden infant death syndrome
   (SIDS), 227
Sugar Blues, 74
Sugar, 31, 74. See also Fruc-
   tose, Galactose, Glucose,
   Maltose, Sucrose
Sulfonamides, 450
Sultan Murad IV, 583
Sun, the, and cancer, 295
Sun protection factor (SPF), 433
Sunburn, 433, 687
Sunscreens, 433
Supernutrition, 100
Superoxide dismutase (SOD), 148
Supplements, dietary, 64ff.
Swank, Roy, 367
Sweat suits, 140
Sweating, 29
   profuse, 39
Sydenhan, Thomas, 327
Sympathetic sickness, 224
Symptoms requiring medical
   care, 670
Syncope, heat, 39
Syphilis, 213

Table sugar. See Sucrose
Taller, Herman, M.D., 115
Tannic acid, 503
"Tanning" pills, 661
Tansy, 534
Tapeworms, 165
Tardive dyskinesia (TDK), 87,
   495
Tarnower, Dr. Herman, 120
Taurine, 69
Tay-Sachs disease, 218
Tea, 51
Teeth, broken, 669
Tempeh, 149
Tendonitis, 40
   rotator cuff, 39
Tendons, 32, 44, 47
   rupture, 47
Tennis elbow, 47–48
Testape test, 91
Testicles, atrophy of, 53
   removal, 189
Testosterone, 10, 52–53, 187
Tetracycline, 209, 210, 451

Tetrahydrozoline, 428
THC (Tetrahydracannabinol),
   561ff.
Theophylline, 51, 415
Thiabendazole, 165
Thiamin, 432.
   See also Vitamin B-1
Thioxanthines, 495
Threonine, 69
Thrower's elbow, 48–49
Thrush, 250
Thyroid drugs, 485
Thyroid gland, 104
Thyroxin, 104
Tin, 109
Tobacco, 564, 582
   amblyobia, 85
   and cancer, 291
   chewing and snuff, 588
   dangers, 585ff.
   history, 582
   how to stop smoking, 588
   nicotine addiction, 583
   withdrawal symptoms, 584
Tocopherol. See Vitamin E
Tofu, 149
Tolnaftate, 428
Tonka bean, 534
Tonometric examination, 405
Tonsillectomy, 391
Toothache, 689.
   See also Dental and gum
   disease
Topical products, 424
TOPS (Take Off Pounds Sensi-
   bly), 138
Toxic shock syndrome (TSS),
   162, 240, 393–95
Toxoplasmosis, 250
Trace elements, 58, 60, 79,
   109–110
Trachoma, 401
Tranquilizers, 495
Transcendental Meditation (TM),
   659
Transient ischemic attacks
   (TIAs), 392
Traveler's diarrhea, 162
Tretinoin, 249
Trichinellosis, 165
Trichinosis. See Trichinellosis
Trichomoniasis, 213
Tryptophan, 69, 71, 135, 352,
   424
Tuberculosis, 250, 395–96
   drugs for, 452
Tulane University, study of Vi-
   tamin E, 96
Tumor, fibroid, 234
*Type A Behavior and Your
   Heart,* 279
Tyrosine, 71, 135

U.S. Center for Disease Control, 316, 349
U.S. Department of Agriculture,
   (USDA), 60
   diet recommended by, 60

U.S. Dept. of Agriculture (cont'd)
   faults, 61.
   See also Dietary Goals for
      the U.S.
U.S. Office of Education, 615
Ulcer drugs, 480
Ulcer. See Peptic ulcers, 373
Ulcerative colitis, 396–98
Ulnar nerve, 49
Ultrasound imaging, 221
Unconsciousness, 670
University of California, 636
University of California, San
   Diego, 633
University of Illinois School of
   Medicine, 642
Unsaturated fats. See Fat, un-
   saturated
Upset stomach, 510
Uremia, 352
Urethritis, 398
Urinary problems, 689
Urinary tract infections (UTIs),
   240, 398–400, 455
Urticaria. See Hives
USDA. See U.S. Department of
   Agriculture
Uterus, prolapsed, 25
Uva-ursi, 535

Vaccines, 389, 464, 498–500
   available, 498
   description, 498
   influenza, 349
   measles, 358, 367
   mixed bacterial, 464
   mumps, 368
   pneumonia, 377
   rabies, 383
   recommended for infants
      and children, 499
Vaginal discharge, bleeding, 689
Vaginal products, 434
Vaginal surgery, 189
Vaginismus, 179
Vaginitis, nonspecific bacterial,
   213, 240
Valerian, 535.
   See also Lady's slipper
Valine, 69
Van Fleet, James, 117
Vanadium, 109

Varicose veins, 400–401
Vegans, 30
Vegetable oils, 288
Vegetables, 60, 70
Vegetarians, 30, 277
Venereal diseases. See Sexually
   transmitted diseases
Veterans' Medical Center, 633
Vibrio cholera, 162
Vinblastine, 529
Vincristine, 529
Viruses, 164
Vision problems, 401–406, 678
Vitamin A, 79–81, 99
Vitamin B-1, 81, 432
Vitamin B-2, 82
Vitamin B-3, 82–83, 471
Vitamin B-6, 83–84, 249, 277
Vitamin B-12, 84–85
Vitamin B-15, 145
Vitamin C, 88–92
   and colds, 305
   and catabolism, 91
   and diabetics, 91
   deficiency, 88, 277
   excessive, 91
   hazards, 91
   megadoses, 90
   RDA, 89
   safe doses, 92
   sources, 89
   supplements, 89, 92
Vitamin D, 92–92
   and osteoporosis, 372
Vitamin E, 94–97, 278
Vitamin K, 97
Vitamin molecules, 100
Vitamins, 58, 59, 79ff.
   megadoses, 99ff., 646
   requirements for exercise, 31
Voll, Reinhold, 604
Vomiting, 39, 677, 690
von Fleischl-Marxow, Ernst,
   550

Warts, 406–407, 434
Water,
   bottled, 169
   and diet, 29
   and exercise, 38
   filters, 169
   and heat stress, 39

Weakness, 679
Weight
   control, 113, 138
   ideal, 112
   loss, 68
   tables, 112
Weight Watchers International,
   139
   Vegetarian Plan, 123
Wheat germ, 82, 149
Wine Diet, the, 123
Wintergreen, 535
Winters, Jason, 531, 633
Wise Woman's Diet, the, 123
*Woman Doctor's Diet for
   Women, the,* 119
Wood, Dr. Peter, 127
Work, as exercise, 28
World Health Organization
   (WHO), 59, 315, 643
Worms, 164–66. See also, Asca-
   ris worms, Fish worms,
   Tapeworm
Wormwood, 536
Wounds, minor, 432

X-rays, 220
   and cancer, 292
   and pregnancy, 220
Xanthines. See Caffeine

Yale, 636
Yeast, 144
Yellow dock, 536
Yerba santa, 537
Yersinia, 162
Yin and yang, 123, 598, 600
Yoga, 662
Yogurt, 60, 149
   recipe, 150
Yogurt Diet, the, 123
Yohimbe, 552, 592
Youth vitamin. See Vitamin E
Yucca, 537

Zicarelli, Joseph (Joe Bayonne),
   639
Zinc, 108–109, 249
Zinc oxide, 431
Zinc pyrithione, 429